MALWA THROUGH THE AGES

(From the Earliest Time to 1305 A.D.)

KAILASH CHAND JAIN M A., Ph.D., D.Litt.
Recipient of the Highest Merit Pay awarded by the Government of Rajasthan for research work, Reader, University School Studies in Ancient Indian History, Culture & Archaeology,
VIKRAM UNIVERSITY, UJJAIN.

MOTILAL BANARSIDASS
DELHI : : VARANASI : : PATNA

Indological Publishers and Booksellers
Head Office : BUNGALOW ROAD, JAWAHARNAGAR, DELHI-7
Branches : 1. CHOWK, VARANASI (U.P)
2. ASHOK RAJ PATH (OPP. PATNA COLLEGE), PATNA-4 (BIHAR)

First Edition : Delhi 1972

Price : Rs. 60.00

Printed in India

BY SHANTILAL JAIN, AT SHRI JAINENDRA PRESS BUNGALOW ROAD, JAWAHARNAGAR, DELHI-7, AND PUBLISHED BY SUNDARLAL JAIN FOR MOTILAL BANARSIDASS, BUNGALOW ROAD, JAWAHARNAGAR, DELHI-7

DEDICATED

TO

THE SACRED MEMORY

OF

My Father

PREFACE

India's history is characterized by unity in diversity. There were different regions in India which possessed separate races, religions, languages, customs and manners. Each region possessed certain characteristics and peculiarities which distinguished it from the other. People of all these regions enriched Indian culture by their contributions. It is desirable to know in what respects, the culture of these regions was different from Indian culture, and how it was one with the whole of India. There do not seem to be provincial or linguistic cultures, as such, quite separate and different from Indian culture, but at the same time, the contributions of these regions can be distinctly marked and traced.

In order to evaluate the contributions made to Indian culture, scholars have written regional histories. R. D. BANERJI, R. C. MAJUMDAR, R. R. DIWAKAR, and DASHARATHA SHARMA have written comprehensive and connected accounts of Orissa, Bengal, Bihar and Rajasthan respectively. In ancient times, Malwa also dominated the history of India, but it is surprising that so far, no comprehensive history of this region has been written. Thus, a history of Malwa is a great desideratum, and I am hopeful that this work will give initiative to others for a detailed study of its different aspects.

In this monogram, I have consulted a long range of scattered material in the form of archaeological antiquities, inscriptions, coins and literature published by several scholars. The material of the neighbouring regions has also been utilised because it either directly or indirectly influenced the history of Malwa. I have sifted and examined this material with a critical eye, and have drawn new conclusions, not only because new facts have been discovered, but also because new aspects have come to light. H. DE TERRA,

T. T. PATERSON, H. D. SANKALIA, A. P. KHATRI, S. G. SUPEKAR, and V. S. WAKANKAR, surveyed and explored the river valleys and collected tools and fossils etc., which are valuable for the study of Stone Age Cultures. A.P.KHATRI has written a thesis on the Stone Age Cultures of Malwa. The reports of these scholars about their survey work have been published from time to time, in the Indian Archaeology—A Review. H. D. SANKALIA, H.V.TRIVEDI, N. R. BANERJI, K. D. BAJPAI and V.S.WAKANKAR have also conducted excavations at the chalcolithic sites of Malwa.

M. B. GARDE carried out archaeological excavations at the historical sites of Pawaya, Mandsor and Ujjain; D. R. BHANDARKAR undertook excavations at Besanagar and D. B. DISKALKAR at Kasrawad. The antiquities discovered in these excavations have been critically studied and utilised in this thesis.

J. F. FLEET, F. KIELHORN, J. BUHLER, E. HULTZSCH, D. R. BHANDARKAR, D. B. DISKALKAR, H. V. TRIVEDI, V. V. MIRASHI and D. C. SIRCAR have edited the inscriptions in the Indian Antiquary and Epigraphia Indica. H. V. TRIVEDI published a number of articles on the ancient coins of Malwa in the Journal of the Numismatic Society, and his work on the Nāga coins is also important.

A. CUNNINGHAM, the great pioneer of archaeological exploration in India, and his assistant, J. D. BEGLAR visited some places of Malwa region between the year 1862 and 1863, and their notes appeared in the Archaeological Survey Reports, Vols. II, VII, X and XX. His work, named Bhilsa Topes, is also noteworthy. JAMES FERGUSSON in 'History of Indian and Eastern Architecture', first published in 1876, reviewed the temples and palaces of the Gwalior fort, the temples at Udayapura and Gyaraspur, and the caves at Bagh. JOHN MARSHALL has written a voluminous work 'Monuments of Sanchi'.

D. R. BHANDARKAR, in the 'Archaeological Survey of Western Reports' has given a description of the archaeological sites. The State Gazetteers, compiled in 1908 under C. E. LUARD, contain brief references to some of the places of archaeological interest. D. R. PATIL in 'The Cultural Heritage of Madhya Bharat' has also given a brief description of the places of archaeological importance. H.V.TRIVEDI's 'The Bibliography of Madhya Bharat Archaeology', serves a useful purpose of being a reference book to research scholars. D. C. GANGULY's book, 'History of the Paramāra Dynasty', and PRATIPAL BHATIA's book, 'The Paramāras (800-1305 A.D.)', have been utilised in writing this work. Some articles published in the Vikrama Volumes also proved to be useful.

This work has been divided into sixteen Chapters. As arranged, Chapters I-IX discuss the Ancient History of Malwa from the earliest times to 700 A.D. while Chapters X-XVI deal with the Early Medieval Period from 701 to 1305 A.D. In Chapter I, the origin, movements and settlements of the Mālavas have been described. The Mālavas of Avanti seem to have assumed the territorial name from about the fifth century A.D., and it included also Eastern Malwa by the seventh century A.D. Chapter II is concerned with the Geographical Background of Malwa, and how it influenced its history.

In Chapter III, the Sources of this work have been critically examined. Chapter IV is related to the Stone Age Cultures of Malwa. Their origin and comparison with other regions has been dealt with. Chapter V is related to the Malwa Chalcolithic Cultures. It differs from the Chalcolithic cultures of other regions in ceramic traditions, but shares a common level of food economy and technology. Its origin, authors and disappearance, have also been discussed. In Chapter VI, the legendary and Traditional History of the very early period of Malwa has been described, and an attempt has been made to correlate it with archaeological evidence.

In Chapter VII, it has been pointed out that Pradyota was one of the most powerful monarchs of North India, and in his reign, Avanti rose to a high position. During the Maurya period, the importance of Avanti was next only to Magadha.

Chapter VIII is concerned with the 'Śuṅga-Sātavāhana-Śaka Period', Vidiśā as a capital of the Śuṅgas became an important cultural centre. The problem of the historicity of Vikramāditya has been thoroughly discussed. Ujjain became the capital of the Śakas, and the Śaka-Sātavāhana struggle began. Though there was a revival of Brahmanical religion, Buddhism reached its highest point of development, as known from the monuments of Sanchi. Ujjain became a seat of learning. Trade and commerce flourished because of the frequent and smooth communications with the outside world. The Nāgas of Padmāvatī became powerful at this time.

Chapter IX is concerned with the Gupta-Aulikara Period. Western Malwa was governed by the Aulikaras, and the Guptas ruled over Eastern Malwa. But the Aulikaras seem to have recognized the suzerainty of the Guptas for a short period. Rāmagupta, as known from the coins and inscriptions found at Vidiśā, seems to have been a local ruler. Ujjain became so prosperous that it is said to have surpassed even Amarāvatī, the city of gods. Art, literature and science developed greatly during the Gupta period. After the decline of the power of the Guptas, the Aulikaras of Daśapura gradually became powerful.

Chapter X is concerned with the Paramāra period. There are different theories about the origin of the Paramāras. Among them, Bhoja was the most famous, and the greatest of the Paramāra rulers of India. Under him, Paramāra imperialism reached its zenith, and Malwa rose to its great glory and renown. In Chapter XI, the Paramāra administration has been discussed. The territorial divisions became systematic and well marked during this period.

Chapter XII is devoted to Religion. During the Paramāra period, Vaishṇavism and Śaivism became dominant. Jainism became popular especially among the merchant classes, and Buddhism gradually began to decline and ultimately disappeared. Chapter XIII is related to Art. The vigorous religious activity contributed to the development of art, and a number of temples were built, and images placed in them. Some of the Paramāra rulers were also patrons of art, and they built beautiful temples. In Chapter XIV, it has been pointed out that Malwa attained greatness and fame in the spheres of education and literature. In Chapter XV, Social Conditions have been dealt with. This period is remarkable for changes in the social set-up; several new castes and *gotras* came into existence. In Chapter XVI, Economic Conditions have been discussed. Malwa became extremely prosperous during this period because of the development of trade and commerce.

This research project was undertaken with the financial assistance of two thousand rupees given by the University Grants Commission in 1967. I received help from numerous persons in one way or another in the preparation and publication of this work. First of all, I want to express my gratitude to Surya Narayan Vyas, at whose initiative, and with whose encouragement, I took up this project.

To D. S. Tatke and Margaretta Pos, I am indebted for their reading the manuscript from the linguistic point of view. I am greatly obliged to H.V.Trivedi for going through the Chapters on the Paramāras, and for giving valuable suggestions, to S. D. Mishra for the Chapter of Geographical Back-ground and to M.L.Dalal and S.M.Pahadia for topics on Art and Buddhism respectively.

I am specially obliged to K. D. Bajpai of Sagar University for sending me the recent report of the excavations of Tumain and Bhim Betika; to V. S. Wakankar for supplying some photographs of Bhim Betika and Kayatha; to R.K.Sethi for supplying coins for photographs, and to Mohan Jhala for preparing maps.

My sincere thanks are also due to B. N. Sharma of the National Museum, New Delhi for the selection of photographs and to Chandra Mohan Srivastav, Librarian, Photo Library of the Archaeological Survey of India, New Delhi, for kindly preparing the photographs in such a short time. These have been published through the courtesy of the Archaeological Survey of India and the photograph of Vāgdevī Sarasvatī of Dhār, through the courtesy of the British Museum, London. I also wish to thank Bhagawat Sahai, Daftari of the Central Archaeological Department Library, New Delhi, for his prompt delivery of necessary books and Research Journals.

I am extremely grateful to Shiv Mangal Simha 'Suman', Vice-Chancellor, and V. Shankaran, Registrar of the Vikram University, for their keen interest in the publication of this book. I also acknowledge my indebtedness to the Vikram University for the grant-in-aid sanctioned towards the cost of publication of this book.

Mohan Niwas, Dewas Road,
Ujjain (M.P.).
15th Aug. 1972 KAILASH CHAND JAIN

ABBREVIATIONS

AAR. Annals and Antiquities of Rajasthan by J. Tod.

ABNUHS. Annual Bulletin of the Nagpur University, Historical Society, Nagpur.

ABORI. Annals of the Bhandarkar Oriental Research Institute, Poona.

AI. Ancient India, Delhi.

AIHT. Ancient Indian Historical Traditions by F.E. Pargiter.

AJGPS. *Apabhraṁśa Jaina Granth Praśasti Saṁgraha.*

AR. Rāṣṭrakūṭas and their times by A. S. Altekar.

ARADGS. Annual Report of the Archaeological Department, Gwalior State, Gwalior.

ARRMA. Annual Report Rajputana Museum, Ajmer.

ASC. Archaeological Survey of India Reports by Alexander Cunningham.

ASI. Archaeological Survey of India, Annual Reports.

Bh. Rep. Bhandarkar's Reports on Sanskrit Manuscripts, 1882-83.

BLUIA. Bulletin of the London University Institute of Archaeology.

CBT. Bhilsa Topes by Cunningham.

CCIM. Catalogue of the Coins in the Indian Museum by V. A. Smith, Calcutta, 1906.

CGD. Catalogue of the Coins of the Gupta Dynasties and of Śaśāṅka, King in the British Museum by John Allan, London, 1914.

CHI. Cambridge History Of India by E.J.Rapson.

CII. Corpus Inscriptionum Indicarum.

DP. *Dravyaparīkshā.*

DV. *Dvyāśrayamahākāvya* of Hemachandra.

EC.	Epigraphia Carnatica.
E.Ch.D.	Early Chauhāna Dynasties by DASHARATHA SHARMA.
EHI.	Early History of India by V. A. SMITH
EI.	Epigraphia Indica.
EMN.	The Excavations at Maheshwar and Navdatoli.
GGVS.	*Guru Gopaladas Varaiya Smṛitigrantha.*
GHPD.	History of the Paramāra Dynasty by D. C. GANGULY.
HC.	Harshacharita, Eng. Trans. by E. B. COWELL and F.W. THOMAS, London.
H.De Terra & T. T. Paterson	Studies on the Ice Age in India and Associated Human Cultures, Washington, 1939.
H.Dh.	History of Dharmaśāstras by P. V. KANE.
HIED.	History of India as told by its own Historians, ed. by ELLIOT and DOWSON.
HMHI	History of Medieval Hindu India by C. V. VAIDYA.
IA.	Indian Antiquary, Bombay.
IC.	Indian Culture, Calcutta.
I.Ar.	Indian Archaeology, Delhi.
IP.	Indian Prehistory, 1964.
IHQ.	Indian Historical Quarterly, Calcutta.
Imp. Gaz.	Imperial Gazetteer.
JA.	Journal Asiatique.
JAOS.	Journal of the American Oriental Society.
JASB.	Journal of the Asiatic Society of Bengal, Calcutta.
JBBRAS.	Journal of the Bombay Branch of the Royal Asiatic Society, Bombay.
JBORS.	Journal of the Bihar and Orissa Research Society, Patna.
JBRS.	Journal of the Bihar Research Society, Patna.
JDL.	Journal of the Department of Letters, Calcutta University.
JGPS.	*Jaina Grantha Praśasti Saṁgraha.*
JGRS.	Journal of the Gujarat Research Society, Bombay.

JIH.	Journal of Indian History, Trivandrum.
JMPIR	Journal of the Madhya Pradesh Itihasa Parishad, Bhopal.
JNSI.	Journal of the Numismatic Society of India.
JRAS.	Journal of the Royal Asiatic Society of Great Britain and Ireland, London.
JRASBL.	Journal of the Royal Asiatic Society of Great Britain and Ireland, London
JSAI.	*Jaina Sāhitya aura Itihāsa* by Premi, N. R.
KB.	*Kharataragachchha Bṛihadgurvāvali.*
MASI.	Memoirs of the Archaeological Survey of India.
Mbh.	Critical Edition of the *Mahābhārata*, Poona.
MI.	Man in India.
MSI.	Studies in Indology by Mirashi, V. V.
NC.	*Navasāhasāṅkacharita* by Padmagupta.
NPP.	*Nāgarī Prachāriṇī Patrikā*, Banaras.
NS.	Numismatic Supplementary.
PC.	*Prabandhachintāmaṇi* of Merutuṅga.
P.Ch.	*Prabhāvakacharita* of Prabhāchandra.
PHAI.	Political History of Ancient India by H. C. Rayachaudhuri.
PIHC.	Proceedings of the Indian History Congress.
PM.	*Pramāṇamañjarī* of Malla.
POC.	Proceedings of the All India Oriental Conference.
PPS.	*Purātanaprabandha Saṁgraha.*
PR.	Peterson's Reports.
PRAS. WC.	Progress Report of the Archaeological Survey of Western Circle.
PV.	*Pṛithvīrājavijaya* of Jayānaka.
PWMI.	Prince of Wales Museum Stone Inscription of Dhar published in Bharatiyavidya, XVII, 1957.
QRHS.	Quarterly Reviews of Historical Studies, Calcutta.
RJSBGS.	*Rājasthāna ke Jaina Śāstra Bhaṇḍāroṁ kī Granthasūchi.*

SACHAU.	Alberuni's India ed. by SACHAU.
SBE.	Sacred Books of the East.
SEHNI.	Social and Economic History of Northern India by M. P. MAJUMDAR.
Sel. Ins.	Select Inscriptions bearing on Indian History and Civilization, Vol. I by D. C. SIRCAR.
SII.	South Indian Inscriptions ed. by E. HULTZSCH.
SILH.	Studies in Indian Literary History by GODE, P. K.
SJS.	Singhi Jaina Series.
SK.	*Sukṛitasaṁkīrtana* of Arisiṁha.
SMK.	*Sṛiṅgāramañjarīkathā* of Bhojadeva.
SP.	*Skandapurāṇa.*
SPPIP.	Prehistory and Protohistory in India and Pakistan by H. D. SANKALIA.
SS.	*Samarāṅganasūtradhāra* of Bhojadeva.
THK.	History of Kanauj by R. S. TRIPATHI.
TM.	*Tilakamañjarī* of Dhanapāla.
TN.	*Tabquāt-i-Nāsirī* of Minhaj-ud-din.
TSS.	Trivandrum Sanskrit Series.
ZDMG.	*Zeitschrift der Deutschen Morgenländischen Gesselschaft.*

CONTENTS

Preface v
Abbreviations xi
List of Maps xxiii
List of Plates xxiii

CHAPTER I

THE MĀLAVAS— 1—14

Origin of the name, 1; Movements and settlements of the Mālavas, 3; Mālavas in the Punjab, 4; Mālavas of Rajasthan, 6; Mālavas in Avanti, 8; Mālava kingdom in the seventh century A.D., 10; Mo-lā-p'o of Yuanchwang, 11; Contributions, 12; Importance of Mālava tribe, 13.

CHAPTER II

THE GEOGRAPHICAL BACKGROUND— 15—20

The Central Malwa Plateau, 16; The North East Plateau, 17; The North-West Plateau, 17; The Narmada Valley, 17.

CHAPTER III

SOURCES— 21—33

(i) Archaeology 21—30

Explorations and excavations, 21; Inscriptions 22; Coins, 27; Monuments, 29.

(2) Literature 30—33

Epics and Purāṇas 30; Mahābhāshya, 31; Pure literary works, 31; Miscellaneous works, 32.

(3) Writings of foreigners, 33.

CHAPTER—IV

STONE AGE CULTURES— 34—62

(1) Lower Palaeolithic Culture 35—49

Sohanian Culture and Hand-axe Culture 35; Exploration of Narmada Valley by DE TERRA and PATERSON, 35; Stratigraphy at Maheshwar, 36; Claim of the Discovery of the Oldwan Culture at Piparia Mahadeo by A. P. KHATRI not justified, 36; Survey of the Narmada and its tributaries by H. D. SANKALIA and S. G. SUPEKAR, 37; Investigation of Pleistocene deposits, 37; Exploration of the Chambal Valley and the Stratigraphy, 38; Different types of tools, 39; Material of the tools and technique, 39; Date and climatic conditions, 39; Controversy among scholars about Sohan Culture, 40; Comparison between the Lower Palaeolithic of the Narmada and the Chambal Valleys, 42; Comparison with Pre-Sohan Culture, 43; Comparison with the Lower Paleolithic Culture of the Provinces 43; Gujrat, 43; Uttara Pradesh, 43; Orissa 43; Maharashtra, 44; Mysore, 44; Andhra, 45; Madras, 45; Comparison with the Cultures of the countries outside India, 45, Africa, 46; Eastern countries of Asia as well as Europe, 47; Habits of the people, 47; Hand-axe man related to the early African man, 48; Sohan-man related to Eastern Asia, 49.

(2) Middle Palaeolithic Culture 49—55

Middle Palaeolithic Industry known by various names, 49; Two types of tools, 50; Exploration of the Narmada Valley, 50; Exploration of the Chambal Valley, 51; Characteristics of the tools, 51; Relation of this culture with other regions, 52; South India, 52; Comparison with the Late Sohan, 52; Climatic condition and Environment, 53; Fauna, 53; Controversy about origin, 54; Foreign 54; Indigenous, 54.

(3) Mesolithic Culture 55—61

General Characteristics, 55; Distribution of Microlithic sites, 56; Peculiarities of Malwa Microliths, 57; Of pre-chalcolithic sites, 57; Microliths of rock-shelters and caves, 58; Comparison with those of other regions, 59; Comparison with those of other regions, 59; Comparison with those of Europe and Africa, 60; Origin, 60; Continued use of microliths by urban and village communities, 61. 61-62.

(4) Neolithic Culture 61—62

CHAPTER—V

CHALCOLITHIC CULTURES— 63—86

General Characteristics, 63; Peculiarities of Malwa Chalcolithic, 63; Distribution of Chalcolithic sites, 63; Settlements, 65; Plan of the houses, 66; Earthen pots of the houses, 67; Kayatha Ware, 67; The Black and Red Ware, 68; Malwa Ware, 68; White Slipped fabric, 69; Jorwe fabric, 69; Other types of pottery, 69; Grey Ware, 70; Designs on the Pottery, 70; Cultivation of Different kinds of grain, 71; Methods of Cultivation, 71; Food, 72; Metal, 72; Ornaments, 72; Terracottas, 73; Relation with the contemporary Chalcolithic Cultures of other regions, 75; Northern Deccan Chalcolithic Cultures, 75; The Neolithic Chalcolithic Settlements of the Deccan, 77; Banas culture, 77; The Chalcolithic Culture of the Gangetic Doab, 78; Chalcolithic Culture of Saurashtra, 79; Origin of the Chalcolithic Culture of Malwa, 80; Western Asiatic influence, 80; Criticism of the theory 81; Origin from Harappan Culture, 83; Chalcolithic Cultures represent the Aryans, 83; Pre-Aryans as authors, 84· Ancestors of some of the Primitive or Aboriginal tribes as authors, 84; End of Chalcolithic Cuture, 86.

CHAPTER—VI

LEGENDARY AND TRADITIONAL HISTORY— 87-97

No mention of Malwa region in Vedic literature, 87; Occupation of Malwa region by the Nāgas and the Haihayas, 88; Controversy among scholars about the date of Vedic Culture, 88; Aryan tribes during the early Vedic period and the position of the Yādavas, 89; P. L. BHARGAVA's views about the early Haihayas, 89; Early Haihaya rulers, 91; Kṛitavīrya, 91; Arjuna, 91 Arjuna's successors and their fall, 92; Haihaya's conquest of Eastern Kingdom, 93; Rulers of Avanti during Bhārata War, 99; Contributions of the Haihayas, 99; Archaeological Evidence confirming the account of the epics and the Purāṇas, 95.

CHAPTER—VII

THE PRADYOTA-MAURYA PERIOD 98-148.

(I) Political History 98-104

Diplomatic relations with Magadha, 99; Vatsarāja of Kauśāmbī, 100; Pushkarasārin of Taxila, 100; The Śūrasenas of Mathura, 101; Pradyota's successors, 101; Defeat of the last Pradyota ruler, 102; Avanti under the Nandas and Mauryas, 103.

(II) Administration 104-113

Nature and ends, 105; Position and functions of the King, 106; The Council of Ministers, 107; Administrative units and officers, 108; Judicial administration, 110; Military administration, 111; Municipal administration, 112 ; Espionage system, 113.

(III) Cultural History 114-148

(a) Religion 114-122

Brahmanism, 114; Buddhism, 115; Jainism, 119; Śaivism, 121; Other sects and religious beliefs, 122.

(b) Art and Architecture 123-134.

Architecture, 123; Town planning, 123; The canal wells of the Pre-Mauryan period, 124; Roads and drainage, 125; Houses, 125; Stūpas, Vihāras and pillars, 126; Ceramics, 129; Terracottas, 131; Seals and amulets, 131; Beads, 132 ; Metal works, 132; stone and bone objects, 133; Symbols on coins, 133; Miscellaneous objects, 134.

(c) Social Conditions 134-140

Structure of Society, 134: Orders or Stages of life, 136; Family life, 137; Marriage and Position of Women, 137; Dress and ornaments, 139; Food and drink, 139; Entertainments, 139; Welfare activities, 140; Funerary customs, 140.

(d) Economic Conditions. 140-148

Currency, 143; Cast Coins, 145; Tribal Coins of Ujjayinī and Eran, 146: Ujjayinī Coinage, 146; The Eran Coins, 147; Inscribed Coins, 147.

CHAPTER—VIII

THE ŚUṄGA-SĀTAVĀHANA-ŚAKA PERIOD— 149-228

Expedition against Vidarbha, 149; Conflict with the Yavanas. 150; Controversy about the identification of Bhāgabhadra, 151; Greek envoy at Bhāgabhadra's Court, 152; Extension of the Kingdom, 152; The Kāṇvas, 152; Rule of Sarvatāta, 153; Occupation of Malwa by early Sātavāhana rulers, 154; Other known rulers, 155; Early Śaka occupation, 155; Vikramāditya Problem, 156; Malwa under the Śakas, 165; Family of Mambarus, 165, The Kshaharāta Satrapas, 166; Arṭa, 166; Bhūmaka, 166, Nahapāna, 167; The Kārdamakas, 169; Jayadāman, 171; Rudradāman, 171; Dāmaghasada or Dāmajadaśrī; Long struggle between Jīvadāman and his uncle Rudrasiṁha for the throne, 173; Rudrasena I, 175; Saṁghadāman and Dāmasena, 175; Yaśodāman, Vijayasena, Dāmajada III and Rudrasena II, 176; Viśvasiṁha and Bhartṛidāman, 177; The rise of a new Śaka House, 178; The fourth Śaka house founded by Rudradāman II and his successors, 179; Śaka dynasty of Māhishmatī, 180; The Nāgas, 182; The Maukharis of Baḍvā, 187; The Mālavas, 187; Other rulers, 188.

Administration 188-192.

Territorial division, 189; Classes of officers, 190. The revenue on the different items, 191.

Culture 192

(a) Religion. 192-202.

Vedic religion, 192; Vaishṇavism, 194; Śaivism, 195; Other minor Brahmanical Sects, 196; Jainism, 197; Buddhism, 198.

(b) Art and Architecture 202-213

Architecture, 202; Sculptures, 207; Terracottas, 210, Pottery, 211; Minor arts, 212.

(c) Education and Literature 213-218.
(d Social conditions. 218-224.
Division of Society, 218; Family, 219; Marriage and Position of Women, 220; Pastime and recreations, 220; Food and drinks, 221; Dress and ornaments, 222.
(e) Economic Conditions. 224-228.
Coinage, 226.

CHAPTER—IX

THE GUPTA-AULIKARA PERIOD— 229-318

Jishṇu, 229; Conquests of Samudragupta. 230; Historicity of Rāmagupta, 231; Chandragupta II, 234; Kumāragupta II, 237; Skandagupta, 239; Kumāragupta II, 242; Budhagupta, 243: Narasiṁhagupta, 246; The Hūṇas, 247; Aulikaras, 250; Latcr Guptas, 259.

Administrative Organization 266-271

Monarchichal government, 266; Ministry, 268; Administrative divisions, 268; City Police, 270; System of justice, 270; Other officers, 271.

Culture 271

Religion— 272-280
Vaishṇavism, 272; Śaivism, 273; Other Brahmanical religions and religious beliefs, 275; Buddhism, 276; Jainism, 279.

Art and Architecture— 280-296.

Architecture, 280; Cave Architecture, 281; Structural buildings, 283; Monasteries and Stūpas, 285; Pillars, 286; Sculptures, 287; Vishṇu, 287; Śiva, 289; Buddhist images, 291; Jaina images, 292; Dvārapāla Mithunas etc. 292; Terracottas, 293; Painting, 294; Pottery, 295; Coins and seals, 295; Other arts 295.

Education, Literature and Sciences— 296-301.
Literature, 296; Sciences, 298.

Social Conditions— 301-313.
Structure of the Society, 302; Other Castes, 302; Lower Castes and tribes, 303; Slaves, 304; Āśrama, 304; Marriage,

305; Position of Woman, 306; Town life, 309; Dress and ornaments, 310; Toilets and Cosmetics, 312; Amusements, 312; Food and drink, 313; superstitions, 313; Living standard, 313.

Economic Conditions— 313-318.

Agriculture, 314: Industries, 314; Trade and Commerce, 316; Guilds, 316; Currency, 317

CHAPTER—X

THE PARAMĀRA PERIOD— 319-377

Arab invasion, 321; Tripartite struggle and the Role of Malwa, 321; Malwa under the influence of the Rāshṭrakūṭas, 321; Mālava kingdom not under the Pratīhāras, 322; Obscure dynasty probably known from the Mahua inscription, 324; Nāga dynasty, 325; Malwa as buffer State, 325; Origin of the Paramāras, 325; Theory of fire-pit, 325; The Paramāras as the Gurjaras, 326; The Paramāras as the Rāshṭrakūṭas, 327; The Paramāras as the Mālavas 328; The Paramāras as the Brāhmaṇas, 328; Vākpati I or Bapparāja, 331; Vairīsiṁha, 332; Sīyakadeva II alias Harsha, 333; Vākpati II, 335; Sindhurāja, 341; Bhoja, 345; Jayasiṁha I, 352; Udayāditya, 354; Lakshmadeva, 357; Naravarmadeva, 359; Yaśovarman, 361; Jayavarman. 362; Ballāla, 363; The Paramāra Mahākumāras, 364; Vindhyavarman, 368; Surbhaṭavarman, 369; Arjunavarman, 370; Devapāla, 371; Jaitugideva, 373; Jayavarman II, 374; Arjunavarman II and Bhoja II, 374; Causes of the decline of the Paramāras, 376.

CHAPTER—XI

ADMINISTRATION— 378-396.

Kingship, 378 ; Duties of the King, 380 ; The law of succession, 381 ; The Queen, 381 ; The Royal Cou t, 381 ; The Ministers, 381 ; Territorial Divisions, 384 ; Feudal system, 386 ; Military system, 389 ; Financial Administration, 391; The judiciary and the Police system, 393; Local Administration, 394.

CHAPTER—XII

RELIGION— 397-421

Buddhism, 397 ; Jainism, 400 ; Śaivism, 405; Vaishṇavism, 414 ; Brahmā, 417 ; Sūrya, 417 ; Śakti worship, 418 ; Minor gods and goddesses, 420; Brāhmanical Tīrthas, 421.

CHAPTER—XIII

ART AND ARCHITECTURE— 422-463.

Post-Gupta architecture, 422; Pratīhāra architecture, 427; Paramāra architecture, 435; Secular architecture, 446; Sculpture; 448; Buddhist sculptures, 449; Brahmanical sculptures, 450; Śiva, 450; Vishṇu, 452 ; Brahmā, 455; Sūrya, 455 ; Mother goddess, 456 ; Vyantara Devatās, 458; Syncretistic Icons, 459; General, 460 ; Jaina Sculptures, 461.

CHAPTER—XIV

EDUCATION & LITERATURE— 364-479.

Education, 464 ; Literature, 468.

CHAPTER—XV

SOCIAL CONDITIONS— 480-496.

Caste system, 580 ; Position of Women, 488 ; Dress, Ornaments and Cosmetics, 490 ; Food and drink, 492 ; Fasts and festivals, 493 ; Means of amusements 496.

CHAPTER—XVI

ECONOMIC CONDITIONS— 497-511.

Agriculture, 497; Industries, 498; Trade and Commerce, 500 ; Guild system, 501; Weights and measures, 502; Coinage, 504.

APPENDICES 512.

GENERAL BIBLIOGRAPHY 514.

INDEX 531.

PLATES

MAPS

LIST OF MAPS

1. Location of Malwa in India.
2. Map of Malwa showing Prehistoric sites.
3. Natural divisions of Malwa.
4. Archaeological map showing important ancient sites of Malwa.

LIST OF PLATES

Plate	Figure	Description
I	1.	Mandsor, Palaeoliths of Series I.
	2.	Nagda, Microliths.
II.	3.	Kayatha, Chalcolithic pottery and other objects.
	4.	Eran, Beads, foot-rubber and other minor antiquities from Chalcolithic period.
III.	5.	Navdatoli, Painted potteries.
	6.	Navdatoli, Copper implements.
IV.	7.	Avara, Chalcolithic pottery.
	8.	Bhim Baithaka, Pre-historic painting form the rock-shelter.
V.	9.	Ujjain, View of a massive brick structure.
	10.	Ujjain, wooden structure in the make up of the rampart.
VI.	11.	Ujjain, Section of roads of different periods.
	12.	Ujjain, Ironsmith's furnace.
VII.	13.	Sanchi, General view of stūpa I.
	14.	Sanchi, Stūpa I North gate.
VIII.	15.	Sanchi, Lion Capital.
IX.	16.	Sanchi, Ajātaśatru and his women meeting Buddha at the mango grove at Rājagṛiha.
	17.	Sanchi, Prasenjit going out of his palace to witness the Miracle of Śrāvasti.
X.	18.	Sanchi, Top bar : Carriage of ashes to Kusinagar. Middle bar : War for relics. Lowest bar : Assault of Māra.
	19.	Sanchi, Śālabhañjikā.

Plate	Figure	Description
XI.	20.	Besanagar, General view of the pillar of Heliodorus.
	21.	Besanagar, inscription of Heliodorus.
XII.	22.	Besanagar, Yakshī.
	23.	Besanagar, Kalpavṛiksha.
XIII.	24.	Besanagar, Palm capital.
	25.	Besanagar, Abacus of *makara*.
XIV.	26.	Pawaya, Fan palm capital.
	27.	Pawaya, Yaksha Maṇibhadra.
XV.	28.	Sanchi, Bodhisattva seated in meditation.
	29.	Sanchi, Bodhisattva Vajrapāṇi.
XVI.	30.	Sanchi, period, Buddha seated in meditation.
	31.	Sanchi, Nāgarāja.
XVII.	32.	Pawaya, Dance panel.
	33.	Sondani, Flying Gandharvas.
XVIII.	34.	Udaigiri, Varāha.
	35.	Udaigiri, Nāga near Varāha.
XIX.	36.	Udaigiri, Vishṇu.
	37.	Udaigiri, Śeshaśāyī Vishṇu.
XX.	38.	Udaigiri, Śivaliṅga.
	39.	Udaigiri, Gaṇeśa.
XXI.	40.	Udaigiri, Gaṅgā and Yamunā.
	41.	Udaigiri, Umā-Maheśvara.
XXII.	42.	Udaigiri, Mahishāsuramardinī.
	43.	Kāyathā, A torso of the Sun image.
XXIIII.	44.	Eran, Varāha.
	45.	Bagh, Head of Dvārapāla.
XXIV.	46.	Udaigiri, Jaina image of Pārśvanātha.
	47.	Vidiśā, inscribed Jaina image of the time of Rāmagupta.
XXV.	48.	Eran, Pillar of the temple.
	49.	Eran, Ruined temple of the Gupta period.
XXVI.	50.	Sanchi, Gupta temple.
	51.	Udaigiri, Gupta temple.
XXVII.	52.	Bagh, Cave IV Chaitya.
	53.	Sanchi, Late Gupta temple.

XXVII.	54.	Sanchi, Buddha standing in *Varada* pose.
	55.	Gyāraspur, Buddha.
XXIX.	56.	Jhalrapatan, Maṇḍapa of Śītaleśvara Mahādeva temple (Chandramauli temple).
	57.	Jhalrapatana, General view of the Sun temple from south-east.
XXX.	58.	Gyāraspur, Hindola toraṇa.
	59.	Gyāraspur, Āṭhakhambā.
XXXI.	60.	Gyāraspur, Bajramaṭha temple.
	61.	Gyāraspur, Maladevī temple, *Śikhara*.
XXXII.	62.	Gwalior, Teli kā Mandir.
	63.	Gwalior, Sāsa bahu temple.
XXXIII.	64.	Surawaya, Vishṇu temple.
	65.	Surawaya, Vishṇu temple, partial view of the maṇḍapa.
XXXIV.	66.	Eran Remains.
XXXV.	67.	Dhar, Bhojaśālā, interior view.
	68.	Dhar, Bhojaśālā, ceiling of the central dome.
XXXVI.	69.	Bhojpur, Bhojeśvara temple, portion of the front doorway.
	70.	Udayapura, Nīlakaṇṭheśvara temple.
XXXVII.	71.	Un, Nīlakaṇṭheśvara temple.
	72.	Udaigiri, Lion Capital.
XXXVIII.	73.	Nemawar, Siddheśvara temple, general view.
	74.	Nemawar, Siddheśvara temple, ceiling..
XXXIX.	75.	Udayapura, Dancing Śiva.
	76.	Ujjain, Naṭarāja Śiva.
XL.	77.	Indore Museum, Umā Maheśvara.
	78.	Gwalior Museum, Bust of Śiva and Pārvatī
XLI.	79.	Dhar, Image of Vishṇu.
	80.	Gandhawal, Harihara.
XLII.	81.	Modī, Brahmā with four heads.
	82.	Torso of a female figure.
XLIII.	83.	Gandhwal, Dancing Kālī.
	84.	Udaipur, Udayeśvara temple sculpture.
XLIV.	85.	Badoh, Yaśodā with Kṛishṇa.
	86.	Dhār, Vāgdevī.
XLV.	87.	Naresar, Indrāṇī.
	88.	Badnawar, A female Jaina deity.

XLVI.	89.	Dhar, A fragmentary sculpture showing Lohapālas.
	90.	Gwalior, Rāhu and Ketu.
XLVII.	91.	Un, Jaina sculpture.
	92.	Gandhawal, Sun.
XLVIII.	93.	Gwalior Museum, Kārttikeya.
	94.	Gwalior Museum, Kubera.
XLIX	95.	Sohania, Skanda.
	96.	Dhar, Iron pillar.
L	97.	Udayapura, Deity of the Udayeśvara temple.
	98.	Nemawar, Dvārapāla at the entrance of the Sabhāmaṇḍapa.
LI	99.	Ancient coins of Malwa.
LII.	100.	Ancient coins of Malwa.

CHAPTER I

THE MĀLAVAS

The territorial unit which we call 'Malwa' was named after the Mālavas, who were an important ancient tribe of India. There were settlements of this tribe in different parts of the country; but the Mālavas of Avanti seem to have assumed the territorial name from about the fifth century A. D., and this name has continued up to the present.

ORIGIN OF THE NAME :—

Both the names Mālava and Mālaya are known from literary, epigraphical and numismatic sources. R. D. DOUGLAS[1] assumes that Mālaya is the older form of the tribal name, but nothing can be stated definitively.

There is a controversy among scholars about the origin of the name Mala, occurring on some coins, which is regarded by R. D. DOUGLAS[2] as the name of a king, the founder of the tribe; but it appears to have been intended for Mālaya or Mālava. A. C. CARLLEYLE[3] and VINCENT SMITH[4], on the basis of the peculiar legends on some coins, hold that these are the names of foreign rulers. It may be concluded from this that the Mālavas were foreigners. But J. ALLAN[5] rightly points out that they are too late for the Śakas and too early for the Hūṇas. These names do not bear any resemblance to any Śaka or Hūṇa name. D. C. SIRCAR[6] suggests that the name of Mālava, like that of the Mālaya mountain range, is probably derived from the Dravidian word 'Malai', meaning hill. Thus originally it meant a Dravidian hill tribe. This is based on speculation, because

1. Numismatic supplement, XXXVII, p. 13.
2. Ibid, p. 45.
3. ASC, VI, p. 174.
4. CCIM, p. 163.
5. A Catalogue of the Indian Coins in the British Museum, p. CVI.
6. The Age of Imperial Unity, p. 163.

there is no concrete evidence of the existence of a hill tribe of this name in the south.

RAJ BALI PANDEY[1] suggests that the Mālavas branched off from the Malla people of the famous Mallarāshṭra situated in the Gorakhpur Division of Uttarapradesh. The first derivative from 'Mall' was Mālaya, or Malāya, which subsequently became Mālava. The Mallas were the descendants of Ikshvāku of the Solar race. According to the Vālmīki *Rāmāyaṇa*, the epithet of Chandraketu, the son of Lakshmaṇa, was Malla, and he founded the Malla-rāshṭra and his descendants were called Mallas. The Solar race of the Mallas is also proved by Buddhist literature[2]. From the Nāndsā inscription[3] of 226 A.D., it is known that they were as famous as the Ikshvākus. But the identification of the Mālavas with Malla does not seem to be reasonable.

On the basis of the peculiar legends of the coins, KALYAN KUMARA DAS GUPTA[4] is of the view that these Mālavas were probably non-Aryan. These are not meaningless attempts to reproduce parts of '*Mālavānāṁ-jayaḥ*', but they mention the names of the Mālava chiefs who belonged to the non-Aryan stock. There is at least one coin in the Indian Museum which definitely bears the name of the tribe Mālava, together with one with the curious expression '*Majupa*'[5]. '*Majupa*' seems to be a Mālava chief who was a non-Aryan. Words of non-Sanskritic origin, like the present legends, are not altogether absent in Indian Numismatics. Words like *Rālimasa*, *Dojaka* and *Aṭakatakā* appear on a group of Negama coins found at Taxila[6]. Scholars regard them as proper names, either of persons, or of places[7]. On this analogy, the outlandish words on Mālava coins may be regarded as proper names, and they seem to be the names of Mālava chiefs probably of non-Aryan origin.

1. Vikramāditya of Ujjayinī, p. 78.
2. The *Mahā-Pariṇivvāṇa-Sutta* and the *Divyāvadāna*.
3. EI, XXVII, p. 265.
4. The Mālavas, p. 19.
5. CCIM, p. 175, No. 70, Class 2, variety B.
6. A. CUNNINGHAM : Coins of Ancient India, p. 19; A Catalogue of the Indian Coins in the British Museum, p. C.XXVI.
7. Coins of Ancient India, p. 65; A Catalogue of the Indian Coins in the British Museum, p. CXXX.

J. ALLAN[1] thinks that these are not personal names, as they are without any normal genitive suffix. Against this, it may be pointed out, that even the Nāga coinage, to which some of the Mālava coins are closely related, has no use of a genitive sign[2]. Hence these legends on the Mālava coins seem to be the personal names of the Mālavas, and they probably lived in the third or fourth century A.D.

Some of the classical writers furnish interesting details about their physiognomy. One of them says that they were of great stature and were amongst the tallest men in Asia. Their complexion was black, and they were very simple in their habits.[3] The *Vishṇudharmottaram*,[4] describing a Mālavya of 104 *aṅgulas* in measure, observes that he is dark like the *mudga* pulse, with a very beautiful body, with a slender waist and arms reaching to the knees. From the account of both these sources regarding their complexion, it may be inferred that they were not Aryans. But from the legends of the coins which belong to the third or fourth century A. D., and the accounts of the classical writers and the literary sources, no conclusion can be drawn regarding their origin. We do not find such names of the Mālavas in the Nāndsā inscription.

The earliest evidence of the exisence of the Mālavas in the fourth century B. C. in the Punjab is found in the works of Greek classical writers who mention them as Malloi. It seems that like many other tribes of ancient India, the Mālavas had their original home in the Punjab; from there they spread in different directions and formed settlements.

MOVEMENTS AND SETTLEMENTS OF THE MĀLAVAS:—

The Mālavas were numerous in Ancient India. It seems that they had separate settlements in the Punjab, Rajasthan, Malwa, etc. As early as the time of the *Mahābhārata*, a two-or-three-fold classification of the Mālavas was known, viz. the

1. A Catalogue of the Indian Coins in the British Museum, p. CVII.
2. CCIM, pp. 162, 164; JRAS, 1897, p. 643; H.V. TRIVEDI : Catalogue of the Coins of the Nāga kings of Padmāvatī.
3. McCRINDLE : Invasion of Alexander, p. 85.
4. III.85; KRAMRISCH'S Translation, p. 32.

Mālavas of the East, North and West.[1] According to E. J. THOMAS[2], the Mālavas of the Jaina *Bhagavatīsūtra* could not have been in the Punjab, and must have been located in Central India. From later literary sources, it is known that the Mālavas were ruling over Malwa in the first century B.C. From epigraphical and numismatic sources, it seems that the Mālavas continued to flourish in south-east Rajasthan from the second century B. C. to the fourth century A. D. D.R. BHANDARKAR[3] and other scholars believe that there were three main stages in the movement and settlement of the Mālavas. First, they were in the Punjab; in the second stage, they were in the south-east Rajasthan, and in the third, they moved southwards and settled in the north-western part of Madhya Pradesh, known as Malwa.

MĀLAVAS IN THE PUNJAB :—

We know about the Mālavas of the Punjab from the classical writers, early Sanskrit Grammarians and the epics. The Greek writers, who wrote on Alexander's Indian campaign, mentioned the Malloi together with Oxydrakoi. These may be identified with the Mālavas and the Kshudrakas respectively. Both formed a confederation which heroically opposed Alexander. According to Arrian,[4] they were the most numerous and warlike of the Indian peoples in those regions of the country. Arrian[5] calls the Malloi a race of independent Indians. Alexander very narrowly escaped in his war with the Mālava-Kshudraka confederacy. The confederate army consisted of 90,000 foot-soldiers, 10,000 cavalry and 900 war chariots. The Macedonians lost heart at the prospect of meeting this army. However, they were defeated, but they survived and sent a hundred ambassadors to Alexander.

There is a difference of opinion among scholars about the

1. Mbh, 106-7.
2. History of Buddhist Thought, p. 6.
3. Carmichael Lectures, pp. 12-13.
4. VI, 4.
5. VI, 6.

location of the Mālavas in the Punjab. V. A. SMITH[1] believes that the Malloi occupied the country below the confluence of the Hydaspes (Jhelum) and Akesines (Chenab), i.e. the country comprising the Jhang District, and the whole, or greater portion, of the Montgomery District. But McCRINDLE[2] thinks that the territory of the Mālavas was of great extent, comprising a part of the modern Doab formed by the Akesines and the Hydraotes, and extending, according to Arrian, to the confluence of the Akesines and the Indus. That is, the modern Multan District with parts of the Montgomery District. H. C. RAY-CHAUDHURI[3] places them in the valley of the lower Hydraotes 'north of the confluence of the river and the Chinab.' Their capital was on Ravi, which is identified by A. CUNNINGHAM[4], with Multan.

Early Sanskrit Grammarians also refer to the Mālava people. Pāṇini,[5] while illustrating the '*Āyudha-jīvī-Saṁgha*' (the republican people living on the profession of arms), showed the Mālava Kshudrakas. The Kāśikā[6] commentary on the *Ashṭādhyāyī* of Pāṇini, clearly states that the Mālavas and the Kshudrakas were most prominent among the *Āyudhajīvī Saṁgha.* While commenting on one of the *sūtras* of Pāṇini, Patañjali[7] refers to the Kshudrakas and the Mālavas together, in the instance of the Kshatriya Janapadas.

In the *Mahābhārata*, in one place, they are mentioned with Trigartas,[8] and in another place, they are referred to with the Śibis and the Ambashthas[9]. From the *Mahābhārata*, it is known that the Mālavas were related to the *Madras* who occupied the territories round about Sialkot. From the context, it appears that the Mālavas were surrounded by the Trigartas and *Madras* in the north-east Punjab, and the Ambashṭhas and the Śibis in

1. JRAS, 1903, p. 631.
2. Invasion of India, App. Note, pp. 351.
3. PHAI, p. 205.
4. Ancient Geography of India.
5. V, 3.144.
6. V, 3.117.
7. VI, 1.68.
8. *Droṇaparva*, (10-17).
9. *Sabhāparva*, 32-7.

the north of Sind. They occupied a great part of the Southern Punjab, including the districts of Firozpur and Ludhiana, and the former states of Jind, Patiala, Nabha, and Maler Kotla which is still called Malwa.[1] During the Mahābhārata war, they fought on the side of the Kauravas.

MĀLAVAS OF RAJASTHAN:—Because of the Indo-Greek invasions, the Mālavas, or at least a large section of the tribe, like other tribes under the pressure, migrated to Rajasthan and other parts of India, and this migration seems to have continued down to the Scythian conquest of India. The occupation of the south-east Rajasthan by the Mālavas from the second century B.C. to the fourth century A.D. is known from both the numismatic and epigraphical evidences. In south-east Rajasthan, the capital of the Mālava republic was Mālavanagara,[2] which has been identified with the modern Nagar.

More than 6,000 Mālava coins were discovered at Nagar. There is a controversy among scholars about the dates and the legends. A. C. CARLLEYLE[3] and A. CUNNINGHAM[4] assigned the Mālava coins to the period between 250 B.C. and 250 A.D., or 350 A. D. at the latest. But to V. A. SMITH[5] and E. J. RAPSON[6] the initial date is not earlier than 150 B. C., and these coins continued up to the fourth and fifth centuries A. D. RAJ BALI PANDEY[7] thinks that these coins were issued by Vikramāditya in order to commemorate his victories against the Śakas in the first century B. C. J. ALLAN[8] seems to be right in assigning these coins to the period between the second century A.D., and the earlier part of the fourth century. These Mālava coins may be divided into three groups. The first group

1. The Imperial Gazetteer, XVII, p. 105.
2. An inscription dated V. S. 1043 (986 A. D.) recently discovered at Nagar calls the place Mālava-nagara and describes its prosperity. (Bhārata Kaumudī I, pp. 271-72; EI, XXXIV, p. 77).
3. ASC, VI, p. 178.
4. Ibid, p. 182.
5. CCIM, p 162.
6. Indian Coins, p. 15.
7. Vikramāditya of Ujjainī, p. 39.
8. A Catalogue of the Indian Coins in the British Museum, p. C VI.

bears the legends, '*Mālavānāṁ Jayaḥ*' or '*Mālava Gaṇasya Jayaḥ*'. The coins have the vase, lion, bull, king's head, fan-tail-peacock and other objects, as their reverse design. The two other groups of coins are ascribed to the Mālavas primarily because they were found along with the Mālava coins, and resembled the latter in fabric. The coins of the second group do not bear any legend, while those of the third category have meaningless legends in which the name of the Mālavas cannot usually be traced.

V. A. SMITH[1] regarded these coins as the most curious and enigmatical in the vast range of Indian coinage. This is partly due to the meaningless legends on the third class of the coins, and partly also to the light weight and small size of many coins. V. A. SMITH suggested that these peculiar legends on the latter group are the names of certain foreign rulers who issued them. J. ALLAN[2] thinks that they are not names but, in most cases, meaningless attempts to reproduce parts of '*Mālavānāṁ Jayaḥ*'. D. C. SIRCAR[3] does not regard these coins as the genuine monetary issues of the Mālavas but they were minted by the local goldsmiths in imitation of the Mālava coins in order to meet the needs of the people. KALYAN KUMAR DAS GUPTA[4] is of the view that these coins were of the Mālava chiefs who belonged to non-Aryan stock.

In Rajasthan and Malwa, the Mālavas were gradually divided into sections and groups known as Sogin, Maukhari, Gardabhilla, etc. ruling over different areas. They carried on a constant and tireless struggle against the śakas. They also brought about the revival of the Vedic religion by performing different kinds of sacrifices.

In the beginning of the second century A.D., these Mālavas are known to have fought with their neighbours, the Uttamabhadras of the Ajmer region, as well as the latter's allies of the Kshaharāta Śakas of Western India. From the Nasik in-

1. CCIM, p. 162.
2. A Catalogue of the Indian Coins in the British Museum, p. CVII.
3. JNSI, XXIV, pp. 3-4.
4. The Mālavas, p. 19.

scription of Ushavadāta[1], it appears that Ushavadāta, the son-in-law of Nahapāna, inflicted a crushing defeat upon the Mālavas. But the Mālavas soon recovered their position. From the Nāndsā inscription, it is known that a Mālava leader of the Sogin clan, whose name has been read as 'Śrīsoma' by A. S. ALTEKAR,[2] and as 'Nandisoma' by M. VENKATARAMAYYA,[3] raised the standard of revolt and celebrated in 225 A.D. the *Ekashashṭirātra* sacrifice to proclaim the independence of his republic. Curiously, this record does not mention the names of the enemies defeated, but it is possible they may have been the Western Kshatrapas. This ruler was the son of Jayasoma, grandson of Bhriguvardhana, and great-grandson of Jayatsena. An undated record of Nāndsā mentions Mahāsenāpati Bhaṭṭisoma. In the Nāndsā inscription, there is mention of '*Mālavagaṇa vishaya*', which, according to A. S. ALTEKAR, extended over a considerable portion of south-eastern Rajasthan, comprising parts of the states of Udaipur, Jaipur, Tonk and Ajmer. A fragmentary record[4] dated K. E. 284 (227 A.D.) from Barnal, mentions a ruler whose name ended in the word 'Vardhana.' It is possible that he also belonged to some clan of the Mālavas.

It seems that the Maukharis of Badwa in the Kota District were a branch of the Mālavas. From the Badwa stone pillar inscription[5], it is known that the Maukharis performed a *trirātra* sacrifice in 239 A.D. The Allahabad pillar inscription[6] also speaks of the Mālavas, together with the tribes Ārjunāyanas and Yaudheyas. The question is where the Mālavas were located at this time. The coin legends are similar to those of the Yaudheyas and the Ārjunāyanas. The places of their inscriptions, at Nāndsā, Badwa and Barnal, and their coins, indicate that they were living in south-east Rajasthan.

MĀLAVAS IN AVANTI :—

That the Gardabhillas were a branch of a wider community

1. EI, VIII, p. 78.
2. Ibid, XXVI, p. 265.
3. IHQ, XXIX, p. 80.
4. EI, XXVI, pp. 118 ff.
5. Ibid, XXIII, p. 52.
6. CII, III, pp. 6 ff.

of the Mālavas is known from a Jaina work, the *Vichāraśreṇi* of Merutuṅgāchārya of the fourteenth century. It is said that they ruled over Ujjain for 135 years. They were dislodged from Avanti by the invasion of the Śakas, but their leader, Vikramāditya, inflicted a crushing defeat on them in 57 B. C. In order to commemorate his victory, he decided to inaugurate a new era.

From the beginning of the fifth century A.D., the Mālavas seem to have settled round about Mandsor. The Mandsor stone inscription[1] of 436 A. D. is, perhaps, the first inscription in Malwa proper dated in the Mālava *Saṁvat* 493. This Mālva era commenced in 58-57 B.C. and was traditionally recorded by the Mālavagaṇa. The Aulikaras, who began to rule, with a capital at Daśapura, from about the close of the fourth century A.D., were probably a clan of the Mālavas.

These Aulikaras seem to be responsible for the name Mālava being applied to the territory from about the fifth century A.D. From the Bālāghāt plates[2] of Pṛithvīsena II, it is known that the Vākāṭaka king Narendrasena, established his suzerainty over the lords of Kośala, Mekala and Mālava. Here, Mālava, together with Kośala, and Mekala, has been used in the sense of territory probably round about Mandsor. The contemporary ruler of Mālava at that time seems to be the Aulikara ruler, who had his capital at Daśapura.

In early times, the Mālava and the Avanti were different territorial names, as known from literary sources, but in later times, the territory of Avanti seems to have been designated the name of the Mālava. The earlier works, such as the *Kāmasūtra*[3] of Vātsyāyana, refer to Avanti and Mālava separately. Bharata in his *Nāṭyaśāstra*,[4] which belongs to about the same period as the *Kāmasūtra*, characterises the people of Avanti, Saurāshṭra and Mālava as having the same style.

1. CII, III, p. 83.
2. EI, IX, pp. 267 ff.
3. VKS, p. 370.
4. XIII, 29.

For the first time in the fifth century A.D., the Mālavas, in the territorial sense, denoted Western Malwa where the Aulikaras, a branch of the Mālavas, ruled, and where the Mālava era was current. The Eastern Mālava was under the possession of the Guptas who introduced Gupta era there.

MĀLAVA KINGDOM IN THE SEVENTH CENTURY A.D.:—

It seems that from the seventh century A.D., the name Mālava territory denoted a wide region, consisting of some part of north-eastern Gujarat, the old territory of Avanti (district round Ujjayinī), and Ākara or Daśārṇa (district round Vidiśā). In the Sanchi inscription of the seventh century A.D., '*Mahāmālava*' has also been mentioned in a territorial sense meaning a big unit of Malwa.[1]

When Prabhākaravardhana is called an axe to the Mālava glory[2], Kumāragupta and Mādhavagupta are called the sons of the Mālava king,[3] the murderer of Grahavarman is called the wicked Lord of Mālava[4], and Rājyavardhana resolves to uproot the Mālavas;[5] in all these different cases, Bāṇa must always have meant it in the sense of some geographical or political entity. Even in his *Kādambarī*, there is a reference to both Avanti and Mālava. In the commentary of the *Kāmasūtra* of Vātsyāyana, we are told that Ujjayinī denoted Western Malwa and where Mālava only is mentioned, it should be taken to mean Eastern Malwa.[6] Relying on these sources, scholars generally believe that in the seventh century A.D., Malwa was comprised of Eastern Malwa. R. S. TRIPATHI[7] observes, "It may not be unreasonable to suggest that Mahāsenagupta, son of Dāmodaragupta, retired to some part of Malwa which was probably Eastern Malwa corresponding to the Bhilsa District on the Vetra-

1. The Monuments of Sanchi, I, pp. 394-95.
2. HC, (CT.), p. 101; HC, Text (Parab), p. 120.
3. Ibid, p. 119; Text (ibid), p. 138.
4. Ibid, p. 173; Ibid (Parab), p. 182.
5. (Text Parab), p. 183.
6. Adhikaraṇa III.
7. History of Kanauj, p. 46.

vatī. H. C. RAYACHAUDHURI[1] remarks that Mahāsenagupta was probably the king of Malwa (Mālava) possibly Eastern Malwa. According to B. C. LAW[2], it is difficult to identify the Mālava kingdom of Māhāsenagupta and Devagupta, but it is probably identical with *Pūrva-Mālava*, that lay between Prayāga and Bhilsa.

D. C. SIRCAR[3] also holds that the application of the name Mālava to Avanti or the Ujjayinī region, does not seem to have been popular before the Paramāra occupation of that area in the latter half of the tenth century A.D. This does not seem to be correct. There are proofs that even in the seventh century A.D., Avanti, with Ujjayinī, was called Mālava. In the *Kādambarī*[4], Bāṇa mentions Ujjain on the Śiprā river, and he also refers to the women of Malwa (Mālavī) associated with Ujjain in such a way, that there is hardly any doubt that the women of Ujjain were known as Mālavīs or women of Mālava in his time. This makes it clear that Mālava of Bāṇa included Ujjain. Bāṇa mentions the beautiful women of Mālava (Mālavī) in the *Harshacharita*, when Harsha inspects the spoils of victory won by his brother from the king of Mālava.[5] We have already seen that Mālavī (or women of Mālava) are associated with Ujjain, and therefore, it is reasonable to hold that Mālavīs of *Harshacharita* also must have included the women of Ujjain. In the Aihol inscription,[6] the Lāṭas, Mālavas and Gurjaras, have been described as feudatories of Pulakeśin II. The name Avanti continued for the Ujjayinī region even when the name Mālava became popular. We cannot conclude from these names that they were separate regions.

MO-LĀ-P'O OF YUANCHWANG :—The Chinese pilgrim Yuan Chwang[7] mentions 'Mo-lā-p'o' country, which was situated near the river Mahi (Chinese Moha) in Gujarat and comprised Kheṭa (modern Kaira) and Ānandapura (modern Vaḍnagar).

1. PHAI, p. 512.
2. Ancient Indian Tribes II, p. 41.
3. Ancient Malwa and the Vikramāditya Tradition, p. 12.
4. Tr. RIDDING, pp. 47 and 59.
5. HC. Text, p. 227.
6. EI, VI, pp. 1 ff.
7. The Life, p. 150; The Records (ii), p. 271; WATTERS (ll), p. 231.

This territory was ruled by Śilāditya of the Maitraka dynasty of Valabhi. He distinguishes it from the country '*Wu-she-yanna*' (Ujjain). He seems to have been confused in taking the provincial seat as a separate principality. At this time, *Molāp'o*, with Ujjain, was governed by the ruler of Maitraka dynasty.

The '*Mo-lā-p'o*' of Yuan Chwang may be identified with Mālavaka *Vishaya* or *Bhukti* mentioned in the two inscriptions[1] of Dhruvasena II, dated 320 and 322 (639-40, 640-641 A.D.). These grants prove that there was a Mālavaka province of the Valabhi kingdom. The first inscription records that the king made a grant on the eastern boundary of Navagrāmaka, in the *Bhukti* of Mālavaka, whereas the second inscription refers to his grant of land on the southern boundary of Chandraputraka in the *Bhukti* of Mālavaka. Navagrāmaka mentioned in the copper plate grant, has been identified with Nogawa in the Ratlam District. Nogawa is actually situated on the Malwa Plateau. This Mālavaka province of Valabhi might have extended so far as Ujjain, which is only 58 km from Nogawa. It is suggested that a branch of the Mālavas might have settled in north and eastern Gujarat, where Yuan Chwang found them, and he therefore called the country 'Mo-lā-p'o'. It is also possible that the Valabhi kingdom had a province which included a portion of Mālava, and hence it was called 'Mālavaka.'

In the post-Gupta period, the Mālavas seem to have gone eastward also. Some copper-plates of Pāla kings refer to the *Kulikas* or cultivators, as consisting not only of the Khasas and Hūṇas, but also of the Mālavas.[2] Their expansion is attested by a late inscription[3] which states that *Daṇḍanāyaka* Anantapāla, a feudatory of Chālukya Vikramāditya VI, subdued the *Sapta-Mālava* countries up to the Himalayas[4], marking the last known state in the movement of the tribe.

CONTRIBUTIONS :—The contributions of the Mālavas to Indian culture are remarkable. Originally, they were *Āyudhajīvī Saṁgha*. They were essentially an army, because they all

1. EI, VII, pp. 188 ff.
2. ABORI, XIII.
3. EI, V, p. 229.
4. For these seven Mālava countries, see PHAI, p. 582, f. n. 5.

adopted the profession of war. They provided heroic resistance against Alexander the Great, and afterwards, they continued their fight against the Śakas and the Kushāṇas for the protection of the freedom of the country. They established strong republican traditions. On their coins, we find the mention of Mālavagaṇa but not the names of their rulers. By the third century A D., they had gradually assumed a monarchical constitution, as we find hereditary rulers mentioned in the Nāndsā inscription. But they still maintained the republican traditions in that they did not assume the title of *Rājā* and *Mahārāja*, but of *Senāpati*. This shows that their State was still primarily a military one.

This Mālava republic revived the Vedic religion by erecting *yūpas* (sacrificial pillars) and performing different sacrifices. From 58 B.C., a new era was recorded which was first known as Kṛita, then Mālava and afterwards Vikrama *Saṁvat*. It has been mentioned in one inscription[1] that it has been traditionally handed down by the Mālava republic.

IMPORTANCE OF MĀLAVA TRIBE

The importance of the Mālava tribe is emphasised by the fact that it has been mentioned in the *Vishṇudharmottaram*[2] and the *Bṛihatsaṁhitā*[3]. These works divide the peoples into five main groupings—Haṁsa, Bhadra, Mālavya, Ruchaka and Śaśaka for purposes of their representation in art and furnish details about the physical peculiarities of each of these types. The territorial units, castes and dialects, were named after the Mālavas. Even today, a large part of the Southern Punjab, comprising the districts of Firozpur and Ludhiana, and the old states of Jind, Patiala, Nabha and Malerkotla, is known as Malwa. The dialect used in the region extending from Firozpur to Bhatinda is known as Malawai. The territory connected with the plateau in Madhya Pradesh has been called Mālava since the seventh century A.D. The name Mālava has also survived in a Brāhmaṇa community, known as Mālavīs.

It seems that from the seventh century A.D., the Mālavas

1. CII, III, pp. 81 ff.
2. III, 85, KRAMRISCH's Translation, p. 32.
3. Chapter C VIII, KERN's Translation, JRAS, 1875, pp. 93-97.

settled in one particular region which became known as Malwa. Both historically and traditionally, Malwa comprises the whole of Western Madhya Pradesh, the Vindhyas in the south, Sagar—Damoh Plateau and Bundelkhand in the east, Guna-Shivpuri region and Rajasthan in the north; and Gujarat and Aravallis in the west. The limits are 21° 50′ N and 24° 30′N, and 74° 30′E–87°′81′E, covering an area of about 47, 760 square km. At present, this region includes eleven western Districts of Madhya Pradesh—Indore, Ujjain, Dewas, Dhar, Mandsor, Ratlam, Rajgarh, Shajapur, Sehore, Vidisha and Raisen. These limits are correct since all the ancient Kingdoms of Malwa—Kuntel (Mandsor), Bagar (Ratlam), Rath (Dhar), Sondwara (Mahidpur), Unaiwara (Rajgarh) and Khichiwara (Raisen) are included within these boundaries.

CHAPTER II

THE GEOGRAPHICAL BACKGROUND

Malwa was one of the most important provinces of India in ancient times, and its influence on Indian culture has been profound. Physically, culturally and politically, we may call it the 'Heart of India'. It is the passageway from North India to the Deccan. 'Malwa' implies the plateau region which formed a political unit like 'Magadha', 'Kaliṅga' and 'Saurāshṭra'. In the sixth century B.C., it became famous under the name of Avanti but from the fifth century onwards it was largely called 'Mālava'. Malwa covers an area of about 47,760 square km and comprises of the districts of Dhar, Jhabua, Ratlam, Dewas, Indore, Ujjain, Mandsor, Sehore, Shajapur, Raisen and Vidisha[1].

Malwa is drained by three main rivers—the Chambal, Betwa and Narmada. To the west and north-west of this plateau are the Arāvalli hills, which is the oldest mountain system on the globe. To the south, it is bounded by the Vindhyas, which are known as mountains but are in fact a series of escarpments overlooking the rift valley of Narmada. South of the Vindhyas and roughly parallel with them, are the Satpura mountains. The Vindhya and Satpura together form the backbone of middle India. To the north-west of Malwa are the Bundi Hills. The Malwa plateau is buckled on the northern fringes, approaching the Ganga valley, with Bundelkhand on its east, and Hāḍauṭī (Rajasthan) on the west. In fact, the Bundeli, Haḍauṭī and Malwi cultures coalesce in Vidisha along the Betwa.

This region is largely covered by black soil, which is very fertile for the cultivation of cotton, wheat, sugarcane, ground-

1. S. D. MISRA : Natural Regions of the Indian Sub-Continent, Typescript, p. 108.

nuts, etc. This black soil was derived from old lava deposits. The area round this region is rich in forests.

This territory of the Malwa region may be divided into the following natural divisions : (1) The Central Malwa Plateau, (2) the North-East Plateau, (3) the North-West Plateau, and (4) the Narmada Valley.

THE CENTRAL MALWA PLATEAU :—

Malwa forms a great triangle based on the Vindhya hills. It is a plateau with a mean elevation of 496 *m* above sea level, interspersed with the Vindhya and Satpura ranges. It lies between 23° 30′ and 24° 30′ N, and 74° 30′ and 78° 10′ E. It is terminated on the south by the Great Vindhya range, on the east by the arm of this same range that strikes north from Bhopal to Chanderi (the Kulāchala *parvata* of the *Purāṇas)*, on the west by the branch which reaches from Amjhera to Chitor (in Rajasthan), and on the north by the Mukandwara range which strikes east from Chitor to Chanderi.[1] It consists of the districts of Rajgarh, Shajapur, Dewas, Indore, Ratlam and Dhar.

Physically, it may be described as high tableland, consisting of a gently undulating and inclined plain, which is open and highly cultivated, and which is varied by small conical and table crowned hills, and low ridges. It is watered by numerous rivers and small streams, and favoured with a rich and highly productive soil and a mild climate, conducive to both the health and happiness of men.[2]

Physically also, Malwa falls into two different divisions which might, indeed, form separate regions. (i) The Vindhya scarplands of the North, and (ii), the Great Deccan Lava Plateau in the South. There is a great contrast between the Vindhya and the Deccan Lava landscapes. The former is arid and more rugged and harder in appearance.[3]

The river system of Malwa is interesting. This region is watered by several rivers which are fed by numerous tributaries

1. Imperial Gazetteer of India, XVII, p. 98.
2. Report on the Province of Malwa and adjoining territories submitted to the Supreme Govt. of British India in 1822 by John Malcolm.
3. India and Pakistan, p. 576.

that intersect and irrigate the area in all directions. Among the principal rivers are the Chambal, the Kali Sind, Śiprā, Parbati, Betwa, Mahi and Narmada. The Chambal, Ken and Betwa rise within 32 km of the Narmada from the Vindhyan escarpments. The Chambal and its tributaries, Kali Sindh and Parbati, have formed a triangular alluvial basin at about 211-271m in Kota, above the narrow trough of the lower Chambal, the present site of Rana Pratap Sagar Barrage.[1]

Malwa's weather is generally mild, except during the latter part of the year when great and sudden changes often take place. The climate on the whole is pleasant and invigorating.

THE NORTH EAST PLATEAU :—

This is narrow outstretch of the great central plateau of Malwa which is made distinctive by the wooded ranges of the Vindhyas encircling it from the east, north and south. With the fertile plateau of Malwa proper easily accessible towards the west, and with its proximity to the fertile Gangetic plains of the east, the region about Vidiśā was always prosperous and flourishing, a fact which is amply reflected in the richness of its monuments.[2] In early times, this region was famous under the name of Daśārṇa.

THE NORTH-WEST PLATEAU :—

This comprises of Mandsor and part of the Ratlam District. It is adjacent to Mewar, the land of Rājpūts, which is full of hills and sandy tracts. It presents some physical features common to the adjoining region. This tract is hilly and rugged, which aids the development of characteristics required for military way of life, and also, affording facilities for the erection of edifices in stone. The Mālavas and the Aulikaras, who ruled over this region, were famous for their heroic deeds. Daśapura (Mandsor) was the famous city of this region.

THE NARMADA VALLEY:—

The low lying narrow valley of this great river is enclosed by the ranges of the Vindhyas and Satpura to the north and south respectively. The country is flat and fertile, and cultiva-

1. India and Pakistan, p. 576.
2. D. R. Patil : Cultural Heritage of Madhya Bharat, p. 5.

tion here is more widespread and flourishing. Along the Vindhya hills, the country becomes wilder, and teak forests predominate in this area. The climate, however, is not as mild as that of the plateau in the north. This region was known as Anūpa in ancient times. On the bank of Narmada the town of Māhishmatī (Maheshwar) once stood, which was one of the most ancient cities of India.

These physical features of Malwa have considerably influenced not only the political, but also the cultural history. They have affected the lives and habits of the people, influenced their character and make-up, and invested them with distinctive characteristics. At times, the natural beauty of this region inspired poets and writers, like Kālidāsa, to write literary works.

In the valleys of the rivers of Narmada, Chambal, Betwa and others, great centres of culture and civilization gradually developed. To begin with, stone age people settled in these valleys. Afterwards, the chalcolithic people made their homes near the banks of the rivers. Among the chalcolithic sites, Maheshwar and Navadatoli are very important. The river bank was convenient to them for making pottery, and for cultivation. In the course of time, the important towns of Ujjain, Maheshwar, Vidiśā, Mandsor, etc., sprang up on the banks of these rivers. Because of the beautiful scenery in the neighbourhood, and the cool breeze, these rivers created a sense of holiness in the minds of the people who, in consequence, used to worship them.

As the climate is good and the soil is fertile in Malwa, most of the people took to agriculture, and other peaceful pursuits such as cottage crafts. There were easy means of livelihood without a hard struggle. The fertile soil and rich resources afforded enough leisure and ease to the people for the development of intellectual pursuits and philosophical speculation, which led to the growth of literature and philosophy. This is one reason for the number of literary giants of this region, who enriched Indian culture by their works. Attracted by the easier way of life, settlers from different parts migrated to this region from time to time.

From the earliest times, this region remained in touch with

the different parts of the country by several routes. From the study of the Stone Age cultures and the Chalcolithic Age cultures, it is clear that there were constant movements of people which led to mutual cultural contacts. There were smooth and frequent communications. Three routes met in Avanti from the western coast, from Deccan and from Śrāvasti. Besides the land route, there was also a water route to the West (the Narmada river passing through Malwa joins the sea). In early times, goods landed at Broach (Bharukachchha of Ptolemy) could be conveniently transported to Malwa by river. These facilities of communication led to the development of commerce and trade. As a result, this region flourished from the earliest times. The general prosperity is evident from the large numbers of ancient monuments, which are excellent specimens of art and architecture, which have been found in this area.

The hills and valleys of Malwa have always been the habitat of the ancient primitive tribes, such as Pulindas, Śabaras, Kirātas, Ābhīras and Bhīlas. Some of these have remained isolated from the civilized world even today. Occasionally, these wild tribes became powerful and defied the central authority. The Pushyamitras mentioned in the Bhitari inscription of Skandagupta, seem to have belonged to the present Shahdol District.

The strategical importance of Malwa was ever significant. In order to control Western India and South India, its occupation was necessary. The Maurya and Gupta rulers conquered it and made it a base for further conquest in this direction. Malwa was always on the crossroads. It also afforded an excellent military base, and its occupation opened the doors for further territorial expansion. The Śaka-Sātavāhana struggle was fought because both the powers wanted to keep this region in their possession.

In the struggle between the Pratīhāras and the Rāshṭrakūṭas, Malwa's position was that of a buffer state which had to bear the brunt of the fighting. Besides, Malwa is very rich and fertile, with no natural protective boundaries. As a result, it was rarely free from foreign invasions. The wealth and power of the people, which could have been used for better purposes, was spent in meeting the dangers from neighbours. Even the powerful rulers like Muñja and Bhoja could not prevent its being attacked. With weaker rulers on the throne, Malwa was the arena where ambitious rulers fought out their battles for supremacy.

Thus, "historically Malwa displays a curious duality. The Deccan Lavas provide the only really extensive agricultural base in Central India, and so it has retained its individuality; yet as a land of passage, it has constantly changed hands. Its frontiers are least persistent in the North. This is, in part at least, inherent in the Geography of Malwa compared to that of its neighbouring regions. As it provides by far the best route from Northern India to the Deccan, it has been regarded as a prized possession by all political powers of Northern India and the Deccan"[1]

Such is the stage of Malwa upon which the drama of history was enacted, which this writer attempts to unfold as he proceeds.

1. India and Pakistan, p. 576.

Chapter III

SOURCES

Malwa has a glorious history, and its contributions to Indian culture are remarkable. Some personalities, such as Vikrama and Bhoja, gained wide fame in India. During the Maurya and Gupta periods, there was all-round progress. Sometimes all political and cultural activities centred around Malwa, and Malwa's history became that of India. Abundant material found scattered in Malwa throws a flood of light on its past history. This vast material may be broadly divided into three classes—(1) Archaeology (2) Literature and (3) Writings of foreigners. For the pre-historic period, we depend on the material obtained from archaeological explorations and excavations, which is limited; but for the subsequent periods of history, the source material gradually becomes richer and richer.

(1) ARCHAEOLOGY

Archaeology may be further sub-divided into (A) Explorations and Excavations, (B) Inscriptions, (C) Coins, and (D) Monuments.

(A) EXPLORATIONS AND EXCAVATIONS:—

In the course of the archaeological explorations conducted in the Narmada valley, potential pleistocene fossils and human artefacts were discovered. In the Chambal valley, Shivna valley, and others also, a large number of different palaeoliths were obtained. These different objects give information about the climatic changes, the environment and habits of the people during the Stone Age. Stone tools were used for digging trees, hunting, and skinning animals.

In the archaeological excavations carried out at some of the sites, such as Maheswar, Navdatoli, Nagda, Manoti, Awara, Eran and Kayatha, different antiquities such as the foundations of buildings, pottery objects, terracottas, some metal objects, grains, beads and ornaments, have been discovered which throw an important light on the material life of the people during the Chalcolithic period. No written record of this period has been discovered as yet.

Trial excavations attempted at the historical sites such as Vidiśā, Ujjain, Mandsor and Pawaya, resulted in the discovery of coins, terracottas, sculptures, pottery and other objects which throw a flood of new light on ancient history.

(*B*) *INSCRIPTIONS*:—

A large number of inscriptions have been found in Malwa, and some of them are very important. They are engraved on rocks, pillars, walls, copper plates, images, etc. These may broadly be classified under two groups—(1) those engraved by or on behalf of the ruling authority, and (2) those incised on behalf of private individuals. The second category is found in large number. Generally, they record donations made in favour of religious establishments, or the installation of images for worship. Sometimes the description is panegyric, and so has to be critically examined before it can be of use.

For the reconstruction of political history, these inscriptions are of great importance. They mention the name of the ruler and his dynasty. Sometimes they give the genealogy of the ruling dynasty. They describe the career and the achievements of the rulers. Indirectly, they help us in the location of the kingdom of the ruler, and in determining the extent of his empire. They give a correct picture of the territorial divisions and the official hierarchy of the different administrations. They inform us about the interstate relations, as also the relations between the suzerain and his feudatories.

The earliest known inscription in Malwa is Aśoka's Sanchi Pillar Edict[1], which proves that Malwa formed a part of the dominions of the Mauryas. From the Besanagar inscription[2],

1. The Monuments of Sanchi, p. 283.
2. Sel. Ins., p. 78.

it is known that Heliodorus was deputed as ambassador by the Greek king Antialcidas, to the Indian king named Bhāgabhadra Kāśīputra of Vidiśā in the 14th regnal year. The Sātavāhana occupation of Malwa may be proved by a votive inscription[1] found on the southern gateway of the great *stūpa* at Sanchi, which records a gift of Vāsishṭhiputra Ānanda, the foreman of the artisans of king Sātakarṇi.

The Eran inscription[2] of Samudragupta proves that Eastern Malwa became a part of his empire. The Udayagiri hill inscription[3] of Chandragupta II's minister Vīrasena, his feudatory chief Sanakānīka Mahārāja[4], and the Sanchi inscription[5] of Āmrakārdava, may indicate his campaign against the Western Kshatrapas, and the occupation of Eastern Malwa. The Mandsor inscription[6] dated M. E. 524 (467-68 A. D.) of Prabhākara, and the Tumain inscription[7] dated 116 G. E. (435 A. D.) inform us that Eastern Malwa was governed by the royal princes, named respectively, Govindagupta and Ghaṭotkachagupta. The Mandsor inscription[8] of M.E. 461 (415 A.D.), the Bihār Koṭrā inscription[9] of M. E. 474 (417-18 A. D.), the Gaṅgdhāra inscription[10] of M. E. 480 (423-24 A. D.), and the Mandsor inscription[11] of M. E. 529 (472 A. D.) give us information of the early Aulikara rulers of Mandsor who ruled over Western Malwa. From the Eran inscription[12] dated G. E. 165 (484-485 A. D.), it is known that sovereignty of Budhagupta was recognized in Eastern Malwa. The Hūṇa occupation of Eastern Malwa is proved from the dated Eran inscription[13] belonging to the first year of Toramāṇa's reign, and the Gwa-

1. EI, II, No. 190.
2. CII, III, p. 18.
3. Ibid, pp. 31 f.
4. Ibid, p. 25.
5. Ibid, pp. 29-34.
6. EI, XXVII, pp. 12-18.
7. Ibid, XXVI, p. 117.
8. Ibid, XII, pp. 320 ff.
9. Ibid, XXXVI, pp. 130 ff.
10. CII, III, p. 74 ff.
11. Ibid, pp. 81 ff.
12. Ibid, p. 88.
13. Ibid, pp. 159 ff.

lior inscription[1] of the fifteenth year of Mihirakula's reign.

Two inscriptions of Yaśodharman, one dated M. E. 589 (532 A.D.)[2], and the other undated[3], furnish information about the military achievements of Yaśodharman. From the Mandsor inscription,[4] and the Chhoṭīsādrī inscription[5] dated M.E. 547 of Gauri, we know that the Māṇavāyaṇīs were ruling as feudatories of the Aulikaras. The Indragarh stone inscription[6] dated V.S. 767 of Ṇaṇṇapa, mentions a new Rāshṭrakūṭa dynasty ruling over the territory round about Indragarh in this early period. The Mahua inscription[7] of about the eighth century A.D., gives a genealogy of the rulers of the dynasty of Vatsarāja.

The copper plate grants issued by Sīyaka[8] II, Vākpati[9] II, Bhoja[10], Jayasiṁha[11], Naravarman[12] and others, record donations of land. The inscriptions on them are important as they mention the territorial divisions and different categories of officers. The Udayapura *praśasti*[13] engraved on a slab of stone of the Nīlakaṇṭheśvara temple, is extremely important and interesting, inasmuch as it furnishes us with much information of great significance for the reconstruction of the early history

1. CII, III, pp. 162 ff.
2. CII, III, pp. 152 ff.
3. Ibid, pp. 146 f.
4. EI, XXX, pp. 127 ff.
5. Ibid, p. 120.
6. EI, XXXII, p. 112; IHQ, XXXI, p. 99.
7. Ibid, XXXVII, No. 11, p. 164.
8. The Harsola grant V. S. 1005 (EI, XIX, p. 236); An Odd copper plate (EI, IX, p. 1. ff.).
9. Gandhwani copper plate, of V. S. 1031 issued from Ujjain (IA, VI, pp. 51-53);
10. Banswārā (EI, XI, pp. 181 ff) and Betmā (EI, XVIII, pp. 320) plates of V. S. 1076 (1020 A.D.) as well as of his Ujjain plates (IA, VI, p. 53 f.) of V.S. 1078 (1021-22 A.D.); Depalpur plates (IHQ, VIII, pp. 305 ff) of V.S.1079 (1023 A.D.); Tilakwada plate, (POC, 1919. p. 319) V.S.1103 (1047 A.D.); Mahudī plates (EI, XXXIII). V. S. 1074 (1018 A.D.), and Moḍāsā plate (EI, XXXIII, p. 192) V. S. 1067 (1011 A.D.).
11. Māndhātā plates (EI, III, p. 46) of V.S. 1112 (1055 A.D.).
12. The Kadambapadraka Grant (EI, XX, p. 105) of V. S. 1167 (1110 A.D.).
13. EI, I, p. 233.

of the Paramāras of Malwa. It is the only available record which supplies a complete genealogy of this family of rulers from Upendra to Bhoja. It is undated and seems to have been issued during the early part of Udayāditya's reign. From a stone inscription[1] of V.S. 1143 (1086 A.D.) found at Jhālrāpāṭan, it may be inferred that this locality was under a sway of Udayāditya. The Nagpur stone inscription[2] of V.S. 1161 (1064 A.D.) is the main evidence which throws light upon the career and the military excursions of Lakshmadeva. The Ingoda inscription[3] dated V. S. 1190 (1133 A.D.) of Vijayapāladeva, shows the disintegration of the Paramāra kingdom from the latter part of the reign of Naravarman. A stone inscription[4] of the Chālukya ruler Jayasiṁha dated V. S. 1138, found at Ujjain, shows that the king, having defeated Yaśovarman, was holding *Avanti-maṇḍala* by force, and that Mahādeva was administering it on his behalf. The copper plate grant inscriptions of Yaśovarmadeva,[5] Jayavarmadeva,[6] Lakshmīvarmadeva[7], Hariśchandradeva,[8] Udayavarmadeva[9] and Devapāla[10] help in building the history of Mahākumāra families.

In addition to political history, these epigraphical records have also proved to be of great value in tracing religious, social and economic history. Several inscriptions record donations, charities, the installation of images, and the construction of temples. From the votive inscriptions[11] found at Sanchi, it seems that Buddhism gained a footing among the common masses of Malwa. The monks and nuns, officers, laymen and laywomen, and the corporate bodies, made donations to the *stūpas*. As these inscriptions constitute the chief means of fixing the dates of the images and temples, they are of incalculable help

1. JASB, 1914, p. 241.
2. EI, II, p. 182.
3. IA, VI, p. 55.
4. Ibid, XLII, p. 258.
5. Ibid, XIX, p. 348.
6. Ibid, p. 349.
7. Ibid, p. 351.
8. JASB, VII, p. 736.
9. IA, XVI, p. 252.
10. EI, IX, p. 108.
11. The Monuments of Sanchi.

in tracing the evolution of art and religion. The Besanagar pillar inscription[1] shows that even the foreigner Heliodorus, became a follower of Vaishṇavism, and erected a *Garuḍa*-staff of Vāsu-deva. A revival of Vedic religion is proved by the Nāndsā inscription[2] dated K.E. 282 (225 A.D.), and the Baḍvā inscription[3] dated K. E. 295 (239 A.D.). The earliest substantial evidence for the existence of Jainism is proved by the Udaya-giri cave inscription[4] of 425-26 A.D., which records the installation of an image of the Tīrthaṅkara Pārśvanātha by Śaṅkara. From the inscription[5] of Jaina images found at Vidiśā, it is clear that they were made by Rāmagupta. From the Mandsor inscription[6], it is known that the guild of silk weavers built the temple of the Sun in M. E. 493 (437-38 A. D.), and restored it in M.E. 529 (473-74 A.D.). The inscription of V. S. 935 (878 A.D.) at Bhilsa[7], is the earliest among the known inscriptions mentioning the temple of Bhāillasvāmin. A Gwalior Museum stone inscription[8] of Paṭaṅgaśambhu, probably brought from Raṇod, and another stone inscription[9] of Raṇod, furnish us with information about the spiritual genealogy of the saints of the Mattamayūra sect of Śaivism, and also their seats at different places.

From the Eran inscription[10] of 510-11 A. D., we get the earliest epigraphical reference to the *Satī* system. This inscription records that Goparāja fought a mighty battle in which he was killed, and his wife cremated herself on his funeral pyre. Some inscriptions mention the castes and gotras of the people who had them engraved. Such information is valuable for social history. The Māndhātā plates of Devapāla[11] and

1. Sel. Ins., p. 78.
2. EI, XXVII, pp. 252 ff.
3. Ibid, XXIII, pp. 42-52.
4. CII, III, No. 61.
5. Journal of the Oriental Institute, Baroda, XVIII, p. 247.
6. CII, III, pp. 81 ff.
7. EI, XXX, No. 36, p. 210.
8. JMPIP, No. 4, p. 3.
9. EI, I, XLI, p. 351.
10. CII, III, pp. 92 f.
11. EI, IX, p. 103.

Jayasiṁha Jayavarman[1] mention the castes, *gotras* and *Pravaras* of the Brāhmaṇas to whom donations were made. From the copper plate grants, it is clear that the Paramāra rulers patronized learning by inviting Brāhmaṇas from different places, and granting lands to them.

From some of these inscriptions, we know how trade and industries were organized into guilds. The Mandsor inscription[2] of 437-38 A. D. and 473-74 A. D., informs us how the members of the silk weavers guild, seeing the better prospects of trade, migrated from Lāṭa to Daśapura. The Shergarh inscription[3] of 1017 A. D. mentions that Thāiyāka was the chief of the guild. Coins in current use are also sometimes mentioned in the inscriptions. The Sanchi inscription[4] of 412-13 A. D. records a grant of 24 *dīnāras* to the Buddhist *Saṁgha* there. In the Paramāra inscriptions[5], there is mention of *dramma*, *varāha*, *vṛishabha*, *rūpaka*, *ardharūpaka* and *viṁśopaka*.

Some of the epigraphic records were composed by poets of great ability and their compositions are of high order. Some of the authors of the epigraphic *kāvyas* are known only from the inscriptions, their other works being lost. Mention may be made in this connection of Vatsabhaṭṭi of the Mandsor inscription[6] of 473 A. D., Vāsula of the Mandsor inscription[7] (532 A. D.), of Yaśodharman and Chittapa of the Bhilsa inscription[8] (1050 A. D.). In some cases, an inscription may embody a *kāvya* or a drama. The *Pārijātamañjarī* of Madana and the *Kodaṇḍakāvya* of Bhoja, have been found engraved on slabs in the Bhojaśālā at Dhāra.

(*C*) *COINS* :—

Next to inscriptions, coins are the most important source of ancient history. Numerous ancient coins have been discovered

1. EI, XXXII, p. 140.
2. CII, III, pp. 81 ff.
3. EI, XXIII, p. 133.
4. CII, III, pp. 29-34.
5. EI, XIV, p. 310; JASB, VII, p. 738; EI, XXIV, p. 131; IA, XLII, p. 78.
6. CII, III, pp. 81 ff.
7. Ibid, pp. 152 ff.
8. EI, XXX, p. 215.

at different ancient sites in Malwa. From the study of their symbols, figures, legends, metal and weight, we may reconstruct not only the political, but also the religious and economic history of Malwa.

The earliest known coins are the punch-marked ones. These punch-marked coins, together with cast coins, have been discovered at Jhalrāpāṭan, Sarangpur, Ujjain, Eran and Maheshwar. This proves that these were old sites. From the study of their symbols, and the layers in which they were discovered in the excavations, it seems that most of them were issued during the Maurya period. Coins of Ujjayinī and Eran found in large quantity in Malwa, were issued by the mints of Ujjayinī and Eran respectively in the third or second century B. C., when this region was a Maurya province. Some towns, such as Ujjain, Eran, Māhishmatī and Vidiśā, started to issue inscribed coins of their own during this period. This proves the autonomous importance of these towns.

Coins are of much help for the reconstruction of the history of the Śakas, because we have only a few inscriptions and literary works giving reference. The Śakas issued coins which not only gave the name of the ruling king and that of his father, but very often the date in the well known Śaka era as well. This has enabled us to reconstruct the history of the Western Satraps for a period of more than three hundred years. In the Gondarman[1] and the Sarvāniā hoards,[2] the coins of Mahākshatrapa Svāmī Rudrasena III are the latest to be represented. It appears that there was a troublesome period in his reign. The counterstruck coins of Nahapāna issued by Gautmīputra Sātakarṇi, prove that he defeated him and occupied his kingdom. The occupation of some portion of Malwa by the Sātavāhanas is clear from the fact that they issued the peculiar local types of coins in this region. The Nāga coins found in large number at Pawaya and Kutwar are useful for the reconstruction of their history.

That Chandragupta II defeated the Śakas, is clear from the fact that he introduced coins in the imitation of those of

1. IAR, 1953-54, p. 63.
2. ASI, 1913-14, p. 227.

the Śakas in the region of Malwa. The Bamnāla hoard[1] of Gupta coins contains coins up to the time of Kumāragupta I, and together with them, a gold bar has been also found. It seems that the hoard was buried during the days of the rebellion of the tribe of the Puśyamitras. From the study of the coins of Jishṇu and Rāmagupta, it seems that they were local rulers.

These coins also throw light on the religious beliefs of the people. Some symbols such as the Sun, bull and elephant found on the punch-marked coins, may have some religious and mythological significance. Śiva, represented on some Ujjain coins, symbolically and anthropomorphically, was probably related to Mahākāla of Ujjain. From the symbols of bull, *triśūla* and peacock on the coins of the Nāga rulers, it seems that they were followers of Śaivism. On the coins of Jishṇu, we find the symbols of *chakra* (wheel) and *śaṅkha* (conch), which may prove his inclination towards Vaishṇavism. Some Gadhiyā coins with the legend *'Śrī Oṁkāra'* on them, appear to have referred to Oṁkāra Māndhātā on the Narmada, and were issued by the ruler in honour of the deity of which he was a follower.

The metal and weight of these coins is valuable from the economic point of view. The punch-marked coins found in Malwa are generally of copper; whereas in other regions, they are of silver. They follow the lighter standard of 42 grams of Kośala. The local currency issued from Ujjain and Eran was also of copper. The cross and balls known as Ujjayinī symbol, is perhaps applicable to Ujjain, indicating it as the junction of trade routes. Most of the coins of the Śakas and the Sātavāhanas found in Malwa are of copper and potin. The coins of Jishṇu and Rāmagupta are of copper and they are very small in size. The Nāga rulers issued their coins to the standard of *kākiṇī*, half *kākiṇī* and a quarter *kākiṇī*. The discovery of a large number of coins of different periods at Ujjain, Vidiśā and Eran, proves that they were centres of trade and commerce in early times.

(*D*) *MONUMENTS* :—

In addition to inscriptions and coins, we have discovered

1. JNSI, V, p. 136.

stūpas, monasteries, temples, sculptures, paintings, etc., of different periods. They are of great importance in tracing the history of evolution of Indian art. These artistic pieces furnish invaluable material on the racial types, on religious beliefs and superstitions, on arms and accoutrements, on dress and personal ornaments, on musical instruments, and on several other subjects.

The remains at Sanchi, and in the neighbourhood, from the third century B.C. to the twelfth century A.D., give us an idea of the evolution of art in a particular locality. The monuments and paintings of Bagh are important artistically. That Vaishṇavism had a great hold at Vidiśā is clear from the ancient monuments. From the archaeological remains at places such as Gyaraspur, Bhojapura, Badoh and Un, it is clear that Jainism and Brahmanism flourished side by side. The old monuments found at Un, Badoh, Gyaraspur, Udayapura, Dhar, Ujjain, etc., give us a glimpse of the main features of Paramāra art. The Śaiva temple known as Nīlakaṇṭheśvara or Udayeśvara at Udayapura, and the temple of Siddheśvara at Nemāwar, are important ancient monuments of India.

(2) LITERATURE

Another important source of the ancient history of Malwa is literature. Though we come across only isolated references to it in literary works, they contribute to our research knowledge. Literature may be further classified as follows :—

(A) EPICS AND PURĀṆAS :—

Only the *Purāṇas* and the epics mention the names of the very old dynasties and kings of Malwa, and the *Vedas* give little information of them. From the *Purāṇas*, we know that in the pre-historic period, the Nāgas and the Haihayas were ruling over this region. As they give mutually confusing and contradictory statements, they cannot be relied upon unless they are confirmed by some independent and contemporary evidence. They give information about Pradyota and his successors. From the *Purāṇas,* we know that the Nāga rulers flourished at Vidiśā, Padmāvatī and Kāntipura. The *Matsya-purāṇa, Narasiṁhapurāṇa, Śivapurāṇa* and *Skandapurāṇa* give description of some holy places like Ujjain. We may call '*Avantikhaṇḍa*' of the *Skandapurāṇa*, an ancient guide book of Ujjayinī. From the *Mahābhārata,* it is known that Ujjayinī became a great seat of learning.

(*B*) *MAHĀBHĀSHYA* :—

Patañjali, whose traditional birthplace was Gonarda[1] in Avanti, is the author of *Mahābhāshya,* a commentary on the *Ashṭhādhyāyī* of Pāṇini. His aim was to discuss grammatical problems, but incidentally he gives information of the social and cultural life prevalent in the second century B.C. He makes repeated references to the personality of Pushyamitra, to the invasion of the Yavanas who besieged Sāketa and Madhyamikā, and to the *yajñas* performed by the Śuṅga monarch.

(*C*) *PURE LITERARY WORKS* :—

There are several literary works written with the motive of displaying literary skill, but they also throw some light on history. The great authors Bhāsa, Vātsyāyana[2], Kālidāsa, Śūdraka, Varāhamihira and Bāṇa, seem to be associated with Ujjain in one way or another. Bhāsa, in some of his plays, speaks of Ujjayinī and gives graphic description of its palaces, mansions, temples, gardens, lakes, pleasures and comforts.

From the *Mālavikāgnimitra* of Kālidāsa, it is known that Pushyamitra deputed his son Agnimitra as his governor at Vidiśā. His son Agnimitra had to fight Yajñasena, the ruler

1. According to the *Sutta Nipāta,* Gonarda stood midway between Ujjain and Besanagar.
2. P. C. Bagchi holds the view that as Vātsyāyana appears to have been thoroughly acquainted with South-Western India, he most probably lived in Ujjain in the fourth century A.D. This town was a great centre of literary activity, and was connected with distant countries both overland and across the sea. This contributed largely to the opulence of the city, and its cosmopolitanism. This type of city must have attracted *nāgarakas* of the type described by Vātsyāyana. (See *Kāmasūtra,* the Hindu Art of Love, Trans. and Edit. by B. N. Basu).

of Vidarbha. This work also refers to the conflict between Vasumitra, son of Agnimitra, and the Yavanas in connection with horse sacrifice. Śūdraka's *Mṛichchhakaṭika*, one of the most interesting dramas in Sanskrit literature, gives a vital and realistic picture of Ujjain. The same is the case with the *Padmaprābhṛitakam* and the *Pādatāḍitakam* which were probably written at Ujjain. Varāhamihira, who belonged to Kapitha now identified with Kāyāthā near Ujjain, is the author of *Bṛihatsaṁhitā* which is a veritable mine of useful information on different subjects. Bāṇa in the *Harshacharita* refers to Prabhākaravardhana's war against the Mālava king.

Padmagupta's *Navasāhasāṅkacharita* is useful for the history of the Paramāras in general, and for the Paramāra king Sindhurāja in particular. Madana's *Pārijātamañjarī* represents in the form of a drama, the course of events leading to the union of his patron king Arjunavarman with the Gurjara princess Vijayaśrī. Dhanapāla's *Tilakamañjarī* sheds valuable light on the contemporary social and religious life of the people. Like the *Tilakamañjarī*, Bhoja's *Śṛiṅgāramañjarīkathā* is also important from the cultural point of view. His *Samarāṅgaṇa-sūtradhāra* is concerned with architecture, and the *Yuktikalpataru* gives us information about the flourishing state of industries.

Legends grew around the great personality of *Vikramāditya*, and a large number of literary works were written. The *Kālakāchārya-kathānaka* informs us not only about Vikramāditya, but also about the early advent of the Śakas into Western Malwa from Seistan via Sind and Kathiawad, in the second century B. C. Besides, the *Kathāsaritsāgara* written by Somadeva, *Siṁhāsanadvātriṁśikā*, *Vetālapañchaviṁśati* and *Śukasaptati*, describe the qualities of Vikramāditya. The Jainas have preserved the traditions of Vikramāditya in many literary works such as *Prabhāvakacharita*, *Jaina Harivaṁśa Purāṇa* and *Paṭṭāvalīs*. As these works are of a later period, written between the twelfth and fifteenth century A. D., they cannot be relied upon.

(D) MISCELLANEOUS WORKS

Besides the above, there are other literary works which

are helpful for the history of Malwa. The *Prabandhachintāmaṇi* is a collection of stories and fables which sometimes contain historical elements. It gives some information regarding the life of Muñja and Bhoja. The *Vividhatīrthakalpa* of Jinaprabhasūri is important both from the literary and historical point of view. It gives a brief history of the Jaina holy places of Malwa. A number of coin types current in Malwa are known from Ṭhakkura Pheru's work *Dravyaparīkshā*, written in V. S. 1375.

(3) *WRITINGS OF FOREIGNERS*

In addition to archaeology and literature, writings of foreigners sometimes give interesting information regarding the ancient history of Malwa. The unknown author of the *Periplus* of the Erythraean Sea, made a voyage to the Indian coast about 80 A. D., and left a record of its ports, harbours and merchandise. Ptolemy wrote a geographical account of India in the second century A. D. The Geography of Ptolemy mentions Ujjayinī as the capital of West Malwa of Trastenes, undoubtedly a Greek corruption of the name Chashṭana. Yuan Chwang describes the political condition and the state of Buddhism, in the kingdoms through which he passed. At the time of his visit, Buddhism was in a state of decline in Ujjain. He mentions only a few Buddhist *stūpas*, but several *deva* temples.

CHAPTER IV

STONE AGE CULTURES

The history of man began when he first appeared on the face of this earth. The geologists and the palaeontologists tell us that this incident took place about two million years ago[1]. After studying the glacial and inter-glacial deposits in India, and having correlated them with the human cultures, PATERSON and ZEUNER came to the provisional conclusion that the earliest man in the Sohan valley lived sometime towards the end of the II Glacial period, or about 435000 years ago[2]. In the opinion of H. D. SANKALIA, the Early Stone Age culture can be dated back about 150000 years[3].

Malwa is an important region for the study of Stone Age cultures. Like the Siwaliks, the Narmada valley yielded potential pleistocene fossils and human artefacts. In the Chambal valley and the Shivna valley also, a large number of different palaeoliths have been discovered. The Hand-Axe culture remained dominant in this area. From the remains of the Lower Palaeolithic, Middle Palaeolithic and Microlithic cultures, it is possible to form some idea of the evolution of the Stone Age cultures. Those of Malwa were related to those of other regions, but they also possessed their own individuality. About the origin of these cultures, nothing can be definitively stated.

1. The Chellena (Abbevillian) at Olduvai in East Africa can now be dated to about 1750000 years by the argon potassium method (LEAKEY, L. S. B. and CURTES, G. H., in National Geographic, October, 1961, p. 564); it is to be seen how this affects the dating of these industries elsewhere.
2. Studies on the Ice Age in India and Associated Human Cultures.
3. SPPIP, Introduction, XXII.

I

LOWER PALAEOLITHIC CULTURE

SOHANIAN CULTURE AND HAND-AXE CULTURE :—

The Lower Palaeolithic culture of India may be divided into two groups with distinct geographical features—(1) The Sohanian culture, or the Pebble culture, or the Chopper-Chopping culture, and (2) The Hand-Axe culture. The Sohanian culture seems to have originated in the Punjab and was generally confined within its boundary, whereas the Hand-Axe culture, though of equal antiquity, is centred in Peninsular India. In Malwa, the Hand-Axe-culture remained dominant, though traces of the Sohanian culture have been noticed at some places. Hand-axes and cleavers were the main components of the Malwian Lower Palaeolithic industry. It is an industry in which core and flake techniques are intimately associated with each other.

EXPLORATION OF NARMADA VALLEY BY DE TERRA AND PATERSON :—

From time to time, the Narmada valley has been explored at different sites. A palaeolithic tool was found at Bhutra in 1873 A. D., in association with fossil mammals[1]. Later, the Narmada basin between Hoshangabad and Narsinghpur was surveyed by De Tarra and Paterson[2] in 1935, and a correlation of the stratigraphy, the tools, and fossil evidence, was attempted. The stratigraphy as reconstructed by them is as follows:—

Black Soil Fine Gravel	Upper Pleistocene and Later Holocene	
Pink Silt Gravel	Upper Group	Middle Pleistocene
Pink Silt Gravel	Lower Group	Middle Pleistocene
Laterite		
Basal Rock		

1. Catalogue of Pre-historic Antiquities in the Indian Museum by J. Coggin Brown; Archaeological Survey of India, Simla, 1917, p. 2.
2. Studies on the Ice Age in India and Associated Human Cultures, pp. 313-26.

De Terra however, tentatively suggests that the Narmada Lower Group represents the true Acheulian and early Sohan, and the Upper Group the Late Sohan industry. But no clear stratigraphical picture, as postulated by De Terra, has been noticed by subsequent observers. Even the laterite was not noticed. No doubt, they discovered the tools and fossils in the gravels, but not in the pink silt. It is difficult to decide which is the 'Lower Group' of gravels, and which the 'Upper'.

STRATIGRAPHY AT MAHESHWAR :—

At Maheshwar, on the contrary, the stratigraphy is much clearer. Though no laterite exists, and though no bed has so far yielded any fossil, the superposition of the two groups is there. The lower gravel is very often eroded, but the second group resting on lower pinkish clay, is mainly well preserved. Between Sahasradhārā and Mandaleshwar, over 400 palaeolithic tools were collected.[1] Among them, there is a large number of flakes, cores, cleavers and a few handaxes. The number of cleavers is, on the whole, large, because it was more convenient to convert flakes into cleavers. These include several types. A few Levallois flakes of quartzite have been found in the second gravel.[2]

CLAIM OF THE DISCOVERY OF OLDOWAN CULTURE AT PIPARIA MAHADEO BY A.P. KHATRI NOT JUSTIFIED :—

In a gravel bed at Piparia, A. P. Khatri[3] found *in situ* over forty artefacts in the block-on-block technique, representing the earliest phase of the Chellean, and illustrating the evolution of the handaxe from the pebble to the earliest Abbevillian stages. They belonged to the pebble industry stage. In the opinion of A. P. Khatri, they were huge, heavy and crude, similar to those found in the basal layer of the second bed at Olduvai Gorge in East Africa. This discovery is important because it proves that the Hand-axe culture evolved independently in India from a basic Oldowan stage, and spread to other parts.

1. EMN, p. 20.
2. SPPIP, p. 53; see also IAR, 1959-60, p. 22.
3. IAR, 1959-60, p. 22.

However no Oldowan horizon or evidence for the evolution of the Hand-axe culture is noticeable. The evolution of the Oldowan culture into hand-axe in Africa took place in pre-Pleistocene times, but it is of the last inter-glacial age. The suggestion of the date of the early Middle Pleistocene for the Mahadevian is speculative. There is no fossil evidence for it and the stratigraphic position of the red grey clay has been questioned by H. D. SANKALIA and SEN. A. P. KHATRI takes this deposit to be pre-Basal gravel while SEN has taken it, to be post-Basal gravel. The preponderance of pebble tools in any given assemblage is an extremely risky criterion for calling it 'Oldowan.' The culture consists of crudely flaked waterworn pebbles, with rough and jagged cutting edges. Among these are also specimens which suggest the form and shape of the crudest type of 'Chellian Hand-axe'. Thus the exact comparison of the Mahadevian lies with the Chelles Acheul assemblage found at the base of the Bed II of Olduvai Gorge, and not with the Oldowan of Bed I. To call it an Oldowan culture is thus inappropriate and misleading[1].

SURVEY OF THE NARMADA AND ITS TRIBUTARIES BY H. D. SANKALIA AND S.G.SUPEKAR :—

Both H. D. SANKALIA and S. G. SUPEKAR surveyed stretches of the Narmada and its tributaries in the districts of Hoshangabad and Narsinghpur, and identified three distinct terraces at Sagunghat on the Narmada. The earlier two respectively yielded Early and Middle Stone Age tools. At Mahadeo Piparia, they laid a cutting in the basal Conglomerate bed of the Narmada river, with a view to ascertaining if the gravel contained only Early Abbevillean tools. In the cutting, several implements, including cores and flakes were recovered.[2]

INVESTIGATION OF PLEISTOCENE DEPOSITS :—

A. P. KHATRI[3] also investigated the Pleistocene deposits with fossil-cum-tools occurring along the Narmada river,

1. IP, pp 9-12.
2. IAR, 1962-63, p. 30.
3. Ibid, 1961-62, p. 22.

between Hoshangabad and the marble rocks at Bheraghat. About a hundred more mammalian fossils were collected. They included the *Bos bubalus*, *Elephas antiquus (namadicus)*, *Elehas-indicus*, *Hippopotamus*, *Equus*, *Cervus* and *Sus*. A preliminary study of surface collection indicates four categories of fossils, according to the degree of their fossilization. But the fossils were found *in situ* in three horizons, accompanied by tools in successive stages, exhibiting a progressive evolution. The change in the faunal content was not marked except in the third gravel, which yielded recent species.

EXPLORATION OF THE CHAMBAL VALLEY AND STRATIGRAPHY :—

On the Chambal basin, the first discovery was of a grey quartzite houcher from Neemuch, in the latter half of the last century, by an unknown geological explorer. V. S. WAKANKAR discovered a number of palaeoliths at Mandsor. Afterwards, the river Chambal and its tributaries, particularly the Shivna, have been carefully surveyed by A.P. KHATRI. The most important sites are the two localities, Ramghat and Shamshan Ghat, at Mandsor and Nahargadh, on the Shivna. The stratigraphy is comparatively simple.

1. Basal trap rock.
2. Cemented pebble gravel.
3. Yellowish silt.
4. Fine well-cemented gravel.

The cemented gravel has yielded large flakes with prominent bulbs of trap, as well as Abbevillio-Acheulian hand-axes. Other collections include a large percentage of hand-axes, cleavers, scrapers, cores with W shaped jagged edges and flakes. The large flakes of trap with prominent bulbs lying right on the rock *in situ* prove the existence of the early clactonian technique, and recall similar flakes on the Narmada.

The area comes under the category of hand axe–cleaver tradition, but pebble tools are found within the basins of the Gambhiri and Chambal, in association with hand-axes and cleavers, but their number is not very large. They are found at Sonita[1] but are absent in the Shivna.

1. IAR, 1956-57, p. 5.

A large number of pebble tools, choppers, hand-axes and cleavers were found on the surface of the Betwa[1]. The tools of brown sandstone pebble were generally old, but the hand-axes and cleavers of red sandstone were fresh. Some cleavers and hand-axes belonging to the Early Stone Age were collected at the top of Shyamala hill in Bhopal.

DIFFERENT TYPES OF TOOLS :—

Besides hand-axes and cleavers, the other components of this culture are scrapers, cores, flakes and pebble tools. The hand-axes are found from the crudest Abbevillian type to the most advanced Acheulian specimens, with complete symmetrical body, straight edges, and controlled, shallow and flat flaking. Their shapes include pear, pick, almond, chordate, ovate, double pointed, single pointed, triangular and sub-triangular. The cleavers are either 'U' shaped, 'V' shaped, or rectangular, with their cutting edges varying from straight, oblique, convex to flaring types. They occur on core as well as on side or end flakes. Sometimes, the nature of the flake is not distinguishable because of the complete chipping of the bulb. The flakes have simple platform and obtuse angles.

MATERIAL OF THE TOOLS AND TECHNIQUE :—

Generally, quartzite of a fine grained variety is the common raw material. Sometimes dolerite, trap and jasper, were also used. Stone-on-stone technique and wood-on-stone technique, or wooden hammer technique, were employed for preparing these implements. In the stone-on-stone-technique, Anvil or Block-on-Block, or direct-rest percussion and direct free hand percussion methods, have been employed.

DATE AND CLIMATIC CONDITIONS :—

The stratification at Narmada helps in fixing the date of the culture, and also explains the climatic changes in the valley. From the work of the Yale Cambridge Expedition, it is known that man had inhabited the Narmada valley between Hoshangabad and Narsinghpur in the Middle Pleistocene Period, that is some 200,000 years ago. The river then flowed almost

1. IAR, 1959-60, pp. 21-22.

3.5m to 4.50m above its present bed. Owing to heavy rain, it used to carry huge boulders in its current. When a drier period followed, these boulders, gravel and sand, were spread in the shape of a fan. Man, who clipped tools with the help of the other stones, lived on its bank. The tools were mainly of three types—huge flakes, hand-axes and cleavers. With these, man dug trees and hunted and skinned animals like the wild ox, wild horse, wild elephant, and hippopotamus. These animals are not existent now and hence are regarded as fossils.

Discovery of similar tools in a similar context at Maheshwar, then at Mandsor and Nahargadh on the Shivna, Basai, Sonita and other places on the Chambal, Morwan, Ratanjana, Kalyanpura on the Kadmali and Gambhiri, enables us to say that this region was also inhabited during the Stone Age, and further, that it had witnessed the same climatic conditions as those existing on the Narmada in the dim past. As known from the types of tools, the man on the Narmada was perhaps not different from that on the Chambal.

CONTROVERSY AMONG SCHOLARS ABOUT SOHAN CULTURE :—

Along with the hand-axes, a few pebbles have been found in the Narmada valley and the Chambal valley[1]. There is a controversy among scholars about them. Some scholars treat them as an intrusion from outside while others consider them to be part and parcel of the hand-axe-cleaver complex. KRISHNASWAMI[2] assumes the meeting ground of the Sohan and the Madras industry in Gujarat. It is also claimed that the Sohanian of the Punjab, and the handaxe cleaver industry of the Peninsula, meet at Chambal.

There are scholars who consider Sohan a part of the Hand-Axe culture on the following grounds :—

(1) According to SUNDAR RAJAN[3], a culture should be the sum total of more than one industry, or a group of techniques

1. IAR, 1956-57, p. 5.
2. Ancient India, No. 3, p. 19.
3. IP, p. 1.

set in an evolving, socio-material matrix. The Sohan culture, on this count, would seem to fall short of the definition, and would at best seem to be an industry displaying the rise, perfection, and degeneration of the 'prepared platform technique'.

(2) It is regional and individualistic, and has lost its contact with the rest of India, and at a later stage, it mixed with the prehistoric culture. On the other hand, the Hand-axe culture displays fulness of evolution and diffusion.

(3) Both hand-axe and Sohan type tools have been found in the same terrace and thus they were contemporary in the same valley, but they never occur together. It is difficult to imagine the two sets of people practising two different traditions in a restricted area.

H. D. SANKALIA[1] holds that the pebble tools are not confined to the Punjab and they are found in different parts of the country. But, the technique of the tools of the Punjab is different from that of rest of the country. It is under slide up Flaking Technique. It is difficult to distinguish the tools of different Sohan types.

Other scholars[2] regard Sohan culture as a separate culture, and advance the following arguments in support of it:

(1) The Sohan culture contains more than one industry and group of techniques. In the early phase, it remained confined to the Beas and Banganga. In the middle phase, it flourished in the Sirsa valley, and in the most developed phase, it is found at Ror. There are three techniques, namely, pebble, clactonian, and Levallois.

(2) P. C. PANT found true pebble tool industry at Lachure, near Hamirapura, and not far from this place, Hand-axe cleaver complex was discovered at Lalitpur by H. D. SANKALIA. This proves that it was not confined only to North West India, but extended to Gujarat and Malwa.

(3) These are two different technological traditions of two different cultures. Sohan tools made on pebbles were used for

1. IP, p. 6.
2. MOHAPATRA, P. C. PANT an d S. P. GUPTA regard Sohan as a separate culture. See their views, IP, 1964, pp. 1-13.

cutting and scraping, while the Madras hand-axes prepared on cores, were meant for digging.

(4) A dozen sites of the Sohan culture have been explored on the Beas, Banganga, Sutlej, etc. A recent survey of the Sutlej near the town of Bilaspur, brought to light a sequence of three implementiferous terraces. No hand-axe or cleaver was found in it. This implied the acceptance of the Sohan as a separate culture of the Chopper-Chopping tools complex, which probably originated in the Sutlaj basin, and remained confined to that area for a very long time.[1]

It is more reasonable to say that the palaeolithic folk need not have been tied down to one single trend only but could have experimented with many techniques simultaneously for the fabrication of tools, particularly in the incipient and early stages of tool making. The reason is that we find different types of tools in the same locality. It is not necessary that they represent different persons.

COMPARISON BETWEEN THE LOWER PALAEOLITHS OF THE NARMADA AND THE CHAMBAL VALLEYS :—

Lower Palaeoliths have been found in both the Narmada and the Chambal valleys. No doubt, they possess similarities, but they are also marked by their own peculiarities. The basal gravel of Shivna, the tributary of the Chambal, yielded exactly the same things as the industry concerned in the lower group, but not the fossil in the state of preservation as found in the Narmada. In the Shivna, no demarcation of the stratigraphic layers into upper and lower groups is noticed. The study of the collection surface, as well as *in situ* from the Chambal and its tributaries, does not reveal any late Sohan characteristic which is noticed in the Narmada tools. There is no proto-Levallois or Levallois element in the lower palaeolithic tools found at Shivna, but a few Levallois flakes of quartzite have been found in the second gravel of the Narmada[2]. Moreover, in the 'make up' of the implements, in the state of preservation and in the quality of quartzite used, Shivna industry is far superior to the Narmada.

1. IP, p. 11.
2. SPPIP, p. 53.

COMPARISON WITH PRE-SOHAN CULTURE :—

This culture can be compared very well with similar Indian cultures found in the valleys of the rivers. In the Shivna valley at Mandsor, large, massive, thick and fresh flakes are found *in situ*. Like the pre-Sohan flakes, these too have prominent cores of percussion, and simple platforms with obtuse striking angles. There are also differences between the two. The pre-Sohan flakes are of the same age as the boulder conglomerate. That conglomerate is contemporary with the second glaciation and is thus of the Middle pleistocene. In the Shivna valley, this sort of dating is not possible as no palaeontological evidence is obtainable so far, and thus only a typological attempt is left. The pre-Sohan flakes occur alone, and no hand-axe or chopper-chopping tools are associated with it, while in the Shivna flakes, they seem to be contemporary with the hand-axe-cleaver industry which is Acheulian in nature.

COMPARISON WITH THE LOWER PALAEOLITHIC CULTURE OF THE PROVINCES :—

GUJARAT :—The Palaeolithic Hand-axe industry of Malwa contains some similar elements to that of Gujarat industry, but there are differences. The former is more fine, is of medium size, and shows more evolved Acheulian work, while the latter is coarser, larger, and less evolved. Moreover, such huge chopper-chopping tools found in the Sabarmati and the Orsang in Gujarat, are completely absent from the collections obtained from the rivers studied in Malwa.[1]

UTTAR PRADESH :—The lithic-tool industries of the Singrauli Basin[2] on the river Rihand in District Mirzapur of Uttar Pradesh, seem to be of the same age as that of the Narmada, because it also contained the fossiliferous Middle Pleistocene patches and Laterite area. The hand-axes may be compared with those of Malwa, but the presence of Levallois and proto-Levallois element, and chopper-chopping tools, is generally alien to Malwa.

ORISSA :—At Mayurbhanj on the river Burhabalang, there

1. Investigations into Pre-historic Archaeology of Gujarat.
2. Ancient India, No. 7, pp. 40-65; IAR, 1959-60, p. 48.

is also a predominance of hand-axe tools[1]. The material utilized is quartzite, which is comparatively coarse grained and not so compact as that of Shivna.

MAHARASHTRA :—The Godavari palaeolithic industry[2] of Maharashtra is Abbevillion hand-axe-cleaver complex, belonging to the Lower or Middle Pleistocene period. The material is basalt. The Lower Palaeolithic industry of Malwa is different from the Godavari in the material used as well as in technique. It is Acheulian. The side-scrapers of the Godavari type are not met with in that region. Moreover, the Levallois trait in the Godavari is not generally present in any of the rivers of Malwa. As the handaxe-cleaver tools have been found at Pravara[3] in association with the *Bos namadicus* fossil, these are of the Middle Pleistocene age, like those of the Narmada. Typologically, the Lower Palaeolithic industry of Malwa is similar to that of Pravara, but the material used in latter is different. They have been made of dolerite.

MYSORE:—As all the tools have been discovered from the same gravel in the Malaprabha Basin[4] of Karnatak, like Malwa, there is no stratigraphical evidence for putting them into different phases. At both Shivna and Malaprabha, pebbles have rarely been used for making the tools. In typological details, both are similar. The main elements are hand-axes, scrapers, cleavers, discoids, cores and flakes. Malaprabha industry, in short, is Acheulian, though Abbevillian tools occur, and the probable age is mid-pleistocene. The Shivna Lower Palaeolithic industry has a similarity with the Malaprabha industry. The one thing which differentiates the industries of the Malaprabha from those of the Shivna and others, is that the former contains flakes, though very few in number.

1. Excavations in Mayurbhanj, (University of Calcutta).
2. Sankalia, H. D., The Godavari Palaeolithic Industry, (Poona, 1952).
3. Sankalia, H. D., Deo, S. B., Ansari, Z. D. and Ehrhardt, S. : From History to Prehistory at Nevasa (Poona, 1960), p. 528.
4. Joshi, R.V. : Pleistocene Studies in the Malaprabha Basin, 1955.

ANDHRA :--Some stone tools of the Kurnool[1] in Andhra Pradesh may be compared with those of Malwa. The industry at Kurnool is Abevillio-Acheulian hand-axes and cleavers, with the accompaniment of pebble element. The one thing which differentiates the Malwian industry from that of Kurnool, is the occurrence of the Levallois and Proto-Levallois flakes in the latter. The material of the tools found on the Penner river in Nellore District of Andhra Pradesh is different[2]. Pebbles were used in making the tools. Because of the large use of pebbles, there is a high percentage of crude pebble tools, but numerically the predominant types are Abbevillian and Acheulian hand-axes.

MADRAS :—One of the most important things in the industry of this region is the presence of the cores. The majority of them are small in size, less than 8 cm. They are chipped symmetrically on both the faces. In Shivna also, such cores are quite common, and they do not seem to be rejects, though it is difficult to guess their use. The hand-axe tools found in the Kortalayar in Chingleput District Madras are very important. The first stone age implement was discovered by FOOTE in 1863 in Pallavaram in this valley and after the place the industry was named Madras Type of tools after the place. In the Malwian rivers, all the Madras Type Lower Palaeolithic tools are represented except the Levallois element. KRISHNASWAMI[3] recognizes four prominent terraces of pleistocene times, but there are no terraces observed so far in Malwa.

COMPARISON WITH THE CULTURES OF THE COUNTRIES OUTSIDE INDIA:—

Outside India, this Lower Palaeolithic culture shows signs of similarity with the upper Acheulians of the Kharga Oasis (Egypt), and Mount Carmel (Palestine). In the same way, exact parallels can be found in the Vaal river (S.Africa), in

1. Antiquity, Vol. IV, 1930, pp. 327-49; Stone Age Cultures of Kurnool, a Ph. D thesis in Archaeology, 1960, Poona University by Prof. ISAAC.
2. Memoir of the Archaeological Survey of India, No. 68.
3. AI, No. 3, p. 34.

the Olduvai Gorge (E.Africa) and in the Uganda 'M' and 'N' horizon.

AFRICA:—The Indian hand-axe-cleaver complex is similar to that in Africa. The basic similarity between the Malwa and South Africa Hand-axe industry is that flake and core element is intimately associated together from the beginning, but afterwards in the Vaal river (S. Africa), there is a trend towards the development of Levallois technique. In the Shivna and other rivers, we do not find any such development. The typological comparison between the two in shape and size continued afterwards.

The sequence exposed at Olduvai Gorge (East Africa) is very important, because we see the stages of evolution of the hand-axe from the pebble stage to the highly Acheulian supported by stratigraphy. The tools found at the lowest level belong to the pebble (Oldowan) culture, and then Chelles-Acheul development is noticed. It passed through eleven stages. No such evolution in the Hand-axe industry of Malwa is noticeable. The specimens from the stage six to the stage eleven are most common. Pebble tools are secured from the Chambal and the Gambhiri, but they seem to be a part and parcel of the hand-axe industry. A. P. KHATRI claims to have discovered some artefacts of the Oldowan culture below an Abbevillio—Acheulian at Mahadeo Piparia near Narsinghpur, but actually it is not the Oldowan horizon.

The earliest tools found at Uganda are termed as Kafuan Pebble culture. There is no question of comparison with Malwa as far as these tools are concerned. It is only in 'M' and 'N' horizon Acheulain tools that we see the closest resemblance. The Acheulain implements illustrated by O' BRIEN have their exact counterparts in the Shivna Lower Palaeolithic industry. It may also be compared with the upper Acheulian of the Kharga basin, one of the largest of the fine principal Egyptian oases. The raw material used in the Kharga Upper Acheulian is chert, while in Malwa, it is quartzite. Along with the Acheulian hand-axes, Abbevillian types also occur, as they do in Malwa. In Malwa and other parts of India one thing is remarkable, that with the advanced Acheulian, the whole development stops, while in Kharga, it continues evolving into Levallois and other industries.

EASTERN COUNTRIES OF ASIA AS WELL AS EUROPE :—

The Lower Palaeolithic industry of Malwa cannot be compared to those from Java, Burma, Malaya and China, because they belong to an entirely different tradition of the Chopper-Chopping tool industry. The Shivna implements may be compared well with the Acheulian type of West Europe, although the material differs. There is a marked difference between the handaxe-cum-cleaver tradition of India and that of Europe. In the former, the flake and core types are integrally associated, while in the latter, their developments run parallel to each other.

HABITS OF THE PEOPLE :—

We should now turn our attention to the method of living and the habits of Lower Palaeolithic Man. The Geographic, climatic and ecological factors are helpful in this direction. European scholars have worked on these lines in Europe and Africa and we should see how far these are applicable generally to India with special reference to Malwa.

Zeunner[1] thought that the hand-axe was an excellent tool for digging up roots, grubs, and other food from the ground (though it can be useful for many other purposes as well, for instance, for making notches in trees to facilitate climbing). Hence the hand-axe (or the Abbevillio-Acheulian) culture was of vegetable and grub gatherers. Desmond Clark has, however, suggested that these were used as meat mattocks, hence the edges of these tools are rarely found blunted.

Likewise Zeunner associated the makers of the large clactonian flakes and hollow scrapers with forests, and the Levallosian and the Mousterians, who made beautiful flakes in a specialized manner, as typical hunters. Such flakes would be extremely suitable for cutting and dressing carcasses.

Macburney[2], after studying the distribution of hand-axes

1. Dating the Past, p. 292.
2. Current Anthropology, 1960, p. 315.
3. The Stone Age of Northern Africa, p. 24 ff.

and flakes in Western Europe, has postulated that the hand-axe makers preferred the low, maritime, and warm regions, whereas the flake fabricators—the Levallosian, for instance, liked the upland which was comparatively colder.

There are difficulties in trying to apply these climatic and ecological considerations to the finds in India. We do not have such sharp climatic and regional differences in India as found in Europe. We have two cultures, namely, (1) pebble and flake culture, and (2) the Hand-Axe culture. Both are of equal antiquity. The former does not belong to a cold phase. The hand-axe people might have avoided thick forests, but it does not seem to be reasonable that they subsisted on vegetables and shrubs alone. They must have been hunters as well. Similarly, the people who used flakes were hunters and forest dwellers. They could not have lived in thick forests and flourished on animal food alone.

The distribution of hand-axe suggests that the Lower Palaeolithic people lived on river banks in the open or on the edge of the forests. They avoided higher altitudes and heavily forested areas, because vegetables, animals and raw material for making tools were scarce at these places and were not easily available. Water was also of prime necessity.

HAND-AXE MAN RELATED TO THE EARLY AFRICAN MAN :—

About the environment and life of the hand-axe man, not much is known. The reason is that no skeleton remains have so far been found in India. The distribution of the stone tools and their great affinity with those from East and South Africa suggest that the Early Man in India was related physically and culturally to the Early African Man. In Africa, early tool makers were called 'Zinjanthropus' and pre-Zinjman dated to 1,750,000 years[1]. His forest arrival in India coincides with a wet phase. He witnessed several wet and dry phases. In the south-east, the great number of sites and their richness, implies that the palaeolithic population was probably much denser in this region than in the west or north. The predominance of this type of tools in Malwa, as well as their

1. National Geographic, October 1961, p. 568.

affinity, shows that people at this time were more in contact with the people of south-east. The mortality rate was high owing to the nomadic nature of life, and the average age of death was forty.

SOHAN MAN RELATED TO EASTERN ASIA :—

A few pebble tools have been found in the Gambhiri and in the Chambal. Most scholars believe them to be part of the hand-axe cleaver complex, while some regard them as alien elements related to the Sohan of the Punjab. Originally, these people worked on pebbles, but gradually took to manufacturing flakes. Whether it was a natural, indigenous development, or due to new influences or arrival of some different man cannot be stated definitively on the present limited evidence.

Who was this Sohan Man racially? In the absence of skeletal remains, nothing can be said definitely. If the tools signify anything, looking at their similarity with those from Java, Burma and China, it may be suggested that they belonged to the Sinanthropus or Pithecanthropus group. If so, he might have known fire, for the Pekin man knew fire. Probably he died very young, at the age of 15 or 16 years[1].

II

MIDDLE PALAEOLITHIC CULTURE

MIDDLE PALAEOLITHIC INDUSTRY KNOWN BY VARIOUS NAMES :—

The evidence for existence of a distinct second Palaeolithic industry was first obtained at Nevasa. Before this it was not recognised, and was known by different names. At Narsinghpur and Hoshangabad, De Terra and Paterson discovered it in the basal gravels of the black soil of Narmada and designated it as the 'Black-Soil Industry or

1. Dutta Jatindra Mohan : "Prehistoric Demography" M. I., Vol. 39, p. 269.

Proto-neolithic'.[1] It was also called 'Proto-microlithic'[2] and 'Epi-palaeolithic'.[3] In order to avoid terminological confusion, the term series II was accepted. As definite proof of independent existence was obtained from Nevasa, it was called Nevasian after the type site Nevasa. From both the chronological and typo-technological significance, it is now known as 'Middle Palaeolithic'.

TWO TYPES OF TOOLS :—The Middle Palaeolithic culture is known from the discovery of two types of tools. One is found *in situ* in the sections exposed on river boundary and another on the surface. The value of the former lies in the fact that they are next to hand-axes. De Terra and Paterson found these tools in the basal gravels of the black soil in the Narmada at Narsinghpur and Hoshangabad.[4] H.D. Sankalia and Subba Rao tried to show that these tools occur *in situ* in terrace II of the Narmada at Maheshwar.[5] Huge factory sites of this culture were discovered at Dongergaon and Choli on either side of the Narmada.

EXPLORATION OF THE NARMADA VALLEY

While exploring the Narmada valley, A. P. Khatri[6] found the tools of this industry deposited with late Acheulian tools at Piparia. It would, accordingly, be contemporary with the Acheulian stage of the Hand-Axe culture, for to derive it from the latter would be out of the question. H.D. Sankalia and S. G. Supekar[7] surveyed stretches of the Narmada and its tributaries in District Hoshangabad and Narsinghpur, and identified three distinct terraces at Sagunghat on the Narmada. The earlier two respectively yielded Early and Middle Stone Age tools. While surveying the upper Narmada region between Amarkantaka and Mandla,

1. Studies on the Ice Age in India and Associated Human Cultures, p. 320.
2. South Western Journal of Anthropology, University of Mexico, IX, No. 4.
3. Journal of Palaeontological Society, India, Lucknow, Vol. II.
4. Studies on the Ice Age in India and Associated Human Cultures, p.320.
5. EMN, p. 37.
6. IAR, 1959-60, p. 22.
7. Ibid, 1962-63, p. 30.

S.G. Supekar[1] also discovered twelve sites out of which five are the factory sites of the Middle Stone Age tools.

EXPLORATION OF THE CHAMBAL VALLEY :—

Middle Palaeolithic tools have been found *in situ* as well as on the surface both at Mandsor and Nahargarh in the Shivna valley[2]. The number of *in situ* tools is very small. Eight have been obtained from the Shamshan Ghat at Mandsor, and three from Nahargarh. Their number is small, but their very occurrence next to Acheulian industry is important.

The surface material may be divided into two categories. One found near the jasper outcrops quite far from the river, is called factory site products, and the other was found on surface in the bed of the river. A factory-site material was found at Mandsor on the Kharki-Mata site. There is a huge Jasper outcrop, and around it are found about five hundred tools.[3] These tools were also obtained from the river-bed of the Shivna throughout its course from Mandsor up to Alvi-Mahadeo. The other rivers are the Retam at Sanjit, the Chambal at Narsing, Khanpura, Nagda and Basai and the Kali Sind at Sonkutch.

These tools were also found at other places in the Chambal valley[4]. At a place five kilometers down the stream from Janod, terrace system and gravels were noticeable. The third gravel yielded tools of series II. On the Undakhal, which pours its water into the Tulsai, hand-axes, cleavers, and occasionally tools of series II were found. Good specimens of tools of series I and II were found in the rivulet near Manoti. Tools of this type were also obtained from Awra. A large number of these tools were found at some sites in the Betwa valley.[5]

CHARACTERISTICS OF THE TOOLS :—

These tools are of typical flake nature. Flakes have simple platforms with obtuse striking angles and hence are clactonian in technique. These are smaller than those of Early Stone Age. No Levallois influence is observed so far. Typologically, the

1. IAR, 1961-62, p. 22.
2. Journal of the Palaeontological Society of India.
3. IAR, 1956-57, p. 11.
4. Ibid, 1959-60, pp. 22-23.
5. Ibid, pp. 21-24.

industry consists of various types of scrapers, points, fluted and irregular cores, flake blades, etc. These are made of new material, such as jasper and chert. The tools found near the factory site are fresh, while those found in the river bed are somewhat rolled. Scrapers were meant for dressing skins and barks of trees, knives for cutting and chopping, and pointed tools for piercing wood and bone.

RELATION OF THIS CULTURE WITH OTHER REGIONS:–

The Middle Palaeolithic culture of Malwa is related to this type of culture in other parts of India, though there are regional variations owing to ecological, geographical, and other factors.

SOUTH INDIA :—At Pravara, the Middle Palaeolithic industry occurs in the upper gravel bed number II. It is from this evidence that this industry, found in the valleys of the Narmada and the Chambal, began to be called Middle Palaeolithic. Stratigraphically and culturally it is related to such industry of Godavari and Pravara in the Deccan, Malaprabha and Ghata-prabha in Karnatak, and Tapti in Khandesh. At all these sites, it succeeds the Hand-axe and precedes the microliths. The tools are generally of flake nature but the raw material differs from region to region. In its early stages, it may be assigned to the latter half of the Pleistocene, and the upper limit may be fixed to the early Holocene period on palaeontological evidence, because the tools of this culture were found associated with the skull of *'Bos namadicus Falconer'* at Kalegaon, on the river Godavari in Maharashtra.

In the basal gravels of Nevasa[1] and Mahadeo Piparia[2] were found Abbevilleo-Acheulean tools, with tools of series II. The juxtaposition of these two industries which are typologically and technologically of a different character, is very important. It is possible that both the cultures might have flourished side by side in these regions for some time.

COMPARISON WITH THE LATE SOHAN :—

De Terra and Paterson[3] compared certain flake

1. EMN, p. 37.
2. IAR, 1959-60, p. 22.
3. Studies on the Ice Age in India and Associated Human Cultures, p. 3.

tools of the Narmada with those of the Late Sohan. R. ALLCHIN and others[1] have suggested that these two cultures are related and fall within the Middle Palaeolithic Period. The tools of these cultures have not been illustrated by anyone and so we are not sure of what we are comparing typologically or stratigraphically. Though the Late Sohan does contain a fairly good percentage of flakes on prepared cores, very few points, awls or borers and various types of scrapers reminiscent of the Middle Palaeolithic culture, are seen. In the absence of a first-hand study of both the assemblages, it would be better to regard the Late Sohan and the Nevasian at the most homotanial and falling within the Middle Palaeolithic period. But both belong to very different environmental, climatic and ecological regions.

CLIMATIC CONDITION AND ENVIRONMENT :—

The climatic condition and environment may be inferred from the study of the nature of deposits found in the rivers. The changes in the deposits may be due to the cycle of a heavy wet phase followed by a drier phase, and then a lighter wet phase. Gradually, the climate became drier. When the Narmada again raised its level and then once again dropped it, owing to a wetter climate, the first Stone Age Man left the valley. When the river rose again for the third time, and shed its load against other deposits, the Middle Stone Man occupied the region. He lived near the foot-hills, a region where raw material in the shape of nodules of agate, jasper and other fine-grained stones, was easily available. He made smaller tools known as scrapers, for dressing the skins of animals, and used wood and bone for handles. There are also points and chisel-edged tools. These imply the invention of the bow and arrow for hunting.

FAUNA :—The vegetational environment in the remote ages remains unknown, but a faint idea of contemporary fauna is formed from several fossils found near Devakachhar and at

1. ALLCHIN : The Indian Middle Stone Age : Some New Sites in Central and Southern India and their implications, BLUIA, No. II, pp. 1-36.

Sanguna ghat on the Narmada.[1] In such an environment, not very humid, and not thickly wooded, ***Bos namadicus Falconer*** (or Lydekher) and even ***Elephas antiquus*** which have hitherto been regarded as characteristic Middle Pleistocene fauna, seem to have flourished, and to have served as game for Middle Stone Age Man.

CONTROVERSY ABOUT ORIGIN :—

FOREIGN :—The question of the origin of this culture is controversial. The tools of this culture are quite different from the Hand-axe culture of the early period. The typical nature of this industry and the use of the new material suggests a basic change in the life of the people. It proves the advent of a different cultural force. It may denote the arrival of a different people from outside, who exercised a new cultural influence. Gradually they spread all over India, and gave individuality to this culture. H. D. SANKALIA[2] and A. P. KHATRI are of the view that these people most probably came from Africa. ALLCHIN[3] thinks that in the early stages, this culture was in contact with similar industries in Central Asia, and later developed in comparative isolation for a long time in the regions southeast of the Sind desert. But it is premature to say that it has affinity with Africa, or Central Asia, or with Europe.

INDIGENOUS :—On the other hand, there are some scholars who are of the opinion that this culture is indigenous. K. D. BANERJEE[4], after his detailed study of Nevasa and North Karnatak material postulated that this culture had evolved out of the earlier Hand-axe-cleaver culture, because techniques like the block-on-block cylinder hammer characterised both, as well the border, which is a type tool of the Nevasian and which is also available, though very rarely, in the earlier industry.

1. IP, p. 42.
2. SPPIP, p. 35.
3. ALLCHIN, "The Indian Middle Stone Age : Some new sites in Central and Southern India and their Implication," BLUIA, No. II, pp. 1-36.
4. Middle Palaeolithic Industries of the Deccan, p. 291.

Similar is the view of SOUNDAR RAJAN[1], who holds that the nature of stratigraphy by which Acheulian tools and Middle Stone Age flakes appear to have been found side by side on the top of the second gravel of the Narmada, together with the nature of occurrence of fossil fauna like *Bos Namadicus*—(Falconer) in the gravels of Godavari, Narmada, etc., both in the Early Stone Age, and continuing in the gravels of the Middle Stone Age, would seem to show an essentially gradual ecological change and a cultural continuum. At Mahadeo Piparia and Nevasa, the Hand-axe culture and the Middle Palaeolithic culture flourished side by side. In Madras, Lower Deccan, Saurashtra and Kutch, Middle Stone Age tools were made of the same material as those of the Early Stone age.

However much more stratigraphic and other data, as well as a comparative study of the Indian, African and Central Asian industries, is necessary before something definite can be said about the origin and relationship of the Middle Palaeolithic culture. At present, however, it would appear to be indigenous.

III

MESOLITHIC CULTURE

GENERAL CHARACTERISTICS :—

The term 'Mesolithic' is used to distinguish a transitional phase from the Palaeolithic to Neolithic culture, and it bridges the gulf between the two. It is different from the early period in climate, technology, in economic and other spheres. The old glacial conditions had more or less gone, and the dry period had started. With the climatic changes, the flora and fauna altered, as also the implements. Technologically, tiny tools known as 'microliths', highly improved upon the earlier ones, were devised. There is the continuation of the Palaeolithic economy, but the emphasis shifted from big game to small game hunting. The occupation of sites was more extensive

1. IP, p. 43.

and intensive than that of any of the two preceding Stone Age cultures. All microliths do not suggest or stand for a Mesolithic stage of culture, but context and stratigraphy can only prove their genuineness. They may be placed between 10000 and 4000 B. C.

DISTRIBUTION OF MICROLITHIC SITES :—

In Malwa, a few sites are known in the districts of Mandsor, Ratlam, Ujjain, Indore, Khandwa and Nimar. There are also microliths in the Vindhya region and Chitor District, in the neighbourhood of Malwa.

A. P. KHATRI[1] collected several microliths from the sites in the valley of the Chambal and its tributaries. A mound at Ashta on Parvati, a tributary of Chambal, yielded microliths.[2] At Parmakheri near Nagda on the Chambal, microliths were found[3]. Microliths were discovered on the mound at Sanjit on the bank of Retam, a tributary of Chambal about forty-eight kilometers from Mandsor in the north-east direction.[4] Suara, on the bank of Shivna, yielded microliths.[5] The microliths were also obtained from Modi in the Chambal region.[6] Sometime they occur side by side with chalcedony and chert nodules, as at Partapgarh, thirty-two kilometers west of Mandsor.[7] They are also located on the bank of the river Mahi and Mahisagar (Banswara).[8]

A. P. KHATRI discovered a very rich microlithic site at Chindwara[9]. The microliths consisted of flakes, backed blades, scrapers and points. Microliths are also available on the Tapti, south west of Burhanpur[10]. Patalpani, twenty-seven kilometers from Indore towards Khandwa, is an open microlithic site.[11] More than two hundred pieces were picked up, out of

1. Stone Age Cultures of Malwa (Ph. D. thesis), p. 182.
2. IAR, 1956-57, p. 80.
3. Ibid, p. 10.
4. Stone Age Cultures of Malwa, p. 182.
5. Ibid.
6. IAR, 1958-59, p. 28.
7. Stone Age Cultures of Malwa, p. 62.
8. Ibid.
9. IAR, 1959-60, p. 69.
10. Ibid.
11. Stone Age Cultures of Malwa, p. 68.

which eighty-seven were selected, and the others rejected. These were also picked up from Kalakunda, a Railway Station between Mhow and Khandwa.[1] A few microliths were also collected from Deoguraria hill ten kilometers south-west of Indore.[2]

Microlithic tools were discovered in the beds of the Agni, Kundala and Machikunda, all tributaries of the Narmada at Jamadhad, Matupur, Chanera, Mojawadi and Garbardi.[3] Microliths consisting of blades, lunates, scrapers and fluted cores, were found at Punaghat Kala, Chalap-Khurd, Borkheda-Khurd, Tosaniya and Karoti in Harsud Tahsil, and Dehgaon, Hutiya and Atud-Khasa in Khandwa Tahsil.[4] Microliths were also discovered on the northern bank of the Narmada river at Nimawar.[5]

PECULIARITIES OF MALWA MICROLITHS :—

These microliths found in Malwa have their own peculiarities. They generally occur on whitish translucent chalcedony or carnelian, and rarely in pure quartz or crystal. They occur in an unstratified context. These are of different types, such as fluted and irregular cores, scrapers, and points, and few blades. Only one backed lunate has been found, at Deoguraria. They have non-geometrical shapes. No pottery has been found in association with them.

OF PRE-CHALCOLITHIC TIMES (EARLIER THAN 2000 B.C.) :—

It is probable that these microliths of Malwa are of the pre-chalcolithic times. As these are surface collections, it is difficult to assign any date to them. These tools occur in the areas where we have a well stratified chalcolithic blade industry. These chalcolithic blade tools, like microliths, were prepared from chalcedony. Hence they bear a genetic relationship with the microliths. Thus, we may call them pre-chalcoli-

1. Stone Age Cultures of Malwa, p. 68.
2. Ibid.
3. IAR, 1959-60, p. 69.
4. Ibid.
5. Ibid, 1962-63, p. 68.

thic. As well, a large number of microliths were located in the Banas Basin of Rajasthan, adjacent to Malwa, and some were excavated at Ahar and Gilund. All these do not belong to the copper or chalcolithic deposits, but to an earlier phase of hunting and forest culture. Besides, they are free from crested technique. The microliths of Malwa seem to be contemporaneous with those of Banas. Like them, they belong to Mesolithic hunter-food gatherers, who occupied the area before the establishment of early peasant settlements there. We may say that in this region too, the Microlithic culture belongs to a period earlier than 2000 B. C.

MICROLITHS OF ROCK-SHELTERS AND CAVES :—

Microliths have also been discovered in rock-shelters and caves. At Pachmarhi in the Mahadeo hills, HUNTER dug a rock-shelter and found microliths, and GHOSH obtained them from Bania Bari cave near Pachmarhi. A large number of microliths consisting of blades, points, triangles, lunates etc., most of them showing geometric shapes, were collected from the rock-shelters at Adamgarh, near Hoshangabad.[1] Tools from this region had been collected earlier by M. GHOSH and D. H. GORDON. They were found in the painted rock-shelters at Kabra Pahar.[2] These were also obtained in the Dharmapuri rock-shelters near Bhopal.[3] A few such tools were also collected from the vicinity of the rock-shelters at Chandigarh in Tahsil Burhanpur, and at Ghatak in Tahsil Khandwa.[4] In the opinion of H.D. SANKALIA,[5] the whole Vindhya range from west to east, is not only a prolific source of microliths, but perhaps holds the key to the microlithic or mesolithic problem in Central India.

Barkhera, thirty-two kilometers south of Bhopal, locally known as Bhim Baithaka, is known for its rock-shelters with paintings. The number of rock-shelters at this site is about six

1. IAR, 1954-55, p. 59.
2. Ibid, 1955-56, p. 69.
3. Ibid, 1959-60, p. 70.
4. Ibid, 1961-62, p. 99.
5. SPPIP, p. 149.

hundred, the largest so far known in any single site in the country, and they cover an area of about thirteen kilometres. The study of paintings reveals a continuous occupation of these rock-shelters by the primitive people, from the prehistoric time to the early historical period.

A few trial trenches in the Auditorium rock-shelters at this site yielded an interesting sequence of the Stone Ages. It is remarkable that this type of sequence in regard to rock paintings has been revealed for the first time in this country. The period I of rock-shelters yielded the palaeoliths. In period II, these tools were replaced by the Middle Stone Age tools. For preparation of these tools, only quartzite stone was selected. The third stage is represented by microliths having geometric and non-geometric forms. These tools were from flint stones.[1]

The man using the early stone age tools lived in river valleys and open forests. In the next stage of Mesolithic culture, man learnt to live in rocky cave-shelters and used tiny tools. Some of these rocky shelters contain paintings. They furnish the idea of the cultural life of the people. The earliest paintings belong to a time when man was primarily a hunter and food-gatherer.

The excavations at the above sites show the evolution of microliths from a non-geometric and non-pottery level at the very lowest, to a pottery using geometric microlithic level. This shows microliths were of early times. Their antiquity is further confirmed because at Adamgarh, numerous microliths were found in black soil.[2] It seems that the microliths found in these rocks probably belong to a period earlier than 2000 B.C.

COMPARISON WITH THOSE OF OTHER REGIONS :—

These microliths found in Malwa do not tally with the microliths found in Gujarat, Uttar Pradesh and Andhra Pra-

1. K. D. Bajpai's letter dated 30-3-1972 informing me about this site. Paper read at the annual Session of Pre-historic Society and Archaeological Society, 1972, Bombay by V. S. Wakankar.

2 IAR, 1960-61, p. 13.

desh. In Gujarat, the most important site is Langhraj.[1] At this place, the tools are geometric and of jasper, and they are found *in situ* with fauna, shells of dentalum, human skeletons, and pottery. In Malwa, these are found generally loose without pottery; they are made of jasper and are non-geometric. This industry was found at the depth of one-and-a-half meter in the Singrauli Basin in the district Mirzapur of Uttar Pradesh.[2] The material is milky quartz, while in Malwa, it is generally chalcedony. It is non-geometric and unassociated with pottery like that found in Malwa. At Tinnevelly,[3] these were found associated with fossil red sand dunes locally called '*teris*' or *teri* industry. Their most distinctive feature is the presence of pressure flaked bificial points. The lunates preponderate and the industry is geometric. From these, the Malwa microliths differ both in raw material and in typology.

COMPARISON WITH THOSE OF EUROPE AND AFRICA ;—

Neither in Malwa, nor in the rest of the country, do we find signs of definite mesolithic cultures, comparable to those of Europe and Africa, either in time, contact or stratigraphy. They do not immediately overlie the Palaeolithic and underlie the Neolithic. In the scale of evolution, we cannot trace in adequate detail the step by step transition from Microlithic to Neolithic culture. There is no doubt that culturally, they are similar to industries classified as Mesolithic in Western Asia, Europe and Africa.

ORIGIN :—It is not exactly clear whether the microliths developed out of the earlier lithic industries, or whether they were the result of the influence of some external stimuli. They might have evolved from the earlier 'blade and burin' industry, or from series II, or Middle Palaeolithic tool complex, but nowhere is such an evolution available stratigraphically. The Kurnool evidence is not from one stratified site, but a typical grouping of the collection from a number of sites. The wide distribution of this industry, not only in India, but all over the world, in Europe, Africa, and Eastern Asia, points to

1. See Sankalia, H. D. in JGRS, Vol. VIII, 1956, pp. 275-84.
2. AI, No. 7, 1951, p. 58.
   Ibid, XII, pp. 4-20.

some cultural link. Probably, a new race of people from Africa entered India with these implements.

CONTINUED USE OF MICROLITHS BY URBAN AND VILLAGE COMMUNITIES :—

Microliths were not only employed by the hunting and food producing Mesolithic people, but were common also among the food producing communities and urban societies. The reason was that there was a short supply of copper and bronze, and these metals were used only by the rich. The common people continued the use of microliths. There was a marked difference between the tool typology of the hunting-food gathering communities on the one hand, and the urban and village communities on the other. The relationship between the Mesolithic stone industries and the Chalcolithic Neolithic blade industries in the different regions, is a problem to be investigated.

IV

NEOLITHIC CULTURE

Neolithic culture means technological and economic changes in society. Technologically, it means the grinding and polishing of stones. Economically, it means the transition from food gathering to food production, involving husbandry. It took place in different areas over a great range of time. Manufacture of pottery and the use of metal, were not the essentials of this culture.

Childe[1] defines this culture in an economic sense, meaning a self-sufficient food producing economy. According to V. N. Misra[2], economy rather than technology is the diagnostic trait of the Neolithic. In this way, he includes the Chalcolithic cultures of Malwa in this culture. He is of the opinion that objects of copper did not change its economy. This view does not seem to be correct. One single copper object is sufficient to classify the culture as Chalcolithic. It means diffusion, and it breaks the isolation. It increases production, and replaces stone axes.

1. Childe, V. G. 1957. "Old World Prehistory : Neolithic" in Kroeber, A.L. (Ed.), Anthropology Today : An Encyclopaedic Inventory, 193-210, Chicago, Fourth Impression.
2. IP, p. 93.

In Malwa, no neolithic find has been discovered so far. Only one polished axe was found at Navada Toli, and one celt was discovered at Maheshwar[1]. One neolithic hand-axe was discovered from the surface at Eran.[2] Whether these celts are intrusions, or whether they indicate the existence of a polished Axe culture, is not yet certain. Probably they travelled from the region of South India, where eight sites have been discovered. The earliest site is Sangankallu, associated with microliths, and the succeeding phase is of polished stone implements. In Northern India, such tools have been found at Burzahom and a few other sites in the Jhelum valley of Kashmir. There are also sites in Orissa, Bihar and Assam.

Nothing can be said positively about the origin of the Neolithic culture. M. WHEELER[3] tentatively suggested that it was a movement from north-east to south-east. He further suggested that the axes might have been derived via China from Central Asia.[4] R. ALLCHIN[5], on the contrary, argues for an Iranian origin. According to B.K. THAPAR[6], the south-Neolithic culture is indigenous, but the Neolithic culture of North and East India, originated from China. V. N. MISRA[7] believes that the Neolithic culture first developed in West Asia in about 7000 B. C.

1. Stone Age Cultures of Malwa.
2. JMPIP, p. 44.
3. AI, No. 4, p. 295.
4. Early India and Pakistan, p. 89.
5. Piklihal Excavations, p. 113.
6. IP, pp. 87-92.
7. Ibid, 94-98.

CHAPTER V

CHALCOLITHIC CULTURES

The transition from Stone Age to Chalcolithic is a great landmark in history, because it laid the foundation of civilization. It brought about great revolutionary changes in economy, from the hunting and food collecting stage to a pastoral and agricultural stage. The self-sufficiency of the Stone Age people was broken, and trade in raw material and finished goods started. As a result of this, relations between isolated regions were established. The discovery of metal is also an important factor, because it led to great technological advancement.

GENERAL CHARACTERISTICS :—

In Chalcolithic culture, a few objects of copper in small quantities, are found together with pottery. Whether these few copper objects were locally made or imported, does not matter. The use of copper is the leading characteristic of Chalcolithic culture. Together with this, painted pottery and lithic industry are found.

PECULIARITIES OF MALWA CHALCOLITHIC :—

Among the different kinds of painted pottery, red pottery painted with black designs is predominent. It is also called Painted Black-on-Red Ware, or Malwa Ware. Generally, it is found in abundance at all sites. It is highly advanced and has various shapes and designs. An invariable concomitant of this pottery was a lithic industry, in which parallel-sided blades predominated. Hence, it is called the 'Short Blade Industry'. Beads, terracotta figurines, etc. are also associated with this culture.

DISTRIBUTION OF CHALCOLITHIC SITES :—

More than forty chalcolithic sites have been discovered in the valleys of Chambal, Narmada and other rivers. This shows the wide spread of this culture in the area which was colonised by people in a period from about 2000 B. C. to 800

B. C. Among these chalcolithic sites, the earliest seems to be Kayatha[1], where a sequence of three cultural periods, with distinct antiquities in the Chalcolithic Age, from 2200 B. C. to 1300 B. C., have been discovered.

Parmar-Kheri, Nagda, Tingni, Metwa, and Takraoda, can be put into one cluster and called Nagda group after the main site.[2] At Koyali, about ten kilometers north-east of Nahargarh, two mounds yielded painted pottery of the type found at Nagda. Again at Koyala, the opposite site of the village produced the same pottery.[3] Ghat-Bilod, forty kilometers from Chambal, yielded a few sherds and microliths.[4] At Pseva or Peva, sixteen kilometers from Sanjit and Maori, and two kilometers to the north-west of Gautampura, are found innumerable black-on-red painted sherds, besides chalcedony microliths.[5] In the village of Khera on the bank of Śiprā, chalcolithic pottery sherds and microliths are found.[6] About five kilometers from Dewas is a village named Bilawali, in which a high mound yielded chalcolithic elements.[7] From Kanwan on the Indore Ratlam road, an incised, and a few painted sherds were obtained from the mound.[8]

There are other chalcolithic sites, such as Ashta on Parvati a tributary of Chambal.[9] Awra and Manoti also produced important chalcolithic pottery.[10] The black-painted red ware of the Malwa chalcolithic assemblage was also found at Mandsor.[11] At Rajota, twenty-nine kilometers west of Ujjain, there is a large mound with black-and-red, burnished red and black-and-red painted wares. On the bank of Chambal, twenty one kilometers to the north of Rajota, a chalcolithic site with

1. IAR, 1967-68, p. 24.
2. Stone Age Cultures of Malwa.
3. IAR, 1959-60, p. 23.
4. Stone Age Cultures of Malwa.
5. Ibid.
6. Ibid.
7. Ibid.
8. Ibid.
9. IAR, 1956-57, p. 80.
10. Ibid, 1959-60, pp. 24-25.
11. Ibid, 1965-66, p. 42.

painted ware was found.[1] The ancient mound of Dharawada in District Indore, produced different kinds of chalcolithic pottery.[2] Bhilsuri and Betwa chalcolithic sites are also well known. There are also chalcolithic sites in Dhar District.

Chalcolithic sites have also been discovered on the banks of the Chambal. The most famous sites are Maheshwar and Navdatoli. Other places are Bhagatrav, Telod, Mehgam and Hasanpur. Eran on the Banganga, a branch of Narmada, was also influenced by the Malwa Chalcolithic culture.

The mounds of the chalcolithic sites are sometimes inhabited, sometimes deserted, or, in some cases, cultivated. Nagda, Kayatha and Ghatiyalod are inhabited, Navdatoli on Narmada, and the sites on Chambal like Paramakheri, Takroda and Pseva, are deserted mounds, while Khera on Śiprā, Maori near Gautampura, and Metwa near Nagda are cultivated. In the furrows of tilled mounds, painted pottery and Chalcedony blades are found.

Excavations at some of the chalcolithic sites such as Kayatha, Maheshwar, Navdatoli, Nagda, Avra, Manoti and Eran, brought to light the stratified chalcolithic layers along with their respective antiquities. These excavated sites have their own peculiar features, but they give a fairly good picture of Chalcolithic Malwa. In comparing the Chalcolithic culture of Malwa with other Chalcolithic cultures of India, it seems that they differ in ceramic traditions but share a common level of food economy and technology.

SETTLEMENTS :—From the excavations of some sites, it would appear that these chalcolithic sites were founded on black soil. The black soil itself is a weathering ***in situ*** of the brownish alluvium owing to thick vegetation which was cleared. These settlements were generally clusters of mud huts though at Gilund[3] and Manoti,[4] we find baked brick structures; at Nagda,[5] the houses were built of mud bricks. At Manoti,[6] a high rectangular platform of sundried bricks of

1. IAR, 1959-60, p. 71.
2. Ibid, 1962-63, p. 68.
3. Ibid, 1959-60, p. 41.
4. Ibid, p. 25.
5. Ibid, 1955-56, pp. 11-14.
6. Ibid, 1959-60, p. 25.

different dimensions was raised in order to protect the habitation from the floods of the Chambal. The people also erected a huge defence wall of similar bricks, nearly eleven feet in width and at least ten to twelve feet in height. Inside the wall, more brick structures were located. At Nagda, there were massive structures of mud and brick, mostly for residential purposes, though one of them is a bastion of a rampart. The discovery of mud defence-wall at Eran[1] is very important. It is made of black and yellow clays. It enclosed the semicircular habitation area from the south, other sides having been enclosed by the river. Originally, the wall had a basal width of about 30.50 meters and the existing maximum height of the wall is 6.41 meters. Discovered immediately to the south of the mud defence wall, and adding another line of defence in that direction, was an ancient moat.

PLAN OF THE HOUSES :—

No regular plan of the houses could be discovered at these chalcolithic sites except at Maheshwar and Navdatoli. The houses here were adjacent to each other. Between a row of four or five houses, there is a narrow passage. These houses were framed by thick wooden posts, and round these were put bamboo screens, which were then plastered with clay from outside and inside. The houses were of different shapes, circular, square and rectangular. The size of these houses varies. Sometimes, a circular hut was only three to four feet in diameter, and it is doubtful if it was meant for habitation. Such small huts have been used for storing grains, hay, etc. The size of the largest rectangular house was twenty feet by forty feet. Normally, the size of a house was ten feet by eight feet, and not more than four persons could live in such a house.

The floor was made of clay mixed with cowdung. They were made smooth, firm, and insect proof by spreading lime on the black soil or yellow silt. If there were depressions, the hollows were filled up with black alluvium, or sometimes the burnt debris of the earlier period was spread and plastered

1. JMPIP, V, p. 23.

with lime. At Avra[1] and Eran[2], the floors were made of rammed yellow clay mixed with *kankar*. Sometimes burnt clods of clay were also crushed into the floor. The charcol pieces found in the floor may indicate their intentional use. The walls of the houses were made of a closely laid series of wooden or bamboo posts, and covered on either side with mud. There was an interwoven bamboo screen between the two principal layers of the mud wall. Wherever the walls were burnt, the impressions of these screens and posts have been left in burnt lumps of clay and lime plaster. The walls were also plastered or washed with lime. How these houses were roofed has not yet been ascertained. They were probably made with bamboos and reeds, traces of which would not be left, as there were repeated destructions. But if they were made of clay and supported by wooden posts or matting, there is some evidence to suggest that some of the debris may belong to the roof as well.

EARTHEN POTS OF THE HOUSES :—

These houses were furnished with small and large earthen pots for storing, cooking and drinking. Generally, these were wheel made. The large storage jars were strong and sturdy but mainly decorated with an engraving or applique work along the neck. The most remarkable pottery vessels are cups, bowls and dishes. A large number of them have stands. The inhabitants had a large number of vessels which, according to their fabric, shapes and designs, fall into distinct groups associated with a particular period.

KAYATHA WARE :—Kayatha Ware[3] is known to be the earliest in this region. It has been dated 2200-2000 B.C., but it is more reasonable to place it between 2000 B. C. and 1800 B.C. It has three distinct ceramic industries. Its principal pottery was a sturdy ware having broad zones of thick chocolate slip, usually from lip to shoulder, sometimes up to the base, and with painted patterns executed in violet. Shapes included jars

1. JMPIP, IV, pp. 13-40.
2. Bulletin of Ancient Indian History and Archaeology I, p. 32.
3. IAR, 1967-68, p. 24.

with globular profile and wide flaring mouth, and bowls having thickened incurved rim and carinated shoulder. The majority of vessels in this ware had ring bases. Vessels with disc bases were also present in small numbers. The red-painted buff ware, of well-levigated clay and fine fabric, was another distinguished industry. The third ceramic industry comprised plain red ware without slip or wash, with incised decorative patterns. Only bowls and dishes were represented in this ware.

THE BLACK AND RED WARE :—The Black and Red Ware seems to be an import from Ahar where it occurs in profusion, and it is dated 1800-1200 B.C. It was made on the inverted firing technique. In Kayatha[1], the people using this ware arrived, and lived from 1800 B.C to 1600 B.C. As Avra[2] and Manoti[3] were not at a great distance from Ahar, it is found at the lowest level and in plenty. At Navdatoli[4], this ware, comprising mostly bowls and cups, was confined only to period I. It has been traced also at Nagda[5] and Eran.[6]

MALWA WARE :—The most common is a Red Pottery painted with black designs. Since this is found throughout Malwa, it is called the 'Malwa Ware'. This occurs at a major pottery fabric from the very first occupation and runs through the entire chalcolithic habitation at Navdatoli[7]. However, in the earliest period only certain designs and shapes figure, both becoming more varied later. At Nagda[8] and Eran[9] also, this pottery remained dominant, and was excavated at the lowest layer. At Kayatha,[10] Manoti[11] and Avra,[12] it appears just underlying the Black and Red Ware of Ahar culture.

1. IAR, 1967-68, p. 24.
2. JMPIP, IV, p. 26.
3. IAR, 1959-60, p. 24.
4. SPPIP, p. 199.
5. IAR, 1955-56, p. 11.
6. Bulletin of Ancient Indian History and Archaeology I, p. 35; IAR, 1960-61, p. 13; 1963-64, pp. 15-16.
7. EMN, p. 83.
8. IAR, 1955-56, p. 11.
9. Bulletin of Ancient Indian History & Archaeology, II, p. 35.
10. IAR, 1967-68, p. 24.
11. Ibid, 1959-60, p. 24.
12. JMPIP, IV, p. 27.

WHITE SLIPPED FABRIC :—Another important fabric is the white slipped one. It was associated with the first two periods only at Navdatoli[1], but disappeared afterwards. It is found in small numbers. Though the white slip is a distinguishing feature, the fabric is not uniform in texture. The shapes are more varied than in Black and Red Ware. In addition to a large number, and varied types of bowls or cups, there are bowls and dishes on stands, and a water vessel like *loṭā*. A band of running antelopes and dancing human figures seem to be characteristic designs in this fabric. A small number of sherds have been also recovered from Avra.[2]

JORWE FABRIC :—In period III at Navdatoli, a new fabric called 'Jorwe,' named after the site in the Deccan, has been discovered. It is a greyish black ware. It has a well backed core with a metallic ring, and a mat red surface. It was in existence along with the Red Ware. A limited number of shapes and designs figure in this ware. The tea-pot like bowls were used probably for some sacrifice or ritual. A vessel identical in size and shape, but in copper or bronze, was found at Parbatsar.[3]

OTHER TYPES OF POTTERY :—The coarse Red and Black Ware sherds have been found all over Malwa in the Deccan. Though small in number, this ware by its finish and peculiar type of vessels indicates some definite and limited use in the Chalcolithic period. The incised ware, though small in quantity, had a definite place in the life of the people. Incised decoration is generally confined to storage vessels, usually of a large size, but it is also found on some small vessels of a specialised type. It remained confined to the two lower most layers at Avra,[4] and about a dozen sherds have been recovered. The Tan Ware appears to be rare both at Maheshwar,[5] Navdatoli[6] and at Avra[7].

1. EMN, p 199.
2. JMPIP, IV, p. 28.
3. SPPIP, p. 199.
4. Ibid, p. 200.
5. JMPIP, IV, p. 28.
6. EMN, p. 84.
7. JMPIP, p. 28.

GREY WARE :—In the Chalcolithic phase, in association with the Black-on-Red and Painted Black and Red wares, Grey Ware in large quantities has also been recovered at Eran.[1] This ware was used continuously by the people from **1750** B.C. to **700** B.C. The thinner sherds of this ware are usually of finer fabric. It seems to be different from the Painted Grey Ware of the Gangetic valley, and it has no similarity with the Neolithic Burnished Grey Ware of South India. From Bhind District[2], some fragmentary sherds of Grey Ware have been collected which seem to have some similarity in fabric, at least with the Chalcolithic Grey Ware at Eran. As the Bhind region has also yielded many Painted Grey Ware sites, it will be worth while to explore some promising sites which may yield both the types of Grey Ware, or at least, on the basis of the excavation, some link may be established between these two regions.

Occasional sherds of the Painted Grey Ware have been discovered in the core of the rampart at Ujjain[3]. It is of the later date because of the paucity and simplicity of painted designs in comparison with the Painted Grey Ware of the Gangetic valley.

DESIGNS ON THE POTTERY :—These various types of pottery were painted with beautiful designs and show the skill of the artists. These designs primarily appear on the outside, above the belly, preferably on the shoulder, neck, or round the rim. The inside decoration is confined to the inside only of the rim of an everted or flaring rimmed vessel, so that it could be seen. The decorative designs are primarily geometric, and include simple bands, lattice, squares and diamonds, hatched triangle and parallelograms, 'ladder' or flag, circles within circles, and circle with rays. Besides this, they have taken the motifs from the animal and vegetable world. They have delineated the different kinds of deer, tigers or panthers, and even a lion, dogs and cats, tortoise and fish, peacock,

1. Bulletin of Ancient Indian History & Archaeology, I, p. 36; IAR, 1960-61, p. 13; 1963-64, pp. 15-16.
2. IP, p. 229.
3. IAR, 1955-56, p. 11.

geese and other birds, a few leaves and flowers, and what looks like a sunrise or sunset.

CULTIVATION OF DIFFERENT KINDS OF GRAIN :

Besides the manufacture of different types of pottery with many designs, the people started to produce various kinds of grains at an early period in this area. This was very significant, and clearly proves that they were not barbarous or semi-nomadic, but had settled at some particular place. That wheat was known to them from the very beginning of their settlement is clear from the excavations at Kayatha and Navdatoli[1], where it was found in large quantity.

From the beginning the inhabitants used five kinds of legumes viz. (i) *masur* or lentil, (ii) *urd* or black grain (iii) *mung or* green grain (iv) *vatana* or mutter or green peas, and (v) lathyrus sp., besides four other leguminous weeds, the identification of which is not certain. The food was probably cooked with linseed oil, the grains of which are found from the earliest phase. Gradually, they seem to have got used to, or discovered the use of, rice, but it seems to be scarce and in short supply. Though wheat was known from Mohenjodaro, these are the earliest examples of rice[2], two kinds of grain, *masur*(lentil), *kulathi* and beans, and oil seeds like linseed. The distribution and antiquity of wheat, lentils and linseed, suggest Western Asiatic contacts, whereas rice is believed by most authorities, to be indigenous to India.

METHODS OF CULTIVATION :—

No plough or other advanced agricultural tool has been discovered, hence the ploughing must have been done with digging sticks. It is quite possible that a number of heavy stone rings which have been found, were used for digging sticks. The stocks of the grains were probably cut with sickles set with stone teeth, as thousands of such stone tools have been found. They crushed them either dry or wet, in deep, basin-shaped stone *pāṭas* called saddle querns, with the help of a

1. SPPIP, p. 200.
2. Rice impression is found at Lothal. See Ghosh, S.S., Indian Forester, 1961, p. 295.

pounder or rubber. A number of such saddle querns were found both at Navdatoli[1] and Avra[2]. They were of the type with concave or depressed surfaces.

FOOD :—The food was cooked on hearths or *chulas*. In the debris of their houses remains have been found of pig, sheep, goat and deer. All these seem to be domesticated and eaten. But since the grains were varied and plentiful, they relied less on animal food, and hence their remains are fewer in number in comparison with those found in other regions. Economically they seem to have been essentially farmers, but they might have lived by hunting and fishing.

METAL:--People knew copper and bronze, but these were used sparingly. At Kayatha[3], two copper axes with bevelled edges and lenticular section, a copper bar and a bracelet, were discovered in the earliest layer. At Avra,[4] the most noteworthy of the excavated finds, is a small bronze celt recovered in the topmost Chalcolithic layer. Some objects in the shape of simple handleless axes, fish hooks, pins and rings, have been found at Maheshwar and Navdatoli.[5] Possibly in a later phase, they used daggers or swords with a mid-rib, as suggested by a fragment found at this place.[6]

With the emergence of metal tools, the blades remained dominant at the expense of the early stone tools, because of their greater utility. They served the daily needs of cutting vegetables, scraping leather, and piercing stones. They were manufactured from nodules of agate and chalcedony. They were made out of long parallel-sided flakes. A special technique was employed for their manufacture. They vary from 1.75 to 0.50 inches. These small, delicate, stone blades, were hafted in a bone or wooden handle.

ORNAMENTS :--People were fond of ornaments which were

1. EMN, p. 233.
2. JMPIP, pp. 13-40.
3. IAR, 1967-68, p. 24.
4. JMPIP, IV. p. 38.
5. SPPIP, p. 201.
6. Ibid.

made of different material. At Kayatha[1] people used copper bangles, round in section, with featureless terminals. Bangles and rings of copper and clay have been found at Maheswar-Navdatoli,[2] and they were used as ornaments. The ear ornament at Navdatoli is simpler in design, with trace of a stem at the back.[3] A thin gold disc (diameter 2.5. cms, weight 20 grams), was found at Eran[4], but the exact purpose of it was difficult to guess. Thousands of beads made of terracotta, shell, steatite, jasper, agate, carnelian and other stones, have been discovered at Maheshwar[5], Kayatha,[6] Avra[7] and Eran,[8] and a few unfinished beads were also recovered. This indicates that bead making was a flourishing local industry at these places. They are of different shapes and sizes, being small, medium and large, and of spherical, biconical, square, cylindrical and barrel shape, in addition to the arecanut-shape. These beads must have been strung into necklaces which were worn by the people. Bangles, rings, lids, amulets and several other fragmentary objects of shell found at Maheshwar and Navdatoli,[9] show that it was a local industry.

TERRACOTTAS :—People decorated their houses with different kinds of terracottas. Besides decoration, they served some other purposes. A large number of unique figurines of bulls discovered at Kayatha,[10] are either naturalistic or highly stylized. The stylized forms, depicting the hump and the horns, had either a rounded or pedestalled base. Such bull forms have no analogues within the country, or elsewhere. At Navdatoli,[11] an interesting specimen of a tiny bull with a tail

1. IAR, 1967-68, p. 24.
2. SPPIP, p. 201.
3. EMN, p. 204.
4. Bulletin of Ancient Indian History & Archaeology, p. 34.
5. EMN, pp. 177-190.
6. IAR, 1967-68, p. 24.
7. JMPIP, IV, pp. 36-37.
8. Bulletin of Ancient Indian History & Archaeology, p. 37; IAR, 1960-61, p. 13; 1963-64, pp. 15-16.
9. EMN, p. 227.
10. IAR, 1967-68, p. 24.
11. EMN, p. 203.

shown in an applique method, has been recovered. Terracotta bulls have been obtained from Avra[1] and Eran.[2] Outside Malwa, they have been discovered at Sind, Baluchistan and the Punjab. They may prove the possible existence of an early and independent cult, revering the bull. The bird figurines from Navdatoli[3] are remarkable. These are flat based beaked figures, which are possibly connected with the dove figurines associated with the cult of mother-goddess, as suggested by E.G.H. Mackay and V.G. Childe[4] on the basis of the evidence from Crete, Sumer and Indus valley.

Pottery discs were found at Navdatoli[5], Avra,[6] and Eran.[7] Of all the terracotta objects, these were the most abundant. They conform to a graded series of fixed weights, and may, possibly, have been used as weights. Some might have been used as skin rubbers. Solid stone balls were found to stand in simple ratios with one another, and perhaps they served the purpose of weights too. People also used skin rubbers, which are actually the barrel-shaped pieces.

Terracotta wheels are also very important. Two specimens came from Navdatoli.[8] One is biconvex in outline. It is important from the point of view of tracing the development of hubbed wheels. It denotes the intermediate stage between single hubbed, and double hubbed wheels. A toy-cart wheel was also available at Eran.[9] Terracotta wheels, with or without hubs, were obtained from Avra.[10] The most important find of this place consists of a perforated wheel showing eight spokes painted on it. The spokes are red. No painted wheel of this kind has so far been recovered from any other of the Indian sites. Though no wooden wheels were found,

1. JMPIP IV, p. 34.
2. Bulletin of Ancient Indian History and Archaeology, p. 37.
3. EMN, p. 203.
4. Mackay : FEM, Vol. I, pp. 295-6.
5. EMN, p. 195.
6. JMPIP, IV, p. 35.
7. Bulletin of Ancient Indian History and Archaeology, p. 37; IAR, 1963-64, pp. 15-16.
8. EMN, p. 192.
9. Bulletin of Ancient Indian History and Archaeology, p. 37.
10. JMPIP, IV, p. 34.

these terracotta specimens should imply the existence of large wooden carts, which served as means of transport and communication.

Other terracotta objects were found such as human and animal figures, seals, spouts and crucible lids. One disc-like object of bone found at Navdatoli[1], seems to be the spindle whorl for the spinning of cotton. Potter's or cloth dyer's stamps recovered from Avra[2], were perhaps meant for dyeing.

RELATION WITH THE CONTEMPORARY CHALCOLITHIC CULTURES OF OTHER REGIONS :—

There existed mutual cultural contacts between the Malwa Chalcolithic and the contemporary Chalcolithic cultures of the other parts of India. If we compare the Malwa Chalcolithic cultures with them, we find that they generally possess a common economy and technology, but differ in ceramic fabrics, designs and forms. This shows that they had inspiration from some common source, but made modifications according to local environments and climate.

NORTHERN DECCAN CHALCOLITHIC CULTURES :—

The Chalcolithic cultures of Prakash[3], Bahal,[4] Chandoli[5], Jorwe and Nevasa,[6] come under the category of Northern Deccan Chalcolithic cultures. This whole cultural complex is characterized by the Jorwe Nevasian Ware, after the name of the site. As both Malwa and the Northern Deccan are adjacent to each other, the mutual influence of the cultures of the two regions was quite natural. The Malwa Chalcolithic culture had spread as far as Narmada, but its outlines had crossed the Tapti Girna valley, and reached as far as the Pravara-Godavari. Pottery and blades of Malwa type have been unearthed at Prakash in the Purna Tapti valley,

1. EMN, p. 224.
2. JMPIP, IV.
3. IAR, 1954-55, p. 13.
4. Ibid, 1956-57, p. 17.
5. Ibid, 1960-61, pp. 26-27.
6. Report on the Excavations at Nasik and Jorwe; IAR, 1954-55, pp. 5-7, and 1955-56, pp. 8-9.

and at Bahal in the Girna valley, as well as at Chandeli and at Nevasa in Pravara valley. The Jorwe Ware occurs at Navdatoli in phase III. These Northern Deccan Chalcolithic cultures do not seem to have taken much from that of Malwa. On the contrary, they seem to have retained the Neolithic features of the Deccan.

Prakash seems to have possessed many fabrics and forms of the Malwa Ware, such as high-necked jars with lines round the neck, vessels with thin, high necks and everted rims, with the rising 'Sun' design, dishes with carrinated bases and clubbed rims, and vessels with short clubbed rims. Certain designs, like the spotted tiger with his neck turned back, and the crane-like birds among reeds and bushes, have not been found at Navdatoli. The Jorwe Ware includes primarily, bowls and large and tiny globular vessels.

Prakash has coarse grey, fine-grey-and-black, and incised ware. However, the fine-grey-and-black inside having occasional faint linear designs in white, seems to be a variant of the Navdatoli, Nagda and Ahar black-and-red with paintings in white. With regard to the fine grey-and-black with linear paintings, the Prakash vessels are slightly bigger than those at Navdatoli, though the latter seem to have a greater variety of bowl forms and designs in white. The incised ware is identical in fabric and design with that of Navdatoli, but some of the designs of Prakash seem to be new. One is a broad and deep chevron covering the entire surface of the coarse, large platter; second a thumb nail, raised, and with deeply incised design round the neck and third circles, and dots in shallow relief round the neck and shoulder. As at Navdatoli and also at Nagda, Prakash and Nevasa, there is also a very small percentage of dull grey ware, having ochre-paint on the rim portion. There is no white-slipped ware, nor the black-and-red with paintings in white.

The lower layers of the Chalcolithic at Bahl yielded a coarse hand-made greyish pottery with a trace of thinner grey ware with painting in red ochre on rimportion. Similar but thicker fabric of this type was found at Navdatoli and Maheshwar. The channel or cut spout, the high or long-necked jar, a burnished grey-and-black ware with oblique paintings in white indicate contact with Navdatoli.

The typical fabric and bowl forms of Jorwe Nevasa occur in the top layers of the Chalcolithic layers at Navdatoli. Even a sort of a tubular spout of Nevasa is found at Nagda in the lowest layer. So also a dull thick grey ware with ochre paint, is found in very small quantities at Nevasa. There is also a small percentage of ochre-paint at Navdatoli.

THE NEOLITHIC CHALCOLITHIC SETTLEMENTS OF THE DECCAN :—

It appears that the Malwa Chalcolithic culture after reaching the Pravara-Godavari, met another Chalcolithic culture which had spread all over Deccan. This cultural complex is known by the Neolithic chalcolithic settlements of the Deccan. Burnished Grey Ware is a distinctive trait of this culture. The painted sherds of this ware occur at Piklihal,[1] Brahmagiri and Maski. By their meeting, they must have influenced each other. The occurrence of copper in the upper strata of the Neolithic occupation indicates, perhaps, the contact of the Southern Neolithic culture, with the Chalcolithic culture of Malwa spreading through the Northern Deccan. The Malwa and Khandesh sites freely borrowed from those of the Deccan, but the latter do not seem to have taken much from those of Malwa. These, on the contrary, seem to have retained the Neolithic features of the earlier cultures of the Deccan.

BANAS CULTURE :—Malwa Chalcolithic culture was also related to Banas culture which was confined to the South-east of Rajasthan. Ahar culture[2] and Gilund culture[3] are the two main constituents of this culture. Fragments of strap handles and cut-spouted bowls have been found at Navdatoli with which Gilund seems to have some contact. The typical Navdatoli Creamslipped Ware, with designs, like dancing figures and spotted animals, are found in the topmost levels of Gilund, whereas at Navdatoli, they figure in the first and second layers. The Banas culture, with its characteristic pottery, also reached

1. Allchin : Piklihal Excavations, No. 1., Hyderabad.
2. IAR, 1955-56, pp. 11-14; 1957-58, pp. 43-45.
3. Ibid, 1959-60, pp. 41-43.

Mandsor, Nagda, Navdatoli, Avra, etc. At Navdatoli, it was confined to the lowest level and it comprised bowls and cups. It is interesting to note that at Avra, sherds of this ware have been found throughout the Chalcolithic period. Certain similarities of forms and fabrics of pottery, at both Ahar and Navdatoli, show their mutual contact. Dishes on stands and long-necked jars have been discovered at both places. The Cream-slipped Ware was noticed at these places in the lowest level.

THE CHALCOLITHIC CULTURE OF THE GANGETIC DOAB :—

Some affinity of the Malwa Chalcolithic culture may be established even with the chalcolithic culture of Gangetic Doab. Ochre Ware is one of the characteristics of this culture, and it has been found in excavations at Bahadrabad,[1] Ambakheri,[2] Hastinapur[3] and Atranjikhera,[4] and in explorations at Manupur, Bhatpura, etc. That this ware is individualistic in types and designs, has been proved by the excavations of Atranjikhera. It comprises bowls, vases, knobbed lids, dishes on stands and handles. The decorations primarily consist of incised designs, such as triangular notches, notches between parallel lines, wavy lines and rectangular lines making a check design. Some scholars hold that this ware has affinity with the Sothi culture of Kalibangan.

At two of the copper hoard sites, namely Bisauli and Rajpur Parsu, this pottery was found, though without the association of any copper objects. Since pottery also occurred in the lowest layer at Hastinapur, below the Painted Grey Ware, it has been tentatively assumed, that the copper hoards might belong to the makers of such pottery of the pre-Grey Ware period.

Some copper objects of the same peculiar types of these hoards, have been discovered at Kayatha and Navdatoli.

1. IAR, 1957-58, p. 30.
2. Ibid, 1963-64, p. 56.
3. AI, Nos. 10-11.
4. Ibid, 1963-64, p. 45; 1965-66, p. 82; 1967-68, pp. 45-47.

It is therefore likely that the pottery of the copper hoard people of the Gangetic Doab, might have some affinity with that of Kayatha and Navdatoli. H.D. SANKALIA[1] observes that the Ochre Ware is distinctive and perhaps a degraded variant of the Malwa Ware.

Besides Ochre Ware, Painted Black and Red Ware was found at many places in the Gangetic valley. At Atranjikhera, it intervenes between Ochre Ware and Painted Grey Ware. Some remote affinity of this ware may be established with the Black and Red Ware found at Ahar and at some other places in Malwa.

CHALCOLITHIC CULTURE OF SAURASHTRA :—

As the Chalcolithic cultures of Malwa and Saurashtra overlap, it is natural to assume that there may have been some cultural contact between the two. The Chalcolithic cultures of Saurashtra stand for some distinct groups, such as Lothal,[2] Rangpur,[3] Somanatha[4] and Rojadi.[5] After the fall of the Harappan civilisation, the Lustrous Red Ware, the Black and Red Ware with paintings in white, and the Prabhas Ware, came on the scene. The Black and Red Ware remained dominant not only at Ahar, but also in Malwa and Saurashtra. There is dissimilarity in the fabric of pottery between these two regions, but they have resemblances in certain specific forms. Carinated bowls, different kinds of dishes, long-necked jars, wine cups, and basins with straight sides and beaded rims, are found in Malwa as well as in Saurashtra.

BENGAL :—Malwa Chalcolithic culture may have some distant relations with those of Bengal. A number of sites have been found in the valleys of the Ajay and Kunoor, and the site of Rajar Dhipi[6] has been excavated. The finds of this chalcolithic site are very interesting. There is a very fine

1. SPPIP, p. 197, f. n. 125.
2. Lalit Kala, Nos. 3-4, pp. 82-89; IAR, 1959-60, pp.16-18; 1958-59, p. 13.
3. IAR, 1953-54, p. 7; 1954-55, pp. 11-12.
4. Ibid, 1955-56, pp. 7-8; 1956-57, pp. 16-17.
5. Ibid, 1958-59, pp. 19-20.
6. Ibid, 1961-62, pp. 59-62; 1962-63, p. 61.

black-and-red pottery with paintings in white, and a red one also which is occasionally painted. Among the shapes, there are bowls and dishes with small open channel-spouts. These remind one of those of distant Navdatoli in Malwa. Actually, the Pandu Rajar Dhibi black-on-red-ware is quite different from the Malwa Ware, so also is its open spout, a jip rather than the long channel spout with which we are familiar in the Malwa Ware.

ORIGIN OF THE CHALCOLITHIC CULTURES OF MALWA :—

The question of the origin of the Chalcolithic cultures of Malwa is full of controversy, and scholars hold divergent views about it.

WESTERN ASIATIC INFLUENCE :—

Some scholars[1] emphasize that this question should be considered along the political and cultural backgrounds of Western Asia. The first quarter of the second millenium B. C. was a time of troubles, and of invasions by Indo-European tribes. These invasions led to the general break up of the Western Asiatic civilization, and resulted in folk movements and migrations of people towards the east. From the cultural point of view, the Chalcolithic cultures of Iran and the Western Asiatic regions are of greater antiquity and are richer and more elaborate. New types of tools, weapons and pottery came into existence, as is known from the archaeological evidence of Western Asia. It seems that the Indus valley civilization and the Chalcolithic cultures of India, especially Malwa, gradually derived a diffusion of influences and people from Iran and other Western Asiatic regions.

I. FORMS AND FABRICS OF POTTERY :—

It seems that the forms and fabrics of the Chalcolithic pottery of Malwa have some Iranian influence.[2] The channel spouted bowls at Navdatoli are matched with those from Necropole B at Sialk and Tepe Giyan I. The pedestalled bowls show close similarity with corresponding forms at Hissar III.

1. IP, pp. 157-173; SPPIP, p. 201; p. 281.
2. Ibid, p. 162.

The theriomorphic 'bull-like' vases from Navdatoli are similar to the vessels from Sialk. The occurrence of dancing human figures on a white slipped piece of pottery at Navdatoli, recalls a similar vessel from the earliest period at Sialk in Iran. Besides, some painted motifs—human, animal, bird or geometric, also have echoes in the Iranian sites.

2. BLADE INDUSTRY :—

The blade industry[1] was a characteristic of the Malwa Chalcolithic culture. This particular technique of making blades is itself an adaptation from West Asia, having originated in the Jericho region, and being transmitted through settlements in the Fertile Crescent and the Iranian Plateau, to the Indian Chalcolithic culture.

3. COPPER OBJECTS :—

Copper objects also form an integral element of the Chalcolithic culture. The comparative rarity of such objects in the Chalcolithic complex, and the rarity of Chalcolithic sites in the northern plains would make it difficult to regard their origin as indigenous, but rather indicate contact with West Asia.[2]

4. BEADS : —

The discovery of faience and steatite beads in the Protohistoric period at Navdatoli[3], having similarities with those found in the Indus valley sites, and sites in Western Asia, tend to indicate a possible contact between these regions.

GRAINS :—

Different kinds of grains found at Navdatoli at so early a period point to West Asia as the source of their origin.[4] The distribution and antiquity of wheat, lentils and linseed, suggest Western Asiatic contacts, whereas rice is believed, by most authorities, to be indigenous.

CRITICISM OF THE THEORY

There are some scholars who do not agree with this theory. According to them, the forms and fabric of pottery found in

1. IP, p. 163.
2. Ibid, p. 165.
3. EMN, pp. 182-183.
4. IP, p. 169.

Chalcolithic period in Malwa are not actually related to those of Iran. The channel-spouted bowls from Necropole B at Sialk are assignable to 1000-800 B. C. At Navdatoli, they are not later than 1200 B. C. Against this, H. D. SANKALIA[1] holds that it was not necessary to copy them from Iran, but from other earlier sites of West Asia. The channel-spout in Western Asia was prevalent in 2500 B. C. This type of vessel from Khiroki Kitia in Cyprus is assignable to about the fourth or fifth millenium B. C.

S. P. GUPTA[2] holds that the channel-spouted vases from Sialk have not only considerably longer channels, but in addition, handles as well. If it is the case of import, influence and imitation, there should also be handles on the bowls at Navdatoli. S. R. RAO[3] is of the opinion that spouted vessels were already known to the Harappans, and there was no question of their imitation from the west. It has been demonstrated at Rangpur how wine-cups evolved from the bowls and dishes on stands, in three stages. At the intermediate stage, the bowls have been found at Ahar. It is not necessary to look for any foreign influence to understand the emergence of wine-cups.

Regarding the designs on the pottery, S.P. GUPTA[4] argues that many designs of the Navdatoli pottery are found on Neolithic Chinese pottery. GRACE MORLEY observes that such a parallelism, is not so real as to indicate any relationship of give-and-take between the two countries. It is not, therefore, a case of diffusion. It also seems to be quite plausible, that at a certain stage of cultural development, men from different places express themselves almost in the same fashion without being much influenced by their contemporaries or neighbours. The decoration of dancing human figures on white slipped pottery is of a general kind and we cannot deduce any conclusion from it.

Iron and Grey Ware were prevalent at Hissar II and Anau III, in Necropole B and Tape Giyan I. Both are absent in Malwa in the early Chalcolithic period. If there was any

1. IP, p. 166.
2. Ibid, p. 170.
3. Ibid, p. 171.
4. Ibid, p. 170.

influence from Western Asia, both iron and Grey Ware would have been adopted. Against this, it may be suggested that its absence was due to selective borrowing.

The blade industry of Malwa did not necessarily originate in Western Asia. It seems that this industry is related to the South Neolithic culture, which according to B.K. THAPAR,[1] is indigenous.

Against the above-mentioned argument about the grains, it may be suggested that wheat was known to the people of Mohenjodaro. Rice is believed to be of indigenous origin. It is possible that the grains cultivated in Malwa in the Chalcolithic period might have been independent in origin and without any influence from the Western Asia.

ORIGIN FROM HARAPPAN CULTURE :—

There is another view[2], that the Malwa Chalcolithic cultures, like other Chalcolithic cultures of India, have their roots in the Harappan culture. After being uprooted from their hearths by the invaders, the Harappans migrated towards Malwa and settled down on the banks of the rivers. While the Harappan culture began to decline from about 2000 B.C., this marks the beginning of the Chalcolithic cultures. We may recognize vague Harappan influences in recurrent forms, and occasional patterns of the pottery, of Chalcolithic Malwa. The dish-on-stand and certain other forms of dishes of Harappa, have been found in Nagda and Navdatoli. The pottery black-on-red, black-on-cream wares, and painted black and red, found at some sites, such as Kayatha and Manoti, have some affinity with the pottery of Harappa.

But there is no clear link between the Harappan culture and the Malwa Chalcolithic culture. There is no stratigraphicaloverlapping. The Harappan culture is urban, but the Malwa Chalcolithic culture is rural.

CHALCOLITHIC CULTURES REPRESENT THE ARYANS:—

One of the theories[3] is that these Chalcolithic cultures might represent the Aryans. From the *Purāṇas*, we know that the Yādavas and their sub-branches, settled down in the

1. IP, p. 70.
2. WHEELER : Early India and Pakistan, pp. 125-26.
3. IP, p. 223; SPPIP, p. 279.

Narmada valley. The chronological estimate on the basis of c-14, goes against this Aryan theory. Generally, scholars place the migration of the Aryans towards India in about 1200 B. C., but the Chalcolithic cultures of Malwa are dated from 2000 B.*C.* The study of Aryan expansion in India is associated with the fully developed iron industry and swift-moving horses, without which the militant race would not have established its supremacy. But on the chalcolithic pottery of Malwa, there is an absence of horses in the painted designs, and no terracottas or bones of horses have been discovered. The theory of an early Aryan movement from Iran is not proved. There is also the question of route, and no remains have been found in the intervening land.

PRE-ARYANS AS AUTHORS :—

If they were not Aryans, they were pre-Aryans,[1] and we should attribute these cultures to the Nāgas, Śabaras and Pulindas, who are, according to the *Purāṇas* the original inhabitants of the Narmada valley. However no much reliance can be placed on *Purāṇas* because they are of a very late period. The archaeological excavations have not proved their genuineness because no written record conforming to the account of the *Purāṇas* has been discovered.

ANCESTORS OF SOME OF THE PRIMITIVE OR ABORIGINAL TRIBES AS AUTHORS :—

Haimendorf[2] has suggested that the authors of these Chalcolithic cultures of India, including Malwa, might have been the ancestors of some of the primitive or aboriginal tribes now confined to the forests or hills, of Madhya Pradesh, Orissa, Bihar and Andhra, tribes like the Gondas, Baigas of Bastar, Śabaras of Chota Nagpur, or the Chanchus of Karnool. It might be held that the Bhīls and Mundas, who are supposed to be some of the Kolarian tribes from the North-West, driven to their present forest habitat by the Aryan-speaking people, were the bearers of the various Chalcolithic cultures of Rajasthan, Madhya Pradesh and the Deccan.

In fact, the *Purāṇas*, and other literature, do speak of the

1. EMN, p. 252.
2. IP, p. 227.

Bhīls, Nishadas, Pulindas and other tribes inhabiting these regions. However, these references are much later than the Chalcolithic culture, which is dated about 2000 B.C.

The second difficulty is that all these tribes are at varying levels of the hunting and food-collecting stage. They practise primitive agriculture by burning forest enclaves, and are ignorant of the real art of ploughing. None of these has any knowledge of fine pottery and grinding of stone implements, which characterize the chalcolithic cultures. This is due to de-socializing and de-culturalizing factors, as argued by some anthropologists. There are certain examples of the tribes, like the Hūṇas and the Gurjaras, who had once been empire builders, but who sank back to the life of shepherds. This is possible also with the primitive tribes under reference, but the links with the past have to be established. For this, excavations are to be carried out in the excluded area of the primitive tribes in order to get an idea of the traces of the culture which their ancestors had carried with them when pushed back by the oncoming Aryans.

ANTHROPOLOGICAL EVIDENCE :—The anthropological evidence[1] from Nevasa indicates an indigenous element in the culture. The limited skeletal data from Nevasa (Ehrhardt, 1960) has shown the prevalence of the native Australoid element among the Chalcolithic people, pointing in the direction of an indigenous folk. The Malwa Chalcolithic cultures are not different from the Northern Deccan Chalcolithic cultures, and hence, like Nevasa, the Chalcolithic culture of Malwa is also native.

All these are purely speculations about the origin and authors of the Chalcolithic cultures of Malwa. In order to say something definite about it, there must be more tangible data, like pottery, particularly abundant skeletal material, and some form of writing if it was there. From the existing material, it seems that this culture is not the result of one particular cause, but its different traits originated in different ways. It seems that the people were indigenous. They adopted new ideas from Iran, and particularly their pottery in its forms

1. IP, p. 189.

and fabric was influenced by that of Iran. The Harappan culture and the other contemporary Chalcolithic cultures, also considerably contributed to the origin and gradual development of this culture.

END OF CHALCOLITHIC CULTURES :—The question then arises of how these Chalcolithic cultures of Malwa came to an end. Nothing definite can be said on this because of lack of sufficient evidence. It is held by some scholars that the iron-using people from Ujjain and Nagda with their weapons and implements, might have been responsible for the destruction of these Chalcolithic cultures in about the eighth or seventh century B.C. At Ujjain, iron was found along with the painted Grey Ware.[1] This Painted Grey Ware has been ascribed by B. B. Lal[2] and others, to the Aryans. This shows that the Aryans in their expansion towards the south from the Gangetic Doab, brought about the destruction of these cultures.

It may be suggested that no one destroyed these Chalcolithic cultures. But in the sixth century B.C. it gradually disappeared when iron, minted money, houses of bricks, and towns, came into existence. All these factors led to the foundation of a new economy. It thus seems that the disappearance of the Chalcolithic cultures was natural.

1. IAR, 1956-57, pp. 20-28; 1957-58, pp. 32-36; 1959, p. 78.
2. IA, Nos. 10-11 (1955), p. 13; IAR, 1954-55, 150-1.

Chapter VI

LEGENDARY AND TRADITIONAL HISTORY

The *Purāṇas* and the epics give us the legendary and traditional history of Malwa before the sixth century B. C. They mention the names of old dynasties, kings, and *ṛishis*. As these are late works, and sometimes they give mutually confusing and contradictory statements, they cannot be relied upon unless they are confirmed by some other independent contemporary evidence. At the same time, we cannot reject this evidence wholesale, because it sometimes gives valuable information.

NO MENTION OF MALWA REGION IN VEDIC LITERATURE :—

The *Vedas*, which were written before the sixth century B.C., give little information about the early history of Malwa. They do not mention this region. The Vindhya hills were unknown and there is no mention of the Narmada river. From this, it may be inferred that the Aryan tribes had not yet begun their advance towards the south. At the same time, it is not necessarily to be presumed that the Aryans did migrate to this region during the Vedic period. The non-mention of the Vindhyas and Narmada in the *Vedas* may be only accidental, and we cannot derive any conclusion about the occupation and expansion of the Aryans from it.

The *Vedas* and the *Purāṇas* contain contradictory views about the expansion of the Aryans in India. Whereas the Vedic literature makes it clear that the Aryans moved eastward and southward from their original home in the Punjab, the *Purāṇas*[1] state that the Aryan dynasties began in the Madhyadesa, Bihar and even Gujarat, and later conquered other parts of India including the Punjab. The *Purāṇas*

1. AIHI, p. 302.

associate the Aryans with Malwa from very early times, but according to the *Vedas*, the migration took place in the later Vedic period.

OCCUPATION OF MALWA REGION BY THE NĀGAS AND THE HAIHAYAS :—

Several *Purāṇas* and the epics unanimously declare that Māhishmatī was situated on the Narmada, and further associate the Haihayas, a branch of the Yaduvaṁśa, with it. The names of the members of the family ending with '*haya*' and '*aśva*' as *Daśāśva* suggest, that these were Aryan-speaking people.[1] The *Purāṇas* also inform us that the previous inhabitants of this area were the Nāgas whom the Haihayas defeated. The Nāg as gave their princess Narmadā to Purukutsa, the ruler of Ayodhyā. They induced him to destroy the Mauneya Gandharvas[2] who had despoiled them. Purukutsa rescued them from the Gandharvas. This indirectly shows the contact of the Aryan culture of the North with that of the Nāgas.

There is another view in some *Purāṇas*,[3] that Muchukunda, the son of Māndhātā, was a famous king. He built and fortified a town on Narmada between Pāriyātra and the Riksha (Satpurā) mountains. Muchukunda's supremacy, however, did not last long, and the Haihaya King Mahishmanta conquered that town and named it Māhishmatī.

CONTROVERSY AMONG SCHOLARS ABOUT THE DATE OF VEDIC CULTURE :—

Scholars hold different views about the date of Vedic culture in India. F. MAX MÜLLER placed the date of Vedic culture, on the basis of Ṛigveda, in 1200 B.C., and the Aryans might have settled down in Malwa in about 1000 B. C. G. WINTERNITZ assigned it to the latter half of the third millenium B.C. P.L. BHARGAVA[4] puts the early Aryan habitation in 3000 B.C. in Saptasindhu, and their migration and settlement in Malwa in 2000 B.C. A.S. ALTEKAR[5] suggested

1. EMN, p. 5.
2. The Vedic Age, p. 278; *Bhāgavata* 9-7 and 1-3.
3. AIHT, p. 262.
4. India in the Vedic Age.
5. PIHC, Presidential Address, Gauhati Session, 1959.

that the Aryan entry into India was 2000 B.C. and within two hundred years i.e. by 1800 B.C., they became successful in carving out their settlement in Malwa. H. D. SANKALIA tentatively places the Aryan civilization between 3000 B.C. to 1000 B.C.[1] B.B. LAL[2] and Y.D. SHARMA[3] regard the Vedic period from 1200 B.C. to 800 B.C. Some scholars, like R.E.M. WHEELER,[4] believe that there were two Aryan movements in India, in 2000 B.C. and 1100 B.C. respectively.

ARYAN TRIBES DURING THE EARLY VEDIC PERIOD AND THE POSITION OF THE YĀDAVAS :—

It seems that during the Early Vedic period, the Aryans settled in the Saptasindhu and were divided into a number of tribal principalities ruled by their chiefs. The *Dāśarājña*, or the battle of ten kings, is an historical battle of note, in which important tribes and personalities participated. Sudāsa, the ruler of Bharatas, emerged victorious after defeating a tribal confederacy of ten kings. Of these, five were well-known tribes, such as Pūru, Yadu, Turvaśa, Anu and Druhyu, along with five of lesser note. The Pūrus were ruled by Purukutsa, and the Yadus lived in the Southern Punjab. H.C. RAYCHAUDHURI[5] on the evidence of one *Ṛigvedic* reference, holds that the Yadus had come from a distant land and were associated with the Persians.

It seems that this battle of ten kings is of great importance, and it led to the migration of the Aryan tribes into different directions. Some small tribes disappeared, while others merged themselves into bigger ones. The confederation of Tritsus, Bharatas and Pūrus, was known as KURUS, which ruled over Hastināpura. The Aryan tribes settled down at Kāśī, Ayodhyā, Mathurā and Saurāshṭra. The Yādavas led by Agastya, migrated to the Narmada valley.

P.L. BHARGAVA'S VIEWS ABOUT THE EARLY HAIHAYAS:-

The *Purāṇas* give valuable information about the Haihayas,

1. IP, p. 226.
2. AI, X and XI, pp. 150-151.
3. IP, p. 233.
4. Early India and Pakistan, p. 28.
5. PHAI, p. 139.

which is not available from the Vedic literature. Their rulers Kṛitavīrya and Arjuna extended their sway far and wide by their conquests, and they became the dominant power of India. In the *Purāṇas*, they have been described as the rulers of Avanti region, but P.L. Bhargava[1] holds the view that they were at this time ruling over the west of Saptasindhu, and he gives the following arguments in support of his view :—

(1) The country of Avanti was named after the Avantis, one of the five branches descended from Arjuna's grandson Tālajaṅgha. The Avantis, therefore, must have been the founders of the Avanti kingdom. It is thus clear that Avanti could not have been under the rule of Arjuna and Jayadhvaja, if founded by their descendants.

(2) The *ṛishi* Jamadagni, with whom Arjuna came into conflict, is said by the *Mahābhārata* to have practised austerities near Kurukshetra, far away from Avanti.

(3) When there was a war between Paraśurāma and the Haihayas, the Haihaya princes took refuge for a long time in the Himālayas. If the Haihayas had been ruling in Avanti, the natural place of refuge would have been the Vindhyas, and not the distant Himālayas.

It is only after their defeat by Sagara, the ruler of Ayodhyā, that the Haihayas left their original home and settled in Central and Western India, as indicated by the *Purāṇas*. The account of the Haihaya kings closes about the time of Sagara. The account of their successors in Central and Western India was not available to the Puranic editors of northern India. The only thing known about them after their migration, was that they divided themselves into five branches.

However, these arguments do not seem to be plausible. There are strong traditions recorded in the *Purāṇas* for the association of the Haihayas and their rulers, Kṛitavīrya and Arjuna, with Māhishmatī, and the Avantis. One of the branches of the Haihayas was ruling over Ujjain. The non-mention of the Haihaya rulers after their defeat from Sagara in the *Purāṇas*, was due to the fact that there was no noteworthy ruler afterwards.

1. India in the Vedic Age, pp. 73 ff.

EARLY HAIHAYA RULERS :

The Haihayas are known to have ruled over the region of Avanti. One of their kings was Sāhañja, said to have founded a city called Sāhañjanī, and his son, Mahishmanta, founded, the town Māhishmatī.[1] This dynasty rose to power under their successsor, Bhadraśreṇya[2] who was an aggressive monarch and conquered the Paurava realm. He also extended his kingdom by conquering the Kāśī territories. The Kāśī King Divodāsa I, recovered his kingdom and capital from Bhadraśreṇya's sons, sparing one young son, Durdama.[3] Durdama re-established himself in it, and he was succeeded by Kanaka.[4]

KṚITAVĪRYA :—The next important ruler was Kṛitavīrya,[5] who was a great monarch, and was called *Samrāṭ* and *Chakravartin*. During his long reign, he extended the Haihaya sway far and wide by his conquests, and raised the Haihaya power to great eminence. He is known by his patronymic, Kārtavīrya, and also as Sahasrārjuna (thousand armed). The thousand arms ascribed to Arjuna were possibly the soldiers of his powerful army.

ARJUNA :—The son and successor of Kṛitavīrya was Arjuna[6] who was a great conqueror. Immediately after his accession, he began his career of conquests, which at once carried the Haihaya empire to great prominence and supremacy. At this time, the Pauravas of Ayodhyā lost their paramountcy, and their place was taken by the Haihayas. Arjuna's contemporary rulers of Ayodhyā, were Triśaṅku and Hariśchandra.

HIS CONQUESTS :—Arjuna fought against the Karkoṭa Nāgas of Anūpa, and after capturing their territory, made Māhishmatī his capital. When Rāvaṇa invaded his territories, he defeated him, and made him captive, but subsequently

1. AIHT, p. 263, Hiralal : *Madhya Pradesh Kā Itihāsa*, p. 4.
2. Ibid.
3. Ibid.
4. Ibid.
5. *Bhāgavata* 9/125; AIHT., pp. 141-2, 144; 151-2, 197, 265.
6. AIHT, pp. 7, 16, 25, 41, 72, 76, 130, 144, 151-3, 155, 171, 199, 206, 229, 242, 262, 265-7, 270.

released him. He appears to have led his victorious campaign from the mouth of the Narmada to as far north as the Himalayas, since in one of his raids, he is said to have come across the hermitage of Āpava Vasishṭha in the Himalayas and burnt it, as a consequence of which, he was cursed. He performed a number of sacrifices in commemoration of his conquests. His victories show that he carried the banner of Aryan conquest far and wide, and that Māhishmatī on the Narmada was an outpost of the Aryan colonies of those days.

Arjuna has been described as an ideal monarch unparalleled in penance, charities, learning and virtues. He ruled over his subjects with perfect justice. He propitiated Dattātreya, a sage regarded as an incarnation of Vishṇu.

HIS TREATMENT TOWARDS THE BHĀRGAVAS :—

In spite of all these virtues, his treatment towards the Bhārgavas was not good and is, actually, a blot on his character. These Bhārgavas were the priests of his father, Kṛitavīrya, who bestowed great wealth on them. Arjuna demanded it back but they refused to give it up, and they fled to other countries for safety. Arjuna or his sons ill-treated their Bhārgava priest Jamadagni, and finally killed him.

ARJUNA KILLED BY RĀMA :—

Jamadagni's son Rāma declared war on the Haihayas. He was supported by the princes of Ayodhyā and Kānyakubja, who were allied to him by marriage. Together they opposed the dangerous raids of the Haihayas. Rāma killed Arjuna and slew many Haihayas. The tradition grew that he destroyed the Kshatriyas twenty-one times.

ARJUNA'S SUCCESSORS AND THEIR FALL :—

Arjuna had many sons and the chief among them was Jayadhvaja.[1] His son was Tālajaṅgha. The *Jātakas* and the *Arthaśāstra* of Kauṭilya preserve the tradition of how the powerful Haihaya prince Kārttikeyārjuna met his terrible fate in consequence of his sinful deeds. The *Arthaśāstra* legend alludes also to a similar fate met by Tālajaṅgha who is

1. AIHT, p. 266.

mentioned in the *Purāṇas* as one of the sons of Kārttikeyārjuna.[1]

HAIHAYA'S CONQUEST OF EASTERN KINGDOM :—

The Haihayas revived and again grew powerful. They comprised five leading groups—Vītihotras, Śāryātas, Bhojas, Avantis and Tuṇḍikeras. and all were called Tālajaṅghas.[2] Their dominions stretched from the Gulf of Cambay to the Ganges-Jumna Doab, and hence to Benaras. They attacked the eastern Kingdoms with the cooperation of north-west tribes. The Kingdom of Kānyakubja fell victim to their raids, and the kingdom of Ayodhyā was open to revolt. Bāhu, king of Ayodhyā, driven from his throne, took refuge in the forest. It seems that all the Kingdoms between north-west and Ayodhyā must have been overthrown. The Haihaya conquests reached the kingdom of Vaiśālī, but they were defeated by the king and his allies. In this way, the Haihaya aggression in the east was checked by the Vaiśāla Kings.[3]

STIFF RESISTANCE BY THE RULERS OF KĀŚĪ AND AYODHYĀ :—

The rulers of Kāśī and Ayodhyā gave stiff resistance to the constant attacks of the Haihayas. They had been carrying on a long struggle from the eastern portion of their territory which adjoined the Vaiśālī kingdom against the Haihayas. Haryaśva, king of Kāśī, fought with the Vītahavya-Haihayas at the confluence of the Ganges and Jamuna. Haryaśva's son was Sudeva, whom the Haihayas defeated. Sudeva's son was Divodāsa, who built a city called Vārāṇasī for the second time. When the Haihayas defeated him, he was forced to leave the city. Divodāsa's son was Pratardana, who attacked and destroyed the Vītahavyas. Pratardana's son was Vatsa, who carried the victory further and annexed the country around Kauśāmbī, which was named after the Vatsa kingdom.

After Bāhu, his son Sagara, the ruler of Ayodhyā, recovered his lost kingdom with the help of the Bhārgavas. He

1. Ujjayinī in Ancient India, p. 12.
2. AIHT, p. 267.
3. Ibid, p. 268.

destroyed the Haihaya power and delivered the people from their devastating raids, and restored peace.

RULERS OF AVANTI DURING BHĀRATA WAR :—

We know about the rulers of Avanti during the Bhārata war. It is said that Rājyādhidevī, a Yadu princess, was married to a king of Avanti[1]. She gave birth to two sons, Vinda and Upavinda, who are most probably to be identified with the heroic Avanti princes Vinda and Anuvinda.[2] At the time of great Bhārata war, Vinda and Anuvinda were the rulers of Avanti. Śrīkṛishṇa defeated Anuvinda, and married his sister Mitravindā.[3] These kings, along with Nīla of Māhishmatī, sided with the Kauravas in the Bhārata war.[4] Anuvinda was killed by Arjuna in that war. Śrīkṛishṇa and Balarāma in their childhood stayed at Ujjayinī, as disciples with Sāndīpani, and gained mastery in the contemporary arts and sciences.[5]

After the Bhārata war, no definite history of Avanti is available, and we do not know the names of its rulers. According to some scholars, the twenty Vītihotras, who are mentined in the *Purāṇas* as having ruled after the Bhārata war, were really the rulers of Avanti.

CONTRIBUTIONS OF THE HAIHAYAS :—

The Haihayas ruled for a considerable time over Avanti and their remarkable contribution is that they aryanised this region to a great extent. For the first time, they carried the banner of Aryan culture with them and spread it far and wide. As they were free from orthodoxy, they freely mixed with the non-Aryans, with whom they had marital relations, and some of whose customs they incorporated. They were not so orthodox in the observance of the Aryan *Dharma*. It is for this reason that the epics and the *Purāṇas* called them Asuras, and classed them with the tribes of the extreme north-west and west, among the Nīchyas and Apāchyas.

1. *Vishṇu Purāṇa* IV, 12; *Agni Purāṇa*, Ch. 275.
2. Ibid; IV, 14.
3. *Bhāgavata* x, 58, 30-31.
4. CHI, p. 274.
5. *Skanda Purāṇa*, V, 27.

ARCHAEOLOGICAL EVIDENCE CONFIRMING THE ACCOUNT OF THE EPICS AND THE PURĀṆAS :—

The question now is how far the traditional and legendary history of Malwa is confirmed by the evidencc of archaeological excavations carried out at Maheshwar, Navdatoli, Kayatha, Eran and Ujjain. This type of archaeological evidence cannot confirm the Puranic account, because no written record was discovered in the excavations. We cannot identify these cultures with certain names of the tribes found in the *Purāṇas* and the epics. These excavations simply confirm the antiquity of the sites about which there are references in the *Purāṇas*. On the basis of pottery and other remains found in the excavations, we know about the movements and cultural contacts of the early tribes.

On the basis of the Puranic traditions, it is believed that the Haihayas, a branch of the Aryans, migrated to the Narmada valley and uprooted the Nāgas. According to some scholars,[1] this incident took place in about 1800 B.C. the period which coincides with the Chalcolithic cultures of India. The Painted-black-on-red-Ware, or the Malwa Ware, found in excavations at places such as Maheshwar, Navdatoli, Avra and Kayatha, remained dominant in Malwa region during this period. The Ochre Ware found at several places in the Gangetic valley is perhaps a degraded form of the Malwa Ware. The Painted Black and Red Ware found both in Malwa and the Gangetic valley is related to the Ahar Ware. Some copper objects also have been discovered along with the pottery. One view[2] is that this Chalcolithic culture probably originated due to Iranian or Western Asiatic influence and contacts, or actual migrations, as it is clear from some pottery forms, fabric and other evidence. The Haihayas are actually a branch of the Yādavas, who according to reference, had come from a distant land and were associated with the Persians. Some scholars regard these people as the first wave of Aryans from Western Asia.

If these are not the Aryans, they may be the Nāgas or

1. IP, p. 223.
2. Ibid, pp. 157-173; SPPIP, p. 201; p. 281.

Pulindas about whom there are references in the *Purāṇas*[1]. They were the original inhabitants of the Narmada valley. As the *Purāṇas* are of a late period, much reliance cannot be placed on their statements. We cannot identify the names of the tribes as mentioned in the *Purāṇas* with the bearers of the Chalcolithic cultures of so early a period. Thus, it is not definite whether the Aryans or the Nāgas were the bearers of these Chalcolithic cultures.

Some scholars[2] advocate that the Haihayas ruled over Malwa in about 900 or 800 B.C., and they ascribe the Painted Grey Ware culture to the Aryans. The Painted Grey Ware has been discovered in the excavations at Ahichchhatra,[3] Hastināpura[4], valley of Sarasvatī and Dṛishadvatī[5], Atranjikhera,[6] Kauśāmbī,[7] Ujjain,[8] etc. This culture seems to have begun from about 1200 B.C. as is clear from the excavations of Atranjikhera. There is a paucity of the Painted Grey Ware found at Ujjain, and it is of simple painted designs, and it has been dated 800-500 B.C.

B. B. Lal[9] attributed this culture provisionally and tentatively to the Aryans because it was generally found on the sites bearing the names mentioned in the *Mahābhārata*. It was discovered in abundance at Sarasvatī and Dṛishadvatī, actually the Junction of the Aryans. This view was further strengthened by the discovery of iron along with the Painted Grey Ware in the excavations of Atranjikhera, and it is dated 1200 B.C. The name '*ayas*' of the *Ṛigveda* has been interpreted in the sense of iron by some scholars[10]. Iron was also found associated with painted Grey Ware at Hastināpura, Alamgirpur,

1. EMN, p. 252; IP, p. 227.
2. AI Nos. 18 and 19, p. 208; XXVI Vol. of Orientalists and Indian Prehistory.
3. AI, No. 1, pp. 58-59.
4. Ibid, Nos. 10 and 11, p. 13.
5. Geographical Journal, No. 39, pp. 173-82; Bulletin National Institute of Sciences in India, No. 1, pp. 36-42.
6. IAR, 1963-64, p. 45; 1965-66, p. 82; 1967-68, pp. 45-47.
7. Ibid, 1957-58, p. 47.
8. Ibid, 1956-57, p. 219.
9. AI, 10 and 11, p. 13.
10. IP, p. 178.

Kauśāmbī and Ujjain. The antiquity of iron has been dated at least 800 B.C. It seems that the Aryans after their entry into India introduced Painted-Grey-Ware and iron.

In the words of Y. D. SHARMA, the study of the Aryan expansion must be made in the light of the fully developed iron industry, and swift-moving horses, without which this militant race would not have established its supremacy over the Asuras, Dāsas, etc. In the *Ṛigveda*, we do not know of any cultural phase other than that of the Painted Grey Ware, which is associated with a fully developed iron industry, and the expansive use of horses, from its very beginning. Finally, the image of culture, which emerges from the study of the *Ṛigveda*, seems to correspond more to the Painted-Grey-Ware Culture. Some scholars, like R. E. M. WHEELER,[1] consider it the second wave of Aryan migration to India from the West.

Besides iron, Eye Goddess[2] was found at the Painted Grey level at Ujjain. It also appeared at Alamgirpur at the same level, along with iron. These are the evolved forms of their proto-types from Harappan sites. A large number of such figurines were found in alabaster in a temple at Tell Basak. It shows a resemblance to the Eye-goddess in West Asia. This goddess seems to be associated with the Aryans of the West.

It is reasonable to hold that the traditional and legendary history known from the literary sources of the epics and the *Purāṇas* about the Haihayas corresponds well with the Painted-Grey-Ware culture of Ujjain. About the early Chalcolithic cultures of Malwa, nothing can be said definitely, unless some written record is found.

1. Early India and Pakistan, p. 28.
2. IP, p. 165.

CHAPTER VII

THE PRADYOTA-MAURYA PERIOD

(FROM 546 B.C. TO 187 B.C.)

I

(POLITICAL HISTORY)

The period of the sixth century B.C. is very important in Indian history because there came into existence for the first time, organised states known as the '*Ṣoḍaśa Mahājanapadas*'[1] (sixteen big States). Some of these were republics or oligarchies, while others were monarchical states. Among these, Avanti, Kosala, Vatsa and Magadha were the most important.

It seems that when the Vītihotras and Avantis passed away, the country or kingdom of the Avantis was divided into two kingdoms, one placed in the Dakshiṇāpatha having Māhishmatī for its capital, and the other, i.e., the northern kingdom, having its capital at Ujjayinī. The southern kingdom, with its capital Māhishmatī, was ruled by Viśvabhū, one of the seven contemporary kings of the line of Bharata.[2] At Ujjain, a minister named Pulika (Puṇika) is said to have killed his master and appointed his own son Pradyota, in the very sight of

1. *Aṅguttara*, I, 213; IV, 252, 256, 260; *Mahāvastu*, I, 34, II, 3; *Vinaya* Texts II, 146 fn; Niddesa II, 37. Jaina *Bhagavatīsūtra*; *Saya* XV, *Uddessa* I (HOERNLE—the *Uvāsagadasāo*, II, Appendix).
   This account is also supported by Pāṇini who lived in the sixth century B. C. Baudhāyana in his *Dharmasūtra* also mentions some of these states.
2. *Dīgha*, II, 236. The *Mahāgovinda Suttanta* also refers to this ruler. See, PHAI, p. 145.

the Kshatriyas.[1] Pradyota thus was Puṇika's son[2], and with him commenced the Pradyota dynasty.

Pradyota was one of the most powerful monarchs of North India in the time of Buddha, and in his days, Avanti rose to a high position. The Buddhist text *Mahāvagga*[3] mentions that he was a great soldier. According to the *Purāṇas*, he reduced many of the contemporary rulers into subjection. The *Purāṇas* do not give a detailed list, but they may be among the rulers of *Ṣoḍaśa-Mahājanapadas*.

DIPLOMATIC RELATIONS WITH MAGADHA :—

The *Purāṇas* wrongly mention Pradyota and Bimbisāra as ruling over Magadha, separated by interval of over a hundred and fifty years. They were, in fact, contemporaries, ruling over Avanti and Magadha respectively, as known to us from Buddhist, Jaina, and other Sanskrit works. The mistake of including the Avanti rulers in the Magadha list probably arose on account of the sovereignty established by Avanti over Magadha.[4]

The relations of Pradyota with Bimbisāra were cordial. Bimbisāra sent his famous physician Jīvaka to cure Pradyota when he fell ill.[5] On the other hand, the Jaina legends mention that Pradyota went forth to attack Rājagṛiha, even during the lifetime of Bimbisāra,[6] but the attempt was foiled by the cunning prince Abhaya.

It is, however, definite that the relations of Pradyota became strained with his son Ajātaśatru. Ajātaśatru is said to have murdered his own father. He adopted an aggressive

1. *Matsya*, p. 272, 1, V. 37. 303.
2. The Tibetans style Pradyota's father Anantanemi. See essay on Guṇāḍhya published in ABORI, 1920-21. This indicates that Puṇika did not install his own son as stated by the *Purāṇas* but the son of his master, the Vītihotra. But this view is wrong as Bāṇa in the H. C. VI, called the youngest son Pradyota as Pauṇakī. This shows that Puṇika was the father of Pradyota.
3. SBE, XVII, p. 187.
4. Hindu Civilization, pp. 235 & 236.
5. Jīvaka was the historical figure and lived during this period because the *Jīvakāmravana vihāra* is attributed to the court physician.
6. ABORI, 1920-21; DPDN, I, 128.

policy of attacking and conquering Vaiśālī. Pradyota was related to Chetaka, the king of Vaiśālī, by some matrimonial alliance.[1] He was himself an ambitious ruler and he could not tolerate the aggressive policy of conquest launched by Ajātaśatru. Both of them wanted to establish their supremacy in Northern India. Pradyota was planning an attack upon his capital at Rājagṛiha.[2] As Ajātaśatru apprehended an invasion by Pradyota, he fortified his capital Rājagṛiha.

VATSARĀJA OF KAUŚĀMBĪ :—Pradyota wanted to consolidate and extend his kingdom. In his neighbourhood, there was the powerful kingdom of Kauśāmbī ruled by his rival, named Udayana Vatsarāja, of the celebrated Bharata family. Pradyota wanted to annex his kingdom, but for this he did not follow a policy of open and direct campaign against such a kingdom. There are legendary traditions[3] about Pradyota and his neighbour Udayana. After critical examination of these legends, we may derive some historical facts. King Pradyota of Avanti and king Udayana of Kośāmbī were believed to have been contemporary rulers of adjoining kingdoms, and to have been connected by marriage, and to have engaged in war.[4] It seems that later on, cordial relations were established between Pradyota and Udayana.[5]

PUSHKARASĀRIN OF TAXILA :—Pradyota engaged in

1. *Majjhima Nikāya*, III. 7.
2. CHI, I, p. 311.
3. The commentary on verses 21-23 of the *Dhammapada* gives a long and romantic story of the way in which Vasula-dattā, the daughter of king Pajjota of Avanti, became the wife of Udayana of Kośāmbī.

   King Udayana was very fond of music and of capturing wild elephants, and Pradyota trapped him by luring him into the pursuit of a faked elephant. Taken captive, Udayana was treated in a right royal manner at Ujjayinī, and was requested to teach music to princess Vāsavadattā. Love arose at first sight, and Udayana soon escaped with Vāsavadattā.

   The Udayana legend has long been very popular and has captivated the hearts of the public. Kālidāsa says that even at his time, there were old people in Ujjain who were proficient in the legend.
4. Buddhist India, pp. 4-7.
5. Vikrama Volume, Eng. ed., p. 478.

hostilitics with Pushkarasarin (Pukkusati) of Taxila, but the cause is not known. Pushkarasārin is said to have sent an ambassador and a letter to king Bimbisāra of Magadha.[1] But Bimbisāra was in no mood to alienate Pradyota. Pradyota was unsuccessful in his war, and was only saved from disaster by the outbreak of hostilities between Pushkarasāri and the Pāṇḍavas.[2] These Pāṇḍavas appear to have been settled in the Punjab.[3]

THE ŚŪRASENAS OF MATHURĀ :—

Pradyota seems to have established close relations with the Śūrasenas of Mathurā. The king at this time was known by the epithet 'Avantiputra', and it seems that there existed a matrimonial alliance between Pradyota and the ruler of the Śūrasenas. He was most probably the son of a princess of Avanti.[4] The *Lalitavistara*[5] gives the personal name of the king of Mathurā in the year of the Buddha's birth, as Subāhu, and this may be the same person. It has also been suggested that Avantiputto of Mathurā was the son of Pradyota.[6]

Pradyota is said to have ruled for twenty-three years. He was cruel as known from his epithet, '*Chaṇḍa*' and he lacked good policy. His younger brother Kumārasena was killed when he tried to put a stop to the practice of selling human flesh in the Mahākāla temple.[7]

PRADYOTA'S SUCCESSORS :—

Pradyota had two sons, Gopāla and Pālaka. Gopāla abdicated the throne in favour of his brother Pālaka. It seems that Pālaka annexed Kauśāmbī to his kingdom and governed it through a prince of the royal blood. He became very powerful by this conquest. Thus Magadha and Avanti were brought face to face with each other. The preparations of

1. Buddhist India, p. 15.
2. Essay on Guṇāḍhya, p. 176.
3. Ptolemy places the Pāṇḍu country in the valley of the Vitastā (Jhelum) See Geography, VII. I.46.
4. *Majjhima Nikāya*, II, 83.
5. Ed. by Rajendra Lal Mitra, p. 24.
6. JBORS, Vol. 1, part I, 1915, p. 78,
7. Pradhan : Chronology of Ancient India, pp. 72,335.

war for supremacy in North India which started between Pradyota and Ajātaśatru, continued even among their respective successors. Though Pālaka had been previously defeated many times by Udāyin or Udayabhadra (519 B.C.), he was successful in devising a plot for killing his rival.[1]

Pālaka is reputed to have been a tyrant. The populace, headed by the president of the merchant guild of the capital, deposed him, and having brought Gopāla out of prison, put him on the throne.[2] Viśākhayūpa, son of Pālaka, ruled over some outlying district of Māhishmatī. He was set aside in favour of Āryaka who occupied the throne, as a result of a popular break, almost immediately after the fall of Pālaka.[3] The *Purāṇas* place after Āryaka, or Ajaka, a king named Nandivardhana or Vartivardhana or Avantivardhana.

There is a conflict of opinion among scholars about the identification of Ajaka and Nandivardhana. K. P. JAYSWAL[4] identifies Ajaka and Nandivardhana of the Avanti list with Aja-Udāyin and Nandivardhana of the Puranik list of Śiśunāga kings. D.R. BHANDARKAR,[5] on the other hand, says that Āryaka or Ajaka was the son of Gopāla, the elder brother of Pālaka. Nandivardhana and Vartivardhana are apparently corruptions of Avantivardhana, the name of a son of Pālaka, according to the *Kathā-sarit-sāgara*;[6] of Gopāla according to the Nepalese *Bṛihatkathā*,[7] or possibly identical with Avantisena, a grandson of Pālaka, according to the *Āvaśyaka Kathānakas*.[8]

DEFEAT OF THE LAST PRADYOTA RULER :—

After Pradyota, the four kings, Pālaka, Viśākhayūpa, Ajaka and Nandivardhana, ruled respectively for 25, 50, 21 and 20 years. The reign period of 138 years ascribed by the

1. *Āvaśyaka-S tra*, p. 690; TAWNEY's *Kathāsaritsāgara*, II, p. 484.
2. JBORS, Vol. I, Part I, 1915.
3. Essay on Guṇāḍhya, p. 115.
4. PHAI, p. 220.
5. Carm Lec. 1918, 64 ft. But J. SEN rightly points out (IHQ, 1930, 699) that in the *Mṛichchhaka ika*, Āryaka is represented as a cow-boy who was raised to the throne after the overthrow of the tyrant Pālaka.
6. TAWNEY's Translation II. 485.
7. Essay on Guṇāḍhya, p. 115.
8. *Pariśish a Parvan*, 2nd ed. p. XII.

Purāṇas to the five Pradyota kings of Avanti, who were contemporaries of the five Bimbisāriyans of Magadha, thus appears to have fallen approximately in the period 546-396 B.C. Even during the reign of Nandivardhana, the traditional hostility continued between Avanti and Magadha. At this time, Magadha was ruled by Śiśunāga (430 B.C.). He maintained the old capital against the continued menace from Avanti, and he also posted his son in charge of Vārāṇasī against both Kosala and Avanti. Finally, Nandivardhana was defeated by Śiśunāga and Avanti was incorporated with the growing kingdom of Magadha. It was the most important achievement of Śiśunāga. The Magadhan victory was doubtless facilitated by the revolution of the subjects of Ujjain against the tyrannical rule of their kings.

AVANTI UNDER THE NANDAS AND THE MAURYAS :—

It seems that Avanti continued under the possession of the Nandas (364-324 B.C.) who became the rulers of Magadha after the fall of the Śiśunāga dynasty. (430-364 B.C.) The subjugation of this region by the Nandas does not seem to be improbable in view of the Puranic statement about the humiliation of the rulers of the neighbouring realm of Avanti, by their Śiśunāga predecessors.

It is also possible that the Nandas themselves might have conquered Avanti. Puranic chroniclers speak of Mahāpadma, the founder of the Nanda dynasty, as the exterminator of the Kshatriyas. This is taken to imply that he uprooted all the Kshatriya families which ruled contemporaneously, viz. the Ikshvākus, Pañchālas, Kāśeyas, Haihayas, Kaliṅgas, Aśmakas, Kurus, Maithilas, Śūrasenas and the Vītihotras. The Haihayas and the Vītihotras seem to have been in possession of a part of the Narmada valley. Jaina writers expressly mention the Nandas among the successors of Pālaka, the son of Pradyota of Avanti.

The rule of the Nandas was uprooted by Chandragupta Maurya (324-300 B.C.). That both Gujarat and Malwa formed integral parts of the Magadhan empire in the days of Chandragupta Maurya, is clear from the Junagarh rock inscription[1]

1. EI, VIII, pp. 42 ff.

of Rudradāman, which refers to Chandragupta's *Rāshṭriya* or Governor, Pushyagupta, who constructed the famous Sudarśana lake at Girnar. The incorporation of Saurāshṭra within the Magadha empire implies control over Avanti.

Avanti remained one of the important provinces of the Maurya empire, with its capital, Ujjain, as the seat of viceroyalty. Tradition associates Aśoka with the viceroyalty of Ujjayinī, and we also know from the inscriptions[1] that it was held by the princes of the royal family. The period of Aśoka's viceroyalty of Ujjayinī was marked by romance. While on his way to the Provincial capital, he halted at Vidiśā and fell in love with Devī, the beautiful daughter of a merchant, and made her his wife. Two children, named Mahendra and Saṁghamitrā, were born of this marriage. Both of them renounced the world and went to Ceylon for the propagation of Buddhism. It is possible that Aśoka founded a Saṁghārāma and erected the *stūpa* at Sanchi because it was the birth place of his beautiful wife Devī.

The Jaina accounts make Samprati, son of Kuṇāla, the immediate successor of Aśoka. Though Pāṭaliputra is mentioned as the seat of his government in some accounts, others, with great probability, make him the ruler of Ujjain. After his conversion to Jainism by Suhastin, he did for Jainism nearly everything that Aśoka did for Buddhism. He is called Jaina Aśoka in the history of Jainism. If Samprati was a grandson of Aśoka ruling at Ujjain, Daśaratha was perhaps another who held sway at Pāṭaliputra.

ADMINISTRATION

The administrative machinery gradually began to develop from the sixth century B. C. onwards, because, for the first time, organized states came into existence, and mutual interstate diplomatic relations started. Among the sixteen Great States (*Ṣoḍaśa Mahājanapadas*), Avanti, with its capital Ujjain, was the most important. King Pradyota, who was the ruling chief of this state, was independent and despotic. He had cordial relations with Bimbisāra of Magadha and the Śūrasenas

1. CII, Vol. I, pp. 160 ff.

of Mathurā, but with Vatsarāja of Kauśāmbī and Pushkarasārin of Taxila, he was on terms of hostility.

The kingship was hereditary. When Nandivardhana, one of the successors of Pradyota, was defeated by Siśunāga, Avanti was incorporated with the kingdom of Magadha. Avanti continued under the possession of the Nandas when they became the rulers of Magadha. It remained one of the provinces of the Maurya empire, with its capital Ujjain, as the seat of Mauryan viceroyalty. Aśoka is said to have acted as viceroy of this province under his father Bindusāra. Some Jaina works mention Samprati, one of the successors of Aśoka, as the ruler of Ujjain.

The administrative machinery became elaborate during the Maurya period. Though the Mauryas ruled from Pāṭaliputra, the government was centralized and there was generally a uniform pattern throughout the empire, which also included Avanti. The main sources of information about the administration are the Megasthenes' *Indica*, Kauṭilya's *Arthaśāstra*, and the inscriptions of Aśoka. If these are correctly interpreted, they supplement one another to a remarkable degree. Megasthenes' *Indica* was written on the personal observation of Megasthenes, who was deputed as ambassador in the court of Chandragupta. Unfortunately *Indica* is lost, but a few fragments of it have been preserved in quotations in the writings of later classical scholars. While writing this book, the author was guided by Greek ideas, and its material must be utilised with caution. The evidence supplied by *Indica* is substantially supplemented and confirmed by evidence from an indigenous source, the *Arthaśāstra* of Kauṭilya. This work, though not definitely dated, may be taken as a document of Mauryan history. The inscriptions of Aśoka throw considerable light on the spirit and the ideals of Mauryan administration, and on the administrative reforms introduced by him.

NATURE AND ENDS :—

Chandragupta, for the first time, established centralized administration on the extensive scale, but it was not a ruthless centralization of policy and complete suppression of all local autonomous bodies. The king was an autocrat, but he also depended for advice on his ministers, and he was guided by law and custom of the country. As he was well-equipped with vast knowledge, he did not misuse this power.

The Mauryan State has been regarded by some scholars as a welfare state because of its control of land and capital, nationalization of mines, state ownership and management of industry, provision of subsistence by the state for those who could not make a living, and of labour for those who were out of employment.

The king adopted a high ideal of kingship. The king will not do whatever he pleases, but what pleases the people. In the happiness of the people lies his own happiness. At another place, Kauṭilya mentions the ideal as follows. 'For a king his *vrata* (religious vow) is constant activity in the cause of people (*Utthānam*), his best religious ceremony is the work of administration (*Kāryānuśāsanam*), his highest charity (*dakshiṇā*) is equality of treatment meted to all." Aśoka also adopted the paternal ideal of kingship as expressed in his edict.

"All men are my children and just as I desire for my children that they may enjoy every kind of prosperity and happiness both in this world and in the next, so also do I desire the same for all men". This idea of paternal responsibility for his people was not confined to the king alone; it belonged to his officers too, to whom he committed the care of his people. Just as a person after making over his child to a skilful nurse feels confident that she would care for the happiness of the child, similarly, Aśoka having placed the people under the charge of officers, was assured that they would look after their welfare and happiness with responsibility.

POSITION AND FUNCTIONS OF THE KING :—

The king was not only the formal head of the empire, but the actual directing head of the government. Kauṭilya enumerates the seven elements of the state—the king (*Svāmī*), the minister (*amātya*), the country (*Janapada*), the fort (*durga*), the treasury (*kośa*), the army (*daṇḍa*) and the friend (*mitra*). He places the king at the top because the progress or downfall of others depended upon the king.

Being the supreme head of the state, the king performed executive, judicial and legislative functions. He personally looked after the administration of the state. He appointed the highest officers of the state, and fixed their wages. Markets were controlled; weight and measures were standardized, and conditions of purchase and sale were determined by the king. He led the army personally, and he could follow an aggressive foreign policy.

The king was the fountain of justice and law. Besides setting up different grades and types of courts, he himself tried cases in an open court. He had to uphold the *Varṇāśrama-dharma* and to punish those who defied its doctrines. Four heads of law are mentioned in the *Arthaśāstra* namely *dharma*, *vyavahāra* (evidence), *charita* (customs) and *rājaśāsana* (royal proclamation). Kauṭilya insists upon the king administering justice efficiently, by taking into consideration *dharma*, *Vyavahāra*, *charita* and *rājaśāsana*. Kauṭilya says that the king should never make any person to wait, but should give an immediate hearing. When the king is inaccessible to the people, there will be confusion and public disaffection.

The king's legislative functions were limited. Generally, laws were the outcome of usage, but the king had the great power of taking executive decisions which had the force of law.

Megasthenes represents the king as a most hard-working official, and gives a time-table of his daily duties. He did not sleep in the daytime. It is interesting to note that Kauṭilya also has similar time-table for the king. Except for few hours of sleep—all his hours are occupied. Aśoka went even further, and declared that messengers might report the peoples' business to him at all hours and places.

THE COUNCIL OF MINISTERS :—

Kauṭilya holds that *Rājatva* (sovereignty) is possible only with assistance. A single wheel can never move. Hence, the king shall employ *sachivas* (ministers) and hear their opinion. Offices were given to them according to their success in the various tests, of religious, monetary, love, and fear characteristics. These ministers possessed the qualifications of belonging to a noble family and having self-control, skill in arts and crafts, a retentive memory, good conduct, good health, courage and an attractive personality. *Amātyas* and *Mantrīs* both constituted the council. The Greek writers refer to its members as councillors and assessors who advised the king in the management of public affairs.

The Council of ministers exercised some sort of check on the authority of the king. Kauṭilya did not want to fix the number of ministers but left it sufficiently elastic as to meet the needs of the state. All administrative measures were discussed in it and were kept secret. The inner cabinet of three or four members constituted the chief advisory body of the king, though the larger body, the *Mantri-parishad* was also often consulted, and had to be consulted in emergencies. Patañjali mentions the *Chandragupta sabhā*, meaning probably the *Mantri parishad*. The Aśokan inscriptions also refer to the *Parishad* which performed two important functions. It saw that the written orders of the king were carried out by the different officials, and it also had the power to scrutinize the oral orders of the king before they were executed. Kauṭilya was the Prime Minister of Chandragupta, while Bindusāra and Rādhāgupta were in turn Prime Ministers of Aśoka.

ADMINISTRATIVE UNITS AND OFFICERS :—

The empire, parcelled out into a number of provinces, was governed by two classes of officers, known as *Kumāra-viceroys* and non-*kumāra* viceroys. The provinces, which were of strategical importance, and required loyal and tactful administration, were assigned to the princes of royal blood, designated *Kumāras*. The province of Avanti, with its capital Ujjayinī, was held by a *Kumāra*-viceroy. The governors of Avanti and Uttarapatha had unfettered power, but this was not the case with other governors. The *Kumāra* governors of Ujjain and Taxila could send on tour a *Mahāmātra* of their own accord, every three years, but in the case of others, they were to be deputed by Aśoka himself. This indicates that Avanti was one of the most important regions of the Maurya empire.

For the convenience of administration, the province was divided into division and sub-divison–*Āhāra* or *Vishaya*, *Janapada*, *Sthānīya*, *Droṇamukha*, *Khārvaṭika*, *Saṁgrahaṇa* and *Grāma*. The administration of the village was carried on by *Grāmika* and

Grāmabhojaka, who were assisted by the village elders. The village enjoyed considerable autonomy, and the king did not interfere in its administration. Above the *Grāmika*, the *Arthaśāstra* places the *Gopa* who looked after five or ten villages, and the *Sthānika*, who controlled one quarter of a *janapada* or District. The administration of the city was under the charge of *Nāgaraka* (city magistrate), with *Sthānikas* and *Gopas* assisting him.

The *Adhyakshas* (superintendents) formed the pivot of the Kauṭilyan administration and they performed the different functions of the state. There were the superintendents of agriculture (*Sītādhyaksha*), of gold and silver (*Suvarṇādhyaksha*), of minted coins (*Lakshaṇādhyaksha*), of weaving (*Sūtrādhyaksha*), of weights (*Paṭvādhyaksha*), of liquor (*Surādhyaksha*), of commerce (*Paṇyādhyaksha*) and of forest and mines. Most of these superintendents have twofold functions to perform—to carry on the administration of the kingdom, and to undertake and manage industries and trades on behalf of the state. These *Adhyakshas* (superintendents) are evidently referred to by Strabo as Magistrates. Of the Magistrates, some have the charge of the market, others of the city, and others of soldiery.

Some categories of officers are known from the inscriptions of Aśoka. THOMAS identifies *Prādeśika* with the officer *Pradeshṭri* mentioned in the *Arthaśāstra*, who was charged with the executive duties of revenue collection and police. S.L.MITRA thinks that these are officials in outlying provinces corresponding to *Rājūkas* in home provinces. V. A. SMITH represents them as District officers.

Rājūka was an officer of a very high grade because Aśoka speaks of having appointed him over hundreds and thousands of men. In Aśoka's time, he was entrusted with the power of giving awards and punishments. In the twenty-sixth year of his reign, Aśoka placed '*Rājūka*' in sole charge of reward and punishment, in order that there would be uniformity in administration and punishment, and also with a view that he would perform his duties with confidence and without fear. He was also to ascertain what gave happiness to the people, and confer favours upon them. *Yukta* was the officer who managed the king's property, and received and kept account of the revenue.

Dharmamahāmātra was an officer like the overseer of the sacred law. He was to satisfy religious hankerings of people for knowledge of truth and practice of piety. He had to encourage the spirit of religious toleration, and to propagate the teachings of religion among the people, both in the dominions of Aśoka and outside.

Nagara Vyavahāraka appears to have been a judge for district tours only. *Anta-Mahāmātra* means high officer of frontiers. *Purusha* was below the rank of '*Rājūka*' and R. K. MOOKERJI refers to him as a civil servant. *Vyuṣṭha* had to undertake tour for the despatch of his business. *Vachabhūmika* was probably an official connected with cattle-herds. *Stryadhyaksha Mahāmātra* was an officer appointed for the protection of the interests of women.

JUDICIAL ADMINISTRATION :—

The *Arthaśāstra* mentions two kinds of law courts—the *Dharmasthīya* (Civil Court of Law) and the *Kaṇṭakaśodhana* (or Criminal Court of Law). Three members acquainted with sacred law and three ministers of the king constituted the *Dharmasthīya* court. Such a court was established in the cities of *Sangrahaṇa*, *Droṇamukha* and *Sthānīya*, to carry on the administration of justice. Kauṭilya lays down the tests which should be passed by the ministers to be appointed as judicial officers. *Kaṇṭakaśodhana* courts consisted of three commissioners (*Pradeshṭāraḥ*) and three ministers who took measures to suppress any disturbance of the peace.

The cases which came before *Dharmasthīya* court for disposal were—(1) contracts and agreements, (2) duties and rights of the employers and employed, (3) loan and deposits, (4) presents and gifts, (5) defamation, (6) laws of marriage, (7) cases of inheritance, etc. In this court, cases were brought by individuals and parties.

In the *Kaṇṭakaśodhana court*, the initiative was taken by state and police. It also performed the function of the Administrative Law Court of France, instituted for the trial of officials. This court also dealt with the anti-social elements. The weavers, washermen, physicians, traders, etc. who did not perform their duties honestly and efficiently, were tried by this court. To remove the obstacles in the way of peace and security was the special function of this court. Those criminals, who destroyed the peace of the country by foul means, were punished by this court.

Capital punishment, imprisonment, fines and the mutilation of limbs, were the main forms of punishment. Prisoners were released on birthdays of the king, and on other such auspicious occasions. Aśoka introduced one important reform in the administration of justice. He granted a respite of three days to men condemned to the sentence of death. The object was to allow time for their relatives to persuade the *Rājūkas* to revise their decision and spare his life, and to afford the condemned an opportunity to think about, and make himself fit for the next world before execution.

MILITARY ADMINISTRATION:—

The vast Mauryan empire rested upon its well organized military force. Kauṭilya mentions *bala* (force) as one of the seven elements of the state. He distinguishes the six kinds of the army, such as (1) hereditary forces, (2) hired troops, (3) soldiers of fighting corporation, (4) troops belonging to an ally, (5) to an enemy and (6) soldiers of wild tribes. The best army should be hereditary, obedient, well contented, ready to take long journeys, ready to bear physical troubles, well trained in weapons, free from duplicity with the king in weal or woe, and composed of the Kshatriya caste. The classical writers also mention a large army of the Mauryas, which consisted of 600,000 infantry, 30,000 horses, 9,000 elephants and chariots. This large army was controlled and administered by a Commission of thirty members, which was divided into six boards, each with five members. These six boards controlled Admiralty, Transport, Infantry, Cavalry, War chariots, and Elephants, respectively. These soldiers were well paid by the king in cash, and they had only military duties to perform.

FINANCIAL ADMINISTRATION :—

The cost of the civil and military administration was

enormous, and it could be only met by the rich treasure which has been mentioned by Kauṭilya as one of the seven elements of the state. The chief sources of revenue from villages were the *bhāga* and the *bali*. The *bhāga* was the king's share of the produce of the soil which was normally fixed at one-sixth, though in special cases, it was raised to one fourth or reduced to one-eighth. *Bali* seems to have been an extra impost for payment. The water tax varied according to the nature of land and crop. There was income from crown lands, from forests, f om mines and manufactures. The revenue from customs at the frontiers and octrois, tolls and ferry dues in the interior levied on merchandise in transport, was considerable. There were profits of coinage and gains from trade operations, carried on by the government. There were other sources of income such as fines levied in law courts, presents to the king, escheat of ownerless property and share in treasure troves. In times of emergency, the rich were forced to pay considerable amounts to the state under one pretext or another.

A considerable part of the revenue was spent on the maintenance of the monarch and his court, and on the members of the royal family and the salaries of ministers, and other officials, high and low. Vast sums were also spent for irrigation, construction of roads, erection of buildings and fortifications and the establishment of hospitals.

MUNICIPAL ADMINISTRATION:—

Megasthenes describes the municipal administration as found in Pāṭaliputra. Paṭaliputra, as controlled by a municipal commission consisting of thirty members divided into six boards of five members each. It is possible that Ujjain was governed on the same principles and by similar methods, as in Pāṭaliputra. The first municipal board looked after industrial arts. The second board took care of the interests of the foreigners. The third board was responsible for the systematic registration of births and deaths. The fourth board supervised trade and commerce. The fifth board looked after manufactured articles. The sixth board was responsible for the collection of a *tithe* (Tax of one-tenth part of any article sold in the market). In their collective capacity, they had in charge their special departments and also matters affecting the general interest, such as the keeping of public buildings in proper repair, the regulation of prices, the care of markets, harbours and temples.

Kauṭilya also indirectly throws light upon the municipal administration of the city. He says a lot about the planning of the city and its gates. He refers to trade, commerce and toll dues. He mentions the hours of market. He emphasizes on stamping of weights and measures. He gives a comprehensive account of census. He gives an account of the care of the foreigners.

ESPIONAGE SYSTEM :—

There were different kinds of spies employed to report to the king about every matter of importance going on in the empire. The classical writers called them overseers or inspectors. Kauṭilya refers to them as *Gūḍhapurushas*. They were known as *Rājapurushān Prativedikas* or News writers. According to Kauṭilya, there were two kinds of spies, viz.

1. *Saṁsthāḥ* or stationary spies, consisting of secret agents styled *Kāpaṭika*, *Udāsthita*, *Gṛihapatika*, *Vaidehaka* and *Tāpasa*, i.e. fraudulent disciples, recluses, house-holders, merchants and ascetics.

2. *Sañchārāḥ* or wandering spies, including emissaries termed *Satri*, *Tīkshṇa* and *Rashada*, i. e. class-mates, firebrands, poisoners, and certain women described as *Bhikshukīs* (mendicants), *Parivrājikās* (wandering nuns), *Muṇḍas* (shavelings) and *Vṛishalīs*. There are also explicit references to courtesan (*puṁśchalī*, *veśyā*, *rūpājīvā*) spies in the *Arthaśāstra*. These were known as dancing girls. Some of these spies knew several languages and could skilfully disguise themselves.

II

(CULTURAL HISTORY)

This was a period of change in the ideas of man, which led him to discard old values and to adopt new ones. The old Vedic religion began to fade, giving rise to new and powerful religious movements. The religious activities gave an impetus to art, which assumed a form and grandeur not known before. Trade and commerce developed because of the beginning of the coinage. The intensive use of iron led to the establishment of many industries. All these led to the prosperity of this region which is attested both by literature and monuments.

(A) RELIGION

The literary records, especially the early Buddhist texts and the *Jātakas* preserve the authentic traditions about the prevailing religions and their practices during the Pradyota-Maurya period. The epigraphical records of Aśoka also give a picture of the religion of the people. From these sources, it is known that Brahmanism, Buddhism and Jainism were the main religions of the people. During the Pradyota period, Brahmanism was the dominant religion of the people, but from the Maurya period onwards, Buddhism became gradually more popular in Malwa.

BRAHMANISM :—During this period, Brahmanism was represented by the Brāhmaṇa priests who were considered to be the custodians of the Vedic lore. These Brāhmaṇas believed in the superiority of their castes and they considered only themselves to be capable of reciting the vedic *mantras*.

These Brāhmaṇa priests were proficient in the *Vedas* and they performed sacrifices and rituals. The kings, nobles and rich people, who were the supporters of this religion, used to perform the sacrifices and rituals with the help of these hired priests. These priests received fees for officiating at sacrifices. The Pali canon mentions some of the Vedic sacrifices by name such as *Aśvamedha*, *Naramedha*, *Sammāpāsa*, *Vājapeya* and *Niraggalam*[1]. The large sacrifices required the immolation of a large number of animals from the herds. Aśoka's reference to the *Deva*-worshippers relates to this class of priests who were engaged in sacrifices.

There were also some other Brāhmaṇa teachers who advo-

1. *Saṁyutta*, p. 299.

cated new ways of religious thoughts and practices which may be traced to Upanishadic origin. They lived a simple life of austerity in the forests, far away from the inhabited localities, striving hard to realise the *'Brahma'* through *Tapasyā* or asceticism. These teachers had a more direct appeal for the common people and attracted people from other classes of society to a life of renunciation. It was probably in the hands of this ascetic class that new theistic movements originated in the Maurya period.

BUDDHISM :—Even in the lifetime of Mahātmā Buddha, Avanti became an important centre of Buddhism. Most of the earnest and zealous adherents of the *Dhamma*, either were born in or resided at Ujjain, e. g. Abhayakumāra[1], Iśidāsī[2], Isidatta[3], Dhammapāla[4], Soṇa Kutikaṇṇa[5] and especially Mahākachchāyana[6]. Soṇa Kutikaṇṇa was declared to be the most eminent of the disciples, distinguished for beauty of expression[7].

Mahākachchāyana was born at Ujjain in the family of the chaplain of king Pradyota. He learned the three *Vedas*, and after his father's death, he succeeded him to the chaplainship. He went to Buddha who taught him the norm with such effect that at the end of the lesson, together with his attendants he was established in *arhantship* with a thorough grasp of letters and meaning. He himself being a native of Avanti, worked with zeal for the diffusion of this faith among his people. He converted the king Pradyota to Buddhism[8]. He used to explain the teachings of Buddhism to householders. He successfully explained in detail the meaning of a stanza mainly dealing with *Kasiṇas* to an *Upāsikā* named Kālī, and she was very satisfied with his explanation. He also explained to a house-

1. Commentary on the *Theragāthā*, p. 39.
2. Commentary on the *Therīgāthā*, pp. 261-264.
3. *Saṁyutta Nikāya* IV, p. 288; *Theragāthā*, p. 120.
4. *Theragāthā*, p. 204.
5. *Vinaya* Texts, II, 32; *Theragāthā*, 369; *Udāna*, V. 6.
6. *Saṁyutta* III, a; IV, 117; *Aṅguttara*, 23; V, 46; *Majjhima* III, 194, 223.
7. Commentary on the *Dhammapada*, IV, 101.
8. Psalms of the Brethren, 238-9.

holder of Avanti named Haliddikāni, a stanza dealing with the question of *Vedānta*, *rūpa*, *Saññā* and *viññāna dhātus* and *Saṁkhāra* and the householder was very satisfied. The same devout and inquisitive householder again approached him for the elucidation of some of the Buddhist doctrine, and he made them clear to him.[1]

Mahākachchāyana is stated to have been called by the Buddha the most pre-eminent of those of his disciples able to expound at length, both as to form and meaning, that which had been said in brief[2]. He was present whenever any sermon was delivered by the Buddha on *Dhamma*. Therefore, the *bhikshus* used to keep a seat for him.[3] Kurara or Kuraghara in Eastern Malwa was a town, which, according to *Vinayapiṭaka*,[4] was for sometime the residence of Mahākachchāyana. It is through his efforts that Buddhism spread far and wide in this province, its followers' number increased, and it became the most powerful religion of this province. At the second council of Buddhism in 443 B.C., the fraternity of Avanti furnished no less than eighty four orthodox *bhikshus* to assist the holy Yaso in suppressing the schisms of the community of Vaiśālī.[5]

Buddha and his disciples propagated Buddhism in the speech of the masses. The peculiar form of this common speech in which the Pali canon was composed, was almost certainly, on historical[6] and philological[7] grounds, the form that was current in Avanti. If that is so, it can be said that Buddhism, born in Nepal, received the garb in which we now know it in Avanti, in the far west of India.[8]

As some of the Buddha's disciples were from Avanti, it is possible that even before Aśoka, there might be some Buddhist

1. *Saṁyutta Nikāya*, IV, pp. 115-16.
2. Commentary on the *Dhammapada*, IV, 101.
3. *Saṁyutta Nikāya*, IV, pp. 115-16.
4. *Vinayapitaka* (Pali Text Society, 1929) Vol. I, p. 194; EI, II, p 96 and B.C LAW : Geography of Early Buddhism, 1932, pp. 22-23.
5. CBT, p. 197.
6. RHYS DAVIDS in Trans. Phil. Soc. 1875.
7. R. OTTO FRANKE, Pali and Sanskrit, 1902.
8. CHI, p. 166.

monastic establishments at Ujjain and Sanchi. In the *Mahāvaṁśa*, there is mention of a beautiful *vihāra* or monastery at a spot called *Chetiyagiri*. The name Chetiyagiri implies a hill with a *chaitya*, and the hill is identified with Sanchi where Aśoka himself set up a *stūpa* and pillar. We have no proof of when the name Chetiyagiri came in use. Before Aśoka's time, the *chaitya* in question is not likely to have been a *stūpa*, because *stūpa* worship was virtually started by Aśoka, but it might conceivably have been some other form of religious edifice or object of cult worship. On the whole, however, it seems more likely that the name *Chetiyagiri* was given to the hill after the erection of Aśoka's own *stūpa* there[1].

It is said that Devī, the queen of Aśoka of Vidiśa, had been a Buddhist even before Aśoka became so. The Buddhist tradition gives all the credit for Aśoka's conversion to Buddhism to Mogaliputra Tishya and other Buddhist saints, but none to the Vidiśā queen. It might be due to the monks dislike of giving any prominence to women in regard to church matters.

Buddhism made striking progress under she patronage of the great Maurya emperor Aśoka. Probably, he built the *stūpa* of brick at Sanchi which underwent subsequent enlargement.[2] According to the *Mahāvaṁśa*, Devī, the queen of Aśoka, erected a sumptuous *vihāra* at Chaityagiri in which he used to live. Before setting out to Ceylon for the propagation of *Dharma*, her son Mahendra stayed in this *vihāra* with her. The existence of the *vihāra* has been proved by the discovery of some structure in the excavation[3]. From the size and fabric of the bricks, the structure seems to have been erected during the Mauryan epoch. The discovery of the steatite seal with the legend '*Basali*' proves that it is not later than 200 B.C.[4] The jewelery recovered in it proves that it was once occupied by royal family. In spite of all this, no inscription has been discovered to identify the structure with the famous Devī's *vihāra*. Probably, after

1. The Monuments of Sanchi, p. 14.
2. Ibid, p. 19.
3. AST, 1936-37, p 84.
4. Ibid.

Devī's death, it was occupied by *bhikshus* and *bhikshuṇīs*. The pillared hall at Sanchi was also erected during this period.[1]

A pillar edict of Aśoka has also been found at Sanchi.[2] The subject matter of the inscription is identical with that of Kauśāmbī and Sārnāth edicts, viz. the penalty for schism in the Buddhist church (*Saṁghabheda*). To Aśoka, who so ever be it, monk or nun, who creates a division in the *Saṁgha*, shall be made to wear white garments and to reside outside the *āvāsa* (quarters). He further directs that this order should be carried out in future by his descendants, as it was his wish that the united *Saṁgha* might long endure. From this edict, it is clear that Aśoka, as a champion of Buddhism and Head of the Buddhist church, was bent upon preventing schism in the order. Some scholars think that the issue of the three edicts was connected with the traditional Third Council of Pāṭaliputra. The object of this council was the suppression of schism (*bheda*) which, according to the *Dīpavaṁśa*, had arisen in the Theravāda during the reign of Aśoka. From this inscriptional evidence, it is clear that Aśoka had to deal with a serious split and that the measures he adopted served temporarily, at any rate, to close the ranks of the orthodox church.

Ujjain remained a centre of Buddhism. The remains of one huge, and two small, *stūpas*, have been discovered.[3] The size of the bricks indicates that these monuments belonged to the Maurya period, and it is further confirmed by the discovery of Punch-marked coins and cast coins.[4] Probably, these *stūpas* were built by Aśoka.

Tumain, known as Tumbavana in early times, is situated on the Vidiśā Mathurā main route. Aśoka built a number of Buddhist *stūpas* on this route, as he did in other parts of the country. Two Buddhist *stūpas* of the Maurya period discovered in the recent excavations by K. D. Bajpai, may be attributed to the great Maurya emperor Aśoka.

1. The Monuments of Sanchi, pp. 64-65.
2. Ibid, p. 283.
3. ARADGS, 1938-39, p. 14.
4. Ibid.

Another place associated with Buddhism was Māhishmatī, now known as Maheśvara. The Third Buddhist Council summoned by Aśoka despatched Mahādeva for propagation of Buddhism to Mahishamaṇḍala, now identified with Maheśvara on the Narmada.[1] Eleven *stūpas* have been discovered at Kasrawad[2], and one *stūpa* is from Maheśvara[3] proper. All these may be placed under the Māhishmatī group.

The names of people found in the inscriptions of the pottery discovered from the *stūpas* prove that they must have been in some way connected with the Buddhist establishment at Kasrawad, either as inmates or as temporary pilgrims. The names of the places Taxila and Ceylon are found recorded on the pottery pieces.[4] There is nothing strange if there was some intercourse between Māhishmatī of the Buddhist records, and other centres of Buddhist worship like Taxilā and Ceylon. The words '*Bhūtaye Saṁghasa*' are found in one of the inscriptions.[5] There were at least eighteen sects of Buddhists, of which about six or seven were already existent in the time of Aśoka. The *Saṁgha* at Kasrawad might be one of them.

JAINISM :—It seems that Jainism arose in Avanti side by side with Buddhism, but it was not so powerful during this period. Mahāvīra is said to have performed some of his penances in the country of Avanti. He visited Ujjaini, where he did penance in a cemetery when Rudra and his wife tried in vain to interrupt him.[6] Jaina traditions ascribe that Pradyota was a follower of Jainism and tried for its propagation. He is said to have installed the Jīvanta Svāmī (life time) images of Mahāvīra at Ujjain, Daśapura and Vidiśā. His son Gopāla was initiated to Jainism by Gaṇadhara Sudharma Svāmī.[7] All these facts are based on traditions, so that they cannot be relied upon.

1. CBT, p. 74.
2. IHQ, XXV, pp. 1 ff.
3. EMN, p. 27.
4. IHQ, XXV, pp. 1 ff.
5. Ibid.
6. The Heart of Jainism, p. 33.
7. *Jaina Tirtha Sarva Saṁgraha*, p. 322.

Jainism appears to have been prevalent even during the Maurya period. Jaina tradition avers that towards the end of his life, Chandragupta Maurya became a convert to Jainism[1]. He was admitted to monkhood at Ujjain, and retired to Śravaṇa-belagolā in Mysore with the saint (Śruta Kevalin) Bhadrabāhu. There he starved to death in the Jaina fashion.[2] Several inscriptions in Mysore dating from about 900 A. D. refer to the pair (*yugma*) Bhadrabāhu and Chandragupta.[3]

Jainism prospered much under the patronage of Samprati, the grandson of Aśoka. He became a devout follower of Jainism because of the discourses of the Jaina saint Ārya Suhastin.[4] He is regarded as Jaina Aśoka in history. Just as Aśoka propagated Buddhism, similarly Samprati took measures for the propagation of Jainism. He is said to have constructed Jaina temples at several places and installed images in them. He organised several *Saṁghas* to holy places.

'*Nigaṭasa Vihāra dīpe*' inscribed on one of the pot sherds found at Kasrawad,[5] proves the existence of the Jaina monastery. It means that the lamp from the Nigaṭa's monastery was used for lighting the rooms. This monastery may be attributed to the Maurya period.

When Ārya Suhastin visited Ujjain in order to worship the image of Jīvanta Svāmī, Avanti Sukumāla took the vocation of monkhood from him.[6] After the death of Avanti Sukumāla, a *stūpa* was erected in order to commemorate him and the image of Parśvanātha was installed in it. After some time, the *stūpa* became barren, and it was known by the name of Kuḍugeśvara (God of the Great Forest).

Being a holy place, Ujjain was frequently visited by Jaina saints such as Chaṇḍarudra, Bhadrakagupta, Āryarakshita and Ārya Āshāḍha.[7] Vajra dwelt at Tumbavanagrāma

1. *Pariśishṭaparvan* (Jacobi), 2nd ed. pp. 415 ff.
2. Ibid, p. 157.
3. Rice : Mysore and Coorge from Inscriptions, pp. 3 ff.
4. IA, XI, p. 246.
5. IHQ, XXV, pp. ff.
6. IA, XI, p. 246.
7. *Jaina Tīrtha Sarva Saṁgraha*. II, p. 318.

(Tumain). After Siṁhagiri had taught him the eleven *aṅgas*, Vajra went from Daśapura to Bhadragupta at Avanti (Ujjayinī) to learn the twelfth viz. the *Dṛishṭivādāṅga*. He was the last who knew the complete ten *pūrvas*, and from him arose the Vajraśākhā.[1] Daśapura (Mandsor) is the birth place of the Jaina saint Āryarakshita who learned from Vajra nine *Pūrvas*, and a fragment of the tenth, and taught them to his pupil Durbalikāpushpamitra[2]. The seventh schism in Jainism occurred at this place. Jaina traditions aver that Vajrasvāmī and other jaina pontiffs, obtained liberation in the hills Kunjarāvarta and Rathāvarta in the neighhourhood of Vidiśā, now known as Bhilsa[3].

ŚAIVISM :—According to traditions, the cult of Mahākāla is of great antiquity. Its temple is said to have been in existence during the time of Pradyota. His younger brother Kumārasena was killed when he tried to put a stop to the practice of selling human flesh in the Mahākāla.[4]

The earliest historical record to mention the worship cf Śiva is that of Megasthenes, the Greek envoy at Pāṭaliputra about 300 B.C. He mentions it by the name of Dionysus, generally identified with Śiva. That Śiva worship was current in the third century B. C. at Ujjain, is clear from the numismatic evidence. Śiva has been represented on the Ujjayinī coinage symbolically and anthropomorphically. A Śiva liṅga on the pedestal placed between two different trees inside railings, is represented on the obverse of variety C of class I coins hailing from Ujjayinī.[5] The tree has in early times generally been associated with the phallic emblem of Śiva.

Śiva appears for the first time in an anthropomorphic form on the coins hailing from Ujjayinī and its environs. The single standing figure on many of these coins can be

1. IA, XI, p. 247.
2. Ibid.
3. *Jaina Tīrtha Sarva Saṁgraha*, II, p. 318.
4. Chronology of Ancient India, pp. 72, 335.
5. A Catalogue of Indian Coins in the British Museum, p. 85, No. 2, XI, 2; p. 233, Nos. 154 and 1549, PI. XXXV, 5 and p. 243, No. 19, PI, XXXVI, 15.

definitely identified with Śiva.[1] The attributes in the hands, viz. a staff in the right and vase in the left, clearly discloses its identity. It is further confirmed by the testimony of another variety of the same series of coins, which shows a bull slightly prancing and looking at the deity. Moreover, the three-headed standing figure on the obverse of a third variety of the Ujjayinī coins, carrying identical attributes, further strengthens it as being the figure of Śiva.[2] A. CUNNINGHAM[3] has identified it with Mahākāla. J. ALLAN[4] is in doubt about the identity of this figure; he proposes that this figure and its variants may stand for both the deities, viz. Śiva Mahākāla and Skanda Kārttikeya. Actually, it seems to be the Siva figure because three-headed Śiva figures are known even from Kushāṇa coins.

OTHER REMAINING SECTS AND RELIGIOUS BELIEFS :—

Besides the above main religions, people worshipped Yakshas, Chaityas, Gandharvas and so forth, about which we know from the Buddhist Pali scriptures, and the inscriptions of Aśoka. A few ring-stones have been discovered in the excavations, and they may prove the existence of the worship of Mother goddess in symbolical form.

That people believed in religious superstitions is known from Rock Edict IX of Aśoka[5] in which he says : "People perform various (lucky) rites in sickness, at marriages, on the birth of sons and on journey." On these and other similar occasions, however, women performed trivial and useless rites. From the sixth century B.C. onwards, to the time of Aśoka, religious schools and sects arose with the doctrine of *Karma*. They maintained that action alone leads to the salvation of the individual. They generally believed in the next world.

1. A Catalogue of Indian coins in the British Museum, p. 168.
2. Ibid.
3. Coins of Ancient India, pp. 97-8.
4. A Catalogue of the Indian Coins in the British Museum, Introduction, pp. CXIiii, 245-52.
5. Sel. Ins., p. 28.

(B) ART AND ARCHITECTURE

The religious movements of this period gave an impetus to the development of art and architecture. The general prosperity of the masses is responsible for its development. The contact with western countries also influenced Indian art. Certain new ideas and features characterize the art of this period. Generally, bricks and stones began to be used for construction in place of wood. Well-planned towns, with ramparts, roads and houses, came into existence. Majestic buildings in the shape of *stūpas* and *vihāras* were built. New ceramic fabrics, with different shapes were devised. A large number of terracotta figures and figurines have been found. Besides, there are also certain images.

ARCHITECTURE

TOWN PLANNING—After the disappearance of the Indus Valley Civilization, towns again came into existence in the sixth century B.C. The archaeological excavations carried out at old sites such as Ujjain, Vidiśā and Maheśvara-Navḍāṭoli, give an idea of the town planning.

The excavations at Ujjain[1] reveal a continuity of occupation on the site from a date prior to 600 B. C. The massive rampart with a moat can be dated back to the earliest period of occupation on the site, which coincides with the Pradyota period. This type of fortification was of mud and belonged to a citadel, but the humbler habitations were situated undefended in the outside area. The rampart enclosed an area approximately two kilometer with a basal width of a little over two hundred feet, and a maximum extent height of forty-two feet. The contours of the area occupied by the rampart show several openings of varying dimensions, suggesting gateways. The rampart was built by the dumping of dug-up yellow and black clays to form a thick wall, with a gentle slope on the inner side and a less pronounced one on the exterior.

The rampart was surrounded on the west, and distantly on the north, by the river Śiprā, while a moat on the eastern side, found to be filled with greenish water-borne silt, added

1. IAR, 1956-57, p. 20; 1957-58, p. 32.

to it a line of defence in that direction, and presumably on the south side as well, completing the circuit of a water-barrier. The moat was found to have a been at least eighty feet wide and twenty-two feet deep.

The fortification on the riverside was breached by floods on at least three occasions during this period. After the first breach, it was repaired by the construction of a fifteen feet wide brick revetment over a raised level of the rampart. The revetment damaged during the second erosion is known from the study of the bricks. The height of the rampart was raised for the second time by the amassing of clay over the damaged remains of the revetment, but even after this, the rampart was eroded for a third and last time. The floods affected some parts of the sheltered areas too. The rampart had a brick platform over its toe, towards the moat, to prevent scouring by water.

The brick fortification could not possibly stand the floods of the river. Hence, during the Maurya Period, fortifications were constructed by a line of timber palisade remnants, which have been unearthed.[1] The existence of such a palisade in the fortification of Pāṭaliputra, the capital of Chandragupta Maurya, described by the Greek ambassador Megasthenes, is well known.

THE CANAL WALLS OF PRE-MAURYA PERIOD :—

The remains of the four masonry walls of the canals have been discovered at Vidiśā[2]. These were possibly of the pre-Maurya period, because they were unearthed at a lower level than the temple of Vāsudeva erected by Heliodorus in the second century B.C. Some time must have elapsed between the destruction of canals and the erection of the temple. As the canal was of solid foundation, it was used for a long time. There are traces of a flight of steps which were found about the middle of the south wall. A slight slope seems to have been deliberately given to all these walls, because in a canal, a batter is needed to counteract the pressure of water.

These canal walls were of lime mortar of superior quality.

1. ARADGS, 1938-39, p. 16.
2. ASI, 1914-15, p. 50.

Their width is seven feet and height five feet six inches. One limb of the canal represented by the north and south walls, was one hundred and eighty-five feet four inches long. Most probably, it must have extended as far as the Betwa river, which is hardly two furlongs from the site, and which alone could have supplied water to this canal. Its water must have been used to irrigate the surrounding area.

ROADS AND DRAINAGE :—

Traces of ancient roads[1] and a drainage system have been found at Kasrawad, but they are not sufficient to give a definite idea of their exact measurements and construction. The roads at Ujjain[2] were usually built of rubble of assorted size, with a clay soling; occasionally black sticky clay was also used, as the semblance of a road through one of the openings across the defences would suggest. The roads of the early period were twenty-four feet wide; those of the later period varied from twenty-three feet to thirty-nine feet in width and were marked with cart-tracks, the gauge being five feet nine inches.

Terracotta soakage-wells, bottomless soakage-jars, and terracotta pipe-drains laid underground, as well as brick drains, represented the sanitary arrangements prevalent at Ujjain[3]. Remarkable evidence of very advanced drainage was found at Avra.[4] At three levels, drains have been recovered of terracotta pipes joined together with elbow bends; and in addition to the terracotta ringwells or soakpits, there are soak-walls made by putting one large pot of cut base over the other, one of the drainage systems tending to fall in the upper pot, and another system joined to a ringwell. In the opinion of B. SUBBARAO, this is the first evidence of its kind in India.

HOUSES :—The houses were made of mud, mud bricks, stone rubble, or burnt bricks. The mud and burnt-brick structures were usually built over a plinth of rubble and clay. The flooring too lay on a bed of rubble, and was made either of

1. IHI, XXV, p. 1 f.
2. IAR, 1956-57, p. 27.
3 Ibid, p. 27.
4. JMPIP, IV, p. 24.

clay, occasionally mixed with mud-bricks or brick-jelly. The mortar and plaster, wherever available, were of a smooth paste of clay. At Avra[1], the walls were of perishable material, like wood or bamboo, posts of which were set in lines at some distance from each other and were thatched with mud mixed with grass. The finds of perforated fragments of tiles and iron nails go to show that the houses were roofed by joining the tiles with nails to keep them in position. At Ujjain[2], the houses appeared to have been roofed generally with oblong tiles, with double perforations for fixing them in position.

A massive underground structure built of large bricks was found at Ujjain[3]. It was found to have been an oblong enclosure measuring approximately 34 X 26 ft. with a low overground parapet-wall. Its use could not be determined, though it appeared to have served as a reservoir.

STŪPAS, VIHĀRAS AND PILLARS :—

The remains of the old *stūpas*, *vihāras* and *pillars* of the period, are beautiful specimens of Indian art and architecture. They are highly polished and are built of huge bricks.

The *stūpa*[4] at Sanchi was probably enlarged in Aśoka's time, by adding a brick casing round an earthen core, i. e. converting a small (*alpeśākhya*) *stūpa* into a large one (*mahāśākhya*). He also enlarged the *Mahāchaitya* by providing a beautiful brightly polished *chhatra Yashṭi* or umbrella, with a post now preserved in pieces in the Sanchi Museum. Originally, this structure was half the diameter of the present *stūpa*. It was roughly hemispherical in shape, with a raised terrace encompassing its base, and a wooden railing and a stone umbrella[5] crowning its summit. Several pieces of an umbrella, probably belonging to *stūpa*, were found in the debris on the plateau. They are relieved by most delicately defined ribs radiating on their under side, the workmanship displaying all the exquisite precision which characterises every known specimen of the mason's craft in the Mauryan age, and which has probably

1. JMPIP, IV, p. 23.
2. IAR, 1956-57, p. 27.
3. Ibid.
4. The Monuments of Sanchi, pp. 19-24.
5. Ibid.

never been surpassed in the stone carving of any country.

The remains of the old *vihāra*[1] built by Devī, the queen of Aśoka, have been discovered. There were an entrance, a hall and a verandah in the building. The pillars and the roofs of the cells and verandah were probably of wood, and must have been burnt down at an early age. On the southern side, there are six cells. The eastern side of the *vihāra* has six cells, and an entrance is facing the western gate.

Building No. 40 known as the Pillared hall[2] was built during the Maurya period. In its original form, it was an apsidal *chaitya*-hall, and is probably the earliest structure of this type of which any remains have been preserved. What is left of the original structure consists of a rectangular stone plinth eleven feet high, and eighty-seven ft. long, by forty six ft. wide, approached by a flight of steps on its eastern and western sides. The plan of these foundations leaves no doubt that the superstructure was apsidal in shape. That the superstructure was mainly of wood and was burnt down at a relatively early age, is evident from the fact that no vestige of it had survived, except some charred remains of timber.

The pillar of Aśoka at Sanchi[3] is an example of the perfection of workmanship. The pillar, when intact, was about 42 feet in height, and consisted of a round and slightly tapering monolithic shaft with a bell-shaped capital surmounted by an abacus, and a crowning ornament of four lions, set back to back. The whole structure is finely finished, and polished to a remarkable lustre from top to bottom. The abacus is adorned with four 'honey suckle' designs, separated one from the other by pairs of geese. The lions from the summit still afford a noble example of the sculptor's art. These animals possess a spirited vitality, and they are marked by the tense development of the muscles, the swelling veins, the strong set of the claws, and the crisp treatment of the mane disposed in short schematic curls. One beautiful specimen of the elephant-capital (broken) of chunār sandstone and the Mauryan polish

1. ASI, 1936-37, p. 84.
2. The Monuments of Sanchi, pp. 64-65.
3. Ibid, 25-27.

has been discovered at Sodhang, a village five kilometers to the north-west of Ujjain.

The remains of three *stūpas* were found at Ujjain.[1] These are of peculiar construction not met with anywhere else so far. Vaiśya Ṭekarī itself consists of a *stūpa*, perhaps the biggest known, being about three hundred and fifty feet in diameter at the base and not less than one hundred feet in height. The hearting is made of local blackish murum rammed hard, while the facing is composed of brick masonry laid in mud mortar. The bricks are large sized. The huge mass of murum has been quarried from the neighbourhood. The quarries have been laid out in such a manner as to form a regular square moat round the *stūpa*, leaving ample space between the moat and the base of the *stūpa*. In the centre of the west side of the moat, there are vestiges of a passage across the moat, for worshippers coming from the city.

The *stūpa* probably consisted of a drum superimposed on a berm or basement. The drum was less than a hemisphere in section. The berm was probably circular on plan. The masonry at the bottom of this *stūpa* is built in the shape of a bowl, which supports the super structure, It is wide at the bottom and gradually narrows as it rises up towards the top. The height of the *stūpa* is slightly less in proportion to its base as compared with other *stūpas* of the period.

Considering the ratio of diameter and height, M.L. Dalal[2] believes the Vaiśyā Ṭekarī *stūpa* to be Pre-Mauryan. From the architectural point of view, this may be placed chronologically between the Piparva *stūpa* and the original Mauryan stūpa of Sanchi.

The two other *stūpas* are smaller. The inner filling of the South-West *stūpa* consisted of black earth, while the western stūpa has never been completed.

From the excavations recently conducted at Tumain by the Department of Ancient Indian History, Culture and Archaeology, University of Sagar, under the direction of K.D. Bajpai, two huge Aśokan *stūpas* have been discovered. These

1. ASI, 1938-39, p. 14.
2. *Mālavā me kalā tathā Sthāpatya*, Typescript, p. 75.

are still intact. One of these is thirty-eight feet high with a radius of about two hundred feet. This *stūpa* has brick covering. The baked bricks are of the usual Mauryan size.

Eleven *stūpas* of the Maurya period were discovered at Kasrawad,[1] a big one in the centre, and ten smaller ones in the eastern part of the mound. Except for the *stūpa* which was built of undressed stones, all of them were built of large bricks. The biggest *stūpa* measures thirty-five feet in diameter. It was paved all round with slabs of plaster and concrete, measuring four feet eight inches in length, three feet three inches in breadth and four and a half inches in thickness. Such pavements are not found in any of the archaeological sites excavated so far. Huge bricks were used in building these monuments. The remains of a *stūpa* have also been found at Maheśvara,[2] at a distance of six kilometers from Kasrawad. But only the traces of a large platform of hard clay, with impressions of large bricks, were found. It was conjectured that the lime platform constituted the circumambulatory passage (*pradakshiṇā-patha*) of *stūpa*, on the basis of a similar narrow platform found around the *stūpas* at Kasrawad. From the nature of the construction, the central drum of the *stūpa* might not have been very high. The *stūpa* remained incomplete because of floods.

M. L. Dalal[3] attributed some remains of the buildings found at Kasrawad to the Jaina monastery which is mentioned on one of the potsherds found at this place. These are lower portions and foundations of some well planned, and well laid-out, residential blocks. They are of the Mauryan period because they are built of huge blocks. One was probably a long assembly hall measuring 75 feet X 20 feet. Another building is eighty feet in length divided into separate compartments.

CERAMICS :—The archaeological excavations conducted at different sites give us an idea of the ceramics used by the people. This period is noteworthy for the introduction of some new fabrics. The most important ware of this period is North

1. IHQ, XXV, p. 1.
2. EMN, p. 27.
3. *Mālwā me kalā tathā sthāpatya*, p. 97.

Black Polished Ware. Smoothness and lustre are the characteristics of this pottery. It originated in the Indo-Gangetic plains where much has been found in the excavations. In Malwa, first only a few sherds have been recovered from Maheśvara, Avra, Eran, etc. and these seem to have been brought by the Buddhist saints. During the Mauryan period, its local preparation started in large quantity, but its quality deteriorated.[1] Bowls of this ware were much in use.

The next most important ware other than North Black Polished Ware, is Black and Red Ware, which was prepared by the 'inverted firing technique.' Only three main shapes, bowls, dishes and basins, have been found. The most abundant ware of this period is the coarse Red. This was much in use because it was not so costly, and it did not require much labour. It served a utilitarian purpose. The thick vessels were hand-made, while others, like bowls and dishes, were wheel-made. This ware bears decorations which are mainly in the form of grooves or incisions.

After this comes the Red Slipped and Burnished Ware. As compared with the coarse red, this ware has a delicacy in the sense that its surface bears a thick-red to orange-brown slip. The least abundant is the coarse black ware. It has globular vessels which were most probably used for cooking. The grey-slipped ware is represented by a few sherds. The shape of the vesiculated ware found at Ujjain[2] is a jar with a flanged rim, and carination at the waist, used for cooking.

Some of the potsherds found in the Kasrawad excavations[3] are ornamented with peculiar patterns of various kinds, such as with Svastika, double cross, fish, cock, leaf, flower and ear ornament. Some geometrical designs are incised on the pots. On many of the potsherds, the solitary letter 'Ma', in large size, is incised. It is also found on some sherds of Maheśvara. This '*Ma*' closely resembles the letter '*Ma*' incised on potsherds found in the excavation at Rairh assignable to the same period.

1. IAR, 1956-57, p, 24.
2. Ibid.
3. IHQ, XV, p. 1 f.

TERRACOTTAS :—Terracottas of different types have been discovered at Ujjain,[1] Avra,[2] Eran[3] and Maheśvara,[4] serving different purposes. Terracotta toys representing human, animal, and bird figures, were meant for the decoration of the houses. Gamesmen of terracotta, dice of terracotta and ivory, pottery discs, balls of stone and terracotta, and wheels of toy carts were used for games and amusements. A torso of a female figure found at Vidiśā[5] is noteworthy. A tortoise figure found at Avra[6] is important, if it is compared to that found at Maheśvara,[7] which is attributable to the Maurya period. Antimony-rods of copper and ivory, pigment sticks, combs of ivory, bangles, plain and decorated, of terracotta, stones, shells, glass and copper, beads of terracotta, ear ornaments in the form of discs of ivory, terracotta and highly polished stone, earrings of copper and hair-pins of ivory represented the toilet articles and ornaments of the people.

SEALS AND AMULETS :—Some seals and amulets found at Ujjain, Vidiśā, Avra and Maheśvara are noteworthy from an artistic point of view. Two seals of ivory from Ujjain[8] inscribed in early Brāhmī script, are attributable to the third or second century B. C. One of the seals reads '*Gosahitakasa*' and the other, possibly, '*Pattilasa*'. One jar found in the excavations at Ujjain[9] contained a clay seal probably inscribed with the name of the person whose remains are among the contents. The seal also bears a figure of a seated bull, or Nandi. The same jar also contained a small clay seal resembling a small coin with a human head on the obverse, and a lotus flower on the reverse. A circular terracotta seal showing a tree in a railing on left, a crescent above at the top, and the Brāhmī letters,

1. IAR, 1956-57, p. 27 and ARADGS, 1938-39, pl. XXII.
2. JMPIP, p. 34.
3. Bulletin of Ancient Indian History and Archaeology, p. 37.
4. EMN, p. 104.
5. ASI, 1914-15, p. 84.
6. JMPIP, pp. 34-35.
7. EMN, p. 104, No. 4.
8. IAR, 1956-57, p. 27.
9. ARADGS, 1938-39, pl. XXVIII.

'Parāyā', of the third-second century B. C. was discovered at Avra.[1] As the first letter is broken and missing, it is tentatively presumed to have been *Aparāya,* meaning the city of Apara. In this case, the name of the once flourishing city might be Apara, which may later on have been corrupted into Avra. One ivory seal of this place represents the mother-goddess,[2] and another is inscribed in Mauryan Brāhmī characters *'Jidhavasa'*.[3] A copper amulet found at Vidiśā[4] is of a much earlier period. A couchant lion in profile is the most artistic piece. Cylindrical copper tubes were used as amulets. One glass seal with an elephant impression was found at Maheśvara[5].

BEADS :—Beads of different shapes, sizes, and designs, were obtained from Ujjain, Maheśvara, Avra and Eran, and some of them are important from an artistic point of view. These are made of agate, carnelian, faience, steatite, terracotta, shell, glass, paste, etc. As unfinished beads have been found at Avra and Ujjain, this proves that there were local industries for the manufacture of beads. A tile-roofed mud house, found in a fallen and damaged state at Ujjain,[6] served as a workshop for the manufacture of beads of agate, arrow heads, and knitting needles of bone. Some large stone beads finished with exquisite polish, generally associated with the Maurya period, were found at Ujjain.[7]

METAL OBJECTS .—Different kinds of metal objects recovered from the old sites in the excavations, give an idea of the state of art during this period. Some objects were used for ornament, while others served domestic purposes. One small gold ornament found at Kasrawad[8] is four inches in diameter, and it weighs seven grains. It is in the form of a wheel with eight spokes, with a hole in the centre. The workmanship is

1. JMPIP, IV, p. 36.
2. Ibid, p. 40.
3. Ibid, p. 23.
4. ASI, 1914-15,p. 84.
5. EMN, p. 220.
6. IAR, 1956-57, p. 27.
7. ARADGS, 1938-39, p. 18.
8. IHQ, XXV, p. 1 f.

beautiful and delicate. At Avra,[1] people used copper in manufacturing antimony rods, bangles and rings. Ivory bangles and rings were worn by the people, and a miniature dagger shaped object was used for decoration. Glass discs were popular at Nagda,[2] Ujjain,[3] and Maheśvara,[4] during the Maurya period. There is no unanimity regarding the possible use of these discs. It is suggested that they were used either as ornaments in the ear lobes, or as weights. It is doubtful whether they could be worn as ornaments with ease and comfort. Bangles of shell, coiled wire, and bone, were prevalent. Steatite lids, circular in shape and pinkish red in colour, discovered at Avra[5] and Maheśvara,[6] were objects of luxury, probably used for keeping precious articles.

Copper was used for the manufacture of bars, rods, and hooks, as known from Avra.[7] The use of iron increased greatly, and it generally replaced the stone and copper objects. The iron objects recovered from the different sites are arrow heads, spear heads, nails, looped hooks, sickles, chisels, etc. They were used as implements for agriculture and weapons for war.

STONE AND BONE OBJECTS :—Stone and bone objects represent the survival of an earlier culture. In spite of the discovery of iron, these stone and bone objects continued to be used by the people. They were flakes, blades, querns, maceheads and hammers.

SYMBOLS ON COINS:—The symbols on the punch-marked coins, the cast coins, and the tribal coins of Ujjayinī and Eran discovered at the old sites of Malwa, reflect the artistic taste of the people. On the Pre-Mauryan Punchmarked coins, there are generally the symbols of the Sun, six armed symbol with three arrow heads and three ovals, a hill above a tank with two fish, a hare on hill, a bull on hill, etc. The main symbols

1. JMPIP, IV, p. 38.
2. IAR, 1955-56, p. 14.
3. Ibid, 1956-57, p. 27.
4. EMN, p. 218.
5. JMPIP, IV, p. 38.
6. EMN, p. 221.
7. JMPIP, IV, p. 38.

found on the punch-marked coins of the Maurya period are the crescented three-arched hill, a peacock on the hill, a caduceus, Triskelis and Taxila mark. In Malwa, the punch marked coins have been discovered at Sarangpur, Bhilsa, Eran, Ujjain, Maheśvara and Kasrawad. The date of the tribal coins of Ujjayinī and Eran is probably the third and second century B. C. when this region was a Maurya province. On the Ujjayinī coinage, there are five symbols on the obverse, but on the reverse, only the single symbol of Ujjayinī (cross and balls). On these coins, the main symbols represented are : a tree in railing, a three-headed deity, possibly Śiva, Abhiṣeka of Lakshmī, a bull before the tree in railing, three human figures, etc. On the Eran coins, the common symbols are those of the Ujjain symbol, the tree in railing, the bull, the horse, the river with fish, the ribbon of svastikas, the taurine symbols, the six armed symbols, and a triangular headed standard in a railing.

MISCELLANEOUS OBJECTS :—There are some miscellaneous objects which give an idea of the art. Cloth-dycr's stamps found at Avra[1] were used for dyeing purpose. Clay spindles prove that weaving was practised at Kasrawad.[2] Pottery discs, which were used either for weights or skin rubbers, have been found at all excavated sites. Ring wells, recovered from the excavations at Ujjain,[3] reveal that they were used for storing grain and other similar domestic things.

(C) SOCIAL CONDITIONS

Some literary works and the inscriptions of Aśoka give a general idea of the social life of India during this period. It may be presumed that the same may have been prevalent even in the region of Malwa. Some antiquities discovered in the archaeological excavations of this area also throw welcome light on the social aspect of the people.

STRUCTURE OF SOCIETY :—

Society was divided into several castes and classes. In the caste series, the Kshatriyas have been mentioned as the first

1. JMPIP, IV, p. 38.
2. IHQ, XXV, p. 1.
3. ARADGS, 1938-39, p. 18.

in the Pali texts, on account of their high status and purity of blood.[1] From the *Jātakas*, it is clear that they used to devote considerable time to the study of the *Vedas* and the other branches of learning.[2]

The influence of the Brāhmaṇas greatly diminished, both in the intellectual and religious spheres. In the *Jātaka* literature, they have been depicted as greedy, shameless and immoral.[3] They performed sacrifices and rituals and received *dāna* in return. They acted as fortune-tellers by reading the symbols of man and by interpreting dreams and other omens.[4] They worked as snake charmers. They began to follow the professions of land cultivation, cattle rearing, trade and hunting.[5] There was no privileged position for the Brāhmaṇas before the law. They were even executed for committing crimes.[6]

The Vaiśyas were not homogeneous and followed different professions. They were conscious of sub-castes rather than groups. The Vaiśyas were known as Gṛihapatis, Kuṭumbikas and Seṭhīs. The most important and aristocratic representative of this class was the *Seṭhī*, who enjoyed a special position of honour in the royal court.[7]

The condition of the Śūdras was miserable because untouchability was in a full-fledged state. For example, the sight of a *chāṇḍāla* aroused contempt. The *Chāṇḍāla* began to be compared to a jackal which is considered low and wretched among animals.[8] A daughter of the *Seṭhī* washed her eyes when she saw a *Chāṇḍāla* at the city gate of Ujjain.[9] This shows that there was not only untouchability, but also unseeability. The wind that had touched the body of *Chāṇḍāla* was considered to be impure. They lived outside the town. Along with the

1. The Social Organization in North-East India in Buddha's time, pp. 83-84.
2. Ibid, p. 93.
3. Ibid, p. 183.
4. Ibid, pp. 229-30.
5. Ibid, pp. 243-247.
6. Ibid, p. 212.
7. Ibid, pp. 253-258.
8. Ibid, p. 319.
9. Ibid, p. 43.

Chāṇḍālas, there were *Paulakasas*, *Nishādas* and others mentioned in the *Jātakas*.[1] They used to pluck flowers, and they lived by hunting and doing the dirty work, such as cleaning temples and palaces. There were carpenters, basket makers, flute makers, weavers and barbers, whose professions were considered to be low.

Some inscriptions of Aśoka mention the Brāhmaṇas and the *Ibhayas*. The *Ibhayas* stand for *Gṛihapatis* or Vaiśyas. The lower strata of society in Aśoka's time are represented by *Bhṛitakas* or hired labourers, and *Dāsa* or bondsmen. Kindness and mercy to such people are stipulated by the king, and form part of the code of moral duties.

Because of the rise of Buddhism and Jainism, the hereditary caste system of the Brahmanical religion received a great setback. It is for this reason that the authors of the *Dharmaśāstras* tried to reorganize the caste system during this period. They fixed the duties, privileges and disabilities of the different castes.

ORDERS OR STAGES OF LIFE :—

Varṇa and *Āśrama* were related terms in early times. The Āśrama system was devised in order to train a person for every stage of his life, so that he might achieve salvation. Though it originated in Upanishadic times, it took final shape during this period. The *Sūtras* and the *Smṛitis* elaborately point out the duties at every stage of an individual's life. The span of human life is one hundred years. It was divided into four parts—Brahmacharya, Gṛihastha, Vānaprastha and Sanyāsa, each of twenty-five years. In Brahmacharyāśrama, a person led a celibate life and lived at his teacher's house for learning. In Gṛihasthāśrama, he married and became a householder, and discharged his debts to his ancestors by begetting sons and to the gods by performing Yajñas. When he became old, he resorted to the forest to become a Vānaprastha. After spending the third part of his life in the forest, he spent the rest of his life as a *Sanyāsin*. How far this scheme actually worked in society, is not known.

1. The Social Organization in North-East India in Buddha's time, p. 321.

FAMILY LIFE :—Generally, the joint family system was prevalent. There were cordial and affectionate feelings between different members of the family, especially between a wife and her husband's parents, brothers and sisters. There was conjugal fidelity and a harmonious relationship between husband and wife. There are examples of serious disagreement, but they are rare.

In early times, the father had extraordinary powers, but during this period, it was gradually curtailed. Some *Dharmasūtra* writers began to recognize the self-acquired property of the son, and an equal share with his father in the ancestral property.

MARRIAGE AND POSITION OF WOMEN :—

Eight forms of marriage were known to the writers of the *Dharmasūtras*, but of these, *Paiśācha*, *Rākshasa* and *Āsura*, unquestionably, belong to the unapproved forms of marriage. There is a difference of opinion about the *Gāndharva*, or love marriage, among the writers. Some approve and praise it, while others regard it with disfavour. In the *Paiśācha* form of marriage, the bride was often induced to drink too much, or was physically overpowered by the bridegroom, in order to make her yield to his passion. The forcible carrying away of the girl is the essence of the *rākshasa*. It is called *kshātra* because the woman was regarded as prize of war. Under *Āsura Vivāha*, the husband gained a bride by paying a reasonable price for her. The *Gāndharva* marriage was a love marriage, pure and simple. In this marriage, the parties fall in love with each other and immediately proceed to consummate their contemplated marriage. Religious rituals etc. do not precede the union.

Ārsha, *Daiva*, *Brāhma* and *Prājāpatya*, were the four approved forms of marriage. In the *Ārsha* form of marriage, the father of the bride was permitted to accept a cow and a bull from his son-in-law, for facilitating the performance of sacrifices which require a cow's milk. According to Megasthenes,[1] the Indian marriage is marked by the gift of a yoke of men. This proves the popularity of the *Ārsha* form of marriage in the

1. Strabo, 15.1.54.

fourth century B.C., when a daughter was offered in marriage to an officiating priest by the sacrificer, and the marriage was designated as a *Daiva* one. There was no distinction between *Brāhma* and *Prājāpatya*, because in both, the father carefully selected the son-in-law, and offered him his daughter according to proper religious rites, together with certain presents. Generally, this type of marriage became popular in the society. As regards the age of the bride at the time of marriage, she was about sixteen years old.

Marriages were usually endogamous, but intercaste marriages were also prevalent. When the bridegrooms of higher castes married brides of lower castes, they were technically known as *Anuloma* marriages; and when the brides of higher class married the bridegrooms of lower castes, these were known as *Pratiloma* marriages. The *Dharmaśāstras* of this age, while recognizing the validity of such marriages, were not prepared to recommend them. The recognition of the legality of inheritance of the sons of mothers of different castes, also proves the existence of intercaste marriages. Aśoka married Devī, the daughter of the banker of Vidiśā. Opinions are not unanimous as to the advisability of *Sapiṇḍa-vivāha*, *Sapravara-vivāha* and *Sagotra-vivāha* during this period. In the *Dharma-śāstra* literature, there is mention of the words '*Punarbhu*' and *Paunarbhava*, '*Punarbhu*' is meant for the lady who is remarried, and '*Paunarbhava*' for the son of the widow. There are examples of widow remarriage even in Buddhist literature.

Some of the women were highly educated and they occupied an honourable position in society. Female students were divided into two classes—*Brahmavādinīs* and *Sadyodvāhās*. The former were lifelong students of theology and philosophy, the latter used to follow their studies till their marriage, at the age of fifteen or sixteen. Women teachers were called '*upādhyāyā*' or '*upādhyāyī*'. The Buddhist and Jaina texts also refer to women of the Brahmavādinī class i. e. those who remained unmarried to carry on their studies. Besides, the women generally received training in fine arts, such as music, dancing and painting.

As against this bright picture of the position of women, there is also a darker one. Aśoka mentions that the people, especially women, performed various rites on occasions of sickness, marriage, and the birth af children.[1] Aśoka condemns them as useless and trivial. It seems that purdah was practised in the high circles of society. Aśoka speaks of his '*avarodhana*', which means a confined female apartment.[2] In consonance with it, is the mention of *antaḥpura* or harem in the *Arthaśāstra*[3] where Kauṭilya gives directions, not only how to build one, but also how to guard it against outsiders.

DRESS AND ORNAMENTS:—People wore upper and lower garments which consisted of dresses like the *dhotī* or the *sārī* and *chādara*. Although cotton was the material generally used, clothes made of silk, linen and wool, were also in great demand, especially among the women and the rich.

People were fond of ornaments, toilet articles and cosmetics. Rings, bangles and necklaces, were the common ornaments worn by the people. A large number of beads of different varieties have been discovered in the excavations, and it seems that there were local industries at different places.

FOOD AND DRINK :—Wheat, rice, and barley, were the chief foodgrains. Milk and its products formed part of the daily diet, and *ghee* was particularly valued as very substantial and nourishing. Various kinds of drinks and liquor were taken, and their manufacture, according to Kauṭilya, was a state monopoly. In spite of the growing tendency of vegetarianism, due to the influence of Buddhism and Jainism, meat and fish were still taken by the people. Aśoka tells us in his R. E. I., that many hundreds of thousands of animals were slaughtered every day in his kitchen for curry. During the reign of Aśoka, peacock meat was much relished by the people.

ENTERTAINMENTS :—People did not lead a dull life, but amused themselves in different ways. Children used to prepare terracotta toys of human beings, animals and birds. There were various kinds of games, both indoor and outdoor. Music and dancing were pastimes of the people. Dramatic performances were also arranged, and entertainments were

1. RE, IX.
2. Ibid, VI.
3. *Arthaśāstra*, p. 40.

provided by buffoons, rope-dancers, jugglers, and wandering bards or heralds (*chāraṇas*). On the occasion of festive assemblies, known as *utsava*, *samāja* and *vihāra*, people were provided with meat and drink, and they enjoyed themselves with music, dancing and singing. In his edicts, Aśoka tells that for a long time past, kings used to go on pleasure tours, in the course of which there was the chase, and other diversions.[1]

WELFARE ACTIVITIES :—Welfare activities promoted by the rulers were concerned with social conditions. In Rock Edict II, Aśoka tells us that in his own dominions, as well as in those of neighbouring potentates, he established two kinds of medical treatment, one relating to man, and the other to animals. He further informs us that medicinal herbs, roots and fruits, wherever they were not found, were imported and planted. Aśoka opened dispensaries for men, and *piñjrāpols* for animals. In addition, he had banyan trees planted along roads, and wells dug, and rest-houses set up. He did so in order to impress upon the people that these were religious duties, so that they might follow the practices of *Dhamma*.

FUNERARY CUSTOMS :—The evidence with regard to the customs about the disposal of the dead, is known from the excavation at Ujjain, of Kumhar-Tekrī,[2] which was a burial-cum-cremation ground. It yielded forty-two skeletons, some of which were more or less complete. They were in numerous poses. There was a custom of burying a large number of earthen vessels and cups with the dead body. Signs of cremation were also unearthed along the lower stratum. Thus the customs of cremation, post-cremation, partial burial, and simple and complete burial, appear to have been in vogue simultaneously during this period at this place. The skeletons with their peculiar postures, might have belonged to a distinct sect which had strange customs for the disposal of their dead.

(*D*) *ECONOMIC CONDITIONS*

At this time, Avanti was one of the most flourishing kingdoms of India. A number of cities and towns, such as Ujjayinī,

1. RE. VIII.
2. ARADGS, 1938-39, p. 15.

Māhishmatī, Vidiśā, Kuraraghara and Sudarśanapura, came into existence. The province produced an abundance of food, and the people were wealthy and prosperous.[1] Several industries, such as cotton and iron, were flourishing. It was rich in quarries. Several trade routes contributed to the general prosperity. It was inhabited by a large number of rich merchants, who worked for its material development.

Agriculture was the main occupation of the people, and there were irrigational works for the development of agriculture. At the Khāmbābā site of Vidiśā,[2] only one canal has been found, but there must have been an intricate network. The river Betwa supplied water to the canals, for irrigating the surrounding area. The Pali work, *Dhammapada*,[3] speaks of *nettikas* forcing water to go where it would not go by itself. It thus appears that irrigation canals and aqueducts were not unknown, even in the pre-Mauryan period when the *Dhammapada* must have been composed. Not only in Avanti, but also in other parts of India, there were irrigational works. The Sudarśana Lake, originally constructed under orders of Chandragupta Maurya, by his provincial governor Pusyagupta, was completed under the orders of Aśoka, by his governor Tushāspha.

These irrigational works increased agricultural production. Different kinds of grain, such as wheat, rice and barley were produced in large quantity. Besides grains, this region also produced an abundance of cotton. The area was rich in quarries, as is clear from their findings at the different places of the excavations.

Because of the agricultural and mineral resources, there was a development of industries and trade. The cotton industry must have been flourishing at important cities such as Ujjain and Vidiśā. The iron industry of Avanti was fairly advanced. Different iron objects have been discovered at Ujjain, Nagda, Eran, Kayatha, etc. Ujjain[4] has yielded evidence of some kind

1. *Aṅguttaranikāya* IV, 252, 256.
2. ASI, 1914-15, p. 50.
3. *Dhammapada*, 80, 145.
4. IP, p. 197.

of bowl furnance for smelting iron. The prevalence of large quantities of argonite and calcite, and deposits of slag, point to the fact that they served as a flux or catalytic agent in the smelting process. The blacksmith's forge consisted of a furnace with an opening for introducing the nozzle of the bellows for the fire. There were miniature iron vessels for drawing water in small quantities, and some finished iron objects. Mammiliated lumps of limonite readily available in the veins of the trap in the neighbourhood, were employed at Ujjain as ores for preparing iron objects.

These different types of iron objects served many purposes. Tools and weapons of warfare were comprised of daggers, knives, swords, arrow heads, spear heads, spikes and caltrops. Those of domestic use were comprised of blades, hooks, nails, chisels, drills, axes, lamps, ladles, bowls and rings. Iron had also penetrated into the sphere of agriculture, in the form of hoes, choppers, hooks and sickles. The limitless potentialities of this new metal led to the quickening and expansion of agriculture, the utilization of forest wealth, and the exploitation of mining. It resulted in a surplus of wealth and prosperity. There are traditions[1] that the iron workers of Avanti became so famous, that they were called to execute the iron works in the palace of a Tamil king. This fact is recorded in the Tamil works *Manimekalai* and *Perungadai*, of the early centuries of the Christian era.

Avanti owed its industrial and commercial prosperity to her situation connecting North India with South India. There were several trade routes linking this region with the coast and the inland marts. Four of her main towns, namely Vidiśā, Gonardā, Ujjayinī and Māhishmatī, were the halting places on the Dakshiṇāpatha. We also hear of merchants travelling from Benaras to Ujjain. The ease of transport and communications in this region greatly increased the number of caravans. Therā Isidattā (Rishidattā) was born in the village of Velugāma (Veṇagrāma) in Avantī, to the family of a caravan guide, of which there were many in his kingdom.

Because of the commercial prosperity, the number of

1. IP, p. 187.

bankers increased. The merchants at Vidiśā were so dominant and influential, that this town later came to be known as Vessanagara (Vaiśyanagara, modern Besanagar). Devī, the queen of Aśoka, was the daughter of a banker of this place. There were other famous bankers at this time. The Buddhist, Theri Isidāsī (Ṛiṣidāsī), in her psalm, describes herself as the only daughter of a virtuous banker of the great city of Ujjayinī.

It seems that in the important towns, such as Ujjain and Vidiśā, both trade and industries were highly organized into guilds, known as '*Śreṇīs*'. The *Jātakas* refer to eighteen guilds, which though a conventional number, show the extensive character of the organizations. The important guilds known to us, were of wood workers, smiths, leatherers, painters, workers in stone, ivory workers, weavers, etc. Their president was known as *Jeṭṭhaka* or *Pamukha*. The chief of the merchant guild was *Seṭhī*. The guilds became hereditary and localized. During the Maurya period, there was state control over them.

CURRENCY :—This period was epoch-making in terms of economic history, because it led to the introduction of currency, which facilitated trade and commerce. The earliest coins are the punch-marked coins which were known as *Kārshāpaṇas*. Along with the punch-marked coins, uninscribed cast coins have been discovered. Ujjain and Eran were the mint towns which issued a peculiar local currency. Some coins inscribed with the names of other towns were also issued during this period. Most of the coins in the region of Malwa, were of copper.

Punch-marked coins have been discovered at Sarangpur,[1] Jhalrapatan,[2] Besanagar,[3] Eran,[4] Ujjain,[5] Maheśvara,[6]

1. ASC, II. p. 288.
2. Ibid, p. 264.
3. ASI, 1913-14, p. 210.
4. ASC, X, p. 37; Bulletin of Ancient Indian History and Archaeology, Saugar.
5. ARADGS, 1940-41, pp. 17 f; JNSI, XVI, p. 117; XIV, p. 41.
6. JNSI, p. 147.

Kasrawad[1] and Badwani.[2] In other regions, silver pieces are more numerous than the copper ones, but the coins of the Malwa region are generally of copper. Copper coins coated with silver were also current. Some coins found at Ujjain are of a metal of yellowish colour. It is an alloy of tin, lead and copper.[3] At Badwani, a large hoard of 3450 silver punch-marked coins has been discovered. These are mostly square and rectangular in shape, but some are circular and oblong.

The normal weight of *Kārshāpaṇa* is sixteen *māshakas*, each *māshaka* being two *ratikas* in weight. The average weight of a well preserved punch-marked coin is in the vicinity of fifty-six grains. In Malwa, like in Kosala, a number of types of punch-marked coins have been found, weighing only forty-two to forty-three grains. It seems, that like ancient Kosala, Malwa was following the lighter weight standard of twelve *māshakas*, or about forty-two grains. The coins between nineteen and twenty-five grains may be *ardhakārshāpaṇa*. To carry on daily transactions, currency of small denominations was required, and it was issued. The repousse coins[4] discovered at Vidiśā are thin and light, weighing only three grains. These are the earliest known specimens of the repousse coinage. The tiny silver punch-marked (*raupya ardha māshaka*) weighing between one and a half grains to two and a half grains, have been discovered at Maheśvara.[5] Coins of small denominations have also been obtained from Kasrawad.[6]

The symbols found on the punch-marked coins have great significance. Generally, five symbols are found on the obverse. The punch-marked coins of Eran are without a stamp of any kind on the reverse. Most of these coins have the Sun and six-armed symbols. The other main symbols known on the punch-marked coins of Malwa, are the Ujjayinī symbol, tree in railing, crescented three or six arched hill, peacock on

1. JNSI, XIV, p. 93; JNSI, VIII, pp. 99 ff.
2. Ibid, V, p. 172.
3. Ibid, XIII.
4. Ibid, XXIII, p. 303.
5. Ibid, XVI, part I.
6. Ibid, VIII, pp. 99 ff.

hill, human figure, elephant with raised trunk, caduceous and fish. On one coin, the Sun symbol was repeated four times.[1] It seems that most of these symbols were introduced during the Maurya Period. There are several conjectures about them but nothing can be stated positively. The crescented three-arched hill symbol, seems to have originally been adopted by Chandragupta Maurya. It is possible that coins having the symbol of the peacock on the hill, might have been issued by Aśoka. The Ujjayinī symbol, human figure and the elephant with the trunk upraised, might have local significance. Some symbols like the Sun and the bull, probably had religious significance. Some were meant purely for decoration.

CAST COINS :—

Early uninscribed cast coins have been found with the Punch-marked coins, at Jhalrapatan,[2] Sarangpur,[3] Besanagar,[4] Ujjain,[5] Eran,[6] Maheśvara,[7] etc. Their frequent association with the punch-marked coins suggests that they were contemporary. Most of these coins are square or rectangular, but some are circular. They are of copper. Their weight standard seems to be the same as that of the Punch-marked coins. One cast copper coin of seventy-four grains found at Maheśvara,[8] and another of ninety-one grains from Pawaya,[9] may be equal to the weight of double *Kārshāpaṇa*. The symbols found on these coins are the elephant, tree in railing, crescented hill, hollow cross, Ujjayinī symbol, etc. The elephant and the other symbols are on the obverse, and the hill symbols are on the reverse. At Pawaya,[10] one coin was recovered with a symbol of horse on the obverse.

1. JNSI, XIV, p. 41.
2. ASC, II, p. 264.
3. Ibid, p. 288.
4. ASI, 1913-14, p. 210.
5. ARADGS, 1940-41, pp. 17 f.
6. ASC, X, p. 37.
7. JNSI, XVII, p. 42.
8. Ibid.
9. Ibid, XVIII, p. 67.
10. Ibid.

Some early single-type silver coins of a weight of about twenty-five grains, have been found at Pawaya.[1] These pieces seem to be half-*Kārshāpaṇas*. They possess a single type on the obverse, and plain reverse. This coinage type proves that it was current in Malwa during this period.

TRIBAL COINS OF UJJAYINĪ AND ERAN :—

Tribal coins of Ujjayinī and Eran found in large quantities in Malwa, were issued by the mint towns of Ujjayinī and Eran respectively, in the third or second century B.C., when this region was a Maurya province. These coins are probably the local issues of the Mauryan governors of the time. They are of copper. VINCENT SMITH[2] ascribed the coins of both Ujjayinī and Eran to Avanti. In spite of a certain similarity of symbols, they have distinct fabrics. Besides, the coins of both the places bear these respective names.

UJJAYINĪ COINAGE :—

These coins were struck on the same principle as the punch-marked coins. Like the punch-marked coins, on the obverse, they have five symbols, some of which change more frequently than others. Unlike the great majority of punch-marked coins, they all have a single symbol of a cross and balls, known as the Ujjayinī symbol, on the reverse.

J. ALLAN[3] has divided the coins of Ujjayinī into six classes of uninscribed coinage according to symbols, and one of inscribed—(1) Tree in railing: (2) deity, three-headed Kārttikeya but possibly Śiva; (3) Ujjayinī symbol absent but from the evidence of provenance ; (4) Abhiṣeka of Lakshmī; (5) bull before a tree in railing; (6) Lion and elephant and (7) inscribed Ujjayinī and elephant on the obverse. N.C. GHOSH[4] thinks that ALLAN's identification of Lakshmī on some Ujjayinī coins, actually portrays the figure of Śiva in sitting posture.

1. JNSI, 1955, p. 13. ALLAN calls them Early single type silver coins in his catalogue B. M. C., p. XVII. Little was known about this type of coins and their findspots.
2. CCIM, p. 145.
3. BMC, pp. cxlii ff.
4. JNSI, XXIV, p. 26.

J. N. BANERJEA[1] has classified these coins under three main heads, viz., standing figure, animals, and inscribed. H.V. TRIVEDI's[2] classification of these coins is as follows : (1) Symbolic types, (2) Animal types, (3) Human beings and deity types and (4), Inscribed types.

The symbols on the Ujjayinī coinage have a certain significance. The tree in railing seems to indicate the halting place on the road. The three-headed deity may well be identified with Śiva Mahākāla whose cult was well known at Ujjayinī. The symbol of a pair of fishes may be interpreted as a representation of the sign of the Zodiac, called Mithuna. The most distinctive, the 'cross and balls', known as the Ujjayinī symbol, seems to have represented a meeting of four cross-roads, which was applicable to Ujjayinī as a junction of trade routes. This symbol became so popular that it was adopted by some succeeding ruling dynasties, such as the Sātavāhanas and the Śakas.

THE ERAN COINS :—These coins of Eran type[3] have affinity with punch-marked coins, and the Ujjayinī coinage. These are large and square, with four or five punches on the obverse and a plain reverse. On some specimens, the symbol of the reverse type belongs to the obverse series. The common symbols found on these coins are the Ujjayinī symbol, tree in railing, bull, horse, river with fish, ribbon of svastikas, taurine symbols, six-armed symbol, a triangular-headed standard, lotus and horse. S. L. KATRE[4] is of the view that the Eran coins are remarkabe for their lotus symbol which is one of the characteristics of these coins.

INSCRIBED COINS : In the third or second century B.C., there were towns in Malwa which began to issue inscribed coins bearing their own names. This proves the commercial importance of these towns. Along with the symbols, name '*Ujenī*' is inscribed on the coins[5]. On such inscribed coins of

1. IHQ, X, p. 723.
2. JNSI, XV, p. 96.
3. BMC, pp. xc-xcii.
4. JNSI, XIV, p. 61.
5. BMC, p. cxlv.

Eran,, the name of '*Erakaṇya*'[1] has been found. On some coins, we find '*Mahisha*' identified with the ancient city of Māhishmatī.[2] The coins with the legend '*Bhāgilāya*', may be the issue of the city of Bhāgila, which has not been identified.[3] The coins bearing the legend, '*Kurarāya*', have been found near the find-spot of the Bhāgilāya coins.[4] This place name, Kurarāya, has been mentioned in the votive inscriptions of Sanchi.[5] As the Bhāgilāya coins have been found in the same region as the Kurarāya coins, it is possible that Bhāgila was situated not far from Sanchi. Coins with the name of the city of Vidiśā have also been recovered. Outside Malwa, Tripuri, Kauśāmbī, Vārāṇasī, Uddahika, Suddvāpa, Pushkalāvatī and Kapiśā are known to have issued such coins.

1. BMC, pp. xci-xcii.
2. JNSI, XV, p. 70; XVII, p. 94.
3. Ibid, XIV, p. 9.
4. Ibid.
5. Ibid, XXIII, p. 303.

CHAPTER—VIII

THE ŚUṄGA-SĀTAVĀHANA-ŚAKA PERIOD

(186 B.C.—318 A.D.)

Soon after the death of Aśoka, the Mauryan empire gradually began to disintegrate. His successors were weak and could not keep the empire intact. The outlying provinces rose in revolt and became independent. But their authority was not acknowledged, even by their ministers and generals. The general Pushyamitra Śuṅga, who probably belonged to Avanti,[1] usurped the throne from Bṛihadratha, the last Maurya emperor in 187 B. C. For a time, he arrested the disintegration of the Mauryan empire.

EXPEDITION AGAINST VIDARBHA :—

Avanti formed a part of the empire of Pushyamitra Śuṅga. From the *Mālavikāgnimitram*[2], it is known that he deputed his son Agnimitra, as his governor at Vidiśā. Agnimitra had to fight against Yajñasena, the ruler of Vidarbha or Berar, who had recently become independent. Yajñasena is stated to have been the relative of a minister of the Maurya emperor, and thus a natural rival of Pushyamitra. The relations between Agnimitra and Yajñasena became further strained, because his friend Mādhavasena, who was a cousin of Yajñasena, was arrested by an *Antapāla* of Yajñasena on his way to Vidiśā. Agnimitra at once called upon Yajñasena for his release. The latter agreed to do so on condition that his relative, the Maurya minister, was released first. Agnimitra gave orders to Vīrasena to invade Vidarbha. Vīrasena defeated Yajñasena and released Mādhavasena. Eventually,

1. CHI, I, p. 512.
2. *Mālavikāgnimitram*, Act V.

Vidarbha was divided between the two cousins, Yajñasena and Mādhavasena, under Pushyamitra their suzerain.

CONFLICT WITH THE YAVANAS

Pushyamitra also came into conflict with the Greeks. This is clear from two references in Patañjali's *Mahābhāṣya* (150 B.C.). The first is *'Iha Pushyamitraṁ Yājayāmaḥ'*, "Here we perform the sacrifices for Pushyamitra." Pushyamitra performed the sacrifices in order to commemorate his victory against the Yavanas. Patañjali[1] also writes of Sāketa or Ayodhyā, and another town called Madhyamikā, (near Chitor), as being besieged by a Yavana king, and refers to it in such a manner as to show that this event took place in his time.

Kālidāsa preserves the memory of this incident, and in his *Mālavikāgnimitram* refers to the conflict between prince Vasumitra, son of Agnimitra and general of Pushyamitra, and a Yavana, on the southern bank of the river Sindhu.[2] According to Kālidāsa, this conflict took place in connection with the horse sacrifice of Pushyamitra, when his troops, escorting the horse under Vasumitra, were stopped by the Yavanas on the south bank of the Sindhu. The Yavanas were defeated and the horse was brought safely back home.

The historical section of the *Gārgī Saṁhitā*, the *Yuga Purāṇa*, mentions that the Pañchāla and Mathura powers, together with the Yavanas who were known for their valour, attacked Sāketa and marched on to possess Pāṭaliputra. They destroyed the city, but because of internal dissension, the Yavanas did not remain in Madhyadeśa for very long.

From the Ayodhyā inscription,[3] we know that Pushyamitra performed two horse sacrifices, and they probably indicate his double victories against the Yavanas. D.C. Sircar[4] holds the view that his first campaign was against Demetrius I, and the second was against Menander. On the

1. *Mahābhāshya*, 3.2.111. *Aruṇad Yavanaḥ Sāketam* and *Aruṇad Yavano Madhyamikām*.
2. IHQ, I, p. 215. The river 'Sindhu' may be taken to be either the river in the Punjab or its namesake in Central India.
3. EI, XX, p. 54 ff; IHQ, 1929, 602 f.
4. The Age of Imperial Unity, pp. 96-97.

other hand, A. K. NARAIN[1] is of opinion that there was only a single expedition, and that it occurred about the middle of the second century B.C. The Greek invader seems to be Menander, whose inscriptions and coins have also been discovered.

Pushyamitra ruled for about thirty years (187-151 B.C.) and was succeeded by his son Agnimitra.[2] He was succeeded by Sujyeshṭha, of whom nothing is known. The fourth king was Vasumitra, the son of Agnimitra. The later Śuṅgas shifted their capital from Pāṭaliputra to Vidiśā. The next important Śuṅga ruler was Bhāgabhadra, who is known to have ruled from capital, Vidiśā. He must have been a powerful monarch among the Indian rulers, to whom the Greek ruler Antialcidas sent an envoy, named Helidorus, who maintained diplomatic relations with him.

CONTROVERSY ABOUT THE IDENTIFICATION OF BHĀGABHADRA :—

D. R. BHANDARKAR[3] identifies Bhāgabhadra of the inscription, with a king of the name Bhāgavata, who is mentioned in the *Purāṇas* as the ninth king of Śuṅga dynasty. V. A. SMITH[4] assigned the date 100 B. C. to this Śuṅga king. But this identification of D.R.BHANDARKAR, and the date assigned by V.A. SMITH, do not seem to be correct, because a second Garuḍa pillar at Besanagar is dated in the twelfth regnal year of king Bhāgavata, and Bhāgabhadra of one pillar cannot be taken to be Bhāgavata on the other. According to R. K. MOOKERJI[5] and D. C. SIRCAR,[6] this Bhāgabhadra was most probably the fifth Śuṅga king, Bhadraka of the *Purāṇas*, known also from the Pabhosa inscription.[7] But actually, there seems to be no reason to identify Bhāgabhadra with Bhadraka, the fifth Śuṅga

1. The Indo-Greeks, p. 84.
2. Also called Vasujyeshṭha. For the Puranic list of Śuṅga kings of D.K.A., p. 70.
3. ASI, 1914-15.
4. The Early History of India.
5. The Age of Imperial Unity, p. 98.
6. Ibid, p. 116, f. n. 2.
7. EI, pp. 242 f.; Sel. Ins., pp. 96-97.

king, because he is credited with a reign of either two or seven years, whereas the inscription is dated in the fourteenth regnal year. Bhāgavata, on the other hand, according to the *Purāṇas*, reigned for thirty-two years. It seems very probable that Bhāgavata and Bhāgabhadra of the two inscriptions found at Besanagar, referring to the twelfth and fourteenth regnal years respectively, are identical.

GREEK ENVOY AT BHĀGABHADRA'S COURT :—

Bhāgabhadra was certainly a powerful king to whom Antialcidās sent an envoy. Antialcidās might have established diplomatic relations with him in order to seek help against his rivals. Bhāgabhadra was given the title '*Trātāra*', equivalent to the Greek '*Soter*'. This is an unusual epithet to be adopted by an Indian king, and must have been given by Heliodorus. The epithet '*Trātāra*', which means 'Saviour', for Bhāgabhadra, may be of special significance. It appears that Bhāgabhadra might have given some help to Antialcidas in a time of need.

EXTENSION OF THE KINGDOM :—

It seems that the kingdom of the Śuṅgas of Vidiśā at this time, extended up to the northern areas of Rajasthan. The Barli inscription[1] seems to be a record of the pious work of an inhabitant of Madhyamikā, incised during the reign of king Bhāgavata of the Śuṅga dynasty.

THE KĀṆVAS:—The tenth and last Śuṅga king, according to the *Purāṇas*, was Devabhūti or Devabhūmi. According to Bāṇa, he was the victim of a conspiracy engineered by his Brāhmaṇa minister Vāsudeva, and was killed by a slave girl who approached him in the guise of his queen. Vāsudeva usurped the throne, and founded a new royal dynasty known

1. JBRS., XXXVI, Parts 1-2, pp. 1-5; Ibid, XL, Part-1, pp. 8-16; Bhāratīya Prāchīna Lipimālā, pp. 2-3; JBORS, XVI, pp. 67-68. G.H. Ojha regards this inscription as of the year 84 of Mahāvīra Nirvāṇa Saṁvat while K. P. Jayaswal agrees with G. H. Ojha in its reading but he refers the year 84 to the Nanda era, which was counted from 458 B. C. and thus the inscription will be of the fifth century B. C. according to Ojha and of fourth century B. C. according to K. P. Jayaswal.

as Kāṇva. Vasudeva, Bhūmimitra, Nārāyaṇa and Suśarman, who ruled respectively for nine, fourteen, twelve and ten years.

RULE OF SARVATĀTA :—J. C. GHOSH[1] is inclined to include among the Kāṇva kings, a ruler named Sarvatāta, who is known from the Ghosūṇḍī stone inscription of about the middle of the first century B. C. It seems to record the construction of a Nārāyaṇa-Vāṭaka, which was a stone enclosure for the worship of Saṁkarsaṇa and Vāsudeva, by a ruler named Rājan Sarvatāta. This ruler is called Gājāyana,[2] which was apparently his family name, and also Pārāśarī-putra, because of his birth to a woman born in a family pertaining to the *Pārāśara gotra*. As the name of Sarvatāta is not included in the list of Kāṇva rulers, it is reasonable to regard him as a local ruler, with his capital at Madhyamikā (Nagarī, near Chitor). He must have been of considerable importance, because he claims to have performed Aśvamedha sacrifice, probably in order to commemorate his victories against his neighbours.

K.D. BAJPAI[3] propounded a theory on numismatic evidence, that the Mitra rulers of Pañchāla, Mathura, Ayodhya and Kauśāmbī, along with the Mitra house at Vidiśā, were related to one another. It appears quite probable that the five branches had their originator in Pushyamitra Śuṅga. However this theory is not convincing. The rule of the Śuṅga rulers of Vidiśā came to an end in the first century B. C, and these rulers are not known to have issued any coin. On the other

1. IA, 1932, Nov., 203 ff; EI, XXII, 198 ff.
2. The identification of the Gājāyana family, to which the king belonged with the gadāyanas or godāyanas (IHQ, 1933, 797 ff) does not seem to be plausible. There seems to be no more reason to identify the Gājāyanas with the Gādāyanas than with the Gahayanas or Gaṅgāyanas of the Śunaka or Kaśyapa group (Baudh, Śrauta Sūtra III, 423-454). It is important to remember the fact that the *Harivaṁśa* refers to a *Kaśyapa dvija* as the reviver of the Aśvamedha in the Kali Age. The Gāṅgāyanas no doubt all recall the Gaṅgas of Mysore who claimed to belong to the *Kāṇvāyana gotra* (A New History of the Indian people Vol. VI, p. 248). But the equation Gājāyana—Gāṅgāyana is not proved.
3. Bulletin of Ancient Indian History and Archaeology, p 4.

hand, the Mitra rulers of Pañchāla, Mathura, Ayodhya and Kauśāmbī, issued coins which, palaeographically, belong to the second or third century A. D. In the Buxar hoard, the coins of these Mitra rulers were found with the Kushāṇa coins of Kanishka and Huvishka. It seems that these Mitra rulers do not seem to have been related to the Śuṅga house of Vidiśā, nor did they have an originator in Pushyamitra Śuṅga.

OCCUPATION OF MALWA BY EARLY SĀTAVĀHANA RULERS :—

This kāṇva dynasty was overthrown by Āndhrabhṛitya of the Āndhra. The Āndhra king not only destroyed the Kāṇyāyanas, but also whatever was left of the power of the Śuṅgas. The Puranic statement[1] probably indicates that even after the death of Devabhūmi, and the overthrow of the Śuṅga dynasty, some members or scions of the family, continued to rule in the Vidiśā region and the other parts.

The Puranic account of Simuka's success against Śuṅgas and Kāṇvas, probably in Eastern Malwa, as well as the discovery of certain coins[2] of the so-called 'Malwa' fabric, with the legend indicative of the illustrious king Sātavāhana in the Telangana region, and the Nevasa excavations,[3] may suggest that the Mālava region was within the sphere of the early Sātavāhana influence. The coins with the legend '*Sātavāhana*' were probably issued by Sātavāhana, the founder of this dynasty.

The Sātavāhana occupation of Malwa may be proved by epigraphical evidence. A votive inscription[4] found on the southern gateway of the Great *stūpa* at Sanchi, records a gift of Vāsishṭhiputra Ānanda, the foreman of the artisans of King Sātakarṇi. This king, whose name points to his descent from Sātavāhana lineage, is usually identified with the Sātakarṇi of the Nānāghāt inscription,[5] but may actually be the second

1. Dynasties of the Kāli Age, p. 49.
2. Rapson—A catalogue of the Indian Coins in the British Museum, XCII-XCIII.
3. Bulletin of Ancient Indian History and Archeology, p. 3.
4. EI, II, No. 190.
5. Buhler : Arch. Surv. West, Ind. V, p. 64; Sel. Ins., p. 190.

king of that name. However it may be said that the Sanchi record can hardly be regarded as proof of the Sātavāhana occupation of Malwa, as the chief artisan of Sātakarṇi may have visited the monastery on pilgrimage.

OTHER KNOWN RULERS :—After the disintegration of the Mauryas, that the eastern Malwa region became independent is clear from the testimony of coins. A coin of king Dharmapāla, with his name written in Aśokan Brāhmī characters, was found by A. CUNNINGHAM at Eran.[1] Recently, the excavations conducted at Eran have yielded a round lead-piece, bearing the die-mark of king Indra-Gupta, and the Brāhmī legend in the die-reading, is '*raño Indragutasa*'.[2] The coin of another ruler, Śivagupta, has also recently been discovered at Vidisā.[3] In any case, these rulers cannot be placed after 100 B.C.Besides the provenance of the coins, from the study of their type and fabric, it would seem that these rulers were ruling in the region.

The name '*Madavika*', either as the name of a person, tribe or republic, has been found on a coin.[4] The group of symbols, Ma-shaped symbols, tree within railing, and V-shaped banner, of this coin, appear on some early uninscribed coins from Eran. It would seem that this type of coin was issued in the second century B.C. in the area round Eran.

Western Malwa seems also to have been ruled by some independent rulers during this period. A few uninscribed coins of the second or first century B. C., found at Ujjain, bear the names of local indigenous rulers. One such was Savita. On another coin, the complete name of the ruler is lost, but the legend is '*raño-datasa*.'[5]

EARLY ŚAKA OCCUPATION :—After the downfall of the Mauryas, India fell a prey to foreign invasions. The early advent of the Śakas into Western Malwa form Seistan via

1. ASC, X, p. 80.
2. IAR, 1960-61, p. 55.
3. JNSI, XXII, p. 132; XXV., p. 104.
4. Ibid, IV.
5. JNSI, XXXII, p. 77.

Sind and Kathiawad, in the second century B. C. is known from the *Kālakāchārya Kathānaka.*[1] After establishing their hegemony in Saurāshṭra Kathiawad, they may have penetrated into Malwa. This late statement of the *Kālakāchārya Kathānaka* has not been corroborated by any substantial or reliable archaeological evidence. However, copper coins of five rulers, viz. Hamugama, Valāka, Mahu, Dāsa and Sauma, are now known from Ujjain and the region round about.[2] On the basis of palaeography, these rulers can be placed in the second and first century B.C. K. D. Bajpai tried to prove that the rulers who issued the coins, were Śakas, the predecessors of the two well known dynasties of Bhūmaka and Chasṭana. The names on the coins resemble those of the Śaka chiefs already known from inscriptions and other coins. On the reverse, there are figures such as frog, moon on the hill, tree within railing, or a double-orbed Ujjain symbol. These symbols are well known from the early *Janapada* coins of Western and Eastern Malwa.

It is not definite that names on these coins are those of the Śakas. There is Brāhmī script, but on the early Śaka coins, there are Greek and Kharoshṭhī legends. It is possible that these are the names of Indian kings.

VIKRAMĀDITYA PROBLEM:—There is a controversy among scholars about the historicity of Vikramāditya. Some writers, like Rajbali Pandey,[3] suggest that there was a ruler of this name in Malwa in the first century B.C. The other view is that there was no king of this name in the first century B.C., and the story is nothing but a myth dating from the ninth or tenth century A. D. There is a group of writers[4] who are inclined to identify the traditional Vikramāditya, with king Gautmīputra Sātakarṇi of the Sātavāhana dynasty. Some writers[5] of the older generation believed that the traditional Vikramāditya, was no other than king Yaśodharman of the

1. JBBRAS, 139 ff; CII, XXVI ff; JBORS, XVI, 233, 293; Brown, the story of Kālaka. The Śāhī chiefs in the story are said to belong to saga kula and their overland is called Śāhānuśāhī.
2. JNSI, XXVIII, pp. 46-50.
3. Vikramāditya of Ujjayinī.
4. See H. K. Deb in *Zeitschrift für Indologie und Iranistic*, 1922, pp. 255 ff.
5. Select Inscriptions, pp. 386 ff.

as Kāṇva. Vāsudeva, Mandsor inscription, one of which is dated in 532 A. D. (V.S. 589). D. R. BHANDARKAR[1], D. C. SIRCAR,[2] and others, identified Vikrama of tradition with Chandragupta II of the Gupta dynasty.

RAJBALI PANDEY and some other scholars, tried to prove that Vikramāditya was not a fiction, but a historical figure and they give the following arguments :—

(1) Both from Indian traditions and Śaka history, it is known that the Śakas ruled over Sind in the first centnry B.C., and they also extended their power up to Malwa. They were defeated by an Indian ruler probably Vikramāditya who became Śakāri. Chandragupta II again defeated the Śakas severely and bore the titles of *Vikrama* and *Śakāri*, in imitation of the former ruler.

(2) Vikramāditya was the personal name of a ruler of Ujjayinī. His *Virudas* or epithets, were *Vishamaśīla*, *Sāhasāṅka* and *Śakāri*. Chandragupta II assumed the title of Vikramāditya in the fourth century A.D., and it presupposes the existence of the name of Vikramāditya in earlier time who set an example to be followed by later kings.

(3) Chandragupta II was not associated with Ujjain or with the Mālava Saṁvat; on the other hand, he was connected with the Gupta Saṁvat and Pāṭaliputra. The ruler Vikramāditya, who remained associated with the Mālava Saṁvat and Ujjain, was a different one, and lived in the first century B.C.

(4) There is a vast volume of literary and oral tradition about Vikramāditya. The earliest reference to Vikramāditya is traced in the lost *Bṛihatkathā*, composed in Paiśāchī Prakrit by Guṇāḍhya, during the reign of a Sātavāhana king of Pratishṭhāna. Guṇāḍhya may be supposed to have flourished between the first half of the first century B.C. and the commencement of the third century A. D., when the imperial Sātavāhanas ruled. Guṇāḍhya describes the great generosity, undaunted valour, and other qualities of Vikramāditya. The other early allusion to Vikramāditya is traced by some writers in the *Sattasai* or *Gāthāsaptaśatī*, as ascribed to a Sātavāhana king named Hāla (Hālavāhana or Sālivāhana). The *Gāthāsaptaśatī* alludes

1. Vikrama Volume, pp. 57-69.
2. Ancient Malwa and the Vikramāditya Tradition, pp. 128-136.

to the unbounded generosity of Vikramāditya. Both Guṇāḍhya and Hāla lived close to the time of Vikramāditya. There are some other literary works of the late period, such as *Kathāsaritsāgara* of Somadeva of Kashmir (1063-89 A. D.), *Vīracharita* of Ananta, *Śālivāhanakathā* of Śivadāsa, etc. One of the stories about Vikramāditya found in the *Kathāsaritsāgara*, represents him as the king of Pāṭaliputra, and as an enemy of the king of Pratishṭhāna,

The Jainas have prescribed the traditions of Vikramāditya in many literary works such as Somaprabha's *Kumārapālapratibodha* (1184 A. D.), Prabhāchandra's *Prabhāvakacharita* (1127 A.D.), Merutuṅga's (*Prabandhachintāmaṇi*) (1304 A. D.), Jinaprabhasūri's *Vividhatīrthakalpa* (1315 A.D.), Rājaśekhara's *Prabandhakosha* (1348 A. D.), Devamūrti's *Vikramacharitra* (1418 A. D.), Rāmachandrasūri's *Pañchadaṇḍachhatraprabandha* (1433 A. D.), Śubhaśīla's *Vikramacharitra* (1442 A, D.) *Kālakāchāryakathā* (before 1279 A. D.) and *Paṭṭāvalīs*. Though these works are of a late period, written between the twelfth and fifteenth centuries, they contain many theories which are in tune with the known facts of history. These works are therefore of value in proving the historicity of Vikramāditya.

(5) Some inscriptions discovered in Malwa and neighbouring areas, throw some light on this problem. At Mandsor, in two inscriptions[1] of Mālava *Saṁvat* 493 and 589, there occurs a significant expression, '*Mālavagaṇasthiti*'. Scholars have interpreted this differently. Kielhorn[2] took it in the sense of *gaṇanā*, or counting of years. K. P. Jayaswal[3] thinks it an era founded to commemorate the republic's constitution. A. S. Altekar[4] translated it as according to the era current in the Mālwa republic, and according to the usage of Mālava republic. The Nāndsa pillar inscription[5] discloses that the '*Mālava-gaṇa-vishaya*' was using the Kṛita era. Thus, the Kṛita, the Mālava and the Vikrama eras, are identical. The era was prevalent in South-east Rajasthan and some portion of Malwa. Though

1. Sel. Ins., pp. 305, 417.
2. IA, 1891, p. 403 ff.
3. Ibid, 1891, XIV, p. 326.
4. JBORS, 1930.
5. EI, XXVI.

these inscriptions are important, they do not prove positively the existence of Vikramāditya, they simply prove the existence of Mālava Gaṇa, and the Mālava era, with which he was associated.

The Mālava tribe was gradually divided into different branches such as Sogin, Gardabhilla, Maukhari and Aulikara. Gardabhilla was a clan of the Mālavas to which Vikramāditya belonged.

(6) At Uniyara,[1] near Jaipur, a large number of small coins were discovered with the legend, '*Mālavānāṁ Jayaḥ*', '*Mālavagaṇasya Jayaḥ* and '*Jayaḥ Mālavānām*' (Victory of the Mālavas). In the opinion of RAJ BALI PANDEY[2], these coins chronologically occupy an intermediate position—later than the Aśokan, and earlier than the Kushāṇa characters, and these were issued by Vikramāditya in order to commemorate his victory against the Śakas. He regards these coins as victory type of coins.

But these coins have not been found in Ujjain, and therefore, they cannot be the issues of Vikramāditya. Besides, some scholars, like J. ALLAN[3] and D. C. SIRCAR[4], are of the view that they were issued between the second and fourth centuries A. D. The Ujjayinī type of coins seems to have remained popular in Malwa from the third century B. C. to the third century A. D. This type might have been current during the reign of Vikramāditya. Hence, we do not find the name of the ruler on the coins, because there was no such practice prevalent.

After examining all this evidence, it may by suggested that Vikramāditya was not a fiction but a historical figure, who lived in the first century B.C. He belonged to the Gardabhilla branch of the Mālava people and was President of the Mālava republic. The capital of the Mālava republic in the first century B. C. was Ujjain, and Vikramāditya ruled from there.

The great achievement of Vikramāditya was the defeat of the Śakas, who invaded India for the first time in the first

1. ASC, VI, p. 178.
2. Vikramāditya of Ujjayinī, p. 38.
3. Catalogue of the coins of Ancient India, p. cvi.
4. JNSI, XXIV, pp. 3-4.

century B. C. This fact is independently established by the ancient history of China, Persia, Central Asia, and the countries to the south of the Hindukush mountains. They were hard-pressed by their Parthian overlord, and they were in search of new territories where they could live in peace. They also occupied Sind. This coincided with the religious disputes between Kālakāchārya and Gardabhilla, king of Ujjain. With the help of the Jaina saint Kālakāchārya, the Śakas defeated Gardabhīlla and ruled for some time in Ujjain. K. D. BAJPAI[1] attributed some coins to those early Śakas. But Vikramāditya inflected a crushing defeat on the Śakas and thus restored the freedom of the country. It was for this reason that Vikramāditya was called *Śakāri*, and this conquest brought peace and prosperity to the country.

In order to commemorate this event, Vikramāditya inaugurated a new era. This era may be the direct, persistent, and living evidence, throwing light on the existence of Vikramāditya. In the early inscriptions from the third century A.D., it was known as Kṛita. According to RAJBALI PANDEY[2], '*Kṛita*' means 'golden age'. The defeat over the Śakas brought prosperity, and hence the name '*Kṛita*'. In spite of being the head of the republic, he could not give his name to this era, because of strong republic traditions. A. S. ALTEKAR[3] is of the view, that it was founded by the ruler Kṛita in the first century B. C. From the fifth century A. D., it began to be called Mālava, because it was associated with the Mālava region. As there were strong traditions of its being founded by Vikrama, it became famous in association with the name of its actual founder, from about the eighth century A. D.

Vikramāditya was a great conqueror. The *Kathāsaritsāgara* describes the victorious camp of Vikramāditya, joined by the king of Śaktikumāra of Gauḍa, Jayadhvaja of Karṇāta, Vijayavarman of Lāṭa, Sunandana of Kashmir, Gopāla of Sind, Vindhyaballa of Bhills, etc. This is mainly regarded as fictitious because these names of these rulers and places, are not

1. JNSI, XXVIII, pp. 46-50.
2. Vikramāditya of Ujjayinī.
3. Vikrama Volume, p. 16.

confirmed by any independent contemporary evidence. It is possible that he might have extended his empire by conquering some neighbouring places.

Vikramāditya embodied in himself an ideal of a kingship. He considered it his prime duty to promote the spiritual and temporal welfare of his subjects. His proverbial sense of justice is well known. His dashing, reckless and adventurous spirit earned him the epithet of '*Sāhasāṅka*'. He is famous for his phenomenal generosity, and his readiness to relieve the misery of his subjects, regardless of their status.

Vikramāditya was a patron of art and literature. According to the *Jyotirvidābharaṇa* (possibly 1242 A.D.) of Gaṇaka Kālidāsa, there were numerous scholars and poets in the court of Vikramāditya, but nine of them were regarded as *ratnas* or jewels of the court. These nine were (1) Dhanvantari (2) Kshapaṇaka (3) Amarasiṁha (4) Śaṅku (5) Vetāla-Bhaṭṭa (6) Ghaṭakarpara (7) Kālidāsa (8) Varāhamihira and (9) Vararuchi. Under him, Ujjain became a great seat of learning.

D.C. Sircar[1] does not regard the above arguments as convincing. He disbelieves that the Vikrama of tradition was a historical figure living in the first century B.C. He tries to identify him with Chandragupta II of the Gupta dynasty.

There is inconsistency in Brahmanical as well as in Jaina legends, in the representation of Vikramāditya as of Ujjayinī. As these are of late date, they are in conflict with known facts of history. The later Śuṅgas and Kāṇvas were, respectively, ruling over the Malwa region; some with Vidiśā as their capital from about the first half of the first century B.C. They were overthrown by the Sātavāhanas, who cccupied East and West Malwa in about the third quarter of that century. There was no room for a mighty emperor at Ujjayinī during this period.

There is no mention of any king of Malwa or Magadha, named Vikramāditya, in the Puranic lists of the rulers of the above regions. It is interesting to note that the *Bhavishyānukīrtana* section of the *Purāṇas*, which brings the prophetic accounts of the so-called future kings of the Kali age down to the

1. Ancient Malwa and the Vikramāditya Tradition.

beginning of Gupta rule in the fourth century A.D., is remarkably silent about the great king Vikrama, even though it mentions the Śakas, Gardabhillas, etc, who are associated in tradition with the said legendary hero. If the mighty emperor Vikramāditya really flourished before the fourth century A.D. the Puranic compilers of Gupta age could hardly have passed over this outstanding figure.

The Śakas ruled in the Ujjayinī region between the second and the fourth century A.D., and Śakāri who extirpated them, could have hardly flourished at an earlier date in the first century B.C. The anti-Śaka policy instituted by Samudragupta, was carried to its successful culmination by his son Chandragupta II, who extirpated the Śaka ruling house, and permanently annexed the Śaka dominions to his empire.

The name, or title, Vikramāditya, in the first century B.C., is not borne by any king as known from epigraphic, numismatic or literary sources. The titles 'Vikrama', Vikramāṅka, and 'Vikramāditya', are known to be applied to the Gupta emperor Chandragupta II (376-414 A.D.). On a coin of Samudragupta, father of Chandragupta II, that monarch is called Vikrama, but this coin has not been regarded by scholars as a genuine issue of the king.[1] From the Gupta period onwards, titles became popular ending in the words, *āditya* and *aṅka*.

In the Cambay and Sangli plates of Rāshṭrakūṭa Govinda IV (929-33 A.D.), Sāhasāṅka is applied to Chandragupta II. This name, Sāhasāṅka, is one of the names applied to the traditional Vikramāditya. This is conclusive proof, that king Vikramāditya of tradition, is no other than Chandragupta II of the Gupta dynasty.

Literary evidence also does not prove the existence of Vikramāditya. The Vikrama legends contained in the *Bṛihatkathā*, according to many scholars, may have actually been interpolated in the work during the post-Gupta age. Even in the *Gāthāsaptaśatī* ascribed to a Sātavāhana king, named Hāla, there are clear signs of later interpolations in that Prakrit anthology.

There is no mention of Vikrama in earlier Jaina litera-

1. A. S. Altekar. Catalogue of Coins (Bayana Hoard) p. LVIII.

ture. H. D. VELANKAR[1] rightly points out that it drew the attention of Jaina writers after the reign of the devout Jaina monarch, Kumārapāla of Gujarat, in order to compare him with the Vikramāditya of old. The Jaina writers were also eager to give their Vikramāditya legends a chronological background. Their statements about Pushyamitra's successors, are opposed to the Puranic lists of the Śuṅga and Kāṇva kings, while the rule of the Gardabhilla dynasty of Ujjayinī from 74 B. C. to 78 A. D. is in conflict with the facts of the history of Malwa under the Sātavāhanas and Śakas. The *Purāṇas* mention the seventy two year rule of seven Gardabhilla kings, and not any king named Gardabhilla, or of the one hundred and fifty-two years of rule of the Gardabhilla dynasty, as mentioned in Jaina works. The Puranic Gardabhillas appear to have been foreigners, akin to the Śakas, while the Gardabhillas of Jaina literature, have been described as a branch of the Mālavas.

The tradition of nine *ratnas* or jewels, in the court of Vikramāditya, is without value because there is no trace of it in earlier literature. There is no reason to believe that all the nine worthies mentioned in the list of the jewels of Vikrama's court, lived at the same time. Varāhamihira can by no means be ascribed to the age of the traditional Vikramāditya, in the first century B. C., as he lived in the fifth or sixth century A. D. Śaṅku and Vetāla-bhaṭṭa are mere names. Kshapaṇaka is identified with the famous Jaina philosopher Siddhasena Divākara, who lived in the fifth century A.D. Ghaṭakarpara is a well known poem, which, according to Abhinavagupta (1000 A.D.) of Kashmir, and certain other writers, has to be ascribed to Kālidāsa. Whether Ghaṭakarpara was meant for the author of the above work, cannot be determined. Vararuchi may be the reputed author of the grammatical work *Prākṛitaprakāśa*, which appears to be a product of the Gupta age. Amarasiṁha, author of *Amarakosha*, seems to have lived about the fifth century A.D. Dhanvantari, author of a Nighaṇṭu or medical glossary, did not live in the first century B.C. but later. Kālidāsa, the greatest writer in

1. Vikrama Volume, pp. 637 ff.

classical Sanskrit, also lived in the Gupta age.

D.C. SIRCAR[1] does not regard the era of 58 B. C. to have been founded by King Vikramāditya of Ujjain. He advocates a theory that the Scytho-Pārthians introduced the use of the East Iranian era of 58 B. C., probably founded by Vonones, in the north-western part of India, including the Punjab, about the beginning of the Christian era. The Mālavas, who appear to have submitted to the Scytho-Parthians in the Punjab, probably carried the use of above era to Rajasthan. The Mālavas were responsible for the popularisation of the era of 58 B. C. in Rajasthan, and ultimately in certain other parts of India. In Rajasthan, at first in the third and fourth centuries, the Mālavas designated their era, borrowed from the Scytho-Parthians in the Punjab, by the name Kṛita. The real significance of this name is as yet unknown. It has been supposed that Kṛita was an illustrious leader of the Mālava tribe. Another probability is that the name Kṛita is a Sanskrit modification of some Scytho-Parthian name or word.

In the fifth century A.D., the Mālava association with the era, is indicated in the records handed down by the Mālava republic, or by the year being counted in accordance with the custom established by, or from, the foundation of the Mālava republic of the Mālavas. When the memory of the Mālava tribe dimmed in the seventh or eighth century A. D,. the era of 58 B. C. came to be associated with Vikramāditya, who may be identified with Chandragupta II of the Gupta dynasty. He annexed Malwa after destroying the power of the Śakas, and Ujjayinī is regarded as the second capital of his empire, besides Pāṭaliputra. He became famous in Indian tradition and folklore, as Vikramāditya Śakāri.

D.C.SIRCAR's theory of regarding the era of 58 B.C. as the East Iranian era of Scytho-Parthian origin founded by Vonones, in the North-Western part of India, seems to be imaginary. There is no evidence that Vonones founded any era, and there is no dated record which can be ascribed to him. There are no records found in the Punjab which can be positively ascribed to the Vikrama era. As far as the

1. Ancient Malwa and the Vikramāditya tradition, p. 163.

Taxila inscription of the time of Moga is concerned, RAPSON[1] ascribes it to the Parthian era, founded in about 150 B.C. About the Panjtar inscription of the year 122, and the Taxila inscription of the year 136, of the early Kushāṇa rulers, nothing can be definitely stated about the era in which they were recorded. Even before the first century B. C., the Mālavas are known to have settled in Rajasthan, from their seals and coins which have been discovered at Rairh. Hence the question of the Mālavas carrying it from the Punjab to Rajasthan does not arise. This era seems to be an indigenous one, and probably originated in Rajasthan.

It is not possible to give any final opinion on the question of Vikramāditya. He should not be regarded as a historical person positively, until more reliable evidence is available. It is more reasonable to accept the existence of this king as a provisional hypothesis, like that of many other kings whose names are known from the Purāṇas.

MALWA UNDER THE ŚAKAS :—

From the first century A. D. onwards, there began a deadly struggle between the Sātavāhanas and Sakas, for the occupation of Malwa. The coins and inscriptions discovered so far, throw considerable light on it. From about the end of the first century A.D., the Kushāṇa emperor Kanishka I, seems to have extended his power up to Malwa, and to begin with, these Śakas acknowledged the suzerainty of the Kushāṇas, but afterwards they became independent. The native powers, both republican and monarchical states, gave heroic resistance to free their country from foreign domination, but their success was temporary. The Śakas ruled over Malwa for about three hundred years, till their power was finally crushed by Chandragupta II.

FAMILY OF MAMBARUS :—From the *Periplus*, we know that Mambarus ruled in Western India in the middle of the first century A. D. At this time, Sandares, the viceroy of the Mambarus, conquered Aparānta from the Sātavāhanas, and he might have penetrated up to Malwa. The ruling house

1. CHI, p. 515.

represented by Mambarus was either subdued or supplanted by the Kushāṇas. It is not known definitely whether the Kshaharātas, who ruled over Western India as Kshatrapas of Kanishka I and his successors, belonged to the same family as Mambarus.[1]

THE KSHAHARĀTA SATRAPS :—

ARṬA :—Arṭa seems to be the earliest known member of the Kshaharāta family who took the title of Kshatrapa. He may have been the predecessor of Bhūmaka. On his two coins[2] so far published, there is, on the obverse, the capital of a pillar consisting of a lion and wheel along with Brāhmī legend '*Kshaharatasa Kshatapas Atasa*'. On the reverse, there is the figure of Nike holding a wreath in both her hands, and a fragmentary Greek legend. He seems to be the viceroy of the Kushāṇas. Arṭa is also known from the coins of his son Kharaosta or Prakharaosta.[3] Both seem to be one and the same person.

BHŪMAKA :—Another Satrap of the Kshaharāṭa family is Bhūmaka. His relation with Arṭa is not known, but we find similar symbols[4] of lion-capital and wheel as found on the coins of Arṭa. He seems to have been the Kshatrapa in charge of the South-eastern part of the empire of the Kushāṇas of Kanishka's house. His coins have been found at Ujjain and Bhilsa in Malwa.[5] They have also been discovered in the coastal regions of Gujarat and Kathiawad, and in the Ajmer region of Rajasthan. They are round and square in shape, and made of copper and lead. The use of both the Kharoshṭhī and Brāhmī scripts in Bhūmaka's coin legends probably points to the fact that the Kshatrapa territories not only comprised such Districts as Malwa, Gujarat and Kathiawad, where Brāhmī was prevalent, but also some regions of Western Rajasthan and Sind, where Kharoshṭhī appears to have been in use. No details of Bhūmaka's rule are known. Whether he issued coins during the lifetime of Kanishka I, or after the latter's death,

1. The Age of Imperial Unity, pp. 178-179.
2. JNSI, XVII, p. 89.
3. The Age of Imperial Unity, p. 134.
4. A Catalogue of the Indian Coins in the British Museum, p. CVIII.
5. JNSI, XVII, p. 89.

when the hold of the Kushāṇas on the outlying provinces of the empire was growing feeble, cannot be ascertained.

NAHAPĀNA:—Bhūmaka seems to have been succeeded by Nahapāna, who belonged to the same Kshaharāta family. The relation between the two is not known. He assumed the title of '*Rājan*', as known from the testimony of coins[1] and inscriptions, and this title was not borne by his predecessor Bhūmaka. No record of Nahapāna refers to his overlord. He therefore seems to have ruled as an independent king.

He is known, however, from the testimony of inscription, to have been Kshatrapa in the Śaka year[2] 41 (119 A.D.), and Mahākshaṭrapa in the Śaka year[3] 46 (124 A. D.). On some of his silver coins[4] on the reverse, there is a tree with large leaves within a railing. This seems to connect it with a coinage which is attributed to the Sātavāhana kings. All this evidence points to the expansion of the power of Nahapāna, at the cost of the Sātavāhanas. He seems to have conquered the Nasik and Poona Districts from the Sātavāhanas of Pratishṭhāna. Realising their strategical importance, he made his son-in-law Ṛishabhadatta, the Viceroy of the Southern province of his dominions. No doubt, the *āhāras* (Districts) of Govardhana (Nasik), and Māmlā (Poona), were in charge of Ṛishabhadatta, but he may have also ruled over Southern Gujarat and the northern Konkan, from Broach to Sopara.

The extent of Nahapāna's dominion may be partially determined by the inscription[5] recording the benefactions of his son-in-law and general, Ṛishabhadatta (Ushavadāta), at different places such as Kāpūr-āhāra (Kapura in old Baroda state), Prabhāsa (Southern Kathiawar), Bhṛigukachchha (Broach), Daśapura (Mandsor in Western Malwa), Sūrpāraka (Sopara in Thana Dist), and Pushkara (near Ajmer), as well as to the rivers Tāpī, Barṇāsa (Banas), Pāradā (Pār in the Surat District), Damana (Damaṅgaṅgā near Daman), and Dāhanukā (near Dāhānu) in the Thana

1. A Catalogue of the Indian Coins in the British Museum, p. CIX.
2. Sel. Ins., p. 164.
3. Ibid, p. 173.
4. A Catalogue of the Indian Coins in the British Museum, p. CIX.
5. Sel. Ins. pp. 167-169; EI, VIII, pp. 78 ff.

District. It is possible that Ṛishabhadatta visited some of the holy places outside the viceregal state as a pious pilgrim. In one of the Nasik cave inscriptions, Ṛishabhadatta is said to have gone at the command of the *Bhaṭṭāraka* to relieve the chief of the Uttamabhadra tribe, who was besieged by the Mālayas (Mālavas).[1] After inflicting a crushing defeat on the Mālayas, the Śaka chief is said to have gone to the Pushkara lake for ceremonial consecration. It is not known whether the word *Bhaṭṭāraka* (lord), indicates the Satrap Nahapāna or his Kushāṇa overlord. His coins have also been discovered in the Ajmer region[2], and in the Nasik District. It seems that Malwa, Kathiawar, Gujarat, the northern part of the Konkan and the Maratha country, the Ajmer region of Rajasthan, and a portion of the lower Sindhu valley, lay within the dominions of Nahapāna.

Soon after the Śaka year 46 (124-25 A.D.), Nahapāna appears to have been defeated and killed by the Sātavāhana king, Gautamīputra Sātakarṇi. Gautamīputra's inscriptions in the Nasik and Poona Districts, show how Nahapāna's viceroy, Ṛishabhadatta, was ousted by him from those regions. The large hoard of Nahapāna's coins discovered at Jogalthembi in the Nasik District, shows how the Sātavāhana king captured the Satrap's treasury and restruck the latter's coins for circulation. On the silver coins[3] of Nahapāna restruck by Gautamīputra Sātakarṇi, Nahapāna's bust is restruck by a six arched *chaitya*, and on the reverse, the Ujjain symbol of the Sātavāhanas. Aparānta, Anūpa, Saurāshṭra, Kukura, Ākara and Avanti, must have been conquered from Nahapāna by Gautamīputra Sātakarṇi.

After conquering Malwa from Nahapāna, Gautamīputra Sātakarṇi issued the current local type of coins, particularly in Malwa, for the convenience of the people. On the obverse, there is the figure of an elephant with its trunk, and on the reverse, the peculiar device of Ujjain symbol.[4] This latter

1. EI, VIII, pp. 78 ff.
2. A Catalogue of the Indian Coins in the British Museum, p. 67.
3. Ibid, p. 68.
4. JNSI, V, p. 25.

is a new feature, not known on any Sātavāhana coinage. It was prevalent only on the coins of Malwa. The Elephant type of coinage was also adopted by Gautamīputra Sātakarṇi. The homo-sign, fairly common on early Ujjain coinage, persisted on the coinage of the Conqueror.[1]

THE KĀRDAMAKAS:—Chashṭana, son of Yaśamotika of the Kārdamaka family, seems to be the contemporary of Nahapāna of the Kshaharāta family. When Nahapāna was ruling over a wide area of the Gujarat, Malwa, and Maharashtra Chashṭana may have been ruling in Kutch and perhaps some adjacent territories, as the Andhau inscription of the year 11 suggests. This inscription of the reign of Chashṭana, records the raising of the pillar in memory of two persons named Palitaka and Māhukāna, apparently belonging to the same family, by the sons of the said persons. That both Nahapāna and Chashṭana belonged to different families is certain; but their use of the Kharoshṭhī alphabet and the character of their names and titles, clearly show that they were of northern origin; while the fabric and epigraphy of their coins—the striking similarity seen in the letters of their Greek-Brāhmī and Kharoshṭhī coin legends, indicate that they cannot have been widely separated, either chronologically or geographically.

D. C. Sircar[2] thinks that both Chashṭana and Nahapāna owed allegiance to some imperial ruling house, which can only be that of the Kushāṇas. Although they enjoyed some position, and were allowed to issue coins in metal other than gold, they were not allowed to date their records in their own regnal reckoning, but in the records of their overlords, which was apparently in the Kanishka era. D. C. Sircar further suggests that Chashṭana was appointed by the suzerain power to rule over such provinces of the Satrapal dominion as remained after the Andhra conquest, and if possible to regain its lost possessions.

The difficulty in accepting this view is that there is no reference in the inscriptions of Nahapāna and Chashṭana that they owed any allegiance to the Kushāṇa suzerain,

1. JNSI, V, p. 25.
2. JIH, Vol. XVIII, Pt. II, p. 255.

Nahapāna could not be so easily defeated by Gautamīputra Sātakarṇi. R. C. MAJUMDAR[1] has recently suggested that Chashṭana was the founder of the Śaka era. Therefore, it is not definite whether the era in the inscriptions of Chashṭana and Nahapāna is the Kanishka era, and on this basis alone, these rulers cannot be regarded as subordinates.

Further, on the evidence of two incriptions[2] of the years 22 and 28 of the reign of Vāsishka[3] (100 A. D. and 108 A.D.), found on the two red sandstone images, some scholars, such as B. N. PURI[4] and D. C. SIRCAR[5], have concluded that the Kushāṇas had some hold over Malwa, and that the Western Kshatrapas recognized their suzerainty. It seems that these two sculptures were executed at Mathura, and the inscriptions were also engraved there. As Mathura was under the suzerainty of the Kushāṇas at this time, the name of the ruling monarch was also engraved on the images. Sanchi being the centre of Buddhism, some of the Mathura images were transported for installation there. From this, it is inadvisable to draw the conclusion that Malwa had come under the sway of the Kushāṇas, because of the name of Vāsishka.

There is evidence to show that the Śakas, under Chashṭana, defeated the Sātavāhana king and recovered most of the northern districts of the latter's dominions which were originally conquered from Nahapāna. On earlier coins[6] of Chashṭana, he is called a 'Kshatrapa', and on later issues, a '*Mahākshatrapa*.' Further, we know that the early coins of Chashṭana bear the type crescent and star, to which a hill symbol was added later. As the hill is intimately associated with the issues of the Sātavāhanas, it signifies some extension of Chashṭana's power at the expense of the Sātavāhanas, i.e. some reconquest of territories previously taken by them from

1. Monthly Bulletin of the Asiatic Society, Vol. IV, No. 7, p. 7.
2. MMS, p. 386, Ins. Nos. 828-29.
3. The characters of the two records are similar, and hence Vāsishka and Vaskushāna may be one and the same ruler.
4. India under the Kushāṇas, pp. 70 ff.
5. Ancient Malwa and the Vikramāditya Tradition, p. 159.
6. A Catalogue of the Indian Coins in the British Museum, pp. CXIII-CXVI.

his predecessor Nahapāna. When the territory of Chashṭana increased because of new conquests, he probably shifted his capital to Ujjain. The geography of Ptolemy mentions Ujjayinī as the capital of West Malwa of Trastenes, undoubtedly a Greek corruption of the name of Chashṭana.

One silver coin[1] of Chashṭana as *Mahākshatrapa*, has been discovered at Ujjain. On the obverse, there is the bust of the king with traces of Greek legend. On the reverse, there is the hill of six arches surmounted by a rayed Sun on the left and a crescent on the right. It differs from the known coins in two respects. There is the interchange of the position of the Sun and the crescent, and the six-arched hill. This symbol was borrowed from the Sātavāhanas by Chashṭana who conquered their territory. But on the coins of the Sātavāhanas, the hill is three-arched. Thus Chashṭana was the originator of six-arched hill, and afterwards it was adopted by the Sātavāhana ruler, Śrī Yajña Sātakarṇi.

JAYADĀMAN :—Chashṭana's son was Jayadāman, who is known to have been only a '*Kshatrapa*', suggesting that the power of the dynasty must have suffered because of the conquest by the Sātavāhanas who were their rivals. The coins attributed to Jayadāman are exclusively of copper and square in form, with two varieties.[2] On the first, on the obverse side, there is a humped bull together with trident and battle axe, and on the reverse, there is a hill of six arches. The second variety bears the Elephant and Ujjainī symbol. Another view[3] is that Jayadāman as *Kshatrapa* under his father Chashṭana died early and was succeeded by his son Rudradāman I. Inscriptions[4] discovered at Andhau in Kachchha show that in the Śaka year 52 (130-31 A.D.) *Rājā* Chashṭana was ruling jointly with his grandson *Rājā* Rudradāman. It seems that at this time, Chashṭana was the *Mahākshatrapa* and Rudradāman, the *Kshatrapa*.

RUDRADĀMAN :—There is evidence to show that Rudra-

1. JNSI, XIV, parts I & II.
2. A Catalogue of the Indian Coins in the British Museum, pp. cxii-cxviii.
3. The Age of Imperial Unity, p. 183.
4. EI, XVI, pp. 23 ff.

dāman as *Kshatrapa* under his grandfather Chashṭana defeated the Sātavāhana king and recovered most of the northern districts of the latter's dominions originally conquered from Nahapāna. In the Junagarh inscription[1] of Rudradāman, that ruler is represented as the lord of many countries including Ākara, Avanti (the whole of Malwa), Anūpa (upper Narabada), Aparānta, Saurāshṭra (Kathiawad) and Ānarta (Northern Part of Gujarat) which had all been conquered from Gautamīputra Sātakarṇi probably when Rudradāman was a *Kshatrapa* under his grandfather. Rudradāman further claims to have twice defeated Sātakarṇi, lord of Dakshiṇāpatha whom he did not destroy as he was a near relative. That Vāsishṭhiputra was the son-in-law of Rudradāman, is clear from the Kanheri inscription. Rudradāman's claim to have reinstated deposed kings may have reference to the (reinstatement of) certain feudatories of Nahapāna, ousted by Gautamīputra Sātakarṇi.

Sometime after 130-31 A. D., Rudradāman succeeded to Chashṭana as *Mahākshatrapa*. All his known coins[2] belong to the period when Rudradāman was a *Mahākshatrapa*. The *Mahākshatrapa's* territories comprised Mālava, Kathiawar, Gujarat, the northern Konkan and the Māhishmatī conquered from Sātakarṇi, the Lord of Dakshiṇāpatha at the time of accession. Later, it included the districts such as Kachchha (Cutch), Śvabhra (the Sabarmati valley), Maru (the Marwar region), Sindhu (Western part of the lower Sindhu valley), Sauvīra (eastern part of the lower Sindhu valley) and Nishāda (about the western Vindhyas and the Aravalli range). Thus Rudradāman appears to have ruled over the whole of the Kshaharāta dominions with only the exception of the Nasik and Poona Districts. He claims to have conquered all these territories by his own valour.

Rudradāman is said to have inflicted a crushing defeat on the republican tribe of the Yaudheyas who inhabited Southern Panjab and the adjoining regions. It is probable that he tried to subdue the insubordinate Yaudheyas on behalf of his Kushāṇa overlords. But that he ruled almost as an independent

1. EI, VIII, pp. 42 ff.
2. A Catalogue of the Indian Coins in the British Museum, p. CXXI.

king is indicated by the absence of any reference to the Kushāṇas in the records of his time as well by his claim that he himself assumed the title of '*Mahākshatrapa*'.

That Rudradāman was a good administrator, is clear from the reconstruction of Sudarśana lake which was destroyed by the excessively swollen floods of the Suvarṇasikatā, Palāśinī and other streams of the mount Ūrjayat in 150 A.D. He appointed Pahlava Suviśākha, son of Kulaipa as the governor of Ānarta and Saurāshṭra and entrusted the task of rebuilding the Sudarśana Lake to him. His efforts were crowned with success and the reservoir was again brought into being. His good rule, we are told, rid his dominions of disease, robbers, wild beasts and other pests.

Besides being a great conqueror and administrator, he was a patron of Sanskrit language. He was himself a great scholar of grammar, polity, music and Logic. He had good command over Sanskrit both in prose and verse. Under him, Ujjainī appears to have become one of the most important seats of learning in the whole of India.

DĀMAGHASADA OR DĀMAJADAŚRĪ :—The son and successor of Rudradāman is Dāmaghasada or Dāmajadaśrī who became the '*Mahākshatrapa*' in about 170 A. D. First he was associated with his father in administration as a *Kshatrapa* and perhaps he took an active part in the campaigns of his father. This type of joint administration by the king as *Mahākshatrapa* along with his son or brother in the junior capacity of *Kshatrapa* became a regular feature of administration in this family. His coins[1] as *Mahākshatrapa* are very rare and the portrait on them shows he was an old man at the time of his accession. His reign therefore probably did not extend beyond 175 A. D. During this short rule, his kingdom seems to have remained undisturbed.

LONG STRUGGLE BETWEEN JĪVADĀMAN AND HIS UNCLE RUDRASIṀHA FOR THE THRONE :—Dāmajadaśrī had two sons namely Jīvadāman and Satyadāman. After Dāmajadaśrī, his elder son Jīvadāman became the '*Mahākshatrapa*' in about 175 A. D. He did not possess much administrative

1. A Catalogue of the Indian Coins in the British Museum, p. cxiii.

experience before his accession to the throne because his coins as '*Mahākshatrapa*' during his father's rule are not found. He seems to be quite young at the time of his accession to the throne. He had the misfortune of having an experienced and ambitious uncle named Rudrasiṁha. In the beginning, he accepted the subordinate position of *Kshatrapa* and professed loyalty to his nephew but, soon, he began to conspire to seize the throne. In his plans, he probably received help from the Ābhīras who were serving the *Kshatrapa* army as generals as it is known from the Gunda inscription[1]. He dethroned his nephew Jīvadāman and became the *Mahākshatrapa* in 181 A.D.

Rudrasiṁha could not enjoy the ill-gotten possession of the throne for long. Soon in 188 A. D., Īśvaradatta, the Ābhira general, deposed him and became *Māhakshatrapa* himself in 188 A. D. and issued the coins[2] during the regnal years 1 and 2. Rudrasiṁha agreed to rule as feudatory in the capacity of a *Kshatrapa*. Rapson[3] ascribes the temporary degradation of Rudrasiṁha to the success of Jīvadāman but actually we have no coins of Jīvadāman in the period of 188-91 A.D. Bhandarkar[4] may be right in associating Rudrasiṁha's degradation in 188-91 A. D. with the rise of Īśvaradatta. However Rapson[5] places the Ābhīra intervention under Īśvaradatta in 231-38 A.D. during which time no coins were issued by the Western Kshatrapas. Since the Ābhīras are known to be serving as generals under the Western Kshatrapas in 180 A.D., it is more probable that the degradation of Rudrasiṁha I during(188-190)was due to their *coup* under Īśvaradatta. It is probable that the success of Īśvaradatta was due to the help he received from the Sātavāhana ruler Yajña Sātakarṇi. Yajña Sātakarṇi also extended his empire at the cost of the Śakas. It is possible that both Īśvaradatta and Yajña combined in order to exploit the situation resulting from the struggle between Jīvadāman and Rudrasiṁha I.

1. EI, XVI, p. 235.
2. A Catalogue of the Indian Coins in the British Museum, pp. 124-25.
3. Ibid, pp. cxxxiii-cxxiv.
4. A.S.I. 1913-4, pp. 227-45.
5. A Catalogue of the Indian Coins in the British Museum, pp. cxxiii-xxxiv.

Anyhow Rudrasiṁha managed to oust Īśvaradatta and again became Mahākshatrapa in 191 A.D. and continued up to 197 A.D. He was succeeded by his dethroned nephew Jīvadāman. Whether a compromise was made between the uncle and the nephew or whether the nephew defeated the uncle and ascended the throne, is not definitely known. The former alternative is more likely because we find Rudrasiṁha's son Rudrasena working as *Kshatrapa* under Jīvadāman towards the end of his reign.

RUDRASENA I :—The next ruler was Rudrasena I. He enjoyed a long reign of twenty-two years from 200 to 222 A. D. He had two brothers Saṁghadāman and Dāmasena, and two sons Pṛithvīsena and Dāmagada. During the reign of Rudrasiṃha I, Malwa, Gujarat, Kathiawar and Western Rajputana continued to be under their rule. Ujjain continued to be their capital.

SAṀGHADĀMAN AND DĀMASENA :—

After the death of Rudrasena, the crown passed on to his elder brother Saṅghadāman. He ruled only for a year and half; for we find his younger brother Dāmasena ruling as *Mahākshatrapa* in 223 A. D. It is possible that Saṁghadāman may have died a premature death. A. S. Altekar[1] is of the view that it is however more likely that he may have died in battle while fighting against the Mālavas of Ajmer-Udaipur tract who made a successful bid for independence at about this time. A Mālava chief Śrīsoma or Nandisoma by name is known to have performed an important sacrifice at Nāndsā near Udaipur to celebrate the liberation of his country. An inscription[2] dated 226 A. D. announces how freedom and prosperity had returned to the country of the Mālavas by this time. The enemies of the Mālavas are not mentioned in the record but they may be the Western Kshatrapas.

Dāmasena became the *Mahākshatrapa* in about 223 A. D. and continued up to 237 A. D. During the first ten years of his reign, Pṛithvīsena and Dāmajada II, sons of Rudrasena I ruled under him as *Kshatrapa*. During the last four years of

1. Vākāṭaka-Gupta Age, p. 49.
2. EI, XXVII, p. 265.

his reign, however his own son Vīradāman was raised to that status. Along with the Ajmer, Udaipur region, soon after Sind also slipped away from the hands of the Western Kshatrapas. During the reign of Dāmasena, the kingdom of the Western Kshatrapas included only Malwa, Gujarat and Kathiawar. Ujjayinī still continued to be their capital.

After the reign of *Mahākshatrapa* Dāmasena, the potin coinage of the Kārdamakas, which is usually attributed to Malwa or some district of that country, seems to have discontinued. This discontinuance of coinage suggests that about this time, Malwa was lost to the Kārdamaka *Mahākshatrapas*. On the other hand, Rapson[1] suggests that potin currency previously circulating in that district was superseded by the more widely used silver coinage. The view of Rapson seems to be reasonable.

About the middle of the third century A. D., there were not only internal dissensions amongst the Śakas of Western India but they were also threatened by the external enemies such aṣ the Mālavas, the Ābhiras, and the Nāgas. The Mālavas took possession of the northern part of the Kārdamaka dominions. In the south, the Ābhiras established a powerful kingdom in the northern Maharashtra and the adjoining regions and started an era of their own in 248-49 A.D. The Nāgas of Vidiśā and Padmāvatī must have become aggressive neighbours of the Śaka Satraps at this time.

YAŚODĀMAN, VIJAYASENA, DĀMAJADA III AND RUDRASENA II (238 A.D. to 279 A.D.) :—

The elder son of Dāmasena named Vīradāman died early so Dāmasena was succeeded by his younger son Yaśodāman as *Mahākshatrapa*. He ruled as *Mahākshatrapa* for about one year (238-239 A. D.). The premature deaths of the two brothers Vīradāman and Yaśodāman in quick succession indicates some trouble in the body politic. Next Vijayasena came to the throne who had a peaceful and prosperous reign of about twelve years (539-51 A.D.) for his coins are found in large numbers throughout Gujarat and Kathiawar. Vijayasena was

1. A Catalogue of the Indian Coins in the British Museum, p. CXXI. See also f. n. 1.

succeeded by his younger brother Dāmajada III in about 350 A.D. Being the youngest of four brothers, he had naturally a short reign of five years and was succeeded in 255 A. D. by Rudrasena II, the son of his eldest brother Vīradāman. He had a long reign of twenty-two years. He seems to have been matrimonially allied with the Ikshvāku king Vīrapurushadatta of Āndhrapatha who probably married Rudra Bhaṭṭārikā described as a daughter of *Mahārāja* of Ujjain.

During the period 239 to 275 A. D., no prince however is known to be associated as *Kshatrapa* with the ruling monarch. This post of *Kshatrapa* seems to have been abolished. It was however revived by Rudrasena II towards the end of his reign, for his son Viśvasiṁha is known to have functioned as a *Kshatrapa* for a short time under his father before death.

It seems that the kingdom of the Western Kshatrapas suffered further contraction at this time. The copper coinage of the Western Kshatrapas, which was current only in Malwa up to 240 A. D., suddenly comes to an end after that year. It seems that soon the Śakas lost Malwa. Vindhyaśakti, the founder of the Vākāṭaka kingdom who ruled from 255 to 275 A.D., seems to have annexed a part of Eastern Malwa.[1] This view does not seem to be correct because an inscribed clay sealing with the names of Kshatrapa Siṁhasena and his father Īśvaramitra, and also two dozen coin moulds of Western Kshatrapas have been unearthed at Eran proving their hold over Eastern Malwa before the time of Samudragupta.

VIŚVASIṀHA AND BHARTṚIDĀMAN (279 A.D. to 304 A.D.):—

As Rudrasena II seems to have had no younger brother, he was succeeded by his eldest son Viśvasiṁha in 279 A.D. He had a short reign of about three years only, for we find his brother Bhartṛidāman ruling as *Mahākshatrapa* in 282 A.D. and his reign extended up to 304 A. D. His son Viśvasena functioned under him as *Kshatrapa* from 294 A. D. onwards. The coins of Bhartṛidāman as *Mahākshatrapa* and of Viśvasena as *Kshatrapa* are found in large numbers; we may assume that they succeeded in retrieving the fortunes of their family to a large extent. Viśvasena is the last *Kshatrapa* belonging to the

1. Vākāṭaka-Gupta Age, p. 51.

family of Chashṭana. It is probable that *Mahākshatrapa* Bhartṛidāman and his *Kshatrapa* Viśvasena were overthrown by the Sassanians but it cannot be regarded as certain, for the interpretation of the Paikuli inscription on which the theory primarily rests, is very uncertain.

THE RISE OF A NEW ŚAKA HOUSE :—

The successor of Bhartṛidāman was not his son Viśvasena who acted as Kshatrapa for about ten years, but one Rudrasiṁha II who is described as the son of Svāmī Jīvadāman, a person mentioned without any royal title like *rājan* or *Kshatrapa*. The relationship of Rudrasiṁha II with Bhartṛidāman is unknown; he seems to have been an upstart or at the most a member of a collateral Śaka branch. Rudrasiṁha II ousted the legitimate heir and occupied the throne in 304 or 305 A.D. He continued to rule up to 316 A. D. when he was succeeded by his son Yaśodāman II who ruled certainly down to 332 A. D. and perhaps for a few years more.

Two facts of this new Śaka house are important. Both Rudrasiṁha II and Yaśodāman II however did not assume the higher title of *Mahākshatrapa* and they were content with the simple title of *Kshatrapa*. After 332 A.D., there is a break in the *Kshatrapa* coinage for sixteen years during which period no ruler is known to have issued coins either as *Kshatrapa* or as *Mahākshatrapa*.

These facts indicate trouble sometimes but any definite cause is not known. One view[1] is that the Sassanian intervention was responsible for this gradual decline and total eclipse of the power of the Western Kshatrapas. This view does not seem to be correct. The Sassanians were involved in war with the Roman emperor and they were not in a position to fight against the Śakas. No coins of the Sassanians of this period have been found in Gujarat, Kathiawar and Malwa; nor does the coinage of Rudrasiṁha II and Yaśodāman II show any Sassanian influence.

A. S. Altekar[2] thinks that the conquests of the Vākāṭaka emperor Pravarasena I were responsible for the decline of the

1. PHAI, p. 428.
2. Vākāṭaka-Gupta Age, p. 55.

Kshatrapa power during the early decades of the fourth century A. D. He, however, is the only Vākāṭaka ruler to assume the title of '*Samrāṭ*' (emperor) and is known to have performed as many as four horse sacrifices (*aśvamedhas*) to celebrate his different conquests. Pravarasena's overlordship over the Kshatrapas is only a theory, no doubt more probable than any other, but still lacking conclusive proof.

V.V. MIRASHI[1], who questioned this theory, ascribes the assumption of the lower title by Rudrasiṁha II and his son Yaśodāman II to the rise of *Mahākshatrapa* and *Rājan* Śrīdharavarman whose inscriptions found at Kānākherā near Sanchi and Eran show that he rose to power in Malwa during this period.

It is also possible that Samudragupta might have exercised some control over the Śakas. There might have been a long-drawn struggle of Samudragupta against the Śakas. D.C. SIRCAR[2] even proposes to identify Rudradeva, one of the nine kings of Āryāvarta exterminated by Samudragupta, with the Śaka Satrap Rudradāman II or his son Rudrasena III. This might well account for the cessation of the coins of western Satraps but such a conclusion can only be regarded as provisional.

At last it may be said that internal dissension might have been the cause or at least one of the causes of the decline in power and authority of the Satraps Rudrasiṁha and his son Yaśodāman II who never assumed the title *Mahākshatrapa*.

THE FOURTH ŚAKA HOUSE FOUNDED BY RUDRADĀMAN II AND HIS SUCCESSORS :—

Rudradāman II, who supplanted Yaśodāman II, may have ruled at least for two or three years before 348 A.D. when his son Rudrasena III ruled as *Mahākshatrapa*. He had a long reign of about thirty-two years but it was not peaceful. Soon after 351 A.D., there occurred a political disturbance of an uncommon nature making life and property unsafe. It was probably due to the rise of the Aulikaras under Jayavarman, who might have seized the territory round about Mandsor in order to establish his kingdom. This situation lasted for thirteen years when we

1. PIHC, 14th Session, Jaipur, p. 16.
2. The Classical Age, p. 8.

find him issuing coins up to 378 A. D. He was succeeded by Simhasena, who was his sister's son and not his own. The succession therefore may not have been a peaceful one. We find Simhasena ruling as *Mahākshatrapa* in 382 A.D. This Simhasena may be identified with Simhaśrī Sena, son of the King Īśvaramitra, mentioned on the clay sealing.

The two Śaka stone inscriptions of Śaka ruler called Śrīdharavarmā discovered at Kānākherā near Sanchi[1] and Eran[2] and at the same time an inscribed clay sealing from Eran[3] written in Brāhmī inscription in well known Kshatrapa style '*Rājña Īśvaramitraputrasya rājño Simha Śrī Senasya*' (King, Simha Śrī Sena, son of King Īśvaramitra) prove that Śakas continued to rule in Malwa in the fourth century A.D. and their power was not crushed in the third century A.D. as presumed by some scholars. They seem to have had several branches ruling over different parts of the vast Śaka kingdom. We do not know of any definite relationship of Īśvaramitra and his son Simhasena with king Śrīdharavarmā ruling over Eastern Malwa.

Simhasena was succeeded by his son Rudrasena IV. In 338 A.D. or soon after, we find Rudrasimha III on the throne ruling as *Mahākshatrapa*. He could not rule for a long time and was completely defeated by Chandragupta II who annexed Gujarat and Kathiawar to the Gupta empire and put an end to the Śaka rule.

ŚAKA DYNASTY OF MĀHISHMATĪ :—

V. V. Mirashi[4] advocates a theory that a Śaka dynasty of Māhishmatī founded by Māna was ruling between 250 A. D. and 450 A. D. The coins of Māna of the types of Elephant, Lion and Svastika have been found in the south and the complete legend on them can be restored as '*Ramño Sagama-*

1. This inscription was first edited by R. D. Banerji (EI, XVI, p. 230) who took it as a record of Jīvadāman. It was re-edited by N. G. Majumdar, JPASB, XIX, p. 337, who rightly pointed out there was no reference to Jīvadāman in the inscription which is a record of Śrīdharavarmā and is dated 13th year of his reign.
2. PIHC, 14th Session, Jaipur, p. 16.
3. Bulletin of Ancient Indian History and Archaeology, Saugar, p. 3.
4. IHQ, 1946, 34 ff.

namahasa (sa). These coins may be attributed to Śaka Māna of the Mahisha dynasty of the *Purāṇas*.[1] It seems that first he was a feudatory or officer of the late Sātavāhana ruler but afterwards he became independent and issued his own coins. He had evidently a fairly extensive dominion, for he is one of the few kings of the historic period to be named in the *Purāṇas*. The family name Mahisha points to his connection with Māhishmatī, the ancient capital of the Anūpa country now identified with modern Māndhātā or *Maheśvara* on the Narmada.

The evidence of the coins and the statement in the *Purāṇas* testify to the rise of this dynasty in about 240 A. D. and it is probable that the Śakas led by their king Māna drove the Western Kshatrapas away for some time from Malwa. *Mahādaṇḍanāyaka* Śrīdharavarman, whose inscriptions have been discovered at Eran and Sanchi, was not an upstart[2] but probably belonged to the dynasty founded by Śaka Māna and like him, might have ruled from Māhishmatī. Śrīdharavarman's descendants continued to rule over Māhishmatī, and Subandhu[3] was probably one of them. The Śaka, who submitted to Samudragupta, as mentioned in the Allahabad Pillar inscription, should be identified with this Śaka dynasty of the Anūpa country.

V. V. Mirashi[4] further suggests that the territory ruled by the Mahisha-Śaka dynasty comprised the southern part of the former Hyderabad State, which in his opinion was called Māhishaka in ancient times. It is also suggested that the said Mahisha-Śaka house of Southern Hyderabad was an offshoot of the Kshaharāta Śaka family of Western India. The device of the thunderbolt and arrow seen on the reverse of the Svastika-type coins of the king Māna was the characteristic of the coins of the Śaka Kshatrapas Bhūmaka and Nahapāna.[5]

Against the reading of the coin-legend and its interpretation, D. C. Sircar[6] has raised the following objections :

1. Pargiter : DKA, p. 51.
2. Majumdar and Altekar : A New History of Indian people, VI, p. 55.
3. EI, XIX, pp. 261 f; IHQ , XXI, p. 80 f.
4. JNSI, XI, pp. 1 ff.
5. EI, XXXVII, pp. 45 ff.
6. Ibid, XXXV, pp. 69-78.

(1) The complete legend of the coin is not '*Raṁno Sagamāna-Mahasasa*' but Sagamāna Mahāsenāpatisa Chuṭukulasa, which means (this coin is) of Chuṭukula, the Mahāsenāpati of Sagamas.

(2) There is no word like '*raṁno*' in the beginning of the legend, near the end of the elephant's tail. It is a six-peaked hill symbol.

According to D. C. Sircar, Chuṭukula, who issued these coins, and enjoyed the official designation '*Mahāsenāpati*' seems to have been the military governor of a district or its sub-division, appointed by some king who cannot be identified. It appears that he flourished as a semi-independent ruler when the Sātavāhana power was fast declining.

It is difficult to agree with the views of V. V. Mirashi. The ruler, to whom these coins are attributed, was ruling only in the south and not in Māhishmatī because no coins of such a ruler have been discovered in Malwa. It is not wise to connect Śrīdharavarman and Subandhu with this dynasty unless we have some evidence. No region in the South is known to be Māhishaka in ancient times.

THE NĀGAS :—According to the evidence of the Purāṇas, Nāga kings flourished, apparently after the decline of the Kushāṇas, at Vidiśā, Kāntipurī, Mathurā and Padmāvatī. The main Nāga rulers, who flourished at Vidiśā, were Śesha, Bhogin and Sadāchandra. Sadāchandra is surnamed Chandrāṁśa who is described as the second Nakhavat (i.e. Nahapāna) and may have been associated with the Śakas.[1]

K. P. Jayaswal[2] holds that the coins usually attributed to kings Śeshadatta, Rāmadatta and Śiśuchandradatta of Mathura are really the issues of the Nāga rulers of Vidiśā mentioned in several *Purāṇas*, bearing the names of Śesha, Rāmachandra and Śiśunandi respectively. The coins of Purushadatta, Uttamadatta, Kāmadatta, Bhavadatta and Śivanandi which also occur in the Mathura series, are also attributed by him to the early Nāga rulers of Vidiśā. The discovery of these coins in the territory around Mathura is attributed by him to

1. The Age of Imperial Unity, p. 169.
2. History of India, 150-350 A. D., pp. 4-16.

the circumstance that Mathura has been a mint for ancient coins from adjoining territories like Ahichhatrā, Padmāvatī and Vidiśā; he has no doubt that these kings were ruling with their capital in eastern Malwa.

A.S.ALTEKAR[1] has proved that there is no evidence to justify the conclusion that Śeshadatta, Rāmadatta, Śiśuchandradatta and other rulers of the Mathura series were ruling at Vidiśā. Their copper coins have been usually found only in the territory round about Mathura and, therefore, they are rightly regarded as being the rulers of that city. They are not found at Vidiśā and some other ancient sites in and near Malwa. The coins of the above Mathura rulers are conspicuous by their absence in Malwa. While the names of the rulers of the later Nāga dynasty like Bhīmanāga, Skandanāga, etc. all end in '*nāga*' the names of none of the rulers of the Mathura series has a nāga-ending. These Mathura rulers belonged to a 'Datta' and not to a Nāga dynasty. K.P.JAYASWAL read as '*dāta*' and not as *datta* or *dāta* meaning donor or liberal sacrificer. Actual y, the last letters are *data* and not '*dāta*'.

K. P. JAYASWAL[2] points out that the Vidiśā Nāga rulers are described as *Vṛishas* 'Bulls' by the *Purāṇas*, and so on their coins 'Śiva's' *Nandi* or bull and *triśūla* are to be seen figuring prominently. The figure of the Nāga or serpent also makes its appearance, often completing the name of the king in a symbolic manner.

A. S. ALTEKAR[3] does not agree with this view. Only some Mss. of the *Vāyu-purāṇa* describe the Vidiśā Nāga rulers as Vṛishas; other Mss. of this *Purāṇa* as well as all the Mss. of the *Brahmāṇḍa Purāṇa* describe them as '*nṛipas*' kings and not as *vṛishas* or bulls. Vṛisha is a scribe's mistake. On the coins of the rulers of Mathura, we do not find the symbols of bull and *triśūla*. The occurrence of a 'wavy line' cannot be regarded as proving the Nāga origin of the rulers.

In the opinion of H. V. TRIVEDI[4], Vṛisha was used not in

1. JNSI, V, pp. III ff.
2. History of India, 150-350 A. D., pp. 4-16.
3. JNSI, V. pp. III ff.
4. Catalogue of the Coins of the Nāga kings of Padmāvatī, pp. V-VI·

the sense of bull as K. P. JAYASWAL advocates but the descendants of Vṛisha as a dynastic appellation. Vṛisha was probably the originator of the Nāga house established at Bhilsa in the latter half of the second century A.D. His coins have been discovered at Bhilsa.[1] On the obverse, we find the rayed Sun and the circular legend '*Mahārāja Śrī Vṛishanāga*'. The prolonged internecine struggle between the Kshatrapa ruler Jīvadāman and his uncle Rudrasiṁha may have offered him an opportunity to rise. This prince originally began to rule at Bhilsa but later because of some political pressure he shifted his capital to Padmāvatī.

According to the *Purāṇas* Navanāgas were ruling when the Guptas rose to power by 325 A.D. K.P. JAYASWAL[2] interpreted this in the sense of New Nāgas who were ruling at Padmāvatī and Kāntipurī as distinguished from an old Nāga House whose members are mentioned in the *Purāṇas* as ruling at Vidiśā. He further holds that its founder was king Nava whose capital was at Kāntipurī[3], modern Kantit in Mirzapur District U.P. Coins, the legends on which have been wrongly read as '*Devasa*' or '*Nevasa*' are to be attributed to this Nāga ruler, the correct reading being '*Nevasa*'. Some of these coins are dated in his regnal year 27. Navanāga was succeeded by Vīrasenanāga, who was a powerful ruler and succeeded in ousting the Kushāṇas from the upper U. P., Mathura and the eastern Punjab. Coins bearing the legend '*Vīrasena*' were issued by this ruler, his tribal name Nāga suggested by the serpent symbol occurring on the reverse of his coins. Some of them bear his regnal year 34. After Vīrasena, the Nāga kingdom was divided into three branches which ruled at Mathura, Padmāvatī and Kāntipurī. Mathura rulers have left no coins. The coins of the Nāga rulers of Padmāvatī are known but the coins of Kāntipurī are not recognized. Barhināga, Chharajanāga, Bhavanāga and Rudrasena belonged to this branch. K. P. JAYASWAL also identifies Bhāraśiva family mentioned in the

1. JNSI, XV, p. 121.
2. History of India, 150-350, pp. 4-16.
3. This place has now been identified with Kutwar in Morena District. It may be the subsidiary capital but not the important capital of the Nāgas.

Vākāṭaka copper plates with the Navanāga family of the *Purāṇas*.

A. S. ALTEKAR[1] rightly holds that there is no evidence in support of the distinction between the old and the new Nāga houses. The coins of Navanāga have no affinity with the coins of the Nāga rulers of Padmāvatī. No coin of Navanāga was found at Padmāvatī. As his coins are found in Eastern U.P., he was probably the ruler of Kauśāmbī. As regards Vīrasena, his coins are much larger in size and do not contain the epithet '*Nāga*' after the king's name. Coins attributed to Hayanāga, Barhināga and Chharajanāga are so blurred that no definite readings can be proposed of the legends partially legible on them. A. S. ALTEKAR[2] tried to prove that the Bhāraśiva rulers were none other than the Nāga kings of Padmāvatī as known to us from the coins such as Bhavanāga, Vasunāga, Skandanāga, Bṛihaspatināga, Vyāghranāga, Devanāga, Prabhākaranāga and Gaṇapatināga.

The *Purāṇas* do not give either names or order of succession of the Nāga rulers of Pawaya. One inscription[3] of the first or second century A. D. inscribed on the pedestal records the installation of the image of Maṇibhadra in the fourth year during the reign of King Śivanandi by the members of an assembly devoted to the deity. King Śivanandi is unknown from any other source but he seems to be the Nāga ruler. H.V.TRIVEDI[4] tried to reconstruct the chronological order of these rulers known from the coins tentatively.

BHĪMA :—The earliest Nāga ruler of Pawaya seems to be Bhīma. The epithet of *Mahārāja* and the way of engraving the legend in two horizontal lines reminds us of the features of early coins found at Pawaya. Thus, it is possible to hold that Bhīma was probably the earliest of the Nāga rulers to have imitated this design. He seems to have ruled from 210 to 231 A.D.

As Bhīma's peacock emblem was adopted by Skanda and

1. JNSI, V, pp. 111 ff.
2. Ibid, V, p. 24.
3. ASC, 1920-21, p. 105,
4. Catalogue of the Coins of the Nāga Kings of Padmāvatī, pp. IX-XI.

Vasu, it seems that Bhīma's immediate successor was Skanda. After him, Vasu became the ruler. The coins of Skanda and Vasu appear to be restruck or counter-restruck. This may go to indicate some political disturbance the nature of which is unknown.

The next member of the house is Bṛihaspati. He also issued coins with the symbol of a couchant bull as issued by Skanda. He closed his reign sometime about the third century A. D. Each ruler beginning from Bhīma issued the coins with the emblem used by his predecessor but added at least one of his own device.

Ravi, Prabhākara, Bhava, Deva and Gaṇapati are known to have been ruling from the third to the fourth century A.D. Of these names only two, viz. Bhava and Gaṇapati figure in the inscriptions but the references are only accidental. A Vākāṭaka record states that Rudrasena I of that dynasty was the daughter's son of Bhāraśiva family. This illustrious Nāga house seized the Gangetic valley by its valour and deserves the credit of performing ten horse sacrifices. If Bhavanāga of the coins is the Bhāraśiva ruler of that name of the inscription, the Bhāraśiva Nāgas must have had their capital at Padmāvatī. They might have become powerful under Bhavanāga who was ruling from 305 to 340 A. D. He gave material assistance to the Vākāṭakas.

It seems that under Bhavanāga and Gaṇapatināga, the political influence of the Nāgas extended even up to Malwa. Among the Nāga coins found at Ujjain[1], those of Gaṇapatināga are overwhelming in number corroborating the statement of *Bhavaśataka* according to which his kingdom extended up to Dhar in the South. He is called 'Dhārādhīśa' in it.

The Gupta emperor Samudragupta claims to have interrupted Gaṇapatināga and Nāgasena. This Gaṇapatināga may be identified with 'Gaṇapatināga' of the coins who ruled over Padmāvatī. No coins of Nāgasena have as yet been discovered; the *Harshacharita* mentions him as the ruler of Padmāvatī. It is not improbable that, after the overthrow of Gaṇaptināga, Samudragupta placed Nāgasena on the throne

1. Catalogue of the coins of the Nāga kings of Padmāvatī, p. XXXIX.

of Padmāvatī as his vassal; but later Nāgasena himself was also interrupted possibly as result of an attempt on his part to assume independence.

THE MAUKHARIS OF BAḌVĀ :—

At Baḍvā, near Kotah, there was a small Maukhari principality during the first half of the third century A.D. *Mahāsenāpati* Bala was at its head in 239 A.D. and he had three grown up sons to help him in the administration[1]. A. S. ALTEKAR[2] thinks that the Maukharis of Baḍvā were probably a feudatory power, owing allegiance either to the Western *Kshatrapas* of Ujjayinī or to the Nāgas of Padmāvatī. D. C. SIRCAR[3] ragards them as a branch of the Mālavas. It is probable that the Maukhari *Mahāsenāpati* Bala owed allegiance to the Mālava republic because he used the Kṛita era of the Mālavas in his inscription. The family seems to have championed the Vedic religion; each of the three sons of Bala had performed a *Trirātra* sacrifice in 239 A.D. They erected the stone (*Yūpas* (*pillars*) to commemorate these sacrifices.

THE MĀLAVAS :—It seems that the Mālavas ruled over the area round about Udaipur in the third century A.D. Some inscriptions of the Sogin branch of the Mālava tribe have been discovered at Nandsa.[4] They are dated in 225 A.D. (V.S. 282) and refer to the achievement of a ruler named Śrīsoma or Nandisoma[5] who was the son of Jayasoma, grandson of Bhṛiguvardhana and great grandson of Jayatvardhana. From this inscription, it is known that a Mālava leader raised the standard of revolt and celebrated the *Ekashashṭirātra* sacrifice to proclaim the independence of his republic. Curiously, this record does not mention the names of the enemies defeated but they may have been none other than the Western Kshatrapas. Nandisoma must have been a very powerful chief. It is quite possible that the village of Nandsa where his records are situated was founded by him and it was evidently his capital. The

1. EI, XXIII, p. 52.
2. The Vākāṭaka-Gupta Age, p. 37.
3. The Guhilas of Kishkindhā, p. 42.
4. EI, XXVII, pp. 252 ff. A. S. ALTEKAR read the name of the Mālava chief as Śrīsoma.
5. IHI, XXIX, p. 80.

name Nandsa might have been a popular corrupt form of Nandisoma or Nandisomaputra. An undated record contains the eulogy of one *Mahāsenāpati* Bhaṭṭisoma who is also described as a Sogin.

OTHER RULERS :—There are other rulers whose existence is known to us in this period from coins. Two coins of Ajadatta[1] are known but their provenance is not definite. These coins bear some resemblance to some of the coins of Ujjayinī or of the Śibis of Madhyamikā. It is not improbable that king Ajadatta may have ruled somewhere in Malwa in the vicinity of Ujjayinī or Chitor in the first century B.C. or A.D.

A few coins of unknown kings belonging to the first-second centuries have been discovered at Pawaya[2]. These coins may prove that the region round about Pawaya was ruled by these rulers. One of them was Sukhadeva whose coin has also been found at Vidiśā[3]. Other rulers known from the coins are Mahata, Sabalasena, Amitasena, and Yatga.

ADMINISTRATION

Under the Mauryas, Ujjayinī was the capital of Avanti Province. With the break up however of the Maurya empire, Vidiśā became the premier city in Malwa and seems to have superseded Pāṭaliputra itself. Though Pushyamitra, the founder of the Śuṅga dynasty, established himself as the successor of the Mauryas with their own capital in Magadha, his son Agnimitra, who had been viceroy at Vidiśā, seems to have shifted the seat of government from Pāṭaliputra to that city. The Śuṅga ruler Bhāgabhadra of Vidiśā must have been the powerful monarch among the Indian rulers to whom the Greek ruler Antialcidas sent an envoy named Heliodorus and maintained diplomatic relations. Under the Śakas, Ujjayinī was the capital.

It seems that monarchical and republican tribes were ruling at this time. The title '*Mahāsenāpati*' (great commander) after the name of the ruling chief shows the military character of the State. An inscription of 226 A.D. discovered

1. JNSI, IV, p. 23.
2. Ibid, XVII, pp. 53 ff.
3. Ibid, XXII, p. 13.

at Nandsa[1] contains the name of *Mahāsenāpati* Nandisoma of the Mālava family, who raised the standard of revolt probably under the Western Kshatrapas. In about the first half of the third century A. D., the Maukharis ruled over the territory of Baḍvā[2] near Kota. *Mahāsenāpati* Bala was at its head in 239 A.D. and he had three grown up sons to help him in the administration.

The Śakas introduced the Persian type of Satrapa government. The titles *Kshatrapa* and *Mahākshatrapa* show that Western Kshatrapas were originally feudatories of the Kushāṇas but gradually, they became independent. The system of joint administration by the king as *Mahākshatrapa* with his son or brother in the junior capacity of *Ksatrapas*, seems to have been a fairly regular practice in the family from the time of Chashṭana. In this type of government, the Crown prince got ample opportunity for training before becoming the ruling chief.

Usually, the crown passed on to the eldest son but among the western *Kshatrapas*, however, a peculiar mode of succession was established from 200 A.D., and the crown passed from the eldest brother to the younger ones in succession. When the youngest brother died after having his turn to rule, he was succeeded by the surviving eldest son of the eldest brother.

TERRITORIAL DIVISIONS :—The kingdom was divided into provinces, districts and villages. *Rāshṭra*, *Āhāra* and *Janapada* seem to have been synonymous terms in this age. The chief officer in a *Rāshṭra* or *Āhāra* was the *Rāshṭrapati*, *Rāshṭrika* (*Rāṭhika*) or *Amātya*. The *Amātya* Suviśākha governed Surāshṭra under the *Mahākshatrapa Rudradāman*[3]. The *Āhāra* of Ujenī is known from the Sanchi inscriptions of the second or first century B.C. in which were included Navagāma and Morajābhikaṭa.[4] The *Āhāra* of Māmāla (Poona District) was under an *Amātya* whose name ended in Gupta. The *Janapada*

1. EI, XXVII, p. 265.
2. Ibid, XXIII, p. 52.
3. EI, VIII, pp. 42 ff.
4. The Monuments of Sanchi, Nos. 164 and 359.

was sometimes placed under the charge of military governor. Part of Eastern Malwa seems to have been governed by a Śaka *Mahādaṇḍanāyaka* named Śrīdharavarman shortly before its annexation by the Imperial Guptas.[1] *Deśa*, too, is often used as a synonym of *Rāshṭra* or *Janapada*. It was under a *Deśādhikṛita*. From the Eran Stone pillar inscription of Śrīdharavarman, it is known that *adhishṭhāna* of Erikiṇa was included in the territorial division of Rāhirikā in *āhāra* of Nagendra.[2]

The next smaller unit was apparently the *Vishaya* governed by the *Vishayapati*.[3] The smallest administrative units were the villages called *Grāma* or *Grāmāhāra*[4] and the smaller towns called *Nigama*. The affairs of a *Grāma* were controlled by officers styled *Grāmeyika*, *Āyutta*[6] who were apparently headed by the Grāmaṇī[5], *Grāmika*[7], *Grāmabhojaka*[8] or *Mahattaraka*. The chief men of the *Nigamas* were the *Gahapatis*.

CLASSES OF OFFICERS :—The designations of some of the highest officers such as *Mahāmātras* and *Rajukas* continued as they were during Maurya period. But side by side with these functionaries, we hear of others who do not figure in inscriptions of the Maurya epoch. The officers most intimately associated with the sovereign were the privy councillors—the *matisachivas* of the Junagarh inscription. Among the prominent court officials must be mentioned the *Rāja Vaidya*[9], (Royal Physician) and the *Rāja Lipikara*[10] (Royal scribe). Among the civil officers, there was another class of *Amātyas* who served as executive officers (*Karma sachivas*). From them were chosen governors,[11] treasurers,[12] superintendents[13] and

1. Sel. Ins., p. 187.
2. CII, IV, Pt. II, pp. 605-609.
3. Luders Ins. 929n.
4. Ibid, 1195.
5. Ibid, 1327.
6. Ibid, 1333.
7. Ibid, 48, 69 a.
8. Ibid, 1200.
9. Ibid, 1190-93
10. Ibid, 272.
11. Ibid, 965
12. Ibid, 1141.
13. Ibid, 1186.

secretaries[1] as in the days of Megasthenes. There was also the *dūta* (envoy or messsenger) who was entrusted with the foreign affairs.

Among treasury officials, mention is made of the *Gaṁja-vara*[2], the *Koshṭhāgārika*[3] and the *Bhāṇḍāgārika*[4] who was one of the principal ministers of state (*Rājāmātya*). The main heads of revenue received into the *Bhāṇḍāgāra* or *Kośa* (treasury) were, as enumerated in the Junagarh inscription, *bali* (extra tribute), *śulka* (duty) and *bhāga* (customary share of the king). These means of revenue filled the treasury of the Mahākshatrapa Rudradāman with *Kanaka* (gold), *rajata* (silver), *vajra*(diamond), *vaidūryaratna*(beryl), etc. Rulers less scrupulous than the *Mahākshatrapa* doubtless oppressed the people with arbitrary imposts, forced labour and benevolences. Besides the *Bhāṇḍāgāra*, we have reference to the storehouse, *Koshṭhāgāra*.[5]

THE REVENUE ON THE DIFFERENT ITEMS :—

The government spent the revenue on the different items. The attempts to provide for '*pānīya*' or drinkable water are specially noteworthy. We know from the Junagarh inscription that Rudradāman had to spend the vast amount of money from his own treasury for the reconstruction of Sudarshan Lake which was destroyed by the excessively swollen flood of the rivers. References to the construction or repair of tanks, wells, lakes and other reservoirs of water, *Pushkariṇīs*, *udapānas*, *hradas* or *taḍāgas* are fairly common.

The important military officials were the *Mahāsenāpati*[6], the *Daṇḍanāyaka*[7] and the *Mahādaṇḍa-nāyaka*[8]. These important functionaries had probably under them subordinates like *Senagopas* (captains), *Gaulmikas*[9] (commanders of platoons), *Ārakshādhikṛitas*[10] (guards), *Aśvavārakas*[11] (troopers), *Bhaṭama-*

1. Luders, Ins. 1125.
2. Ibid, 82.
3. EI, XX, 28.
4. Luders, Ins. 1141.
5. Ibid, No. 937.
6. Ibid, Ins. No. 1124, 1146; EI, XXVII, p. 265, EI, XXIII, p. 52.
7. ASI, 1914-15, p. 82.
8. Sel. Ins., p. 187.
9. Luders, Ins. No. 1200.
10. Ibid.
11. Ibid, 381, 728.

nushyas[1] (mercenaries), *haya-hasty-adhikārī*[2] (the officer in charge of horses and elephants, etc.)

CULTURE

This period is noteworthy in the cultural sphere because it witnessed the revival of Vedic religion, and the evolution of Vaishnavism, Śaivism and other minor sects. Buddhism still continued to be followed by a large number of people. The religious activities led to new trends in art and architecture; temples and images began to be constructed. The contact with the foreigners like the Greeks and Śakas was important in influencing the Hindu society in many ways. There was a considerable development of trade and commerce. The local nd the punch-marked coins were gradually replaced by the new ones having some foreign influence.

(A)
RELIGION

VEDIC RELIGION :—It is well known that Aśoka discouraged sacrifices, rituals and the slaughter of animals; but they were revived, and perhaps with greater enthusiasm, in the time of Pushyamitra. In the *Mahābhāshya*[3] Patañjali refers to sacrifices performed for this Brāhmanical ruler *iha Pushyamitraṁ Yājayāmaḥ* : 'here we perform the sacrifices for Pushyamitra.' This is supported by the Ayodhya inscription[4] of Dhanadcva, which records the performance of two *Aśvamedha* sacrifices by Pushyamitra and the *Mālavikāgnimitra* of Kālidāsa[5]. The *Mahābhāshya* also refers to different types of sacrifices—*Agnishṭoma*, *Rājasūya*, *Vājapeya*, and the domestic ones—*Pākayajña* or *Pañchayajña*, accessories needed in such sacrifices, their duration, the benefits that accrued from their performances, and lastly, the priests required for them, who received handsome *dakshiṇās*. Patañjali also mentions the *Yūpas*, which were associated with Vedic sacrifices.

1. Luders. Ins. No. 1200.
2. ASI, 1914-15, p. 82.
3. III 2.123 p. 123 L. 3.
4. JBORS, X, p. 203 L.2.
5. Act V.

During this period, sacrifices were performed, and the *yūpas* (sacrificial posts) were erected at important places. These religious activities created a national awakening among the people in facing the foreign invasions. Sometimes the ruling chiefs performed sacrifices in order to commemorate their victories. In the second or first century B. C., Gājāyana Sarvatāta performed an Aśvamedha sacrifice at Madhyamikā.[1] From the Nāndsā yūpa inscription[2] of V. S. 282 (226 A. D.), it is known that the Mālava leader Nandisoma of the Sogin clan, performed the *Ekashashṭirātra* sacrifice to proclaim the independence of his republic. From the Barṇāla inscription[3] of 228 A.D., it is known that a king, whose name ended in Varddhana, erected seven *yūpas*. The reference to the group of seven yūpas may show that the king had performed seven sacrifices. Another *yūpa* inscription found here, commemorates a sacrifice performed fifty-one years later. This inscription, of 279 A. D., commemorates the performance of five *Trirātra*, or perhaps *Gargatrirātra*, sacrifices by a Brāhmaṇa. The Maukharis of Baḍvā also championed the Vedic religion. In 239 A.D, Mahāsenāpati Bala and his three sons performed a *Trirātra* sacrifice.[4] From the inscriptions of Vākāṭaka copper plates, it is known that the Bhāraśivas under Bhavanāga performed as many as ten *aśvamedhas* and won the Ganges water by their prowess. K.P. JAYASWAL[5] rightly concluded that they must have flourished from about the beginning of the third century A. D., and celebrated their *Aśvamedhas* to commemorate their conquest of the Gangetic valley, after the expulsion of the Kushāṇas.

At Vidiśā, the remains[6] of some old *Yajñakuṇḍas* or sacrificial pits of the second or third century A. D., have been discovered, and they prove that Vidiśā was a great centre of the Vedic religion. These are of exceptional interest be-

1. EI, XVI, p. 27; EI, XXIII, p. 198.
2. Ibid, XXVII, pp. 252 ff; IHQ, XXIX, p. 80.
3. Ibid, XXVI, pp. 118 ff.
4. EI, XXIII, pp. 42-52.
5. History of India, 150-350 A. D.
6. ASI, 1914-15, p. 75.

cause nowhere else have such remains been found. Near them, two drains were found, connected with the sacrificial pits. On the levels of the *Kuṇḍas* and the brick pavement, the walls of two structures were discovered, which were intended to be spacious halls constructed for accommodating a large number of people gathered for sacrifice. These sacrifices instituted by kings or wealthy *Yajamānas* of the ancient times lasted for months, and some for years, and for their adequate performance, halls of permanent structure were as much a necessity as the *kuṇḍas* themselves. A sacrificial site was always a meeting place of *Ṛishis*, *Yājñikas* and distinguished guests of the sacrificer. The hall excavated in the south of the *Kuṇḍas* served the purpose of a dining hall or for feasting, and the other huge and extensive hall was meant for the carrying on of philosophical debates.

Some seals connected with the sacrificial site have been discovered. On some of them, the words *hotā*, *potā* and *mantra*, which are technical to sacrificial literature, have been carved. The sealings have been classified under four heads, viz—(1) rulers, (2) officials (3) private individuals, and (4) passport. Only two seals of the first class were found. One of these gives the name of Viśvāmitra as the name of a ruler not so far known from any epigraphic or literary source. Of the three sealings of the second class, two belong to two different *daṇḍanāyakas* or police officers, and one to an officer *haya-hasty-adhikārī* (in charge of elephants and horses). There are also seals of private individuals. All these persons were followers of the Vedic religion. The seals of passport were meant for admitting persons to the sacrificial hall.

VAISHṆAVISM :—In the last quarter of the second century B.C., Vaishṇavism became a popular religion at Vidiśā. The Besanagar *Garuḍa* pillar inscription,[1] informs us that the *Garuḍa*-staff of Vāsudeva, God of gods, was erected by Heliodorus, the son of Dion, an ambassador from Antialkidas, the Greek king at Taxila, who had come to the court of the king Bhāgabhadra in the 14th year of his reign. He calls himself a Bhāgavata i.e. a worshipper of Bhāgavata (Vāsudeva-Vishṇu).

1. JBBRAS, XXIII, p. 104; ASI, 1913-14, p. 190.

The fact that foreigners such as the Greeks were embracing the cult of Vishṇu, is a positive proof of its vitality and popularity. Another inscription[1] from Besangar, speaks of the erection of the Garuḍa column of an excellent temple (*prāsādottama*) of the Bhāgavata (Vāsudeva), by Gautamīputra, a Bhāgavata. These two records prove that there were some Vaishṇava temples at Vidiśā. The remains of such temples have also been discovered in the excavations. That Pavanaputra, an inhabitant of Aparārka, was a Bhāgavata, and erected a pillar of Vishṇu, is known from a recently discovered inscription of the second century B.C, found at Anvalā near Mandsor.

The Ghosuṇḍī (Nagarī) inscription[2] of the second or first century B. C. records the installation of the images of Vāsudeva and Saṁkarshaṇa in a temple which has been named Nārāyaṇavāṭikā. It proves definitely that there were followers of Vaishṇavism at Madhyamikā (Nagarī) near Chitor.

It informs us that the followers of Vāsudeva followed the cult of Saṁkarshaṇa, and the latter came to be regarded as Vāsudeva's elder brother. From the study of the sculptures and other remains, it is clear that Vaishṇavism was flourishing at Pawaya during the third century A.D.[3]

ŚAIVISM :—Ujjayini continued to be a great centre of Śaivism, and its temple of Mahākāla remained famous. The *Mahābhārata* refers to Mahākāla, Koṭitīrtha, Bhadravaṭa, etc. as the sacred sites of Ujjayinī[4]. The medieval Jaina writers[5] have recorded a repeated tradition, that Gardabhilla, the father of Vikramāditya, was a Śaivite and that Vikramāditya himself followed his ancestral faith till he was converted to Jainism by a Jaina sage. It was about the same time that the cult of Paśupati was followed by Lakulīśa in Lāṭa, and it spread to the areas nearby.

The name of the Bhāraśiva dynasty of the Nāga rulers of Pawāyā, indicates that it was staunchly Śaiva. The Śiva

1. ASI, 1913-14, p. 190.
2. EI, XXIII, p. 198.
3. ARADGS, 1924-25, p. 9.
4. *Mahābhārata*, Cr. Ed. III, 80, 68-9.
5. Jainism in Rajasthan, p. 14.

symbol (liṅga) which the Bhāraśivas carried on their shoulders, is not necessarily the phallic one, for it may have been *triśūla*, which occurs on the coins of some of the rulers of Padmāvatī. The peacock, which figures on the coins of Bhīmanāga and Skandanāga also points to Śaiva leanings; for it is the vehicle of Skanda, the eldest son of Śiva. The symbol of the bull associated with Śaivism is also found on the coins of some Nāga rulers.

OTHER MINOR BRAHMANICAL SECTS :—The preponderance of the Yaksha statues[1] at Vidiśā indicates the Yaksha worship among the people during this period. The inscription[2] of the first or second century A. D. records the installation of the image of the Yaksha Maṇibhadra during the reign of the king Śivanandi, by the members of an assembly devoted to the deity.

Vidiśā was also a centre of Nāga worship. The Nāga rulers appear to have been the worshippers of the Nāgas, and they patronized this. Various statues of Nāgas and Nāgīs, both in the human and the serpent form, from the first to the third century A.D., have been found at Vidiśā.[3] It appears that during this period there were some temples of Nāgas at this place, such as the temple of Dadhikarṇa at Mathura.

G. BUHLER[4] has shown that the names of the donors mentioned in the votive inscriptions, furnish valuable information regarding the existence of the Purāṇik worship at the time that they were inscribed. Some names, such as Agisimā (Agniśarmā), (Agidocde) va, Bahadat (Brahmadatta), Mahida, Mitā, Vesamanadatā, Visvadeva and Yamarakhitā, are closely connected with the ancient Vedic worship; and some, Nāga, Nāgila, Nāgadatta and so forth, bear witness to the existence of the snake worship. Finally, the names Vinhukā (Vishṇudatta or Vishṇurakshitā), Upidadata or Opedadata (Upendradatta), Balaka and Balamitra (Kṛishṇa, Baladeva or Balarāma), furnish evidence for the development of Vaishṇavism, while Nadiguta (Nandigupta), Nandigiri Sāmidata (Svāmī i.e.

1. JMPIP, 1960, pp. 19 ff.
2. ASI, 1915-16, p. 105.
3. JMPIP, 1960, pp. 19 ff.
4. EI, II, p. 95.

Kumāra-datta), Samika and Samikā (Svāmika and Savamikā), Sivanadi (Śivanandi), do the same service to Śaivism. It is also possible that Isadata and Himadata are likewise Śaiva saints. To these groups of names distinguished by G. BUHLER, JOHN MARSHALL[1] added another, consisting of such names as Yakhadāsī, Yakhadina, Yakhi and Yakhila, which point to the existence of Yaksha cults.

The occurrence among the Buddhists of the names connected with ancient Vedic religion, as well as with Vaishṇavism and Śaivism, in these early inscriptions, proves that their bearers or their ancestors, adhered to these creeds before their conversion, and that they received their names in accordance with the established custom of their families. There was no restriction by any religion in keeping the names. These names are of great historical value because they form a link in the chain of evidence which enables us to trace the existence, indeed the prevalence of Vaishṇavism and Śaivism, not only during this period, but during much earlier times.

JAINISM :—From the traditions recorded in the *Jaina Nibandhas*, we know that Jainism was associated with Saurāshṭra and Avanti in the first century B. C. The great Jaina saints and scholars like Kālakāchārya, lived and propagated Jainism in this area. At this time, it was a living and active religion, and it influenced the life of the people. Some of the Jaina sources[2] claim Vikramāditya as a convert to Jainism. It is claimed that Siddhasena Divākara, having caused the breaking of the phallic symbol of Mahākāla in Ujjayinī, and the appearance of the image of Pārśvanātha, enlightened Vikramāditya. According to the Digambara Jaina Paṭṭāvali[3], Vikramāditya played as a child for eight years, for sixteen years he performed sacrifices following a false doctrine; for forty years he was devoted to the religion of the Jaina, and then reached heaven. It seems that the ancestral and personal religion of Vikramāditya was Śaivism but he was also under the influence of Jainism and patronized it. The temple of Avanti-

1. The Monuments of Sanchi, p. 299.
2. The Paṭṭāvali Samuchchaya, p. 46, 106
3. IA, XX, p. 247.

sukumāla was probably in existence at Ujjain during this period.

BUDDHISM :—After the death of Aśoka, Buddhism received a setback during the reign of Pusyamitra Śuṅga, who was a staunch follower of Brāhmanical religion. The Buddhist tradition is not complimentary to Pushyamitra, and describes him as a cruel persecutor of Buddhists. He is said to have destroyed monasteries and killed the monks in course of his march to Sākala (Siālkot in the Punjab), where he declared a prize of one hundred gold coins on the head of each monk.[1] JOHN MARSHALL[2] is of the view that the early Buddhist *stūpas* and monasteries of the time of Aśoka at Sanchi, and in the neighbourhood, might have been destroyed by him; but actually there is no definite contemporary independent evidence to prove it.

The successors of Pushyamitra Śuṅga seem to be tolerant towards Buddhism. The Great *stūpa* at Sanchi was encased in stone during the reign of either Agnimitra or his immediate successor. The second and third *Stūpa* at Sanchi, belong to the Śuṅga period. Queen Vākala, mother of Ahimita, who may have belonged to the ruling family of Vidiśā, made donation to the Buddhist establishment of Sanchi.[3] The names of two kings, viz. Aṅgarāja and Dhanabhūti, are known to us from the inscriptions engraved on the gateway of the Bharhut railing.[4] It is known from some inscriptions from Bharhut, that king Revatimitra of Vidiśā, and his queens, made donations to the stūpa at Bharhut.[5]

It was under the Kāṇvas and the Sātavāhanas that Buddhism reached its zenith in this area, because the most splendid of the Sanchi structures, namely the four gateways of Great *stūpa* and the single gateway of the third *stūpa*, were erected under them. On the southern gateway of the Great stūpa is a donative inscription, recording the gift of one of its architrave by a certain Vāsishṭhiputra Ānanda, the foreman of the

1. *Divyāvadāna*, pp. 429-34.
2. The Monments of Sanchi, p. 23, p. 67.
3. Ibid, Ins. No. 364.
4. IA, XXI, p. 227.
5. CBT, Introduction, p. VII.

artisans of king Sātakarṇi[1].

Buddhism continued to survive under the Western Kshatrapas, who seem to have recognized the suzerainty of the Kushāṇas. A few sculptures in the Kushāṇa style from Mathura have been discovered at Sanchi, one of which bears an inscription of the year twenty eight, in the reign of the Rājātirāja Devaputra Shāhī Vāsashka. The object of the inscription is to record the installation of an image of the Bhāgavata (Śākyamuni) in the Dharmadeva *vihāra* by Madhurikā, daughter of Vera.[2] It may be noted that although the term Bhāgavata is used in the inscription, the image to which it is applied, is that of the Bodhisattva, and not of Buddha. The name Vāsashka is identified with Vāsudeva.

A piece of a railing with an inscription '*Dāmasya putrasya Rāño*' has been found at Ujjain. It is probably of the Buddhist stūpa built during the Western Kshatrapa period.

From the votive inscriptions of this period found at Sānchi, it seems that Buddhism gained a footing among the common masses of Malwa. The monks and nuns, officers, laymen and laywomen, and the corporate bodies, made pious donations to these *stūpas*. The specific titles of some monks have been given[3], such as—*Aya*, i. e. the Noble Master *Thera* i. e. Venerable; *Bhadata*, i. e. Most gentle; *Bhāṇaka* i. e. Reciter of texts; *Dhamakathika* i. e. Preacher of the Law; *Sadhivihārī* i. e. co-resident monk; *Vināyaka* i. e. Teacher, *Sutātika* and *Sutātikinī* i. e. one who is versed in the Suttantas; *Pañchanekayika* i. e. one who is versed in the Five *Nikāyas* and *Sapurisa* i. e. Saint.

People of all castes and classes made grants to this holy establishment[4]. The *gahapati* or village landholder, Seṭhī, *Seṭha* or alderman, *Vaṇija*, *Vāṅka* or trader. *rājalipikāra* or royal scribe, *lekhaka* or professional writer, *āvesanī* or forman of artisans, *asavārika* or trooper, *karmika* or humble workman, *sotika* or weaver, *vaḍaki* or carpenter, *rajjuka* or revenue settlement officer, *pāvārika* or a cloakseller, etc. gave different kinds of contributions. The mention of professional writers is of some

1. The Monuments of Sanchi, Ins. No. 398.
2. Ibid, p. 386.
3. The Manuments of Sanchi, p. 297.
4. EI, II, p. 87 and p. 366; The Monuments of Sanchi, p. 297.

importance on account of the great age of the inscriptions. The frequent mention of the merchants as donors proves that Buddhism had a great hold on this class.

Besides individual donations, collective subscriptions were raised from particular families, associations, and from the inhabitants of particular places[1]. The ivory-workers(*daṁtakāras*) of Vidiśā, and the *Dhamakas*, *Magalakaṭīyas*, *Sāphinayakas*, *Tāpasiyas* and the *Vākiliyas* of Ujjayinī, gave contributions. Gift was made by the Buddhist assembly of Dharmavarddhana, and by the guild of *Barulamisas* of Vidiśā. The villages e. g. Vejaja, Asavatī, Morajabhikaṭa, Pāḍukulikā and Chudamoragiri, made their contributions to the Buddhist establishment. The lay-worshippers of Kaṁtakanūya record a joint donation.

Sanchi at this time became a place of pilgrimage. People from neighbouring as well as far away places, visited it.[2] Devotees from Erakaṇa (Eran), Mahisati (Maheśvara) Ujeni, Kuraraghara (Kuraghara), Tubavana (Tumbavana), Sonara (Sonārī), Pāḍāniya (Parana), Naṁdinagara (Nandner), Kāpāsigāma (Kapasi), Madhuvana (Madhuban), Ububaraghara, (Umner), Vidiśā, etc. were attached somehow with this place. The frequent occurrence of these place-names in the Sanchi inscriptions, show that the cost of erecting the adjuncts to the *stūpas* was defrayed largely by the people of Malwa. Pilgrims outside Malwa had also intimate contact with this place. The donations of the pilgrims of Pokhara (Pushkara), Pratiṭhāna and Aboḍa (Abu), have also been recorded. People even from Kīkaṭa, or the Magadha country, also visited this place. Even a foreigner, a Greek Yona from Śvetapatha, participated in these donations.

About the end of the second century B. C., the Haimavata School of Buddhism became powerful, because it collected from various sources, the corporeal relics of the former Āchāryas from Kāsapagota down to Vāchisuvijayita, and enshrined them in a *stūpa* at Sanchi and the places in the neighbourhood[3]. The saints represent at least three generations of teachers. Goti-

1. The Monuments of Sanchi, pp. 297-298.
2. EI, II, p. 87; The Monuments of Sanchi, p. 299.
3. The Monuments of Sanchi, pp. 289-295. A. Cunningham ascribes the

puta, who was a kinsman and heir of Dudubhisara, must have flourished after him. Kāsapagota, Dudubhisara and Majhima, who formed the first group of teachers, were followed by Gotiputa, and Gotiputa by his disciples Mogaliputa[1] and Vāchiputa, or Vāchiya Suvijayita. As regards the position of Mahavanāya, Āpagira and Koḍiniputa, nothing can be said definitely. But they probably came sometime before Vāchiya, who is to be reckoned as the last of the *Vināyakas*. These three or four generations of teachers might easily have covered a span of a century or a little more, and they flourished from the reign of Aśoka (250 B. C.) onwards.

Gotiputa appears to have held a highly dignified position in the Buddhist church of Eastern Malwa, as suggested by the fact that his relics were enshrined at no less than three places, namely at Sanchi, Sonāri and Ander. It seems that he was given the title of '*Kākanāva Prabhāsana*',[2] the light of Kākanāva.

The relics[3] of Mahāmogalāna and Sāriputa, the disciples of Buddha, have been enshrined in the *stūpa* at Sanchi and Śatadhārā in the second century B.C.

The Buddhists of Sanchi were Theravādins, but in the first century B.C., the Buddhist church probably took a more serious turn. From the inscriptions, it is known that *aña-āchariya-kula* i.e. *anyāchārya kula*, came into existence.[4] The Theravādins

stūpas of the relics of these saints to the third century B. C. He interpreted the saints of Himavanta in the sense of country, but not as school, of Buddhism. See CBT.

1. A CUNNINGHAM has identified him with Mogaliputra Tissa who presided over the Third Buddhist Council in 241 B. C. MARSHALL thinks it improbable, as Mogaliputra was the pupil of Gotiputa, the heir of Dudubhisara. The latter can be identified with Dundubhisāra in the *Dīpavaṁśa* (VIII.10) as one of the five missionaries sent by Tissa to the Himalayan country after the conclusion of the third Council, in the reign of Aśoka.
2. CUNNINGHAM identified Kākanāva Prabhāsana, who was a donor at Sanchi, with a sea captain named Kākābhāsā who traded with Taxila in the reign of Aśoka. As both were contemporaries of Aśoka, it is quite possible that they were the same person. See CBT, pp. 185-187 This view is not correct, see The Monuments of Sanchi, p. 294.
3. The Monuments of Sanchi, p. 296.
4. Ibid, p. 298.

even apprehended dismemberment of their sacred edifices. Later on, the inscribed Buddha and Bodhisattva images of Kushāṇa period clearly testify that an alien school had already established itself at Sanchi.

The Buddhist monks Mātaṅga Kāśyapa and Dharmaraksha, who belonged to central India, made great efforts for propagation of Buddhism in China in the first century A. D.[1] Mātaṅga Kāśyapa visited China in 64 A. D. and completed translation of *Bayālisa Parichchhedīyasūtra*. Dharmaraksha accompanied Mātaṅga Kāśyapa to China, and helped him in his translation work. After the death of Mātaṅga Kāśyapa, Dharmaraksha translated several other *sūtras* into Chinese.

(B)
ART AND ARCHITECTURE

The great religious movements of this period gave an impetus to art and architecture. The use of stone increased in large scale. Big *stūpas* and temples began to be constructed. We get the idea of sculpture from the statues of Yakshas, Nāgas, and other folk deities, on the one hand, and from the study of the motifs of great variety and richness carved on the gateways of the *stūpas* at Sanchi,[2] on the other hand. Some terracottas of this period have been discovered in the excavations at Avara, Vidiśā, Pawaya, etc. The pottery of this period is peculiar in form and fabric. Some other minor arts also developed.

ARCHITECTURE :—Some Buddhist *stūpas* and temples discovered at Sanchi give an idea of the architecture of this period. The original brick *stūpa* built by Aśoka was later encased during the Śuṅga period. The new structure was about twice the original Mauryan stūpa covering an area one hundred and twenty feet in diameter with a total height of fifty-four feet. This offers the first instance of true masonry used for constructional purposes in any ancient building.

1. *Chīnī Bauddhadharma Kā Itihāsa*, pp. 21-22.
2. The Monuments of Sanchi, p. 29.

The great *stūpa* is a semi-circular dome truncated at the top. It is surrounded at a height of 16 feet by a lofty terrace (*medhi*), which served as the upper *Pradakshiṇāpatha*, and was girdled by a smaller railing. On the flattened summit, there was a small square pavilion (*harmikā*), surrounded by a railing from the centre of which rose the shaft of the umbrella discs. On the ground level, there is a second processional path, paved with stone, encircling the *stūpa*. Round this is a great railing in plain design. It consisted of the upright pillars, rail bars, and coping stones.

In the first century B.C., the four elaborate and richly carved gateways were built in the four directions of the *stūpa*[1]. They are similar in design, and thirty-four feet in height. Each gateway was composed of two square pillars surmounted by capitals, which in turn supported a super-structure of three architraves with vaulted ends decorated beautifully by spirals. The architraves were separated from one another by four square blocks set in pairs above the capitals of the square pillars. Between each pair of square blocks, there were three short uprights.

In size and construction, *stūpa* II[2] was almost a replica of *stūpa* I, the main difference being the decoration of the ground railing. *Stūpa* III is smaller in size and the ground railing has almost entirely disappeared. There was a stairway with balustrade similar to that of *stūpa* I in style, decoration, and structural form. One gateway was probably added in the early part of the first century A.D. It is enriched with reliefs in the same style as those on the four gateways of the Great *stūpa*.

The apsidal temple[3] No. 18 belongs to the Śuṅga age, and its plan is similar to that of the rock-cut *chaitya* halls at Karli. The apse of the temple No. 18 is enclosed not by columns, as in the cave temples, but by a solid wall. The inner and outer walls around the apse were constructed by dry stone masonry. The older pillars and pilasters of the nave are monoliths, square in section, and seventeen feet

1. The Monuments of Sanchi, pp. 36-37.
2. Ibid, pp. 79-82.
3. Ibid, p. 55.

high, slightly tapering towards the top. Within the apse of the temple, there once stood a *stūpa* which contained a steatite vase.

Outside the town of Besanagar, remains of a Buddhist stūpa of the Śuṅga period such as railings inscribed with short records of the donors, rail-bars, broken bell-capitals and pillars, have been found. According to A. CUNNINGHAM,[1] this *stūpa* must not have been more than eighteen feet or twenty feet in height. The reliefs carved on the railings are concerned with incidents in the life of Buddha, and some of them are important from a social point of view.

Even at Udayagiri, the remains of a Buddhist *stūpa*, such as railings, bell-capitals, lion-capitals and pilaster, have been discovered.[2]

In the neighbourhood of Sanchi, at the sites such as Sonārī, Śatadhārā, Bhojapur and Āndher, some Buddhist *stūpas* and monasteries of the Śuṅga period have been found. Like the Sanchi *stūpas*, they are also made of stone. Most of them are small in dimensions, and hence, artistically, they are not so important as those of Sanchi.

There are about eight *stūpas* preserved at Sonārī.[3] Among them, the No. 1 and the No.2 *stūpa* are important. *Stūpa* No. I is solid hemisphere. Its base was surmounted by railings, of which nothing now remains but a few broken pillars and two or three fragments of coping. The coping was different from that of the Sanchi railing. The pillars were ornamented on the outer face. The second of the Sonārī tope is also of the same type. No trace of railings or pinnacles but five relic caskets were found. The remaining topes of this place are all of small dimensions.

At Śatadhārā[4] also, a group of about seven topes has been preserved. The biggest of them is now a vast mound of brick ruins, that once was faced with stone, like the Great Tope at Sanchi. It was crowned by railings of which several

1. ASC, X, p. 37.
2. Ibid, p. 46.
3. CBT, pp. 200-206.
4. Ibid, pp. 207-210.

pillars still remain, lying together upon the terrace. A circular railing surrounded its top. Tope No 2 is also in a ruined condition. Tope No. 7 is in somewhat better condition, but the remaining topes are little more than mere circles of stone. Two of them are hollow in the centre. Around the biggest tope, there are three solid masses, which were probably the remains of the residence of the Buddhist monks.

The remains of about fifty small *stūpas* have been found at Bhojapur.[1] Among them, tope No. 2 is the most perfect. This is built of dry stones without any mortar or mud. Two buildings, which were probably the residences of the *bhikshus*, have been found.

At Andher,[2] there are three *stūpas*. *Stūpa* No. 1 has a railing standing. The base of its dome rests in a cylindrical plinth. Its terrace has a stone coping. This is the only instance of terrace-coping that now exists. The coping resembles the terrace. The pillars are ornamented with full and half medallions, formed of lotus and other flowers. Tope No. 2 is of much smaller dimension, but in a much more perfect state. Tope No. 3 is the most complete in its preservation, and one of the most interesting in its contents.

In the second century B.C., an elliptical temple was in existence at Vidiśā.[3] It was earlier than the Heliodorus pillar, which, in turn, is contemporary with another Vishṇu temple constructed on a raised platform after the destruction of the elliptical temple, and was enclosed and strengthened by a rubble retaining wall.

There are structural remains which no doubt pertained to temple of Vāsudeva,[4] referred to in the Heliodorus inscription. Now only three retaining walls of an old platform, on which the old shrine of Vāsudeva was erected facing the east, are extant. Close to the shrine platform was the foundation of an old dwelling. Both this house and the shrine platform were found enclosed by what may be called a solid railing,

1. CBT, pp. 211-220.
2. Ibid, pp. 221-225.
3. IAR, 1965-66, pp. 43-45.
4. ASI, 1914-15, p. 66 f.

which was of a unique type not previously found anywhere else in India.

The Besanagar pillar[1] of Heliodorus is different from the Aśokan pillar, from the architectural point of view. It is not round and polished like the Aśokan pillar and the shaft of the column is a monolith octagonal at the base, sixteen sided in the middle, and thirty-two sided above, with a garland dividing the upper and middle portions. The capital is of the Persepolitan bell-shaped type, with a massive abacus surmounting it.

A second *Garuḍa* pillar at Besanagar is dated in the twelfth regnal year of king Bhāgavata. Two fan-palm capitals and a crocodile (*Makara*) capital, apparently derived from other pillars discovered here, belong to this period. The pillar with the inscription of the second century B. C. found at Anvalā near Mandsor, is also of the same type from the architectural point of view. The *yūpa* pillars found at Baḍvā and Nāndsā are square at the bottom and octagonal above.

Two fan-palm capitals obtained from Pawaya are of white sandstone and fairly well polished on the surface. The capital is shaped like a cylinder tapering towards the top, covered with three courses of palm leaves, with a closed bud at the top and bunches of fruit in the intervals between the leaves. The top-bud and the uppermost course of leaves, point upwards, while the two courses point downwards. A lion rampant is seated on a leaf in the lowermost course.

An idea of secular architecture is gained from the study of the residential buildings discovered in the excavations. Besides following the earlier tradition of having foundations of coarse rabbles, people introduced the use of foundations of large bricks, arranged on pebbles mixed with sticky black clay and resting on rammed earth, in building the structures. The brick foundation may be placed in this period. A number of patchy brick constructions appear to be the remains of some structures belonging to this period. The frequently encountered debris of brickbats, and the way of laying the foundations, suggests the existence of some well-thought out

1. The Monuments of Sanchi, Vol. I, p. 49.

plan. The use of bricks was also adopted in the construction of ovens in place of earth.

SCULPTURES :—The sculptures on the four gateways with their architraves and pillars of the first *stūpa*, on the balustrade of the second *stūpa*, and the railings and gateway of the third *stūpa*, at Sanchi[1], are marked by simplicity and naturalness. There is diversity in style and in technique. This sculptural art has its root in the faith of the people, and gives eloquent expression to their spiritual beliefs.

The bas-reliefs relate to Buddha's life showing his birth (*jāti*), enlightenment (*Sambodhī*), first sermon (*Dharmachakra-pravartana*), and death (*Mahāparinirvāṇa*). Each is represented by its own peculiar symbol : the lotus, the *pipal* tree, the wheel, and the *stūpa*. They also depict the miracles of the master, e.g. his walking in the air, on water, and the miracles in the hermitage of Kaśyapa. Among the characteristic Buddhist emblems others than those already mentioned, are the *tri-ratna*, *nandipada*, *śrīvatsa*, and pillars crowned by lions or elephants.

During this period, sculptural art became narrative. Scenes from the *Jātakas* of *Vesantara*, *Chhadanta*, *Śyāma* and *Mahākapi* have been beautifully carved in reliefs on gateways and railings. Historical scenes, such as the visit of Ajātaśatru and Prasenjit of Kosala to the Buddha, of Prasenjit visiting the mango tree at Śrāvasti, Ajātaśatru visiting the Āmravana of Jīvaka, king Śuddhodana going to meet the Buddha, the war of the relics which the chiefs of seven other clans waged against the Mallas of Kuśinaras, and Aśoka's visit to Bodhi-vṛiksha, and Nāga *stūpa* at Rāmagrāma, have been well depicted.

Figures of animals or birds are, as a rule, arranged schematically in pairs (*Saṁghāṭa*). The animals are both real and legendary, sometimes with riders and sometimes without them. They include goats, horses, bulls, camels, elephants, deer and winged lions. Among birds, the peacock, the goose and the *sārasa* are prominent. Among plants, the

1. The Monuments of Sanchi.

favourite is the lotus.

There are female figures, or caryatids, standing under the dense foliage of trees on the *toraṇas*, and they are known as *toraṇaśālabhañjikā*. There are also figures of Yakshas. The artists depicted the scenes of the Uttarakuru country where happy *mithunas* enjoy dance, music and drink, under the Kalpavṛiksha trees. The figure of Śrī-Lakshmī, and also that of *Pūrṇakumbha*, are remarkable.

A few free-standing statues of Yaksha and Yakshī of the Śuṅga period found at Besanagar,[1] are massive in size. They are peculiarly Indian in their dress and ornamentation, and also in spirit and outlook. They reflect primitiveness in art, and indicate the earliest phase of the indigenous art of India.

The statue of Yaksha measures over twelve feet in height, and is decidedly the biggest Yaksha image of an early period so far discovered in India. The figure wears *dhotī* tied with a heavy waistband. The upper part of the body is carved with an *uttarīya*. A number of ornaments, such as torque, earlobes and armlets, are seen on the figure. In the left hand he is holding a purse, which indicates that the figure is that of Kubera, the lord of the Yakshas.

The Yakshī figure is seven and a half feet high. Besides the usual garments, she is wearing various ornaments, like necklaces, ear rings, armlets and wristlets. She has a heavy nine-beaded *mekhalā* on her waist. Her coiffure is tastefully decorated, reminiscent of some Yakshī figurines at Sanchi and Bharhut. She holds the branch of a tree in her right hand, and bunch of fruits in the left. Recently, a few more figures of Yaksha and Yakshī have been discovered.

All these images exhibit archaicness coupled with burliness and sheer volume, yet the treatment and modelling appear to be earlier and freer. Each of these displays more rounded features, including the arms, breasts and abdomen. The linear contour at the sides is less harsh, and has a smoother movement. These features distinguish them from the Parkham image.[2]

1. JMPIP, No. 2, 1960, p. 19.
2. A Survey of Indian Sculpture, p. 54.

An image of the Yaksha Maṇibhadra of white sandstone in the round, standing on a pedestal, of the first or second century A.D., was found at Pawaya.[1] The modelling of this figure is ungraceful and the execution rough. Its height, from neck to foot is four feet, and ten inches; the head however, is missing, and in other respects also, the image is somewhat mutilated. The left hand is lowered and is grasping a money bag. A well-defined fold of flesh is portrayed around the throat, and another fold below the chest, both treated in a very conventional manner. The dress consists of a waist cloth and a scarf. The sacred thread (*Yajñopavīta*) passes across the belly. The ornaments comprise of a rich necklace, consisting of a number of jewel or pearl strings, knotted, and hanging down in tassels on the back, an armlet on the right arm, and a bracelet on the left-wrist. There was a plain nimbus round the head which has left its traces on both sides of the neck.

S. K. Saraswati[2] has compared it with that of the Parkham image. According to him, this image exhibits a greater sense of modelling, and a greater co-ordination of volumes. The artist here appears to have overcome the conflict between the rounded forms and the flattened surface. There is nothing primitive or archaic in this figure.

Some statues of Nāga and Nāgī, both in the human and the serpent form, have been found at Vidiśā[3] and Sanchi.[4] There is also the statue of Nāga at Sanchi. It is six feet and seven inches in height from the bottom of the pedestal, and of grey-white sandstone. The Nāga, which possesses seven hoods, holds an uncertain object (lotus) in the right hand, and a flask in the left. Its style proclaims it to be a clumsy work of the first or second century A.D. Nearby Nāga is a smaller figure, of a Nāgī of the same age and style.

Some sculptures of Buddha and Bodhisattva images of the Kushāṇa period, originally executed in sandstone were

1. ASI, 1915-16, p. 105.
2. A Survey of Indian Sculpture, pp. 54-55.
3. JMPIP, No. 2, 1960, p. 19.
4. The Monuments of Sanchi, p. 244.

discovered at Sanchi. One of them is the statue of a standing Buddha, of which, unfortunately, only the feet and pedestal remain.[1] Its donors have had themselves represented on the cycle, and all of them—men, women and children—are wearing the characteristic dress of the barbarian invaders, who came down from the North-West; the boots, breeches and belted cassocks of the men, and characteristic jackets of the women, leave no room for doubt on this point. Another statue is of Bodhisattva Maitreya.[2] What is left of the carving consists of a seated figure of Buddha, and on his left two female devotees bearing garlands in their right hands.

The early image of Balarāma of the second or third century A.D. found at Tumain[3] is interesting from the artistic point of view. It represents the god standing under the canopy formed by the seven hoods of the snake, holding *mūsala* and *hala* in his right and left hands respectively, and wearing *kuṇḍalas* differing from one another in form, his eyes being shown rolling, In later art, *hala* and *mūsala* are his constant emblems.

TERRACOTTAS :—Some ancient sites, such as Ujjain,[4] Eran[5], Vidiśā[6], Maheśvara[7] and Avara[8], yielded a large number of terracottas which are easily distinguishable by the local features of form and style of particular periods. These terracottas were either fashioned directly out of clay by hand, or shaped and modelled by moulds. They are of different varieties and served different purposes—decoration of houses, objects of worship, play objects for children, and magical and totemic objects.

The elaborately decorated female figures found at Ujjain are noteworthy. Both male and female figures of the Ksha-

1. The Monuments of Sanchi, p. 253.
2. Ibid, p. 253.
3. ASC, 1918-19, p. 22.
4. IAR, 1056-57, p. 28.
5. JMPIP, V, p. 19 f.
6. ASI, 1915-16, pp. 66 f.
7. EMN, pp. 191 ff.
8. JMPIP, IV, pp. 34-36.

trapa period were recovered from Avara. They are well baked, and some of them are moulded. Elephants and horses, with or without riders, have been found. These seem to be the characteristics of the Śaka-Kushāṇa period.

Terracottas of mother and child unearthed in the excavations at Ujjain and Maheśvara, are concerned with the worship of the Mother goddess. Terracotta votive tanks of the Kshatrapa period found at Maheśvara, Ujjain and Avara, were associated with older-cult of the Mother goddess, whose worship was introduced by foreigners. From the Kshatrapa period was recovered a terracotta plaque at Avara. It is round in shape and on the obverse, the plaque represents a goddess standing on a full blown lotus, with a couple on either side, and on the reverse, is a floral design consisting of a lotus in the centre, encircled by a coiled garland with a beaded border separating the two. A miniature representation of a mother-goddess in ivory found at this place, is also of interest.

Among the animal figurines of Avara, those of bulls are the most important, representing all types as found in Malwa, even to this day. The next animal represented is the elephant; then there are two figures of a dog and one of a horse showing an exquisitely carved mane. Another horse figure recovered from a layer ascribable to the Kshatrapa period, appears to betray a foreign contact, which the site had during this period. A tortoise figure was obtained at Ujjain, Avara, and Maheśvara. Toy animals and carts were also unearthed in the excavations at Besanagar.

POTTERY:—This period is marked by the disappearance of the Black and Red Ware, and its replacement by the Red polished Ware. It has been found extensively in the excavations at Ujjain, Avara, Eran and Maheśvara. As it was invariably associated with the Kshatrapa or the late Sātavāhana layers, it belonged to the early centuries of the Christian era. It was made of an extremely fine levigated clay, and was burnt uniformly to a brick red colour. It closely resembles the Roman Samian ware, and the other red wares of the Eastern Mediterranean area. As a result of extensive commercial trade with the Mediterranean region, the technique of the Roman Samian wares was successfully copied. A few small fragments were recovered in the excavations. Some however, appeared to be distinctly Roman and were imported from the Mediterranean. Besides Malwa, this ware is available at sites in Gujarat, Rajasthan and in the Deccan.

The fabric is the same and the forms of vessels are dishes, bowls, beakers, cups, jugs, sprinklers, spouted vessels, globular and gourd-shaped pots and storage jars, sometimes with moulded, embossed, or applied decorations, and finger tips designs.

MINOR ARTS :—Among the minor miscellaneous arts of this period, the jewellers' art occupies a prominent place. This is clear from the representations in stone sculptures, terracottas and ivory. We get the idea of jewelry from the images of Yaksha and Yakshī of Vidiśā, and of Maṇibhadra of Pawaya. Reference may also be made to an ivory Yakshī figure from Avara. The bas-reliefs at Sanchi also throw light on the ornaments of the people. They wore earrings, necklaces, rings, bracelets, anklets, girdles, etc. These were made of gold, silver, copper, ivory, shell, etc., with great skill.

Copper and ironsmiths held an important place amongst the artisans. Every ancient city site excavated so far reveals considerable attention given to metallurgical works. Some metal wedges used at the bottom of the *Garuḍa* pillar and other pillars at Vidiśā, are actually of steel, and they prove that even in the second century B.C., the process of steel making was known to the metal workers.[1] Similarly with the carpenters' art, the lithic monuments such as gates, rails of *stūpas*, *chaitya* facades, halls, etc. at Sanchi are but translation into stone from wooden originals, which proves the efficiency of carpenters. The carpenter is referred to in the inscriptions of Sanchi.

Ivory carving was another prosperous art. It is well known that the ivory carvers of the city of Vidiśā, imparted something of their fine skill to the reliefs of the Sanchi gates and

1. Vikrama Volume (Eng. ed.), p. 378 f. n. 1.

to the figure of Yakshī which was made of ivory, found at Avara. Ivory was used in making ornaments. Beads of different shapes and sizes were prepared and some of them are of artistic merit.

Two crystal reliquaries found at Bhojapur and Sonārī, respectively display splendour and remarkable workmanship. The reliquary from Bhojapur is made from a well-chosen transparent crystal, and is shaped like a miniature *stūpa*, complete with a pedestal base, the *aṇḍa* with *harmikā*, *chhatra-daṇḍa* and a parasol at the top. The overall height of the *stūpa* is eleven and a half centimeters and the lower reel-shaped pedestal base is seven centimeters. All the constituent parts of the *stūpa* are symmetrical and well proportioned and their compactness enhances their beauty. The second reliquary found at Sonārī consists of a small bowl, about five centimeters in diameter, and 2.7 centimeters high. This bowl has a flat cover with levelled edges.

(C)

EDUCATION AND LITERATURE

From the *Mahābhārata*, it is known that Ujjayinī became a great seat of learning because of the existence of the *Āśrama* of Sāndīpani in the second century B.C. There were traditions at that time that it was founded by the ancient *Ṛishi* Sāndīpani, who was the tutor of Śrīkṛishṇa and Balarāma. Such was the name and fame of this institution, that students from distant places came for higher studies. The subjects taught were the *Vedas*, *Dharmaśāstra*, religion, Philosophy, *Nītiśāstra*, Accountancy, Archery, etc. The students lived under the guidance of their teachers, and they led a celibate life. They served their teachers by performing several duties. Some *Purāṇas* and other literary works also, describe this ancient educational institution of Ujjain.[2]

1. JMPIP, p. 52.
2. *Brahmāṇḍa-Purāṇa, Padmapurāṇa, Vishṇupurāṇa, Skandapurāṇa, Bhāgavata,* etc.

Patañjali, whose traditional birthplace was Gonarda[1] in Avanti, indirectly refers to the prevalent educational system in his *Mahābhāshya*. Emphasis was laid on the study of Grammar which was necessary for the preservation of the *Vedas*.[2] Besides Grammar, the other subjects of study were four *Vedas*, with six *Aṅgas*, their mysteries, a hundred *śākhās* of *Yajur-veda*, and the *Sāma-veda* with its thousand *pāṭhas*, treatises on dialogue, or the science of Logic, Epics, *Purāṇas* and Medicine.[3] Other studies included *Saṁgraha*, Metrics,[4] *Dharmaśāstra*[5], Astrology[6] and a comparative study of all doctrines (*sarva-tantra*)[7], and popular subjects like the tales of *Sumanottarā* and *Vāsavadattā*.[8] The *Smṛitis*, Chiromancy and the science of animals are also mentioned.

Patañjali refers to *gurukula* or the 'teacher's house', where the pupils lived under the guidance of the preceptor.[9] The boarders were known as '*ante-vāsin*[10]' and the teacher providing lodging was called '*anteguru*'.[11] Generally, the relations between the Preceptor and his pupils were very cordial. With begging bowl in his hands, the pupil went out on rounds[12] to the householders for food and other necessities.[13]

The method of the study was the rote system, but there was scope for discussion and interpretation for a proper understanding of the texts. Emphasis was laid on pronunciation and recitation. Despite insistence on rote method, writing was

1. IHQ, 1926, 267. According to the *Sutta Nipāta,* Gonarda stood midway between Ujjain and Besanagar.
2. 1.1.1, p. 1.L.15.
3. 1.1.1, p. 9.LL.21-23.
4. 1.2.32, p. 208.L.19.
5. 1.2.64, p. 242.L.25.
6. VI.3.79, p. 170.L.17.
7. IV.2.60, p. 284.L.12.
8. IV.2.60, p. 284.L.12.
9. IV. 2.62, p. 333.L.1.
10. IV. 3.104, p. 315.L.22.
11. IV. 3.10, p. 145.L.16.
12. 1.4.84, p. 347.L.17.
13. 1.1.55, p. 133.L.25.

in use. It is certain that Greek, *Kharoshṭhī*, and *Brāhmī*, were popular scripts in that period.

Patañjali also refers to female education. According to him, terms *Upādhyāyā* and *Upādhyāyī*[1] denoted a female teacher. He also mentions a young girl of the *Aupagavī* school[2], and a Brāhmaṇī studying *Kāsakṛitsnī* doctrines.[3]

There was *Parishad*[4] of the learned persons who knew the *Vedas*, the *Dharmas* and the *sciences*. It appears that it regulated the academic activities of different groups or schools, and served as a means for the development and propagation of learning. The pupils were known after the *gotras* and the *chāraṇas* of the teachers.

The question of fees, it seems, was not very important, because the diffusion of learning had no mercenary motive. It was the duty of the householders to meet the requirements of the preceptor and his family, as well as of his pupils. The students were expected to pay fees in cash or in kind, so that the teacher could maintain himself and his family.

LITERATURE:—This period is noteworthy for the revival of Sanskrit literature and literary creation. Patañjali, the great Grammarian, author of the *Mahābhāshya*, lived in this period. He was probably the chief priest in the *yajña* performed by Pushyamitra Śuṅga.

Ujjayinī became a great centre of learning, and it attracted a large number of scholars. Rājaśekhara[5] records a tradition that Viśālā was an examination centre where poets used to be examined. It is said that Kālidāsa, Meṇṭha, Amara, Rūpa, Sūra, Bhāravi, Hariśchandra and Chandragupta were examined at Ujjain. However, about the period in which these writers flourished, nothing can be definitely stated.

Bhāsa in his plays *Avimāraka*, *Chārudatta*, *Pratijñā-Yaugan-*

1. III.3.21, p. 147.L.20.
2. IV.1.93, p. 247.L.24.
3. IV.1.14, p. 206.L.9.
4. III.3.108, p. 155.L.10.
5. *Kāvyamīmāṁsā*, 3rd., ed. p. 55.

dharāyaṇa and *Svapnavāsavadatta*, speaks of Ujjayinī, and gives graphic description of its palaces, mansions, temples, gardens, lakes, pleasures, comforts and licenses, which indicate a close contact of the dramatist with the city. U.L. PUSALKER[1] places Bhāsa in the fifth or fourth century B.C., but some scholars ascribed him to the second or third century A.D.

Vikramāditya, who is said to have lived in the first century B.C., was a great patron of learning. Under him, Ujjayinī became a synonym for culture. Great poets, dramatists, philosophers, astronomers, scientists and artists flocked to Ujjain. Gaṇaka Kālidāsa, who belonged to 1164 Śaka era, recorded them in the *Jyotirvidābharaṇa*. According to this work, there were nine *Sabhāsads* or court *Pandits* in the court of Vikramāditya. They were Śaṅka, Vararuchi, Maṇi, Aṅgadatta, Jishṇu, Trilochana, Hari, Ghaṭakarpara and Amarasiṁha. Besides these, there were seven *Kālatantra kavis* or poets conversant with the science of time. Under this head are given the names of Satya, Varāhamihira, Śrutasena, Bādarāyaṇa, Maṇittha and Kumārasiṁha. In addition to these two lists, Gaṇaka Kālidāsa gives a further list of Nine Gems in which the prominent names of the two previous lists are incorporated. The names of nine Gems are—(1) Dhanvantari (2) Kshapaṇaka (3) Amarasiṁha, (4) Śaṅku (5) Vetālabhaṭṭa (6) Ghaṭakarpara (7) Kālidāsa (8) Varāhamihira and (9) Vararuchi. It is possible that all these great scholars may not have flourished at one and the same time, but it seems that they were attached somehow with Ujjain.

Under the Western Kshatrapas, Ujjayinī became one of the important seats of learning in India. During this period, Prakrit was gradually giving place to Sanskrit. The Girnar epigraph is one of the earliest records written throughout in Sanskrit, and displays clearly the existence of an elaborate Sanskrit Literature. It was written in prose, but it also depicts in a most interesting manner, the development from the simple epic to that of the *Kāvya*.[2] Rudradāman him-

1. Bhāsa—A Study.
2. KEITH ; A History of Sanskrit Literature, p. 49.

self was well-versed in Grammar, Politics, Music and Logic. He also seems to have been equally well versed in prose and poetry. The inscriptions of the successors of Rudradāman are also mostly written in Sanskrit. On the contrary, the inscriptions of the contemporary Sātavāhanas are written in Prakrit, which seems to have been the language of the common folk. The later coins of Dāmaghsada, son of Rudradāman, are in pure Sanskrit, and the use of Sanskrit legends on the coins was also continued by his son Satyadāman.[1]

Besides the development of classical Sanskrit literature, Levi[2] points out that it was at Ujjayinī, and during the sway of the Śakas, that drama began to develop. Levi[3] points out further, that Śakāra, i. e. king's brother-in-law (Śyālaka) of the Sanskrit drama, is in reality a picture of a Śaka, who were Scythian princes ruling for nearly four centuries in Western India. In the drama, Śakāra is a ridiculous figure, a brawling scoundrel, provoking laughter and contempt from the audience. Such a figure was evidently introduced to bring the alien Śakas into low estimation with the public. The earliest drama in which '*Śakāra*' appears is probably the '*Chārudatta*' of Bhāsa. It is not known what led the great dramatist to bear such a hatred against the Scythians.

Together with the Indian theatre, they must have done a good deal also for the development of Indian musical art, for drama and music are inseparably connected with each other. In the Girnar record, Rudradāman is credited as having mastered the *Gāndharva vidyā*. Mataṅga, in his *Bṛihaddeśī*, refers to music of foreign extraction, and incidentally mentions '*Śakamiśrita*' and *Śakākshya*'. The three branches of this art, *gīta* or music, *vādya* or playing on instruments, and *nṛitya* or dancing, are mentioned by Vātsyāyana, who enjoins that an ideal citizen must be acquainted with at least a rudimentary knowledge of these *kalās*.

It was in Ujjayinī, possibly the capital of the Western Kshatrapas, that Greek astronomy was translated into

1. Rapson : Catalogue, p. 82.
2. JA, 1902, pp. 95-125.
3. *Le Theatre Indian*, p. 361.

Indian soil, which was ultimately recast and remodelled by the Indians.

(D)

SOCIAL CONDITIONS

DIVISION OF SOCIETY :—Society was, no doubt, divided into the usual four *Varṇas*, but mixed marriages, whether among the higher or lower groups, had resulted in the creation of some new castes, such as *Vṛishalas*[1], *Varuḍas*[2], *Ugras*[3], *Nishādas*[4], *Chāṇḍālas*[5] and *Mṛitapas*.[6] Some of these, like the *Vṛishala*, *Chāṇḍāla* and *Nishāda*, have been mentioned in Vedic literature. *Varuḍas* belonged to one of the seven low castes called *antyaja*, whose occupation was the splitting of canes. The *Ugra* traced his origin to a Kshatriya father and a Sūdra mother, and was noted for his cruel disposition and rude conduct. The *Mṛitapas* belonged to that class of persons who took care of the dead, who collected deadmen's clothes, or who executed criminals. Persons belonging to these groups had an inferior position in the social setting, partly because of their professions, and partly because of their lineage.

Because of the revival of the Brāhmanical religon, the status of the Brāhmaṇas increased in society, but emphasis was still laid on their purity. Besides literary and spiritual attainments, they began to follow other professions. Śuṅga and Sātavāhana rulers were Brāhmaṇas by caste. The caste system was rigid and fixed in the society, as seen in one of the inscriptions of Gautamīputra Śrī Sātakarṇi, who boasts of having prevented the contamination of the four castes and as being the true supporter of the Brāhmaṇas.[7] But a curious fact to note, is that Gautamīputra Sātakarṇi and Rudradāman were related to each other. Rudradāman, who was a Śaka and of

1. Patañjali's *Mahābhāshya*—1.1.7, p. 59, L.18.
2. IV.1.97, p. 253.L.5.
3. IV.1.14, p. 257.L.15.
4. V.4.36, p. 435.L.8.
5. II.4.10, p. 475.L.6.
6. Ibid.
7. EI, VIII, p. 71.

foreign extraction, gave his daughter in marriage to the son of Gautamīputra Sātakarṇi.

At this time, there was a continuous influx of foreigners. Though Hindu society was rigid, it gradually absorbed these foreign elements. The foreigners adopted Hindu names, manners and customs. The son-in-law of Nahapāna bears the Indian name Ushavadāta, and her daughter's name is Dakshamitrā. Further, they adopted Brāhmanism and Buddhism, and championed them zealously.

A number of sub-castes and *gotras* also came into existence. In the votive inscriptions of Sanchi, there is mention of *Dhamakas*, *Magalakaṭiyas*, *Sāphineyakas*, *Tāpasiyas* and the *Vākiliyas* of Ujjayinī, who made gifts to the Buddhist establishment of Sanchi[1]. The *goṣṭhī* of the *Barulamisas* of Vidiśā also participated in donations.[2] At Sanchi, there is mention of a gift by Dharma Rakhitā of the Mādhava community[3], to *stūpa* I, and gifts from Āryagrāma and Buddha Pālita, the Śreshṭhi of the race of Pāṇḍu[4], to *stūpa* II.

A ruler named Sarvatāta, who is known from the Ghosuṇḍī inscription,[5] belonged to Gājāyana family. He was the son of a lady of the Pārāśara Gotra. Sogin,[6] Sohartrī[7] and Maukhari[8], seem to be the sub-clans of the Mālavas in the third century A. D.

FAMILY :—The family was a homogeneous unit consisting of blood relations, and the authority of the head of it was recognized. There was a joint family system, because sometimes the donation from a whole family is recorded in the inscriptions[9] of Sanchi. They record the family of Dhamu(tara), and the family of Ajitiguṭa. Among the epithets given to

1. The Monuments of Sanchi, p. 297.
2. Ibid.
3. CBT, p. 152.
4. Ibid, p. 180.
5. EI, XVI, p. 27.
6. Ibid, XXVII, pp. 252.
7. Ibid, XXVI, p. 118.
8. The Guhilas of Kishkindhā, p. 42.
9. EI, II, p. 87 f.

females in the Sanchi inscriptions, the repeated occurrence of the old Pali title '*Pajāvati*', literally a mother of children, is not without interest, and the fact that some females are named as being merely 'the mother of', and that others proudly proclaim the names of their sons without mentioning their own names, is worthy of note.

MARRIAGE AND POSITION OF WOMEN :—

A lawfully wedded wife is called '*bhāryā*'[1] in the *Mahābhāshya*, but a synonymous term, '*Ūḍhā*',[2] is also mentioned. Generally marriages were arranged by parents, who took into consideration the *gotra* and family of the other party. *Sagotra* marriage was not permissible, and one finds references to marital alliances between different *gotras* : the Atri with Bharadvāja, Vasishṭha and Kaśyapa, Bhṛigu and Aṅgirasa, Garga and Bhārgava, and Kutsa and Kuśika.

Women occupied a respectable position in society. There are many epigraphs at Sanchi which record gifts from nuns and other ladies. An inscription on the pillar of the *stūpa* at Andher records the gift of Dharma Śiva's mother.[3] It seems that women joined hands with men in the construction of the *stūpas* and gateways. In the sculptures at Sanchi, women worshipping Buddhist emblems are often depicted in assemblies, playing on instruments, enjoying music and dance, and entertaining guests together with their husbands. That the Purda system did not exist in the society, is known from the sculptures of Sanchi.

PASTIME AND RECREATIONS :—

The pastimes and recreations were many, and were universally enjoyed. Patañjali has mentioned the term '*Samāja*',[4] meaning festive gatherings for which there were numerous items of entertainment, like, music, dancing and acting. Dramatic performances accompanied by music and dancing were arranged. The story of Kaṁsa and his slaughter,

1. IV.1.52, p. 22, L.17.
2. 1.1.1, p. 42, L.16.
3. CBT, p. 222.
4. 1.1.50, p. 123, L.3.

and the binding of Bāli were shown on the stage[1]. In these performances, it was not merely the show, but the speech of the narrator, and the dialogues, which were enjoyed.[2] The actor used different types of head-dresses.[3] Dancing was also performed, the movements in a rhythmical manner, and the hands expressing themes through gestures. This art is confined to ladies alone. Patañjali refers to female dancers[4], and the Bharhut sculptures show only women dancing. Vocal and instrumental music was common. Certain gestures and postures in the Bhārhut sculptures[5] suggest the practice of vocal music. Patañjali has mentioned some musical instruments[6]—drum (*mṛidaṅga*), conch (*Śaṅkha*), flute (*tūṇava*), and another instrument of the guitar type (*vīṇā*), having seven strings. Wrestling,[7] walking[8] and fire displays[9] were other recreations. The indoor recreations included the game of dice,[10] which was probably meant for the old and rich, who had the time and money to do so.

FOOD AND DRINKS :—

Patañjali[11] gives exhaustive information about food and drinks, with vegetarian and non-vegetarian items, solid and liquid food, arrangements for meals, milk preparations, sweets, wines and fruits, and even dinner etiquette. Rice, wheat, barley and pulses were used by the people. The sweet balls popularly known as *Modaka* were liked by children. Generally, the meat of deer, goat, sheep, and the *sāraṅga* bird, was popular. Different kinds of drinks, both soft and alcoholic, were enjoyed.

1. III. 1. 26, p. 36, L. 15.
2. I. 4. 26, p. 329. L. 8.
3. II. 1. 69, p. 403, L. 8.
4. VI. 3. 42, p. 158, L. 16.
5. BARUA : Bharhut fig. 34, 69, 136.
6. II. 2.34, p. 435, L. 11.
7. III. 4. 47, p. 181, L. 18.
8. VIII. 1.7, p. 370, L. 1.
9. III. 2. 124, p. 125, L. 17.
10. I. 4. 2, p. 310, L. 4.
11. *Mahābhāshya*.

DRESS AND ORNAMENTS :—

Some literary works, the sculptural representations of Sanchi, and some figures of Yaksha and Yakshī, give us some idea of the dress and ornaments of the people. The lower garment was called '*upasaṁvyāna*[1]', corresponding to the modern *dhotī*-loin, which was generally white. The upper cloth for covering the shoulders, was called *paṭa*'.[2] Patañjali also refers to the use of cotton[3] and wool[4]. Clothes were sewn with a sharp needle.[5] Patañjali refers to leather shoes as well as to wooden sandals.[6] Women wore a skirt, generally white in colour[7]. The dyeing of clothes was very common. Patañjali[8] has referred to blue (*nīla*), yellow (*pīta*), green (*harit*) and brown red (*kāshāya*) colours.

The Yaksha figure of Besanagar of this period, wears a *dhotī* tied with a heavy waist band, and the upper part of the body is carved with *uttarīya*. The dress of the Yaksha, Maṇibhadra of Pawaya, consists of a waist-cloth and a scarf. From the study of the sculptures of Sanchi, we know that both men and women used upper and lower garments. The head dress for men was generally of *śaṁkhākāra* (shape of conch) fashion. On rare occasions, women put on the lower garments in '*Sakachchha*' fashion, i.e. by passing one end of it between the legs and tucking it up behind at the waist. The cloth was fastened at the waist by a girdle. Soldiers, body-guards, charioteers (*sārathī*), standard-bearers (*dhvajavāhaka)*, Brāhmaṇas and saints put on their own peculiar dress.

The Scythians are represented as wearing trousers and big overcoats, and this was imitated by the Indians. Women too began to wear blouses, jackets and frocks, in imitation of the Greeks and the Scythians, but the fashion did not become a general one.

1. I. 1. 36, p. 93. L. 12.
2. I. 4. 21, p. 321, L. 16.
3. IV. 1. 55, p. 224. L. 14.
4. V. 1.3, p. 338, L. 19.
5. II. 12, p. 373. L. 20.
6. V. 1.2, p. 337, LL. 6-7.
7. II. 2.5, p. 410, L. 21.
8. IV. 2.2, p. 271, L.10 f.

Patañjali[1] mentions four kinds of ornaments *ruchaka* (necklace), *kaṭaka* (bracelet), *svastika* (triangular piece), and *kuṇḍala* (ear-ring). Both men and women wore these ornaments. The forehead pieces, like *latika* or the fastened leaf, long collars, garlands, zones or girdles, and anklets, were exclusively meant for women. The Yakshī figure of Besanagar wears ornaments like necklaces, ear-rings, armlets and wristlets. She has a heavy nine-beaded *mekhalā* on her waist. The ornaments on the Yaksha Maṇibhadra of Pawaya, comprise of a rich necklace, consisting of a number of jewel or pearl strings, knotted and hanging down in tassels on the back, an armlet on the right arm, and a bracelet on the left-wrist. There was a plain nimbus round the head, which has left its traces on both sides of the neck. An idea of these ornaments is also gained from the sculptures of Sanchi. Rings, ear-rings, strings of beads, girdles of beads, bangles, necklaces, bracelets made of gold, silver, copper and ivory, have been discovered in the excavations of old sites.

The figures at Bhārhut and Sanchi, however, show different methods of arranging the hair. The loose hair is allowed to fall at the back, and then the end is looped and knotted.[2] It is arranged in a top-knot when the lady has a head dress.[3] The hair falling down the back is divided into two halves, and that into tassels, and then plaited.[4] Men generally had long hair tied in a top-knot, around which the folds of the turban were arranged[5]. The fashion of plaited hair, of the women, coiled around the head in a top-knot, is also observed in sculptures.[6] In some cases, the hair is fastened by an ornament.[7] Curly locks touching the neck are favoured by musicians, charioteers, and soldiers.[8] The arranging of hair

1. I. 1. 1, p. 7, L. 15 f.
2. BARUA ; Bharhut, Vol. III, P. XXIII-top.
3. Ibid, pl, XXX, 23, left side.
4. Ibid, pl. XXXIX, 34.
5. Ibid, III, pl. XXX. 23.
6. FERGUSSON : Tree and Serpent Worship, Pl. XXX. fig. 1. XXXII, fig. 2.
7. Ibid, pl. XXXV, flg. 2.
8. Ibid, pl. XXXIV, fig. 1. 22.

needed oil, combs and mirrors, while collyrium sticks, unguent vases and pots, were required for the make-up of the face. Patañjali mentions *chandana*-sandal, *gandha*-perfume, and *añjana* or black pigment[1] applied to the eye lashes.

Names of persons were kept in different ways. From some votive inscriptions[2] of Sanchi, it is known that a considerable group of proper names, e.g. *Asāḍa*, *Mūla*, *Mūladatā*, *Phaguṇa*, *Poṭhak*, *Pusa*, *Pusaka*, *Pusani*, *Pusagiri*, *Pusarakhita*, *Poṭhādevā*, *Rohiṇī*, *Sātila*, and *Svatiguṭa*, have been derived from the names of the *Nakshatras*, and point to the conclusion that the rule of some *Gṛihyasūtras*, which recommends the use of *Nakshatranāmānī*, was observed.

(E)
ECONOMIC CONDITIONS

There was ample production of raw material in Avanti. The case of communications during this period led to the development of trade, both internal and external. A large number of professions came into existence, which were organized into guilds. The prosperity of this region is also evident from the fact that most of the donors who built the *stūpas* at Sanchi and in the neighbourhood, came from this area.

This region produced an abundance of cotton. The village of Kāpāsigāma[3], mentioned in three inscribed labels on the railing of Sanchi stūpa I, is a proof of its vast production, because the village was named after it. Cotton industries must have been flourishing at important cities, such as Ujjain and Vidiśā. In fact, the region was famous for the export of fine muslins.

The area was rich in quarries, as is clear from their findings at different excavations. It is for this reason that the region was known as Ākarāvanti in the second century A.D., s is known from the Girnar inscription[4] of Rudradāman.

1. VIII. 2. 48, p. 408, L. 23.
2. El, II, pp. 87 f.
3. CBT, p. 160, No. 99.
4. EI, VIII, pp. 42 ff.

It may be inferred from the account of the commercial importance of Uzene in the *Periplus*, that Avanti was a country which abounded in quarries of stones like onyx.

The iron industry was also gradually developing. On examining a specimen of some metal wedges used at the bottom of the *Garuḍa* pillar of Besanagar, ROBERT HATFIELD, an authority on steel in England, proved that it was of real steel.[1] Thus Avanti knew the process of steel-making as early as the second century B. C. This was an important fact in the future economic progress of the Province.

Communication was smooth and frequent, as seen in the benefactions at Sanchi made by persons coming from different parts of India. This must have given impetus to internal trade. In Avanti, the three routes from the western coast met, from the sea-ports Surpāraka(Sopara)and Bhṛigukachchha (Broach), from the Deccan and from Śrāvasti. It seems that there was a brisk trade with the two important marts, namely Paithana and Tagara in the Deccan. It was also carried on with the important trade centres of the Gangetic valley. Avanti exported its main products, such as onyx-stones, cotton and grains.

Trade was not only internal, but also external. The unknown author of the '*Periplus*' of the Erythraean Sea, of the second half of the first century A.D., gives information about the external trade. Merchandise from Ujjain and other remote places in the north, were brought to Bhrigukachchha for export to foreign countries. The chief articles were onyx-stones, porcelain, fine muslins, mallow tinted cotton, etc.

As a result of commercial and industrial development, a large number of professions and crafts came into existence. Some are mentioned in the votive inscriptions[2] of Sanchi, such as Sotika. i.e. *Sautrika* (weaver), *vaḍaki* i.e. *Vardhakin* (carpenter) and *daṁtakāra* (worker in ivory). Besides these, there were hunters, trappers, fishermen, butchers and tanners. Their existence is proved by the manufactured objects unearthed in the archaeological excavations.

1. Vikrama Volume (Eng. Ed.), p. 378 f. n. 1.
2. EI, II, pp. 87 f.

Some of the crafts and industries were organized into guilds. The guild of the ivory workers of Vidiśā was well known, and it made a gift to the *stūpa* at Sanchi. The foreman of the artisans was known as *āvasenī* and his name is mentioned in the inscription at Sanchi.[1] The head of the merchant guild was known as *śreṣṭhī* who is frequently mentioned in the votive inscriptions of Sanchi.

COINAGE :—

During this period, punch-marked coins, and Ujjayinī coins continued for some time; but gradually, they were replaced by other coins. In form, character, and standard of weight, they were influenced by the Graeco-Bactrian and Roman coins. This was inevitable, because of the trade and commerce with the west. Even foreign names like *dīnāra* and *dramma* were applied to them. Yet in spite of the foreign influence, some elements of the early coinage were retained.

The Śaka silver coins have the bust of the king together with meaningless traces of circular Greek legend, borrowed from the Indo-Bactrian prototype on the obverse. The circular Brāhmī legend on the reverse of these coins, carefully mentions the name and the title, not only of the ruler, but also of his father. From the reign of Jīvadāman (175 A.D.), each coin issued from the mint bore the date. The crescented three-arched hill with the sun and the moon on either side, is the reverse symbol on the Kshatrapa coins. In course of time, the hill in the centre dominated the other two, which dwindled into insignificance. The average weight of the silver coins of the Western Kshatrapas is about thirty-five grains. They are obviously hemidrachms of the Persian weight standard.

The lead, potin and copper coins of the Western Kshatrapas have been found in abundance in the Ujjain-Bhilsa region. One silver coin of Chashṭana as Mahākshatrapa, was found at Ujjain.[2] On the obverse, there is a bust of the king with the traces of Greek legend. On the reverse, there is a

1. EI. II, pp. 87 f.
2. JNSI, XIV, p. 20.

haitya of six-arches surmounted by a rayed Sun on the left, and a crescent on the right. Coins with the figures of bulls are also found in this area. Potin coins of the Western Kshatrapas having on the obverse the figure of an elephant and on the reverse a *chaitya*, seem to be restricted to this area.

A hoard of Kshatrapa coins was found during the excavations at Sanchi. Another hoard of fifty-one silver coins of the Western Kshatrapas was obtained from Gondarman[1], eleven Kilometers north-west of Bhopal. The hoard consisted of five coins of the Mahākshatrapa Vijayasena, six coins of the Mahākshatrapa Rudrasena II, seventeen coins of Bhartṛidāman both as Kshatrapa and Mahākshatrapa, ten coins of the Kshatrapa Viśvasena, three coins of the Kshatrapa Rudrasiṁha II, and one coin of the Mahākshatrapa Svāmī-Rudrasena III. The attribution of the remaining nine coins is uncertain. All the coins were dated, the legible dates ranging from Śaka 157 to 270 (235 A.D. to 348). Like the the Uparkot and Sarvaniā hoards, this hoard appears to have been buried at the end of the earlier reign-period of the Mahākshatrapa Svāmī Rudrasena III, whose coins are the latest to be represented.

The Sātavāhana rulers issued their own distinctive coinage, with the hill and the Ujjain symbol as permanent features. There are metronymics together with personal names in Brāhmī. These are of lead, potin, copper and silver.

Early coins in lead and potin have been found with the legend '*Rāño Siri Sātasa*.' On the obverse, there is a figure of an elephant, and the symbological representation of a river with fishes, and on the reverse, there is the Ujjayinī symbol. These coins may be attributed to the Mālava region from the consideration of their type.[2]

After capturing this Malwa region from the Śaka ruler Nahapāna, Gautamīputra Sātakarṇi counterstruck his silver coins. On these, there is the *chaitya* of three arches on the obverse, and the Ujjayinī symbol on the reverse. He also

1. IAR, 1953-54, p. 63.
2. Rapson; Catalogue of the Indian Coins in the British Museum, p. xcii.

issued the coin types which were already current in this region, such as the homo-figure, the Elephant and the Lion, and the Svastika between the taurine symbols. His son Vāsishṭhīputra Pulumāvī, began the practice of issuing silver coins with the royal portrait. His successors, Vāsishṭhīputra Sātakarṇi and Yajñaśrī Sātakarṇi, continued this.

At Pawāyā in the first or second century A. D., symbolic types of coins were current.[1] These coins are triangular in shape, with the symbols of a triangle, a Sun, a monkey, a Nāga, a tree within a railing, a trident, a lion standing, a bull walking, etc. On the early coins of this area, the names of the rulers, such as Amitasena, Sabalasena, Yagata, etc.[2] are inscribed.

In the third and fourth centuries A. D., the Nāga coins, which are similar to Mālava coins in fabric, were issued in the regions of Pawaya (Padmāvatī) and Kutwar (Kāntipurī)[3]. These coins are die-struck. Most of them are round, but some are rectangular. On one side of the coins, there is a symbol in a circle of pellets, one group bearing the figure of a peacock, and the other of a humped bull. Some of the Nāga rulers issued coins with an additional recurring symbol. These symbols are—a trident, a crescent, a lion and a wheel. Excepting the last one, all are Śaivite emblems. The other side has a fragmentary Brāhmī legend-*Mahārāja*, *Adhirāja* and *Śrī*. These are of copper and conform to the standard of thirty six, and eighteen nine grains, representing respectively, a *kākiṇī* a half *Kākiṇī*, and a quarter *kākiṇī* respectively.

1. JNSI, XVIII, part I, p. 67; part II, p. 163.
2. Ibid, xvii p. 53.
3. Catalogue of the Coins of the Nāga kings of Padmāvatī.

CHAPTER—IX

THE GUPTA-AULIKARA PERIOD

(319—700 A. D.)

When the foundation of Gupta empire, with Pāṭaliputra as the capital, was laid by Chandragupta I in about 319 A.D., there were several independent petty states in this region of Malwa. The Mālavas settled in the region now known as Mewar, Tonk and Kota; the Sanakānīka, Ābhīra, Prārjuna, Kāka and Kharaparika ruled in the area around Bhilsa; the territory around Pawāyā was in the possession of the Nāgas, and western Malwa was ruled by the Śakas.

JISHṆU :—

From the evidence of coins, it seems that Jishṇu ruled over Malwa in the fourth century A.D. On the obverse of these coins, there is the legend, '*Jishṇu*', and on the reverse, there are conches, or wheels or *nandipada*, or vases with foliage. In size, shape and fabric, these coins are similar to the Mālava coins. To which dynasty this ruler belongs is not known. P.L. GUPTA[1] identified the coins of Jishṇu of Malwa and of the Punjab, and attributed them to one of the successors of Yaśodharman and Vishṇuvardhana, who ruled over an extensive dominion from the Punjab in the north to Malwa in the south. Jishṇu coins of the Punjab are quite different from those of Malwa, and V. A. SMITH is right in ascribing them to the ruler of the local Hūṇa dynasty of the sixth century A.D. Jishṇu is not known to be one of the successors of Yaśodharman and Viṣṇuvardhana.

H.V. TRIVEDI[2] has pointed out that the conch (*śaṅkha*) and the wheel (*chakra*) which are the motifs on the coins described by him, are the symbols of Vishṇu, and has ad-

1. JNSI, XV, p. 89.
2. JNSI, XIII, p. 150; 192.

vanced the view that the issuer of these coins was a devotee of Vishṇu, and suggested the possibility of his being connected with the Gupta dynasty; but no king named Jishṇu is known in the Gupta dynasty. It seems that Jishṇu was a local ruler of Malwa in the fourth century A. D.

CONQUESTS OF SAMUDRAGUPTA :—

After Chandragupta I, Samudragupta became the emperor after 330 A. D. He was an ambitious and powerful ruler. First of all, he seems to have conquered the rulers of Gangetic Doab, and annexed their territory to his empire. He defeated the Nāgas and crushed their power. Gaṇapatināga, whose name has been mentioned in the Allahabad inscription,[1] was ruling over Pawāyā where his coins have also been discovered.

Later, Samudragupta probably turned his attention to the petty chiefs ruling in the forests of Central India on the flanks of the Vindhya range in the Jabalpur division. Their subjugation was obviously an initial step for the grand campaign of the Deccan, which the emperor was contemplating. In the south, this expedition of Samudragupta was confined mostly to Madras Presidency. No Districts of that area however were annexed to the Gupta empire; but their rulers were uprooted and replanted in their dominions obviously on their acknowledging the overlordship of the conqueror, and agreeing to pay him a tribute.

This powerful ruler naturally inspired awe among his neighbours. As a consequence, the Ābhīras, the Prārjunas, the Sanakānīkas, the Kākas and the Kharaparikas, ruling in the region of Eastern Malwa, and in the neighbourhood, vied with each other in offering him their submission in a variety of suitable ways.

That Samudragupta annexed Eastern Malwa is clear from his Eran inscription.[2] This refers to his good deeds and to his virtuous queen and also refers to Eran as a pleasure-town (*svabhoganagara*).

1. CII, III, p. 6 ff.
2. Ibid, p. 18.

HISTORICITY OF RĀMAGUPTA :—

Till 1925, it was unanimously believed that Samudragupta was succeeded by Chandragupta II. The passages of the lost drama '*Devīchandraguptam*' in the *Nāṭyadarpaṇa*, written by Rāmachandra and Guṇabhadra, brought Rāmagupta to light. Similar references are noted in the *Harshacharita*, the *Śriṅgāra-prakāśa Kāvyamīmāṁsā*, *Majmaluttavārikha* and the Sanjan, Cambay and Sangli copper Plate inscriptions of the Rāshṭrakūṭas. From these scattered literary and late epigraphical sources, it is argued that Samudragupta was succeeded by his son Rāmagupta, whose wife was Dhruvadevī. In the course of war with the Śaka king, he was defeated and he agreed to surrender his wife. His younger brother, Chandragupta, was successful in defeating the Śakas. Afterwards, he killed his elder brother Rāmagupta. He not only seized his kingdom, but also married his widow.

There is a keen controversy[1] among scholars about the historicity of Rāmagupta of literary traditions. Some scholars doubt his historicity. No official Gupta genealogy ever mentions the name of Rāmagupta as the son of Samudragupta and the predecessor of Chandragupta II. The *Devīchandraguptam* drama of Viśākhadatta, cannot be considered to be a trustworthy source of history, at it was composed for purpose of drama. All the later evidences, being based on the *Devīchandraguptam*, cannot be relied upon. At the same time, there is some discrepancy in these works, which do not relate the same thing.

The other view is that Rāmagupta preceded Chandragupta II. The name of Rāmagupta is not in the official records, which give only the genealogy but not the succession, of kings. Viśākhadatta is a contemporary, or near contemporary, of the

1. Levi. S. JA; CCII, I, p. 201 ff; Sarasvati, IA, LII, pp. 181 ff; Altekar A. S. JBORS XIV, pp. 223 ff., Ibid, XV, pp. 134 ff; Banerji, R.D. AIG, pp. 26 ff; Bhandarkar, D.R., Malaviya Commemorations Volume, pp. 189 ff; Jayaswal K.P. Jbors, XVIII pp. 17 ff; Winternitz, Aiyangar Commemoration Volume, pp. 359 ff. Ibid; IA. LXII, pp, 201 ff., Das gupta, N. IC.V. pp. 216 ff. Raghavan V, BHU Magazine II, pp. 23 ff. Raichaudhari H.C, Phai. p. 405. n. 1. Chhatopadhyaya. S, The Early History of North India, pp. 164.

events narrated. This occurrence shows the persistence of a historical tradition which must have its foundation in reality. Further, it is confirmed by different literary sources, and the later epigraphs of the Rāshṭrakūṭas. When Chandragupta and Dhruvadevī of the drama are historical names, there should not be any doubt in regarding Rāmagupta as a historical person. When the literary evidence is correlated to the epigraphical, it tends to show that Dhruvadevī, wife of Chandragupta, was originally the wife of his elder brother Rāmagupta.

In the Poona copper plate[1] of Prabhāvatī Gupta of the year 13, her mother Kuberanāgā is called *Mahādevī*, but in the Riddhapur plates[2] of Pravarasena II of the year 19, she has been mentioned as simple '*Devī*.' In the Gupta inscriptions of the successors of Chandragupta II, Dhruvadevī has always been called '*Mahādevī*'. Two *Mahādevīs* of the emperor at one time were not possible. Either Kuberanāgā was degraded or she died, and afterwards. Dhruvadevī became *Mahādevī*. From the mention of two Mahādevīs, it appears that Dhruvadevī was originally the wife of Rāmagupta, but after his death his younger brother Chandragupta II married her. Because of the political and social pressures of the time, Dhruvadevī could not be made *Mahādevī* earlier. The Nāgas were very powerful, and the claim of Kuberanāgā could not easily be set aside. Socially, Dhruvadevī could not be accorded the same regard and position at the same time as Kuberanāgā.

Interest in this problem was revived by the discovery of copper coins of Rāmagupta at Vidiśā, Eran, etc., in Malwa. These are mainly of two types, namely the Lion type, and the Garuḍa type. P.L. Gupta[3], A.S. Altekar[4] and K.D. Bajpai[5], attribute these coins to Rāmagupta of literary tradition on the following grounds :—

1. EI, XV, p. 30.
2. Ibid, XIX, pp 100-104.
3. JNSI, XII, p. 3.
4 Ibid, p. 106.
5. Ibid, XVIII, pp. 340-344.

(I) No Rāmagupta other than the Gupta ruler referred to in the literary tradition, is known to us so far.

(2) Eastern Malwa was already conquered by Samudragupta, who might have appointed Rāmagupta as the Governor of Eran, and allowed him to issue tiny copper coins in imitation of the local coins for the Mālava subjects.

(3) The presence of the lion on the coins of Rāmagupta has its own obvious significance when considered together with its presence on the seal of his wife, Dhruvasvāminī.

(4) The fabric and weight of these coins are similar to the Mālava coins. They also resemble the coins of Chandragupta II issued in Malwa.

(5) There was the practice of governing Malwa through royal princes. In the time of Kumāragupta, Ghaṭotkacha was the governor of Malwa. During the reign of Chandragupta II, his son, Govindagupta, ruled h ere. The practice probably started in the time of Samudragupta, who deputed his son, Rāmagupta, to govern Eastern Malwa.

(6) Palaeographically, the legends are of the early Gupta period, and belong to the time of the Rāmagupta of literary tradition.

(7) *Garuḍa* was the crest of the Imperial Guptas, and it is also found on their coins. Therefore Rāmagupta, who issued *Garuḍa* type of coins, belonged to the Imperial Gupta Dynasty.

(8) A battle was fought between the Śaka chief and Chandragupta II at Vidiśā, for the protection of Dhruvadevī. This seems to be so from fact that Śaka coins and inscriptions have been found in this area.

D.C. SIRCAR[1], A. K. NARAIN[2] and NISAR AHMAD[3] are of the view that these coins do not belong to Rāmagupta of the literary traditions.

(1) These copper coins were issued after the fall of the Gupta empire in the fifth century A.D., by Rāmagupta, a local ruler.

1. JIH, XL, p. 533.
2. JNSI, XII, p. 41.
3. Ibid, XXV, p. 105.

(2) The type, fabric, weight, and provenance, indicate that these are local coins, and Rāmagupta may have been an independent local ruler.

(3) The *Garuḍa* crest is not the monopoly of the Guptas. The gold coins of Mahendrāditya also have the figure of *Garuḍa*.

Three Jaina sculptures have recently been discovered at Vidiśā. The inscription on them records that these were made by *Mahārājādhirāja* Rāmagupta on the advice of Chelukshamaṇa, son of Gokyantī, and pupil of *Āchārya* Sarppasena Kshamaṇa, who was the grand pupil of the Jaina teacher, Chandra Kshamāchārya. K. D. BAJPAI,[1] G. S. GAI,[2] and others, have identified this Rāmagupta with the Gupta ruler of the Imperial Dynasty because he assumed the title of *Mahārājādhirāja*.

It seems that Rāmagupta of the inscription is identical with Rāmagupta of so many of the coins found in Malwa. This Rāmagupta seems to have been a local ruler of some collateral branch of the Gupta dynasty, ruling in the fourth or fifth century A.D., with his capital at Vidiśā. He cannot be identified with the imperial ruler of the literary tradition merely because of the title '*Mahārājādhirāja*'. The local ruler of Malwa could assume this title. No gold coin of this Rāmagupta has so far been found, and the Imperial dynasty of the Guptas is famous for the issuing of gold coins. It cannot be assumed that Rāmagupta ruled for a short time, when large number of his copper coins have been found, and his inscription is available. His coins and inscriptions have not been discovered outside Malwa. The region of Vidiśā was conquered for the first time by Chandragupta II, and Rāmagupta seems to have come afterwards. Rāmagupta in the above mentioned inscription does not give a genealogy in the fashion of the inscriptions of the Imperial Gupta rulers.

CHANDRAGUPTA II :—

Chandragupta II, who became the ruler in about 375 A.D.,

1. *Hindi Weekly Hindustan Sāptāhika* dated 30-3-1969, p. 10.
2. Journal of the Oriental Institute, Baroda, XVIII, p. 247.

emulated the military career of his father, Samudragupta. He was also a diplomat, and tried to strengthen his position by matrimonial alliances. He himself was married to the daughter of Kuberanāgā, a daughter of the Nāga family, and their daughter, Prabhāvatī, was married to the Vākāṭaka king, Rudrasena II. It is not an unreasonable assumption that these alliances were made deliberately with the motive to safeguard the kingdom against foreigners.

Scholars generally identify Chandra of the Meharauli iron pillar inscription with Chandragupta II.[1] This inscription records that Chandra inflicted a crushing defeat on his enemies in the Vaṅga country. He also defeated the Vāhlikas in battle, having crossed the seven mouths of the river Sindhu. Scholars have identified Vaṅga with Eastern Bengal, and Vāhlika with Bactria, beyond Hindukush. K.D.Bajpai[2] tried to identify Vāhlika with modern 'Balis' in the Western Punjab, and Vaṅga with the region of the Makaran coast in Baluchistan. Chandra also defeated the Kushāṇas and the Pahalavas of this region.

As well, Chandragupta II launched an attack against the Saka Kshatrapas of Western India. The Udayagiri hill inscription[3], near Vidiśā, of one of his ministers, states that the latter had accompanied his royal master to Udayagiri, when he was seeking to conquer the world. This undoubtedly refers to a military campaign undertaken by Chandragupta towards the south western part of the empire. In addition to the record of the minister of Vīrasena, we also have the inscription of Sanakānika Mahārāja[4], a feudatory of Chandragupta II, and also of Āmrakārddava,[5] who was an official of Chandragupta II. The presence of a minister, a feudatory and a military officer, of Chandragupta II, for a prolonged time in the same locality of Eastern Malwa, clearly indicates

1. JIH, p. 13.
2. Mirashi Felicitation Volume, p. 355.
3. CII. III, pp. 31 f.
4. Ibid, p. 25. This inscription gives the genealogy of the Sanakānika dynasty ruling in this area—the *Mahārāja* Dhala, the son's son of *Mahārāja* Chhajalaga and the son of the *Mahārāja* Vishṇudāsa.
5. CII. III, pp. 29-34.

his campaign against the Western Kshatrapas. The campaign was signally successful, for Chandragupta II not only defeated the Western Kshatrapas, but completely annihilated their power, and annexed to his empire dominions, consisting of Eastern Malwa, Gujarat, and Kathiawar.

The great success achieved by the Gupta emperor is indirectly attested to by the coins. The long series of coins testifying to the almost unbroken rule of the Western Kshatrapas, for more than three hundred years, comes to an end between 388 and 397 A. D., and is replaced by the coin of a similar design, issued by Chandragupta II. The earliest silver coins of Chandragupta are of the year 409 A.D., issued to replace the coins of the Western Kshatrapas in Malwa. This leaves no doubt that Chandragupta II extinguished the power of the Western Kshatrapas, and annexed their dominions.

The assumption of the title '*Vikramāditya*' by Chandragupta II, indicates his success against the Western Kshatrapas. It is held by many scholars that Chandragupta's exploits must have recalled those of King Vikrama, and he might have assumed this title after his conquests, in imitation of the legendary hero.

From 402 A.D., Chandragupta II seems to have had a residence in Malwa, possibly at Vidiśā at first, and later on, after his western conquests, at Ujjain. Certain chiefs of the Kanarese Districts, who claimed descent from Chandragupta (Vikramāditya), refer to their great ancestor as lord of Ujjain and Pāṭaliputra.[1] In the *Kathāsaritsāgara*,[2] Vikramāditya is represented as ruling at Pāṭaliputra as well as at Ujjayinī. Sāhasāṅka of Ujjain is even said to have ordered the exclusive use of Sanskrit in his harem.[3] Among the *Kāvyakāras* tested in Ujjain, mention is made of Chandragupta along with Kālidāsa, Amara, Bhāravi and others.[4] In the *Pādatāḍitakam*, there is mention of *Sārvabhauma Nareśa* and *Sārvabhauma-*

1. PHAI, p. 556.
2. VII, 4. 3
3. *Kāvyamīmāṁsā*, 3rd ed., p. 50.
4. Ibid, p. 55.

Nagara. Baro has identified the *Sārvabhauma Nareśa* with Chandragupta II, and the *Sārvabhauma Nagara* with Ujjain.[1]

There is no solid contemporary evidence, either archaeological or literary, to prove that Eastern Malwa, along with Ujjayinī, was in the possession of Chandragupta II. On the other hand, the Aulikara ruler, Naravarman, was an independent ruler at this time with his capital at Daśapura.

It seems that Chandragupta II deputed his son Govindagupta, to govern Eastern Malwa. Govindagupta is known from a clay seal of his mother, Mahādevī Dhruvasvaminī found in the excavations at Basarah (Vaiśālī)[2]. From this seal as well as from others, it appears that he was the eldest son of Chandragupta. He was *yuvarāja* (heir apparent) during the reign of his father. The Mandsor inscription[3] of V.S. 524 (467-68 A.D.), describes Govindagupta as a paramount sovereign, to whom obeisance was paid by feudatory princes. His general's name has been mentioned as Vāyurakshita. No conclusive evidence is available so far, to show when exactly, he ruled as emperor. The above inscription does not state whether he was the contemporary ruling emperor. D. R. Bhandarkar is of the opinion, that Govindagupta probably ruled as emperor between his father, Chandragupta II, and his younger brother, Kumāragupta I. His reign cannot have exceeded three years—the interval between the last known date of Chandragupta II and the earliest known date of Kumāragupta I (G.E. 93-96). As he ruled for such a short period, he left no coins. Being a collateral, Govindagupta does not appear in the genealogy of the inscriptions of Kumāragupta and his successors.

KUMĀRAGUPTA :—Kumāragupta, who ascended the throne in about 414 A.D., appoined Ghatotkachagupta to govern Eastern Malwa. The Tumain fragmentary inscription[4] dated 116 G.E. (435 A.D.), records the construction of a temple by five brothers residing in Tumbavana, during the

1. *Chaturbhāṇī, bhūmikā*, pp. 4-6,
2. ASI, 1903-04, pp. 102-107.
3. EI, XXVII, pp. 12-18.
4. Ibid, XXVI, p. 117.

reign of Kumāragupta, when Ghaṭotkachagupta was holding the office of governor of the province Airikiṇa (Eran), which included Tumbavana. Ghaṭotkacha was probably the son or younger brother, of Kumārgupta. He is known from a clay seal and also from a coin. A square copper coin with the legend, '*Satyagupta*', in gupta characters, was discovered at Tumain[1]. He seems to be the chief of the Gupta dynasty ruling over the area round about Tumain.

The Aulikara chiefs, either Viśvavarman or Bandhuvarman, ruling over Western Malwa, with Mandsor as the capital, for the first time seem to have recognized the suzerainty of the Guptas. The Mandsor inscription[2] of V.S. 493 (436 A.D.), refers to the reign of Kumāragupta, and to Viśvavarman's son, Bandhuvarman, who was the governor at Daśapura under him. It narrates how a number of silk weavers emigrated from the Lāṭa *Vishaya*, or Central and Southern Gujarat, into the city of Daśapura. Some took up other occupations, while others continued as weavers. The guild of the silk weavers built the Temple of the Sun in 437-38 A. D.

Towards the very end of the reign of Kumāragupta, the peace of the empire was rudely disturbed by the invasion of an enemy, whose identity is not yet definitely established. It is generally believed, that the hostile forces in the Bhītarī inscription[3] were of the Pushyamitra tribe, but the reading of this name is uncertain. K. D. BAJPAI[4] thinks that the Pushyamitras mentioned in the Bhītarī pillar inscription, were somehow connected with Senāpati Pushyamitra Śuṅga. It is presumed that some of Śuṅga-mitra-chiefs of Ahichchhatra,

1. IAR, 1967-68, p. 62.
2. CII, pp. p. OI ff.
3. CII, pp. 53 ff. FLEET read the crucial expression as '*Pushya-mitrāṁscha* but noted the second syllable of the name as damaged. DIVEKAR proposes to read the compound as '*Yudhy-amitrāṁs-cha* (ABORI, I, pp. 99 ff.) A tribe called Pusyamitra is referred to in the *Vishṇupurāṇa* which associates it with the region near the source of the Narmada valley.
4. Bulletin of Ancient Indian History & Archaeology, No. 1. p. 3. Fxcept for the name, there is no definite evidence to associate the clan of the Pushyamitras of the fifth century A.D. with Pushyamitra the founder of the Śuṅga dynasty.

Mathurā, Ayodhyā and Kauśāmbī, after their defeat at the hands of Samudragupta, took refuge in the forest area of the present Shahdol District of Madhya Pradesh, near the source of the river Narmada. Taking advantage of the Hūṇa invasion, and the internal dissensions of the reign of Kumāragupta, the Pusyamitra rose in revolt. Kumāragupta deputed his son Skandagupta, to put them down. From the Bhītarī inscription[1] of Skandagupta, it is known that he had to spend the whole night sleeping on the bare earth when fighting against the Pushyamitras.

That there was a critical period during the reign of Kumāragupta, is further substantiated by numismatic evidence. The Bamnālā hoard[2] of Gupta coins found in the Nimar District of Malwa, contains coins up to the time of Kumāragupta I, and a gold bar has also been found. A. S. ALTEKAR[3] has rightly pointed out, that the hoard was buried during the days of the Pushyamitras' rebellion, and the gold bar might have been the result of melting gold ornaments, always a common practice in times of stress in India, even today. Another hoard of gold coins found at Bayana in the Bharatpur District of Rajasthan, according to A.S.ALTEKAR[4], was buried towards the end of the reign of Kumāragupta, or the beginning of that of Skandagupta, when nothing and no one was safe. In other words, the empire immediately before, and after, the death of Kumāragupta I in 455 A.D., was under stress, and Skandagupta saved it from disintegration.

SKANDAGUPTA :—

Some scholars are of the opinion that there was a war of succession after the death of Kumāragupta in 456 A.D., between Purugupta and Skandagupta. Kumāragupta was succeeded by Purugupta, and not by Skandagupta. This is clear from the fact that he is referred to as *Pādānudhyāta* in the Bihar stone pillar inscription,[5] and that his mother was

1. CII, III, pp. 43 ff.
2. JNSI, V, pp. 135 ff.
3. Ibid, p. 136, note 1.
4. Ibid, VIII, p. 179 ff.
5. CII, III, pp. 49 f.

Mahādevī. In the Junagarh inscription[1] of Skandagupta, it is suggested that the goddess Lakshmī chose Skanda, after discarding all other rivals. The same conclusion may also be confirmed by his coin type, namely the king and Lakshmī. ALLAN[2] rightly associates this picture with the statement in the Junagarh inscription, that the goddess of sovereignty, of her own accord selected him as her husband, having discarded all other princes in succession. It seems that Skandagupta obtained the throne by a *coup d'ètat*.

The early years of Skandagupta must have been both busy and disturbed. He had to face both internal and external dangers. Early on, he had to fight against the invading Hūṇas, a savage tribe living in Central Asia. This was a terrible invasion. In the Bhītarī pillar inscription,[3] he is said to have shook the earth (*dharākampitā*) in subduing the mighty Hūṇas, with whom he came into close conflict, and destroyed the pride of his enemies at its root. This achievement was no mean one, for the Hūṇas were at the height of their power, and had crushed a number of kingdoms in Asia and Europe. Besides the epigraphical evidence, the victory of Skandgupta over the Hūṇas is confirmed by literary evidence. Both the *Kathāsaritsāgara* and the *Chandragarbhaparipṛichchhā* indirectly refer to this invasion.

By 460 A.D., troubles had been subdued and in order to safeguard his kingdom from both internal and external dangers, Skandagupta established an efficient administration. He appointed capable viceroys who enjoyed his confidence. These viceroys were endowed with wisdom, truth, straightforwardness, civility, and one of them was Parṇadatta, who was the Viceroy of Saurāshṭra. Parṇadatta appointed his son, Chakrapālita, to govern Girnar.

Skandagupta's administration was both moral and just, as it is clear from the Junagarh rock inscription. The Sudarśana Lake burst in his time, and it was rebuilt by Chakrapālita under Skandagupta's orders. It testifies to the care of the

1. CII. III, pp. 58 ff.
2. CGD, p. xcix.
3. CII, III, pp. 53 f.

Gupta emperor, towards irrigation works in the remote dominions. He was always concerned about the prosperity of the people.

According to V.SMITH[1], R.D.BANERJI[2], ALLAN,[3] and other scholars, there was a second Hūṇa invasion in the later years of his reign when he lost some of his territories. A numismatic argument is advanced in support of it. The heavy-weight coins issued during the critical years later in his reign were debased. The depreciation in the purity of the gold was possible due to the financial loss caused by the Hūṇa wars. But this hypothesis was proved wrong by the British Museum Laboratory's report[4] on the coins of Skandagupta, and there is therefore no question of a Hūṇa invasion during the later years of his reign, to explain the alleged debasement of the heavy-weight coins. The last years of Skandagupta's reign seem to have been peaceful and prosperous, as is clear from the Junagarh rock inscription.

The theory that the last years of his reign were not peaceful has been backed by the Mandsor inscription[5] of Prabhākara, dated in the Mālava year 524(467-68 A.D.). The inscription mentions the early Gupta emperor Chandragupta II and his son Govindagupta. It records a donation by Prabhākara's Commander-in-chief, Dattabhaṭa, son of Vāyurakshita, the general of Govindagupta. The non-mention of Skandagupta's reign in the inscription has been interpreted as his loss of sovereignty in Western Malwa. The other view is that the way in which Prabhākara is mentioned, suggests that he was a feudatory of the Guptas, and the non-mention of Skandagupta's reign is only accidental.

It has also been suggested, that during the last years of his reign, Skandagupta lost Mālava to the Vākāṭakas. The source of this inference are the Bālāghāṭa plates of Pṛithvīsena II. The Vākāṭaka king Narendrasena, is said to have established his suzerainty over the lords of Kośala, Mekala and

1. EHI, p. 328.
2. The Age of the Imperial Guptas, p. 220.
3. CGD, p. XLIX.
4. The Decline of the Kingdom of Magadha, p. 61.
5. EI, XXVII, pp. 12-18.

Mālava.[1] V.V. MIRASHI[2] places the accession of Narendrasena in 450 A.D. It is possible that during the invasions of the Hūṇas, and the internal dissensions in the Gupta empire immediately after the death of Kumāragupta I, Narendrasena might have seized Malwa temporarily from the Guptas. But after his success against the Hūṇas, and the rivals to his throne, Skandagupta must have recovered the western province of Malwa. That the Vākāṭakas lost their power, is clear from the Bālāghāṭa inscription of Pṛithvīsena, who raised his family status. R.C. MAJUMDAR[3] placed Narendrasena in the period after 480 A.D. and thus makes him a contemporary of Budhagupta. Anyway, it should be accepted that there is no evidence that Eastern Malwa was lost to the Gupta powers in the later years of Skandagupta.

An inscription[4] found at Mandsor refers to the period between 436 and 472 A.D. as one of troubles, and one which saw the reigns of several kings. According to some scholars, it suggests the invasions of Hūṇa kings, and Vākāṭaka rulers over Malwa, and as a consequence, the Sun temple was destroyed. It was later repaired in 472 A.D. But it is possible to suggest that the temple had been neglected and it might have needed some repairs after the thirty-six years since its construction. The last years of Kumāragupta were critical, and the years following his death were full of internal and external troubles. The neglect of the temple was, therefore, natural. The reference to many kings does not necessarily suggest Hūṇa and Vākāṭaka rulers. The phrase may refer to Kumāragupta I, Purugupta (and possibly Ghaṭotkachagupta), and Skandagupta.

KUMĀRAGUPTA II :—

Skandagupta was succeeded by Kumāragupta II of the Sāranātha inscription[5] dated 473 A.D. He is different from

1. EI, IX, pp. 267 ff.
2. ABNUHS, Oct., 1946, pp. 8 ff.
3. JASB, 3rd series, XII, pp. I ff.
4. CII, III, No. 18, pp. ff.
5. ASI, 1914-15, p. 123.

Kumāragupta III as is known from the Bhītarī[1] and Nālandā[2] seals. The relation existing between Skandagupta and Kumāragupta II is not known, but the latter may have been his son. B.P. SINHA[3] attributed the coins of class I of ALLAN's Catalogue[4], to Kumāragupta II. These coins are better in style, clearer in legend, lighter in weight and purer in metal, than class II which is of very rude workmanship and base metal.

The Mandsor inscription[5] relates the history of the building of the Sun temple in M.E. 493, and its repair in M.E. 529 (472-73 A.D.). It has been suggested with good reason, that Kumāragupta II is also referred to in the opening line, as well as Kumāragupta I. As both the building of the temple and its repairs were completed in the reign of two kings each bearing the name of Kumāragupta, the author saved repetition and also introduced an element of intelligent imagination by mentioning Kumāragupta only once. D. C. SIRCAR[6] holds that the name of the reigning Gupta emperor is not given in the Mandsor inscription of Mālava year 493 and 529, and therefore, he suggests that in about 473 A.D., a struggle for Gupta imperial throne took place, and the author avoided mention of the reigning Gupta emperor, owing to the confusion caused by it. However in the year 473-74 A.D. Kumāragupta II was ruling, and it is not likely that any contest for the throne had begun.

BUDHAGUPTA :—

The reign of Kumāragupta II must have ended before 476 A.D., when Budhagupta is referred to as ruling the earth. Therefore, it is clear that Budhagupta followed Kumāragupta II in or before 476 A. D. It is not known as to how the reign of Kumāragupta II ended, and that of Budhagupta began. The allusion to Budhagupta seizing the throne after Śakrāditya

1. JASB, LVIII, pp. 84. ff.
2. MASI, No. 66, p. 64.
3. The Decline of the Kingdom of Magadha, p. 65.
4. CGD, pp. 140-143; p.c. IV.
5. CII, III, pp. 81 ff.
6. SII, p. 295, note 4.

(Kumāragupta II) in *The Life*,[1] may suggest, that Budhagupta acquired the throne after a *coup d'etat*. He was the son of Purugupta, as known from the Nālandā seal. The change of line effected by Budhagupta may have been preceded by a struggle. He may have overthrown Kumāragupta II whose short reign then becomes explicable.

Budhagupta was undoubtedly the last of the great imperial Guptas. The find spots of the inscriptions, seals, and coins, prove that the territories over which Budhagupta ruled were fairly extensive. His empire extended from the Himalayas to the Eastern Malwa, and from the Eastern Punjab to Bengal. He tried to maintain the whole of the Gupta empire of the period of Skandagupta except Saurāshṭra, but elements of decadence had already set in.

From the Eran inscription dated G. E. 165 (484-85 A. D.), it is known that the sovereignty of Budhagupta was recognized in Eastern Malwa. While Budhagupta was king, *Mahārāja* Suraśmīchandra was the governor of the country between the Kalindi and the Narmada. This inscription records the erection of the column which is called a '*dhvaja-stambha*' or flag-staff of the god Vishṇu, under the name of Janārdana, by a *Mahārāja* named Mātṛivishṇu. His sovereignty in Eastern Malwa is confirmed by numismatic evidence.[2] His silver coins follow the style of those of the Śakas of Saurāshṭra, which was used by his predecessors. On the obverse of these coins, there is the head to the right, with the date in front, and on reverse is a peacock with wings and tail outstretched, and the inscription '*vijita-vanira-vanipati* (h) *Śrī Budhagupta* (*divam*) *jayati*'. The type of these silver coins proves that his authority was recognized in Eastern Malwa.

Budhagupta maintained influence in Eastern Malwa, but there were ominous signs of the decline of his power and authority in the outlying provinces. Parivrājaka Mahārāja ruled in Bundelkhand (Nagod and Jaso States). *Mahārāja* Hastin[3] (475-517) A. D.) of this family, issued land grants without

1. *The Life*, p. 110.
2. CGD, p. 153.
3. EI, XXI, pp. 127 ff.

mentioning Budhagupta and making only a general reference to Gupta sovereignty. Adjacent to the Parivrājaka kingdom, was another principality, with Uchchakalpa as the capital. King Jayanātha issued land grants in the year 174-177, which probably refer to the Gupta era. As Jayanātha's grants[1] do not contain any reference to the Gupta sovereignty, it is probable that by 493 A. D., he had ceased to owe any allegiance to it. A dynasty called the Pāṇḍuvaṁśa[2] rose into importance in the neighbourhood. The Aulikaras of Mandsor under Ādityavardhana appear to have become independent.

The copper grants giving the names of Svāmidāsa (year 67), Bhulunda (year 107), and Rudradāsa, are, according to R.C. MAJUMDAR,[3] dated in the Gupta era. The rulers mentioned in the grants ruled over the Anūpa region. They are known to have recognized the suzerainty of some ruler, but his name has not been mentioned. However V.V. MIRASHI[4] accords them to the Kalachuri era, founded in 249 A.D. According to him, in the fourth century A.D., these rulers ruled not over Anūpa, but over some district of Northern Maharashtra, with the capital at Valka, which may be identified with Vāghli, about ten kilometers northeast of Chalisgaon in the East Khandesh District.

Similarly, *Mahārāja* Subandhu, who issued land grants from the ancient town of Māhishmatī (Maheshwar) on the Narmada, makes no reference to any Gupta suzerain. One of the grants found at Barwani[5] is dated in the year 167. R.R.HALDAR[6] referred its date to the Gupta era, and took it as equivalent to 468 A.D. He thought that *Mahārāja* Subandhu was a subordinate of the Gupta emperor Buddhagupta, whose Eran stone inscription is dated in the Gupta year 165(484-85). This view, however, presents several difficulties. If *Mahārāja* Subandhu was a feudatory of the Guptas, it is strange

1. CII, III, 117, 121; EI, XXIII, pp. 171 ff.
2. Bhārata-Kaumudī, I, p. 215; EI, XXVII, p. 132.
3. EI, XV, pp. 286.
4, CIII, IV, Part I, pp. 5-12.
5. EI, XIX, p. 261; CII, IV, Part I, p. 17; See also the Bagh cave plate of Subandhu, CII, IV, Part I, p. 19.
6. EI, XIX, p. 261.

that he does not name his liege-Lord, or generally refers to the suzerainty of the Guptas. As a matter of fact, Gupta suzerainty seems to have received a setback in Central India in the second half of the fifth century A. D., for there are several records from Mandsor and the adjoining places in the ancient Daśārṇa country, which are dated not in the Gupta era, but in the Mālava *Saṁvat*. Further from Balaghat plates of Pṛithvīsheṇa II (470-90 A.D.), it is known that the king of Mālava was one of the vassals of his father, Narendrasena. If Daśārṇa and Mālava had broken away from the Gupta empire, it is not likely that Anūpa, which lay further to the west, would continue to acknowledge Gupta supremacy. V.V. Mirashi thinks that the year 167 is not of Gupta era, but Kalachuri Chedi era, founded in 249 A. D. Thus the date of the grant would be 417 A. D.

The Hūṇas occupied Eastern Malwa either after the death of Budhagupta or, shortly before it. Toramāṇa's undated Eran inscription,[1] belonging to the first year of his reign, must be placed after Budhagupta's dated inscription,[2] 484-85 A.D. As it belongs to the same period, it may be put in the last years of Budhagupta's reign, or soon after his death. R.C. Majumdar[3] placed the Vākāṭaka ruler, Narendrasena, in the period after 480 A.D., and placed him as a contemporary of Budhagupta. Narendrasena might have taken advantage of these Hūṇa raids. While Toramāṇa made himself master of Eastern Malwa, the Aulikaras of Western Malwa might for a while have surrendered to Narendrasena.

NARASIṀHAGUPTA :—

Budhagupta was succeeded by his younger brother Narasiṁha gupta in about 496 A. D. He has been rightly identified with the ruler who issued gold coins of the Archer type, on the *Suvarṇa* standard, with the legend '*Nara*' on the obverse and '*Śri Bālādityaḥ*' on the reverse.[4] It is certain that Bālāditya was also known by the name of Narasiṁhagupta. No

1. CIII, III, pp. 159 f.
2. Ibid, III, p. 89.
3. JASBL, XII, pp. 1 ff.
4. CCIM, I, pp. 119-20.

silver coins of Narasiṁhagupta have been discovered, and this suggests that he did not control Eastern Malwa.

In the history of Malwa, the death of Budhagupta marks the end of one epoch and the beginning of another. The rule of the Imperial Guptas was over in Eastern Malwa, and there was disorder and confusion. Taking advantage of this situation, the Hūṇas invaded and occupied this area. The local feudal dynasty of the Aulikaras gradually became powerful, and gave a final death blow to the tottering Gupta empire.

THE HŪṆAS :—The Hūṇas became very powerful and conquered Western and Central Asia. They invaded India under their leader Toramāṇa, who conquered the Punjab, Part of Rajasthan, and Eastern Malwa. An undated inscription of the reign of Toramāṇa Śāhī or Śāh-Jauval, was discovered at Kura, in the salt range in the Punjab.[1] This title '*Jauval*' is also found on the silver and copper coins issued by Toramāṇa[2]. According to Uddyotanasūri, author of the *Kuvalayamālā*, the headquarter of Toramāṇa's Indian possession, was Pavvaiyā on the Chenab.[3]

Taking advantage of the weakness of the Gupta empire, the Hūṇas occupied Eastern Malwa. Two records found at Eran indicate unmistakably the transfer of sovereignty. The earlier one,[4] dated 165 G.E. (485 A.D.), records some pious construction by *Mahārāja* Mātṛivishṇu and his younger brother Dhanyavishṇu, during the reign of Budhagupta. The later one[5] records the construction of a temple by Dhanyavishṇu, after the death of his brother Mātṛivishṇu, in the first year that the *Mahārājādhirāja*, the glorious Toramāṇa of great fame, was ruling over the earth.

Making this area his strategic base, Toramāṇa seems to have invaded Magadha, the cradle of the Guptas. Besides, directly or indirectly, he encouraged the rival claims of the royal princes to the throne, and thus brought about disruption which weakened the Gupta empire. He is said to have

1. EI, I, pp. 238 ff.
2. JASB, 1894, p. 188.
3. JBORS, XIV, pp. 28 ff.
4. CII, III, p. 88.
5. Ibid, pp. 159 f.

installed Prakaṭāditya as a king in Kāśī.[1] He encouraged Vainyāditya to assume independence, and he began to issue seals[2] with the imperial title, and coins[3] with the *Āditya* title '*dvādaśāditya*'.

The authority of the Hūṇas was recognized for some time, but the Guptas continued their struggle to free Eastern Malwa from the clutches of the foreigners. From posthumous inscription[4] of Goparāja of Eran, it is known that a chieftain named Goparāja came to this place in the company of Bhānugupta. He fought a mighty battle in which he was killed, and his wife cremated herself on his funeral pyre. As the inscription is dated in 510-11 A. D., the battle was certainly fought against the Hūṇas, who were in possession of the area. This inscription is silent about the result of the battle. We do not know what happened to Bhānugupta and who won the battle. It is not unlikely that Bhānugupta freed Eran from the yoke of Toramāṇa, for the Gupta sovereignty was acknowledged by Parivrājaka Mahārāja, who ruled in the adjoining Province from 510 to at least 528 A.D. It seems that Toramāṇa's power suffered a decline, and he was forced to retreat.

But, if Bhānugupta had really achieved such a great victory, it would have been expressly stated in the record referring to him. It is also possible that Bhānugupta was defeated in this battle, after making futile attempts to free Eastern Malwa. It would seem to be only the unsuccessful battle of the Guptas against the Hūṇas.

After Toramāṇa, his son Mihirakula became the ruler. He revived the ambitious project of his father, and overran a large part of Northern India. An inscription[5] dated in the fifteenth year of his reign (530 A.D.), shows that his sovereignty extended up to Gwalior, and his authority was probably acknowledged further beyond that territory as well. According to Yuan Chwang, he subdued the whole of India,

1. CII, III, p. 284.
2. MASI, No. 66, p. 67.
3. CGD, p. 144.
4. CII, III, pp. 92 f.
5. CII, III, pp. 162 f.

and Cosmos also describes the Hūṇa chief at this time as the Lord of India. Yuan Chwang mentions that Bālāditya acknowledged the formal suzerainty of the Hūṇas, and agreed to pay tribute.

Mihirakula was a cruel persecutor of Buddhism. According to Yuan Chwang,[1] he wanted to be a Buddhist, but, the Buddhist priest told him that his servant could be his teacher. He felt deeply insulted and issued an order for the persecution of the Buddhists and destruction of the monasteries. Bālāditya revolted against this anti-Buddhist policy, and refused to pay tribute. When Mihirakula invaded his territory, he was defeated by Bālāditya. Besides this defeat of Mihirakula by Bālāditya as related by Yuan Chwang[2], there is epigraphical evidence[3] that Yaśodharman also defeated him.

It has been a problem for scholars to reconcile the statements of Yuan Chwang and the Mandsor stone pillar inscription of Yaśodharman. V. A. Smith[4] advocated the theory that, the native princes under the leadership of Yaśodharman, a *Rājā* of Central India, appeared to have formed a confederacy against the foreign tyrant, and further concludes that the weight of evidence is now decidedly in favour of the rejection of Yuan Chwang's story. J. F. Fleet[5] was of the view that Mihirakula was overthrown by Yaśodharman in the west, and by Bālāditya in the direction of Magadha. R. Hoernle[6] supposed that Yaśodharman-Vishṇuvardhana was a feudatory of Narasiṁhagupta, and defeated Mihirakula in latter's reign, and thereupon took advantage of his great success to found an empire for himself. But in fact, the defeats of Mihirakula by Bālāditya and Yaśodharman were two different events which were not synchronous. According to B. P. Sinha,[7] the victory of Bālāditya may be put in 520 A.D., while the

1. Watters, I, p. 288.
2. The Records I, p. 169.
3. CII, III, pp. 152 ff.
4. EHI, p. 337, note 2, p. 330.
5. IA, 1889, p. 228.
6. JASB, XVIII, p. 96.
7. The Decline of the Kingdom of Magadha, p. 110.

success of Yaśodharman over Mihirakula should be placed in, or shortly before, 533 A.D.

The constant invasions of the Hūṇas harassed the Gupta empire both financially and politically. The royal treasury was exhausted against the powerful Hūṇas. As a result of this, coins of pure metal of different varieties disappeared, and Gupta rulers only issued the single type of debased coins. Politically, it weakened the Gupta empire and gave opportunities to the feudatories and provincial governors to establish independent kingdoms. Yaśodharman, the Later Guptas, the Maukharis, and the Gauḍas, became independent, and they gave a shattering blow to the tottering Gupta empire. In spite of this, they themselves did not occupy any permanent place in Indian politics.

AULIKARAS[1] :—The Aulikaras, who ruled from about 350 to 550 A.D., occupy an important place in the history of Malwa. For some time they appear to have recognized the nominal sovereignty of the Guptas, otherwise they remained independent. Some Aulikara rulers, like Ādityavardhana and Yaśodharman, were powerful, and extended their empire by conquests. Their coins are not available but we know about them from their inscriptions.

In the Bihar Kotra Inscription[2] dated 417 A.D. (474 M.E.) of Naravarman, and the Mandsor inscription[3] dated 532 A.D. (589 M.E.) of Yaśodharman, the name of the dynasty, Aulikara, has been mentioned. These Aulikaras seem to have been a branch of the Mālavas, because they always used the Mālava era in their inscriptions. Even in the Bihar Kotra inscription, this era has been called the 'Aulikara *Saṁvat*'. These Aulikaras seem to have been responsible in giving the name of this territory as Mālava.

Generally, scholars[4] believe that the early Aulikaras were feudatories of the Guptas but there is no solid evidence for it. Like the Vākāṭaka rulers, they assumed the simple title

1. I am grateful to M. L. Dalal for giving valuable suggestions in writing on the Aulikaras.
2. EI, XXXVI, pp. 130 ff.
3. CII, III, pp. 81 ff.
4. The Classical Age, p. 39.

'*Mahārāja*', or '*Narendra*, but it does not mean that they were dependent rulers. The founder of the Aulikara dynasty was Jayavarman. No achievement has been described in the inscriptions of his successors, except that he has been called '*Narendra*' in the Mandsor inscription dated 404 A. D. (461 M.E.) of Naravarman.[1] This proves that the Aulikaras gave up republican traditions and assumed a monarchical constitution.

Jayavarman seems to be a ruler of note. Taking advantage of the confusion created during the reign of Mahākshatrapa Rudrasena III, for thirteen years, from 351 to 364 A.D., the Aulikaras under Jayavarman seized the territory near Mandsor from the Śakas. As the Aulikaras have not been mentioned in the Allahabad inscription of Samudragupta as vassals, Jayavarman seems to be an independent chief.

Jayavarman was succeeded by Siṁhavarman in about 375 A.D. Nothing important is known about him. The son and successor of Siṁhavarman was Naravarman. He is known from the Mandsor inscription[2] dated 404 A. D. (461 M.E.), which refers to the reign of Naravarman, who was the son of Siṁhavarman and grandson of Jayavarman. The Bihar Kotra inscription[3] dated 417-18 A.D. (474 M.E.) describes the reign of Jayavarman. He is also mentioned in the Gangdhar inscription[4] dated 423-24 A. D. (480 M.E.), of his son Viśvavarman.

Naravarman appears to have been a powerful monarch who extended the Aulikara dominions by fresh conquests. He is known by the epithets of *Devendra Vikrama* and *Siṁha-Vikrāntagāmin*. D. R. BHANDARKAR[5] and other scholars have interpreted the expression in the sense that Naravarman was a feudatory of Chandragupta II. On the Lion Slayer type of coins, the legend '*Siṁha Vikrama*' is the epithet of Chandragupta II. This interpretation of the expression is not convincing. Here

1. EI, XII, pp. 320 ff.
2. Ibid.
3. Ibid, XXXVI, pp. 130 ff.
4. CII, III, pp. 44 ff.
5. IA, XLII, p. 161.

the word is *'gāmin'*, but not *'anugāmin'*. It seems that the author of the inscription compared Naravarman to a lion for his heroic deeds. Naravarman seems to have been an independent ruler, for there is no reference to his suzerain in his inscriptions.

Both Siṁhavarman and Naravarman were contemporary to Chandragupta II. Bihar Kotra, where an inscription of Naravarman was found, gives an idea about the extent of the latter's empire in the east. Bihar Kotra is situated at a distance of two hundred forty-one Kilometers from Mandsor and about sixty four Kilometers from Vidiśā. In his inscriptions, that neither the name of the Gupta suzerain has been given, nor have these inscriptions been recorded in the Gupta era, shows an independent status for Naravarman. It is also possible that Naravarman joined forces with Chandragupta II in the national cause in his fight against the Śakas. It seems that Western Malwa remained under the possession of Naravarman.

Naravarman was succeeded by his son Viśvavarman. He seems to have been independent up to 423 A.D. (480 M.E.), because in his Gangdhār inscription,[1] the name of a suzerain has not been mentioned. In this inscription, Viśvavarman has been described the bravest among kings. This inscription records how his minister, Mayūrākshaka, built a temple of Vishṇu, a temple of the divine mothers, and also a large drinking well. In the Mandsor inscription[2] dated 436 A.D. (493 M.E.) and 473 A.D. (529 M.E.), he has been described as equal in intellect to Śukra and Bṛihaspati.

Either Viśvavarman or his son Bandhuvarman, seem to have recognized the suzerainty of the Guptas, as known from the Mandsor inscription dated 436 A. D. and 473 A. D., wherein the name of the reigning emperor, Kumāragupta, has been given. This inscription records that the temple of the Sun was built by the guild of the silk weavers in 436 A.D., when Bandhuvarman was governing the city of Daśapura.

There is no definite information about the Aulikara rulers

1. CII, III, pp. 44 ff.
2. Ibid, pp. 81 ff.

who succeeded Bandhuvarman. The Mandsor inscription[1] states that within thirtysix years (436-73 A. D.) three kings ruled at Daśapura, but their names have not been mentioned. One of these may have been Dāśeraka Rudravarmā, who has been mentioned in the *Pādatāḍitakam*, written in about the fifth century A.D.[2] H.V. Trivedi[3] has discovered several coins at Mandsor with the legend "*Rudra* or *Rudrila*" in Gupta script. Some scholars attributed them to this ruler, Rudravarmā, but nothing can be said positively. They may be the coins of some other ruler of this name.

Prabhākara is known to have ruled at Daśapura in 467 A.D. (524 M.E.).[4] He probably belonged to the Aulikara family though it is not stated so explicitly. He is said to have fought with the enemies of the Guptas. Dattabhaṭa was the commander of his forces. Who the enemies were, is not known. V.V. Mirashi[5] identified the enemies of the Guptas with the Vākāṭakas but during the reign of Skandagupta, they seem to have been the Hūṇas. In about 467 A. D., Skandagupta died and there was a dispute about the succession to the Gupta throne. Taking advantage of this situation, Prabhākara seems to have become independent, and therefore he did not give the name of his sovereign in the inscription of 467 A. D.

After the death of Skandagupta, Western Malwa seems to have ceased to have been part of the Gupta empire. It was a period of turmoil and confusion. In the Mandsor inscription[6] at the time of the renovation of the Sun temple, in 473 A.D., even the name of the local ruling authority has not been mentioned. Taking advantage of this situation, the Vākāṭakas appear to have increased their own influence. In the Bālāghāṭa plates of Pṛithvīsena[7], Narendrasena is said to have been honoured by the kings of Kosala, Mekala and Mālava, although the actual extent of his political influence in these

1. CII, III, pp. 44 ff.
2. *Chaturbhāṇī*, p. 9.
3. Ibid.
4. EI, XXVII, pp. 12-18.
5. ABNUHS, Oct. 1946, pp. 8 ff.
6. CII, III, pp. 81 ff.
7. EI, IX, pp. 267 ff., XXII, pp. 207-12.

territories cannot be determined. The Mālava ruler may be identified with Prabhākara.

BUDHA PRAKASH[1] suggests that the old Varman line of kings was dismissed and the new Vardhana line of Ādityavardhana, was set up. This view does not seem to be correct. In the Bihar Kotra inscription dated 417 A. D. of Naravarman, and the Mandsor inscription dated 532 A. D. of Yaśodharman, the family was known as Aulikara. Hence no distinction can be made between these two families.

Ādityavardhana seems to have been the successor of Prabhākara. Though his dynasty is not known, he seems to be Aulikara from his name. The undated Mandsor inscription[2] of Gauri of the Māṇavāyaṇi family of the Kshatriyas, records the excavation of a tank in the suburbs of Daśapura for the merit of his deceased mother when his maternal grandfather, *Narendra* Ādityavardhana, was ruling at Daśapura. This inscription also indicates that Gauri was a relative or a feudatory, ruling round about Chhoṭī sādrī. In the Mandsor inscription, Ādityavardhana has been described as the conqueror of the enemies. These enemies do not seem to be the Guptas and the Hūṇas. He might have defeated the Vākāṭakas, who had established their sway over Malwa. The Vākāṭaka ruler Pṛithvīsena II, the son and successor of Narendrasena, claims to have twice retrieved the fallen fortunes of his family[3]. It seems that Western Malwa became independent of the Vākāṭakas under Ādityavardhana, at this time.

As the known date of this feudatory, Gauri, is V.S. 547 (490-91 A.D.), Ādityavardhana may be referred to the period V. S. 532-552 (475-495 A. D.). From the Mandsor and the Chhoti sadri[4] inscriptions of Gauri, we know about his predecessors. Puṇyasoma was the first king in the family of the Māṇavāyaṇis. His son and successor was Rājyavardhana. Rāshṭra was the son of Rājyavardhana. Rāshṭra's son and successor was Yaśagupta. King Gauri was the son of *Mahārāja* Yaśagupta. The prince Gobhaṭa is also mentioned in the

1. Aspects of Indian History and Civilization, p. 98.
2. EI, XXX, pp. 127 ff; XXXIII, pp. 205 ff.
3. Ibid, XXII, pp. 207-212.
4. Ibid, XXX, p. 120.

Chhoti Sadri inscription. It is very probable that he was a son of the Māṇavāyaṇi king Gauri. In the Chhoti Sadri inscription dated 491 A.D. (M.E. 547), *Mahārāja* Gauri does not mention his sovereign, either by accident or through ambition.

The next Aulikara ruler seems to have been *Mahārājādhirāja* Dravyavardhana, who has been mentioned by Varāhamihira in the *Bṛihatsaṁhitā*[1]. For the purpose of writing this work, Varāhamihira consulted on *śakuna* among others Dravyavardhana's work, which was composed after consulting Bhāradvāja's work. Since Dravyavardhana bore the name ending in Vardhana, it can be conjectured that he also belonged to the Aulikara family. AJAY MITRA SHASTRI has proved that Varāhamihira's *Pañchasiddhāntikā* was written in 505 A. D[2]. Varāhamihira therefore belonged to the first half of the sixth century A.D. King Dravyavardhana, whose work he consulted, must have ruled sometime in, or before, the beginning of that century. According to V. V. MIRASHI,[3] Dravyavardhana was an Aulikara king who ruled from about 495 to 515 A.D. (552 to V. 572) and was thus a predecessor of Yaśodharman Vishṇuvardhana, and probably his father.

BUDHA PRAKASH[4] holds a different view. He regards *Mahārājādhirāja* Dravyavardhana of Avanti as the successor of Yaśodharman Vishṇuvardhana of Malwa. He inherited from him a vast empire, as well as the position of paramountcy, implied in the title of *Mahārājādhirāja*. Living in an age of comparative peace, he devoted his attention to literature and science, and wrote something on omens and astrology. His work was of a fairly high standard, so as to be considered fit for acknowledgement by a gifted astronomer of the calibre of Varāhamihira. BUDH PRAKASH regards 505 A. D. as the year of the Varāhamihira and that he died in 587 A.D. These views do not seem to be plausible. V. V. MIRASHI has proved that both Varāhamihira and *Mahārājādhirāja* Dravyavardhana flourished

1. *Bṛihatsaṁhitā*, LXXXV.2.
2. India as seen in the *Bṛihatsaṁhitā* of Varāhamihira, p. 505.
3. IHQ, XXXIII, pp. 314-20; Studies in Indology, Vol. I, pp. 206-12; Vol. II, pp. 180-84.
4. Aspects of Indian History and Civilization, pp. 94-95.

in the first half of the sixth century A.D.

Harisheṇa, the ruler of the Vatsagulma branch of the Vākāṭakas, who lived in the first quarter of the sixth century A.D., is probably described in the Ajanta record[1] as having spread his influence in Kuntala, Avanti, Kaliṅga, etc. The exact relations of Harisheṇa with the above countries cannot be ascertained. It is possible that either during the end of the reign of Dravyavardhana, or at the beginning of the reign of Yaśodharman, Harisheṇa might have tried to establish some sort of sway over Avanti.

Yaśodharman, who became the ruler in about V. S. 589, was not an upstart. His predecessors, Ādityavardhana and Dravyavardhana, had assumed imperial titles, and made the Aulikara family famous. Yaśodharman further increased the prestige of the family by his conquests, and he may be called a national hero.

Yaśodharman is found mentioned in the two Mandsor inscriptions written by Govinda. One is dated V.S. 589, while the other is undated and written in the present tense. It is definite that both belong to the same period, because their author is Govinda. In the dated inscription, Yaśodharman is mentioned after Vishṇuvardhana who defeated many kings. The Mandsor stone inscription of Yaśodharman and Vishṇuvardhana, describes Yaśodharman as '*Janendra*', and Vishṇuvardhana as '*Narādhipati*', and speaks highly of both. Yaśodharman is said to have plunged into the array of his enemies: Vishṇuvardhana is referred to as having brought into subjection, with peaceful overtures, and by war, the mighty kings of the east, and many kings of the north, and is described as *Rājādhirāja*, and *Parameśvara*, and having conquered the earth with his own arms.

There is a controversy about the relationship between Yaśodharman and Vishṇuvardhana. J.Allan[3] held that Yaśodharman was the suzerain of Vishṇuvardhana. J.F.Fleet[4] was

1. Hyderabad Archaeological Survey, XIV.
2. CII, III, p. 146 f.
3. CGD, pp. LVII-LVIII.
4. CII, III, p. 151.

also of the same opinion. HOERNLE,[1] K.P. JAYASWAL[2] and D.C. SIRCAR[3] are of the opinion that Vishṇuvardhana and Yaśodharman were identical. If they recognized them as different kings, then the historical facts cannot be reconciled. It could not be possible for both of them to have acquired sovereignty over the same area, and that too within a few years. Both are mentioned in the one record of the same place. It is possible that because of his popularity, Yaśodharman was also given the honorific title '*Janendra*'

The undated inscription[4] of Yaśodharman found at Mandsor, gives information about the military achievements of Yaśodharman. His sovereignty was acknowledged over the vast area bounded by the Himalayas in the north, the Mahendra mountains (Ganjam District) in the south, the Lauhitya (Brahmaputra) river in the east, and the ocean in the west. He conquered those countries which had not submitted even to the Guptas or to the Hūṇas. Further, it is claimed that homage was paid to him, even by the famous king, Mihirakula.

The general and conventional description of universal conquest given in the inscription, cannot be accepted at its face value. It is not possible to regard Yaśodharman as the sole and undisputed monarch of Northern India. At the same time, such bold claims would not have been made in a public record, unless there was some basis of fact. There is no doubt that Yaśodharman was a great conqueror.

It is possible that Yaśodharman first extended his empire by his conquests at the cost of the Guptas; but the exact limits of his empire cannot be defined. It is certain, however, that he could not finally annihilate the Gupta empire. According to B.P. SINHA[5], Kumāragupta III, known from the Bhītarī and Nālandā Seals, was the Gupta emperor. It is quite possible that in this struggle, Kumāragupta III perished, and the event may be dated as 530 A.D. It may have been the news

1. JASB, LVIII, p. 96.
2. IA, XLVI, pp. 145.
3. SII (old Ed.) p. 386, note 2.
4. CII, III. p. 147.
5. The Decline of the Kingdom of Magadha, p. 117.

of his death that induced Bālāditya, father of Kumāragupta, to commit suicide[1].

Yaśodharman also defeated Mihirakula, and freed Malwa and the neighbouring region from the Hūṇa depredations. B.P. Sinha[2] is of the view that after his successful *digvijaya* in the East and Madhyadeśa, Yaśodharman proceeded to the North where he forced Mihirakula to pay obeisance, and broke the power of the Hūṇas in India. Cosmos[3] refers to Mihirakula about 530 A.D., as a powerful and proud king but he was forced to bow to Yaśodharman before 533 A. D. Therefore, the defeat of Mihirakula may be placed in 531-32 A.D.

From the Mandsor inscription[4] of V. S. 589, it is known that the country between the Vindhya and Pāriyātra (Arāvalī) mountains, was governed by one Nirdosha, of the Naigama family, who was a *Rājasthānīya* appointed by Yaśodharman, and who had his headquarters at Daśapura. This post of *Rājasthānīya* seems to be *hereditary*, because the predecessor of Nirdosha, Abhayadatta, was his father. He protected the region comprising of many countries, which were presided over by his own councillors. A fragmentary inscription[5] of about the sixth century A. D. discovered at Chitor, records certain pious deeds (probably the building of some shrines), of Varāha's grandson, who was the *Rājasthānīya* (governor), of Daśapura and Madhyamā. If Varāha is the same as Varāhadāsa, who was the ancestor of *Rājasthānīya* Abhayadatta, the *Rājasthānīya* of the Chitor inscription also belonged to the Naigama family. The Chitor inscription may prove the rule of the Aulikaras over Madhyamikā.

Scholars are not unanimous about the capital of the later Aulikaras. V. V. Mirashi[6] suggested that the later Aulikara kings, Ādityavardhana, Dravyavardhana and Viṣṇuvardhana,

1. IHI, p. 33.
2. The Decline of the Kingdom of Magadha, p. 117. The Rev. Father Heras held that Yaśodharman defeated Mihirakula in Malwa earlier than his defeat by Bālāditya. (IHQ, pp. 1 ff.)
3. IA, XXXIV, pp. 73 ff.
4. CII, III, pp. 146 f.
5. EI, XXXIV, p. 55.
6. IHQ, XXXIII, No. 4, p. 315.

ruled not from Daśapura, but from Ujjayinī. A stanza from Varāhamihira's *Bṛihatsaṁhitā* mentions *Mahārāja* Dravyavardhana as an *Avantika nṛipa*, i. e. a king of Avanti. Avanti is a synonym of Ujjayinī. From the Mandsor inscription (V.S. 589)of Yaśodharman, we know that his *Rājasthānīya* had his headquarters at Daśapura. This clearly indicates that Yaśodharman himself was not ruling from Daśapura, but from some other place, such as Ujjayinī.

D. C. SIRCAR[1] holds that Daśapura continued to be the capital of the Aulikaras. Avanti does not indicate Ujjayinī, but the country or the people. The Mandsor inscription does not mention the headquarters of Nirdosha being at Daśapura, which he could have had. The two inscriptions of the Aulikaras were found at Mandsor, and others in its neighbourhood, but not at Ujjain. From the two stanzas in the inscription of Bandhuvarman and Ādityavardhana, it is clear that their capital was Daśapura.

It seems that Yaśodharman was in power for short duration. He rose and fell in meteoric fashion between 530 and 540 A. D., and his empire perished with him. Shortly after the great *coup* of Yaśodharman, and perhaps as an inevitable consequence of it, the rise of several powerful feudatory principalities can be traced in the very heart of Gupta empire. Among them, the later Guptas and the Maukharis are of importance.

LATER GUPTAS :—

The lineage and the ancestral home of the Later Guptas is not definitely known. Some connect them with the Imperial Guptas, because all the names of the kings except Ādityasena, bear the suffix, Gupta. Most of their inscriptions are found in Magadha; but in their inscriptions, they do not claim imperial dynasty. The name ending may be accidental, or as a result of imitation, and without much significance. As the early rulers, namely Kṛishṇagupta and Harshagupta, were called by simple titles, '*nṛipati*' and '*Śrī*' respectively, this proves that the family had modest origins. They might have been distantly related to the Imperial Guptas.

1. IHQ, XXXV, p. 10.

D. C. Sircar[1] holds the view that the Later Guptas are Mālavas by nationality. This view does not seem to be correct. As the Later Guptas ruled over the Mālava territory, they were known as Mālavas after the name of the region.

There is no doubt that the Later Gupta rulers, from Ādityasena to Jīvitagupta, ruled from Magadha, but the place of the early rulers, from Kṛishṇagupta to Mādhavagupta, is full of controversy. R. Hoernle[2] is of the view that they were a branch of the Imperial Gupta family ruling over Eastern Malwa. C. V. Vaidya,[3] R. K. Mookerji[4], Ray Chaudhuri[5] and Edward A. Piers[6] advocate that Malwa was the home of the Later Guptas. R.N.Saletore[7] also thinks that the Later Guptas had their centre in Malwa, and extended their influence eastward coming into conflict with the Maukharis. This theory is based on two main conclusions :—

(1) Mādhavagupta of the Aphsad inscription,[8] is identical with Mādhavagupta, the Mālava *Rājaputra* of Bāṇa[9], and therefore his father and predecessors were kings of Malwa.

(2) The Imperial Guptas were the masters of Magadha and Northern Bengal down to the sixth century A.D. Afterwards, the sovereignty of the Maukharis in Magadha is proved by epigraphical evidence, thus showing that the Later Guptas were gone.

J. F. Fleet[10] believes that the Later Guptas originally belonged to Magadha. The same is the view of R. S. Tripathi[11] and B. P. Sinha[12], and they give the following arguments :— (1) The victory of Mahāsenagupta on the banks of the

1. Ancient Malwa and the Vikramāditya Tradition, p. 17.
2. JRAS, 1903, p. 551 ff.
3. HMHI, I, p. 24.
4. Harsha, pp. 53-56.
5. PHAI, 4th Edn, pp. 492-93.
6. The Maukharis, pp. 152-53.
7. Life in the Gupta Age, p. 53.
8. CII, III, No. 42, pp. 201 ff.
9. Harshacharita (CT), p. 119.
10. CII, III, No. 42, pp. 205 ff
11. Malaviya Com. Vol., pp. 261 ff.
12. The Decline of the Kingdom of Magadha, pp. 133-156.

Lauhitya gives rise to strong belief, that he was already master of Magadha and North Bengal. The Maukhari rule over Magadha was established in the later years of Mahāsenagupta. It was not possible for Mahāsenagupta to extend his authority up to Lauhitya from his centre in Malwa at the cost of Maukharis, who dominated Uttara Pradesh. His control of Magadha and Gauḍa was necessary before the Maukharis could conquer Magadha in the time of Sarvavarman.

(2) There is also the positive testimony of epigraphy. The Aphsaḍ inscription of Ādityasena, describes the exploits of Jīvitagupta on the seashore, and the Himalayan region. This clearly shows that the centre of his activity was near Bengal rather than in far off Malwa.

(3) The Later Guptas could not have ruled over Malwa at this time, because the Aulikaras were very powerful.

(4) Harsha awarded his friend Mādhavagupta with the kingdom of Magadha after it came into his possession. It confirms that Magadha was the ancestral home of the family of Mādhavagupta.

The Later Gupta dynasty starts with Kṛishṇagupta (490-505 A.D.). The Aphsad inscription[1] gives some information about him and his successors. He was victorious over his foes, who may be identified with the Hūṇas. He was a contemporary of Harivarman, the founder of the Maukhari line of Kanauj. Both established mutual relations; Kṛishṇagupta married his daughter with Ādityavarman, son of Harivarman. Kṛishṇagupta was succeeded by Harshagupta (505-525 A.D.). As a loyal feudatory of Imperial Guptas, he participated in the terrible contests against the Hūṇas.

Jīvitagupta I (525-545 A.D.) was more important than his predecessors, and he assumed the title '*Kshitīśa-Chūḍāmaṇi*'. His campaigns in the Himalayan regions, and in south-western Bengal, were probably made ostensibly in the name of the emperor, though really they increased his own power and prestige. His exploits were referred to as superhuman deeds.

1. CII, III, pp. 201 ff.

The son and successor of Jīvitagupta was Kumāragupta (540-560 A.D.) He had to fight against Īśānavarman who by defeating the Āndhras, the Śulikas, and the Gauḍas, had increased his power and prestige.[1] He assumed the title of *Mahārājādhirāja*. Kumā agupta was also ambitious. The families of the Maukharis and the Later Guptas, which were friendly, became bitter rivals. Īśānavarman was decisively defeated after 554 A. D., the date of the Harah inscription. Kumāragupta assumed independence and the imperial titles.

Kumāragupta was succeeded by his son Dāmodaragupta, who fought against the Maukharis, as known from the Aphsaḍ inscription. Dāmodaragupta's father, Kumāragupta, fought and defeated Īśānavarman. It is possible that after the death of Kumāragupta, he might have made another attempt to recover his lost prestige. It appears more likely that the Maukhari ruler, whom Dāmodaragupta fought, was Sarvavarman. R. S. Tripathi[2] and N. Ray[3] hold that after this defeat, the later Guptas retired to Malwa. R. G. Basak also holds that Dāmodaragupta was defeated by the Maukhari king. The inscription clearly mentions that the Maukhari army was defeated. The death of Dāmodaragupta does not mean that he was defeated. If Mahāsenagupta retired to Malwa immediately after the alleged defeat and death of his father, his victory over Susthitavarman, king of Kāmarūpa, cannot easily be explained.

In order to consolidate his position against the repeated invasions of the Maukharis, Mahāsenagupta contracted matrimonial alliance with the Vardhanas of Thāneśvara. He married his sister *Mahāsenaguptā* with Ādityavardhana. This alliance was advantageous to both. He felt reassured of the Western frontier for some time, and it acted as a deterrent on the Maukhari policy of aggression. After making his position secure in the west, he marched against Susthitavarman, the king of Kāmarūpa, and defeated him, as is known from the Aphsaḍ inscription.

1. EI, XIV, pp. 110 ff.
2. THK, pp. 44-45.
3. Calcutta Review, 1928, pp. 201 ff.

But Mahāsenagupta soon fell on hard times. From the Deo-Baranārk inscription[1], it is clear that Sarvavarman succeeded in making himself master of at least a part of the kingdom of Magadha. His successor, Avantivarman, is also referred to as *Parameśvara* in the same inscription. The seals of Sarvavarman, his son Avantivarman, and the latter's son, Śuva or Śucha, have been found in Nalanda.[2] Thus, Mahāsenagupta lost Magadha to the hereditary enemy, the Maukharis.

The Mahākūṭa pillar inscription of Maṅgaleśa attributes to Kīrtivarman the victory over Magadha. Kīrtivarman's rival in Magadha might have been Mahāsenagupta. Thus, pressed on all sides by powerful enemies, like the Maukharis, the Chālukyas and the Gauḍas, Mahāsenagupta left the ancestral country of Magadha, and retired to Malwa in about 582 A.D.

According to R. S. TRIPATHI[3], RAY CHAUDHURI,[4] D.C. SIRCAR[5] and B. C. LAW[6], the 'Mālava' of Mahāsenagupta denoted eastern Malwa. This view is based on the commentary of the *Kāmasūtra* of the late period. B.P. SINHA[7] tried to prove that Mālava of the *Harshacharita* and the *Kādambarī* should be identified with the kingdom of Ujjain as described by Yuan Chwang. It probably extended to Eran in the East.

When the Later Gupta king, Mahāsenagupta, retired to Malwa, he was certainly the king of Malwa, with its capital of Ujjain. Ujjain was one of the most famous cities of the Gupta empire. It might have served as a capital for sometime. After Yaśodharman, there was no barrier for the Later Guptas. There was no hostility between the Maitrakas and the Guptas. There was no political or geographical barrier to Mahāsenagupta's retirement to Malwa, because

1. CII, III, No. 96, p. 218 f.
2. EI, XXI, pp. 73 ff; Ibid, XXIV, pp. 283 ff.
3. THK, p. 46.
4. PHAI, p. 512.
5. JASBL, XI, pp. 69 ff.
6. Ancient Indian Tribes, II, p. 41.
7. The Decline of the Kingdom of Magadha, pp. 179-88.

Malwa was traditionally the Gupta province, and Ujjain the Gupta city.

Ray Chaudhuri[1] thinks, that as the Kalachuris were in possession of Ujjain, and after them the Maitrakas held it, there was no place for Mahāsenagupta there. But the view appears to be erroneous. The Kalachuris came into possession of Ujjain in 595 A.D., and were masters of Vidiśā in 608-9 A.D. There can be no contradiction involved in holding that Mahāsenagupta ruled Mālava, with Ujjain as the capital, from 582-95 A.D.

Mahāsenagupta was not allowed peace in his new home at Malwa. From the Abhonā plates[2] of Śaṅkaragaṇa, dated 347(595-96 A.D.), it is known that the Kalachuri king, Śaṅkaragaṇa, occupied Ujjain. In his plate, and that of his successors[3], he is referred to by epithets traditionally peculiar to Samudragupta, and the Imperial Guptas in general. These epithets were assumed by Śaṅkaragaṇa after the conquest of Ujjain, where the Gupta traditions were still continuing. The ruler defeated by Śaṅkaragaṇa was Mahāsenagupta.

B. A. Saletore[4] thinks that Mahāsenagupta was victorious over Śaṅkaragaṇa, or at any rate, the latter was not completely successful against the king of Malwa, because Buddharāja, the son of Śaṅkaragaṇa, issued a grant from the victorious camp Vidiśā in 608-09 A. D. That Buddharāja was defeated by the Chālukya ruler Maṅgaleśa, is known from the Mahākūṭa pillar inscription.[5] Prabhākaravardhana, the ruler of Thāneśvara and nephew of Mahāsenagupta, might have joined the Chālukyas against the Kalachuris, identified with the *Lāṭas* of the *Harshacharita*. He made efforts to restore the country of Mālava to Mahāsenagupta, but was unsuccessful.

However, the misfortunes of the Kalachuri king Budharāja, at the hands of the Chālukyas, offered a godsent opportunity to Devagupta, who was a relative of Mahāsenagupta, to

1. PHAI, pp. 534-35.
2. EI, IX, pp. 296 ff.
3. Ibid, VI, pp. 294 and XII, pp. 30.
4. Life in the Gupta Age, pp. 60, 68.
5. IA, XIX, pp. 7 ff.

declare himself as king of Mālava. This destroyed the chances of Kumāragupta and Mādhavagupta, sons of Mahāsenagupta, and cousins of Prabhākaravardhana. The latter, therefore, waged a war against the king of Malwa, who was Devagupta and not Budharāja, as supposed by D. C. GANGULI[1], nor Śilāditya of *Molā-po*, as believed by R. HOERNLE.[2] Prabhākaravardhana, though failing to gain the throne of Mālava for his cousins, succeeded in rescuing them, and appointed them as companions to his sons Rājyavardhana and Harshavardhana. Bāṇa refers to Prabhākaravardhana's war against the Mālava king in clearly exaggerated terms. He is described as an axe to the creeper of Mālava glory.[3] This Mālava campaign may be dated in about 603 A .D.

Devagupta, with the help of Śaśāṅka, the king of Gauḍa, invaded the Maukhari kingdom and killed its ruler Grahavarman. When Prabhākaravardhan's son, and successor of Thāneśvara, heard this news, he rushed forward with his forces to take revenge on the enemies of his brother-in-law Grahavarman. He defeated the forces of the Mālava king, Devagupta, and perhaps killed him; but he was treacherously slaughtered by the latter's ally, the king of Gauḍa, Śaśāṅka.[4] It seems that the defeat of Devagupta of East Malwa, in his struggle with the Pushyabhūtis, about 605 A. D., facilitated the Kalachuri conquest of that country. It is possible to think that shortly afterwards, Harsha succeeded in extending his power over East Malwa, although the extirpation of the Kalachuri rule from the Western part of that country seems to have been mainly due to the Maitrakas.[5]

There is evidence to show that it was the Maitrakas of Valabhi who ousted the Kalachuris from Western Malwa. Yuan Chwang speaks of the rule of Maitraka Śīlāditya (i.e. Śīlāditya Dharmāditya whose known dates range between 605 and 609

1. JBORS, XIX, pp. 399 ff.
2. JRAS, 1903, p. 551 ff.
3. HC (CT), p. 101, Text (Parab.), p. 120.
4. This is known to us from the *Harshacharita* as well as from the Copper-plate grants of Harsha.
5. WATTERS : On Yuan Chwang, II, p. 242.

A.D.) over *Mo-lā-po*. Dharmāditya's younger brother and successor, Kharagraha I, issued two grants from Ujjayinī in 616 A. D.[1], while two charters of his son, Dhruvasena Bālāditya, found in the former Ratlam state in Malwa, and dated 639 and 640 A.D., record the grant of land in the *Mālavaka bhukti*[2]

ADMINISTRATIVE ORGANIZATION

When Chandragupta II conquered Eastern Malwa from the Western Kshatrapas, he annexed this region and it became one of the provinces of his empire. It is said that besides Pāṭaliputra, the Guptas made Ujjain a second capital, in order to control the Western provinces which lay far off from Pāṭaliputra. During this period, Daśapura was the capital of the Aulikaras. Eran remained associated with the Guptas from the time of Samudragupta.

MONARCHICAL GOVERNMENT :—

During this period, the republics gradually disappeared, and a monarchical type of government was established. There was hereditary monarchy, and the doctrine of the divine right of kings became more and more popular. The king was now regarded as a divinity[3]—*Achintya Purusha* 'the Incomprehensible Being', *Dhanada-Varuṇendrāntaka-Sama* the equal of Kuvera, Varuṇa, Indra and Yama, *loka-dhāma-deva*, a god dwelling on earth and *Paramadaivata*, 'the supreme deity'. Divinity does not invest the king with infallibility. The king can become a successful ruler, only if he waits upon the elders, studies the art of government, cultivates religious precepts and protects his subjects. Great emphasis was laid on the training of princes in political science and in military art.

The emperor gave up the modest title of '*Rājan*' and adopted a title of high-sounding style. From the Udayagiri cave inscription[4], Chandragupta II is known to have assumed the title of '*Paramabhaṭṭāraka Mahārājādhirāja*.' The Jaina

1. CII, IV, p. 47.
2. Bhandarkar's List, Nos. 1346-47; EI, VII, pp. 188 ff.
3. PHAI, p. 559.
4. CII, III, p. 25.

inscriptions[1] of Vidiśā, refer to *Mahārājādhirāja* Rāmagupta. The Eran Stone Boar inscription[2] refers to the reign of *Mahārājadhirāja* Toramāṇa. The Aulikara king, Yaśodharman Vishṇuvardhana in his inscription[3] dated 532 A.D. (V.S. 589), represents himself as enjoying the title of *Rājādhirāja Parameśvara*. The feudatory and vassal rulers were known by the simple title of *Mahārāja*. The ruler of the Sanakānika tribe, who was a feudatory of Chandragupta II, assumed the title of '*Mahārāja*'. The Aulikara ruler, Naravarman, has been given the title of *Mahārāja* in the Bihara Kotra[4] inscription, and Prabhākara has been called '*Bhūmipati*' in the Mandsor inscription.[5]

Next in rank to the Emperor stood the Crown Prince. The crown usually passed to the eldest son, who was installed to the office of the heir-apparent when he came of age and finished his training. Younger brothers of the crown prince were usually appointed to the posts of Provincial governors. Govindagupta, a brother of Kumāragupta I, was the governor of Malwa under his father Chandragupta II.[6] Ghaṭotkachagupta held the office of governor of the province of Airikiṇa, which included Tumbavana.[7] He was probably either the son or younger brother of Kumāragupta.

There were some feudatory states in Malwa owing allegiance to the Guptas. The ruler of the Sanakānika tribe was a feudatory of Chandragupta II.[8] The early Aulikara rulers, such as Viśvavarman aud Bandhuvarman of Daśapura, seem to have been feudatories of the Gupta emperors, but later they became independent, and made land grants without the permission of the imperial power. The Aulikaras had their own feudatories. King Gauri of the Māṇavāyaṇi family, who ruled

1. Journal of the Oriental Institute, Baroda, XVIII, p. 247.
2. CII, III, pp. 159 f.
3. Ibid, pp. 152 ff.
4. EI, XXXVI, pp. 130 ff.
5. Ibid, XXVII, pp. 12-18.
6. Ibid.
7. Ibid, XXVI, p. 117.
8. CII, III, p. 25.

in V.S. 547 (490-91 A.D.) over Chhoti-Sādari, recognized the suzerainty of Ādityavardhana of the Aulikara family.[1] During the reign of Budhagupta, his feudatory, Suraśmichandra, was governing the country lying between the river Kālindi or Yamunā, and Narmadā.[2] *Mahārāja* Mātṛivishṇu is known to have exercised his authority under the gupta Provincial Governor. When this area was occupied by the Hūṇa ruler Toramāṇa, Dhanyavishṇu, younger brother of Mātrivishṇu, continued in the post of his brother.[3] It shows that Toramāṇa left intact, not only the old system of provincial administration, but also the ancient official families.

MINISTRY :—

The king carried on the administration with the help of a ministry. Ministers were known as *Mantrins* or *Sachivas*, whose offices were often hereditary. One such minister was Śābha, who was the '*Sāṁdhi-vigrahika*', Minister for Peace and War, of Chandragupta II, and who accompanied the emperor in his campaign against the western Kshatrapas.[4] There was no clear division between civil and military officials. The same person could be *Sāṁdhi-Vigrahika*, *Kumārāmātya* (cadet minister), and *Mahā-daṇḍa-nāyaka* (Great Commandant of the Army) and a *Mantrin* could become a '*Mahā-balādhikṛita*' Chief Commander of forces. Mayūrākshaka, who built the temples of Vishṇu and the Divine Mothers, and a huge well in 423 A.D. at Gaṅgadhāra, was a minister of the Aulikara king Viśvavarman.[5]

ADMINISTRATIVE DIVISIONS :—

The empire was divided into a number of provinces, styled *Deśas*, *Bhuktis*, etc., which were sub-divided into Districts, called *Pradeśas* or *Vishayas*. Among *Deśas*, one embracing Eastern Malwa was known as '*Kālindī Narmadayor Madhya*', the territory lying between the Yamunā and Narmadā.[6] Among *Pradeśas* or *Vishayas*, mention is made of Airikiṇa in Eastern Malwa,

1. EI, XXX, pp. 120 ff.
2. CII, III, p. 89.
3. Ibid, III, pp. 159.
4. Ibid, III, pp. 31 f.
5. Ibid, p. 74 ff.
6. Ibid, p. 89.

called *Pradeśa* in Samudragupta's Eran inscription,[1] and *Vishaya* in that of Toramāṇa.[2]

In the Barwani plate[3] of the year 167 and the Bagh plate[4] of Subandhu, the *pathakas* of Udumbaragartā and Dāsilakapatha have been respectively mentioned. Udumbaragartā may be Umarbar, now a small village on the western border of Barwani District, and Dāsilakapalli may be identical with Deswālia, which lies about twenty two kilometers south of the Bagh caves. Daśapura *Vishaya* of Mālavaka, has been mentioned in the Ratlam plates[5] of Dhruvasena II in the (Gupta) *Saṁvat* 321.

The *Deśas* were governed by officers called *Goptṛis*, or wardens of the Marches, as suggested by the passage, '*Sarveshu Deśeshu Vidhāya Goptṛīn*' or having appointed *Goptṛis* in all *Deśas*. The *Bhuktis* were usually governed by *Uparikas* or *Uparika Mahārājas*, who were apparently sometimes princes of the Imperial family e.g. *Rājaputradevabhaṭṭāraka*. Govindagupta, governor of Tirabhukti, has been mentioned in the Basārh seals[6]. Ghaṭotkachagupta mentioned in the Tumain inscription, probably held such a post. The office of *Vishaya-pati* or District officer, was held by Imperial officials like the *Kumārāmātyas* and *Āyuktakas*, as well as feudatory *Mahārājas* like Mātṛivishṇu of Eran[7].

Rājasthānīya was the governor of the Province. A record[8] of King Vishṇuvardhana mentions a certain Abhayadatta, who as *Rājasthānīya* (Viceroy), governed the tract bounded by the Eastern Vindhyas, the Pāriyātra (Western Vindhyas), and the Ocean. Abhayadatta was assisted in the administration of his many districts (*Deśas*) by his own Ministers (*Sachivas*). It thus appears that the governor of Vishṇuvardhana was at liberty to select his own subordinates in charge of

1. CII, III, p. 20.
2. Ibid, pp. 159 f.
3. Ibid, IV, p. 17.
4. Ibid, p. 19.
5. ASI, 1902-03, p. 232.
6. Ibid, 1903-04, pp. 102-107.
7. CII, III, p. 89.
8. Ibid, pp. 152 ff.

districts. A fragmentary inscription[1] of about the sixth century A.D., discovered at Chitor, records certain pious deeds, (probably the building of some shrines) of Varāha's grandson, who has the *Rājasthānīya* of the Aulikara family ruling over the territory around Daśapura and Madhyamā. Nagarī appears to have been the head quarters of a district of the Aulikara kingdom in the sixth Century A. D.

The governors and district officers were no doubt helped by officials and dignitaries,[2] like the '*Dāṇḍika, Chauroddharaṇika* and *Daṇḍapāśika* (apparently judicial and police officials), *Nagara-śreshṭhī* (President or Alderman of a city guild), *Sārthavāha* (caravan-leader or merchant), *Prathamakulika* (foreman of artisans), *Prathama-Kāyastha* (the chief scribe), *Pusta-pāla* (record keeper), and others. Every *Vishaya* consisted of a number of *grāmas* or villages, which were administered by headmen and other functionaries, styled as *Grāmikas, Mahattaras* and *Bhojakas.*

CITY POLICE :—

The city police (*Nagara-rakshādhikṛita*)[3] was charged with the duty of patrolling the streets for maintaining law and order. At convenient points in the city, there were stations for the policemen, and there were inspectors in charge of police-posts. The Chief Police Officer of the city seems to have been the '*Nāgarika*', who was connected with the work of the police within the precincts of the city[4]. In the *Śakuntalā* of Kālidāsa, this official is depicted leading a criminal to the court of justice with the help of guards. In the *Vikramorvaśīya*, he is connected with the city administration. He is entrusted with his police-work by the king, who commands him to search out offenders. There are references also to negligence of duty.

SYSTEM OF JUSTICE :—

There was an elaborate system of justice[5]. The seat of

1. EI, XXXIV, pp. 53 ff.
2. PHAI, p. 561.
3. B. C. Law Volume I, p. 400 f., Ujjainī in *Mṛichchhakaṭika.*
4. India in Kālidāsa, p. 142.
5. B. C. Law Volume, p. 400. 'Ujjaini in *Mṛichchhakaṭika*'.

justice was known as *Vyavahārāsana*, *Dharmāsana* and *Dharmasthāna*. The Court of justice was presided over by a judge, known as *Adhikaraṇika*, assisted by a body of assessors, among whom were a Kāyastha, clever in recording the proceedings in court, a *Śreshṭhin* or President of the Merchants' guild, expert in mercantile law and the practices of commerce, and perhaps one or more interpreters translating the various dialects used by the miscellaneous people who resorted to the court of justice. There do not appear to have been any lawyers on behalf of either party in the suits. The judge's duty consisted in taking evidence, ascertaining the facts, applying the law to the case before him, and giving his findings on the issues. He could not however pass final judgement, which was in the province of the king. But the judge could submit his recommendations to the king.

OTHER OFFICERS :—

There are some literary works[1] which throw interesting sidelights on the administrative organization, because they mention several officers—*Dharmāsanika* (judge), *Prāḍvivāka* (*dharmādhyaksha*), *Pradhyāti* (judge), *Śāsanādhikṛita* (one who issued the charters of the king), *Balādhikṛita* (military officer), *Mahāpratīhāra* (the great Chamberlain), *Senāpati* (Commander-in-chief), *Adhikaraṇa* (judge), *Śrāvaṇika* (one who serves summons), *Mahātalavara* (chief general or local chief), *Baladarśaka* (one who received debts by force) and *Mahāmātra* (civil officer). These names, as mentioned in literary works, prove that these offices were actually held.

CULTURE

The Gupta age brought in an era in which Malwa regained a new political consciousness and solidarity, after a long period of political disintegration and foreign domination. Some of the rulers of the Gupta dynasty were great conquerors, who tried to bring about the unification of the country by their conquests. In order to consolidate their empire, they established an efficient administration, which was well orga-

1. *Padmaprābhṛitakam* and *Pādatāḍitakam*, see *Chaturbhāṇī*, p. 84.

nized both at the centre and in provinces. Peace and security made possible by the Government, led to a remarkable development in trade, art, literature and the sciences, which in turn, marked the Golden Age of India.

RELIGION:—

This period is important for the history of religion, because it is marked by many important changes. The old Vedic *Saṁhitās* and the *Brāhmaṇas* ceased to be the popular religious literature, and their place was taken by the *Purāṇas*. The old Vedic pantheon and sacrifices gradually disappeared, and Vaishṇavism and Śaivism became very popular. There was a diversion from the abstract to the concrete in the form of worship. This led to the construction of many images of different gods. Vishṇu and Śiva established their unquestioned supremacy over other gods, and the rest became subsidiary to them. Even the austere and rigid morality of Buddhism and Jainism gave way to devotion, and images of Buddha and the Jaina Tīrthaṅkaras began to be constructed. There was religious toleration among the followers of the different religions, which flourished side by side. The rulers showed reverence and respect to all religions.

VAISHṆAVISM:—

Vaishṇavism became popular because of the patronage extended by the Gupta rulers, who took pride in calling themselves *Paramabhāgavata*. An important feature of this religion was the popular worship of *Avatāras*, or the incarnations of Vishṇu, so their temples were constructed and images were placed in them.

The Eran Stone inscription[1] of Samudragupta, most probably, refers to the construction of a Vaishṇava temple or image in the fourth century A. D. The Udayagiri inscription[2] of 401-402 A.D. records the gift or dedication, to a Vaishṇava cave, by a Mahārāja of the Sanakānika tribe or family, who was a feudatory of Chandragupta II. The Gaṅgadhāra inscription[3] of 423-24 A.D. records that Mayūrākshaka, minister

1. CII, III, p. 20.
2. Ibid, p. 25.
3. Ibid. p. 74 ff.

of the Aulikara ruler Viśvavarman, built a temple of Vishṇu. The Eran stone inscription[1] of 484-85 A. D. records the erection of the column called a *dhvaja-stambha* of the god Vishṇu under the name of Janārdana, by Mātṛivishṇu and Dhanyavishṇu, for the merit of his parents during the reign of Budhagupta, whose feudatory, Suraśmichandra, was governing this region. The Eran inscription[2] of the first year of Toramāṇa, refers to the temple in which the Boar stands, built by Dhanyavishṇu, younger brother of the deceased *Mahārāja* Mātṛivishṇu. From these inscriptions, it is clear that Vaishṇavism was prevalent at Eran and Bhilsa. Some existing monuments at these places also confirm its popularity. At Tumain,[3] an old structure, originally a Vaishṇavite temple, and the interesting image of Balarāma, have been found. A stone sculpture of Vishṇu in the Gupta style, was discovered in the excavations at Pawaya.[4]

Ujjayinī was an important centre of Vaishṇavism. From the *Padmaprābhṛitakam* and the *Pādatāḍitakam*,[5] it is known that there were followers of Vaishṇavism known as *Chauksha*. This sect was also known by the name of *ekāyana*. There were temples of Kāmadeva and Pradyumna; it is possible that both names might be the name of one and the same temple. For the Vaishṇava devotees, Aṅkapāda was a sacred shrine, linked with the memory of Śrīkṛishṇa and Balarāma in their childhood.[6]

ŚAIVISM :—

Śaivism became more dominant than Vaishṇavism in Malwa. Kālidāsa[7] refers to Jyotirliṅga, called Mahākāla, at Ujjain, where people assembled in the evening for worship. He also mentions the holy place of Chaṇḍeśvara, the Lord of three worlds. The *Matsyapurāṇa*, *Nṛisiṁhapurāṇa*, *Śivapurāṇa*

1. CII, III, p. 89.
2. Ibid, pp. 159 f.
3. ASI, 1918-19, p. 22.
4. ARADGS, 1940-41, p. 17
5. *Chaturbhāṇī*, p. 82.
6. *Skanda Purāṇa*, V, 27.
7. *Meghadūta*, 33-34.

and *Skandapurāṇa*, deal in detail with the glorification and mythological accounts of the deity of Mahākāla of Ujjain. The old temple was vast and massive, and there was much of gold and jewellery. From the *Avantikhaṇḍa* of the *Skandapurāṇa*,[1] it is clear that Śaivism became so popular that the entire area of Ujjain was full of Śiva-liṅgas. Eighty four liṅgas, however, have been enumerated as the principal Śiva-liṅgas at Ujjayinī, also called Siddha liṅgas and yoga liṅgas, which rose into prominence during the past eighty-four *Kalpas*, and each liṅga is known as *Īśvara*.[2] There are also six *Guhya liṅgas* or *Guhyasthānas* viz. *Śukreśvara*, *Chūḍāmaṇīśvara* and *Chaṇḍīśvara*.[3] Besides these *Īśvaras*, there were eight Bhairavas, eleven Rūdras, twelve Ādityas, six Vināyakas and twenty-four Mātrīs, in the sacred Avanti.[4] There were guardian deities of the different quarters—Piṅgaleśvara to the east, Kāyāvarohaṇeśvara to the south, Bilveśvara to the West and Durdarśeśvara to the north, with Mahākāleśvara as the principal deity (Kshetrādhipati) at the centre.[5]

One Udayagiri cave inscription[6] records the excavation of the cave as a temple of the God Śiva under the name of Śambhu, by the order of a certain Vīrasena, otherwise called Śobha, one of the ministers of Chandragupta II. From the Mandsor inscription[7] of Yaśodharman, it is clear that he was a follower of Śaivism. At Mandsor, a large and imposing sculpture of Śiva has been discovered.[8] The original temple to which it belonged, has disappeared. That the Hūṇa ruler Mihirakula was a follower of Śaivism, is known from the Mandsor inscription[9] of Yaśodharman. Mihirakula, who did not bow his head to any one except Sthāṇu, saluted him.

1. S.P.V, 39.3; also 70.88.9.
2. Ibid, 48, 46-7.
3. Ibid, V.43.
4. Ibid, V.1.14-15.
5. Ibid, V.81, 29-33.
6. CII, III, p. 35.
7. Ibid, pp. 146 f.
8. M. B. Garde : Archaeology in Gwalior, p. 24.
9. CII, III, pp. 146 f.

On his coins,[1] we find the symbols of Trident and Bull, and the legend, '*Jayatu Vṛishaḥ*', 'victory to bull, the mount of Śiva'.

OTHER BRĀHMANICAL RELIGIONS AND RELIGIOUS BELIEFS :—

Sun worship was prevalent in some areas of Malwa. From the Mandsor inscription[2] it is known that the guild of silk weavers who migrated from Lāṭa, built the temple of the Sun in V.S. 493 (437-38 A.D.). A part of this temple fell into disrepair, and was restored by the same guild in V. S. 529 (473-74 A.D.). The Gwalior stone inscription[3] of the fifteenth year of the reign of Mihirakula, records the building of a temple of the Sun by a person named Mātṛicheṭa, on the mountain Gopā, for increasing the religious merit of his parents and himself. At Kapithaka (Kayatha), there was a Sun temple of Varāhamihira's time. A torso of the Sun recovered from Kayatha may belong to this temple.

Temples or images of Mahishāsuramardinī, another form of Durgā, have been found at Udayagiri and Bhumara[4]. The Gaṅgdhāra inscription[5] of 423-24 A.D. of the Aulikara ruler Viśvavarman, mentions the temple of the Divine Mothers built by Mayūrākshaka, minister of Viśvavarman. This inscription proves the prevalence of a Tantric form of religion at this place. There was worship of Sapta Mātrikas at Pathari in the fifth century A.D. Two images of Gaṅgā standing on *Makara* were found at Vidiśā. The temple of Harasiddhidevī of Ujjain was well-known. The *Māhātmya* of this goddess has been described in the *Avanti-Khaṇḍa*, where the sacrifice of a buffalo for the goddess has been prescribed. Vikramāditya is said to have practised austerities in this temple for several years.

The worship of Nāgas, as also of Yakshas, continued during this period. There was a Yaksha temple at Padmāvatī,

1. CCIM, I, p. 236.
2. CII, III, pp. 81 ff.
3. Ibid, pp. 162 f.
4. ASC, X, p. 50.
5. CII, III, p. 74 ff.

near Gwalior. The Pūrṇabhadra Śriṅgāṭaka Chaitya was in existence at Ujjain.[1]

The *Mṛichchhakaṭika*[2] also throws light on the religious beliefs of the people. They performed daily worship of the domestic deity. In rich families, priests were employed for worship. They offered an oblation of water with a prayer to the rising Sun at early dawn. People believed in superstitions such as faith in *Dākinī* (malignant female spirit), omens like the trembling of eyelids or throbbing of limbs, the crowing of crows on dry branches, or seeing snakes on the wayside. The omnipotence of fate was a universal belief, as also belief in the predictions of *siddhas*.

BUDDHISM :—

Though Gupta rulers were followers of Brahmanical religion, they were tolerant in matters of religion. Therefore Buddhism continued to prosper during this period. The new Mahāyāna sect of Buddhism was growing popular and began to attract the attention of the people. Sanchi and Bagha were the strongholds of Buddhism, where *stūpas* and temples were built and images placed in them. The Buddhist monks endeavoured to propagate their ideas.

Chandragupta II was himself a Vaishṇava, but his military officer Āmrakārdava, who accompanied him on his expedition to Malwa, was a Buddhist. The inscription[3] dated 412-13 A.D. of the *Mahārājādhirāja* Chandragupta II, records the grant of a village or a plot of land, called Īśvaravāsaka, and of a sum of twenty-five *dīnāras* or gold coins, to the Buddhist Saṁgha at the monastery of Kākanādaboṭa, i.e. Sanchi, by Āmrakārdava, son of Undāna, for the purpose of feeding mendicants and burning lamps at the *Ratnagṛiha*. The grant was made partly on behalf of the king and partly on behalf of Āmrakārdava himself. An inscription[4] of the fifth century A. D. on the pedestal of a standing figure at Sanchi, records the installation of an image by one belonging to the *Śūra-kula*.

1. *Chaturbhāṇī*, p. 82.
2. B. C. Law Volume, I, '*Ujjain in Mṛichchhakaṭika*', p. 406.
3. The Monuments of Sanchi, p. 388.
4. Ibid, p. 387.

A Copper plate inscription[1] of about 416-17 A. D. discovered in the debris of cave II at Bagh, records the grant of village Dasithakapalli, which king Subandhu of Māhishmatī, made to Buddhist monks for their maintenance, upkeep of the monastery, and worship of the Lord Buddha.

The Bihāra Koṭrā inscription[2] of 417-18 A. D., records the digging of a reservoir in the name of the Bhikshusaṁgha of the four quarters, for the quenching of the thirst of all beings. The gift was made by Vīrasena, son of Bhaṭṭimahara, in 417-18 A.D., during the reign of *Mahārāja* Naravarman of the Aulikara dynasty, Buddhism was prevalent at Tumain, because a *stūpa* was built during the Gupta period and it is still extant.

The Sanchi inscription[3] of 450-51 A. D. records an endowment of sixteen gold coins (*dīnāras*) to the Buddhist community residing in the monastery at Kākanāda-boṭa (sanchi). This was to be subdivided with twelve coins for feeding a monk each day, three coins for the jewel-house (*Ratna-gṛiha*), and one for the place of the four Buddhas (*Chatur-Buddhāsana*), in both cases for maintaining lamps. The grant was made by the *Upāsikā* Harisvāminī, the wife of the *Upāsaka* Sonasiddha. The four Buddhas are the four images in the *Pradakshiṇā-patha* adjoining the ground balustrade, one opposite each entrance. Another Sanchi inscription[4] of the fifth century A.D., records the gift of a Vajrapāṇi-pillar, two pillars of a gateway *maṇḍapa* or pavilion of a monastery, and a gateway, by one Rudrasiṁha, son of Gośūrasiṁhabala, the superintendent of a monastery.

Buddhism was followed by people even at Daśapura, the capital of the Aulikaras. The Mandsor inscription[5] of 467-68 A.D. records the construction of a *stūpa* by Dattabhaṭa, the commander of the forces of king Prabhākara. There was also the Lokottara *vihāra*, which was possibly the proper name of some local Buddhist monastery, probably named after the

1. IHI, XXI, No. 2.
2. EI, XXXVI, pp. 130 ff.
3. The Monuments of Sanchi, pp. 389-90.
4. Ibid, p. 390.
5. EI, XXVII, pp. 12-18.

Lokottaravādin sect of the Hīnayāna form of Buddhism.

Buddhism was also practised by people at Sanchi in the sixth century A.D. An inscription[1] records the gift of an image by Rekhagupta, and another[2] records an image donated by a person named Kulāditya.

Literary works throw an indirect light on the condition of Buddhism. From the *Mṛichchhakaṭika*[3], it is known, that Buddhism, though no longer the dominant religion, was still prevalent at Ujjain. The monastic discipline of Buddhism was still strict. The Buddhists still had their own religious establishments inhabited by monks and nuns. There was no ban on Buddhists attaining high honour and position in the State. The *Padma-Prābhritakam*[4] gives indirect references to the Vajrayāna form of Buddhism. The Dharmāraṇya *vihāra* existed at Ujjain.

The importance of Buddhism in Malwa is clear from the fact that a large number of Buddhist scholars[5] visited China between the fifth and the seventh century A.D. from this region, to study Buddhist lore. They also took with them a large collection of Buddhist texts, and translated some of them into the Chinese language. Guṇabhadra[6] was a noted Buddhist scholar who had specialized in *Abhidharma*. Originally he belonged to Central India, but went to China in 421 A. D. He remained there till his death in 468 A.D. and translated seventy-six texts into Chinese.

Both Upasūnya and Paramārtha[7] were from Ujjayinī, which was in that period a great centre of Sanskrit learning. Upasūnya went to China by the sea route. He worked there during half of the sixth century A.D. Paramārtha, who came to China in the same period (546-69), was also known as

1. The Monuments of Sanchi, p. 392.
2. Ibid, p. 394.
3. B. C. LAW Volume I, *Ujjainī in Mṛichchhakaṭika*, p. 400.
4. *Chaturbhāṇī*, p. 83.
5. Catalogue of the Chinese Translation of the Buddhist Tripiṭaka by BUNIGU, NANGIO, pp. 411, 416, 423 and 437.
6. India and China, p. 212; *Chīnī Bauddhadharma Kā Itihāsa*, p. 82.
7. Ibid, p. 43. Ibid, p. 94.

Guṇaratna. He was well-trained in all branches of Buddhist literature. He translated seventy Sanskrit texts into the Chinese language. Nālandayaśasa, Vinītaruchi and Atigupta of Ujjain,[1] visited China in the sixth century A.D. for the propagation of Buddhism. They are also credited with the translation work of some Buddhist texts from Sanskrit into Chinese.

Some Chinese scholars, such as Fahien, Hsuain-tai[2] and Yuan-Chwang, visited India to study Buddhism. Hsuan-tai is known to have come to Central India. At the time of Yuan Chwang's visit, Buddhism was in a state of decline at Ujjain. He noticed just one Buddhist *stūpa* in the neighbourhood of Ujjayinī, and saw *Deva* temples occupied by different sects.[3]

JAINISM :—

Jainism was not so prevalent as Buddhism in Malwa during this period. The earliest substantial evidence for the existence of this religion, is known from the three stone images[4] of Jaina Tīrthaṅkaras of the fourth or fifth century A.D. discovered at Vidiśā. From the inscriptions of these images, it is clear they were made by *Mahārājādhirāja* Rāmagupta at the preaching (*upadeśa*) of Chelukshamaṇa, son of Gokyāntī, and pupil of *Āchārya* Sarppasena Kshamaṇa, who was the grand pupil of the Jaina teacher Kshamāchārya. Though Rāmagupta was a follower of Brāhmanical religion, he extended his patronage to Jainism also, by erecting statues of the Jaina Tīrthaṅkaras.

The Udayagiri cave inscription[5] of 425-26 A.D. records the installation of an image of the Tīrthaṅkara Pārśvanātha by Śaṅkara, the disciple of saint Gośarman, who was the ornament of the image of *Āchārya* Bhadra. This inscription was found inside the cave which may have been a Jaina temple during

1. *Chīnī Bauddhadharma Kā Itihāsa*, pp. 128-134.
2. *Chavannes-Meimore 'Compose'* a *liepoque de la grande dynastie Tang* etc., p. 34.
3. Watters : On Yuan Chwang, II, p. 250.
4. Journal of the Oriental Institute, Baroda, XVIII, p. 247.
5. CII, III, No. 61.

the Gupta period. It seems that the region round about Vidiśā was a stronghold of Jainism. It is believed that the great Jaina philosopher, Siddhasena-divākara, lived at Ujjain.

ART AND ARCHITECTURE

The Gupta period is the golden age in the history of Malwa because the different forms of art, viz. architecture, sculpture, painting and others, attained a maturity, a balance, and a naturalness of expression. This art is marked by a parting of the ways. In one way, it is the age of the culmination and perfection of earlier phases and forms of art, but in another, it marks the ushering in of a new age, which is connected with the evolution of temple art. Thus it is a formative and creative period in the sphere of art.

ARCHITECTURE :—

Some literary works give information about the prosperous conditions of Ujjain and its ancient buildings, which are no longer in existence. Śūdraka speaks of the monasteries, parks, tanks, temples, wells and sacrificial posts of Ujjayinī. He gives eloquent description of the palace of Vasantasenā, the famous courtesan of this city, which consisted of eight courts. It is actually the picture of a typical mansion of a wealthy person. Kālidāsa[1] says that the city was like radiant piece of heaven on earth, where the gods had appeared from the upper region in order to enjoy the fruits of their merits.

The *Kathāsaritsāgara*,[2] which is the work of a later period, claims to describe the city as it existed in the time of Vikramāditya, who can be identified with Chandragupta II. The description in the *Kathāsaritsāgara* appears to have been handed down to its author by some existing Indian tradition. According to this work, the city was an ornament of the earth. It excelled even over Amarāvatī, tha city of gods, owing to its huge mansions, which were white like nectar.

In the *Kādambarī* of Bāṇa, Ujjayinī has also been noticed as prosperous city. According to this work, it was situated on

1. *Meghadūta*, 30.
2. *Kathāsaritsāgara*, 11, 31.

the bank of the river Śiprā, and was chief among the cities.[1] It was strongly fortified by a deep moat[2] and a high wall.[3] In the city, there were picture houses which were ornamented by the portraits of demons and gods, as also of celestials, like Siddhas, Gandharvas and Vidyādharas. By the great beauty of the palatial buildings, it had clearly surpassed even Amarāvatī, the city of gods, which was famous in Indian legend for its loftiness and splendour of appearance[4]. It also possessed an adjoining sub-town on its border, known as Śākhānagara, in order to accommodate the surplus population. Yuan Chwang[5] saw several *deva* temples at this place. Some *Purāṇas*[6] mention that the temple of Mahākāla was vast and massive, and there was much of gold and jewellery. The *Skandapurāṇa* describes a large number of temples of this place. Vatsabhaṭṭi, the author of the Mandsor inscription,[7] describes that the city of Daśapura was adorned with many beautiful temples and buildings.

Most of the ancient buildings have perished, but the remaining bulidings may be classified under two heads—(1) Caves and (2) Structural buildings.

(1) CAVE ARCHITECTURE :—

Specimens of cave architecture have been found at Bagh and Udayagiri. The Bagh caves are sacred to Buddhism, and those of Udayagiri are related to Brahmanical religion and Jainism. The architectural peculiarities of the Bagh caves, consist of large pillared halls, with small cells on both sides, porticos in front and chapels at the back. The pillars are massive and bear a variety of carved patterns. The architectural features of the Udayagiri caves, however, consist only of small cells with richly ornamented doorways, but the walls of the verandah bear sculptures.

1. *Kādambarī*, p. 88.
2. Ibid, p. 99.
3. Ibid, p. 99.
4. Ibid, p. 108.
5. Watters : On Yuan Chwang, II, p. 250.
6. *Matsyapurāṇa*, *Nṛisiṁhapurāṇa*, *Śivapurāṇa* and *Skandapurāṇa*.
7. CII, III, pp. 81 ff.

The Bagh caves situated at a distance of one hundred and forty-five kilometers from Indore by metal road, were excavated in a hill overlooking the Bagh river. Originally there were many caves, but owing to the weakness of the rock, they have been seriously damaged. As a result, only nine have survived, in a half-ruined condition, while the rest are either mere wreckages, or have totally disappeared. These caves are varied in character. Cave No. 3 is a pure *vihāra*, cave Nos. 2 and 4 are combinations of the *chaitya* and the vihāra, but cave No. 5 is neither a *chaitya* nor a *vihāra*, but is, perhaps, either a refectory or an oratory.

Scholars hold different views[1] about the date of these caves, which, from the point of view of architecture, occupy an intermediate position between the Nasik and Ajanta caves. On the basis of the copper plate grants of Subandhu, V.V. Mirashi[2] tried to fix the date at the end of the fourth century A. D. at the latest. This is also confirmed by the form of the object of worship in the *vihāras* excavated at Bagh.

In general plan and arrangement, these caves are similar to the Ajanta caves, but they have certain distinct features. They are, however, of a plainer and simpler type. Like the earlier *vihāras* at Nasik, the sanctuaries of the Bagh caves at the innermost end of the hall generally contain a *chaitya* instead of an image of the Buddha. They possess pillars along with the usual colonnade, inside the central hall, as additional support for the roof.

The most important cave is the Great *vihāra* (No. IV), known locally as the *Raṅgamahala*. It consists of a central hall, about ninety-six ft. square with a range of cells on all its sides except the front. The most interesting feature of the cave is supplied by a highly ornate porch, consisting of a

1. J. Fergusson and J. Burgess say in one place (The cave temples of India, p. 186) that the caves were excavated about 350 A. D. to 450, and in another (Ibid, p. 366) about 450 A. D. to 500. Vincent Smith thought that they belonged to the Later Gupta period. He referred them to the period from the middle of the sixth to that of the seventh century A. D. (A History of Fine Art in India and Ceylon, p. 295). This was also the opinion of M. B. Garde. (ARADGS, 1928-29, p.28)
2. IHQ, XXI, No.2.

deep entablature, supported on two circular columns. The ornamental feature inside a monastic hall is singular in its appearance in this cave, and is not known to occur anywhere else. Close to it is a long rectangular hall known as *Śālā*.

Two small caves of the Gupta period cut in laterite were found at Tumain.[1] The Udayagiri caves, situated in Bhilsa, are twenty in number. They are partly rock-cut and partly stone built. As some of the caves contain inscriptions, they may be dated about the beginning of the fifth century A. D. Except one or two Jaina caves, all are Brahmanical. Out of these caves, only Nos. 1,2,4,6,7,16,17, and 19, show distinct features of architectural value. The rest are simple cuttings, and of little value.

The architecture of these caves indicates a gradual evolution and development. Cave No. 1 is the most simple and primitive in appearance. It has no door ornamentation, and the design of its pillars is simple but impressive. Cave Nos. 4 and 6 have shrines which are much large and more ornate. The cells appear more spacious. Cave No. 19 represents a still further stage in the growth of architecture. Its cella is more spacious and its portico has become almost a large *maṇḍapa* or pillared hall. Along with the evolution of temple architecture, we also notice changes in the decorative motifs.

The caves were not suited to the ritualistic needs connected with the worship of images. The earlier small shrines and sanctuaries could not provide proper space for the deities. In order to fulfil religious needs, the building of the structured temples started.

(2) *STRUCTURAL BUILDINGS*:—

The temples at Sanchi[2], Tigawa[3] and Eran[4] are the earliest examples of structural temples. These resemble the rock-cut shrines of Udaigiri, built during the beginning of the fifth century A. D. The flat roof, the plain square or

1. ASI, 1918-19, p. 22.
2. ASC, X, 60-62; The Monuments of Sanchi, pp 56-58.
3. Ibid, IX, pp. 42-46.
4. Ibid, pp. 82-89.

rectangular form, and the stern simplicity of the wall are the characteristics of these temples. This is the basic form of the temple, which led to elaboration in course of time.

The temple of Sanchi appears to be the oldest structural temple. It is a tiny and unpretending shrine, consisting of nothing more than a simple square flat-roofed chamber with a pillared porch in front. Though modest in dimensions, its structural propriety, symmetry and proportion, appreciation for plain surfaces, and restraint in ornamentation, may very well be compared with Athenian architecture.

At Eran, the temples of Vishṇu and Varāha, though in dilapidated condition, are rectangular in plan. Before the sanctum, there was a shallow porch with four columns supporting the architrave on which the roof rests. The inter columnation is slightly greater in the middle than at the sides. The walls of the temple are quite plain, but there is decorative richness on the pillars and door frames. At Sanchi, there is the 'plain reeded bell' without turnovers of any kind. Every pillar in the Eran temples shows a highly ornate 'bell' with elaborate turnovers below the corners of the abacus. In the Tigawa temple, there is just the beginning of these turnovers. A buttress-like projection also appears in the temple of Vishṇu at Eran. Thus, the nucleus of a temple, viz. a cubical cella (*garbhagṛiha*) with a single entrance and a porch (*maṇḍapa*), appears for the first time in this archaic group of structural temples.

Gradually, there are the additions in the structural temples. The excavations at Pawaya[1] revealed an interesting terraced-brick structure consisting of three platforms placed one above the other. It appears to be a flat-roofed structure made up of timber, brick and lime. The two platforms below it served the purpose of a path ('*Pradakshiṇāpatha*') around the structure. Only at Ramnagar (Ahichchhatra) in the Barelly District of Uttar Pradesh, was such a terraced-brick temple found. As a few sculptures unearthed in the excavations are of Brāhmanical nature, it seems to be a Vaishṇava temple.

1. ARADGS, 1940-41, p. 17.

In the excavations at Mandsor[1], the foundations of a large brick building, which, judging from the slump of a huge *Sahasra liṅga* found lying half-buried in the mound, appears to have been a temple of Śiva. A beautifully carved *toraṇa* pillar, standing half-buried in the ground, was also found. The brick building, to which the *toraṇa* was related, was probably a Śaiva temple. Some ruins of the shrines of the Gupta period have been discovered at Morwan[2] (Mayūravana) about twenty-four kilometers north of Neemuch. Platforms of buildings of the Gupta period have been found at Paṭhāri.[3]

MONASTERIES AND STŪPAS:—

Some *stūpas*[4] and monasteries[5] of the Gupta period have been found at Sanchi. *Stūpas* Nos. 28 and 29 are of the Gupta period. Each of these small *stūpas* was provided with high square base, cornice and footings, characteristics of the early Gupta age to which they belonged, and each has the same outward appearance. Their interior construction, however, is not identical; the one to the west is built throughout of stone, but the one to the east has a core of large-sized bricks.

Monasteries Nos. 36, 37 and 38, appear to belong to the Gupta Period, and they were built approximately on the same plan. They consist of a square court surrounded by cells on the four sides (*chatuḥ-śāla*), with a verandah supported on pillars around the court, a raised platform in the centre of it, and in some cases, an additional chamber outside. The entrance passed through the middle chamber in one of the sides, and was flanked without by projecting turrets. The upper storey was probably constructed largely of timber or mud, the lower storey being of dry stone masonry. They belong to the sixth or seventh century A. D.

The structures of this period followed the earlier tradition of brick constructions over rubble plinths. Terracotta soakage wells, bottomless soakage jars, and terracotta pipedrains laid

1. ASI, 1922-23, p. 185.
2. Ibid.
3. ASC, VII, p. 64.
4. The Monuments of Sanchi, pp. 47-48.
5. Ibid, pp. 68-69.

underground, as well as brick drains, represented the sanitary arrangements of the period.

PILLARS :—

Some pillars of the Gupta period have been found at Sanchi, Mandsor, Eran, Pathari and Bhopal, and they have peculiar characteristics. At Sanchi[1], there are three pillars of this period. Pillar No. 26 is of the early Gupta period. It is distinguished from other pillars on this site by the unusual quality and colour of its stone. At Sanchi, this particular type of stone was freely used in the construction of the monuments of the Gupta period. It is twenty-two feet six inches in height and was composed of two pieces only, one comprising the the circular shaft and square base, and other the bell capital, lions and crowning wheel. Pillar No. 35 is massive. The shaft is circular and smooth, and the remainder, constituting the base square, is rough dressed. The bell capital and square abacus ornamented with a balustrade in relief, are entirely cut from a single stone. This pillar was surmounted by the statue of Boddhisattva Vajrapāṇi.

The peculiar feature of the pillars found at Mandsor, Eran and Pathari, is that they have been crowned with human figures back to back. The two huge monolithic pillars at Mandsor[2] were erected by Yaśodharman in the sixth century A. D. These pillars constitute a monument of the most outstanding archaeological interest. Each pillar is three feet six inches in diameter, and was over forty feet in height when entire. The discovery of a double head with two faces looking in opposite directions, near the base of one of the columns, proves beyond doubt that the crowning pieces consisted of double human figures, standing or seated back to back.

At Pathari[3], the entire shaft, pedestal and base, are of one stone. The capital consists of a disk which is surmounted by a square abacus. On it, there are two human figures placed

1. The Monuments of Sanchi, pp. 49-51.
2. M. B. Garde : Archaeology in Gwalior, p. 24.
3. ARC, VII, p. 64.

back to back, armed and bearing shields. The total height of the pillar is forty-seven feet of which more than forty-two feet is one piece of stone.

The monolithic pillar of Eran[1] is square below and octagonal above. The square portion is twenty feet high, and a large portion is buried in the ground. It is two feet nine inches square, and is surmounted by a corrugated cap. This is further surmounted by a four armed lion bracket and abacus. On the abacus, there are two human figures, placed back to back, facing east and west.

A stone pillar placed at Bhopal,[2] District Sehore, is roughly ascribed to the Gupta period. The polish and material of the pillar has a striking similarity with those of the Mauryan times, but the shaft, which bears an inscription in shell characters, lacks the characteristic taper of the Mauryan pillars.

SCULPTURES :—

During the Gupta period, artists gave visible expressions to the Puranic concepts through the medium of stone, clay or painting. A number of Hindu deities, such as Vishṇu, Śiva, Brahmā, Sūrya, Skanda, Gaṇeśa, Kubera, Gaṅgā, Yamunā, Pārvatī and Mahishamardinī, have been found in Malwa. There are sculptural representations of the epic stories from the *Rāmāyaṇa* and the *Mahābhārata*. The lithic evidence of the iconographic development is in agreement with the recorded literary traditions of this period.

The Malwa specimens of the Gupta period are invariably heavy, round, and tough in comparison with the eastern ones, which are soft, slender and delicate. The heavy consistency, and concentrated roundness of the sturdy body, are found in those sculptures which are formed out of the rock of the Udayagiri caves. These qualities are indicated by local ethnic legacy on the one hand and vigorous social thought of puranic integration on the other.

VISHṆU :—

That the worship of Vishṇu became very popular is clear

1. ASC, VII, p. 88.
2. IAR, 1957-58, p. 68.

from the several images found at different places. At Udayagiri, many images of Vishṇu have been noticed. In cave No. 6, two figures of Vishṇu represent standing Vishṇu. The right hand figure is armed with a heavy ringed club. To his left is the *chakra* mounted on a drum like box. Both are four armed. The jewellery of these figures consists of a garland, armlets and necklace. The standing image of Vishṇu is also found in the caves No. 5,9,10,11 and 12. In the cave No. 13, the colossal statue of *śeshaśāyī* Vishṇu is twelve feet long. The god is sleeping on the coils of the primeval snake with his head resting on the palm of one of his four hands. He is attended by his vehicle Garuḍa, represented in his purely animal form, and by eight other figures, all of them somewhat indistinct. One image of Vishṇu has also been recovered from Pawāyā.[1]

Some images of the incarnations of Vishṇu are noteworthy. In cave No. 19 of Udayagiri, the scene depicting the well-known story of the *Amṛitamanthana*, i. e. churning of the ocean for obtaining nectar, is a remarkable one. The sculpture of the famous *Varāha* incarnation of Vishṇu in cave No. 5 is an important monument and shows the genius of the Gupta artists. This colossal figure is twelve feet and eight inches in height. His right tusk supports a woman personifying *Pṛithvī*, the earth goddess, raised from the depths of the primeval sea. Kālidāsa makes an appropriate reference to Vishṇu rescuing the earth from cosmic convulsions. The two flanking scenes are of unusual significance, representing the birth of the twin rivers Gaṅgā and Yamunā, their confluence at Prayāga, and the final merging into the ocean. Its symbols were the twin river goddesses Gaṅgā and Yamunā standing on their respective vehicles, crocodile and tortoise. The combination of the scene of the descent of the Ganges and Yamunā with Varāha is not found anywhere else.

This carving shares the average plastic qualities of the Malwa idiom in general characterized by sturdiness. Yet, it seems to stand apart. While comparing it with the reliefs of Indra and Sūrya at Bhaja, Stella Kramrisch[2] recognizes

1. *Vikrama Smṛiti-grantha*, p. 694.
2. Indian Sculpture, pp. 68-69.

forces more vital, and at the same time, more ancient and deep in the gigantic appearance.

The scene of Bāli's sacrifice, and Vishṇu taking the three strides, has been found carved on a big lintel of a *toraṇa* gateway found at Pawāyā.[1] One image of Varāha, and another of Narasiṁha, have been obtained at Eran.[2] An image of Naraṣiṁha discovered at Besanagar is a remarkable one.[3]

ŚIVA :—

Next to Vishṇu, the worship of Śiva images became popular. Both the *Liṅga* form and the anthropomorphic image of Śiva existed in the Kushāṇa period, but their combination as evolved in *Ekamukhī*, *Chaturmukhī* and *Ashṭamukhī* Śivaliṅga, was a characteristic feature of Gupta iconography. An image of Ekamukhī Śivaliṅga at Udayagiri in cave No. 4 is two feet five inches in height, and one foot two inches in diameter. The face is round and not elongated. The arrangement of the hair is a most striking feature of this sculpture. The top-knot, i. e. an '*ushaṇīsha*', in the centre on the head, is shown tied round with a fillet, with the hair curling out of the knot and some flowing down in locks on to the shoulders. The only decoration on the figure is an ornamental inset with a diamond at the centre. An image of *chaturmukhī* Śivaliṅga has been recovered from Makanganja,[4] and of *Ashṭamukhī* liṅga from Mandsor.[5] One Śiva image found at Tumain,[6] and another at Badoh,[7] are in broken condition. A colossal sculpture of Śiva discovered at Mandsor[8] is an excellent specimen of Gupta art.

The worship of Brahmā images was not so popular as that of Vishṇu and Śiva, and therefore only two sculptures of this period, have so far been discovered, one Chatur-

1. ARADGS, 1924-25, p. 24.
2. ASC, VII, p. 88.
3. *Vikrama Smṛitigrantha*, p. 697.
4. ARADGS, 1929-30, p. 19.
5. *Vikrama Smṛiti-grantha*, p. 698.
6. Ibid.
7. Ibid.
8. ARADGS, 1925-26, p. 4.

mukha at Besanagar,[1] and another in a seated pose at Pawāyā.[2] A beautiful torso of the Sun has been discovered at Kayatha.

The images of minor gods and goddesses have also been found. There is probably a figure of Skanda in the Udayagiri cave No. 3. It has a *daṇḍa* in the right hand. The left hand is damaged but rested on the hip. It has two hands and one face. It has put on a lion-cloth and a turban-like head-dress, with tufts coming down on shoulders. The image carved in cave No. 6 is of Skanda. Though the image of Skanda discovered from Tumain[3] is small, it is artistic. The image of Skanda obtained from Kota[4] is very beautiful. An image of Kārttikeya was found carved on a lintel of a *toraṇa* gateway at Pawāyā[5]. Two images of Gaṇeśa were found in caves No. 6 and No. 17 respectively. The figure of Gaṇeśa in cave No. 6 is crudely carved, and has an elephantine face. The image of Gaṇeśa in cave No. 17 is found wearing a sort of cap-like headdress, probably indicating its slightly later date.

At Udayagiri in cave No. 6, the figure of Mahishamardinī (i. e. the goddess Durgā killing the buffalo demon or Mahishāsura) has been shown as having twelve arms holding different objects. With her foot, she is shown treading upon the head of the buffalo. A similar figure of Mahishamardinī was found in cave No. 17. The image of Umāmaheśvara in amorous mood found at this place, is also noteworthy. The images of Pārvatī found at Tumain[6] and at Pawāyā[7] are important from the artistic point of view. There are images of Saptamātṛikās in caves No. 4 and No. 6. These images have been carved on the rock at Paṭhārī.[8] Such images are also noticed at Bagh.

It is only in Gupta art, as well as in literature, that the two rivers Gaṅgā and Yamunā make their appearance for the

1. *Vikrama Smṛiti-grantha*, p. 700.
2. Ibid.
3. Ibid, p. 701.
4. Ibid, p. 701.
5. ARADGS, 1924-25, p. 24.
6. *Vikrama Smṛiti-grantha*, p. 700.
7. Ibid.
8. Ibid.

first time in the scheme of temple architecture. Kālidāsa, making a pointed reference to them as attendants of the temple deity, refers to a principal feature of contemporary art. The goddesses Gaṅgā and Yamunā assumed visible forms, and with *chauries* in their hands, took up positions as attendants of the great God. On the doorways of cave No. 6 at Udayagiri, these deities are found as attendants. Independent sculptures of Ganges and Yamunā are also found. Mention may be made of a broken statue of Gaṅgā standing gracefully on *makara* found at Vidiśā. A similar statue already discovered at this place has now been placed in the Boston museum. The image of Ganges at Tumain[1], and of Yamunā in a panel on[2] the toraṇa pillar at Khilchipura, are excellent specimens of art.

The lower part of a pot-bellied figure (*Kubera*), sitting cross-legged on a pedestal, was unearthed in excavations at Pawāyā[3]. A scarf is tied round the belly with a knot in front. An image of Kubera was found in cave No. 4 at Bagh[4]. The images of Kubera found at Tumain[5], Besanagar[6] and Terahi[7] are beautiful. The flying demigods (*Gandharvas*) of Mandsor[8], are excellent from the artistic point of view. An image of Yaksha and Yakshī back to back found at Vidiśā,[9] is artistic.

BUDDHIST IMAGES :—

The Buddhist images of this period were discovered at Bagh and Sanchi. The sculptures of Buddha and Bodhisattvas of Bagh[10] are larger than life size. Some detached sculptures of Buddhism found at Sanchi are stereotyped and artificial, and hence are not artistic. In *stūpa* No. 14, the statue repre-

1. *Vikrama Smṛitigrantha*, p. 702.
2. ARADGS, 1930-31, p. 14.
3. Ibid, 1924-25, p. 24.
4. Bagh Caves, p. 40.
5. *Vikrama Smṛiti grantha*, p. 702.
6. Ibid.
7. ARADGS, 1934-35.
8. Ibid.
9. *Vikrama Smṛitigrantha*, p. 702.
10. Bagh Caves, pp. 28-29.

sents Buddha seated cross-legged in *dhyānamudrā*.[1] It is of Mathura sandstone and a product of the Mathura school. The features of the face, particularly the lips and eyes, the highly conventionalized treatment of the hair, and the highly stylised disposition of the drapery, proclaim it to be of the early Gupta period. The statue of Bodhisattva Vajrapāṇi standing erect, clad in *dhotī* and adorned with bracelets, earrings, bejewelled necklace and headdress, is noteworthy.[2] An image of Buddha of reddish brown sandstone was found seated on a lotus.[3]

JAINA IMAGES :—

The image of the Jaina Tīrthaṅkara Pārśvanātha was installed in cave No. 20 at Udayagiri, but only a snake canopy behind the head of the figure has survived. Another image of Jaina Tīrthaṅkara is seven feet in height with a halo behind. There are two *chaurī* bearers flying on both the sides.[4] Recently three stone images, two of Jaina Tīrthaṅkara Pushpadanta, and one of Chandraprabhu were discovered[5]. These are in meditative mood seated in *padmāsana* on the pedestal. The *Śrīvatsa* symbol is noticed on the chest. There is a lotus halo with scalloped border behind. Down below, on both sides, can be seen attendant *chaurī* bearers.

DVĀRAPĀLAS, MITHUNA etc. :—

In caves Nos. 4,6,7,17 and 18, the images of *dvārapālas* or door-keepers on both sides of the doors have been found. Two big sculptures of *dvārapālas* of this period have been found at Khichlipur near Mandsor.[6] A scene of music and dance has been beautifully carved on a piece of a big lintel of a gateway of Pawāyā.[7] Sculptures of Nāgas are seen in the Bagh caves. A remarkable statue of Nāgarāja (Nāga king), with umbrella at the back has been recovered from Pawāyā.[8]

1. The Monuments of Sanchi, p. 47.
2. Ibid, p. 254.
3. Ibid, p. 250.
4. *Vikrama Smṛiti grantha*, p. 704.
5. Journal of the Oriental Institute, Baroda, XVIII, p. 252.
6. ARADGS, 1925-26, p. 4.
7. Ibid, 1924-25, p. 24.
8. Ibid, 1940, p. 17.

TERRACOTTAS

That the plastic art of clay modelling developed to a high level during this period is proved by the finds of Pawāyā, Ujjain, Maheshwar and Besanagar, in Malwa. They may be compared with similar terracottas unearthed in the excavations at Rajaghat near Benaras, Ahichchhatra, Bhitargaon and Basaṛh.

Among the terracottas found in Malwa, those of Pawāyā,[1] are the most beautiful from the artistic point of view. The findings are mostly busts and heads of human figures with beautiful expressions and fine arrangements of hair. Some have laughing faces, and others weeping ones. There are some fragments showing the different poses of hands and feet, and a torso showing the modes of dress and ornaments. The figures of animals and birds are also among the finds.

A beautiful head of the Gaṇa figure discovered at Pawāyā has been recently acquired by the National Museum, New Delhi.[2] The grotesque face, with wide open mouth and protruding eyes, recalls to mind the contemporary figures from Ahichchhatrā[3]. From the face, it appears that after making a holocaust of Daksha's sacrifice, he is laughing derisively. The head, showing all the characteristics of classical art, may be considersed as one of the finest examples of the Gupta period.

The notable terracotta objects discovered in the excavations at Ujjain[4] are the figures of mother and child, elaborately decorated female figures in the round, tortoises, elephants, horses with or without riders, bas-relief carvings on thin stone slabs, fragments of sculpture in sandstone, and soapstone caskets with lids. A group of six fragmentary and headless figurines was found at Maheshwar.[5] Of these, there are distinctly mother and child figurines, one male, and two, though fragmentary, are probably female figurines belonging to the mother and child group. The terracotta toys found consist

1. ARADGS, 1924-25, p. 24; 1940, p. 17.
2. Journal of Indian Museums, New Delhi, Vol. xxv-xxvi, p.130, fig. 35.
3. AI, No. 4, PI, LXI-LXIII.
4. IAR, 1956-57, p. 21.
5. EMN, p. 200.

of figurines of birds, bulls, rams, elephants, horses, and a fragmentary sword.

A number of terracotta figurines was unearthed from the excavations at Besanagar.[1] Of the human figures, nearly half are male, and half female. The backs of most of them are flattened. Of other living beings, figurines of the duck, parrot, elephant, horse, ram, bull, tortoise and fish have been found which must have served as playthings for children. Of these, the neck of the tortoise, and the mouth of the horse are each pierced with a hole, no doubt for passing a string through it, and pulling the animal with it. The bull is represented as squatting, and through the knees of its forelegs a similar perforation has been made. Five miniature wheels were discovered which must have originally formed part of toy carts.

PAINTING

The art of painting reached a high point of development during the Gupta period. In Malwa, there are the specimens at Bagh. Out of the several caves at Bagh, paintings on the walls, pillars and ceilings[2] are preserved only in four.

The subjects covered by the paintings are varied and numerous, such as the representation of the Buddha and Bodhisattvas, decorative scroll works, friezes and other patterns. The *Jātaka* stories have been beautifully illustrated. There is a scene of a lady in lament probably being vainly consoled by her lady friend. The next scene of discourse is laid out in a park or forest, having amongst its four participants, two princely or godly figures on one side, and the rest much simpler on the other, who are seriously engaged in a discussion over a topic concerning the most touching aspect of life, viz. sorrow. In two of the groups, the subject is pleasant, illustrating the performance of the '*hallīśaka*' a musical dance, acted by a troupe of women led by a man. They are elaborately dressed, singing and dancing with considerable freedom. The last two scenes represent a pageant of two festive processions.

1. ASI, 1914-15, p. 209.
2. Bagh Caves.

These paintings of Bagh correspond to those of the Ajanta caves. They belong to the same period and the same style. They are related to Buddhism and illustrate the *Jātaka* stories. In spite of these similarities, there is a slight difference. The paintings of Bagh are more earthly and human than those at Ajanta. They are secular and depict contemporary life.

POTTERY

The important pottery finds of this period found at Ujjain, Maheshwar, Eran, Avara, etc. testify to a very high standard of pottery. The Red Polished Ware, which was the characteristic of the Kushāṇa and Ḳshatrapa period, continued. Generally, the pottery of the period was wheel-made, except for the large soakage or storage jar. Mould-made pots are also noticed and the period is famous for this technique. The common shapes are dishes, bowls, jars, lids, basin caskets etc., and some of them are richly and elegantly decorated by several designs, such as lotuses, rosettes and small vegetable patterns, rectilinear or curvilinear geometrical patterns, spirals, girds, zigzags, fan-shaped or ornate *nandipada* pendants, etc. A large number of pottery spouts of this period, designed in the form of animals' heads, such as boar, elephant, lion, and *makara* are of note.

COINS AND SEALS

The gold and silver coins of the Guptas are marked by refinement and elegance. The figures of kings, animals, and deities, wearing dress, and ornaments in different poses, are very beautiful to look at. In Malwa, there have been only two finds, one at Nimad[1] and the other at Sehora[2] in Guna.

The seals of the Gupta period have been discovered at Besanagar, Eran Avara, etc. in Malwa. These are not in large number, as those from Bhīṭā, Basārh and Kosam and they are not of artistic merit.

OTHER ARTS

No gold, silver or precious jewellery of this period, has been discovered in the excavations. From the eleborate and vivid description in contemporary literary works, and from

1. JNSI, V, pp. 135 ff.
2. ARADGS, 1924-25, p. 17.

the specimens of the sculptures at Udayagiri, and painting at Bāgh, it is clear that the art of jewellery had reached a high standard during this period. The Gupta gold and silver coins also suggest that the jeweller's art in these metals was fairly well advanced in design and execution. Beads of different kinds showing high artistic skill have been found in plenty. The excellence of the carpenter's art can be presumed, because wood was still used in the construction of forts, palaces, and in the civil architecture of the upper strata of the people.

EDUCATION, LITERATURE AND SCIENCES

Under the liberal patronage of the Guptas, education, literature, and sciences developed greatly. Capital cities and holy places became famous seats of learning. In Malwa, such places were Ujjayinī and Padmāvatī. From some *Purāṇas* and literary works, it is known that Ujjayinī became a well-known centre of learning, to which students and scholars from distant parts of the country flocked. From the *Mālatīmādhava* of Bhavabhūti, it seems that Padmāvatī (Pawāyā) was an important seat of learning.

During this period, there was no organized system of education, and the private teacher was the pivot of education. He taught the students and received the honorarium voluntarily paid by their guardians. His income was supplemented by his professional earning as priest, and by the grants and donations from the State and wealthy citizens. The students had to study the *Vedas*, *Purāṇas*, *Smṛitis*, Logic, Metaphysics, Grammar, and Astronomy cum Astrology.

LITERATURE :—

There was all round development of Sanskrit literature. From the literary works and inscriptions of this time, it is clear that language had become polished. The *Kāvyamīmāṁsā*[1] says that king Sāhasāṅka of Ujjain ordered the extensive use of Sanskrit in the royal sergalio. Sāhasāṅka has been identified with Chandragupta II of the Gupta dynasty. It seems that Sanskrit attained the position of the *lingua franca*.

The chronology and the habitat of most of the Sanskrit authors remains unsettled. Scholars generally hold the view

1. *Kāvyamīmāṁsā*, p. 50.

that Bhāsa, Kālidāsa, Śūdraka, Bhāravi, etc. flourished during this period. From their literary works, it seems that they were somehow associated with Malwa. The names of some authors are known only from their epigraphs, which are actually beautiful specimens of classical poetry.

Bhāsa has been praised by both Kālidāsa and Bāṇa. Scholars generally believe that Bhāsa lived about a century or so before Kālidāsa, about 300 A. D. There is a divergence of opinion among scholars[1] about the attribution of his works. One view is that the thirteen trivandrum plays do not belong to Bhāsa. The opposite school ascribes all these plays to Bhāsa. This view seems to be more probable. From the *Pratijñāyaugandharāyaṇa*, the *Svapnavāsavadatta* and the *Chārudatta*, it seems that Bhāsa was well acquainted with Ujjain.

The date of Kālidāsa has not yet been finally settled. One school holds the view that he lived in the first century B. C. and was a contemporary of Vikrama, the founder of Vikrama era. The other school maintains that he lived in the Gupta period, and that he was a contemporary of Chandragupta II. Literary tradition states that Kālidāsa had revised the poem *Setubandha* of the Vākāṭaka king Pravarasena II. A close perusal of his works shows that he was probably a native of Ujjain.

Kālidāsa has been regarded as the best poet in Sanskrit literature. His poetry is marked by grace, simplicity and sentiment, and is decorated by striking figures of speech. He is also famous for his similies. The *Ṛitusaṁhāra*, the *Mālavikāgnimitra*, the *Kumārasambhava*, the *Meghadūta*, the *Śakuntalā* and the *Raghuvaṁśa* are his main works.

Śūdraka, author of the *Mṛichchhakaṭika*, seems to have lived in the fourth century A. D. His work asserts that its author was a king, but no author of this name is so far known to be a king. It is one of the most interesting dramas in Sanskrit

1. For arguments in favour of the authenticity of the plays of Bhāsa, see T. Ganapati Sastri, Bhāsa's works: a critical study; Keith, Sanskrit Drama; Pusalkar, Bhāsa, a study. For the contrary view, consult Barnett, JRAS, 1919, pp. 233-4; Levi, 2D MG. LXXII, 203-08; Kane, *Vividhajñānavistāra*, 1920, pp. 97-102 and Pisharoti, IHQ, V, 552-558.

literature, and it gives a living and realistic picture of Ujjain. Śūdraka is also a writer of the *Padmaprābhṛitakam*[1] which was written in Ujjain. *Pādatāḍitakam*[2] was composed in Ujjain by Syāmilaka.

Rājaśekhara[3] records a tradition of Ujjain being a seat of learning where *Kāvyakāras*(poets) were tested by Chandragupta along with Kālidāsa, Bhāravi and others. Bhāravi, author of the *Kirātārjunīya*, flourished towards the middle of the sixth century A.D. Bhartrihari, author of the three *Śatakas*, is known to have been associated with Ujjain in the sixth century. A.D. Some scholars have identified him with Bhaṭṭi, author of the *Rāvaṇavadha*, popularly known as the *Bhaṭṭikāvya*. Whether the grammarian Bhartṛihari, author of the *Vākyapadīya*, is to be identified with the author of the *Bhaṭṭikāvya* and the three Śatakas, is still a moot question.[4] Amarasiṁha, the author of the *Amarakosha*, the most popular Sanskrit dictionary, lived during this period.

Important religious and philosophical works were written during this time. The famous Jaina philosopher Siddhasena Divākara, author of the *Sanmatitarka*, who lived in the fifth century A.D., was perhaps a native of Ujjain. He is the father of Jaina Logic. His *Nyāyāvatāra* is the first systematic work on Jaina Logic. Some *Smṛitis* probably belong to this period. The authors of some *Purāṇas* seem to have remodelled them while staying at Ujjain.

Some epigraphs of this period composed by Sanskrit poets of great ability, who are not known to us from any other source, are actually specimens of classical poetry. Mention may be made in this connection of Vatsabhaṭṭi of the Mandsor inscription[5] of 473 A.D., and Vāsula of the Mandsor inscription[6] of 532 A. D..

SCIENCES

The science of Mathematics made great progress. The most epoch-making achievement of this age was the discovery of the

1. *Chaturbhāṇī*, Int. pp. 5-6.
2. Ibid.
3. *Kāvyamīmāmsā*, p. 55.
4. Keith : History of Sanskrit Literature, pp. 116, 176
5. CII, III, pp. 81 ff.
6. Ibid, pp. 152 ff.

decimal system of rotation, which simplified arithmetical calculations and processes. Āryabhaṭa was a great Mathemātician who wrote the *Āryabhaṭīyam*. In the realm of Geometry, this work refers to some of the important properties of circles and triangles. The method of finding square roots and cube-roots was known to them. In Algebra, simultaneous equations, with four unknown quantities, were solved and the problem of finding a general solution of the interminates of the first degree was successfully touched. Trigonometry was also cultivated at this time.

Astronomy made striking advances during the Gupta period. Ujjayinī became a great centre[1] of astronomy, and many of the *Siddhānta* works in Indian astronomy were composed there. After contact with Greek astronomy through the Śaka rulers, there was an interchange of some of the principles leading to the inclusion of *rāśis* etc. in the Indian astronomical works. The technical terminology of Hindu astronomy contains some words, like, *kendra*, *hārija*, *drekkāṇa*, *lipta*, etc., which are clearly adoptions of the Greek words. The *Romaka Siddhānta* clearly betrays Greek influence both in its name and contents[2] Bhāsa, the first Sanskrit Dramatist, refers to the observatory at Ujjayinī where records were taken of the rise of the Sun etc.[3]

This age produced some well known astronomers. Among them, Āryabhaṭa was the greatest, who wrote the *Āryabhaṭīyam*. His conclusions were independent, based upon his own observations and researches. He was the first Indian astronomer to discover that the earth rotates around its axis. He was also the first to find out sine functions and utilise them in astronomy.

Dravyavardhana, who seems to have been the Aulikara ruler of Daśapura, and who lived in or before the beginning of the sixth century A.D., was fond of Astrology. He compos-

1. Ujjayinī is the Indian Greenwich, the first meridian of Indian astronomers. It is said that there was a well at Ujjayinī in which the Sun was reflected vertically upwards at a certain moment. (ANNIE BESANT quoted in OKE'S Vikramāchārya Ujjayinī, p. 85.)
2. Varāhamihira himself pays handsome tribute to Greek astronomers. They are, he says, no doubt Mlechchhas but nevertheless good experts in astronomy and therefore worthy of as high a respect as the sages of yore.
3. Bhāsa—A Study, p. 434; cf *Svapnavāsavadatta*, p. 81.

ed a work on *Śakuna* after consulting Bhāradvāja's work.

The next astronomer of note is Varāhamihira, who was born at Kapitthaka,[1] (Kayatha) near Ujjain, and lived during the first and second quarters of the sixth century. He wrote the *Bṛihatsaṁhitā* after consulting, among others Dravyavardhana's work. He is the author of a number of works, such as the *Pañchasiddhāntikā*, the *Laghujātaka*, the *Bṛihajjātaka*, the *Vivāhavṛindāvana*, the *Yogayātrā*, the *Samāsasaṁhitā* and several others. In the *Pañchasiddhāntikā*, he gives a concise account of the five *siddhāntas* namely *Vaśishṭha Siddhānta*, *Pauliśa Siddhānta*, the *Romaka Siddhānta*, and the *Sūrya Siddhānta*. It is believed that the *Pañchasiddhāntikā* and the *Bṛihatsaṁhitā* originated from Ujjain. There was an old observatory built under the supervision of Varāhamihira, but it cannot be identified.[2]

Varāhamihira was a man of genius and versatility. He was a scientist with encyclopaedic interest, and his *Bṛihatsaṁhitā* is a veritable mine of useful information. He was well acquainted with the science of metallurgy, as seen in his methods for sharpening swords. He was well versed in the science of jewellery, as he knew how to ascertain the nature, and value of gold, emeralds, pearls, diamonds, etc.[3] He was a botanist and discussed topics of gardening and how to produce fruit-trees and fruits out of season.[4] He gave useful information to ascertain the nature of good and indifferent horses, elephants, dogs etc.[5] He was a student of civil engineering, and his book contains valuable information about the nature and structure of temples, palaces, mansions and houses.[6] He took great interest in water divining, and his work supplies useful information on this topic.[7] He also had a mastery over the science of meteorology. He knew and explained what kind of clouds

1. Ajaya Mitra Shastri has identified Kapitthaka with modern Saṁkāśya in Farrukhabad District of U. P. See India as seen in the Bṛihatsaṁhitā of Varāhamihira.
2. Vikrama Volume, p. 470.
3. *Bṛihatsaṁhitā*, Chaps. 80-3.
4. Ibid, Chaps. 55.
5. Ibid, Chaps. 62-4.
6. Ibid, Chaps. 53.
7. Ibid, Chaps. 54.

bring rain, when accompanied with what kind of wind, coming from what quarter.[1]

The science of medicine made advancement during this age. The *Charaka-saṁhitā* and the *Suśruta-saṁhitā* continued to enjoy a supreme reputation and confidence among the people. A systematic summary of these two works is given in the *Ashṭāṅgasaṁgraha* by Vāgbhaṭa I, who seems to have lived in the sixth century A.D. Another work composed on this subject is the *Navanītakam*. Veterinary science was not neglected. The *Hastyāyurveda* of Pālakāpya was probably composed during the later Gupta period. It deals with the diseases of elephants, their diagnosis and treatment, both medical and surgical. The great achievement of this period in the medical sphere, was the discovery of a metallic preparation which was applied to cure different diseases. In big cities like Ujjain, there were well-managed hospitals where students were given regular practical training.

The science of Chemistry and Metallurgy did not lag behind. The preparation of colour and its blending was well known to the people. This is indicated by the paintings of Bagh and Ajanta. The metallic preparations prove that there was a close association of medicine and Chemistry, and it led to great progress in Chemical knowledge. That the science of metallurgy was in an advanced state is clear from Varāhamihira. The name of the region round Vidiśā, Daśārṇa, clearly indicates that it was famous for its sharp-edged swords.[2] The progress of metallurgy at Ujjain is known from a large number of metal objects unearthed in the archaeological excavations.

SOCIAL CONDITIONS

The Gupta period is marked by significant changes in the social sphere. Foreigners, like the Greeks, Śakas, Pārthians and Kushāṇas, merged themselves in Hindu Society by adopting the Hindu religion, customs and manners. The rise of Vaishṇavism and Śaivism greatly influenced society. The development of industry and commerce led to prosperity,

1. *Bṛihatsaṁhitā*, Chaps. 21-26.
2. Vikrama Vol. (Eng. Ed.) p. 378.

which gave birth to a cultured society. The people became wealthy and were able to entertain themselves in different ways.

STRUCTURE OF THE SOCIETY

The traditional divisions of society into the four Varṇas, namely the Brāhmaṇas, the Kshatriyas, the Vaiśyas and the Śūdras, continued during the Gupta period, and they became more and more rigid. The fourfold division of the means of earning money, described in the *Kāmasūtra*,[1] according to birth, shows that in Vātsyāyana's time, occupation was controlled by the caste in which one was born. In connection with another important matter of life, viz. marriage, Vātsyāyana[2] speaks of four castes, of higher and lower castes, and also on the advisability of the union between men and women of the same caste. Varāhamihira[3] in his *Bṛihatsaṁhitā* assigns the different quarters of a city to the Brāhmaṇas, Kshatriyas, Vaiśyas and Śūdras. The Brāhmaṇas enjoyed special privileges. That the old law of exempting the Brāhmaṇa from capital punishment and confiscation of property, was followed in actual practice, is to be seen from the concrete examples in the dramas and prose romances of the period. Chārudatta, though found guilty of murder by the presiding judge, is recommended for exemption from the death penalty because of his Brāhmaṇa birth.[4]

OTHER CASTES:—Because of intercaste marriages and the intermingling of people of different races, several other castes came into existence. Among the ruling communities, the Gupta, the Aulikara and the Māṇavāyaṇi were important. The name ending in '*Gupta*' indicates that they were Vaiśya. The other view is that they may be Jāts and Kshatriyas[5]. The Aulikaras, probably a branch of the Mālavas, were ruling over Mandsor. A Māṇavāyaṇi *Kula* of the Kshatriyas is known

1. KSI, IV, Sūtra 1, p. 42.
2. H. Chakladar : Social Life in Ancient India, p. 75.
3. 89, 94-95.
4. *Mṛichchhakaṭika*, IX.
5. Jayaswal : JBORS, XIX, 1933, p. 113.

from the Mandsor inscription,[1] and the Chhoti Sādrī inscription[2] dated 490-91 A. D. An inscription of the fifth century A.D. engraved on the pedestal at Sanchi seems to record the installation of an image by one belonging to the *Sūra-Kula* i.e. the Sūra family.[3] From the Mandsor stone inscriptions of Yaśodharman and Vishṇuvardhana, it is clear that the *Rājasthānīyas* of the Aulikara rulers of Daśapura, were of the Naigama caste.[4]

Several subcaste and gotras also came into existence. From the Ratlam plates[5] of Dhruvasena II, it is known that Brāhmaṇa Dattasvāmin and Kumārasvāmin were the sons of Budhasvāmin, and they belonged to the *gotra* Parāśaras, and to the School of the Mādhyandina Vājasaneyas. Dattasvāmin and Kumārasvāmin were respectively Trivedins and Chaturvedins of Daśapura.

LOWER CASTS AND TRIBES :—

Chāṇḍālas occupied the lowest rank among the low castes. They performed the most menial work, such as carrying unclaimed corpses and executing criminals. They lived outside the towns and villages. From the literary works of the Gupta period, it is known how the Chāṇḍālas, who were confirmed meat-eaters, were habitually engaged as public executioners, and were regarded as untouchables.[6] Other sub-castes known from Varāhamihira, are Ḍombas, Nishādas, Pāraśava, Śvapacha and Ugra.[7]

There were tribes inhabiting the region of Malwa, some of them savage. The Allahabad inscription[8] gives us information about some, such as the Ābhīras (Bhilsa Jhansi area), the Prārjunas, the Sanakānikas (near Sanchi) and Kharaparikas (Damoh District). The Pushyamitras[9] took refuge in the dense area in the present Shahdol District. These aboriginal tribes were living in the forests and mountains, and they led a

1. EI, XXX, pp. 127 ff.
2. Ibid, pp. 120 ff.
3. The Monuments of Sanchi, p. 387.
4. CII, III, pp. 152 ff.
5. ASI, 1902-03, p. 232.
6. Mri. X.
7. India as seen in the Bṛihatsaṁhitā of Varāhamihira, pp. 198-99.
8. CII, III, pp. 6 ff.
9. Ibid, pp. 63 ff; Bulletin of the Ancient Indian History and Archaeology, No. 1, p. 3.

savage life and lived on hunting.

The professions do not seem to have been rigidly determined by the castes. From the Mandsor inscriptions[1] of 437-38 A.D. and 473-74 A. D., it is clear that the members of the silk guild migrated from Gujarat to Mandsor, where they adopted different professions, such as those of archer, story teller, exponent of religious problems, astrologer, a warrior, and ascetic. Mātṛivishṇu, who was a Brāhmaṇa by caste, gave up the priestly life, joined the army and founded a principality near Eran.[2] The Gupta emperors are said to be Vaiśyas, but they were great conquerors. It seems that a large percentage of the army was recruited from the Vaiśyas and the Śūdras.

That the rules of the castes were not so rigid is clear from intercaste marriages. In the contemporary Sanskrit dramas and prose romances, we find Brāhmaṇas and Kshatriyas even marrying the daughters of courtesans and female slaves. In the *Mṛichchhakaṭika*, Brāhmaṇa Chārudatta has been shown marrying Vasantasenā, and Brāhmaṇa Śarvilaka marrying her slave Madanikā.

SLAVES :—

From the *Mrichchhakaṭika*, it is known that generally wealthy persons had one or more slaves. Slavery was an established social institution in Ujjain. The slave masters exercised considerable power over them. The treatment they received at the hands of the masters, depended upon the latter's nature. Madanikā is regarded by her high-minded mistress as a friend and confidante. Sthāvaraka is beaten and put in fetters by his brutal master. As soon as a slave girl was liberated, she took her rank as a free citizen, and could be married as a free citizen in gentle society.

ĀŚRAMA

Along with *Varṇa*, the idea of the division of individual life into Āśramas was known to the people, because Varāhamihira[3] and Vātsyāyana both mention it. How far this system was in actual practice, nothing can be said definitely.

1. CII, III, pp. 81 ff.
2. CII, III, p. 89.
3. India as seen in the Bṛihatsaṁhitā of Varāhamihira, p. 199.

Vātsyāyana[1] emphasizes that the scheme of life of the individual was to be so devised that *Dharma*, *Artha* and *Kāma*, may harmonize together and not clash in any way. He strictly enjoins that until a man finishes his education, he should practise Brahmacharya. Afterwards, he should enter into the life of the householder (*Gārhastya*) that is, he should marry and settle down. It seems that the third Āśrama of Vānaprastha was going out of vogue in the Indian society by the time that Vātsyāyana wrote his book, because there is no reference to it. He mentions different types of ascetics which belong to the fourth stage of life. As the *Kāmasūtra* is the work of different nature, Vātsyāyana has very little occasion to speak of the third and fourth Āśramas of the Vānaprastha and the Yati respectively.

MARRIAGE

Marriage is the foundation of family life and it was considered to be necesssary for man. In the society depicted by Vātsyāyana, no marriage could take place until a youngman had completed his education. To him, a good marriage secured the end of *Dharma* and *Artha*—that is, both spiritual as well as social and economic welfare. Marriage, to be happy, must be between equals in social status.[2] Though early marriages had started among the Kshatriya families as known from the Sanskrit dramas, generally, the custom of postpuberty marriage was followed.

Vātsyāyana[3] has mentioned four forms of marriage, as approved in society, in the order of Brāhma, Prājāpatya, Ārsha and Daiva. He describes the Gāndharva, Paiśācha and Rākshasa forms; of these, the first he mentions by name, and of the last two forms, he gives only the description. He mentions altogether seven forms, leaving out Āsura marriage, in which the bridegroom receives maiden after having given as much wealth as he can afford, to the kinsmen and the bride herself, according to his own will. Most probably,

1. H. Chakladar : Social Life in Ancient India, pp. 80-81.
2. Ibid, pp. 85 ff.
3. Ibid, p. 101.

it was very much looked down upon in cultured society in his days. According to him, the Gāndharva form of marriage is the most respected, because love is the fruit of all the forms of marriage. Love is more in evidence in the Gāndharva form,[1] whereas considerations of birth, money, or other qualities, are the deciding factors in other forms of marriage.

Among the eight types of marriage, Kālidāsa has referred to *Gāndharva*,[2] *Āsura*[3] and *Prājāpatya*.[4] He has mentioned also the *Svayaṁvara* form of marriage which was sometimes resorted to by royal families. The Gāndharva marriage was not prevalent during this time. Generally, Prājāpatya marriage was popular, and it was considered to be the ideal one.

Although man in general wedded a single wife, plurality of wives was not unknown. Nobles and rich men often had several wives. Ordinarily, it was expected that a man should marry a woman of his own caste, but intercaste marriages were not unknown. Chandragupta II's daughter, Prabhāvatī gupta, was married to Rudrasena II of the Vākāṭaka dynasty, who was Brāhmaṇa by caste. Kukusthavarmā, a Brāhmaṇa of the Kadamba dynasty, married his daughter with someone in the Gupta dynasty.

Great preparations were made for celebrating marriage. On this occasion, houses and roads were decorated with auspicious articles. Brides and bridegrooms were adorned with dress, ornaments and other articles. A number of rituals were necessary to be performed in order to unite them in wedlock. The custom of giving a dowry to bridegrooms existed, although it was not a condition preceding the marriage. The presents and ornaments received by the bride from her relatives became her *strīdhana*.

POSITION OF WOMAN :—

From literary sources, it is clear that woman occupied a high position in society. The ideal wife attended on her husband

1. KS, III, V, Sūt. 29-30, p. 238.
2. Śaku, 3.20.
3. Raghu, 11.38.
4. Ibid, 7.13, 15-28.

with all the love and devotion that a devotee shows to the deity he worships. She ministered to his personal needs, looked after his food and drink, as well as his toilets and his amusements; she tried to appreciate his likes and dislikes, welcomed his friends with proper presents, respected and loved his parents and relatives, and was liberal to his servants. On his return home, she hastened to meet him and wait upon him herself; in his games and sports, she followed him; even when offended she did not speak too bitterly to him. She may attend a festive assembly only with his permission. She should do nothing that might rouse his suspicion against her fidelity. She should avoid the company of women of questionable character.[1]

Service and self-restraint were the main qualities of woman. With the permission of her husband, the wife took upon herself the care and management of the family. She prepared the budget for the whole year and regulated the expenditure in proportion with the annual income. The joint-family system seems to have been prevalent because parents, brothers and sisters and their families lived together.

Ordinarily, women were literate, but higher education was not common among them. The daughters of kings and nobles, as also the *Gaṇikās*, were highly educated and had their intelligence trained and sharpened by the *Śāstras*. Moreover, from Vātsyāyana's work, as well as from contemporary literature, it is clear that a knowledge of the arts was considered necessary for all women. They were usually trained in the arts of singing, dancing, and the like. The *Amarakośa*[2], a work of the Gupta age, refers to words meaning female teachers (*Upādhyāyā*) and *Upādhyāyī*) as well as female instructors of Vedic *mantras*, known as *Āchāryas*. Varāhamihira[3] alludes to a *brahmavādinī* woman well-known for her proficiency in all the sciences. Poor women earned a living by spinning and weaving.

1. H. Chakladar : Social Life in Ancient India, p. 122.
2. 11.6.14.
3. India as seen in the *Bṛihatsaṁhitā* of Varāhamihira, p. 208.

The widow generally led a life of strict chastity and self-restraint. The custom of *satī* was known, but only on rare occasions did widows become *satīs*. It was occasionally referred to by Bhāsa, Vātsyāyana, Kālidāsa, Śūdraka, and Varāhamihira in their works. There, is, however, only one historical case of *Satī*, which took place when king Goparāja died on the battlefield in 510 A.D., and his wife immolated herself on the funeral pyre.[1] The remarriage of widows, though disfavoured, was not absolutely forbidden. There is the example of Chandragupta marrying Dhruvadevī. The practice of polygamy was confined to kings and rich people.

From some literary works[2], it is clear that there were a large number of prostitutes living at Ujjain. Some of them were even from outside India. A separate quarter was assigned to them in the city. They were renowned for their beauty, wit and other accomplishments. They were also notorious for their greed. They possessed enormous wealth which they spent lavishly on comforts and luxuries. They lived in magnificent palaces. From the *Meghadūta*[3] of Kālidāsa, it is known that these prostitutes were employed for dancing purposes in the temple of Mahākāla at Ujjain.

Vātsyāyana[4] states that only the courtesan, who is versed in sixty-four arts (*Kalās*), is endowed with an amiable disposition, personal charms and other winning qualities, acquires the designation of a *Gaṇikā*, and receives a seat of honour in the assemblies of men. Though belonging to the class of 'public women', she occupied a peculiar position in town and was treated with special consideration.

From the study of the sculptures of this period, it seems that there was no *purdā* system in the modern sense, and women could move about freely. Some ladies of the royal families lived in a portion of the place known as *antaḥpura*[5],

1. CII, III, pp. 92 ff.
2. *Mṛichchhakaṭikam, Padmaprābhṛitakam* and *Pādatāḍitakam.*
3. 1.36.
4. H. CHAKLADAR : Social Life in Ancient India, p. 138.
5. Raghu, 16.59; kumāra, 1.2, Śaku, p. 104; Mālavikā, 2, 24.

varodha[1] and *śuddhānta*,[2] guarded against intrusion from any tranger. From literary sources, it is known that out of nodesty, women sometimes covered their bodies with shawls or other mantles and put on a veil.

TOWN LIFE :—

Vātsyāyana paints the picture of a *nāgaraka* (city-bred nan) of a particular and limited section of the urban people, who possessed ample wealth and leisure at their disposal.[3] This type of *nāgaraka* was a product of prosperous cities which came into existence during the Gupta period. He was a man of varied culture. In addition to a healthy physique, good birth and an independent means of livelihood, he possessed a knowledge of various arts. He was learned and eloquent, and was, moreover, a poet, and well skilled in telling stories.

After finishing his education, he was expected to lead a life of comfort and pleasure with the help of self-acquired or inherited property in a city. He was to possess aesthetic taste to a high degree, and should exhibit it in the construction of his house, in laying out gardens and in other spheres of life. His house was to be decorated with painting and sculptures, and he should be fully acquainted with such arts as singing (*gīta*), playing instruments(*vādya*), and dancing(*nṛitya*). He must have a taste for dress and ornaments.

As far as the daily life of the *nāgaraka* was concerned, he rose in the morning, and after taking his bath, decorated his body with different toilets. He put on dress and ornaments. He took his meals in the morning and evening. After his evening meal, he amused himself in various ways. He also went out fully dressed to attend social gatherings and in the evening, he enjoyed music. He sat on the bedstead in his well decorated and perfumed drawing room, to discourse with his friends, and to await the arrival of his beloved ones.

Besides the daily round of pleasures, the *nāgaraka* also took part with his friends in outdoor amusements periodically, on holidays and on other occasions. These are of five types.

1. Raghu, 1.32; 4.68; 16.25; 58.71; Śaku, 6-12.
2. Raghu, 3.16; 6.45; Śaku, 1.15.
3. H. Chakladar : Social Life in Ancient India, pp. 103 ff.

In the first place, he mentions the festivals in connection with the worship of different deities (*samāja*, *yātrā* and *ghāṭa*), sometimes attended with grand processions; then come the *Goṣṭhīs*; or social gatherings of both sexes; next *āpānakas* or drinking parties, and *uddyānayātrās* or garden parties, and last of all, various social diversions in which many persons take part (*samasyākrīḍā*).

Such a type of *nāgaraka* is found in the character in the *Mṛichchhakaṭika*. In the inner portion of his house lived his devoted wife, while he himself spent his times with his companions, mostly in the outer portion to which was attached a garden. In his outer house, there were large and small drums, a flute, a lute, reed-pipes and manuscripts. Though reduced to poverty, he wore a perfumed upper garment. He also attended a musical concert in the evening and returned late at night with sweet memories of the song and music.

DRESS AND ORNAMENTS :—

From contemporary literary works, sculptures and paintings, some idea is gained of the dress and ornaments of the people during the Gupta period. Generally, men wore three articles of dress—a turban (*veshṭana*), and then two pieces of cloth (*dukūlayugmam*), namely the upper-scarf (*uttarīya*) and loin-cloth (*dhotī*). Women put on three garments—an upper one, a lower garment, and a shawl. The upper garment was a bodice (*Kūrpāsaka*, *Stanāṁśuka*). The lower garment was a type of petticoat (*ghāgharā*). From the use of the words *nīvī* and *nīvī-bandha*, it can be inferred that it hung to the ankles and was held up by a cord (*nīvī*). Lastly, there was a long shawl used by women, which covered them almost from head to foot and serving even for a veil. Foreigners introduced coats, overcoats and trousers. Jackets, blouses and frocks were used by the Scythian ladies.

Cotton garments were used for daily purposes, but silken ones were worn by rich and fashionable persons on festive occasions. The silk cloths of Mandsor[1] were famous, as they

1. CII, III, pp. 81 ff.

were delicate and of different varieties.

People of different classes put on different types of dresses. The dress of a statue of Nāga king[1] found at Pawāyā, and some portraits of kings in the caves at Bagh[2], indicate the apparel of the princes who wore a simple *dhotī*, an upper garment and a simple *mukuṭa*. The statue in cave No. 5 at Udayagiri gives an idea of the dress of upper class people, which consisted of loin cloth, upper scarf and head dress. The upper garment and a lower *dhotī* continued to be the costume of the majority of the people. The *dvārapālas* of Udayagiri wore a simple *dhotī* with an under garment, and left the rest of the body uncovered. The torso of a female found at Pawāyā[3] has a close fitting *lahaṅgā*, and a jewelled girdle. In one cave at Bagh, horse riders with their dresses have been depicted.[4] In another, some ladies in dress riding elephants have been shown.[5] Both at Pawāyā[6] and Bagh[7], there are dancing and music scenes in which ladies have been depicted with their peculiar dresses.

People used several types of ornaments.[8] Ornaments worn on head were *chūḍāmaṇi*, *ratnajāla* and *muktājāla*. Ears were adorned with various sorts of ear-rings called *Karṇa-bhūshaṇa*, *Karṇapūra*, *Kuṇḍala* and *maṇikuṇḍala*, made of rubies and other precious stones. On the neck was worn what was called '*nishka*'. Various kinds of long necklaces were worn, falling in strings on the breast. Of these, *muktāvalī* was a string of pearls; *tārahāra*, a necklace of big pearls; *hāra*, an ordinary necklace; *hāraśekhara*, a snow-white string; *hārayashṭi*, an only string of pearls—*śuddha ekāvali*—with a gem in the centre, and *vaijayanti* is a necklace composed of a successive series of groups of gems, each group wherein has five gems in particular order. *Hemasūtra* was a chain gold with a

1. ARADGS, 1940, p. 17.
2. The Bagh Caves.
3. ARADGS, 1924-25, p. 24.
4. The Bagh Caves.
5. Ibid.
6. ARADGS, 1924-25, p. 24.
7. The Bagh Caves.
8. India in Kālidāsa, p. 202

precious stone in the centre. *Prālamba* and *mālā* were long garlands of flowers. *Aṅgada* or *keyūra*, armlets of gold with gems set in them, were frequently used by both men and women. *Valaya* bracelets adorned the forearm of the two sexes, and rings of various designs decorated the fingers. Girdles made of gold, and precious stones were worn by women on their waist, and these were known by several designations, like *mekhalā*, *hemamekhalā*, *kāñchī*, *kanakakāñchī*, *kiṇkiṇī* and *raśanā*. *Nūpuras*, producing sweet sound, adorned the ankles of women. Both men and women wore ornaments. The *dvārapālas* of Udayagiri put on ornaments such as armlets and necklaces. A necklace and armlet adorned the figure of Nāgarāja of Pawāyā. The girdle of ornamented chains round the waist of the goddess *Pṛithvī* in the Varāha scene at Udayagiri, may be suggestive of its use by high class ladies.

TOILETS AND COSMETICS :—

The prosperous condition of the people produced different kinds of toilets and cosmetics, which were refined, delicate and elegant. These included painting long nails, scenting the body, face and hair, with *aguru* incense, and other perfumes, powders and pastes, massaging the body and the face, with scented oils and pastes, elaborate arrangements of the hair in elegant curls and coiffures etc. Some terracottas of men and women found in the excavations at Pawāyā[1] are important for the study of hair dressing.

AMUSEMENTS :—

There was enough wealth for people to entertain themselves in different ways. Dice and chess were favourite indoor pastimes; and hunting, ramfights and cockfights were the principal outdoor amusements. Both boys and girls played with balls. Swings (*ḍolā*) were a common means of merriment, especially enjoyed by women. Fairs, shows and dramas provided a variety of entertainments.

Some of girls' sports as well as some of their playthings have been described by Vātsyāyana. The girls took delight in making garlands of flowers, building small houses of earth and wood, and playing with dolls. They sometimes played games

1. ARADGS, 1924-25, p. 24.

of 'odd and even', of 'close fists', hide and seek, etc. Among the games of men, wrestling matches were important.

Both from Kālidāsa[1] and Bāṇa[2] we know that story-telling was another sort of diversion for the people. They took keen interest in narrating the stories from religious works, like the *Mahābhārata*, *Rāmāyaṇa* and *Purāṇas*. Music and dancing scenes depicted on the wall of a cave at Bagh, on a lintel of the temple at Pawaya, display a particular artistic taste on the part of the people of the region. Gambling was favourite pastime of the people, both high and low and there was a gamblers' association, (*Dyūtakara maṇḍalī*), which wielded considerable powers over the life and person of the gamblers.[3]

FOOD AND DRINK :—

The society was partly vegetarian and partly non-vegetarian. People used to take rice, wheat, barley, pulses, butter, sugar, etc. The wealthy drank rich liquor and wine, and prepared varieties of different dishes.

SUPERSTITIONS :—

The literature[4] of the Gupta period contains repeated references to popular superstitions. People believed in charms and spells, as well as Astrology and Divination. They had a belief in omens, portents, and other such superstitious things.

LIVING STANDARD :—

The wealth and prosperity produced a high standard of living among people. From the *Bṛihat-saṁhitā*,[5] we know that clubs, umbrellas, elephant goads, canes, bows, canopies, halberds, standards and chowries were in general use. At this time, Ujjain became a cosmopolitan city because people from different places settled there. In the *Pādatāḍitakam*, there is a reference to *sārvabhaumanagara*, meaning supreme city, which has been identified with Ujjain.[6]

ECONOMIC CONDITIONS

After defeating the Śakas, Chandragupta II annexed the

1. *Meghadūta*.
2. *Kādambarī*.
3. *M ichchhakaṭika*.
4. Ibid, IX.
5. LXII.3.
6. *Chaturbhāṇī*, Intro.

region of Eastern Malwa to the Gupta empire. The peace and order secured by the efficient administration led to the development of agriculture, industry and commerce. The literary sources describe the great prosperity of this region, which is further confirmed by the monuments of the Gupta period.

AGRICULTURE :—

Agriculture was based on traditional methods. In spite of the richness of the soil, agriculture depended upon the rainfall. Varāhamihira[1] gives numerous references to rains and rainfall, and in particular, to careful forecasts of excessive, scanty or sufficient rain, in the light of astronomical and metrological data, as well as observations of omens and portents. The agriculture implements and lines of agricultural operations appear to be of traditional type. The *Amarakośa*[2] gives synonyms for these component parts, the harrow for loosening the soil, the hoe and the sickle. There were two principal harvests, namely the summer and the autumn crops, although a minor spring crop was also known.[3]

There were different kinds of agricultural crops, and products of trees and plants. The *Amarakośa*[4] and the *Brihatsaṁhitā*[5] refer to rice, wheat, barley, lentils, oil seeds of many different kinds, ginger and other vegetables, pepper and other species, medicinal and other herbs. Sugar trees were grown for the production of raw, as well as refined, sugar. It seems that all these were cultivated in the region of Malwa.

Varāhamihira[6] gives rules for the preparation of the soil, for grafting a tree branch on another tree, and for watering trees at the proper season, for spacing trees, for treating their disease, and for promoting the growth of fruits and flowers of trees, creepers and shrubs. Tree-growing was to be practised for aesthetic effect as well as for piety.

INDUSTRIES

There was enough production of raw materials, and

1. *Bṛihat-saṁhitā*, XXI, 32, 34 etc. XXIII, 2.
2. II, 9, 6 f.
3. *Bṛihat-saṁhitā*, 21 f, IX.42, X.18.
4. III, 9.
5. V 21 f; IX, 42, X, 18, XXV, 2, XXVII, 1 and XL.
6. Chapter 55.

skilful artisans and craftsmen were also available. It was, therefore, natural that there should be a vast development of different industries. There was a large variety of clothing material, which consisted of cotton, silk, wool and linen, as well as barks of trees.[1] The textiles were of various types. From the *Amarakośa*, it is discovered that different terms were in the use for finer and coarser varieties of cloth, as well as for unbleached and bleached silk and the like[2]. Different weaving techniques were used for gold and silver brocade, weaving after separate dying of the warp and the woof, and for spotted muslin. At Mandsor, silk cloths, which were delicate and of different colours, were manufactured.

Among the metals, iron was the most important. The sharp-edged swords of Vidiśā were famous[3]. There were iron industries at Ujjain. Gold and silver were obtained in exchange for raw material. The literary works of this period contain numerous references to the wear of gold and silver ornaments by the people.

Technical sciences were utilised for the manufacture of metals. These were *Rūparatnaparīkshā* (the testing of precious stones), *Dhātuvāda* (the melting of metals) and *Maṇirāgakara-jñānam* (technology of the jewels), and so forth. The art of the jeweller seems to have been in an advanced condition. The *Bṛihat-saṁhitā*[4] mentions no less than twenty-two jewels. The list includes diamond, sapphire, emerald, ruby, beryl, amethyst, crystal, etc. Varāhamihira[5] deals successively with varieties of diamonds, pearls, rubies and emeralds. Literary evidence[6] proves that jewels were used for a large variety of purposes—for being set in gold ornaments and seals, for adorning dresses, for covering couches and seats as well as mirrors and lamps, for decorating doorways, and for inlay of the floor of a house. Jewels were worn as good omens.

1. *Amarkośa*, II, 6, 110-11.
2. Ibid, 115-16.
3. Vikrama Volume, Eng. Ed.
4. 80, 4-5.
5. Ibid, 81.
6. Śaka : V, *Raghu*. XVI, 43; XVII, *Bṛihatsaṁhitā* LXXX. 2, 15-17; LXXI, 30; LXXXII.6; LXXXIII.

Pearls were used for inlay work in the manufacture of ornaments, sword handles and drinking vessels, as also for ornamentation of ladies' dresses.[1] There is a vivid picture of jewellers at work in a rich household, in a famous description of the heroine's palace in the *Mrichchhakaṭika* drama. Semi-precious stones were also used. Beads and other small objects of jasper, agate, carnelian, quartz, etc. have been discovered from the Gupta strata in the archaeological excavations at Ujjain, Vidiśā, Eran, etc.

TRADE AND COMMERCE :—

The main towns of Malwa, which flourished during this period, were Ujjain, Daśapura, Vidiśā, Eran, etc. These towns and villages in the neighbourhood, were connected by routes. Outside Malwa, these places were linked with Bharoch in the west, Paithan in the south, Mathura, Prayaga, Kāśī and Pāṭaliputra in the east. The routes were well protected during the Gupta rule. Goods were transported in carts and on the backs of animals.

Trade was not only internal, but also external. Malwa had brisk commercial relations with the Western countries through Bharoch. The principal items of export were pearls, precious stones, cloths, perfumes and ivory articles and the main imports were gold and silver. The trade was highly profitable and Malwa became a prosperous region.

From the *Pādatāḍitakam*, it is clear that Ujjain was a great commercial centre. Goods were bought by land and sea routes for purchase and sale from different places both inside and outside India. A large number of merchants from different countries settled there. People of Magaḍha, Kirāta, Kaliṅga, Vaṅga and Kāśya from the east, and of Cholaka, Pāṇḍyaka and Kerala people from the south, settled at Ujjain. Even the Śakas, Yavanas, Pārthians, etc. established their settlements. Ujjain became a cosmopolitan city.

GUILDS :—

Because of the development of trade and commerce, a

1. *Bṛihatsaṁhitā*, LXXI, 31-36; *Amarakośa*, II, 6, 105-06.
2. *Chaturbhāṇī*, p. 29.

large number of industries and crafts came into existence; which were organized in guilds. The affairs of the guild were managed by a President, and a small executive council of four or five members. It had its own rules and regulations.

From the Mandsor inscription[1] of 437-38 A. D., and 473-74 A. D., it is clear that the members of the silk weavers' guild, seeing better prospects of trade, migrated from Lāṭa to Daśapura. They were both rich and cultured. Besides their profession, some were well versed in folklore, some in astrology, and some in the military profession. In case of emergency, they could raise a militia from among their own members to afford protection to the person, property, and merchandise of their members. These members were so rich that they built a temple of the Sun at Daśapura, and later repaired it when needed from their own contributions. There might have been some other guilds of this type performing these functions.

CURRENCY :—

The coins of the Guptas are rarely found in Malwa. So far there is record of only two finds, one at Bamnāla[2] in Nimad, and the other at Sehora in Guna. All these coins are of gold. The Bamnāla hoard contains twenty-one specimens, and the rulers represented are Samudragupta, Chandragupta II, and Kumāragupta I. The coins obtained from Sehora are the issues of Chandragupta II. It seems that after the conquest of Eastern Malwa, the Guptas introduced silver coinage similar to those of the Kshatrapas in size, weight and fabric, especially in Malwa. The artistic value of the local coinage decreased, as it is clear from the coins of Rāmagupta and Jishṇu, which have been discovered at several places. These are copper coins and similar to those of Mālava coins in weight and fabric. The coins of Jishṇu are of different types, such as conch, wheel, Nandipada, vase with foliage, etc. The main types of Rāmagupta, are of lion and Garuḍa.

From literary and epigraphical sources, the names of the

1. CII, III, pp. 81 ff.
2. JNSI, V, p. 136.
3. ARADGS, 1924-25 p. 17.

current coins are known. In the *Pādatāḍitakam*,[1] *Suvarṇa*, *māshaka*, *māshakārdha* and *kākiṇī* have been mentioned. In the Sanchi inscription[2] of 450-51 A. D., there is a reference to *dīnāras* which were used for charitable purposes. Varāhamihira refers to the coin denominations *Kārshāpaṇa* and *rūpaka*, while giving the tariff of prices of precious stones. *Kārshāpaṇa* and *rūpaka* are used by Varāhamihira as two different names of one and the same coin. Most probably, he referred to late Gupta silver coins.

1. *Chaturbhāṇī*, p. 86.
2. The Monuments of Sanchi, p. 388.

CHAPTER—X

THE PARAMĀRA PERIOD

Before the Paramāras, the Mauryas and the Rāshṭrakūtas seem to have been ruling in Malwa in the seventh or eighth century A. D. It is possible that they owed allegiance to Harsha, but after his death, they became independent. The Mauryas are referred to in a record[1] at Jhālarāpāṭan, dated 690 A.D. At this time, Durgagaṇa was the ruler. He has been described as the chief of kings. Another inscription of the seventh or eighth century A.D. records the name of Śaṅkaragaṇa.[2] Śaṅkaragaṇa of this inscription, may belong to the same family as the princes Durgagaṇa and Śivagaṇa of the Kaṇaswā inscription of 738 A. D.[3] The Mauryas were probably ruling with their capital at Chitor in the seventh or eighth century A.D. The Ḍabok inscription[4] of V.S. 701 (644 A.D.) mentions the Guhila chief Dhanika of Dhavagarta, and the latter's overlord, *Paramabhaṭṭāraka Mahārājādhirāja Parameśvara* Dhavalappa. D. R. BHANDARKAR[5] identified Dhavalappa, of this inscription with the Maurya king, Dhavalātman, of the Kaṇaswā inscription.

In the Sanchi inscription[6] of about the seventh century A. D., the Lord of Mahāmālava has been mentioned, and also a certain ruler Vappakadeva, and his son *Mahārāja* Sarvva. The name of the son of Sarvva has been given in the inscription, but it has disappeared. To which dynasty these rulers belonged is not known. Voppaka, as a great courtier or general, who played an important part in the

1. IA, V, p. 182.
2. ARRMA, 1912-13, p. 2.
3. IA, XIX, p. 55.
4. EI, XXXV, p. 100.
5. IA, XIX, p. 57.
6. The Monuments of Sanchi, I, pp. 394-95.

political games of the feudatories of Durgagaṇa, has been mentioned in the Jhālarāpāṭan inscription[1] of 689 A. D. Vappakadeva of the Sanchi inscription may be identified with Voppaka of the Jhālarāpāṭan inscription.

The Indragarh inscription[2] refers to king Naṇṇappa, who was ruling in 710-11 A. D. His father was Bhāmāṇa. A Rāshṭrakūṭa prince, Naṇṇarāja, is mentioned in the Multai plates[3] dated 709-10 A. D., and the Sangaloda plates[4] dated 693-94 A.D. The dates provided for Naṇṇarāja by the Multai plates and the Sangloda plates (693-94 A.D.), came very close to the Mālava year 767 (710-11 A. D.). One is tempted to identify Naṇṇappa of the Indragarh stone inscription with Naṇṇarāja. There is only the discrepancy of the name of the father. The Berar records give the name Svāmikarāja, while that of Naṇṇappa is mentioned as Bhāmāṇa. Yudhāsura was the name of Naṇṇarāja. It is possible that Bhāmāṇa might be the *biruda* of Svāmikarāja. If this identification of Naṇṇappa is accepted, it seems that the kingdom of the Rāshṭrakūṭas of Vidarbha extended as far as the Chambal in the North. Dhavalappa mentioned in the Ḍabok inscription, as overlord of the Guhila Chief Dhanika, might be related to Rāshṭrakūṭa Naṇṇapa, bearing a similar *appa* ending name. Dhavalappa assumed the title *Paramabhaṭṭāraka Mahārājādhirāja Parameśvara*.

V. V. Mirashi[5] suggested that the prince mentioned in the Indragarh record was probably a petty ruler accepting suzerainty of the Mauryas, who were supreme in this region. But there is no conclusive evidence to show that the region actually formed part of the dominions of the Mauryas whose suzerainty was recognized by Naṇṇappa. This inscription does not mention the overlord of Naṇṇappa. Naṇṇappa seems to be an independent ruler. This record, though not referring

1. IA, V, p. 182.
2. EI, XXXII, p. 112; The Journal of the Bihar Research Society 1955, p. 1.
3. IA, XVIII.
4. Ibid, XXIX, p. 109.
5. IHQ, XXXI, No. 2, p. 99.

to any specific exploit of this ruler, mentions him as a prince of great valour, who made his enemies leave the battlefield.

ARAB INVASION :—

Next came the Arab aggression. Sindh was conquered by them in 712 A.D. Between 724 and 738 A.D., Janaid, or his successor Tamin[1], tried to extend Muslim dominion over interior parts of India. They conquered Bailmān and Jurz, and his lieutenants proceeded as far as Ujjain, overrunning Marmad, Mandal, Dahnaz, Burwas and Malibah. Malibah and Uzain no doubt stand for Mālava and its capital city Ujjayinī. It appears that the Arabs advanced through Rajasthan, and proceeded as far as Malwa in the east, and Bhroach in the south. From the Navsārī inscription[2] also, it is learnt that the Arabs defeated the kings of the Saindhavas, the Kachchhelas. Saurāshṭra, the Chāvoṭakas, the Mauryas and the Gūrjaras, and advanced as far south as Navsārī. But the success of the Arabs was shortlived, and they were defeated by the Pratīhāra king Nāgabhaṭa,[3] and the Chālukya ruler of Lāṭa (S. Gujarat), Avanijanāśraya Pulakeśīrāja[4].

TRIPARTITE STRUGGLE AND THE ROLE OF MALWA :—

In the first half of the eighth century A.D., there emerged three imperial dynasties—the Pālas, the Pratīhāras and the Rāshṭrakūṭas. They played an important role in succeeding generations. The 'tripartite struggle' began between these powers, which, from time to time, continued for generations. These dynasties wanted to increase their respective power and influence. In this struggle, Malwa played a large part because of its economic and strategic importance. The independent but friendly state of Malwa was an asset to the power concerned. Its occupation opened the doors for further territorial expansion.

MALWA UNDER THE INFLUENCE OF THE RĀSHṬRAKŪṬAS :—

In this struggle, Malwa first came under the influence of

1. HIED, Vol. I.
2. ABORI, X, 31.
3. EI, XVIII, p. 87.
4. ABORI, X, 31.

the Rāshṭrakūtas. From the Samangad plates[1] dated 754 A.D., and the undated Daśāvatāra cave inscription[2] at Elora, of Dantidurga, it is clear that he fought on the bank of Mahi, Mahānadī and Revā, and won victories over Kāñchī, Kalinga, Śrī Śaila, Mālava, Lāṭa and Ṭaṅka. He made liberal rewards to various rulers at Ujjayinī. A later record[3] celebrates this by stating that Dantidurga performed *Hiraṇyagarbhadāna* in which the Gurjara lord and other kings were doorkeepers (*Pratīhāras*). The use of the phrase that the Gurjareśa was posted as the *Pratīhāra*, has led D. R. Bhandarkar[4] to conclude that a member of the Gurjara Pratīhāra family was ruling at Ujjain at this time. On this basis, some other scholars, like R. C. Majumdar,[5] A. S. Altekar,[6] R. S. Tripathi[7] and D. C. Ganguly,[8] think that Ujjain was the Pratīhāra capital before it was shifted to Kānyakubja. According to them, it is further confirmed by the verse of the *Harivaṁśapurāṇa*,[9] in which Vatsarāja has been mentioned as the ruler of Avanti.

MĀLAVA KINGDOM NOT UNDER THE PRATĪHĀRAS :—

The above views do not seem to be convincing. From the Daśāvatāra temple inscription, it is clear that the Mālava kingdom and the Gurjara kingdom were different.[10] The Gurjara kingdom of this inscription, lay somewhere on the sea-coast, and after its conquest, Dantidurga occupied the beautiful palace of Gurjareśvara. It is the Gurjara kingdom of Bharoch and the ruler of this kingdom who acted as door-keeper along with others in the *Hiranyagarbha* ceremony.

The Gurjara king acting as *Pratīhāra* in the *Hiraṇyagarbha*

1. IA, XI, 111.
2. PRAS, WC, V, 92.
3. EI, XVIII, 252. The Sanjan Plates of Amoghavarsha.
4. Ibid, XVIII, p. 239.
5. The Age of Imperial Kanauj, p. 22.
6. AR.
7. THK.
8. GHPD, p. 10.
9. *Harivaṁśapurāṇa*, p. 806, V. 52.
10. ASOI, Vol. V, p. 84.

ceremony should lead to the conclusion that he alone was the ruler of Malwa, when other Kshatriyas also participated in *Hiraṇyagarbhadāna* ceremony. It seems that Ujjain was already a sacred place, and Dantidurga, after its conquest, chose it for performing this ceremony in which he invited the different rulers, along with Gurjareśa, to participate.

As far as the verse of the *Harivaṁśa Purāṇa* is concerned, it is ambiguously worded and its meaning is not certain. It has given rise to a keen controversy.[1] From the literary and epigraphical source, it is clear that the kingdom of Vatsarāja was somewhere in Rajasthan, but not in Malwa. From the *Kuvalayamālā* of Uddyotana Sūri, it is clear that Vatsarāja was ruling at Jalor in 778 A.D. The inscriptions of Vatsarāja have been discovered in Rajasthan but not in Malwa. After his defeat at the hands of the Rāshṭrakūta ruler Dhruva, Vatsarāja retired to Maru in Rajasthan.

That Mālava was not a Pratīhāra kingdom, but was ruled by some other different chiefs, is clear from certain other facts. The Nesārikā grant[2] of Govinda III dated 805 A.D. mentions the Gurjara and Malwa kings separately. The king of Malwa was different from the Gurjara king. The Baroda copper plate[3] of Karkarāja dated 812 A. D. bears clear testimony to the fact that the Gurjara lord made a severe attack on the Malwa king, who was saved from ruin by the help of Karkarāja. The inscription of the Khālimpura plates[4] of Dharmapāla of Bengal, also mentions the king of Malwa among those rulers who acclaimed the succession of Dharma-Pāla's protege, Chakrāyudha to the throne of Kanauj. This role cannot be that of the Gurjara Pratīhāra ruler Vatsarāja. The Malava ruler, who was present at Kanauj in the ceremony of accession, actually allied himself with the enemies of the Gurjara Pratīhāra ruler, Vatsarāja. It was perhaps, to punish the ruler of Avanti for his hostile activities, that Nāgabhaṭa II, the son and successor of Vatsarāja, attacked Malwa and

1. For various opinions, JDL, X, 23-25; also IC, XI, 161 ff.
2. EI, XXXIV, p. 131.
3. IA, XII, p. 163.
4. EI, IV, p. 243.

captured some outlying forts.[1] This very Malwa ruler, or his father, may have been the one who aided Govinda II against his brother, Dhruva Dhārāvarsha.[2]

OBSCURE DYNASTY PROBABLY KNOWN FROM THE MAHUA INSCRIPTION :—

The family which ruled over Malwa during the beginning of the tripartite struggle, is not definitely known. The Mahua inscription[3] of the latter half of the eighth century A. D., records the genealogy of the family of Vatsarāja, the hero of *Praśasti*. It is said that there was a king called Āryabhāsa, alias Vyāghrahela. He was followed by his son, Nāgavardhana. After him, came Tejovardhana, who was followed by Udita. The latter's son was Vatsarāja. The family name has not been mentioned. It simply states that the body of Vatsarāja was divided by his sacred thread (*Yajñopavīta*). He bore in his body faculties (*tejas*) of both Brāhmaṇas and Kshatriyas. It seems that Vatsarāja of this inscription belonged to a family with Brāhmaṇa-Kshatriya intermarriage.

It appears that the ancestor of Vatsarāja of this obscure dynasty was ruling over Avanti in the eighth century A.D., when Ujjayinī was conquered by the Rāshṭrakūṭa king, Dantidurga (735-755 A. D.). Jinasena, who completed his Jaina *Harivaṁśa* in Vardhamānapura or Wadhwan in Kathiawad, refers to one Vatsarāja, the king of Avanti, as ruling over the eastern region in 783-84 A. D. This Vatsarāja may be identified with Vatsarāja of this inscription. The *Kuvalayamālā* written in 778 A. D., refers to the ruler of Malwa as Avantivardhana. This Avantivardhana was probably meant for the ruler of this dynasty, because the names of some rulers end in Vardhana.

The absence of reference to any overlord in the Mahua inscription probably suggests that this Vatsarāja was an independent, or at least a semi-independent ruler. He continued to maintain his independent position, but sided with the Rāshṭrakūṭas and the Pālas against the Gurjara Pratīhāras in the

1. EI, XVIII, p. 118.
2. Ibid, XII, p. 184.
3. Ibid, XXXVII, No. 11.

tripartite struggle. The dynasty probably perished in the struggle.

NĀGA DYNASTY :—

A Nāga dynasty was ruling near Shergarh in the eighth century A.D. An inscription[1] found at Shergarh refers to *Sāmanta* Devadatta ruling in 790 A. D. As the names of the three ancestors, namely Bindunāga, Padmanāga and Sarvanāga, nd in Nāga, it may be taken that a Nāga family was ruling n this region in the eighth century A.D., if not earlier.

MALWA AS BUFFER STATE :—

In this struggle between the Pratīhāras and the Rāshṭrakūṭas Malwa's position was that of a buffer state which had to bear the brunt of the fighting, whenever these two imperial powers clashed with each other. D. C. GANGULY[2] thinks that Malwa remained a Rāshṭrakūṭa dependency up to the time of Mahipāla Pratīhāra (918-33 A.D.). This view does not appear to be convincing. Mihira Bhoja of the Pratīhāra dynasty had effective control over Malwa, and it continued even in the reign of Mahipāla. In the tenth century A. D., the power of the Pratīhāras began to decline, and the Rāshṭrakūṭas occupied themselves in the affairs of the South. This gave an opportunity to the Paramāras. In the struggle between the Rāshṭrakūṭas and the Pratīhāras, they sided with the former and thus they gradually gathered strength.

ORIGIN OF THE PARAMĀRAS

THEORY OF FIRE-PIT :—

The origin of these Paramāras, like the other Rājapūta clans, is lost in obscurity. The *Navasāhasāṅkacharita* of Padmagupta, the commentary of Abhayatilakagaṇi on the *Dvyāśrayamahākāvya*, and most of the Paramāra inscriptions[3], declare the origin of the Paramāras from the fire-pit of *Ṛishi* Vasishṭha at Abu. The bardic tales, some of which have been recorded

1. EI, XXIII, p. 132.
2. GHPD, pp. 32-33.
3. Udaipur Praśasti, EI, I, pp. 222-38; Nagpur *Praśasti* EI, II, pp. 180-95; Vasantgarh inscription, EI, XVI, pp. 183 ff, Paṭanārāyaṇa inscr., IA XLV, pp. 77 ff. and Jainad Inscr. EI, XXII, pp. 66 ff., etc.

by J. Tod[1], and the *Prithvīrājarāso*,[2] also give this version of the origin of the Paramāras.

According to G. H. Ojha,[3] the theory of the fire-origin of the Paramāras became popular because in some of their inscriptions, Dhūmarāja has been mentioned as the first ancestor of the family. Dhūma, the first half of the name meaning smoke, was enough to suggest to the *Praśasti* writers and bards to build up a theory of the fire-origin of this royal family. But actually, the inscription in which the name Dhūmarāja occurs, is of a comparatively late period. Padmagupta and the early inscriptions of the Paramāras, give 'Paramāra' as the name of the dynasty after whom the family was named. It seems that when the *Agnikula* theory became popular enough, the later *Praśasti* writers made Dhūmarāja as the progenitor of the family in place of Paramāra. Thus it is not the name Dhūmarāja that gave rise to the *Agnikula* theory, but the theory which gave rise to the name of Dhūmarāja in place of Paramāra.

THE PARAMĀRAS AS THE GURJARAS :—

Watson, Campbell, Forbes, D. R. Bhandarkar and H.C. Ray, hold that the Paramāras were an offshoot of the Gurjaras, who are believed to have entered India with the Hūṇas during the fifth and sixth centuries A.D., after the downfall of the Imperial Guptas.[4] As one of the *Agnikulas*, named Pratīhāras, was named Gurjaras in some of their records, so the remaining three i.e. the Chahamānas, the Chālukyas and the Paramāras, should be assumed to have been the Gurjaras.[5] The Chāpas, one of the branches of the Paramāras, are known as the Gurjaras.[6] Some of the Osavālas, who were Paramāras,

1. AAR, p. 79.
2. Part, I, pp. 45-51.
3. *Rājaputānā kā Itihāsa*, p. 67.
4. IA, L, pp. 145 ff; Bomb. Gaz., Vol. IX, PL.II, pp. 485 ff; IA, XL, p. 30; JRAS, 1909, Pt. I, pp. 53-54; Bomb Gaz., Vol. I, Pt. I, p. 2; Journal of the Royal Anthropological Research Institute of Great Britain (1911) pp 39 ff.; AA, Vol. III p. 1445; JDL, Vol. X, p. I; Smith EH I, p. 138; THK, pp. 221-23; JRAS, 1904, p. 640; Ibid, 1907, p. 988, ASC Vol. II, pp. 72-73.
5. IA, XL, p. 30.
6. Ibid. IV, p. 145.

are well known as the Gurjara Osavālas[1].

These arguments do not seem to be logically conclusive. It is illogical to regard four *Agnikulas* as the Gurjaras, when only one is known so. It is against literary and epigraphical evidence. This *Agnikula* theory of the four clans is based on the *Pṛithvīrājarāso* written in the fifteenth or sixteenth century A. D. Besides, '*Gurjara*' is not only the name of the people, but also of the territory. Those who lived in the Gurjara land, were known as Gurjaras. Hence, the Pratīhāras, the Chāpas and the Osavālas were known as the Gurjaras, after the name of the territory.

THE PARAMĀRAS AS THE RĀSHṬRAKŪṬAS :—

D. C. GANGULY[2] thinks that the Paramāras were the descendants of the Imperial Rāshṭrakūtas of Mānyakheṭa. According to Harsola Copper Plate grant[3] of Sīyaka II, dated V.S. 1005 = 949 A.D., Bappairāja (Vākpatirāja 1) was descended from the family of the Rāshṭrakūṭa king Akālavarsha Kṛishṇa III, (939-66 A.D.). Vākpati Muñja, the son of Sīyaka II, assumed the Rāshṭrakūṭa titles of *Amoghavarsha*, *Śrīvallabha* and *Pṛithvīvallabha*. D. C. GANGULY further argues that the original home of the Paramāras must have been in the Deccan. He tries to find support in the statement of the *Āin-ī-Akbarī*, that Dhanañjaya, the founder of the Paramāra family, transferred his seat from the Deccan to Malwa.

The arguments of D. C. GANGULY are not very convincing. The Harasola Copper Plate inscription refers to Bappairāja's relations with the Rāshṭrakūṭa house on his mother's side as otherwise; if the Paramāras were direct descendants of the Rāshṭrakūṭa emperors, the Paramāra rulers would have continued to mention the fact even in their later records. The Harasola copper plate inscription mentions two Rāshṭrakūṭa kings, Amoghavarsha and Akālavarsha. If the Paramāras had been the descendants of the Rāshṭrakūṭas, Sīyaka II in the Harasola plate grant would have drawn the pedigree of his family from the early members of the Rāshṭrakūṭa family, and

1. Bomb. Gaz. IX, Pt. I, p. 485.
2. GHPD, p. 9.
3. EI, XIX, p. 236.

not simply mentioned his own, and his father's, contemporary Rāshṭrakūṭa rulers.

It is not possible to draw any definite conclusion in this respect from the Harasola copper plate grant. Even Sīyaka II used Rāshṭrakūṭa titles in his Gaonari grants. It is possible as well, to suggest that even Vākpati II considered himself the successor of the departed glory of the Rāshṭrakūṭas. He was doing what the Rāshṭrakūṭas had done when they appropriated some of the imperial Chālukya titles.

As far as the evidence of *Āin-i-Akbarī* is concerned, it is of very late period. No name of Dhanañjaya is found in the genealogy of the Paramāra rulers.

It is unlikely that Padmagupta, the courtier of Vākpati Muñja would forget the origin of the Paramāras and give a false view—within the short space of twenty-five years or so. It would have been the proud privilege of the Paramāras to trace their lineage from the Rāshṭrakūṭas, who were one of the most powerful ruling dynasties of the time. We cannot bypass the evidence supplied by Padmagupta, and the inscriptions (which unanimously speak of the Paramāras as born of the sacrificial fire at Mt. Abu), in favour of the vague and stray reference in the Harasola grant.

THE PARAMĀRAS AS THE MĀLAVAS :—

D. C. Sircar[1] is of the view that the early Paramāras, who ruled over Mālava country near the Mahi river, were Mālavas by nationality. There is no evidence that in the beginning these Paramāras were called the Mālavas. In course of time, when they occupied the Mālava land, they began to be called Mālavas.

THE PARAMĀRAS AS BRĀHMAṆAS: A theory of the Paramāras as Brāhmaṇas originally advocated by Dasharatha Sharma[2] was followed by Pratipala Bhatia.[3] Halāyudha,[4] the

1. Ancient Malwa and the Vikramāditya Tradition, p. 12.
2. Rājasthāna Bhāratī, Vol. 3, No. 2.
3. The Paramāras—(800—1305 A.D.), p. 19.
4. *Brahma-kshatra-kulīnaḥ samasta-sāmanta-chakra-nuta charṇaḥ* |
sakala-sukrit-āika—puñjaḥ śrīmān Muñja—śchiraṁ jayati || This Verse

court-poet of Vākpati-Muñja, has used the word '*Brahmakshatra*' for his patron in his *Piṅglasūtravṛitti*. The expression means, perhaps, that Muñja belonged to a family which had the attributes of Brāhmaṇas as well as of Kshatriyas, i.e. the learning of the former and the valour of the latter. The Paramāras, like the Śuṅgas, the Sātavāhanas and the Kadambas, were descended from an ancestor who though originally a Brāhmaṇa, through adopting the profession of arms, came to be regarded as a Kshatriya. In the case of the Paramāras, the possibility increases still further as it is known that their *gotrochchāra* was *Vasishṭha gotra*. It is probable that they were originally Vasishṭha Brāhmaṇas, but later on came to be regarded as Kshatriyas on account of adopting *Kshatradharma*.

This view also is not free from difficulties. The expression '*Brahmakshatra*' means that Vākpati Muñja, in spite of being a king, was also a learned scholar. He possessed the qualities of learning and valour. It does not mean that he was descended from some Brāhmaṇa ancestor. Some priest seems to have transmitted his gotra to the Paramāras, and therefore they were known as of Vasishṭha *gotra*. It does not mean that they were Brāhmaṇas.

It is difficult to be definite about the origin of the Paramāras. Both from literary and epigraphical sources, it is clear that the early Paramāras were connected with Abu in one way or other, and they followed the profession of arms. The *Agnikula* myth signifies, perhaps, that some sort of religious rite was performed in the presence of the sacred fire, by a priest to inspire them to fight for the protection of religion and culture.

The Paramāras of Malwa may have at sometime settled near Abu. Taking advantage of the confusion caused by the struggle between the Pratīhāras and the Rāshṭrakūṭas, they occupied Malwa. The knowledge of the early Paramāra rulers from Upendra to Vairisiṁha is scanty; there are no records, and they are known only from later sources.

Both the *Navasāhasāṅkacharita* and the Udaipur *Praśasti*

clearly states that the Paramāras belonged to the Brāhmaṇakshatra family, meaning thereby, that by birth, they were Brāhmaṇas, and because they took to arms by profession, they were Kshatriyas.

regard Upendra as the founder of this dynasty. Some scholars[1] believe that Upendra had another name i.e. Kṛishṇarāja. In Muñjā's land grants,[2] the pedigree begins with Kṛishṇarāja. Even in some inscriptions, it starts from Sīyaka. It does not mean that Sīyaka is the founder of the branch. The synonymity of Upendra and Kṛishṇa can, no doubt, be put forward in favour of proposed identity, but it is not based on sound arguments.

Vākpati Muñja, the seventh king of the dynasty, commenced his reign about 972 A.D. D.C.Ganguly and Pratipala Bhatia, regard Upendra as a king of Malwa, and they place him either in the last quarter of the eighth century A. D., or in the first quarter of the ninth century A.D. Pratipala Bhatia assigns twenty-five years of rule to each. She further holds, that the ruler of Avanti who took part in coronation ceremony of Chakrāyudha at Kanauj in 791 A.D, was Upendra. Upendra was the Malwa vassal of the Rāshṭrakūṭa ruler Govinda III, who commissioned Karkarāja, the chief of Lāṭa, to defend Malwa against the incursion of the Pratīhāra ruler, Nāgabhaṭa II. These views are only conjectures, and not based on solid evidence. It is doubtful whether Upendra was the ruler of Malwa. The time assigned to him and his successors is not correct. At this time, Malwa was under the control of the Rāshṭrakūṭas and Pratīhāras, and there was no room for the Paramāras to occupy this region.

A. S. Altekar and K. A. N. Sastri identify Upendra Paramāra with Upendra of the Begumra plates (also called the Nansārī plates) of Indra III[3]. On the basis of this inscription, they make Upendra as adversary of Indra III, and they put his reign between 900 and 915 A.D. and regard him as the grandfather of Sīyaka II[4]. This creates many difficulties, the most important of which is chronological. It goes against the evidence provided by the Udaipur *Praśasti* and the *Navasāhasāṅkacharita*.

1. H. C. Ray, G. H. Ojha, Bühler, Cunningham and Hall.
2. IA, VI, p 51; XIV, p. 160.
3. EI, IX, pp. 24 ff. JBBRAS, XVIII, pp. 254 ff.
4. AR, p. 100 and
   Dr. Lakshmana Swaroop Commemorative Volume, p. 297.

It seems that Upendra was the ruler of the territory in Gujarat in the ninth century A. D. He was ambitious and adventurous. From the Udaipur *Praśasti*, it is known that he gained the high order of kingship by his own valour. He was particularly famous for performing many sacrifices. He lightened the burden of taxes borne by his subjects, and patronized learning. The poetess Sītā, who made him subject of her song, may have been at his court. His queen was called Lakshmīdevī.

Upendra had two sons, Vairisiṁha I and Dambarasiṁha. Dambarasiṁha and his successors ruled in Vāgaḍa and Dungarpur until the early part of the twelfth century A.D. Vairisiṁha succeeded his father. His name is omitted in the *Navasāhasāṅkacharita*, and the Udaipur *Praśasti* says that he composed his own eulogy by erecting pillars of victory on the earth bounded by four oceans. He might have extended his empire by some new conquests. Vairisiṁha was succeeded by Sīyaka I. Sīyaka I was succeeded by another ruler, whose name is omitted in the Udaipur *Praśasti*, but whose existence may be assumed by the statement of the *Navasāhasāṅkacharita*.

VĀKPATI I OR BAPPAIRĀJA :—

Vākpati I or Bappairāja must have been an important ruler, for he is mentioned not only in the Udaipur *Praśasti*, but is also the first ruler to be mentioned by name, after Upendra, in the *Navasāhasāṅkacharita*. In the Harasola grant, Sīyaka II traced his descent from Bappairāja.[1] He has been given the imperial titles "*Parama Bhaṭṭāraka Mahārājādhirāja Parameśvara*" in the land grants[2] of Vākpati Muñja.

The Udaipur *Praśasti*[3] also describes Vākpati as the Sun for water lilies and the eyes of the maidens of Avanti. This probably depicts his hold over Avanti. It seems that from the time of Vākpati I, the Paramāras began to exercise some sort of control over Malwa. He has been also described as resembling *Śatamakha* (Indra), and whose armies drank the

1. EI, XIX, pp. 236 ff.
2. Dharmapuri grant IA, VI pp. 51 ff. and Ujjain grant, XIV, pp. 160.
3. EI, I, p. 234, Verse 10.

waters of Gaṅgā and of the ocean. It seems that as a feudatory chief of Mahendrapāla II, he took part in the latter's conquests of Magadha and Vaṅga, and in the course of these expeditions, he might have reached as far as the Bay of Bengal. Bards[1] also credit him with a campaign in Kāmarūpa (Assam), in which he is said to have been successful after twenty-seven days. The conquest of Assam is not possible, but the reference is probably to his eastern campaign.

H.C.Ray[2] and D.C.Ganguly[3] hold that during Vākpati's reign, Rāshṭrakūṭa Indra III probably halted at Ujjain, while advancing with his army against the Pratīhāra Mahipāla. It is not likely that Vākpati I accompanied Indra in that expedition. The Udaipur *Praśasti* mentions that he led his army up to the banks of the Gaṅgā. It is difficult to agree with the above view. The only basis is the mention of the courtyard of *Kālapriya* as the place where Indra stabled his elephants on his way to Kanauj. They identified '*Kālapriya*' with Mahākāla of Ujjain. V. V. Mirashi[4] suggested that *Kālapriya*' is identical with Kalpi in Central India, and lies on the road from Mānyakheṭa to Kanauj. Thus there is no basis for Indra's march through Malwa. It is doubtful whether Vākpati was ruling at this time, and whether his rule was comprised of Malwa.

VAIRISIṀHA II :—

From the Udaipur *Praśasti*[5], it is known that Vairisiṁha is also known as Vajraṭasvāmin. He increased Paramāra influence and power by occupying Dhāra. D. C. Ganguly[6] and Pratipala Bhatia,[7] make him a contemporary of Mahipāla. Pratipala Bhatia assigned him the dates 919-945 A.D. This view does not seem to be reasonable. Mahipāla's hold over Malwa was very strong, and there was no chance of

1. The Paramāras (c. 800-1305 A.D.), p. 36.
2. DHNI, II, p. 846.
3. GHPD, pp. 32 ff.
4. Studies in Indology, Vol. I, p. 41.
5. EI, I, Verse 11.
6. GHPD, p. 33.
7. The Paramāras (c. 800-1305 A.D.), p. 36.

success for Vairisiṁha. The people in the Vindhyan territories bowed before him. He was the axe to the Kuntalas i.e. the Rāshṭrakūṭas. He also attacked the Ramaṭhas.[1] From the Kalha plates[2], it is known that Bhāmana, the grandson of Bhoja I's feudatory Guṇambodhideva, distinguished himself by the conquest of Dhāra. As he was a petty local chief of the Kalachuris of Gorakhpur, he could have occupied Dhāra only as a feudatory of Bhoja's grandson, Mahipāla. The Pratapagarh inscription[3] also mentions that both Mandu and Ujjain were ruled by the Pratīhāra officials in **946** A.D. It seems that Vairisiṁha II occupied Dhāra only after 946 A.D., when the Pratīhāra empire was dismembered.

SĪYAKADEVA II ALIAS HARSHA :—

Vairisiṁha II was succeeded by his son Sīyaka II, who was also known as Harsha. The *Prabandhachintāmaṇi*[4] called him Siṁhadantabhaṭṭa. He was the greatest among the early Paramāra rulers of Malwa. He assumed the titles of *Mahārājādhirājapati* and *Mahāmaṇḍaleśvara Chūḍāmaṇi*.[5] He increased his power to a considerable extent at the cost of both the Gurjara Pratīhāras and the Rāshṭrakūṭas. Actually, he was the real initiator of Paramāra imperialism, and strengthened his position by new conquests.

From the Harasola grants[6] dated V.S. 1005 (949 A. D.), it seems that in alliance with the king of Kheṭakamaṇḍala, Sīyaka II attacked Yogarāja and inflicted a crushing defeat on him. This Yogarāja has been identified with Avantivarman II of the Chālukya family. According to D. C. Ganguly,[7] Yogarāja was the vassal of the Rāshṭrakūṭas. PRATIPALA BHATIA[8] thinks that both Sīyaka II and Yogarāja were, perhaps, the feudatory chiefs of the Pratīhāras, and they wanted to extend their power.

1. JDL, X, p. 73.
2. EI, VII, pp. 85; CII, IV, No 74.
3. EI, XIV, pp. 176 ff.
4. *Prabandhachintāmaṇi*, p. 21.
5. EI, XIX, p. 236.
6. Ibid, p. 242.
7. GHPD, p. 39.
8. The Paramāras—(c. 800-1305 A. D.), p. 39.

According to the *Navasāhasāṅkacharita*[1], Sīyaka II defeated a Hūṇa chief who was ruling over Hūṇa *Maṇḍala*. As to the locality of the Hūṇas, nothing is known. On the basis of the Gaonari plates[2] of Vākpati II, scholars locate the Hūṇa *Maṇḍala* in the region adjoining Indore and Mhow. This is not correct, and H. V. TRIVEDI rightly identified it with northern part of Mandsor District.[3]

Sīyaka's other achievement, according to the *Navasāhasāṅkacharita*,[4] was the defeat of the lord of Ruḍapāṭī. A territory called Rodapadi is mentioned in a fragmentary inscription[5] from Bhilsa, wherein Vāchaspati, the minister of king Kṛishṇa, is said to have restored the chiefs of Rālamaṇḍala and Roḍapadi to their dominions. D.C. GANGULI[6] thinks that Ruḍapāṭī was identical with Roḍapaḍī, a province which was supposed to be in the neighbourhood of Ḍāhalamaṇḍala and Malwa. It was probably somewhere near the eastern boundary of the Paramāra Kingdom.

The conquest of Ruḍapāṭī by Sīyaka led to the extension of his kingdom in the east, and it touched the Chandela kingdom. Yaśovarman Chandela was ruling at this time. Both Sīyaka and Yaśovarman were ambitious rulers. As they both wanted to extend their respective empires, a struggle between the two was inevitable. The Khajurāho inscription[7], dated 956 A. D. (V.S. 1013), claims that Yaśovarman Chandela was like the God of death to the Mālavas. The same inscription also registers the fact that in 956 A. D, the Chandela kingdom extended as far as Bhāsvat (i.e. Bhilsa). In this struggle, it seems that Sīyaka II had to acknowledge defeat at the hands of the Chandela Yaśovarman of Khajurāho. Yaśovarman pushed the boundary of his kingdom up to the Mālava river, which is probably identical with the Vetravatī, modern

1. NC, XI, v.90.
2. EI, XXIII, pp. 101 ff.
3. A Paper contributed to the Archaeology Section of the Oriental Conference, Ujjain.
4. NC, XI, V.89.
5. PRAS.WC, 1913-14, p. 59.
6. GHPD, p. 42.
7. EI, I, p. 128, v.23.

Betawa.

Sīyaka II's greatest achievement by the end of his reign was the capture and sack of Mānyakheṭa, the capital of the Rāshṭrakūṭas. By his aggressive policy Sīyaka II had alienated the Rāshṭrakūṭa ruler Kṛishṇa, but he was now busy in his southern campaigns. After the death of Kṛishṇa III, his son, Khoṭṭigadeva, became the ruler, but was weak and incapable. This gave a golden opportunity to Sīyaka II to give a blow to the tottering power of the Rāshṭrakūṭas. We learn from the Udaipur *Praśasti*[1] that Sīyaka, equalling the snake-eater (*Garuḍa*) in fierceness, took the wealth of king Khoṭṭiga from him in battle. In this bold venture, he was helped by the Paramāra Kaṁka or Chachcha, the ruler of Vāgaḍa. He captured and sacked Mānyakheṭa in 972 A.D. (1029).[2] The poet Dhanapāla, in the concluding verses of his *Paiyalachchhi*[3], states that he completed his work when one thousand years of the Vikrama era, and twenty nine besides, had passed, and at the time when Mānyakheṭa was plundered as the consequence of an attack by the Lord of Malwa.

Sīyaka II was a successful general. By dint of his sword, he was able to enlarge his small principality into a strong well-knit kingdom which extended from Banswara in the north, to the river Narmada in the south, from Kheṭaka-maṇḍala (i.e. modern Kaira and part of Ahmedabad District) in the west, to Bhilsa in the east.

Sīyaka's queen's name was Vaḍajā,[4] and she had two sons, Vākpatirāja II and Sindhurāja. He seems to have abdicated his throne in favour of his son, Vākpatirāja II, shortly after his return from his southern expedition.

VĀKPATI II :—

Vākpati II, also known as Utpalarāja and Muñja, became the ruler in 972 A.D. He assumed the titles of *Pṛithvīvallabha*, *Śrīvallabha* and *Amoghavarsha*. The Paramāra kingdom at this time was surrounded by many strong powers.

1. EI, I, V.12.
2. Ibid, XIX, p. 242.
3. Ed. by Bühler, Intro., p. 6, V.276, 277 and 278.
4. NC, XI, V.86.

In the south, there were the Chālukyas of Kalyāṇī under Tailapa II; in the east, there were the Kalachuris and the Chandelas and the Chahamānas of Śākambharī and Nāḍol and the Guhilas of Mewar, and the Chālukyas of Gujarat were ruling on the Western border. Vākpati II pursued the successful imperialistic policy initiated by his father in dealing with most of these powers, but he failed against the Chālukyas of Kalyāṇī.

In the beginning of his reign, Vākpati II came into conflict with the Guhilas of Mewar. He destroyed the elephant forces of the king of the Guhilas who was either Naravāhana or his son Śaktikumāra, and plundered his capital of Āghāṭa, modern Ahar in Udaipur. The vanquished chief saved his life by taking shelter with the Rāshṭrakūṭa Dhavala of Hastikuṇḍi in Marwar,[1] As a result of this victory, the eastern part of Mewar and the territory adjoining Malwa, was annexed to the Paramāra dominion.

Another ally of the Guhila ruler defeated by Vākpati II, was the Gurjara ruler, whose plight was specially pitiable. Hard pressed by the victors, the Gurjara king left the battlefield and sought refuge with the Rāshṭrakūṭa Dhavala of Hastikuṇḍi.[2] D.C.Ganguly[3] and Dasharatha Sharma[4] think that the Gurjara ruler defeated by Vākpati II was Mūlarāja Chālukya of Gujarat. In the tenth century A.D., the word 'Gurjara' was used for the Pratīhāra rulers. He should be identified with Mahipāla's weak successor Vijayapāla, who ruled between 954 and 989 A. D. Pratipala Bhatia[5] holds that Vākpati II, after defeating the Gurjara Pratīhāra ruler Vijayapāla, occupied Ujjain, which was under the possession of the Gurjara Pratīhāras by 946 A.D. It seems that Ujjain was already conquered by his father Sīyaka II, and soon after his accession, Vākpati II issued his land grants[6] from Ujjain in 973 A.D.

1. EI, X, p. 20.
2. Ibid, X, p. 20, v.10.
3. GHPD, pp. 53-54.
4. E. Ch. D., pp. 122-23.
5. The Paramāras (c. 800-1305 A. D.), p. 49.
6. IA, VI, p. 51.

Vākpati II's victory over the Guhilas of Mewar brought the boundary of his kingdom close to that of the Chauhānas of Marwar. As a consequence, conflict between the two powers was natural. Padmagupta[1] sang of Vākpati II's fame, as causing the pearls in the necklaces of Marwar women to dance. This evidence is corroborated by the testimony of Kauthen grant of Vikramāditya V.[2] It says, "The people of Marwar trembled at the approach of Utpala." On the other hand, the Sevāḍi plates of Ratnapāla, call Śobhita Chāhamāna of Nāḍol by the Lord of Dhāra[3]. Śobhita's successor, Balirāja, also claims to have defeated the army of Muñja[4]. The question is how to reconcile these two contradictory facts. It seems that in the early phase of the struggle, the Chauhānas gained some success against the Paramāras. Vākpati II soon recovered his position, and pushed them back from his frontiers. Three rulers of the Chahamīna family of Nāḍol, viz. Śobhita, Balirāja and Vigrahapāla, died within the short period of fourteen years, while Vākpati II was on the throne of Malwa. It seems that their deaths might not have been due to natural causes, but through conflict with the Paramāras of Malwa.

Vākpati II also conquered the Hūṇas, who seem to be the same people as defeated by his father. The Kauthen grant[5] of Vikramāditya V, describes Vākpati II as the destroyer of the Hūṇas. From the Geonri inscription[6] of Vākpati II, it is clear that he granted the village Vaṇika, situated in the *Hūṇamaṇḍala*, to certain Brāhmaṇas. Vākpati's conquest over the Hūṇas does not seem to have been final because his successor, Sindhurāja, also had to deal with them.

D. C. Ganguly[7] builds up the ingenious theory of the partition of the kingdom among the Paramāra princes, by Vākpati II, simply on the similarity of the names of the

1. JBBRAS, XVI, p. 174.
2. EI, XVI, p. 23.
3. Ibid, XI, pp. 308 ff.
4. Ibid, IX, p. 75, V. 7.
5. IA, XVI, p. 23; EI, XII, p. 276.
6. EI, XXIII, pp. 101 ff.
7. GHPD, pp. 22, 52 and 298.

ruling chiefs. While marching towards Marwar, Vākpati II conquered Abu, Jālor, Kirāḍu, etc. He divided the newly acquired territory among the princes of the Paramāra royal blood. He is believed to have appointed his sons, Araṇyarāja and Chandana, to look after the administration of Abu and Jālor respectively, while his nephew, Dūsala, was assigned the government of Kirāḍu.

Though this theory has been accepted by some scholars, such as H. C. RAY[1] and K. M. MUNSHI,[2] it has been proved to be fallacious by PRATIPALA BHATIA.[3] The conquest of Abu cannot be inferred from Vākpati II's expedition to Marwar. It is not on the direct route. Abu was ruled by another line of the Paramāras. The conquest of Abu by Vākpati II, also known as Utpala, cannot be established on the grounds that many Abu inscriptions mention Utpalarāja as the founder of the Abu line of the Paramāras.[4] This Utpalarāja was the fourth in lineal ascent from Dharaṇivarāha,[5] who was ruling over Abu sometime between 967 and 1002 A. D. As Araṇyarāja, who was the grandfather of this Dharaṇivarāha, would have lived about two generations earlier than Vākpati II of Malwa, it is obviously impossible to endorse D.C. GANGULY's view that Araṇyarāja was a son of Vākpati II.[6] Sindhurāja was actually the founder of the Paramāra family of Abu, and not Utpalarāja.

It is also not known whether Chandana was a son of Vākpati II. Neither epigraphy nor tradition proves that he had any son. Most probably, he died without any male issue, and for this reason was succeeded first by his younger brother, and then by his nephew Bhoja.

D. C. GANGULY puts forward the view that Vākpati II appointed his nephew Dūsala, a son of Sindhurāja, as the chief of Kirāḍu. He based his conclusion on the Kirāḍu inscription of Someśvara dated 1161 A. D., wherein the genea-

1. DHNI, II, pp. 854, 909 and 924.
2. The Glory that was Gurjaradeśa, III, p. 113.
3. The Paramāras (c. 800-1305 A. D.), p. 51.
4. EI, IX, pp. 10-15.
5. Ibid, XXXII, p. 137.
6. IHQ, 1958, pp. 174-76.

logy of the Paramāras of Kirāḍu starts from Sindhurāja, who has been taken as the brother of Vākpati II.[1] It is incorrect that the name of the successor should be read as Dūsala, for it is Utpala. Even if the reading is accepted, Sindhurāja of the Kirāḍu inscription, known as the *Mahārāja* of *Marumaṇḍala*, is different from Sindhurāja of Malwa, who ruled between 997 and 1010 A. D. On the other hand, Sindhurāja must have lived in the last quarter of the ninth century A. D. and his son (whether he was Dūsala or Utpala) somewhat later, i.e. about 900 A. D.

Vākpati II also tried to extend his empire in the east. The Udaipur *Praśasti* describes that he vanquished Yuvarāja, slew his generals, and raised his sword high in Tripuri. It means that he defeated the Kalachuri Yuvarāja II and plundered his capital of Tripuri. He could not annex any part of the Kalachuri kingdom. V. V. MIRASHI suggests that Vākpati II may have made peace with the Kalachuris, and returned their kingdom.

It seems that after his victories and conquests in the north, Vākpati II turned his attention towards the south. The Udaipur *Praśasti* asserts that he subdued the *Karṇāṭas*, *Lāṭas*, *Keralas* and *Cholas*.[2] But it is rather too general a statement to carry conviction. He could not have reached the country of the Kerals and Cholas which lay beyond the Karṇāṭa dominions. It is possible that the Cholas and the Keralas sought Vākpati II's help against their enemies.

It is certain that Vākpati II fought against the Lāṭas and the Karṇāṭas. Lāṭa was not only close to Malwa, but it was ruled by the Chālukya Bārappa, the general of the Chālukya Taila II, the life-long enemy of Vākpati II. Naturally, Bārappa owed allegiance to his master Taila II. Vākpati II attacked Lāṭa and defeated its ruler, Bārappa, or his son Goggirāja. A.K. MAJUMDAR[3] maintains that Lāṭa was already seized by Mūlarāja as evidenced from the Gujarat chronicles. Vākpati II came into conflict with the Chālukya ruler over

1. GHPD, p. 23.
2. EI, I, p. 234, V. 14.
3. Chālukyas of Gujarat, pp. 28-29.

the possession of that province. It is this Paramāra Chālukya conflict which is referred to in the Udaipur *Praśasti*.

Vākpati's war with the Karṇāṭas, i. e. the Chālukyas of Kalyāṇī, was natural, because he defeated their general Bārappa, the chief of Lāṭa. Besides, after the decline of the power of the Rāshṭrakūṭas, Tailapa Chālukya became powerful in the south and Vākpati II himself also adopted an aggressive policy. According to Merutuṅga[1], Vākpati II defeated Tailapa more than once before he himself was finally defeated at the hands of Karṇāṭa king. The Udaipur *Praśasti* also records the victory of Vākpati II over the Karṇāṭas. It seems that Vākpati II gained some success against his rival in the beginning. Tailapa continued the struggle in spite of some reverses. In order to get rid of this menace once and for all, Vākpati decided upon an aggressive campaign. His veteran minister, Rudrāditya, did not approve of this policy, and tried to prevent him from following it. On being unsuccessful, he requested his master not to cross the Godāvarī under any circumstances. Vākpati II led his army to the Deccan and crossed the Godavari in pursuit of the enemy, totally disregarding the advice of his minister. He was soon entrapped in his enemy's country, and taken prisoner. Taila II took possession of the southern part of the Paramāra kingdom, possibly up to the banks of the Narmadā. Muñja was tormented in several ways and finally executed on the orders of Taila. Such was the tragic end of a great king.

Vākpati II was a gifted general, but he is even more famous as a poet and a patron of art and literature. He was no mere nominal '*Vākpati*' (i.e. lord of speech), but a '*Vākpati*' in fact. The Udaipur praśasti[2] praises him for his learning, eloquence and poetical gifts. Because of his royal patronage, scholars from all parts of India flocked to his court. The most famous among them were Padmagupta, Dhanañjaya, Dhanika, Dhanapāla, Śobhana and Halāyudha. His inscription[3] of

1. *Prabandhachintāmaṇi*, p. 22.
2. EI, I, p. 234, V. 13.
3. IA, VI, p. 51.

Dharmapuri records a grant to Vasantāchārya, a philosopher who migrated to Malwa from Ahichchhatrā. The Gaonri inscriptions[1] of Vākpati II record the names of various Brāhmaṇa donees who migrated from different parts of India, such as from Bengal, Bihar and Assam. Vākpati II beautified Dhāra with many buildings. He also built a big tank called Muñjasāgara, and temples and embankments at Ujjain, Maheśvara, Oṁkāra, Māndhātā and Dharmapurī. A town in Gujarat bore his name, i.e. Muñjapura[2].

SINDHURĀJA : 995-1000 A. D.

The tradition recorded by Merutuṅga and others, that Vākpati Muñja, also called Utpala, was succeeded not by his younger brother Sindhurāja, but by the latter's son Bhoja, is contradicted by the *Navasāhasāṅkacharita* as well as by epigraphic evidence. PRATIPALA BHATIA[3] assigns the period of his reign from 997 to 1010 A. D., but this view is doubtful. Merutuṅga has assigned a reign of fifty-five years to Bhoja. We find the latest reference to Bhoja in 1055 A. D.[4] If we place Bhoja's reign between 1000-1055 A. D., it is natural to assign his predecessor's reign from 995 to 1000 A. D.

Sindhurāja assumed the titles of *Kumāranārāyaṇa* and *Navasāhasāṅka*. No inscription of Sindhurāja has yet been discovered, but the *Navasāhasāṅkacharita* and the later Paramāra inscriptions, give information about his career and achievements. The Udaipur *Praśasti*[5] records the single fact that he conquered a king of the Hūṇas. The *Navasāhasāṅkacharita*[6] mentions the same victory, and in addition, others over the prince of the Kosalas as well as the inhabitants of Vāgaḍa and Lāṭa and the Muralas. As Padmagupta, the author of the *Navasāhasāṅkacharita*, was the court poet of Sindhurāja, it is only natural that he should give an exaggerated account of his

1. EI, XXIII, pp. 101 ff.
2. The Glory that was Gurjaradeśa, Vol. III, p. 117.
3. The Paramāras (c. 800-1305 A. D), p. 58.
4. Daśabalīya Chintāmaṇi Sārṇikā—Śaka 977 (1055 A. D.), (JOR) Madras, Vol. XIX, pt. ii Supplement. Int. p. 1.
5. EI, I, p. 234, V. 16.
6. NC, X, 14-20.

master. It is not fully reliable unless it is confirmed by some independent evidence.

Both D. C. GANGULY[1] and PRATIPALA BHATIA[2] think that soon after his accession, Sindhurāja led an expedition against the Kuntalas, the great enemies of his brother Vākpati II, in the south, and recovered the Paramāra territory lost by his predecessor. The Kuntaleśvara was most probably Tailapa II's successor Satyāśraya, who, soon after his accession in 997 A.D. , found himself involved in a protracted struggle with the Chola king Rājarāja the Great (985-1014 A. D.). Sindhurāja prabably took advantage of the situation. The success of Sindhurāja is not confirmed from any other independent evidence. His successor Bhoja also fought against the Kuntalas, and he might have recovered the territory.[3]

After consolidating his position, Sindhurāja attacked the Huṇas ruling in the neighbourhood. His victory over the Hūṇas is confirmed by the Udaipur *Praśasti* and the *Navasāhasāṅkacharita.* This victory was decisive, and the Hūṇa territory was annexed to the Paramāra kingdom.

Padmagupta speaks of his master's victory over the people of Vāgaḍa. D. C. GANGULY[4] thinks that it was against the Guhila territory of Vāgaḍa, that Sindhurāja led his army. PARTIPALA BHATIA[5] is of view that his contemporary ruler of Vāgaḍa, might have been Chaṇḍapa. It is not unlikely that Sindhurāja attacked Vāgaḍa, situated quite close to the Paramāra kingdom, but it is not confirmed by any other evidence.

Sindhurāja's victory over Kosala is also narrated in the *Navasāhasāṅkacharita*, but it is not confirmed by any other independent evidence. This Kosala must have been south Kosala i.e. modern Chhatisgarh and the adjoining territory.[6] Sindhurāja's contemporary ruler in Kosala might have been

1. GHPD, pp. 64 ff.
2. The Paramāras (c. 800-1305 A. D.), p. 59.
3. It is possible that Bhoja's expedition as the prince against Kuntalas has been ascribed to Sindhurāja.
4. GHPD, p. 106.
5. The Paramāras (c. 800-1305 A. D.), p. 61.
6. CII, IV, Intro. p. cxv.

Kaliṅgarāja.[1] The king of Kosala has been also identified with the Somavaṁśī ruler, Yayāti Mahāśivagupta.[2]

Goggirāja, the son of Bārappa Chālukya, might have seized his father's kingdom after the defeat of Vākpati II at the hands of the Chālukyas of Kalyāṇa. He soon had to confront the invading army of Sindhurāja, whose victory over the Lāṭas is sung by Padmagupta. Sindhurāja may have reduced the Lāṭa chief to subordination, but it is not confirmed by any other evidence.

Sindhurāja pushed his army further towards Aparānta, then ruled by a Śīlāhāra family,[3] where he is said to have won a victory. V. V. Mirashi[4] has suggested that Sindhurāja invaded Aparānta in order to help Arikesarin, alias Kesideva, against his younger brother Vajjaḍa, who had superseded the former's rightful claim of succession after the death of their father Aparājita, the Śīlāhāra ruler of Koṅkaṇa. Pratipala Bhatia[5] is of view that Sindhurāja's contemporary ruler in Koṅkaṇa, most probably was not Arikesarin, but his father Aparājita, who issued the land grant in 997 A.D. The occasion for this attack might have been provided by the fact that while Satyāśraya was fighting against the Cholas in the south, Aparājita was attacked by Sindhurāja and forced to accept latter's supremacy. This view is doubtful, because if it had been actually conquered by Sindhurāja, there would have been no need for Bhoja to conquer it.

The *Navasāhasāṅkacharita* speaks of Sindhurāja's victory over the Muralas. N. L. Dey[6] and B.C.Law[7] identify Murala with Kerala. Pratipala Bhatia[8] tried to locate it between Kerala and Aparānta. According to her, after his victory over Aparānta Sindhurāja pushed further south and defeated the Muralas. It is possible that the Muralas might have come in

1. CII, IV, No. 77.
2. QRHS, Vol. I, No. 3, 1961-62, p. 128; MSI, II, p. 59.
3. IC, II, p. 402.
4. IA, LXII, pp. 102-3; MSI, II, pp. 61-62.
5. The Paramāras (c. 800-1305 A. D.), p. 63.
6. Geographical Dictionary, pp. 98, 134.
7. Historical Geography, p. 163.
8. The Paramāras (c. 800-1305 A. D.), p. 66.

conflict with Sindhurāja, as feudatories or allies of the Chālukyas or Śīlāhāras of Koṅkaṇa. The victory of Sindhurāja against so many powers in the south is not possible because he was not a daring soldier. It is only a panegyric account of the court poet for his master.

The *Navasāhasāṅkacharita* describes how Sindhurāja gained the Nāga princess Śaśiprabhā, the daughter of the Nāga king Śaṅkhapāla, after destroying the Asura Vajrāṅkuśa, who resided in Ratnavatī. The whole story seems to be mythological, but it is likely as some scholars have suggested, that it has some historical basis. The Nāga chief Śaṅkhapāla, has been identified with a ruler of Chakrakoṭya in Bastar.[1] At this time, Nāgas were ruling over this area, and bore the proud title of Lord of Bhogavatī.[2] They often engaged in hostilities with the Kalachuris of Ratnapur.[3] The Nāga ruler Śaṅkhapāla, might have not been in good terms with Vajjuka, a Kalachuri ruler, and sought the aid of the Paramāra king Sindhurāja against him. Sindhurāja found a good opportunity to strengthen the south-eastern frontier of his kingdom.[4] Together with the Śīlāhāras, he marched against Vajrāṅkuśa whom he slew in battle, placed a Nāga prince in charge of his territory, and married the daughter of the Nāga king.

The *Navasāhasāṅkacharita* is silent about Sindhurāja's conflict with the Chālukyas. On the basis of Vaḍanagara *Praśasti*, G.H. OJHA thinks that Sindhurāja was killed on the battlefield at the hands of Chāmuṇḍarāja.[5] He finds support for his conclusion in the *Kumārapālacharita*,[6] wherein we are told that Chāmuṇḍarāja killed Sindhurāja in the battle. On the basis of Vaḍanagara *Praśasti*, it is held that Sindhurāja was not killed on the battlefield. It seems that Sindhurāja's armies came into conflict with the Chālukyan armies, but the Paramāras were defeated.[7]

1. CII, IV, Intro, p. cxx; MSI, II, p. 66.
2. Hiralal, Ins. of C. P. and Berar, p. 146.
3. MSI, II, p. 60.
4. EI, XXXIII, p. 253, f. n. 2.
5. *Ojhā Nibandha Saṁgraha*, p. 175.
6. *Kumārapālacharita*, 1.31.
7. The Paramāras (c. 800-1305 A. D.), p. 73.

BHOJA

In about 1000 A.D., Sindhurāja was succeeded by his son Bhoja, the most famous, and the greatest, Paramāra ruler of Malwa. Under him, Paramāra imperialism reached its zenith, and Malwa rose to its greatest glory and renown. He ruled for about fifty-five years, and his kingdom extended to Chitor, Banswara, Dungarpur, Bhilsa, Kandesh, Konkan, Sabarkantha, Ahmedabad region, and the upper courses of the Godavari.

As Bhoja seems to have been quite young at the time of his accession[1], he thought it better to consolidate his kingdom for a few years. Later by his aggressive policy, he involved himself in a life and death struggle with his neighbours.

To avenge the death of his uncle, Bhoja's first expedition was probably directed against the Chālukyas of Kalyāṇī. He made a confederation with the Kalachuri Gāṅgeyadeva and Rājendra Chola[2] of Tanjore for the invasion. Both Gāṅgeyadeva and Rājendrachola also were not on good terms with the Chālukyas of Kalyāṇī, because of their imperialistic policy. The Udaipur *Praśasti*[3] and the Kalvan[4] inscription record Bhoja's victory over the Karṇāṭas. Gāṅgeyadeva has been also described as defeating the king of Kuntala.[5] On the other hand, the Chālukya inscriptions claim Jayasiṁha II's victory over the Paramāras.[6] His vassal, Bachirāja, is also eulogised for having put the Mālavyas to shame by his victorious arms.[7] The battle between two rival forces was fought on the bank of the Gautama-Gaṅgā i. e. Godāvarī. It seems that the outcome of the Mālava-Chālukya struggle at this time remained indecisive.

During his southern campaign, Bhoja inflicted a defeat on Indraratha,[8] who was probably a Somavaṁśī ruler, whose capital was at Ādinagar, modern Mukhaliṅgam, in the Gan-

1. *Paramāravaṁśadarpaṇa*, p. 70.
2. Kulenur ins. EI, XV, pp. 330 ff.
3. EI, I, p. 235, V. 19.
4. Ibid, XIX, pp. 71-72.
5. CII, IV, No. 50, p. 256.
6. The Belagamva inscription, IA, V, pp. 17 ff; The Kulenur Inscr. EI, XV, pp. 330 ff.
7. Hyderabad Arch. series No. 8, p. 20.
8. EI, I, p. 234, V. 18.

zam District of Orissa[1]. He fought this battle in association with Rājendra Chola, who also claims to have defeated the ruler of Ādinagara[2].

The Udaipur *Praśasti* records Bhoja's victory over the Lord of Lāṭa. His contemporary ruler on the throne of Lāṭa was Kīrtirāja, whose Surat grant[3] is dated in 1018 A.D. An inscription of Kīrtirāja's grandson Trilochanapāla, states that Kīrtirāja's fame was temporarily taken away by his enemies.[4]

The conquest of Lāṭa by Bhoja brought his kingdom close to Koṅkaṇa, the territory of the Śīlāhāras. He seems to have attacked Koṅkaṇa, but the cause for which is not known. D. R. Bhandarkar[5] suggested that Bhoja undertook this expedition to avenge the murder of his uncle Muñja. This view does not seem to be correct. They were not responsible for the murder, and they also were not friendly disposed towards the Chālukyas of Kalyāṇa. V. V. Mirashi[6] is of the view that a nephew of Arikesarin usurped the throne after the death of the latter, setting aside the rightful claimant, Arikesarin's son. It seems that the imperialistic policy of Bhoja compelled him to attack Koṅkaṇa early in 1020 A.D. He occupied it and may have reduced the Śīlāhāras to vassalage.

Bhoja celebrated this victory by issuing two land grants i. e. Banswara copper plate[7] grant issued on third January, 1020 A.D. and Betma copper plate[8] grant issued in September, 1020 A. D. The occasion for the first was the *Koṅkaṇa-vijaya-parva* and for the second *Koṅkaṇa grahaṇa parva*.

Scholars have interpreted these expressions differently. Some think that as there is a difference of seven months and ten days between the two grants, the expressions cannot refer to one and the same festival observed on a certain fixed day

1. PIHC, 1940, pp. 66-67.
2. SII, Vol. III, p. 424.
3. Pathak Comm. Vol., pp. 287.
4. IA, XII, pp. 204 ff.
5. Ibid, XLI, pp. 210 ff.
6. Ibid, LXII 1933, pp. 101 ff and MSI. II, pp. 71-72.
7. EI, XI, p. 182.
8. Ibid, XVIII, p. 320.

of the year, but to the two different events. E. HULTZSCH[1] translated '*Koṅkaṇa vijaya*' of the Banswara plates, as the anniversary of the conquest of Koṅkaṇa. D. R. BHANDARKAR[2] translated it as 'on the festival day (*parvaṇi*) in consequence of the conquest of Koṅkaṇa'. The expression in the Banswara grant, means that Bhoja conquered 'Koṅkaṇa', and in the Betamā grant, perhaps that he occupied it[3]. DASHARATHA SHARMA[4] thinks that the '*Koṅkaṇa-vijaya-parva*' of the Banswara grant may mean the '*Koṅkaṇa-vijaya-yātrā-parva*' i.e. the day on which the Parmāra forces started on their expedition for the conquest of Koṅkaṇa. Seven months and ten days later, followed the '*Koṅkaṇa-vijaya-grahaṇa parva*' i.e, the day on which the farces of Bhoja occupied the whole of Koṅkaṇa. D. C. SIRCAR[5] rightly thinks that both the expressions mean the same event. viz. 'Bhoja's conquest of Koṅkaṇa'.

H. V. TRIVEDI[6] suggests that if the grants refer, respectively, to the conquest of Koṅkaṇa and its later annexation, then in the reading of the Betma grant, the word *Vijaya* should have been placed before *grahaṇa* and not after it. It would appear that the same victory was celebrated at either of these places at different times, and hence the difference of seven months between their dates.

Bhoja does not seem to have come into a direct clash with the Muslims, who led many expeditions under Mahmūd of Ghaznī. In 1008 A. D., he sent an army to help the Shāhī Ānandapāla against Mahmūd of Ghaznī. About 1019 A. D., he gave shelter to Ānandapāla's son Trilochanapāla who was hard pressed by Mahmūd. After sacking the temple of Somanātha (1024-26 A. D.), Mahmūd Ghaznī lacked the courage to return by the way he came, because on that side lay the armies of the great In dian ruler Param Deo, an encounter with whom might have meant defeat and disaster for the

1. EI, XI, p. 182.
2. IA, XLI, pp. 210 ff.
3. EI, XVII, p. 320.
4. Journal of Ganganath Jha Institute, V, pp. 61 ff.
5. EI, XXXIII, p. 215.
6. Inscriptionum Indicarum of the Later Dynasties of Central India, XVI, Typescript.

Muslim forces. Param Deo probably refers to the great Paramāra ruler, Bhoja, who was known to be the champion of Hinduism. Perhaps, Mahmūd's avoidance of Bhoja has been construed by the Udaipur *Praśasti*[1] into a defeat of the *Turushkas.* The chief 'Toggala', said to have been defeated by Bhoja, might have been a Ghaznavite general.[2] In 1043 A.D., he seems to have joined a confederacy of Hindu chiefs and conquered Hansi, Thaneshwar, Nagarkot and other dependencies of the Muslims, and besieged the fortress of Lahore for seven months.

There is no Paramāra inscription mentioning Bhoja's relations with the Chandellas, but the fragmentary Mahoba inscription[3] of the Chandellas refers to both Bhoja and the Kalachuri ruler, Gāṅgeya. On the basis of the Mahoba inscription, V.V.Mirashi[4] holds that both the Paramāra king Bhoja and Kalachuri Gāṅgeya, fought under the leadership of Vidyādhara in his expedition against Rājyapāla of Kanauj. D.C. Ganguly[5] thinks that Bhoja attacked the Chandella kingdom but with no favourable results. In the absence of any corroborative evidence, it is difficult to agree with the views of either V.V. Mirashi or D. C. Ganguly. Bhoja tried to capture Gwalior, but was stoutly resisted by the Kachchhapaghāṭa Kīrtirāj, a feudatory of Vidyādhara, as known from the Sāsabahu inscription[6]. The proud claim to success made for Vidyādhara might have been related to this incident.

However, Bhoja made an alliance with Abhimanyu of the Kachchhpaghāṭa dynasty of Dubkuṇḍa, who was the sworn enemy of the Pratīhāra ruler of Kanauj.[7] He wanted to secure help for the invasion of Kanauj. The Udaipur *praśasti*[8] tells us that Bhoja conquered a Gurjar king. As Bhīma, the Chālu-

1. EI, I, p. 234, V. 18.
2. The Paramāras (c. 800-1305 A D.), p. 83.
3. EI, I, p. 222.
4. CII, IV, Intro. p. xc.
5. GHPD, p. 104.
6. IA, XV, p. 30, V. 10.
7. EI, II, p. 238.
8. Ibid, I, p. 235, V. 19.

kya ruler of Gujarat has been referred to separately in the same line, the Gurjara king defeated by Bhoja might have been a Pratīhāra chief of Kanauj.

At first Bhoja had cordial relations with the Kalachurīs, but later, he defeated the powerful Chedi ruler Gāṅgeya Vikramāditya. Both the Kalvan[1] and the Udaipur inscriptions[2] refer to Bhoja's victory over a Chedi king whose identity with Gāṅgeya is disclosed by a verse of the *Pārijātamañjarī*[3] of Madana.

As regards his relations with the Guhilas of Mewar, Bhoja exercised suzerainty. In 1031 A.D., the fort of Chitor was honoured by the presence of the Paramāra ruler Bhoja.[4] From the Chirva inscription,[5] it is known that he built the Śiva temple at Chitor. Some scholars think that his control over the Guhila territory is implied by his Ujjain copper plate inscription,[6] dated 1021 A.D., which records a grant made by the king in '*Nāgadraha-paschima-pathaka*' and it has been identified by them with Nagda near Udaipur in Rajasthan. According to H. V. Trivedi, Nagda in Ujjain grant may be Nāgajharī near Ujjain.

Bhoja led his forces against the Chahamānas. The *Pṛithvīrāja Vijaya* tells us that the glory of Vīryarāma of Śākambharī, was destroyed by Bhoja, the ruler of Avanti.[7] In his war with the Chahamānas, Bhoja was helped by his general, Surāditya. The inscription of V. S. 1103 (1045 A.D.) on the Tilakawāḍā plates,[8] records that Surāditya was helpful to Bhojadeva in strengthening his rule, by slaughtering enemy warriors in the battle with Sāhavāhana, as well as the warriors of other princes. D.C. Ganguly[9] has identified this Sāhavāhana with

1. EI, XIX, p. 69.
2. Ibid, I, p. 235.
3. Ibid, VIII, V. 3.
4. *Vividhatīrthakalpa* (SJS. No. 10), p. 16.
5. EI, XXII, p. 288.
6. IA, VI, p. 53.
7. PV. Canto, V, p. 117, V. 67.
8. EI, XXI, p. 157.
9. GHPD, p. 109.

a Chamba prince, Śālivāhanadeva. D. B. Diskalkar[1] rightly holds that the Sāhavāna stands for the word Chāhamāna. The Paramāra forces perhaps occupied Śākambharī for a while as a result of this victory.[2] Aṇahila, the Chāhamāna chief of Nāḍol, soon came to the rescue of Chāmuṇḍarāja, the successor of Vīryarāma. Aṇahila seems to have killed the Paramāra commander Sāḍha, who might have been stationed in the Chahamāna dominions by Bhojadeva.[3]

Bhoja's relations with the Chālukyas of Gujarat were not cordial. In the beginning of his reign, he humiliated the Chālukya Chāmuṇḍarāja, son of Mūlarāja, by forcing him to give up his royal robe when the latter was passing through Mālava in the course of a pilgrimage to Banaras. Chāmuṇḍarāja's two sons, Vallabharāja and Durlabharāja, assumed a hostile attitude towards the Paramāras. From Merutuṅga,[4] it is known that Bhoja maintained friendly relations with the Chālukya Bhīma, son of Durlabharāja, for sometime but then made designs to conquer Gujarat. When Bhīma was engaged in a war in Sindh, he sent his general Kulachandra to attack Gujarat. Kulachandra sacked Aṇahilapāṭaka, the capital, and returned to Malwa, taking with him a *jayapatra* or letter of victory. Bhoja's victory over Bhīma, the king of Gujarat, is confirmed by the Udaipur *Praśasti*.[5] Bhoja even seems to have incited his kinsman Dhandhuka, the ruler of Abu, against Bhīma, who was his master. Bhīma seized Dhandhuka's kingdom, and the latter took refuge with Bhoja.

For a long period, when Bhoja was at the height of his power, he must have controlled the destinies of his contemporary rulers either directly or indirectly. Some of them were conquered, and others looked to him for guidance. Ultimately, his imperialistic policy did not prove to be beneficial, and it created enemies all round. He devoted more and more time to cultural pursuits and left the actual fighting to the generals, and this policy proved to be disastrous. In the diplo-

1. EI, XXI, pp. 158-59.
2. E. Ch. D., p. 34.
3. EI, IX, p. 75; E.Ch.D., p. 35 fn. 16.
4. *Prabandhachintāmaṇi*, pp. 32-33.
5. EI, I, p. 235, V. 18.

matic sphere, the friend of poets failed to become the friend of rulers, and he antagonized them by his imperialistic policy.

As a result of this policy, a series of calamities overtook the Paramāra empire about the middle of the eleventh century. About 1047 A.D., Someśvara, the Karṇāṭa ruler, defeated Bhoja and sacked Dhāra.[1] He burnt both Dhāra and Ujjain, and one of his *daṇḍanāyaka*, Guṇḍamaya, captured Māndu.[2] Though Bhoja recovered Dhāra, this attack of Someśvara had important repercussions. It meant not only the loss of the Paramāra kingdom in the Deccan, but it also exposed the weaknesses and deterioration of Bhoja's kingdom. Taking advantage of this situation, his enemies raised their heads. Karṇa, the son and successor of Gāṅgeya, and Bhīma I, attacked Malwa. Bhoja made preparations but he became ill, and died. The invaders attacked Dhāra and captured it.

Bhoja was one of the greatest sovereigns of ancient India. He was great as a ruler, as a conqueror, as a poet, as a patron and as a builder. For his versatile genius and wonderful achievements in different spheres, he occupies a place second only to that of Vikrama, of the legendary traditions.

Bhoja was a great military leader. Though he ultimately failed, he made his power felt among his contemporaries. He was still greater as a scholar. A large number of works in different branches have been ascribed to him. He wrote a commentary on the *Yogasūtras* of Patañjali. The '*Kūrmaśataka*' found engraved on slabs at Dhāra was composed by him. The *Samarāṅgaṇasūtradhāra* and the *Yuktikalpataru* are voluminous treatises on art. The *Sarasvatīkaṇṭhābharaṇa* and the *Śṛiṅgārapprakāśa* are two comprehensive works on rhetorics composed by him. Besides these, he wrote on astronomy, medicine, religion, lexicography, grammar, music and *subhāshitas*. It is difficult to believe that so many works were written by him, when he was devoted not only to literature, but to many different pursuits in life. It is possible that many works bearing his name were written by scholars under his personal

1. Hydra. Arch. Series No. 8, p. 13.V.43.
2. Ann. Report of Mysore Arch. Dep. 1928, pp. 68-69.

guidance. He was a patron of learning and extended a liberal patronage to scholars, poets, philosophers, artists and scientists.

Bhoja was also a great builder and he put into practice the principles of architecture that he enunciated in his treatises, the *Samarāṅgaṇasūtradhāra* and the *Yuktikalpataru*. He rebuilt Dhāra, adorning it with temples and the finest of buildings. The old fortification of Dhāra and Māndu is also attributed to him. From the Udaipur *Praśasti*,[1] it is known that he built temples dedicated to Kedāreśvara, Rāmeśvara, Somanātha, Saṁḍūra, Kāla, Anala and Rudra. He founded a town named Bhojapur. Not far from it is a Bhojapur Lake. The *Rājataraṅgiṇī*[2] records that he built the Pāpasūdana *tīrtha* at Kapoteśvara, modern Kothār in Kashmir.

JAYASIṀHA I : 1055-1070 A. D. :—

The era of Paramāra ascendancy ended with the death of Bhoja. His imperialistic policy created many enemies and plunged Malwa into wars. Henceforth, the Paramāra rulers mainly played a defensive role in Indian politics. His death produced a chaos in Malwa, and there were both internal and external dangers. Malwa was besieged by the forces of the Chālukyas from the west, and the Kalachuris of Ḍāhala from the east. As Bhoja had left no son, there were internal dissensions over the throne. Jayasiṁha, who is known from the Māndhātā plates[3] issued from Dhāra in V. S. 1112 (1055 A. D.), was, according to A. S. ALTEKAR, probably his son[4] and the immediate successor of Bhoja, and perhaps one of the claimants who fought for the throne of Malwa after the demise of Bhoja the Great.

The invaders not only captured Dhāra but they threatened the very existence of the Paramāra kingdom. Under these adverse circumstances, Jayasiṁha I was compelled to seek the aid of Someśvara I, the Chālukya king of Kalyāṇa, the erstwhile

1. EI, I, p. 235, V. 20.
2. *Rājataraṅgiṇī*, VIII, pp. 190-93.
3. EI, III, p. 46.
4. Ibid, XXIII.

invader and arch enemy of Malwa. Someśvara sent his son Vikramāditya II to help Jayasiṁha. Vikramāditya repulsed the enemies of Jayasiṁha.[1] All these encounters took place before 1055 A.D., for the Mandhata plates dated in that year, show that Jayasiṁha I was firmly established.

Sometime before 1059 A.D., Jayasiṁha I came into conflict with a general Kāṇha. The Panhera inscription[2] of his feudatory (*Māṇḍalika*) of Vāgaḍa, records that he took general Kāṇha prisoner with his elephants and horses, and handed him over to Jayasiṁha. Who this commander really was, and how he came in conflict with the Paramāra chief is not known.

As Jayasiṁha regained his kingdom with the help of Vikramāditya, he became his staunch ally. D. C. GANGULY[3] holds the view that he accompanied the Chālukya prince in his invasion of the Andhra country, and occupied Veṅgī sometime after 1062 A.D. He further states that the Eastern Chālukyas, with the help of the Chola Vīrarājendra, defeated the Karṇāṭas and the Paramāras, and the younger brother of Jayasiṁha I, together with many other generals, lost his life.

D. C. GANGULY's theory of Jayasiṁha's conflict with the Eastern Chālukyas and the Cholas is subject to criticism. Scholars[4] are at variance regarding the reading, which has been interpreted by some as, 'younger brother of Jananātha of Dhāra'. In the light of different readings, it is not possible to identify Jananātha of the Chola inscriptions with Jayasiṁha I of Dhāra with any degree of certainty. The younger brother of Jananātha cannot be identified with Jagaddeva. However Jagaddeva may not be the cousin of Jayasiṁha I, because we do not know the relationship bet-

1. *Vikramāṅkacharita* of Bilhaṇa.
2. EI, XXI, p. 48.
3. GHPD, pp. 125-26.
4. K. A. N. SASTRI interprets the expression as the younger brother of Dhārāvarsha (The Cholas, p. 325, f. n. 18). K. B. SUBRAMANYA AYYAR prefers to read 'tār' instead of Dhāra and translates the whole phrase as the 'younger brother of Jananātha adorned with wealth, (EI, XXI, p. 242).

ween Jayasiṁha I and Udayāditya.[1] PRATIPALA BHATIA[2] thinks that the Jananātha defeated by Vīrarājendra Chola was one of the *Daṇḍanāyakas*, and must have been a chief of some small state of the south.

Jayasiṁha I was not destined to rule in peace for long. As long as Someśvarva, the Chālukya ruler of Kalyāṇī, was alive, his enemies could not rise against Jayasiṁha I. But afterwards, there were both internal and external dangers for the Paramāra kingdom. It seems that Udayāditya was also an aspirant for the throne. Someśvara II, the Chālukya king of Kalyāṇī, suspected that his younger brother Vikramāditya, was conspiring against him with Jayasiṁha I. In order to punish Jayasiṁha, king Someśvara II made an alliance with Karṇa. F. KIELHORN[3] identified Karṇa with the Kalachuri king who was a contemporary of Udayāditya, and he is followed by V. V. MIRASHI. D.C.GANGULY and some other scholars[4], are of the view that he was the Chālukya king, Karṇa of Gujarat, the successor of Bhīma. This view is open to objection. The Udaipur *praśasti*[5] credits Udayāditya with the total destruction of the lord of Ḍāhala. This shows that the king Karṇa, who brought about the destruction of King Jayasiṁha of Malwa, and was later defeated by Udayāditya sometime after 1068 A.D. and a little before 1071 A.D., was the Kalachuri Karṇa and not the Chālukya king.[6] Thus the defeat and death of Jayasiṁha I took place in 1068-1069 A.D.

UDAYĀDITYA : 1070-1086 A.D.

During the time of his predecessor, Jayasiṁha, conditions had not improved. Udayāditya made efforts to bring about peace and order. In this task he was probably helped by the

1. Udayāditya is the father of Jagaddeva.
2. The Paramāras (c. 800-1305 A.D.), p. 101.
3. EI, II, p. 181.
4. GHPD, p. 130.
5. EI. I, pp. 232-38.
6. Udayāditya fought against Karṇa of Gujarat in the reign of Vigraharāja III of Śākambharī i.e. after 1079 A.D., the date of Vigraharāja's accession (E. Ch. D., pp. 36-37).

naulas, or the hereditary servants of the state, who are referred to with respect by the Udaipur *praśasti*[1]. The conditions in the south were good. There was no danger because Someśvara II was engaged in dealing with the Chola monarch, Vīrarājendra.[2] This gave Udayāditya an opportunity to regain his position and stabilize his authority in Malwa.

On the authority of the *Pṛithvīrājavijayamahākāvya*,[3] some scholars, like G.H. OJHA, D.C. GANGULY and K.M. MUNSHI, think that Udayāditya obtained the throne with the help of the Śākambharī Chauhāna ruler, Vigraharāja III. This view is not tenable because Vigraharāja succeeded to the throne many years after the accession of Udayāditya. Udayāditya was already in a well established position when Vigraharāja III presented a horse to him called Sāraṅga.

Scholars do not agree as to the relationship of Udayāditya with Bhoja. D. C. GANGULY[4] thinks that Udayāditya was a distant cousin of Bhoja, and that he belonged to a minor branch of the Paramāra clan which was ruling in a feudatory capacity. He relies on a Udaipur stone inscription,[5] which states that Udayāditya was the son of Gyāta, grandson of Goṇḍala, and great grandson of Suravīra of the Paramāra family. The Nagpur Museum stone inscription[6] dated 1104 A.D. (V.S. 1161), refers to Udayāditya as a '*bandhu*' of Bhoja. The Jaināḍ inscription[7] of Udayāditya's son, Jagaddeva, mentions Bhoja as the '*Pitṛivya*' (uncle), and Udayāditya as the father of Jagaddeva. The Doṅgargāon inscription[8] of the time of Jagaddeva, dated śaka 1034 (1112 A.D.), describes Udayāditya as the '*bhrātā*' of Bhoja. On the basis of these sources, V.V. MIRASHI[9] and PRATIPALA BHATIA[10] regard Udayāditya

1. EI, I, pp. 232-38.
2. The Cholas, pp. 333-34.
3. Canto V., vv. 15-18.
4. GHPD, pp. 134-35.
5. JASB, IX, pp. 546.
6. EI, II, p. 185.
7. Ibid, XII, p. 60.
8. Ibid, XXVI, p. 183, v. 5.
9. PIHC, Vth Session, 1941, pp. 37 ff., MSI, II, pp. 77-78.
10. The Paramāras (c. 800-1305 A.D.), p. 108.

as the brother of Bhoja. This view does not seem to be tenable. If we regard him as the real brother of Bhoja, it is not possible that he was still ruling in 1086 A.D. Most probably, he was a near relative of Bhoja.

The task before Udayāditya, soon after his accession to the throne, was not an easy one. His own feudatories revolted against him. Māṇḍalika of Vāgaḍa served Jayasiṁha I, but Māṇḍalika's son, Chāmuṇḍarāja, turned against Udayāditya, the successor of Jayasiṁha I. It seems that Udayāditya and Jayasiṁha were rivals. Chāmuṇḍarāja claims to have defeated the lord of Malwa many times in the *sthalī* land, i.e. Vāgaḍa.[1] It seems that Udayāditya could not effectively control the refractory feudatory of Vāgaḍa.

The greatest danger which Udayāditya had to face, was from the Chālukya ruler, Karṇa of Gujarat. His invasion took place sometime after 1079 A.D. Karṇa achieved some success against the Paramāras in the initial stages. He is said to have carried away an image of Nīlakaṇṭha after defeating the ruler of Malwa.[2] Another Gujarat chronicler states that Karṇa overran the whole of the Malwa kingdom.[3] The fragmentary Chitorgarh inscription[4] of the time of Chālukya Kumārapāla, records that Karṇa defeated the Malwa (king) in the Sudakūpa pass. With the help of the Chauhānas of Śākambharī and Nāḍol, Udayāditya was successful in defeating Karṇa. Vigraharāja III of Śākambharī sided with Udayāditya.[5] Pṛithvīpāla of Nāḍol, who claims to have defeated the armies of Karṇa, might have done so as an ally of Udayāditya.[6]

Like his predecessors, Udayāditya tried for the cultural advancement of the people. He was a great builder. He founded the town of Udaipur and adorned it with beautiful temples. The temple of Nīlakaṇṭheśvara or Udayeśvara, one of

1. JASB, IX, p. 546.
2. SK, II, V. 23.
3. *Surathotsava Kavi Praśasti*, V. 20.
4. PRAS. WC. 1905-06, p. 61.
5. P.V., V, vv. 76-78.
6. EI, IX, p. 76.

the superb specimens of Hindu architecture of this place, was probably built by him. He also built the Udayasamudra tank.[1] Some of the temples at Un are assigned to his reign.[2] He also loved literature. In the *Pāṭhaśālā* of Bhoja, there is an inscription of two verses in the *Nāgabandha* figure, perhaps composed by Udayāditya. Similar verses are also found engraved at Ujjain and Un.[3]

Udayāditya was a follower of Śaivism. He granted the village of Vilapadraka to the temple of Somanātha, which was situated in the fort of Kośavardhana, i.e. modern Shergarh.[4]

Udayāditya is known to have issued gold coins. They bear the image of a seated goddess on one side and the name of the king on the obverse.[5]

LAKSHAMADEVA : c. 1086-1094 :—

Udayāditya was succeeded by his eldest son Lakshamadeva. On the other hand, H. V. Trivedi thinks that Udayāditya was immediately succeeded on the Paramāra throne by Naravarman, and Lakshamadeva did not come to the throne at all. The Nagpur stone inscription[6] dated V.S. 1161 (1104-05), is the main source of information about his career and achievements. It says that Lakshamadeva went out with a large army for a *digvijaya*, and subjugated the earth in all directions. It records the following achievements :—(1) Conquest of Bengal; (2) defeat of the armies of Aṅga and Kaliṅga; (3) occupation of Tripuri; (4) subjugation of the Cholas and other southern tribes; (5) invasion of the Pāṇḍya country and Ceylon; (6) victory over the Timiṅgilas and others who resided in the Maiṇaka mountains in the west and (7) defeat of the Turushkas and the Kīras.

Much of the description of the Nagpur *praśasti* is mere poetic panegyric without any foundation of facts. Lakshama-

1. PRAS. WC, 1914, p. 66.
2. ASI, 1918-19, pp. 17-18.
3. JBBRAS, XXI, p. 350.
4. EI, XXIII, pp. 131 ff.
5. JASB, XVI, p. 84.
6. EI, II, pp. 180 ff.

deva was not so powerful as to conquer all these places, and besides, he did not rule for very long.

Lakshamadeva never conquered the Pāṇḍya country and Ceylon. It is difficult to believe that he succeeded in defeating the powerful Cholas. In the extreme North, it is difficult to believe that he led his army on to the banks of the river Vaṅkshu and to the Kīra country i.e. Kāngra valley in the Punjab. Some scholars, like D.C. GANGULY,[1] believe in the possibility of his raid on Aṅga, Kaliṅga and Gauḍa, as the struggle of the Kaivartas and the Pālas had rendered Bengal vulnerable.[2] It is difficult to believe that he could move so far to the east.

In the Nagpur *praśasti*, the author appears to have modelled his description on that of Raghu's *digvijaya* in the *Raghuvaṁśa*. In this account, the only tangible and probable facts mentioned, are an expedition undertaken against Tripuri, the well-known capital of the Chedi kingdom, and some fights with the Muslim invaders. Lakshamadeva might have won a victory over the Kalachuri Yaśaḥkarṇa, who was ruling over Chedi kingdom.[3] In the encounter with the Muslims, he does not seem to have been successful, for the invaders, led by a Ghaznavite ruler, Mahmūd, occupied Ujjain and destroyed thousands of temples.[4]

The Nagpur *praśasti*[5] informs us that Lakshamadeva had granted at the time of a solar eclipse two villages in the Vyāpuramaṇḍala, and that his brother, king Naravarmadeva, afterwards assigned the village of Mokhlapaṭaka instead.

D.C. GANGULY[6] identified Lakshamadeva with his younger brother Jagaddeva, and attributed Jagaddeva's conflict with the Hoyasālas to Lakshamadeva; but this view is not correct. Jagaddeva and Lakshamadeva were two different princes. Lakshamadeva never came into conflict with the Hoyasāla chiefs.[7]

1. GHPD, p. 144.
2. History of Bengal, I, pp. 152 ff.
3. CII, IV, Intro. p. ciii.
4. History of India as told by its own Historians, Vol. IV, p. 524.
5. EI, II, p. 186, verses 55 and 56.
6. GHPD, pp. 148-49.
7. The Paramāras (c. 800-1305 A.D.), p. 113.

NARAVARMADEVA : 1094-1133 A.D. :—

Lakshamadeva was succeeded by his younger brother Naravarmadeva about 1094 A.D. He assumed the title of *Nirvāṇa-Nārāyaṇa*. He was not a general of high rank, because he was not successful in his expeditions. On the other hand, he was a talented poet, and was devoted to religion.

Naravarman lost some of his territory to the Chandellas. The Ajayagarh inscription[1] of the time of Vīravarman Chandella, states that the sword of Salakshanavarman, (1110-1115 A.D.), took away the fortune of the Mālavas and the Chedis. From the Banda plates[2] of Madanavarman Chandella, it is known that he made a land-gift in 1134 A.D. (V.S. 1191) while he was encamped near Bhaillasvāmin (Bhilsa). As Bhilsa was under the possession of the Paramāras, the Chandellas seized this territory from them.

Naravarman had to fight against the Chauhānas of Śākambharī, and was defeated. The Chauhāna ruler Ajayavarman, defeated Naravarman on the borders of Avanti, and captured alive the latter's general Sollana.[3] He killed the three warriors, Chachiga, Sindhula and Yaśorāja, probably after storming the fort of Śrīmārga.[4] It seems that Chachiga, Sindhula and Yaśorāja, were the warriors associated with the fort. The Bijauliā inscription refers to the defeat of Naravarman at the hands of Arṇorāja of Śakambharī.

The struggle of Naravarman with Jayasiṁha Siddharāja, the Chālukya ruler of Gujarat, was a dangerous one. Jayasiṁha Siddharāja was more powerful, skilful and determined. The Gujarat chronicles[5] record the defeat of Naravarman at the hands of Jayasiṁha Siddharāja. The account of the chronicles is corroborated by epigraphic evidence. An inscription in the Gaṇapati temple of Talavāḍā, a village in the Banswara District, states that Jayasiṁha humbled Naravar-

1. EI, I, pp. 326 ff.
2. IA, XVI, p. 208.
3. EI, XXVI, p. 104, V.15; PV. Cant. V, V. 85.
4. Ibid, p. 104, V. 15 of the Bijaulia Inscription.
5. Jayasiṁha Sūri's *Kumārapāla Bhupāla Prabandha*, Jinamaṇḍana's *Kumārapāla Prabandha* and Hemachandra's *Dvyāśrayamahākāvya*, XV.

man's pride.[1] Jayasiṁha Siddharāja was also helped by his feudatories. The Nanana Grant[2] of Ālhaṇa Chauhāna states that Āśārāja Chauhāna of Nāḍol went to Dhāra to fight. This struggle was a prolonged one, and continued for twelve years. It started during the reign of Naravarman, and went on until the time of Yaśovarman. Naravarman was defeated, but the final defeat took place in the reign of his successor, Yaśovarman. By this, the independent existence of the Paramāra kingdom was threatened.

The existence of the independent kingdom as known from the Ingnoda inscription,[3] dated 1133-34, in the neighbourhood of Ujjain, reveals that the Paramāras did not have a strong hold during the reign of Naravarman. This inscription records that *Mahārājādhirāja* Parameśvara Vijayapāladeva, son of Tribhuvanapāla and great grandson of Pṛithvīpāla, after worshipping Śiva, granted the village of Agasiyaka, situated to the south of Iṅganapat, (Modern Ringod now in Ratlam District), to the god Gohadeśvara. To judge from his titles, this prince seems to have been independent and to have established an independent kingdom. From the undated inscription of Lakshmīvarman found at Bhopal, it is known that the above rulers belonged to the dynasty of Adhi-Droṇāchāryānvaya.[4]

The fragmentary and the undated Avanti inscription[5] mentions a king named Nirvāṇa-Nārāyaṇa who, according to it, made conquests as far as Sāketa in the east, Dvārikā in the west, Malayāchala in the south and the Himālayas in the North. However, this description is conventional and cannot be relied upon. When Naravarman, alias Nirvāṇa Nārāyaṇa, was not in a position to protect his kingdom from enemies like the Chandellas, the Chauhānas and the Chālukyas, it is unlikely that he could go for a *digvijaya* as mentioned in the *praśasti*.

1. ARRMA, 1914-15, p. 2.
2. E.Ch.D., p. 186.
3. IA, VI, pp. 55-56.
4. JMPIP, II, p. 3.
5. Ed. by S. N. Vyas.

On the basis of the *Vikrama-Cholānula*, D. C. GANGULY[1] thinks that Naravarman came into conflict with Vikrama Chola and suffered a reverse. But this is not corroborated by any other evidence, either literary or epigraphic.

Naravarman himself was a great scholar, and was devoted to his religion. He is credited with the composition of the *Nagpur praśasti*[2] and the Dhāra inscription.[3] Besides these, he is said to have composed many other hymns and verses. He was a patron of learning. He was also a builder of temples and tanks. From the *Kharataragachchha Bṛihadgurvāvali*[4] of Jinapāla, it is known that he honoured the Jaina teacher Jinavallabhasūri, for his skill in poetry.

YAŚOVARMAN : 1133=1142 A.D. :—

The reign of Yaśovarman was a most tragic one. The misfortunes which began in the reign of Naravarman, overshadowed the Paramāra kingdom during the short period of Yaśovarman. The main reason was the Chālukya invasion of Jayasiṁha Siddharāja of Gujarat. The causes of this invasion have been differently stated. One reason was want of free access to the temples of Kālikā and other Yoginīs at Ujjain.[5] Yaśovarman of Malwa invaded Gujarat while its ruler Jayasiṁha was away on pilgrimage with his mother Mayanalladevī[6]. In retaliation, on his return, Jayasiṁha invaded Malwa with his forces.

That Jayasiṁha Siddharāja inflicted a crushing defeat on Yaśovarman is confirmed both by the old Gujarati chronicles and epigraphical sources. Arisiṁha[7] tells that Jayasiṁha imprisoned Yāśovarman, the king of Dhāra. The *Surathotsava*[8] and the *Kīrtikaumudī*[9] of Someśvara, relate that Jaya-

1. GHPD, p. 161.
2. EI, II, p. 181.
3. Ibid, XXXI, p. 25 ff.
4. KB, p. 13.
5. DV, XIV, VV. 5-74.
6. PC, 58-59; *Kīrtikaumudī* of Someśvara, II, V. 30-32. Forbes, '*Rāsamālā*', pp. 111 ff.
7. *Sukṛitasaṁkīrtana*, XI, V. 34.
8. *Granthapraśasti*, V. 31-33.
9. *Sarga* II, VV. 31-42.

siṁha defeated the Paramāras, conquered Dhāra, and threw its lord into a wooden cage. That Yaśovarman was thrown into prison is borne out by a Dohaḍ inscription.[1] From the Ujjain stone inscription[2] of V.S. 1195 (1136 A.D.), it is clear that Jayasiṁha was holding *Avantimaṇḍala* after vanquishing Yaśovarman. He placed it under the charge of his governor, Mahādeva.

The defeat of Yaśovarman at the hands of Jayasiṁha Siddharāja was of great political significance. As a consequence of it, a great part of the Paramāra dominions was seized by the Chālukyas. Both Ujjain and Dhāra came under the possession of Jayasiṁha Siddharāja, who, for nearly seven years (i.e. from 1136 to 1143 A.D.), became the *Sārva-bhauma* ruler of western India.

However, Yaśovarman escaped from Jayasiṁha's prison and with the assistance of the Chauhānas of Ajmer, regained some portion of his kingdom and perhaps came to the terms with Jayasiṁha. He may have ruled as a Chālukya feudatory up to 1142 A.D. if the date of the Jhālarāpāṭan inscription[3] is correct, and *Mahārāja* Yaśovarman is the same person as Yaśovarman Paramāra.

JAYAVARMAN : *1142-1143 A.D.* :—

After the defeat of Yaśovarman at the hands of Jayasiṁha Siddharāja, there was some confusion in the political affairs of the Paramāra kingdom. His son, Jayavarman, also called Ajayavarman,[4] ruled for a short while and succeeded in reoccupying Dhāra.[5] His Ujjain plates[6] were issued from Varddhamānapura, otherwise Badnawar, sixty-four kilometres to the south-west of Ujjain.[7] In the undated ins-

1. IA, Vol. X, p. 159.
2. Ibid, XLII, (1913), p. 258.
3. PRAS. WC, 1905-06, p. 56. Some think that the Jhalrapatan inscription need not be taken as belonging to Yaśovarman's reign. At any rate, its date V.S. 1199 is uncertain, since the last number 9 is based on conjecture.
4. GHPD, p. 81.
5. EI, XXIV, p. 229.
6. IA, XIX, p. 350.
7. Indian Culture, Vol. XI, p. 166.

cription of these plates, he assumed the title of *Paramabhaṭṭāraka Mahārājādhirāja Parameśvara*. It also records the grant of a village to a Brāhmaṇa. About his relations with the Chālukyas, we do not know.

It appears that Malwa was once again plunged into chaos during the reign of Jayavarman. Some scholars, like D. C. GANGULY[1] and PRATIPALA BHATIA,[2] are of the view that Chālukya Jagadekamalla of Kalyāṇa, together with the Hoyasāla Narasiṁha I, invaded Malwa, destroyed Jayavarman's power, and seems to have placed one, Ballāla, on the throne. This event must have taken place before 1143 A.D. But this cannot be accepted, as the Hoyasālas had revolted against the Chālukya Jagadekamalla, and could not have been trusted by them as allies. Narasiṁha himself was hardly nine years old in 1142 A.D., as he is stated to be three years old in 1136 A.D. in one inscription.[3] That the Chālukya Jagadekamalla II of Kalyāṇī had a victory over Mālava is known from a number of inscriptions.[4] But whether the Chālukyas set Ballāla up over Malwa, is difficult to say.

BALLĀLA :—

After Jayavarman, Ballāla ruled in Malwa. There are different views about his identification. A. K. MAJUMDAR[5] thinks that he was perhaps a local chief or a former feudatory of the Paramāras, who, during the period of confusion, declared himself the ruler of Dhāra. D. C. GANGULY[6] suggests that Ballāla might have been a Hoyasāla chief, who after the death of Jayavarman was left by the Hoyasāla invaders as the master of Malwa. As the Hoyasālas had not invaded Malwa at this time, Ballāla could not have been a Hoyasāla chief. He appears to be a southerner, but his identity cannot be precisely established.

Ballāla made an alliance with the Śākambharī Chauhāna ruler Arṇorāja, in order to defeat Kumārapāla, the successor

1. GHPD, p. 172.
2. The Paramāras (c. 800-1305 A. D.), p. 124.
3. Epigraphia Carnatica, III. T. N. No. 129.
4. EI, XVI, p. 254; Epigraphia Carnatica, Vol. VII, S. K. No. 123; Vol. XI, DI. Nos. 35 and 43.
5. Chālukyas of Gujarat, pp. 454-55.
6. GHPD, pp. 172-73.

of Jayasiṁha Siddharāja.[1] When Kumārapāla heard this, he himself marched towards Ajmer and sent his general, Kaka, and his feudatories, Alhaṇa Chauhāna[2], and Yaśodhavala Paramāra, the Ābū chief[3] against Ballāla. Both of them claimed to have slain Ballāla. Hemachandra,[4] however, gives the credit of killing Ballāla to some Brāhmaṇa soldiers of Kumārapāla's army. The defeat and death of Ballāla seems to have taken place in about 1150 A.D. or 1151 A.D.[5]

During the reign of Kumārapāla, Malwa once again became a Chālukya province. From the Udaipur stone inscription[6] dated V. S. 1220 (1163 A.D.), it is clear that a certain Rājyapāla, who is described as *mahā-sādhanika*, and who had been appointed by Kumārapāladeva, was governing Udayapura. Another Udaipur stone inscription[7] of V. S. 1229 (1171 A.D.), refers to the reign of the Chālukya king Ajayapāladeva of Aṇahilapāṭaka, and at this time, Lūṇapāsaka was an officer appointed by the king to govern Udayapura in the *Bhaillasvāmī Mahādvādaśaka* province.

THE PARAMĀRA MAHĀKUMĀRAS :—

After the death of Jayavarman and Ballāla, a large part of the Paramāra kingdom passed into the hands of the Chālukyas. Their ruler, Kumāra, assumed the title of *Avantinātha*, and appointed officers for its administration. But even during this period, a junior branch of the Paramāra family, designated as the 'Mahākumāras', ruled at Bhopal, Bhilsa and Hoshangabad, the south east portion of the Paramāra kingdom. The ruling members of this family styled themselves as '*Samadhigata-paṁcha-mahāśabdālaṁkāra- virājamāna-mahākumāra*'. Their status and relations with the Chālukyas are not known.

The history of these Paramāra Mahākumāras is complicated because different genealogies have been given in their

1. DV, XIX, V. 13.
2. EI, VIII, p. 201.
3. Ibid, VIII, p. 216.
4. DV, XIX, V. 126.
5. EI, I, p. 29, V. 15.
6. IA, XVIII, p. 342.
7. Ibid, p. 81.

inscriptions. However, an attempt has been made to reconstruct their history with the help of their inscriptions.

According to PRATIPAL BHATIA,[1] Yaśovarman probably had four sons, Jayavarman, Ajayavarman, Lakshmīvarman and Trailokyavarman. D. C. GANGULY[2] suggests that Jayavarman and Ajayavarman were the one and the same prince. After Yaśovarman, Jayavarman succeeded to the throne, but probably fell fighting against the Chālukyas, sometime before 1143 A.D. As a consequence of this, the major portion of the Paramāra dominions came under the possession of Ballāla, and then under the Chālukyas.

After the death of Jayavarman, there was chaos in Malwa. Lakshmīvarman, the younger brother of Jayavarman, carved out a small principality in the region of Bhopal. The Bhopal plates[3] of Udayavarman, dated 1199 A.D., state that Lakshmīvarman obtained his kingship through the valour of his own sword. It shows that he did not obtain this principality from Jayavarman, either through inheritance or as a gift.

The Ujjain copper plate grant[4] of Lakshmīvarman's reign dated V.S. 1200 (1144 A.D.), states that on the occasion of the eclipse of the moon, Lakshmīvarman reaffirmed the grant made by Yaśovarman in 1134 A.D., and made a grant of the villages of Vaḍaūda and Uthavaṇaka, in the *Mahādvādaśaka maṇḍala* adjacent to Bhaillasvāmin. Obviously, this territory which had been lost by the Paramāras and had passed into the hands of the Chandellas by 1134 A.D., was reconquered by Lakshmīvarman, and this necessitated the reissuing of the grant, which had originally been made by his father, Yaśovarman, in 1134 A.D.

Another undated inscription[5] of Lakshmīvarman found at

1. The Paramāras (c. 800-1305 A.D.), p. 130.
2. GHPD, p. 81.
3. IA, XVI, p. 253.
4. Ibid, XIX.
5. JMPIP, II, p. 3—This inscription describes the genealogy of a feudatory family named as Adhi-Droṇāchāryānvaya. The first prince of the family was Mahārājaputra Ajayapāladeva. His name is followed by that of his son Mahārājaputra Prīthanadeva. His son Mahārājaputra Tejjovarmmadeva and his younger brother's son Vijayasiṁhadeva.

Bhopal, shows that he ruled in the Bhopal region and not over Ujjain and Dhāra. This inscription confirms that he acquired the kingdom through his own arms. It mentions that a feudatory of Lakshmīvarman, named Vijayasiṁhadeva, of the Adhidroṇāchārya family, politically and matrimonially allied himself with the Rāshṭrakūṭa Rājaputra Vāddiga, and gained victory over his enemies in battle. It is difficult to identify the enemy. S. L. KATARE[1] suggests that he may be Ballāla, who is called the ruler of Avanti, Dhāra and Mālava. It is possible that he might be the Chandella ruler who was expelled from the region around Bhopal by Lakshmīvarman.

Another son of Yaśovarman, named Trailokyavarman established a principality near the territory of his brother, Lakshmīvarman. A fragmentary inscription[2] of Mahākumāra Trailokyavarmadeva has been discovered at Gyaraspur thirty-nine kilometres from Bhilsa. This inscription refers to the consecration of an image of the God Chāmuṇḍasvāmīdeva, and records the grant of a village for the god's worship, by Mahākumāra Trailokyavarmadeva, when he was encamping at Harshapura, now a village called Harsauda in the Nimar District. The tract over which he ruled extended from Gyaraspur region in Bhilsa District, to the District of Nimar.

N. P. CHAKRVARTI[3] suggested that Trailokyavarman was possibly ruling as regent during the minority of Hariśchandra with the full power of a chief. This is further confirmed by his recently discovered Vidiśā stone inscription, dated V.S. 1226, in which he is called a king. This inscription proves that he also enjoyed titles connected with the princes of the Mahākumāra line.

Hariśchandra was Lakshmīvarman's son and Udayavarman's father. He has been described as having received his principality through Trailokyavarman's favour, even though he was Lakshmīvarman's son. It is possible that Hariśchandra

These rulers are also known from the Ingnoda inscription dated 1133-34 A.D.

1. JMPIP, II, p. 3 ff.
2. EI, XXXIII, p. 93.
3. Ibid.

might have been adopted as the successor to his territory by Lakshmīvarman's younger brother, Trailokyavarman. Thus the territories of these two brothers might have been combined under their common successor, Hariśchandra. The Bhopal plates[1] dated 1157 A.D. record the grant of the village of Dādarapadra, belonging to Vikhilapadra-twelve, and situated in the *Mahādvādaśakamaṇḍala*, by Hariśchandra.

Sometime after 1157 A.D., the Chālukyas seem to have conquered this area from Mahākumāra Hariśchandra, as is proved by the Chālukya records dated 1163 A.D.[2] and 1172 A.D.[3] The Chālukya ruler Ajayapāla, (1172-75 A.D.), had to face dangers both from inside and outside his kingdom. Perhaps during this period, taking advantage of the situation, Hariśchandra recovered his territory sometime before 1178 A.D. as is clear from his Piplianagar grant.[4] Its object is to record that Hariśchandra, having bathed in the holy waters of the Narmada, near the temple of the four-faced Mārkaṇḍadvāra, made some grant to the learned Brāhmaṇas.

Hariśchandra had two sons, Udayavarman and Devapāla. From the Bhopal plates[5] of Udayavarman V.S. 1256 (1199 A.D.), it is clear that he was the son of M. K. Hariśchandra and the successor of M. K. Lakshmīvarman. The inscription records that Udayavarman, after worshipping many gods for the increase of the religious merit of his parents and of himself, granted the village of Guṇaūrā to the Brāhmaṇa Māluśarman, the son of Yajñadhara. Two inscriptions, dated 1184 A.D. (V.S. 1241) and 1185 A.D. (S 1108),[6] referring to a ruler named Udayāditya, probably refer to Udayavarman, for no other Udayāditya is known to have ruled in the area at this time.

As Udayāditya probably died without any male issue, he was succeeded by his younger brother Devapāla. By succeeding

1. EI, XXIV, p. 225.
2. IA, XVIII, p. 341.
3. Ibid, XV, p. 344.
4. JASB, VII, pp. 736 ff.
5. IA, XVI, No. 171. Guṇaūrā seems to be undoubtedly the modern 'Ganora', 11 kilometres south-west of Hoshangabad.
6. Journal of the American Oriental Society, VII, p. 35.

also to the throne of the main branch, he reunited all the houses of the Paramāras of Malwa.

VINDHYAVARMAN : 1175-1194 A.D. :—

During the last quarter of the twelfth century A.D., the Imperial Paramāras reasserted their independence. After the death of Chālukya Kumārapāla of Gujarat, his immediate successors were not competent enough to hold Malwa under control for long. Taking advantage of the weakness of the Chālukyas, Vindhyavarman, the successor of Ajayavarman or Jayavarman, decided to drive the Chālukyas out of Malwa.

According to D. C. GANGULY[1], the Gurjara king, in whose time Vindhyavarman achieved independence, was Mūlarāja, who ruled up to 1178 A.D. On the other hand, PRATIPALA BHATIA[2] thinks that Malwa remained under the Chālukyan legions until 1187 A.D. The Gurjara ruler defeated by Vindhyavarman was Bhīma II, the successor of Mūlarāja II. Malwa appears to have attained its independence between 1187 and 1190 A.D.

The task of Vindhyavarman in freeing his country from the clutches of the Chālukyas was not an easy one. In 1187 A.D., the Chālukya armies, commanded by their general Jagaddeva Pratīhāra, were in Malwa.[3] Vindhyavarman is said to have been defeated at Goggasthāna by Kumāra, the Chālukya general.[4] In spite of these reverses, he recovered Dhāra, and liberated the greater part of Malwa from the Chālukyas of Gujarat before 1190 A.D. This is known from the commentary on *Vṛittaratnākara* by Vindhyavarman's court poet, Sulhaṇa, who wrote it in 1190 A.D.[5] It is further confirmed by the inscription of the Māndhāta plate of Devapāla,[6] and the inscriptions of Arjunavarman.[7] This fact is also corroborated by the statement of Āśādhara that he left

1. GHPD, p. 189.
2. The Paramāras (c. 800-1305 A.D.), p. 138.
3. KB, pp. 8 and 34.
4. *Surathotsava*, V. 136.
5. *Vṛittaratnākara.*
6. EI, IX, pp. 108-09.
7. JASB, Vol. V, p. 378; JAOS, VII, p. 26; IA, XIX, p. 346.

Māṇḍalgarh in Sapādalaksha, after its subjugation by the Turks, and took shelter in the kingdom of Malwa, which was ruled by Vindhyavarman.[1]

Vindhyavarman was unable to rule his newly conquered ancestral kingdom in peace. He came into conflict with the ruler of the Deccan. The Chālukyas of Kalyāṇa were no longer powerful, and their place was taken by the Hoyasālas of Dorasamudra, and the Yādavas of Devagiri. The Yādava ruler Bhillama, is said to have defeated one Vindhyabhūbhṛit[2], who is the Paramāra ruler Vindhyavarman. The Mutgi inscription[3] of Bhillama, dated 1189 A.D., describes him as a great nuisance to the Mālavas. An inscription[4] of Gaṅga Narasiṁha, a feudatory of the Hoyasāla chief Ballāla II, states that at the command of his master, he subdued the united kings of Mālava, Lāṭa, Gurjara and Chola.

Vindhyavarman was a patron of scholars in spite of his engagement in wars. His Prime Minister was a great scholar and was a friend of the Jaina scholar Āśādhara,[5] who wrote several works. Sulhaṇa was probably his court poet. During his reign, Dhāra, Ujjain, Nalakachhapura (Nalcha) and Maṇḍapadurga (Māndu), were centres of learning.

SUBHAṬAVARMAN : 1194-1209 A.D. :—

The son and successor of Vindhyavarman was Subhaṭavarman. The condition in Gujarat had further deteriorated because of the weak rule of Bhīma II. Subhaṭavarman was an ambitious man, and this gave him the opportunity for invasion.

Subhaṭavarman led his armies against Lāṭa and Gujarat. He destroyed the city of Dabhoi completely. He did not even spare the gold cupolas of the temples.[6] During this campaign, he seems to have reached as far as Cambay, where a mosque

1. *Sāgara Dharmāmṛita* of Āśādhara, p. 1.
2. EI, XXXII, p. 31.
3. EI, XV, pp. 34-35, v. 9.
4. EC, VI, Kd No. 156.
5. EBORI, Vol. XI, pp. 49-53.
6. *Sukṛitasaṁkīrtana* of Arisiṁha, p. 135. V. 33., Sukṛitakīrtikallolinī of Jayasiṁha; *Vasantavilāsa* of Bālachandra, p. 20, V.U.

is said to have been destroyed by the raiding Malwa army.[1] He forced the Chālukya feudatory, Siṁha of Lāṭa, to transfer his allegiance to him.

After despoiling Lāṭa, the Paramāra forces appear to have marched against Aṇahilapaṭṭana, the capital of the Chālukyas of Gujarat. Merutuṅga[2] mentions that Sohaḍa advanced up to the boundary of Gujarat in order to devastate the country. From Śrīdhara's Devapattana *praśasti*[3], it is known that Śrīdhara, governor of Bhīma II, checked their progress. Eventually, his powerful feudatory, Lavaṇaprasāda of Dholka, rescued the country of Gujarat and forced Sohaḍa to withdraw. From the Managoli inscription[4] dated 1200 A.D. it is clear that Subhaṭavarman suffered a defeat at the hands of the Yādava Jetugi.

ARJUNAVARMAN : *1210-1215 A.D.* :—

Subhaṭavarman was succeeded by his son Arjunavarman. He fought successfully against Jayasiṁha, the Chālukya ruler of Gujarat. Merutuṅga[5] calls Arjunavarman the destroyer of Gujarat, and states that Arjuna completely overran the realm of Gujarat. The Paramāra inscriptions[6] also confirm it. The drama *Pārijātamañjarī*[7] narrates the victory of Arjunavarman. over Jayasiṁha. It says that king Arjunavarman defeated the Chālukya king in the valley of Parva mountain, and captured Jayaśrī.

Another enemy against whom Arjunavarman had to fight, was the Yādava ruler Siṁhaṇa, (1210-47 A.D.). Siṁhaṇa invaded Lāṭa which formed a part of the dominions of Arjunavarman. In this struggle, Arjunavarman was helped by his feudatory, Salakhaṇasiṁha Chāhamāna. The Māndhātā plates[8] of Jayasiṁha Jayavarman, mention that the Chāhamāna leader

1. JOI (Baroda), Vol. X, No. 4.
2. PC pp. 97-98.
3. EI, II, pp. 439 ff.
4. Ibid, V, p. 31.
5. PC, p. 97.
6. JAOS, VII, p. 26; JASB, p. 378, V. 17.
7. EI, VII, p. 103.
8. EI, XXXII, V. 60.

of the Paramāra forces defeated the army of Siṁhaṇadeva, no doubt the Yādava king of this name. Again, after making full preparations, the Yādava ruler invaded Lāṭa. The Yādava commander of this expedition was a Brāhmaṇa general named Kholeśvara, who secured a victory in the battle that ensued.[1] The Bāhl inscription[2] of 1222 A.D. records Siṁhaṇa's victory over Arjuna. He was probably killed in the battle while fighting against Siṁhaṇa.

Like his predecessors, Arjunavarman was not only a patron of scholars, but was himself a poet of high calibre. He assumed the epithet of *Trividhivīrachūḍāmaṇi*.[3] His *guru* was Mādhava, who was the author of the *Pārijātamañjarī*.[4] This drama shows the high standard of culture and civilization during the period. Govind was his family minister. Bilhaṇa and Salakhaṇa were his ministers for peace and war, and Nārāyaṇa was his Chief Minister.[5]

DEVAPĀLA : 1218-1239 A.D. :—

Sometime about 1218 A.D., Arjunavarman was succeeded by Devapāla, the son of Mahākumāra Hariśchandra. He also succeeded his elder brother Udayavarman as Mahākumāra. Thus, under Devapāla, two or three different lines of the Paramāras were united.[6] His dominions extended as far as Udaipur in the north, Hoshangabad and Nimar Districts in the south, and possibly Bhroach in the west.

Devapāla was not an astute diplomat, and he followed an unfortunate foreign policy. The fight with the Chālukyas of Gujarat and the Yādavas of Devagiri continued in his reign. Siṁhaṇa, the Yādava king, attacked Lāṭa and took prisoner Devapāla's vassal, Saṁgrāmasiṁha, also known as Śaṅkha. The Chauhāna chief of Lāṭa, Siṁha, seems to have changed

1. CITD, p. 52.
2. EI, III, p. 113.
3. JAOS, VII, p. 26.
4. EI, VIII, p. 96.
5. *Sāgara-dharmāmṛita* of Āśādhara, p. 2; EI, VIII, pp. 100 ff. EI, IX, p. 107; JASB, V, pp 378-79.
6. Whether there were two or three lines only is a matter of discussion for which see EI, XXIV, p. 225. M.P.CHAKRAVARTI regards only two Mahākumāra families.

allegiance to the Chālukyas of Gujarat. Śaṁkha, the nephew of Siṁha, was released from Yādava captivity, perhaps with a view of fomenting trouble for the Chālukyas. He formed a strong confederacy, consisting of himself, the Yādava ruler Siṁhaṇa, and Devapāla, the ruler of Malwa. Vāstupāla brought about dissension between Devapāla and Siṁghaṇa. Thus Lāṭa was finally lost to the Paramāras of Malwa through the lack of diplomacy on the part of Devapāla, who could not form a strong confederacy against the Chālukyas of Gujarat. Even against the Yādavas of Devagiri he was unsuccessful. Siṁhaṇa's inscriptions[1] generally describe him as a destroyer of the fortunes of the Malavas.

During Devapāla's reign, the greatest danger came from the Muslims, who invaded Malwa. In 1234 A.D., Iltutmish captured Bhilsa and plundered Ujjain.[2] He put Bhilsa under the control of his governor. But the Muslim occupation was only for a temporary period, as known from the Māndhātā plates of Jayasiṁha.[3] The inscription mentions that Devapāla killed an *adhipa* of the mlechchhas (i.e. a governor of the Muslims) in a battle fought near the city of Bhāillasvāmin. This might refer to his attack on Bhilsa, which he seems to have recaptured.

Devapāla's end was probably inglorious. When Iltutmish captured Raṇathambhor in 1226, its ruler Vāgbhaṭa, sought refuge in Malwa. He was even assigned a fief for his maintenance by Devapāla. The *Hammīramahākāvya*[4] states that Vāgbhaṭa put Devapāla to death when he came to know that the latter was conspiring in a plot to kill him at the instigation of the Sultan of Delhi, and he made himself the master of the Malwa kingdom. This fact is further confirmed by the genealogy given at the end of the *Prabandhakośa*, wherein Vāgbhaṭa is mentioned as the conqueror of Malwa. Thus Devapāla seems to have died at the hands of Vāgbhaṭa Chauhāna, sometime before 1239 A.D., which is the earliest known date of his successor.

1. EC, VII, No. 91.
2. *Tabquāt-i-Nāsirī*, p. 622.
3. EI, XXXII, Verses 46-48.
4. HMK, IV, VV. 107-23.

Literary activities continued under the royal patronage of Devapāla. Āśādhara wrote during his reign. Bilhaṇa, the great scholar, remained his minister for peace and war.[1] The royal preceptor Madana, composed his Māndhātā inscription. The town of Depālapur was probably founded by him.

JAITUGIDEVA : *1239—1255 A.D.* :—

Devapāla was succeeded by his son Jaitugideva, before 1239 A.D. No inscription of this Prince has been discovered, but his dated references are found in Āśādhara's works.[2] He is also referred to in the inscriptions of his younger brother and successor, Jayavarman II. He assumed the title of *Bālanārāyaṇa*.[3]

From his time onwards, the deterioration of the Paramāra power was clearly visible, and Jaitugi completely failed to face external invasions. The Yādavas of Devagiri continued to raid. Siṁhaṇa's successor, Kṛishṇa Yādava, invaded Malwa about 1250 A.D.[4] The invasion of Balban[5] also took place at this time. The Muslims failed to establish a permanent authority in Malwa, but their raid hastened the decline of the Paramāra regime in Malwa.

Vīsaladeva, the Vāghela prince of Gujarat, attacked Malwa and sacked the city of Dhāra. His success against Jaitugi is clear from the testimony of inscriptions.[6] Nṛivarman, the son of Chehad of the Yajvapāla family, is said to have defeated the king of Dhāra and exacted tribute from him.[7] This statement according to H. U. TRIVEDI, cannot be verified, because the last year of Nṛivarman's father, Chehad, is also V.S. 1311, the first year of the accession of his grandson Āsala.[8]

1. EI, IX, pp. 103 ff.
2. He finished his *Sāgara-dharmāmṛita* in V.S. 1296—1239 A.D. and his *Aṅgāra-dharmāmṛita* in V. S. 1300—1243 A.D.
3. EI, IX, p. 121, V. 22.
4. Ibid, XIX, p. 27.
5. TN. I, pp. 690-91.
6. EI, I, p. 28, (Vīsaladeva's Dabhoi inscription dated 1253 A.D. Kādi grant dated 1253 (IA, VI, p. 212); ASI, 1936-37, p. 98 (An inscription of the time of Karṇa dated 1297 A.D.).
7. EI, XXIII, p. 69.
8. MPIP, II, p. 26.

JAYAVARMAN II: *1255-74* A.D. :—

Jaitugi was succeeded by his younger brother Jayavarman II, before 1255 A.D. He was also known by the name Jayasiṁha. The relations with the Yādavas of Devagiri were not cordial. Hemādri's *Vratakhaṇḍapraśasti* states that the ruler of Malwa was frightened by Mahādeva, the ruler of Devagiri.[1] On the other hand, verse fifty-four of the Māndhātā plates[2] refers to Jayavarman's success against a Dākshiṇātya king, whose kingdom lay to the south of the Vindhyas.

Jayavarman had also to fight against Jaitrasiṁha, the Chauhāna ruler of Raṇathambhor. The Balavāna inscription[3] of Hamīradeva, dated 1284 A.D. states that his predecessor, Jaitrasiṁha, gained victory over Jayasiṁha. Jaitrasiṁha is also said to have captured at *Jhamphaithaghaṭṭa* (Jhampaitghāṭ on Chambal), one hundred of the soldiers of the ruler of Malwa, who were thereafter thrown into prison at Raṇathambhor, and enslaved. It seems that Jayavarman received reverses in the battle against the Chauhāna ruler.

Jayavarman's Sādhanika was Anayasiṁha, who constructed tanks and lakes with the permission of his master.[4] Ajayadeva was his *Mahāpradhāna*,[5] and his *Sandhivigrahika*[6] was Maladhara. Ṭhākura Nārāyaṇa was a famous poet, called *Mahākavi Chakravartin*, and the Atru grant was made in his favour in 1257 A.D. by Jayasiṁha Jayavarman II.[7]

ARJUNAVARMAN II and BHOJA II—

After Jayavarman II, Arjunavarman II became king. He was very weak, and it was his misfortune that he was not only surrounded by enemies but his own minister also turned against him.

During his reign, the Yādava ruler Rāmachandra, raided Malwa once again. The Udari stone inscription[8] of Rāma-

1. Bomb. Gaz. I, Pt. II, p. 274.
2. EI, XXIII, p. 140.
3. Ibid, XIX, pp. 49-50.
4. Ibid, XXXII, p. 152.
5. Ibid, IX, p. 120.
6. Ibid.
7. PRAS. WC. 1905-06, p. 56.
8. An. Rep. Arch. Survey Mysore, 1929, p. 143.

chandra describes his success against Arjuna, the king of Malwa. Next, Hammīra, the Chauhāna ruler of Raṇathambhor, defeated Arjuna.[1] He captured Arjuna's elephant force and also a great deal of the wealth of Malwa.[2] The Vāghelas from the west could not resist the temptation of striking a blow at their tottering hereditary enemy. Sāraṅgadeva, with the help of Vīsaladeva, defeated the Lord of Mālava,[3] who was Arjunavarman II and not Jayavarman II as supposed by H.C. Ray.[4]

Arjuna II's chief minister turned against him and thus increased his difficulties. He is known as Goga or Koka. He made himself the master of some portion of Malwa. Sāraṅgadeva Vāghela is said to have defeated one *Goga*.[5] A late inscription[6] dated 1439 A.D., praises a Guhilot prince named Lakshmasiṁha of Mewar, for having defeated Gogadeva, the ruler of Malwa. Firishta[7] states that when Āin-ul-Multāni was sent by Allāuddīn Khiljī to subjugate Malwa, he was opposed by Koka, the Rājā of Malwa. Amir Khusrau,[8] the court poet of Allāuddīn, states that when Malwa was invaded by the Khilji army, it was opposed by Rai Mahlak Deo of Malwa and Koka, his *Pradhāna*, who was even stronger than Rai. It means that Goga or Koka became independent of his master.

The *Hammīramahākāvya*[9] describes Hammīra's victory over Arjuna, the king of Sarasāpur and Bhoja, the master of Dhāra. It is possible that Goga might have put Bhoja II on the throne of Dhāra, and ruled in his name.

The Paramāra kingdom of Malwa, with internal dissensions and external dangers, could not survive for long as an independent entity. The Slave Sultans of Delhi raided more

1. HMK, VII, VV. 53-56.
2. EI, IX, p. 50.
3. Asiatic Researches, XVI, p. 311; IA, XIV, p. 79. V. 42.
4. DHNI.
5. ASI, 1935-36. p. 98; Ibid, 1907-08, p. 214.
6. ASI, 1907-08, p. 214.
7. T.F. Vol. I, p. 361.
8. E and D III, p. 76; Khazāin-ul-Futūh, pp. 42 ff.
9. HMK, IX, p. 73.

than once, but they returned leaving it to the Native rulers. Things changed with the coming of imperialistic Khiljī dynasty. Its first ruler, Jalāluddīn Khilji, captured Ujjain in 1291 A.D. His successor Allauddīn, started with a large army against Malwa in 1305 A.D., and defeated Koka or Goga and his master Mahlak Deo with great slaughter. In this way, the independent existence of the kingdom of the Paramāras came to an end in 1305 A.D.

CAUSES OF THE DECLINE OF THE PARAMĀRAS :—

The Paramāra power flourished in Malwa for nearly five hundred years. It reached its zenith during the reign of Vākpati Muñja and of Bhoja. Politically, they made their power felt as contemporary rulers who looked to them for guidance. At this time, the Paramāras were highly prosperous through trade and commerce. In the sphere of art and literature, there was no one to compete with them in India. But in the course of time, their power began to decline.

There is some confusion among scholars as to the actual causes of their decline. We cannot regard lack of vigour in the Paramāra chiefs as a cause of their downfall. The Paramāra rulers were great warriors. It is equally difficult to agree with those scholars who ascribe the fall of the Paramāras to the lack of astute generalship among the kings. Nor can the Paramāra failure be accounted for, for want of religious fervour among their leaders. The Paramāra rulers were devout followers of Brahmanical religion and culture, and by their efforts they brought about great religious enthusiasm among the people.

Partly, at least, the extinction of the Paramāra sovereignty must be ascribed to the geographical situation of the region they ruled over. It is very rich and fertile with no natural boundaries for protection. As a result of this, Malwa could never remain free from foreign invasions. The wealth and power, which should have been used for better purposes, was spent in meeting the danger from neighbours. Even the powerful rulers, like Muñja and Bhoja, could not prevent it being attacked. With weaker rulers on the throne, Malwa became the arena where ambitious rulers fought out battles for supremacy. The Chālukyas of Kalyāṇa, the Chālukyas of Gujarat, the Chauhānas of Śākambharī and Raṇathambhor, the Kalchuris, the Chandellas and the Yādavas of Devagiri, all in their turn tried to draw Malwa within the sphere of their political influence. When they could, they sacked the rich cities and brought considerable destruction to the Paramāra kingdom. Whatever the strength of a dynasty it cannot constantly face the loss of man, money and power, in facing invasions. It was therefore but natural, that the Paramāras, because of their geographical position, could not remain in power for ever.

There were also other causes for the downfall of the Paramāras. To some extent, the caste system was responsible. It kept a large section of society from joining the military profession. Brāhmaṇas, Vaiśyas and Śūdras were normally not allowed to do so. The number of the soldiers in the army was thus very small.

In some measure, the downfall of the Paramāra power was due to the existence of strong feudatory families, whose power and ambition constituted a perpetual threat to the stability of the Central Government. The internal dissension among the Paramāras is also responsible. Sometimes, the ministers and officers did not remain loyal, and even formed their own kingdoms and became independent. The masses remained ignorant of the internal weakness of the Paramāra Government and the danger of external invasion.

An equally important cause of the decline of the Paramāra power was their over-ambitious foreign policy and the equally over-ambitious policy of their neighbours. As a consequence, mutual struggles continued and brought about their fall. Lastly, the Paramāras were not far-sighted, and they did not make adequate preparations to meet the coming danger of the Muslims, who finally removed the independent existence of the Paramāra kingdom.

CHAPTER—XI

ADMINISTRATION

In the seventh and eighth century A.D., Malwa remained under the political influence of the Rāshṭrakūṭas and the Pratīhāras. It is only from the ninth century onwards, that the Paramāras established an independent state and extended their territory by conquests. The king became powerful. With the growth of the state, its functions also increased. This necessitated the appointment of a number of ministers and officers. The territorial divisions became systematic and well marked. They were governed by Governors and feudatories who were responsible to the king. The local bodies also functioned efficiently. The Government introduced many innovations to meet the needs of the time.

THE KINGSHIP :—The Government at this time was monarchical. The titles of the ruling chiefs indicate their political status. The Rāshṭrakūṭa ruler, Ṇaṇṇapa, of the Indragarh inscription[1] dated V.S. 767 (710-11 A.D.), the Nāga ruler Devadatta,[2] ruling in 790 A.D. over Shergarh, and Vatsarāja[3] of the Mahua inscription, seem in fact to be feudatories from their titles. The Maurya ruler[4] Dhavalappa, of the Ḍaboka inscription, assumed the title '*Parama Bhaṭṭāraka Mahārājādhirāja Parameśvara*[5]. It indicates that he was an independent ruler. Similarly, the early Paramāra rulers assumed simple titles, such as *Mahārāja*, *Nṛipa* and *Bhūpa*, because to begin with they were feudatories. But from the time of Vākpati II onwards, the Paramāra rulers of Malwa

1. EI, XXXII, p. 112.
2. Ibid, XXXII, p. 132.
3. Ibid, XXXVII, No. 11.
4. Ibid, XXXV, p. 100.
5. IA, VI, pp. 55-56.

assumed the imperial title of *Parama Bhaṭṭāraka Mahārājādhirāja Parameśvara*. But it is not necessary so that these imperial titles always meant an independent position. From the Ingnoda inscription dated 1133-34 A.D., it is known that Vijayapāladeva assumed the title of '*Mahārājādhirāja Parameśvara*'. Actually he was not an independent ruler, but a feudatory of the Paramāras.

The Paramāra rulers assumed other epithets which have both political and cultural significance. Vākpati II assumed the titles of '*Śrīvallabha*, *Pṛithvīvallabha* and *Amoghavarsha*' of the Rāshṭrakūṭas, because he considered himself to be the successor of the departed glory of the Rāshṭrakūṭas, and he was also their relative. As he was a patron of poets, he took the title of *Kavibāndhava*. His brother Sindhurāja, bore the title of '*Navasāhasāṅka*'. Bhoja was called a '*Sārvabhauma Chakravartin*', and because of his cultural accomplishments, he was known by the titles, '*Tribhuvananārāyaṇa*', *Śishṭaśiromaṇi* and *Sarasvatīkaṇthābharaṇa*. Naravarman took pride in calling himself *Nirvāṇa Nārāyaṇa*.

The authority of the king was supreme. He was both the constitutional and the executive head of state. He appointed all the important officers of the state, transferred them from one place to another, and dismissed them if he thought fit. He was the commander-in-chief of the army and himself led various campaigns. Many of the grants of the Paramāra rulers were issued when they were in victorious camps in the course of their military campaigns.[1] He was the chief justice, and the lord of the exchequer. In theory he was an absolute ruler.

The bards and poets have described the king as divine. They identified him and compared him, with one god or another. Vairisiṁha II is said to be one who humbled Indra and surpassed Śesha. Bhoja was compared to Kṛishṇa, the epic hero. Naravarman called himself by the title '*Nirvāṇa Nārāyaṇa*.' However, the king's authority was controlled by checks and balances which were of a constitutional type.

1. The Harsola grant of Sīyaka II was issued in 949 A.D., when he was returning from his expedition against Yogarāja and was encamped on the banks of the river Mahi. EI, XIX, p. 236.

Before taking the burden of the state on their shoulders, the Paramāra princes received proper training in different branches of learning. They possessed high and noble ideals of self restraint, charity and impartiality. They seem to have been like the philosopher kings of Plato's republic, and they did not misuse the power entrusted to them.

Customs and traditions exercised a check on the power of the king. He was expected to govern his people strictly in accordance with the civil and criminal law contained in the *Smṛitis*. The ministers and other high officers exercised considerable influence over the king.[1] His power was limited by the influential feudatories known as the *Māṇḍalikas*, and the *Sāmantas*, who enjoyed many privileges. His authority was also checked by local bodies such as the guild, *pañchāyata*, town committee etc.

DUTIES OF THE KING :—The first and foremost duty of the king was the protection of his subjects against both internal and external dangers.[2] He had to punish thieves and dacoits, and to safeguard the public against social injustice. Sometimes, he himself led the army against the enemies.

The king was considered to be the upholder of the *Varṇāśramadharma*. He had to see that the people were following the respective duties of their castes. He honoured all sects and promoted a feeling of mutual toleration and respect among the followers of these sects.[3]

The king carried on the administration of the state. Being a scholar, he promoted art, literature and sciences. His heavy burden of administration was lightened by his hobbies, and alleviated by the amusements provided for him. His hobbies were horse-riding, witnessing elephant fight, archery, and the use of other arms. The king spent his leisure hours in hunting, water-sports, with his wives, and witnessing dramatic performances.

An ideal king, according to Dhanapāla, was one who was a *Sārvabhauma-chakravartin*; who was proficient in the six-fold

1. When Vākpati II marched to the south in disregard to the sage advice of his minister, he perished.
2. TM, p. 244.
3. Ibid, p. 11.

policy; who had brought all the *Sāmantas* under his sway; who had his *Mantrimaṇḍala* under control; who had the confidence of his friends and who had appointed trusted men in his forts.

THE LAW OF SUCCESSION :—The kingship was hereditary and the principle of primogeniture was followed. In the life-time of the ruler, the eldest son was made heir-apparent and was called *Yuvarāja*, *Mahākumāra* or *Mahārāja kumāra*. He helped his father in running the administration. The title *Yuvarāja* was given at sixteen, and he ascended the throne after the death of his father. In the absence of a son, a younger brother succeeded to the throne. Vākpati II made his nephew Bhoja his *Yuvarāja*, though his younger brother Sindhurāja was alive. Mahākumāra Lakshmīvarman's principality was inherited by his grandson Udayavarman, though his son Hariśchandra was alive. If the king died in the battle-field without leaving any male issue, his nearest relative could claim the throne. This was the case with Jayasiṁha I, who became the successor of Bhoja. Sometimes, the king abdicated in favour of his heir-apparent. In his old age, Sīyaka II abdicated in favour of his heir-apparent, Vākpati II. There are instances of wars of succession among the kinsmen of the king after his death. Udayāditya had to fight against his relatives for the throne.

THE QUEEN :—The queen had a special position of honour. She lived in an inner apartment. Generally, the name of queen is referred to in connection with charities and donations.

THE ROYAL COURT :—The royal court consisted of two types of courtiers; those who helped the king in the work of administration, and others who simply adorned the court by their presence. The ministers, generals, *pratīhāras*, etc. came in the first category. The great poets, learned Brāhmaṇas, bards, astrologers, the king's relatives and friends, were the courtiers of the second type.

THE MINISTERS :—Next to the king were ministers. They were experienced and well-versed in *Dharmaśāstras* and the other branches of learning. Their posts were generally hereditary. Their number and importance depended upon the state and its ruler. They helped the king in running the administration of the state. They tried to promote the welfare of the state in different ways. Unlike the modern cabinet, there was no principle of collective responsibility, but of individual responsibility.

It seems that there were two types of ministers[1] *Buddhisachiva* and *Karmasachiva*. The duty of the former was to give counsel to the king on state matters, and of the latter, to assist the king in the execution of the state policy. In the inscriptions and contemporary literature of this period, the designations of ministers and high officers are as follows :—

(i) *Mahāpradhāna* was the chief minister of the state. He was the highest officer who supervised the general administration of the state. He held the charge of the Royal seal and was specially concerned with revenue administration. He was the most trusted and influential member of the state. Some of the *Mahāpradhānas* were Rudrāditya[2], the chief-minister of Vākpati II, Purushottama[3] who was the *Mahāpradhāna* of Yaśovarman, and Ajayadeva[4] who served Jayavarman II.

(ii) *Mahāsandhivigrahaka* was the minister of peace and war. He had to draft royal charters and despatches. Generally good officers were appointed to this post. Bilhaṇa and *Rājā* Sallakhaṇa[5] were the ministers of war and peace for king Arjunavarman.

(iii) *Mahādaṇḍanāyaka and Daṇḍanāyaka* : Scholars are not unanimous as to the nature of this post.[6] At this time, he seems

1. TM, p. 13.
2. PC, p. 22.
3. IA, XIX, p. 349.
4. EI, IX, p. 120.
5. JASB, V, p. 378. Magistrate (Prinsep); the great leader of forces (Fleet), Prefect of Police (Auriel Stein), the Chief Judge or Chief Officer of Police (Marshall) and military officer. (Mirashi & Altekar)
6. TM, p. 148.

to be a military officer, though he was entrusted with other duties. The *Tilaka Mañjarī* speaks of a *Daṇḍanāyaka* for North and a *Daṇḍanāyaka* for Dakshiṇāpatha.[1] Bhoja, in whose time the *Tilakamañjarī* was written, might have appointed two *daṇḍanāyakas*, one in the north and the other in the south. He might have adopted a system of zonal command.

TANTRAPĀLA :—The Maser inscription[2] of the Śulki chief refers to one *Tantrapāla* of Muñja. He seems to be the officer of the borders, and his duty was to look after the interests of the state.

MAHĀPRATĪHĀRA :—This officer is also known as *dauvārika*.[3] Because of his constant attendance on the king, he wielded considerable influence over his master.

RĀJAGURU :—The office of Rājaguru was one of great status and respect. He was consulted in important matters and was often entrusted with various kinds of work as befitting his position. Madana was the *Rājaguru* of Arjunavarman.[4]

MAHĀPUROHITA OR PUROHITA :—He was the adviser of the king on religious matters. He was expected to ward off the evils of the state by means of rites and incantations.[5]

Besides these, there were a large number of officers who are known from contemporary literature and inscriptions.

Dharmastheya[6] :—He was the Judicial officer and his main duty was to advise the king on judicial matters.

Akshapaṭalika[7] :—He was the keeper of the accounts. He kept full account of the income and expenditure of the state.

Dūtaka[8] :—He was a high officer who conveyed the royal

1. TM, p. 66.
2. EI, XIV, pp. 176-83.
3. TM, p. 58.
4. JASB, p. 37.
5. TM, p. 55.
6. Ibid, p. 12.
7. Ibid, p. 84.
8. Sometimes, this office was combined with that of a *Mahāpradhāna* or *Mahāsandhivigrahaka*. *Mahāpradhāna* Rājaśrī Ajayadeva was the *dūtaka* of the Māndhātā grant of Jayavarman II (EI, IX, p. 120). *Mahāsandhivigrahaka* Pandit Bilhaṇa was the *dūtaka* of the Māndhātā plates of king Devapāla, (Ibid, p. 103).

sanction of charters to local officials. The duty of *Lekhakārika*[1] was to carry the king's letters. *Kośarakshaka* was perhaps the keeper of the royal treasury.

Other officers were associated with the Royal Court. *Mahāvaidya*[2] was concerned with the health of the ruler, his household, and any one in whom the king might be interested. *Aṅgarakshaka*[3] was the body-guard of the king. *Śayyāpālaka*[4] was to guard the bed of the king. *Vandiputra*[5] was the royal bard. *Narmasachiva*[6] was perhaps to entertain the king.

The *Aṁtarvaṁśika*[7] was in charge of the royal Seragalio. *Paṭṭabandha*[8] may have helped the king in his dressing. The state astrologer was also an important official because he lived near the king's palace.

There were some local officers[9] who are known from inscriptions, such as *Deśaṭhakkura*, *Adhishṭhānaka*, *Karaṇapurusha* and *Bhaṭṭaputra*. *Paṭṭakila* was the village headman. He has been frequently mentioned in connection with the grant of villages. *Vishayika*[10] was the head of the District.

TERRITORIAL DIVISIONS :—

For the convenience of administration, the empire was divided into territorial units known as *Maṇḍalas*, such as *Pūrṇapāthakamaṇḍala*,[11] *Ardhāshṭamaṇḍala*,[12] *Vyāpuramaṇḍala*,[13] *Rūṇamaṇḍala*,[14] *Upendramaṇḍala*,[15] *Sthalimaṇḍala*,[16] *Vindhyamaṇḍala*,[17]

1. TM, p. 156.
2. IHQ, XXIII, p. 120.
3. TM, p. 12.
4. Ibid, p. 156; IA, 18, p. 81.
5. Ibid, p. 12.
6. Ibid.
7. Ibid, p. 59.
8. Ibid, p. 109.
9. IA, XVIII, p. 81.
10. Ibid.
11. EI, III, p. 48.
12. Ibid, XXXIII, p. 197.
13. Ibid, II, p, 192.
14. Ibid, XXIII, p. 108.
15. Ibid, XX, p. 106.
16. Ibid, XI, p. 182; IA. XLI, p. 201 (The area round about Banswara).
17. IA, XVI, p. 252.

Mahādvādaśakamaṇḍala,[1] *Saṅgamakheṭakamaṇḍala*,[2] *Avantimaṇḍala*,[3] *Nīlagirimaṇḍala*,[4] *Siharāmaṇḍala*,[5] *Uparahāḍamaṇḍala*,[6] *Chachuroṇimaṇḍala*[7] and *Sellukamaṇḍala*.

These *Maṇḍalas* were further divided into territorial units known as *Vishaya*, *Bhoga*, *Pathaka* and *Pratijāgaraṇaka*. PRATIPALA BHATIA[8] tried to distinguish them, but they are the names of one and the same unit. In the Māndhātā plates[9] of Devapāla, Mahuḍa has been mentioned as *Pratijāgaraṇaka*, and in that of Jayavarman II, as *Pathaka*.

From the copper grant[10] of the Mahākumāra Lakshmīvarmadeva, it is known that *Rājasayaṇa bhoga* was situated in the *Mahādvādaśaka Maṇḍala*. From the Banswara plates[11] (V.S. 1076=1020 A.D.) of Bhojadeva, it is clear that Vaṭapadraka was included in the *ghāghradora bhoga* of the *Sthalī Maṇḍala*. From the Copper Plate Grant[12] of the time of Ajayapāla, it is known that the village of Ālaviḍagāṁva belonged to *Pūrṇa Pathaka*. The stone inscription[13] of Ajayapāla dated V.S. 1239, informs us that the village of Umarathā was situated in the *Pathaka*, called *Bhṛiṁgārikā Chatuḥshashṭi* in the *Mahādvādaśaka Maṇḍala*.

The *Pratijāgaraṇaka* seems to have been the common name used for the territorial unit of a district. The inscriptions speak of a number of *Pratijāgaraṇakas*. From the Kadambapadraka grant of Naravarman,[14] it is known that Kadambapadraka was situated in the *Pratijāgaraṇaka Maṇḍāraka* of the *Upendra-*

1. Ibid, XIX, p. 35?. (The Great group of twelve) The area of Udaipur and Bhilsa.
2. Ibid, XXI.
3. EI, XXIII, p. 112.
4. IASB, VII, p. 735.
5. IHR, 1961, p. 163.
6. IA, XX, p. 84.
7. EI, XXIII, p. 135.
8. The Paramāras—(c. 800-1305 A. D.), p. 215.
9. EI, IX, pp. 103-117.
10. IA, XIX, p. 352.
11. EI, XI, No. 18.
12. IA, XVIII, p. 81.
13. Ibid, XV, p, 344.
14. EI, XX.

pura Maṇḍala. In the Māndhatā[1] plates of Paramāra Jayasiṁha Jayavarman (V.S. 1331), mention is made of *Vardhanā-pura-Pratijāgaraṇaka* (Badanawar, near Ujjain), *Saptāśīti-pratijā-garaṇaka*, literally a *paraganā* consisting of 87 villages, *Nāga-daha pratijāgaraṇaka* (Nagda, near Ujjain) and *Śākapura Pra-tijāgaraṇaka* (Shujalpur). Besides, *Mahuḍa Pratijāgaraṇaka*[2], *Narmadāpura Pratijāgaraṇaka*[3] and *Pagāra Pratijāgaraṇaka*[4] are also known.

Each *Pratijāgaraṇaka* was a group of villages. Sometimes, it was known after the number of villages constituting the group, for instance, *Vikhilapadraka*—twelve, *Nyāyapadra*[5]—seventeen, *Vaṭakheṭaka*[6]—thirty-six, *Mākhulagāṁva*[7]—forty-two, villages, *Voḍasirāsakta*[8]—forty-eight villages, and *Chatuḥshashṭi*[9]—sixty-four villages.

The *grāma* or village was the lowest territorial unit. The villages granted to Brāhmaṇas were known as *Agrahāra* villages, and the villages inhabited by the Brāhmaṇas were known as *Brahmasthāna* or *Brahmapurī*.

FEUDAL SYSTEM :—

Territory ruled by feudal princes was known as *Māṇḍali-kas*, *Maṇḍaleśvaras*, *Mahāsāmantas*, *Sāmantas*, *Rājaputras* and *Ṭhakkuras*. The Paramāra court was full of feudatory chiefs and the Paramāra kings are described as the ones at whose feet the feudatories bowed down.[10] The feudatory chiefs took their seats in the royal court according to their grades.

The feudatories may be divided into certain categories according to their status, and their relations with the Central Government. The first category consisted of those who were

1. EI, XXXII, p. 140.
2. Ibid, IX, p. 109.
3. IA, XVI, p. 252.
4. JAOS, VII, p. 27.
5. EI, XVIII, p. 320,
6. IA, XIX, pp. 349-50.
7. Ibid, XVIII, p. 81, EI, III, p. 48.
8. Ibid, XVI, No. 171.
9. Ibid, XV, p, 345.
10. EI, II, p. 192.

rewarded with land in consideration of valuable services. The Chauhāna Anayasiṁha was the *Sādhanika* (military governor) of Jayasiṁha Jayavarman posted at Maṇḍapadurga.[1] He seems to be a hereditary feudatory because we know that his father Salakhaṇasiṁha, and his grandfather Palhaṇadeva, owed allegiance to the Paramāras, and assisted them in battles. His father Salakhaṇasiṁha, the Chauhāna leader of the Paramāra forces, gave military assistance to his master and defeated the army of Siṁhaṇadeva, no doubt the Yādava king of that name who ruled in 1210-47 A.D. Salakhaṇasiṁha has been mentioned as *Mahāsandhivigrahika* in Arjunavarman's Bhopal Plates. That Anayasiṁha granted four villages with the permission of the Paramāra king Jayavarman, alias Jayasiṁha, in favour of the Brāhmaṇas, points to his special power and prestige.

To the second category belonged the feudatories of Junior line. The Paramāras of Vāgaḍa were of this type. They were kith and kin relations of the Imperial Paramāras of Dhāra, to whom they acknowledged supremacy, and enjoyed their good-will.

The third category was comprised of those feudatory princes who carved out principalities by the force of their own arms, during the period of decline of the Central authority of the Paramāras. In this class are the Paramāra Mahākumāras, who, though they used the subordinate titles of Mahākumāra and *Pañchamahāśabdālaṁkṛita*, were for all practical purposes independent, and did not even bother to mention the name of the contemporary Paramāra overlords in their public records.

To the fourth category belonged those chiefs who, when defeated, accepted the suzerainty of the king. They can be called vassal chiefs. The Guhilas of Mewat may be placed in this category, because when they were defeated by Vākpati II, they accepted the Paramāra suzerainty.

The mutual relations between the sovereign and the feudatories depended upon circumstances, and their relative strength. They had their own duties and responsibilities

1. EI, XXXII, p. 142.

towards each other.

The feudatories mentioned the name of the suzerain when the central authority was strong, but not when it was weak. In the Arthūṇā inscription[1] and in the Paṇherā inscription,[2] the Paramāra rulers of Vāgaḍa referred to their sovereign. In the inscription of Vijayarāja, the feudatory Paramāra ruler of Vāgaḍa, the name of the sovereign Lord and his family has been omitted because he was weak.

These feudal lords attended the imperial court on ceremonial occasions. Many had their own houses in the Imperial capital. They paid regular tribute to their sovereign and gave presents to him on festive occasions. They not only sent a certain number of troops to the aid of their master, but they themselves led the armies in the battle-fields. The Paramāras of Vāgaḍa fought several times on behalf of the Imperial Paramāras of Dhāra.

The internal autonomy enjoyed by these feudal lords varied according to their status. The Paramāras of Vāgaḍa and the Paramāra Mahākumāras enjoyed a large amount of internal autonomy. They could create their own sub-feudatories and appoint their own officers. They could assign taxes, alienate villages, and exempt certain people from taxation, without any reference to the Imperial power. Smaller feudatories enjoyed less autonomy. Anayasiṁha, the Chauhāna Sādhanika of Maṇḍapadurga, could not grant land without the permission of his Master.[3] The king could grant land even from the territory of the feudatories. King Sīyaka II is said to have granted the two villages of Kumbharohaka and Sīhaka in *Mohaḍāvasak*, which was a part of *Kheṭakamaṇḍala*, then ruled by a subordinate chief of Sīyaka I1.[4]

The king honoured these feudal lords in different ways. He invited them to his coronation, and to other such occasions. These feudal lords participated in ceremonial dinners given by the king. The king gave them gifts of dress and

1. EI, XIV, p. 295.
2. Ibid, XXI, p. 46.
3. EI, XXXII, p. 142.
4. Ibid, XIX, p. 236.

rewarded them with honours. The title of *Pañchmahāśabda*[1] was conferred on very powerful feudatories, but sometimes it was used by them of their own accord, without its being conferred.

In the absence of a male heir to the throne after the death of the sovereign, the throne was sometimes offered to one of the scions of the royal family. In the case of an invader after conquering the kingdom, he did not annex it, but installed one of these scions of the royal family to subordinate rulership.

Sometimes, the existence of so many powerful feudal lords tended to weaken the central Government, for they incited centrifugal forces. Generally, they were opportunists, and took advantage of the Central authority. When the great Paramāra emperor Bhoja died, the difficulties of the Paramāra dynasty increased because of the selfish interests of the *Sāmantas*. They could not keep the old bonds of permanent relationship, but were prepared to transfer their allegiance to the invader Ballāla, in return for greater privileges.

MILITARY SYSTEM :—

The army consisted of two types of soldiers, namely *maulas* and *bhṛitas*. The '*maulas*' were hereditary, and depended for their livelihood on land grants made by the king. The *bhṛitas* were paid wages for their services. Of these two, the *maulas* were more reliable and were preferred to the *bhṛitas*, who changed sides when they received higher wages from the other party.

The army at this time was divided into three main branches, namely infantry, cavalry, and elephants. Bhoja, in his *Yuktikalpataru*, mentions the importance of these different branches of the army. According to him, foot soldiers are the main source of strength on all occasions.[2] He was not ignorant of the importance of cavalry, as he refers to the

1. According to the *Vivekachintāmaṇi*, *Pañchamahāśabda* stood for five instruments i.e. *Śṛiṅga* or horn, *tammaṭa* or taliage; *Śaṅkha* or conch; *bheri* or kettledrum and *Jayaghaṇṭia* or bell of victory (IA, XII, p. 96)
2. Yukti, p. 7.

horses from Tajikistan and Tushāra countries as the best.[1] Elephants formed an important source of military strength, and they accompanied the army on almost all important occasions. Chariots, though not important, were still in use, as they are referred to in the *Yuktikalpataru*.[2]

As Malwa is a land-locked region, there was no necessity of keeping a fleet. Boats were frequently required for crossing rivers. When the Paramāras conquered Lāṭa, the importance of maintaining a navy was felt. It is for this reason that Bhoja, in his *Yuktikalpataru*[3], gives elaborate directions for constructing different types of ships. He further says, that the king, who has boats, wins the war, and the king who through ignorance does not keep boats, loses his prestige, vigour and treasury.

The army was under the charge of military officers *Mahādaṇḍanāyaka* or *Daṇḍanāyaka* was probably the highest military officer, identifiable with a Commander-in-chief. *Balādhikṛita*[4] was put in charge of the military town. *Sādhanika*[5] appears to have been in charge of cavalry and, was perhaps stationed at important forts. *Mahāmātra*[6] was the commander of the elephant forces.

For the protection of the civic population, proper attention was given to the construction of forts and walled cities. The famous forts of this time were Dhāra, Maṇḍapadurga and Koshavardhana. The well garrisoned cities baffled the enemy, and there was no alternative but for a long siege. Jayasiṁha Siddharāja had to fight for twelve years against Naravarman and Yaśovarman, and in the end, was able to break the gate of Dhāra due to the treachery of a Malwa soldier. Bhoja, in his *Samarāṅgaṇasūtradhāra*[7], suggests methods of constructing various types of forts.

1. Yukti, p. 182.
2. Ibid, p. 7.
3. Ibid, pp. 224-229.
4. TM, p. 97.
5. Ibid, p. 150.
6. Ibid, p. 149.
7. I, p. 36.

The soldiers had peculiar dresses and weapons. They were heavily clad, with helmet and iron nets protecting separately, the belly, thighs, arms, and other parts of the body. They also wore *pugrees*, made up with multi-coloured scarves arranged in layers. They used swords, discs, daggers, spears, bows, *śūla* and parigha as their weapons. Their methods and weapons of warfare proved to be outdated in their struggle against the Muslim invaders. They relied on frontal attack without the use of stratagem or tactics.

The Yātrā, or march, of the army, was an occasion of great significance. The particular day was fixed in consultation with an astrologer. People celebrated this event with great rejoicings, as is clear from the Banswara Copper Plate of Bhoja[1]. Dasharatha Sharma[2] thinks that the '*Koṅkaṇa-vijaya-parva*' may mean the *Koṅkaṇa-vijaya-yātrā-parva* i.e. the day on which the Paramāra forces started on their expedition for the conquest of Koṅkaṇa. Dhanapāla[3] gives a vivid account of the army on march. The royal camp was an elaborate affair. The wives of the big chiefs, their concubines and prostitutes, all accompanied them. The merchants supplied everything for the soldiers at the camp in order to make their lives comfortable.

FINANCIAL ADMINISTRATION :—

The financial administration was efficiently organized. A large number of taxes were levied by the State. There were also other sources of revenue. Consequently, the treasury became rich and the rulers could spend a large sum of money on public works. They extended patronage to literature by rewarding men of letters.

Most of the Paramāra inscriptions record the grant of villages with *bhāga*, *bhoga*, *Uparikara* and *hiraṇya*. *Bhāga* was the king's share of the produce which was fixed one sixth, but it could be altered when required. *Bhoga* denoted the periodic offerings of fruits, firewoods, flowers, milk and curd, which the subjects had to make to the king or to his local agents.

1. EI XI, p. 182.
2. Journal of Ganganath Jha Institute V., pp. 61 ff.
3. TM, p. 96.

Uparikara meant an additional tax, which might have included miscellaneous taxes in kind. *Hiraṇya* was perhaps a tax on some of the land produce which was paid in cash.

Śulka was also an important source of revenue. It was charged on goods brought for sale. It was of two types, namely *maṇḍapikādāya* and *ghaṭṭadāya*. *Maṇḍapikādāya* was levied on goods carried by land and collected at *maṇḍapikā*.[1] *Ghaṭṭadāya* was levied on goods carried by water in riverine areas. The Arthūṇā inscription[2] of 1080 A.D. enumerates the separate duties levied on different goods brought in the market for sale, and the whole income was granted to the deity. The Bhopal inscription[3] of Arjunavarman refers to the ferry duties which may have been collected by an officer known as *Ghaṭṭapati*.[4]

There were also other taxes charged by the State. The Arthūṇā inscription[5] refers to the excise duty of four *rūpakas* on each *viṁvaka* of the distillers. That *Mārgadāya* (Road cess) was imposed is clear from the Paṇherā inscription, which records that King Jayasiṁha I assessed one *viṁśopaka* coin on every bull that passed along the road.[6] The Shergarh inscription[7] states that Varaṅga, who was *Mārgadāyī Kauptika*, made a donation of five *Vṛishbhas* (a type of coin) out of *mārgadāya* in 1018 A.D., in favour of the God Somanātha, for the purpose of providing incense and sandal in the temple.

The Arthūṇā inscription[8] records that some other taxes were prevalent at this time. The trade tax of one *dramma* was levied on shops and houses of traders in the local *bazār* on the occasion of the *Chaitra* festival, and the festival of the sacred thread. This type of tax of one *dramma* was also imposed on

1. EI, XXIII, p. 136 (Shergarh inscription)
2. Ibid, XIV, pp. 295 ff.
3. JAOS, VII, p. 27.
4. CII, p. cxlii., Ibid No. 74, p. 34.
5. EI, XIV, p. 302. 74.
6. Ibid, XXI, p. 48.
7. Ibid, XXIII, p. 137.
8. Ibid, p. 392, V. 75.

each trader's association. The gambling tax[1] of two *rūpakas* was levied on each gambling house. Every house in the state was taxed at the rate of one *dramma* each.[2] House tax is referred to in the Bhopal inscription of King Arjunavarman.[3] Salt tax is also known from this inscription.[4] *Shamhalāṭam* (*Ka*)-*Samanvita* is a new revenue term which occurs in Devapāla's Māndhātā inscription.[5] Its meaning is not definite.[6]

Besides these different taxes, there were other sources of revenue for the king. He received tribute from the feudatories and from defeated enemies. War booty was an important source of income. The king received money by way of fines on the wrong doers. The property of persons who died without male heirs, and without making any adequate alternative arrangement, was annexed by the state. The state had a share in treasure troves. It also got the considerable income from the forests and mines.

Under expenditure comes the maintenance of the monarch and his royal court, and the members of the royal family. The state had to pay the salaries of the ministers and officers, high and low. The kings had to spend considerable amounts in war activities. They also founded cities, and constructed forts, palaces and temples, which are beautiful specimens of art and architecture. They patronized literature by rewarding intellectuals. They also spent money for welfare of the people.

THE JUDICIARY AND THE POLICE SYSTEM :—

The king was the highest judicial authority in the state and his decisions were final. He did not give arbitrary judg-

1. EI, p. 392, V. 75.
2. Ibid.
3. JAOS, VII, p. 27.
4. Ibid.
5. EI, IX, p. 103.
6. The space between *ta* and *ta* is larger than is generally left between two *aksharas* in other places in this record. This phrase was unintelligible to F. Kielhorn. H. V. Trivedi reads '*Samastatālaka Samanvita*'. While editing this grant, he suggested that it should mean, 'all ponds or tanks.' See, Corpus Inscriptionum Indicarum of the Later Dynasties of Central India, Vol. XVI, Typescript.

ment but was assisted by learned Brāhmaṇas who were well versed in the *Dharmaśāstras*. The judicial officers were known as *Dharmastheyas*[1] and *Rājādhyakshakas*[2], whose main duty was to determine justice impartially.

It seems that in the villages, cases were decided by village councils and the village elders. The *Pañchakulas* had a considerable say in the judicial matters of the town. In towns and villages, there were police officers, like the *Talāras*[3] or the *Daṇḍapāśikas*, whose duty was to detect crimes and to keep a check on unruly elements and on new-comers.

The penal code was very severe. Hands and feet were cut off for the slightest offence. Death by execution or torture was the usual punishment. Sometimes the criminal was hanged. Theft was a serious crime. Adultery was heavily punished. In the *Sṛiṅgāra-mañjarīkathā*[4], an oilman was arrested for adultery. Though he paid the fine, he was not freed, but was tortured and given other heavy punishments. Criminals were sometimes bound with iron chains and put into gaols. Resort to ordeal was common enough during this period.

LOCAL ADMINISTRATION

In the villages and towns, whether they were under the charge of rulers and *sāmantas* or not, considerable power lay in the hands of the people. There were a number of local bodies carrying on the administration. The official element was also represented in the local administration, but its influence was not very effective.

The village council, known as *Janapada*, carried on the administration of the village. It was mostly concerned with local affairs. The village headman, known as *Grāmakūṭa* or *Grāmaṭaka*, presided over the meetings of the council. The most important officer in the village was *Paṭṭakila* or *Paṭel*. There is hardly a land-grant of the Paramāras which does not refer to

1. TM, p. 12.
2. EI, XXXIII, p. 197.
3. IA, LVI, p. 12.
4. SMK, p. 45.

a *Paṭṭakila*. His main duty seems to have been the assessment of the land and the fixation of the boundaries.

The town council was known as *Pañchakula*, or the committee of five. It was the most important committee which managed the civil affairs of the town. The *Pañchakulas* registered land grants and were associated with the administration of justice. From the Indragadh inscription of Naṇṇappa[1] dated V.S. 767 (710-11 A.D.), it is clear that the city council was charged with the responsibility of carrying out repairs to the shrine and maintaining worship therein. The government officers, such as *Mahattama* and *Balādhikṛita*, assisted this council in the discharge of its duties. An inscription from Shergarh[2] refers to three merchants as making a grant to the Bhaṭṭāraka Nāganaka of the Somanātha temple in the year 1017 A.D., out of the *maṇḍapikā* tax. These merchants seem to have constituted the town committee in charge of the collection, as well as of the disbursement of local taxes.

There were a number of guilds functioning in cities and towns. In the inscriptions of this period, there is reference to the guilds of goldsmiths, *śreshṭhins*, *sthapatis* Nāga Baniyās, Lāra Baniyās, *telīs*, etc. These guilds managed the affairs of their communities and looked after the interests of their members. The chiefs of these guilds could make endowments on behalf of their communities, and were influential in the administration of the town. The Shergarh inscription[3] records grants made by Tailakarāja Ṭhākura Devasvāmin, which consisted of oil for the lamp in the Somanātha temple, a daily gift of a *voḍi* for providing incense at the Parṇasālā, and the monthly payment of two *varāhas* on the occasion of *Saṁkrānti*. As suggested by A. S. ALTEKAR,[4] Tailakarāja made these gifts, not in an individual capacity, but most probably on behalf of the guild of the *Telīs*, of which he might have been the chief representative, and was therefore connected with the city administration at that time.

1. EI, XXXIII, p. 112.
2. Ibid, XXIII, p. 138.
3. Ibid, XXIII, p. 1$8.
4. Ibid, p. 137.

In the Moḍāsā plates[1] of Paramāra Bhoja dated 1011 A.D., a Brāhmaṇa donee named Derdda has been given the epithet of *Chāturjātakīya*. D.C. Sircar thinks that the epithet *Chāturjātakīya* means that Derdda was a member of *Chāturjātaka*, which according to him, was an administrative board of four. According to Pratipala Bhatia,[2] the word *jātaka*, however, means *Jyotisha* i.e. astronomy and not committee, and the epithet *Chāturjātakīya* may, therefore, mean one who was the member of an assembly of those who were well-versed in astronomy. This explanation is doubtful, because we rarely find an assembly of astronomers.

The above discussion shows that the administrative organization was headed by the king, working through various agencies, both official and non-official. The *Mantrins*, *Daṇḍanāyakas*, *Sādhaṇika* and *Balādhikṛita* were the officials of the Government, and *Mahattaras*, *Pañchakulas*, *Janapadas* and *Śreṇīs* were the representatives of the people. The impact of these local bodies was greater than that of the officials on the general administration. One noteworthy feature of this administration, which distinguishes it from others, is its cultural and benevolent spirit. Muñja and Bhoja set a model not only for their contemporaries, but also for their descendants to emulate.

1. EI, XXXIII, p. 197.
2. The Paramāras—(c 800—1303 A.D.), p. 239.

CHAPTER—XII

RELIGION

No doubt the religious ideas and practices of the previous period continued during this age, but the relative importance of religion underwent change. Image worship became very popular among the masses, and images of the different gods and goddesses in various aspects have been found. The number of temples increased, and they are massive and grand from the architectural point of view. The liberal outlook of religion is clear from the fact that images of different gods and goddesses are found in the same temple. The ruling chiefs showed an attitude of toleration by honouring all religions. These mutually influenced one another in their ideas and practices. The Jainas and the Buddhists began to worship images with devotional songs and rites and ceremonies of the Brāhmanical religions. The Jainas influenced the Brāhmanical religions by the doctrine of Ahiṁsā.

The Puranic Brahmanical religion in the forms of Vaishṇavism and Śaivism became dominant because of royal patronage, and the influence of their saints. Jainism became specially popular among the people of merchant classes. As a result of Tantric practices, Buddhism gradually began to decline, and from the twelfth century disappeared.

BUDDHISM

Buddhism was in existence, but was in a state of decadence. In the eighth century A.D., the region around Shergarh was ruled by the Nāgas who were probably feudatories of the Mauryas. As these Nāga rulers were followers of Buddhism, it seems that the Buddhist monuments of this period were erccted under their patronage. The ruler Devadatta, who was of the Nāga family, built a monastery and temple at Shergarh in 770 A.D.[1] There are also Buddhist caves found at Kholvi[2] Binaika[3] of this period, but the most important centre in this area was Dhamnār.[4] The seventy Buddhist caves excavated prove that there was a great Buddhist monastic establishment in the eighth century A.D. That Dhamnār was known as Chandanagiri mahāvihāra during this period, is clear from the discovery of an inscribed clay seal.[5] A series of the Buddhist caves of the eighth century A.D. were found at Khejaria Bhop,[6] which is thirty-two kilometres south-east of Dhamnār, and sixteen kilometres west of Kholvi.

About twenty kilometres south-east of Garoth, there is a place known as Polāḍuṅgara, where there are about a hundred Buddhist excavations.[7] Most of the caves have suffered great damage; ceilings and pillars of several of them have given way. All these are Vihāras except two which are *chaityas*. Of these, one is in ruins and the other is well preserved. As not a single figure of Buddha and Boddhisattva has been discovered, this Buddhist establishment must have belonged to the Hīnayāna sect which survived in this area up to the eighth century A.D.

The vestiges of the last activities of Buddhism are found at Gyaraspur.[8] A few ruined platforms built of dry rubble masonry might possibly be the remanants of *stūpas*. A seated image of Buddha has been also discovered. There are two images of Buddha carved in the face of a hill about three kilometres to the west of Gyaraspur. The Buddhist *stūpa* at Rajpur[9] probably belonged to the ninth century A.D. About two kilometres to the north of the *stūpa* lies an old deserted site called '*Buddhon*', a name which suggests its association with Buddhism.

1. IA, XIV, p. 45.
2. ASC, II, p. 187.
3. ASI, 1922-23, p. 124.
4. Ibid, 1905-06.
5. I. Ar. 1960-61, p. 60.
6. ASI, 1916-17.
7. PRAS. WC, 1913.
8. The Cultural Heritage,
9. Archaeology in Gwalior,

The name of the place Bihār in the Persian inscription dated 1440 A.D. in the Maszid, proves that it was a centre of Buddhism. The monument called '*Solākhambhā*' of this place, is the ruin of a Buddhist temple. Sculptures relating to Buddhism have been found.[1]

Sanchi continued to be a centre of Buddhism even in the early medieval period. There are Buddhist monasteries, temples and images, from the eighth century to the twelfth century A.D.[2] An enshrined figure of Buddha with an inscription of the seventh or eighth century A.D., has been found at Bhojapura.[3] All these facts indicate that Buddhism lingered in this area.

Lui-pā, the famous Tantric teacher, was born in Ujjain. He was a writer of a king called Sāmantaśubha[4] who cannot be identified. He was initiated into the *Chakrasambhara maṇḍala* by Śmaśānapati, and reached Bhaṅgala (Bengal). He initiated the king of Uḍivisa (Orissa), Dārika,[5] and his minister Ṭeṇgi, into Trantric rites. In the Tibetan Catalogue, the following works are attributed to Lui-pa, besides the *Yoginī-saṁcharyā*, *Śrībhagavadabhisamaya*, *Vajrasattvasādhana*, *Abhisamayavibhaṅga* and *Buddhodaya*.

In the first half of the twelfth century A.D., an enterprising adherent, Dāna-Śrījñāna, styled himself differently, as Bodhisattva, Āchārya Bodhisattva, and Mahāchārya Bodhisattva, in his various books.[6] Sometimes represented as Mālavahi Paṇḍita,[7] he was more popularly known as Dhārī-Śrī-Jñāna, implying his residence at Dhāra, the capital of Malawa under the Paramāras, and it may be that he enjoyed the patronage of the contemporary Paramāra king.

1. PRAS. WC., 1921,
2. The Monuments of Sanchi.
3. CBT.
4. Mystic Tales of Lāmā Tāranātha, 11,
5. There were more than one Dārika, and the Dārika initiated by Lui-Pā was different from Dārika of Dohākosha.
6. CORDIER, P. : Catalogue *Du fonds Tibetain* de la Bibliotheque Nationale, II, pp. 368; 284 and 358.
7. Ibid, III, p. 120, for his works sec II, pp. 212, 213, 216-17, 230, 294, 358, 368, 385; III, pp. 83, 120 etc.

JAINISM

As in Gujarat and Rajasthan, Jainism made considerable progress in Malwa also during this period, as is clear from literary and archaeological evidence. Though the ruling chiefs were followers of Brahmanical religion, they took an active interest in the development of Jainism. They patronized Jaina scholars, and promoted Jainism in their kingdom. Ujjayinī and Dhāra became the Seats of Jain Āchāryas, and they converted a large number of people. Several Jaina temples were built, and images were placed in them. There were also the Jaina holy places of pilgrimage.

Even before the Paramāras, Jainism had begun to develop in this area. The *Paṭṭāvalīs*[1] of the Mūlasaṁgha, tell that the first twenty-six pontificates took place in Bhaddalapura. According to the four *Paṭṭāvalīs*, Bhaddalapura is in Malwa, while the fifth *Paṭṭāvalī* tells us more correctly, that it was in the south. After that, the twenty-seventh Pontiff transferred his seat from Bhaddalapura to Ujjain, as according to all the *Paṭṭāvalīs*. From Ujjain, Māghachandra II, the Fifty-third Pontiff shifted his seat to Baran in Kotah District in about 1083 A.D. Down to the sixty-third or sixty-fourth, the pontificates were held in Bāran. From here, fourteen pontificates were held in Gwalior, down to the seventy-seventh, according to the four *Paṭṭāvalīs*, but the fifth *Paṭṭāvalī* states that ten pontificates were established at Chitor and four at Baghera. From Ujjain, Sarasvatīgachchha and Balātkāragaṇa originated, and they were mentioned along with Mūlasaṁgha.[2] Thus it is clear that Jainism must have prospered by the efforts of these Jaina Saints. Siṁhanandi is also known as the Bhaṭṭāraka of Malwa.[3]

It is known that various Gachchhas originated in the north with the disciples of Uddyotanasūri, who remained attached with this area because he died in about 937 A.D. on a pilgrimage which he had undertaken from Mālavadeśa to Śatruñjaya,

1. PR, 1883-84 ; IA, XX; IA, XXI, p. 58.
2. JSAI, p. 391.
3. Ibid, p. 371.

to worship Ṛishabha.[1] Devasena wrote the *Darśanasāra* in V.S. 990 (933 A.D.) in the Jaina temple of Pārśvanātha at Dhāra.[2]

The Jaina *Āchāryas* Amitagati, Mahāsena, Dhanapāla and Dhaneśvara, were patronized by Vākpati Muñja.[3] Amitagati, who belonged to Māthura *Saṁgha*, was the disciple of Mādhavasena Sūri and grand-disciple of Nemisheṇa[4] Mahāsena[5] was of the Lāḍa Bāgaḍa Saṁgha, and he was the pupil of Guṇākarasena, who was the pupil of Jayasena. Mahāsena was the Guru of Parpaṭa who was the *Mahattama* of Sindhurāja. Māṇikyanandi, the author of *Parīkshāmukha*, probably lived during his reign at Dhāra. His predecessors are Padmanandi, Vishṇunandi, Viśvanandi, Vṛishabhanandi, Rāmanandi and Trailokyanandi. They might have been living in the area of Malwa.[6]

The great Jaina writer Prabhāchandra was honoured by Bhojadeva.[7] Dhanapāla wrote his *Tilakamañjarī* at the request of Bhoja who conferred on the author the title of *Sarasvatī*. Under his influence, Bhoja is said to have inclined towards Jainism.[8] From the Dubkuṇḍa inscription of V.S. 1145 (1088 A.D.), it is known that Śāntisheṇa defeated the learned scholars in discussions in the court of Bhoja.[9] Surāchārya also adorned his court. Devabhadra also perhaps received the favour and patronage of Bhoja.[10]

The famous Jaina *Āchāryas*, Jineśvarasūri and Buddhisāgara of Dhārānagarī, must have lived during Bhoja's time. Another contemporary Jaina poet was Nayanandi, who composed his *Sudarśana-charita* in 1043 A.D. while staying in

1. The Age of Imperial Kanauj, p. 295.
2. Catalogue of Sanskrit and Prakrit Manuscripts in C. P. and Berar, p. 652.
3. PR, No. 4, Intro., p. 3.
4. JSAI, p. 278.
5. GGVS, p. 543.
6. GGVS.
7. Ibid.
8. Tilakamañjarī, Intro. pp. 4-5.
9. JSAI, p. 274.
10. *Bhāratī*, 1955, p. 119

the *Jinavara-vihāra* of Dhāra.[1] Śrīchandra, pupil of Śrīnandi, who, under Bhojadeva of Dhāra, wrote the *Purāṇasāra*, and commentaries on the *Padmacharita* of Ravisheṇa, and the *Mahāpurāṇa* of Pushpadanta.[2] Nemichandra Saidhānika wrote the *Laghudravya Saṁgraha* at Āśramanagara (Keshoraipatan) during the reign of Bhoja, when Śrīpāla was *Māṇḍalika.*[3]

The inscription engraved on the pedestal of a colossal image of a Jaina Tīrthaṅkara in the old Jaina temple at Bhojapura, refers to Chandrārdhamauli (i.e. the God Śiva), and its consecration by the Jaina house-holder Sāgarnandin, through the Jaina monk Nemichandra Sūri, in the reign of Bhojadeva.[4] Bhoja was succeeded by Jayasiṁhadeva, who was also patron of Prabhāchandra.

The Jaina temples at Un ascribed to the eleventh and twelfth centuries, appear to have been built during the reign of the later Paramāra kings of Malwa. This is confirmed by the two inscriptions of Udayāditya, and a Sarpabandha inscription of Naravarman.[5]

Jainism prospered greatly during the reign of Naravarman. Samudravijaya, who studied *Tarkaśāstra* in Malwa, was one of the famous figures of the court of Naravarman.[6] When Jinavallabha Sūri came to Dhāra, Naravarman invited him to listen to his religious discourses. So pleased was he with his extraordinary poetic talent, that he offered him the choice of accepting either three villages or three lac *pāruttha drammas*. Jinavallabha accepted neither. He requested instead, that Naravarman should grant two *pāruttha drammas* daily from the customs house of Chitor, for the maintenance of its two Kharatara temples.[7] Jinavallabha's successor Jinadatta Sūri, sent his pupils to Dhāra to study *Vṛittipañjikādi Lakshaṇaśāstra.*[8]

1. JGPS, No. 3.
2. GGVS.
3. Ibid, p. 550.
4. EI, XXXV.
5. ASI, 1918-19.
6. Bhāratī, 1955, p. 122.
7. KB, p. 13.
8. Ibid.

Jinadatta himself visited Ujjain, Dhāra, Vāgaḍa and Chitor to propagate Jainism.[1]

Many Jaina temples were built, and images were installed, during the reign of Naravarman. The inscription of V.S. 1157 on the pedestal of an image of the Jaina Tīrthaṅkara Pārśvanātha at Bhojapura, records that it was installed by Chillna of the Vemaka family during the reign of Naravarman.[2] The Arthūṇā inscription[3] of V.S. 1166 (1109 A.D.) records the construction of a Jaina temple and the consecration of an image of Vṛishabhanātha at the town of Uthūṇaka, during the reign of Vijayarāja, the Paramāra ruler of Vāgaḍa, by Bhūshaṇa. An inscription of 1134 A.D. in the Jaina temple of Sheragarh,[4] records how a great festival of the Jaina Tīrthaṅkara of Neminātha was celebrated at the new *chaitya* during the reign of Naravarman. Devapāla ordered the *ratnatraya* (images of three Tīrthaṅkaras Śantinātha, Kuntanātha and Arhanātha), and performed their installation ceremony in association with his son, parents, relatives and *goshṭhīs*, at Kośavardhana.

Jainism gradually became a powerful force because of the literary, missionary and reformist activities, of the Jaina scholars and saints in the Paramāra dominions. Dharasena lived in Dhāra, and his disciple was Mahāvīra, a learned *Āchārya*, well-versed in different branches of Jainism, and who received the patronage of king Vindhyavarman.[5] When Āśādhara migrated to Dhāra from Māndalgarh in about 1192 A.D., he was taught by Mahāvīra. Āśādhara[6] was a profound scholar of Jainism. He lived for a long time, to the middle of the thirteenth century A.D., and wrote a number of books on Jainism. He makes mention of five kings during his life-time, Vindhyavarma, Subhaṭavarma, Arjunavarma, Devapāla and Jaitugideva. Probably, his father Salakhana,

1. KB, p. 13.
2. EI, XXXV.
3. Ibid, XXI.
4. Ibid, XXI, p. 80.
5. JSAI, p. 347.
6. Ibid, p. 342.

was *Saṁdhivigrahika* (minister of peace and war) of Arjunavarman, and Āśādhara's son also served the same ruler in some capacity. Āśādhara has been highly praised by the great poet Bilhaṇa, who was also the *Saṁdhivigrahika* of Vindhyavarmadeva, and Bāla Sarasvatī Mahākavi Madana learnt *Kāvyaśāstra* under his guidance. Āśādhara left a number of Jaina disciples, such as Viśālakīrti, Arhadāsa and Devachandra, who advanced the cause of Jainism by their literary contributions.

In 1197 A.D. (V.S. 1264), Jinapati Sūri visited Dhāra and propagated *Vidhimārga* in the temple of Śāntinātha.[1] In the middle of the thirteenth century, Devadhara seems to have been the head of a Jaina monastery at Ujjain.[2] He died in V.S. 1327 (1270 A.D.) in Malwa, and thirteen days later, his appointed successor, Vidyānandasūri, also passed away at Vidyāpurī. After that the brother of the latter, Dharmakīrti Upādhyāya, received the *Sūripada* under the name of Dharmaghosha. He died in V.S. 1357 (1300 A.D.).

The considerable progress and growing popularity of Jainism is reflected in the numerous temple remains at Badoh, Gyāraspur, Bhilsā, Buddhi Chanderi, Narwar, Padhaoli, Bithla, Rakhetra, Suhania, Dubkund, Gandharwa and Badwani. The old holy places of Jainism existing before the fourteenth century A.D. are known from the *vividha-tīrtha* of Jinaprabhasūri, who mentions Kuḍuṁgeśvara of Ujjain, Abhinandanadeva at Maṅgalāpura Supārśva at Daśapura and Mahāvīra of Bhāilasvamī gaḍha.[3] The *Śāsanachatustriṁśatikā* of Madanakīriti also refers to Abhinandana Jina of Mārigalapura in Malwa.[4] Jayānanda, in the '*Pravāsagīti*', mentions Lakshmī, which is situated in the forest near Nimbara.[5] The remains of Jaina images and temples have been also discovered. At a distance of one hundred and seventeen kilometres from Dahod, there is a holy place named Tālanpur. A number of

1. KB.
2. IA, XI, p. 255.
3. *Vividhatīrthakalpa*; 32, 47 and 85.
4. JSAI, p. 347.
5. *Jaina Tīrtha Sarva Saṁgraha*, pp. 313, 320.

images and temples have been found, and one inscription dated V.S. 1022 on an image, bears the name Tungipattan.[1] The Jaina holy place of Bāvanagajā, named after the big image at Badawani, is also well known. The temples of this place were renovated in V.S. 1233 and V.S. 1388.

Some inscriptions engraved on the images throw light upon the Jaina Saṁghas and their Āchāryas, who performed the installation ceremony of images. The Mūlasaṁgha and its Āchārya Ratnakīrti have been mentioned in the inscription of V.S. 1323.[2] Kalyāṇakīrti of the Vāgaḍa Saṁgha is known to have installed images at Vardhanāpura now known as Badnawar, in V.S. 1308.[3] The temple of Śāntinātha existed at this place, as is known from the inscription[4] of V.S. 1229. Khaṇḍelāgachchha, which originated from Khaṇḍelā in Rajasthan, has been mentioned in the inscription of V.S. 1326.[5] The Māthura Saṁgha and its Āchāryas, are known from the inscription of V.S. 1308.[6]

ŚAIVISM

There was a rapid growth of Śaivism during this period. Even before the Paramāras, Śaivism began to prosper, as most of the earlier medieval temples of the seventh to ninth century at Jhalrapatan, Indargarh, Modī, Mahua, Terahi, Badoh, Kagpur, Gyaraspur, etc. were dedicated to Śaiva deities. It began to flourish and become powerful from the tenth to the twelfth century A.D., during the reign of the Paramāras, as is clear from the remains of the temples and images of Śaivism found at Udayapur, Māndhātā, Nemawar, Shergarh, Ujjain, Bhojapura, etc. Besides temples, monastic order evolved, and the Mattamayūra sect became popular at Kadwāha, Terahī, Rāṇod, etc.

The Mauryas and the Rāshṭrakūṭas, who were ruling

1. *Jaina Tīrtha Sarva Saṁgraha*, pp. 313, 320.
2. See Appendix No. 1 for the text.
3. ,, ,, No. 2 ,, ,, ,,
4. ,, ,, No. 3 ,, ,, ,,
5. ,, ,, No. 4 ,, ,, ,,
6. ,, ,, No. 5 ,, ,, ,,

before the Paramāras, encouraged Śaivism. The temple of Śītaleśvara Mahādeva at Jhālarāpāṭan of the seventh century A.D., was probably built during the reign of the Mauryas. In about 689 A.D., Voppaka, brother of Deva, built a Śiva temple at this place, during the reign of the Maurya ruler Durgagaṇa.[1] Voppaka was a great court officer or general of Durgagaṇa. Another inscription[2] of the eighth century A.D., on a pillar in the temple of Śītaleśvara Mahādeva, records the visit of Śaṅkaragaṇa, probably the successor of Durgagaṇa. He might have granted some donations to this temple. Mainchuka, son of Mosuka, came to worship this shrine in the ninth century A.D.[3] In one inscription, there is mention of the name of the sage Iśānamu, who has been compared to Lakulīśa.[4]

The Indargaḍha inscription[5] of 710-11 A.D. (V.S. 767) records the re-erection of a temple of Śiva, called here Svayambhū, and also as Guheśvara by a Pāśupata teacher of the name of Dānarāśi. He was a disciple of an ascetic teacher of the name of Vinītarāśi during the reign of the Rāshṭrakūṭa king Naṇṇappa. Vinītarāśi was well versed in Grammar, and he commanded great respect. Durgāditya, son of Śaṅkara from Gauḍadeśa, was the first to perform worship. This inscription also records the endowments made to Guheśvara, which appears to be the name of the deity enshrined in the temple by Deullika, Takshullika and Bhoginikā, daughters of one Kumāra of the Prāgvāṭa caste. There was also the city council charged with the responsibility of carrying out repairs to the shrine, and the maintenance worship. The old temple of Lakulīśa of the eighth century A.D. at Modi, situated eleven kilometres from Indragadha, proves that this area was a centre of Śaivism.[6]

The inscription[7] of the latter half of the eighth century

1. IA, V, p. 182.
2. ARRMA, 1912-13, p. 2.
3. PRAS. WC, 1905-06, p. 56.
4. JBBRAS, XXII, p. 158.
5. JBRS, 1955, Sept., p. 1, IHQ, XXXI, p. 99.
6. PRAS. WC. 1912-13, p. 56.
7. EI, XXXVII, No. 11.

A.D. engraved on an architrave of the porch in a temple at Mahua, records that the *Paṇḍāla* (*maṇḍapikā*) of Dhūrjaṭi, i.e. Śiva, was constructed by some Vatsarāja, for the increase of the religious merit of his parents, whose family name has not been mentioned.

The God that found the greatest acceptance in the Paramāra dominions was Śiva, who was worshipped under various names, derived either from the achievements ascribed to him or from the locality where his image was set up, or after the name of the builder of the temple. Śiva seems to have been the tutelary deity of the Paramāra kings, whose inscriptions invariably begin with the formula *'Oṁ Namaḥ Śivāya !'* Of the famous twelve *Jyotirliṅgas*, two were situated in the territory of the Paramāras, viz. Mahākāla at Ujjain, and Oṁkāramāndhātā on the banks of the Narmada. Of these two, the most famous was the Mahākāla of Ujjain, who enjoyed wide fame.

The Paramāra ruler Sīyaka, was a follower of Śaivism. According to the *Prāyaśchitta Samuchchaya*, his spiritual teacher was Lambakarṇa of the Mattamayūra sect.[1] He has been described as one who heard the whole of the Śaiva *Siddhānta*, and was like a Śiva on Kailāśa.[2] The *Purāṇas* mention Lambakarṇa as a Bhairava at Avanti.[3] The line of Lambakarṇa continued through Īśvaraśiva, whose disciple, Hṛidaya Śiva, composed the *Prāyaśchitta Samuchchaya*.

Vākpati II had inclinations towards Śaivism. His Ujjayinī plates begin with an obeisance to Girija, i.e. Pārvatī and Śrīkaṇṭha, i.e. Mahādeva.[4] The king is said to have worshipped Bhavānīpati at the time of making his land grant.[5] The inscription also refers to a Śiva lake, which was excavated by Vākpati II, perhaps to commemorate Śiva.[6] The Gaonri plates of this king also start with two verses in praise of Śiva.[7]

1. Notices of Sans. Manuscripts and Select Palm Leaf in Durbar Library, p. 215.
2. Ibid.
3. The Śākta Pīṭhas, p. 7.
4. IA, VI, p. 51.
5. Ibid.
6. Ibid.
7. EI, XXIII, p. 108.

King Sindhurāja was also a devotee of Śiva. From the *Navasāhasāṅkacharita*, it is known that Sindhurāja worshipped at the temple of Hāṭakeśvara after his marriage with the Nāga princess Śaśiprabhā. He is also said to have established a Śiva liṅga, which was presented to him by Śaṅkhapāla in his *Kularājadhānī* Dhāra.[1]

Śaivism spread greatly in Malwa under the patronage of Bhoja, who was not only a follower, but also an exponent of Śaivism. One of his works, *Tattvaprakāśa*, deals with Śaivism. The Udaipur *praśasti* tells that Bhoja made the world (*Jagatī*) worthy of its name by covering it all around with temples dedicated to Kedāreśvara, Rāmeśvara, Somanātha, Suṁdīra (?) Kāla, Anala and Rudra.[2] The Bhojeśvara temple of Bhojapura[3], and the Saṁdhīśvara temple[4] at Chitor, were also built by Bhoja. The Tilakawada copper plate refers to Bhoja's grant to a Śaiva ascetic, Dinakara, for the worship of the god Ghaṇṭeśvara, at the village Ghaṇṭoli.[5]

Śaivism continued to flourish under his successor Jayasiṁha. The Pāṇāherā inscription[6] of 1059 A.D. (V.S. 1116) records the foundation of the temple of Maṇḍaleśvara (Śiva) at Pāṃśulakheṭaka (Pāṇāherā), and various endowments in that connection by the Paramāra ruler Māṇḍalika. Jayasiṁha also seems to have made some grant to meet the expenses of this temple. The Paramāra ruler Dhanika of Arthūṇā, built the temple of Dhaneśvara near Mahākāla of Ujjain.[7]

King Udayāditya's reign may be regarded as a golden age in the history of Śaivism in Malwa. He is said to have fathered his son Jagaddeva, after worshipping Hara i.e. Śiva. He founded the town of Udayapura, where he built the temple of Nīlakaṇṭheśvara between the years 1059 and 1080 A. D.[8] That the famous Śaiva temples of Un, namely Mahā-

1. NC, p. 304.
2. EI, I, pp. 236-37.
3. Imp. Gaz. VII, p. 121; ASI, 1926-27.
4. NPP, III, pp. 1-18.
5. Bhandarkar's List, No. 120.
6. EI, XXI, p. 42.
7. Ibid.
8. ASI, 1923-24.

kāleśvara, Nīlakaṇṭheśvara and Valleśvara, were built during the reign of Udayeśvara, is clear from the inscriptions of the temples. The Shergarh inscription[1] of Udayāditya records that he visited the temple of Somanātha, and granted a village to meet the expenses of worship. The village seems to have been Vilāpadraka, since its inhabitants even now pay dues to this temple.

The example of the ruler was followed by the masses who also constructed Śaiva temples. A temple dedicated to Śiva was erected at Doṅgargāon by a Brāhmaṇa named Śrīnivāsa in the time of Jagaddeva.[2] The Jhālarapāṭan stone inscription of V.S. 1143 (1086 A.D.) records that Janna, the head of a guild of oilmen, built a temple of Śiva and dug a *vāpi* in the reign of Udayāditya.[3]

King Naravarman offered obeisance to Sambhu and Karttikeya, though he might have been a Vaishṇava.[4] A Mahākāleśvara temple inscription[5] records either the construction or the restoration, of a Śiva temple at Ujjain, by the Paramāra king Naravarmadeva. In verse 3 of the Jainad inscription of Jagaddeva, Śiva is worshipped in his *Tripuradahana* form.[6] Śaiva temples were also constructed at Devapālapura, Śakapura and Oṁkāra, during the reign of Jayasiṁha Jayavarman II.[7] The Siddheśvara temple at Nimar was also built during this period.[8] Vijayapāladeva of the Adhi-Droṇāchārya dynasty, probably a feudatory of the Paramāras, in the presence of councillors, gave the village of Agāsiyaka south of Inganapat to the god Gohadeśvara in V.S. 1190 in the presence of the councillors.[9]

During the period of the occupation of Malwa by the Chalukyas, Śaivism continued to develop. Certain donations were

1. EI, XXIII, pp. 131 ff.
2. Ibid, XXVI, p. 184.
3. JASB, 1914, p. 241.
4. EI, II, p. 182.
5. Ibid, XXXI.
6. Ibid, XXII, p. 70.
7. Ibid, XXXII. ; PRAS. WC, 1912-13, p. 56.
8. PRAS. WC.
9. IA, VI.

made to the temple of Udayeśvara from time to time. A person named Vasantapāla, during the reign of the Chālukya king Kumārapāladeva, made donations on the occasion of an eclipse of the moon in V.S. 1220 (1163 A.D.).[1] Another inscription[2] of V.S. 1222 on a pillar, records that Ṭhākura, the illustrious Chāhaḍa (one of the generals of Kumārapāla) for the spiritual benefit of his deceased parents, gave half the village of Saṁghavaṭṭa to the temple at Udayapura on the occasion of *akshayatṛitīyā*. Another inscription[3] of V.S. 1239 of the reign of the Chālukya king Ajayapāladeva in this temple, mentions that Lūṇapāsaka was an officer appointed by the king to govern Udayapura in the Bhaillasvāmin. On the occasion of *Yugādi*, which coincides with the *akshaya-tṛitīyā*, he gave the village of Umarathā to the god Vaidyanātha (Śiva) for the spiritual benefit of the deceased *Rājā*, the illustrious Solaṇṣdeva, a son of Rājaputra of Muhilaūndha family.

The Paramāra Mahākumāras were devotees of Śiva, and gave land-grants to the Brāhmaṇas. The Gyāraspur inscription[4] of Mahākumāra Trailokyavarman, records the construction of an image of the god Chāmuṇḍasvāmideva, and a grant of a village for the god's worship. The king made the grant from his camp at Harshapura. Udayavarman is said to have worshipped Śiva at the time of making his land-grant.[5]

The four main sects among the Śaivas were Śaiva, Pāśupata, Kāladamana and Kāpālika. Not much is known about their distinctive beliefs and practices. Among these sects, the Pāśupata sect became very popular after the seventh century A.D., in the region roughly comprising of Gujarat, Malwa and Rajasthan. The saints of this sect resorted to the use of ashes, barks, and matted hair. They were conversant with Pāśupata Yoga, and worshipped the God Ekaliṅga. The temples and monasteries were under the charge of the saints

1. IA, XVI.
2. Ibid, XVI.
3. Ibid, XV.
4. EI, XXXIII, pp. 93-94.
5. IA, XVI, p. 252.

of this sect. The Indargaḍha inscription[1] of V.S. 767, mentions only two generations of the spiritual teachers of the Pāśupata sect, namely Dānarāśi, a disciple of an ascetic teacher Vinītarāśi, who was well versed in Grammar, and who commanded great respect. Some of these ascetics lived naked. *Bhaṭṭāraka* Nāganaka, who lived in the temple of Somanātha at Shergarh, did not wear clothes.[2]

The Kapālikas professed to have their supernatural powers sharpened by drinking wine and eating a special kind of food and always being embraced by the power (*śakti*) of Kapālin i.e. Bhairava who is said to have been established at Ujjain.[3] The Kapālikas used human skulls as their bowls, and bones as ornaments. They moved around naked.[4] The Kapālika system was extremely tantric. The Tilakawādā inscription[5] of Bhoja refers to an ascetic who had taken a *Mahāvrata*. This copper plate describes *Mahāvrata* as Śaṅkara in Kapālī form.

The Pāśupatas and the Kapālikas did not believe in the caste system, and admitted people freely to their ascetic orders.[6]

During this period, there were a number of Śaiva monasteries, which also acted as educational institutions, where religious scriptures were studied. At the head of each monastery was a Superintendent, who was highly distinguished for his learning. There was a Śaiva monastery of established repute at Ujjain, known as Chaṇḍikāśrama,[7] where the following Achāryas were successively Superintendent—Tāpasa, Vākalarāśi, Jyeshṭajarāśi, Yogeśvararāśi, Maunirāśi, Yogeśvarī, Durvāsārāśi and Kedārarāśi. The succession was spiritual i.e. from the teacher to the disciple. Even women could become heads of monasteries, by virtue of merit, such as Yogeśvarī in the above list.

1. JBRS, 1955, Sept., p. 1; IHQ, XXXI, p. 99.
2. EI, XXIII, p. 134.
3. Śākta Pīṭhas.
4. *Ṣaḍdarśanasamuchchaya* of Haribhadra.
5. Bhandarkar's List, No. 120.
6. Vāmana Purāṇa, VI, 86-89.
7. IA, XI, p. 221.

Śaivism received a great impetus at the hands of Śaṅkarāchārya, who was a great revolutionary leader. By his teachings and writings, he brought about reforms, and a great awakening among the people. He was a Śaiva by birth, and composed several hymns in glorification of Śiva as the God of gods. Though he was born in the south, he went from place to place for the propagation of his views. In the course of his *digvijaya*, Śaṅkara met in argument several groups of pseudo-Śaivas, who were responsible for the prevalence of left-handed practices, and by quelling them freed the followers of Śaivism from their baneful influence. At Ujjain, which was famous for the worship of Mahākāla, he is said to have vanquished a Pāśupatāchārya[1] in argument.

The Mattamayūra sect of Śaivism became dominant in Malwa and in its environs, during this period. The saints of this sect were the *Rājagurus* of the Kalachuri rulers, and the name of this sect became Mattamayūra, after Avantivarman's capital town, where he invited Purandara from Upendrapura. Upendrapura, Mattamayūrapura, Kadambaguha (Kadwāha), Terambī (Terahī), Āmardakatīrtha (Ujjain), Raṇod, Siyadoni, Bilhari, Surwaya, Chanderi and Kuṇḍalapura were the main centres of this sect, where Śaiva temples, monasteries and images have been found.

No personal names of the early Śaiva *Āchāryas* of this sect are known but they are called after the localities of their origin. Both from the Raṇod inscription,[2] and the Gwalior Museum stone inscription of Paṭaṅgaśambhu,[3] it is known that the *Āchāryas* of this sect promoted Śaivism by constructing temples and monasteries which became seats of learning. They excavated tanks and wells. The first three *Āchāryas* were—Kadambaguhādhivāsin (the inhabitant of Kadambaguha), Śaṅkhamaṭhādhipati (the Superintendent of Śaṅkamaṭhika and Terambipāla (the protector of Terambī).

The fourth *Āchārya* mentioned in the Gwalior Museum stone inscription is Rudraśiva, who is the same as the Śaiva

1. The Age of Imperial Kanauj, p. 303.
2. EI, I, p. 351.
3. JMPIP, 1962, p. 3.

Āchārya Āmardakatīrthanātha, mentioned in the Raṇod inscription. Rudraśiva adorned Āmardaka for a long time. Āmardaka-tīrtha is identified with Ujjayinī. This Śaiva Āchārya lived in Malwa. A verse in the *Pañjikā* of Brahmaśambhu, states that Āmardakādhīśa (lord of Āmardaka i.e. the same as Āmardakatīrthanātha), lived in Mālavaka where he had a number of disciples.

After Rudraśiva, Purandara became the head. In the Bilhāri inscription,[1] he has been described as Mattamayūranātha. When the king Avantivarman, who was desirous of being initiated in the doctrines of Śaiva faith, heard of the great holiness of the sage, he resolved to bring him to his own country. Accordingly, he went to Upendrapura, induced the sage to accede to his request, was initiated by him in the Śaiva faith, and duly rewarded him. Upendrapura, where Purandara was performing penance, and from where he was invited to Mattamayūra by king Avantivarman, was probably situated in Malwa; for Upendrapura is mentioned as the head quarters of a *Maṇḍala* in a grant of the Paramāra king Naravarman, dated V.S. 1167 (1110 A.D.).[2] Purandara founded a *maṭha* or monastery at Mattamayūra, the prince's town. He also established another *Maṭha* at Araṇipadra,[3] and not Rāṇipadra, as taken by Kielhorn[4] and others.

Next came Kavachaśiva; his disciple was Sadāśiva, and he was succeeded by Hṛidayeśa, who adorned the penance grove, the Araṇipadra. Hṛidayeśa's disciple was Vyomaśiva. He was renowned for his knowledge of the six *darśanas*. He wrote the *Vyomavatī*, a commentary on the *Padārthasaṁgraha* of Praśastapāda. He is referred to by Udayana in his *Kiraṇāvalī*, and is also cited by later writers like Guṇaratna, Vardhamāna and others.[5] The Bilhārī inscription also mentions Sadāśiva and Hṛidayaśiva.

1. ASC, XIII, p. 8.
2. EI, XX, p. 105.
3. JMPIP, 1962, p. 3.
4. EI, I, p. 351.
5. Keith : Indian Logic and Atomism, p. 32.

Hṛidayaśiva was followed by Paṭaṅgaśambhu, who was well-known for his piety and charity. He was handsome in form, obliging, liberal, serene, and full of spiritual graces. The temple, monastery, tanks and wells, built by Paṭaṅgaśambhu, probably belonged to Raṇod.

VAISHṆAVISM

That Vaishṇavism was prevalent even before the Paramāras, is known from the ancient temples, images and inscriptions, which have been found at Gwalior, Gyaraspur, Tumain, Dhamnar, etc. The ruling chiefs of the Rāshṭrakūṭas, Mauryas and the Pratīhāras, of this period, tried to encourage Vaishṇavism.

A large monolithic pillar inscription[1] of V.S. 917 (861 A.D) at Paṭhārī, records that a temple of Vishṇu known under the different names of Murārī, Kṛishṇa and Hari, was constructed by Parabala, a king of the Rāshṭrakūṭa dynasty.

The excavations[2] carried out at Hindola in Gyaraspur brought to light the remains of a huge temple of the tenth century A.D. The inscription in it records the construction of a temple of Vishṇu. The genealogy of the dynasty is given as Śivagaṇa, Chāmuṇḍarāja and Mahendrapāla. It was by a scion of this dynasty, or one of their dependents, that the temple seems to have been built. The dynasty is not definitely identified, but it may be the Maurya, because Śivagaṇa is known to be the ruler of Maurya dynasty from the Kaṇaswa inscription[3] of 738 A.D. The Udayagiri Amṛita cave inscription[4] of V.S. 1093, records the visit of a pilgrim named Kaṇha to this cave of Vishṇu which was originally made by Chandragupta.

At Dhamnār[5], the temple of Dharmanātha is a Vaishṇava one of the eighth or ninth century A.D. There is a statue of Vishṇu holding in his hands the *gadā*,, *mālā*, *Chakra* and *Śaṅkha*.

1. EI, IX, p. 248.
2. ARADGS, 1932-33.
3. IA, XXX, p. 55.
4. Ibid, VI.
5 ASI, 1905-06.

The Chaturbhuja temple dedicated to the four armed Vishṇu, as known from the inscription[1] at Gwalior, was constructed in 875 A.D. by one Alla, during the reign of Rāmadeva of the Imperial Gurjara Pratīhāra dynasty of Kanauj. The *Telī kā Mandira* of this place, originally dedicated to Vishṇu, may be safely assigned to a period between the eighth and tenth centuries A.D.[2] From an inscription[3] in the entrance porch of the Sāsbahu temple, it is clear that the construction of the temple was started sometime before 1093 A.D., and completed in that year by the Kachchhavāha Rajput prince, Mahipāla of Gwalior. The inscription[4] of V.S. 1082 at Tongra, records the construction of the temple of Hari.

The cult of Vishṇu was widely prevalent in the Paramāra kingdom. Vishṇu was worshipped in different incarnations i.e. Nṛisiṁha, Matsya, Boar, Tortoise, Paraśurāma, Rāma and Kṛishṇa. The Paramāra kings adopted Garuḍa, the vehicle of Vishṇu as their state emblem.

The Paramāra rulers were generally followers of Śaivism but they also promoted Vaishṇavism in various ways. Sīyaka II was a devotee of Vishṇu. In his Harsola Copper plate[5] grant, Sīyaka invokes the blessings of Vishṇu in his *Nṛisiṁha* incarnation. His son and successor, Vākpati II, makes obeisance to 'Rādhā-Virahā-tura-murārī, i.e. Kṛishṇa.[6] From the Udaipura *praśasti*[7], it is known that he restored a temple of Vishṇu in the boar incarnation.

Naravarman was a follower of Vaishṇavism, because he took pride in adopting the title of 'Nirvāṇa-Nārāyaṇa.' H.V. TRIVEDI[8] suggests that Naravarman adopted the title of Nirvāṇa Nārāyaṇa, possibly in view of the fact that he was the protector of his subjects, in the same way as Vishṇu is regarded

1. The Cultural Heritage of Madhya Bharat.
2. Ibid.
3. Ibid.
4. ARADGS, 1928-29.
5. EI, XIX, p. 236.
6. IA, XIV, p. 160.
7. EI, I.
8. See Vol. XVI, Corpus Inscriptionum Indicarum of the Later Dynasties of Central India, Typescript.

as the protector of the world. The Nāgpura praśasti[1] of Naravarman's time, pays homage to the different incarnations of Vishṇu. Verse 2 of the inscription declares that Vishṇu is the sole lord of the fortune of the three worlds, from whose middle stride even the sun and the other luminaries yonder, shine forth, and verse 7 invokes the protection of Vishṇu in the guise of a fish and other creatures.

King Arjunavarman is said to have worshipped Vishṇu at the time of making his land-grant[2] and to have paid homage to *Śesha*, Paraśurāma, Rāma and Yudhishṭhira as well as to the conqueror of Kaṁsa viz. Kṛishṇa[3] There is a highly poetical description of god Vishṇu in his different incarnations in a fragmentary inscription from Māndu, composed by Bilhaṇa, the poet minister of King Vindhyavarman.[4] He speaks of having strung together his flowery verses in a wreath for Vishṇu, and has thus by word of mouth offered his deep and lasting devotion at his feet.[5]

King Subhaṭavarman donated two gardens (*Vāṭikā*) for the use of the temple of Vishṇu.[6] King Jaitugi is called a Young Nārāyaṇa,[7] and King Jayavarman II makes obeisance to Paraśurāma, Rāma and Kaiṭabhajit.[8]

Of the temples of Vishṇu in the Paramāra territories, there is a reference to the existence of the temple of Daityasūdana near Māndhātā.[9] At Nimār, there is an incomplete temple of Vishṇu which belongs to the period.[10] A black sculpture at Arthūṇā belonging to the eleventh or early twelfth century A.D., represents a sleeping female and a child sprawling on

1. EI, II, p. 182, v. 2.
2. JAOS, VII, p. 27.
3. JABS, V, p. 378.
4. ABORI, XI, pp. 49-53.
5. Ibid, pp. 50-52.
6. EI, IX, p. 109.
7. Ibid, p. 121.
8. Ibid, XXXII, pp. 148-49.
9. EI, IX, p. 109.
10. PRAS .WC, 1920-21, p. 98.

a cushion beside the mother.[1] This sculpture represents Yaśodā reposing with her infant Kṛishṇa.

BRAHMĀ :—

The worship of Brahmā was not popular. However there are Brahmā images on the friezes of the door lintels of the temples of Nimar[2] and Girwar.[3]

SŪRYA :—

During this period, there was a great centre of Sun worship at Bhilsa, where the famous temple of Bhāilasvāmī was, the existence of which goes back to 878 A.D. The inscription[4] of V.S. 935 (878 A.D.) found at Bhilsa records the grant of an *Akshayanīvikā* (which means a permanent endowment), to the temple of Bhāilasvāmī by Haṭiāka, a merchant of the Poravāḍa community. The grant was made by the libation of curds and water at various *Tīrthas*, or bathing '*ghāṭas*', of the locality. The endowment consisted of the income derived from three *vithis*, meaning shops.

The second inscription[5] is a *Khaṇḍakāvya* in the praise of the Sun-god, composed by Chittapa, who was a *Mahākavi Chakravartin.* He was a contemporary and a court poet of Bhoja, who conferred the title of '*Mahākavi Chakravartin*' on him. This poet might have been the inhabitant of the area.

Mahākumāra Hariśchandra is said to have made a land-grant in presence of the god Bhāilasvāmin, situated on the banks of Vetravatī i.e. Betwa at Bhilsa.[6]

In the Jainād inscription[7] of Jagaddeva, the first two verses are devoted to the praise of the god Sūrya, and it also refers to a temple of Nimbāditya,[8] constructed by the wife of Lolāraka, the minister of Jagaddeva.

1. IHQ, XXX, p. 343.
2. PRAS. WC, 1920-21, pp. 106 ff.
3. Ibid, 1906-07, p. 27.
4. EI, XXX, p. 213.
5. EI, XXX.
6. Ibid, XXIV, p. 225.
7. Ibid, XXII, pp. 59-60.
8. Ibid.

The Bhilsa inscription[1] dated V.S. 1320, refers to the reign of king Jayasiṁha, and to Bhāilasvāmīdevapura where a pious act was performed by a lady named Sādhumati for the Śreyas of Paṇḍita Ṭhākura Madanasiṁhadeva, chief of the territory called Pubhāni. The queen has been described as '*Kuptakāstha*', meaning resident of a locality called Kupatākā. Sādhumati granted Dooramela which appears to be the name of a locality. The donee has not been mentioned, but it seems to be the temple of Bhāilasvāmin.

Bijamaṇḍala or *Ghaḍliyalan Kā-Makān*,[2] is perhaps a remnant of the Sun temple close to the temple of Udayeśvara, at Udayapura. This is corroborated by an unfinished Sanskrit inscription on the building, which opens with praise of the Sun-God.

At Gyāraspur near Bhilsa, there are ruins of a temple called Vajramaṭha, with a figure of the Sun driven by seven horses.[3] Out of the six temples of tenth or eleventh century at Tongra, thirteen kilometres to the south-west of Shivapuri, two have been dedicated to Sūrya.[4] Sometimes Sun images have been noticed in Brahmanical temples.

ŚAKTI WORSHIP :—

Śakti was visualised as the Prime Power which pervades the whole world. It was through her that every god was powerful. The Śakti of Vishṇu was called Śrī or Lakshmī; Sāvitrī and Sarasvatī were associated with Brahmā, and Śakti of Śiva is known as Durgā or Bhagavatī. The *Purāṇas* describe two aspects of Śakti, the pacific and the terrible. Śiva's consort in her benedictory form was Gaurī or Pārvatī, and as the consort of Rudra, she was Kāli, Chaṇḍikā and Chāmuṇḍā.

The popularity of Devī worship is clear from the fact that she is referred to along with Śiva in various Paramāra

1. EI, XXXV, p. 187.
2. The Cultural Heritage of Madhya Bharat.
3. ASR, X, pp. 73 ff.
4. ARADGS, 1928-29.

inscriptions.[1] From the inscription[2] of V.S. 1331 of the Māndhātā plates of Paramāra Jayasiṁha Jayavarman, it is known that Abhayasiṁha built a temple for the goddess Ambikā at Śakapura. According to the *Skanda Purāṇa*, Devī Vindhyavāsinī (i.e. Durgā) resided at Avanti.[3] Ujjain was the famous Śāktapīṭha, i.e. the centre of the worship of Śakti and Bhairava.

A number of temples and images of Devī are known to have been in existence during this period. An inscription on the image of Pārvatī at Dhāra, records that a person of Lāra class dedicated it in Saṁ. 1138=1081 A.D., probably during the reign of Udayāditya.[4] The antiquity of the temple of Kālikādevī at Mandu, also goes back to this period.[5]

The Bijaimaṇdal mosque[6] was built from the old Hindu temple of Charchikā or Vijayā. The goddess had probably another name, Vijayā, after which the temple was called Vijayamandira. One of the inscriptions begins with a panegyric of a goddess called Charchikā, in which we are told that the Lord of Dhāra became master of the earth through her favour, and that when properly worshipped, she conferred upon her devotee the supernatural power of flying in the sky. It seems to have been constructed by the Paramāra ruler Naravarman. Some inscriptions on the pillars mention the names of the pilgrims who visited this temple.

The Maladevī temple at Gyāraspur[7] appears to have originally been a temple of a goddess, because a figure of a goddess occupies the dedicatory block on the outer door frame. The Gadharmal temple at Badoh[8] was dedicated to *Devī* as there is a fine large sculpture of a goddess with a *baby* found lying in the debris. An image of a goddess has beed carved on the dedicatory block of the door lintel, and

1. EI, II, p. 182.
2. Ibid, XXXII.
3. *Avantikhaṇḍa*, LXVI, 27.
4. ABORI, IV, pp. 99 ff.
5. Ibid.
6. ASI, 1935-36.
7. Ibid.
8. ARADGS, 1923-24.

several images of goddesses have been installed in this temple. There is an old temple of Mohijamātā of the tenth or eleventh century at Terahi.[1] The old temple of the Goddess Ambikā at Suhania,[2] is of the tenth or eleventh century A.D.

A number of stone images of mother goddesses, with unusual names, like Vigrā, Bhayavati, Maghavatī, etc. as stated in inscriptions on their pedestals, datable to the twelfth century A.D. have been discovered at Naresar.[3] There is a ruined temple of Devī at Kāgpur. An inscription[4] of V.S. 1306 records the installation of an image of Śrī Maṅgalā goddess in V.S. 1306.

SOME OTHER GODS AND GODDESSES :—

This period is characterized by the multiplicity of the gods and goddesses, many of them of minor cadre, and yet important enough for those who worshipped them. With the growth of literary activities under the patronage of the Paramāra rulers, the worship of the goddess of learning i.e. Sarasvatī, became very popular. She was also known as Vāgdevī Bhāratī.[5] An inscription in the praise of the goddess of learning was found at Mandu.[6] She is invoked in a number of Paramāra inscriptions. Bhoja was a great devotee of Sarasvatī which was the presiding deity of his famous Bhojaśālā of Dhāra, which is now in the British Museum, in London.

The worship of Gaṇapati became popular, because he helps to attain the desired objectives of life. People worshipped Kārttikeya, Madana, Soma, Agni, Hanumāna, etc. The worship of Navagrahas was prevalent. Bhoja in his *Samarāṅgaṇa-Sūtradhāra*,[7] prescribes rules for the images of Brahmā, Vishṇu, Balabhadra, Śiva, Kārttikeya, Lokapālas, Aśvinas, Śrīdevī, Kauśikī, etc.

1. ARADGS, 1934-35.
2. Archaeology in Gwalior.
3. The Cultural Heritage of Madhya Bharat,
4. ARADGS, 1931-32.
5. EI, II, p. 182.
6. ABORI, VIII, pp. 142-44.
7. S.S. II, Chap. 77.

BRAHMANICAL TĪRTHAS :—

Pilgrimage to holy places was considered a religious act in early times. Of the *tīrthas* during this period, the most famous was Ujjain, on the banks of river Śiprā, with its famous temple of Mahākāla. It was a famous Śākta centre. It had Devasthānas and places of pilgrimage called after the names of Ṛishis.[1]

In 1055 A.D., the Paramāra ruler Jayasiṁha, granted a village to the Brāhmaṇas of the holy Amareśvara.[2] The deity there, Oṁkāreśvara, situated on the island of Māndhātā in the river Narmada, was a famous Jyotirliṅga. The Kalvān inscription of King Yaśovarman refers to Kālakāleśvara *tīrtha*.[3] The Vindhyan hills were considered sacred, being the abode of the goddess Vindhyavāsinī. Another sacred place referred to by the inscriptions is Māhishmatī.[4] A manuscript called *Pramāṇapallava* of Narasiṁha, composed in the thirteenth century, refers, among others, to Dhāreśvāra as *tīrtha*,[5] which has been identified with Dhārā *tīrtha*. The Revākhaṇḍa of Skandapurāṇa refers to Haṭṭakeśvaratīrtha near the river Narmada.[6]

A dip in the river on some auspicious occasion was considered to be sacred. The Betwā, Śiprā and Kapilā, besides Narmadā, were regarded as sacred rivers. Most of the Paramāra grants were made after the king had bathed in one river or the other.

Tīrthayātrās were not merely just the physical action of moving from one sacred place to another, and bathing in a number of ponds, tanks and rivers; strict mental discipline was ordained for the *Tīrthayātrī*. The *Śāstras* laid down that only the *Yatrī* who had full control over his organs, secured the merit of the *Tīrthayātrā*.

1. IA, IV, p. 266.
2. EI, III, p. 49.
3. Ibid, XIX, p. 72.
4. Ibid, IX, p. 109.
5. SEHNI, p. 326.
6. Kalyana, Skandapurāṇāṅka.

CHAPTER—XIII

ART AND ARCHITECTURE

Because of its situation in the heart of the country, Malwa was open to influences on all sides. After the Guptas, the Nāgas and the Mauryas appear to have occupied some region of Malwa, and then the Imperial Pratīhāras ruled over most of Northern India, with Kanauj as their capital. After their decline, the Paramāras became powerful in Malwa, the Chandellas in Jejākabhukti, the Kalachuris in Dāhala, and the Kachchhapaghāṭas established their kingdom in the region of Gwalior. These ruling dynasties were inspired by the rich traditions of Gupta art, and vied with one another in building temples.

The temples built during the rule of these dynasties have some common features, as regards plan, design, and decorative scheme. The common constituents of the plan are the sanctum, vestibule and *maṇḍapa*. In the more developed temples, the *maṇḍapa* has lateral transepts and a porch is added in the front. The entrance is partly enclosed by an ornamental balustrade which is canopied by overhanging eaves. The *sukanasa*-antefix is of the stepped and gabled design. The *śikhara* over the sanctum is of five or seven *rathas*, of which the central one is surmounted by two *amalasarakas*, crowned by a pot-finial. The decorative designs are stencil-like incised scrolls.

POST-GUPTA ARCHITECTURE :—

The earliest dated temple of this period is the Śītaleśvara Mahādeva at Chandrāvatī, near Jhālarāpāṭan, founded in 689 A.D. It has been demolished and crudely rebuilt, but it still retains some original parts, such as the pillars of the porch, basement mouldings, and perhaps some parts of the lower portion of the shrine-walls. The pillars of the temple are minutely carved. These are unique examples of such intricate stone-work. The male and female figures of *dvārapālas* on the doors upholding the structure, are life-like. J. FERGUSSON[1] considers this temple to be one of the most elegant specimens of architecture in India.

Another temple of this age at the same place is dedicated to Kālikādevī.[2] It consists of two rooms—the ante-chamber and the sanctum. The sculptured entrance to the sanctum shows that the temple is an old one, and also that it was originally dedicated to Vishṇu, whose four armed figure holding a shell, occupied the central niche over the doorway. It would seem that it was built as a pair with the temple of Śītaleśvara. They are parallel and the centres of both shrines are upon the same line.

The remains of the ruined Śiva temple at Kansua, dated by an inscription[3] in 738 A.D., indicate that this temple was similar to the Chandrāvatī temple in plan and in design.

The temple of Dharmanātha at Dhamnar,[4] originally dedicated to Vishṇu, belongs to the eighth century A.D. It stands in the middle of a pit in the plateau, a few yards north of the caves. This pit measures one hundred and seventy feet long by sixty-six feet wide, and is about thirty feet deep. This monolithic temple is of the same general style as that of the famous Kailash temple at Ellora. The architecture is of the same heavy character. But it is less decorative on account of the spongy nature of the rock, which forbade any attempt at fine work. What was lacking in the rock was probably supplied by superimposed plaster. This is in the Nagara style, while the Kailash temple is in the Dravidian style.

This temple consists of porch, hall, and sanctum, surmounted by its *śikhara*, and seven small shrines around it acting as its satellites. One peculiarity noticeable in the decoration of the roof of the *maṇḍapa*, is the half *chaitya*-arch ornament, seen on either side of the little central *śikhara* over the porch.

1. HIEA, p. 449.
2. PRAS. WC., 1905-06, p. 56.
3. IA, XIX, p. 55.
4. ASI, 1905-06.

The interior of the temple is comparatively plain, the pillars being both simple and substantial. The ceilings have been decorated to some extent. There are back doors leading out of the *maṇḍapa* in the south-west and north-west corners, into the surrounding courtyard. Five shrines girdle the principal shrine. The two corner shrines at the back, are square, while the other three are oblong. This temple is surrounded by seven minor shrines, five around the main shrine, and one in each of the north-east and south-east corners of the courtyard. These shrines contain image slabs.

Along with Brahmanical temples, Buddhist monuments of this period have also been found. They were erected during the reign of the rulers of the Nāga and Maurya dynasties, who were followers of Buddhism. At this time, Buddhism was in decline.

The temples, monasteries and *stupas* of this period, found at Sanchi, are massive structures. As known from the model of Sanchi,[1] the Buddhist temple of the eighth or ninth century A.D., consists of a square sanctum (*arbhagṛiha*) approached through a small ante-chamber. It stands on a raised terrace, and round three sides of it runs a processional path (*pradakshiṇā*). It has been constructed of massive blocks well dressed on their outer faces.

There are corner pilasters in the sanctum and ante-chamber. The upper half of the former is richly decorated on both faces, with pot and foliage design set over a *kīrtimukha* head, and surmounted by a band of floral ornament with a border of palmlettees above. The capitals are moulded and fluted, and provided with a narrow necking adorned with a conventional garland pattern. The spire (*śikhara*) with which the temple was roofed, was of the usual curvilinear type which distinguished the Brahmanical temple. Its summit was crowned with a massive *āmalaka* and *kal aśa* of the usual form. The majority of the decorative carvings are in the medieval style. The door-jambs, the ceiling of the sanctum, the spire and the niches on the outside wall, all have sculptures.

1. The Monuments of Sanchi.

At Gyaraspur,[1] there are four ruined rectangular platforms, which can be presumed to be *stūpas*, because some sculptures of the Buddha of the ninth or tenth century were found in the neighbourhood. The *stūpas* appear to be of the same period. This is not improbable because vestiges of Buddhism of this era, exist at Sanchi, not far from Gyaraspur.

The *solākhambā*,[2] or the sixteen pillars at Bihar, is actually a part of a Buddhist temple. The shape of the platform indicates the shape of the structure which once stood on it. The space where the pillars are standing, must have been the porch in front of the *maṇḍapa*. Behind the *maṇḍapa* itself, was a *garbhagṛiha*, but the remains of the *maṇḍapa* and the *garbhagṛiha*, with the tall *śikhara*, seem to have been used for building the Muslim tomb and the Mosque close by. The carving on the pillars was elaborate. The sculptures on the shafts of the pillars could not be properly identified. The Buddha has been illustrated seated with an attendant on each side. The figure holds a staff in the left hand, which is also held by an attendant to the left.

At Rajpur,[3] there is a Buddhist *stūpa* locally called 'Kuthila Maḍh'. The *stūpa* is built of severely plain rubble masonry. It consists of a hemispherical dome super-imposed upon a tall, shaped drum, which is indicative that it is of the ninth or tenth century. It possesses no epigraphical record nor sculptural representation.

A large number of rock-cut caves or temples have been discovered at Dhamnar,[4] Kholvi,[5] Binaika,[6] Khejaria Bhopa and Poladungari. From the style of the carvings and from the general features of their plans, the Buddhist caves belong to the eighth or ninth century A.D. These monuments are found in the area which was ruled by the Nāgas at this time, who were followers of Buddhism.

1. ARADGS, 1931-32, p. 3.
2. PRAS. WC., 1921, p. 110.
3. Archaeology in Gwalior, p. 117.
4. ASI, 1905-06, p. 107.
5. ASC, II, p. 187.
6. ASI, 1922-23, p. 124.

Among the rock-cut caves found at Dhamnar, *Bhīma Bazāra* and *Baḍī Kacherī* are the most interesting. The *Bhīma Bazāra* is the largest of the Dhamnar caves, and it is a combination of the *chaitya* and *vihāra*. It consists of a large rectangular court with a *chaitya* in the centre, enclosed on three sides by ranges of small cells, each side having a smaller chapel in the central cell. Few carvings or figure sculptures are found in the cave. But in the central hall to the west, there are two rock-cut images of seated Buddha.

In the group of smaller caves known as *chhoṭā* or small *bazār*, a number of rock-cut images of the Buddha have been badly mutilated. The *Baḍī Kacherī* is, in fact, a large *chaitya* hall, square in plan, with a pillared portico in front enclosed by a stone railing. The other caves are not of interest, either artistically or architecturally.

One peculiarity about the Dhamnar caves, is that the *dāgobas* formed in *chaityas* and *vihāras* are standing out in the floor in the open air, as the principal objects of worship. They are high in comparison with their diameter, and this shows a late date for the caves.

From the study of the various monuments, it seems that the *stūpa* of this period has particular features. Originally, the dome of the *stūpa* was hemispherical, it now became bulbuous and flattened. Then a low drum or cylindrical portion was added below, to give height to the dome. Later, the drum grew in height compared with its diameter, until the whole object became a tall cylinder with a small dome on the top. In later ones, it was a common practice to place an image of Buddha in a niche carved out of the front of the cylinder. Mouldings were added round the drum, which became more elaborate. Square pedestals in later times were placed beneath the cylinder, and ribbing was introduced into the vaults of the *chaitya*.

The excavations at Polāduṅgara[1] (literally the hollow hills) which is situated about twenty kilometres south-east of Garot in Mandsor District, consists of one large cave and a number

1. PRAS. WC., 1913, p. 55; PRAS. WC., 1920-21, pp. 81-82.

of small ones. These are on the three faces of the hill. As the stone of the hill is laterite, of a soft kind, the caves have suffered great damage, ceilings and pillars of several of them having given way. Some of them are filled with debris, and in consequence the interior is not accessible. All these *vihāras* or residences, were meant for monks, except two which are *chaityas* or worship halls.

The large excavation faces south, and consists of a porch and *antarāla*, and a large room with a *chaitya* in its centre. To the west of the *chaitya* hall, there is a monastery, which consists of a courtyard in the centre, with rows of cells on three sides.

The *chaitya* cave has three openings in front, a long narrow door, and two windows of the same pattern on each side. Mortice boles for wooden window frames are still visible. To the west of this *chaitya*, there is another monastery. These both belong to a Hīnayāna sect, because not a single figure of Buddha or Boddhisattva has been discovered.

There are a series of Buddhist caves situated near the village of Khejadia Bhop[1] in the Mandsor District. The hills are thirty-two kilometres south-east of Dhamnar, and sixteen kilometres west of Kholvi. These caves are cut out of a very coarse lateritic rock, and devoid of any refined ornamentation. The excavated facade is a horse-shoe bay, nearly five hundred yards in length. About the middle of the line stands a *stupa* in an open court; the rest of the excavations consist of cells, of which originally there were not less than thirty, though only twenty of them are reasonably well preserved now. The *stūpa* is composed of two cylindrical drums, one above the other, and is nine feet and ten inches in height. The date of the *vihāra* at Bhop appears to be approximately the same as that of the Dhamnar caves, namely the seventh century A.D.

EARLY MEDIEVAL ARCHITECTURE

PRATĪHĀRA ARCHITECTURE :—

The surviving temples of the eighth and ninth centuries

1. ASI, 1916-17.

in Malwa and in the neighbourhood, have certain common features which distinguish them from the preceding and the following temples. As most of this region was under the sway of the Gurjara Pratīhāras at this time, this style may be called Pratīhāra. Since the Pratīhāras ruled over an extensive empire, from Kanauj, the style spread over vast tracts of North India, with certain regional variations.

The Pratīhāra temples of Malwa are characterized by a low socle, a simple and relatively stunted spire, a wall decorated with a single band of sculptured niches crowned by tall pediments. There is an unpretentious plan, generally consisting of only the sanctum and vestibule, which in a few cases, is preceded by a porch.[1]

The group of temples at Naresar,[2] near Gwalior, forming the earliest examples of the Pratīhāra style in this region, show a square sanctum with a curvilinear *tri-ratha* spire of a stunted shape and a constricted vestibule with a simple gabled roof. Their doorway is of the overdoor design, usually with three simple bands decorated with scrolls, pilasters, and serpents whose tails are held in the hand of *Garuḍa* represented centrally on the lintel. The lintel shows short pediments, surmounted by a frieze of chain-and-bell design, which continues round the shrine. The wall is plain except for sculptured niches on the central offsets, depicting deities like Gaṇeśa, Kārttikeya, Lakulīśa, Sūrya and Pārvatī. The site also has an interesting rectangular shrine showing two major offsets on the longer rear side, with the usual sculptured niches and a wagon-vault roof. The group of temples at Batesara and the Mahādeva temple at Amrol, both situated not far from Gwalior, are similar in plan, with the latter being slightly larger and more elaborate in ornamentation.[3] These temples are roughly datable to the eighth century A.D.

At Mahua[4] in District Shivapuri, there are two Śiva temples

1. Temples of North India, p. 21.
2. The Cultural Heritage of Madhya Bharat, p. 79. D. R. Patil considers these temples to be of the eleventh or twelfth century but these are of the eighth century A.D.
3. Temples of North India, p. 22.
4. ARADGS, 1923-24, p. 5.

of about the eighth century A.D. The smaller of these is the more important owing to a contemporary Sanskrit inscription, which is engraved on the front lintel of its portico. The temple consists of a shrine and a porch. The *śikhara* on the shrine has totally disappeared. This temple is comparable in plan and date with the Amrol temple, but shows divergence in details of design and ornamentation. There is some good and vigorous arabesque work and figure sculpture on the exterior faces of the shrine. The bigger Śiva temple is in a better state of preservation. The *śikhara* still exists, though the hall and porch have disappeared.

A small shrine at Terahi,[1] not far from Mahua, is slightly later in date, with an advanced plan showing a *pañcha-ratha* sanctum with a porch in front. The wall shows pilasters of an early Pratīhāra order, on the offsets flanking the central one, and *dikpāla* figures in niches crowned by pediments in the corner offsets. The recesses of the wall are all decorated with tall thin pediments.

The *Teli-Kā-Mandir*[2] at Gwalior is the grandest temple of the Pratīhāra style, and is exceptional in design. It consists of a rectangular sanctum and vestibule, the former surmounted by a lofty wagon-vault superstructure. The podium mouldings are simple and bold, but include a recessed frieze of sculptures, representing gods and goddesses in niches surmounted by richly carved scrolls. The wall at cardinal offsets displays elaborate niche-shrines surmounted by a large pediment or *śikhara* motif. The wall also shows smaller replicas of the same design on the corner buttresses. The *śikhara* portion is composed of two storeys, indicated by lateral *āmalakas*, which are crowned by a wagon-vault roof of two components. On the shorter sides, the central offsct of the *śikhara* shows a progressively widening series of *chaitya*-dormers, surmounted by an enormous sun-window, crowned by an ornate arch. However, on the longer sides, the oblong superstructure is decorated with a monotonous design of a double row of niches. The temple is entered by a grand flight of steps leading to an

1. Templcs of North India, p. 22.
2. Ibid, pp. 22-23.

elaborate doorway of fine bands, in the lower part elegant figures of river-goddesses are carved, flanked by attendants and Śaiva *dvārapālas*. The doorway of the sanctum proper differs only in the introduction of '*śākta dvārapālas*' in the place of the Śaiva ones, indicating the dedication of the temple to Śakti. This temple appears to have been founded by the Pratīhāra ruler, Mihira Bhoja.

Another temple[1] at Gwalior, known as Chaturbhuja, is dedicated to the four armed Vishṇu. This temple, hewn out of living rock, consists of a square shrine, with a spire and a portico. It was constructed in 875 A.D. by one Alla, in the reign of Rāmadeva of the Imperial Gurjara Pratīhāra dynasty.

The modern temple of the goddess Vindhyavāsinī at Tumain, is built on the site of the Vaishṇava temple. M. B. Gadre[2] assigns this temple to the ninth century A.D., though it seems a little earlier. The only portion surviving of the early temple is the shrine, carved doorways and pillars of the verandah. Many sculptures now built up in the walls are vestiges of the old temple. At Kāgpur,[3] there are remains of old temples of the eighth and ninth century A.D.

The above temples are followed by the Godarmal temple at Badoh[4] (District Vidisha). It consists of two distinct parts—the basement which is a remnant of the original magnificent temple of about the ninth century, and the spire, which is composed of a heterogenous collection of pieces, evidently a later repair. The temple stands on a spacious platform, and is surrounded by seven attendant shrines which are all in ruins. There was originally a fine carved *toraṇa* gateway over the stepped entrance to the platform. The plan of the principal temple is rather unusual. It consists of an oblong shrine room, and an entrance porch without *sabhāmaṇḍapa*, and in this respect, this temple is somewhat similar to *Teli-Kā-Mandir*. The interior of the basement has usual mouldings and niches inset with images

1. Archaeology in Gwalior, p. 78.
2. Ibid.
3. ASI, 1922-23, p. 185; 1923-24, p. 133.
4. Ibid.

of gods and goddesses of the Brahmanical pantheon. The attendant shrines sheltered subsidiary gods. The sculptures and carvings of this temple are usually fine, and the entrance porch is particularly imposing.

There are also some other remains of archaeological interest at Badoh. The *Solākhambā*, as its name implies, is an open hall with a flat roof supported on sixteen pillars arranged in four rows on a high plinth. On architectural grounds, it may be assigned to the eighth or ninth century A.D. It was probably a pleasure resort.

The Daśāvatāra temple is a group of shrines dedicated to one or another of ten incarnations of Vishṇu. There is also a temple in the shape of a hall which once sheltered the image of all the ten incarnations. These shrines range in date from the eighth to the tenth century A.D.

The name of the temple Sat Madhi implies the existence of seven shrines in this group of which only six are standing. The ruins indicate the existence of many more. The sculptures in the ruins indicate that some of the shrines were Vaishṇavite and others Śaivite. At least one shrine was sacred to Gaṇeśa.

The Jaina temple of Badoh forms a group of some twenty-five different shrines, placed so as to enclose aṇ oblong courtyard. The individual shrines are not all contemporary with each other, but appear to have been constructed at different times between the ninth and twelfth centuries. Some of these shrines are flat roofed, others have domes, while the rest are crowned with *śikhara*.

At Gyāraspur[1] (District Vidisha), the Maladevī temple, which is partly rock-cut and partly structural, is a mature example of Pratīhāra style. From the decorative motifs and architectural features, this temple appears to be of the ninth century A.D. It consists of a porch, hall, vestibule and sanctum with an ambulatory. Each of its shorter sides shows a pair of non-functional balconied windows, while the longer sides show three such windows, two projecting from the *maṇḍapa*, and one from the sanctum proper. The sanctum

1. ARADGS, 1932-33.

is *tri-ratha* on plan with a *pañcha-ratha śikhara* of nine turrets. The buttress of the *śikhara* extends to the neck which is surmounted by a pair of *āmalakas* and a pot-finial. The roofs of the porch and the hall are pyramidical, composed of horizontal tiers. The hall doorway shows a figure of Chakreś-varī as the tutelary image, while the sanctum door-frame is carved with a row of standing Jinas on the lintel.

There are also other monuments at Gyaraspur which are remarkable from an architectural point of view. The *Aṭhakhamba*, or eight pillars, are the remains of a once magnificent temple. Four of these belong to the *sabhāmaṇḍapa* and two to the porch. The remaining two are pilasters and pertain to the *antarāla*, or shrine vestibule. Of the shrine, nothing except the door now remains. The pillars are exquisitely carved. On the lintel of the door the figures of Śiva, Brahmā, Vishṇu, Gaṇapati and Saptamātrīs are carved. From one of the pilgrim's inscription, it is clear that the construction of the temple cannot be later than 982 A.D.

The Bājrā Maṭha is an example of rare class of temple, containing three shrines in a row. It is now occupied by Jaina idols, but it was originally a Brahmanical temple, in which three shrines dedicated to the gods of the Hindu Trinity are combined. The central shrine is sacred to Brahmā, the southern to Vishṇu, and the northern to Śiva. The carv-uing of the doorway is exceptionally fine and vigorous. The *śikhara* of the temple is equally unusual in its plan and design. The central shrine is crowned with a spire of the curvilinear type, and the side ones with roofs formed by low semi-pyramids rising in tiers and meeting the spire. On the top of the hill immediately to the west of the Mānasarovara, are the remains of temples which seem to have belonged to the eighth or ninth century A.D.

Hiṇḍolā is one of the *toraṇas* or entrance-arches connected with a large temple of the tenth century A.D., dedicated either to Vishṇu or to Trimūrti, the remains of which have been discovered in excavations. It consists of two pillars carrying two horizontal beams supported on brackets, and having two small ornamental arches placed between the two beams. At a distance of forty feet from the Hiṇḍolā gateway is a group of four other pillars, forming a square on plan, and carrying a set of four beams also supported on brackets. It was a huge temple one hundred and fifty feet in length, east to west, and some eighty-five feet in breadth, north to south. It probably consisted of a shrine room, a hall with two projecting balconies on either side, and a porch with one principal entrance and two side entrances, each having a *toraṇa* gateway in front of it. It had a *śikhara* or spire, crowned wilh *āmalaka*, and decorated with medallions and miniature repetitions of the spire. The temple faced east, and the surviving gateway was related to the southern entrance. The four pillars are evidently the central pillars of the hall, and the plinth of the temple was about eight feet high above the pavements.

After the Pratīhāras, the Kachchhapaghāṭas and the Paramāras ruled side by side over their kingdoms. Their buildings have many features in common, despite some regional variations. The Kachchhapaghāṭ temples[1] are distinguished by a low plinth, a double register of sculptures on the wall, low pillars decorated with a pot-and-foliage motif, a doorway of five bands, of which one is carved with a stylized design of serpents and another with a pilaster design with spiral decorative bands, and a frieze of square rafter ends, embellished with monkey-heads below the *śikhara*, which is normally of a medium height.

The earlier phase of the style is represented by the temples at Surwaya[2] (District Shivapuri). Among them, the Brahmanical monastery built in the tenth century A.D. is famous. It is built around a rectangular courtyard surrounded by pillared corridors on three sides, and a spacious hall on the fourth. This hall may have served as dormitory for the monks. Some carvings consisting of vases and palmettes, gods and goddesses are of striking interest.

The middle phase is noticeable for the Kakamadha temple of Suhania,[3] built by Kākanvati, queen of the Kachchhavāha

1. Temples of North India, p. 54.
2. ASI, 1934-35, p. 25.
3. Ibid, 1925-26, p. 122; Archaeology in Gwalior, p. 122.

king, Kīrtirāja, in 1000 A.D. Standing on a lofty platform and surrounded by subsidiary shrines, this temple is notable for its size and sculptural wealth, and comprises a sanctum with an ambulatory, roofed by a tall *śikhara*, a grand hypostyle *maṇḍapa*, and a porch approached by a flight of steps.

The principal temple of Padhavali,[1] ten kilometres north west of Kutwal (Kantipuri) consists of a shrine, a hall and an entrance porch. It is a tenth century Śaiva temple, and the most interesting feature is that the faces of the architraves and the friezes in the interior, are adorned with panels of sculptures. The subjects depicted include various gods and goddesses of thc Brahmanical pantheon, and mythological scenes from the *Rāmāyaṇa* and the *Bhāgavata*, Śiva and his attendants, Sūrya, and the three principal gods of the Hindu Trinity.

Kadwah[2] possesses the remains of a Śaiva monastery, and of no less than fourteen Brahmanical temples, all belonging to the tenth and eleventh centuries. Most of these temples are dedicated to Śiva. One of the temples is very well preserved, and represents some of the best characteristics of medieval temple architecture. It is built on a raised platform, and consists of a sanctum or shrine proper, with an ornate porch in front surmounted by a well carved pyramidal roof. It has no pillared hall or *sabhāmaṇḍapa*, which is usually found in the temples of the period.

The twin Vaishṇava temples known as the Sās-bahu, at Gwalior,[3] mark the climax of this style. Of these two, the larger one was completed by the Kachchhavāha ruler Mahipāla, in 1093 A.D. With a simple plan comprising of sanctum, vestibule and a closed hall with three entrance porches, the temple has grand dimensions and an impressive design showing a two-storied elevation for the vestibule and the entrance porch, and a three-storied elevation for the hall proper, which has a lofty bell roof. The *śikhara* over the sanctum, which must have been loftier, is lost. Internally, the closed hall is a spacious structure of twelve sides with a circular

1. ASI, 1925-26, p. 87.
2. Archaeology in Gwalior, p. 94.
3. Temples of North India, p. 55.

ceiling supported on four massive pillars and twelve plasters. The temple is noted for extravagance of ornamentation, both plastic and decorative, which covers its exterior and every inch of its interior. The smaller temple is a modest replica of the larger one, with the difference that it has a ceiling roof resting on octagonally planned pillars, and has totally lost the sanctum but for its highly ornate door-frame.

PARAMĀRA ARCHITECTURE :—

The temples built during the reign of the Paramāras in Malwa are known as the *Bhūmija* style of architecture. As the Paramāras had intimate contact with Khandesh and Konkan, they are affiliated more to this style than the Northern one. This style was not confined to Malwa, but spread to Rajasthan, Gujarat, Maharashtra and Deccan.

The most distinctive feature of the Paramāra temples[1] is its *śikhara* of *Bhūmija* class, which shows four spines decorated with the usual mesh of *chaitya*-dormers on the central *rathas* (offsets), but the quadrants between these spines are filled with miniature shrine-models of diminishing heights, arranged in three to five horizontal and five to seven vertical rows. Another characteristic of these temples is the prominent *sukanasa*-antefix exhibiting a sculptured medallion within a conspicuous *chaitya*-dormer at the base of the spine on each side. The *maṇḍapa* usually shows a nascent form of bell-roof. The pillars are squat and highly ornamented and show a few circular mouldings. The wall faces of the temples are richly ornamented. Though most of the temples are *pañch-rath* in plan and in elevation, many of them have a star-shaped layout and are built by rotating a square round a central axis. The temples do not, as a rule, possess an ambulatory, and consist of a sanctum, a vestibule and a *maṇḍapa* with three cardinal porches. Triple-shrined temples are not unknown, and always possess a common *maṇḍapa* and a porch.

This style originated in Malwa in the tenth century, as is attested by the nucleus of the Amareshwara temple[2] at Omkar Mandhata. This place became a prolific centre for Bhūmija

1. Temples of North India, p. 15.
2. ASI, 1935-36, p. 80.

temples. The later Amareshwara temple built of this plan and design is dated 1063 A.D.

The Paramāra ruler Bhoja was a great patron of art, and he is said to have established a college known as Bhojanaśālā, now converted into a mosque at Dhar. This consists of a large open court with a porch in front, colonnades on all sides, and a large prayer hall at the back in the west. The carved pillar used over the building, and the delicately carved ceilings of the prayer hall, seem to have belonged to the original Bhojanaśālā. There are numerous slabs of black slate stone carved with the writings of the *Pārijātamañjarī* and the *Kumārastotra*. Similarly, the Lata Maszid of this place is planned with carved pillars and brackets of older temples. The colonnades and the beautifully carved facing of the ceiling was utilised for the interior of the dome of the Prayer hall.[1]

A magnificent temple of Śiva was built in the tenth century during the reign of Bhoja at Bhojapur.[2] This temple, situated on a low rocky hill to the north-east of the great Bhojapura Lake, is square in plan. Four massive and monolithic columns surmounted by flowered capitals, support a circular ceiling, constructed of corbelled rings, the lowermost of which is decorated with figures of musicians and demi-gods. Beneath this copy is a *liṅga* about seven and a half feet in height, resting on a *yonī* some twenty-one feet square. The entrance to the temple is flanked by male and female figures carved on either side. The figures on the extreme right and left are those of Kubera, the god of wealth. Alongside the entrance steps are pillared niches containing images of Śiva, and other niches adorn the plinth of the platform. The three facades, to the north, east and south of the temple, are relieved by pillared balconies supported on brackets. The temple is remarkable for its massive strength. North-east of the temple are several ponderous, but incomplete sculptures, such as capitals, pillars, plinth stones, etc.

At Bhojapur,[3] there are also the ruins of a Jaina temple

1. The Cultural Heritage of Madhya Bharat, p. 115.
2. ASI, 1926-27, p. 48.
3. Ibid, 1922-23. p. 49.

containing a sanctum and an *antarāla*, attributable to the reign of Bhoja, though its outer facades appear to have been rebuilt at a later date. Owing to the collapse of the *śikhara* and roof of the sanctum, it is now open to the sky. Inside, is a colossal standing image of Ādinātha, about twenty feet in height, flanked on either side by images of Pārśvanātha accompanied by figures of Indra.

The ruins of Modī,[1] situated twelve kilometres to the west of Bhanpur, consist of a number of temples, only one of which is now standing. This temple, dedicated to Śiva, stands on the brink of a large stepped tank. Only the *garbhagṛiha* of the temple is intact. The lintel of the door leading to the interior of the sanctum bears the figure of Śiva as Lakulīśa, and some of the large stones of the basement bear inscriptions of the twelfth century. Close to this shrine are the remains of three other temples. The one nearest to the temple of Śiva must have been one of the finest medieval shrines of Malwa. The portion that remains is a part of the *maṇḍapa* and consists of four magnificently carved pillars supporting square brackets on which lintels are placed. A short pillar stands on the top of each of the pillars, which support square bracket capitals. Close to the ruins of this *maṇḍapa*, there are two large rectangular platforms which are evidently plinths of temples.

Kohla,[2] which is at a distance of eight kilometres. from Bhanpur, possesses antiquarian remains of considerable importance. The largest and most pretentious temple is that of Varāha, which stands at the end of the village. The temple consists of a *maṇḍapa* and a *garbhagṛiha*, of which only the former is standing. The *maṇḍapa*, which is the only part of the ancient temple left intact, stands on twelve pillars. The *maṇḍapa* is cruciform in plan. Twelve pillars arranged in the form of a hollow square support the dome of the *maṇḍapa*, and the lower part of the shaft of each pillar is sixteen sided. Over this there is a projecting octagonal band containing a row of fine Kirttimukhas. The temple of Lakshmī Nārāyaṇa

1. PRAS. WC, 1918, pp. 55-56; 1920, p. 94.
2. Ibid, p. 83.

of this place is one of the best preserved ancient monuments of Malwa. It stands on a stone platform. It faces the south and consists of a *maṇḍapa* and a sanctum. The porch has three small projections. The *maṇḍapa* is square in form, and its dome is supported by eight pillars. The old temple of Mahādeva at Vithalpur, near Bhanpura, consists of a small porch, two old pillars and door frame, which are exquisitely carved. It is now in a dilapidated condition.

The temple of Chaturbhujanātha of Sandhāra,[1] situated near Bhanpura, is important from an architectural point of view. The interiors of the *maṇḍapa* and *garbhagṛiha* are intact, but a large portion of the original structure seems to have perished. The only door of the *maṇḍapa* is richly ornamented. The *maṇḍapa* rests on twelve pillars which bear six domes on them. The domes are minutely carved. The presence of an image of Lakulīśa in the centre of the lintel of the door frame, probably indicates that this temple was originally dedicated to Śiva. The ancient Jaina temple of this place is called '*Tambolī Kā Mandir*', or 'the temple of the betel leaf-seller'. The interior, with its exquisitely carved pillars, is intact. The temple consists of a large *maṇḍapa*, and a small cell behind it is the *garbhagṛiha*. The roof of the *maṇḍapa* is supported by four stone pillars which bear capitals, cruciform in shape, with figures of dwarfs (gaṇas) sprawling on each arm. Some of the lintels bear arabesque patterns on them. The interior of the shrine is neat and plain. The stone door-frame of the entrance to the sanctum is plain, but the lintel has a small niche in centre containing a seated jina figurine. The roof of the empty sanctum is traberate. In the roof of the sanctum, there are three small carved panels, the central one being the largest. The large panel bears the figure of a male in relief, seated with a female on each thigh.

The temple of Śeshaśāyin at Kethuli[2], consists of a small *maṇḍapa* and *garbhagṛiha*. The *maṇḍapa* rests on sixteen pillars and the *śikhara* is intact. There are three niches on the three sides of *garbhagṛiha*, which once contained images. This temple,

1. PRAS. WC., 1920, pp. 88-91.
2. Ibid, p. 92,

though very small in size, is perhaps one of the best specimens of medieval carving in Malwa. Its *maṇḍapa* and *garbhagṛiha* bear a dado which is extremely beautiful and well proportioned. The Vishṇu temple of Kukdeśvara is of the twelfth century. The porch, the *maṇḍapa*, and the *garbhagṛiha* of the original temple, are still intact. The Jaina temple of this place consists of a porch, a verandah, closed *maṇḍapa*, a small *antarāla* and a *garbhagṛiha*. The lintel of this temple is a magnificent piece of carving and bears three figures in high relief.

There are two old temples at Jharda,[1] near Mahidpur, of which one is dedicated to Hanumāna. This temple rests on four finely carved pillars, the carving of which appears to belong to the tenth century A.D. There are several fragments of old sculptures lying scattered in front of the temple of Hanumāna. The second temple is dedicated to the worship of Śiva. The ancient *maṇḍapa* of the building consists of four rows of finely carved stone pillars, with four pillars in each row. Six kilometres from Jharda is Makla, where ancient remains are more numerous. A large number of pillars, lintels, capitals and carved roofing slabs of ancient temples have been found. The *maṇḍapa* and *garbhagṛiha* of the Gaṇeśa temple are intact, and this is a good example of Hindu temple architecture of the eleventh and twelfth centuries in Malwa.

From the architectural point of view, the Chaubīsa Khambā of Ujjain is a part of an eleventh century building. It was possibly one of the gates in the outer compound wall of the early medieval temple of Mahākāla, a portion of which still exists a few hundred feet to the west of the gate, and is traditionally known as kot, or fortification wall. The *Binā Nīmakī Maszid* of this place is a mosque situated in the Anantpetmohallā not far from the river. It has been constructed on the foundations, and with the material of an old Hindu or Jaina temple. A portion of a porch of the original temple still exists almost intact, and it was utilised as the entrance porch to the mosque.

1. PRAS. WC., 1920, p. 100.

There are important archaeological remains of the Paramāra period found at some other sites. At Khor, on Ajmer Khandwa line near Neemuch, there stands a *Nau-toraṇa* temple. It is so called because there are the remains of ten arches. The sanctum and pillared hall of this temple are also intact. A hill called Bandar pekhada of Bijawada,[1] eighty kilometres east of Indore, contains the ruins of a very large Jaina temple of the tenth or eleventh century. The ruins now consist of architectural fragments, dressed and undressed slabs of stone, and images of the Tīrthaṅkaras. On the door road from Bolia to Kothadi, there is a small village, Pura Gulana,[2] which possesses an ancient Jaina temple of the eleventh or twelfth century A.D. Of this temple, one door-jamb and some images are left.

The temple of Nīlakaṇṭhesvara or Udayeshvara, after its royal author Udayāditya, at Udayapura[3] is the grandest specimen of Paramāra architecture and was started in 1059 and completed in 1080 A.D. It is stellate in plan and consists of a *saptaratha* sanctum, and a hall with three porches. The temple is surrounded by seven subsidiary shrines, and stands on an extensive platform terrace which was originally approached through a stepped entrance flanked by large figures of Śaivā *dvārapālas* (door keepers). Great ingenuity has been employed in designing the *śikhara* of the sanctum, which is decorated with seven vertical, and five horizontal, rows of miniature *śikharas* in each quadrant, providing a picturesque for setting the play of light and shade. The sculptured medallions, inset in bold *chaitya*-dormers, on each side of the base of the central *ratha* (offset) of the *śikhara*, form a conspicuous feature of this monument, which vibrates with sculpture and ornaments of exquisite elegance and vivacity. The voluptuous figures of *apsarās* represented on the balustrade decorating the three entrance porches, are notable or their grace and expressiveness. This monument is remarkable for its rich ornamentation, the elegance of its accentuated

1. PRAS. WC., 1921, p. 106.
2. Ibid, 1920, p. 81.
3. Ibid, 1914, p, 64.

śikhara design, and for the organic unity and proportion of its constituent elements.

Un[1] has group of about a dozen Bhūmija temples but none of them are in a good state of preservation. Except two Jain temples, all the others appear to be Śaiva. Architecturally, they all belong to a cognate style, and essentially have the same plan and *śikhara* design as the Udayeśvara temple, but they are simpler. They seem to have been built in the eleventh and twelfth century A.D., during the reign of the later Paramāra rulers.

Among the Brahmanical temples, the most important is Chaubara Derā, which is the largest and most elaborately carved. It consists of a *maṇḍapa* with a large porch in front. The porch is exquisitely carved, and the style resembles that of the Sāsbahu temple on the Gwalior fort. In the *maṇḍapa*, four carved round pillars support four large stone lintels, and these in their turn support the dome, which is carved elaborately in the style of the domes of the temple of Vastupāla and Tejapāla on Mt. Abu. There are carvings and figure sculptures on the two door-frames, one giving entrance to the hall and other to the shrine proper. From the examination of the figures, it seems that the temple was dedicated to Śiva.

To the north of this is a large Śiva temple called Mahākāleśvara, which is important for its graceful *śikhara*, and its size. The style of its *śikhara*, now much shattered, has much in common with the Paramāra temples, as it is adorned with clusters of miniature *śikhara* on all sides. The *maṇḍapa* of this temple was probably the largest in Un, of which the only remains are three huge bases of pillars which supported the dome.

To the north-west is the Valleśvara temple, rebuilt with a round dome of Mohammedan type in place of a *śikhara*. The jambs and lintels of the door leading to the shrine and the lower parts of its walls are old. The name Valleśvara suggests that it was built by Rājā Vallāla.

1. PRAS. WC., 1919, p. 62; ASI, 1918-19, p. 17.

The temple of Nīlakaṇṭheśvara standing in the middle of the village, is the best among these Brahmanical temples. It has a very graceful *śikhara* of the Paramāra style. The door-frames bear beautiful figure sculptures. The carvings of the *śikhara*, and the wall of *garbhagṛiha*, are equal to those of the Khajurāho temples. Close to the temple of Nīlakāṇṭheśvara is a small underground temple of Śiva, called Gupteśvara. The shrine, of which only a small underground chamber remains, must have originally been below ground level. Near it is another temple of Śiva called Mahākāleśvara. The *maṇḍapa* in front has disappeared, but the larger portion of the *śikhara* is still standing.

Of the Jaina temples that stand at the northern extremity of Un, the most notable is the temple locally called Chaubara Derā II. Its plan is similar to that of the Chaubara Derā No. I, except that here there are no side porches. Its *śikhara* was partly dismantled. It consists of a porch in front, a spacious *maṇḍapa*, a small *antarāla* and *garbhagṛiha*. The *maṇḍapa* is spacious, having eight beautifully carved pillars to support the roof. The carvings are of high order, and it is a good specimen of Paramāra architecture.

At a short distance from this Jaina temple, there is another Jaina temple called Goleśvara, because cowherds (gvālas) take shelter in it during inclement weather. With the exception of a portion of the *āmalaka* and a crest jewel (*chuḍāmaṇi*), the temple is almost perfect. The plan is similar to that of Jaina Chaubara Derā. The porch was most probably omitted. The *maṇḍapa* is square in shape and has four doors, three of which lead outside, and the remaining one leads to the interior. The level of the door of the *garbhagṛiha* is about ten feet below that of *maṇḍapa*.

The Mahādeva temple at Jamli (District Dhar) is the only Bhūmija temple in Malwa which is not stellate in plan. It is also the smallest and plainest shrine of a *pañcha-ratha* plan and five-storeyed elevation, and appears to be later than the Udayeśvara temple by a decade or so.

Nemawar[1] contains one unfinished, and one finished

1. PRAS. WC., 1921, p. 98.

temple, both of them exquisitely carved. The finished temple of Siddheśvara is one of the most important ancient monuments of India. The temple stands on the bank of the river and has been built on a massive platform of stone.

In plan, it consists of a shrine surmounted by a lofty *śikhara* or spire, with a pillared-hall in front approached by three porches. The pyramidal roofs of the hall and porches show signs of later repairs or additions to their pinnacles, as they are covered with an unseemly coat of white lime plaster. The interior of the main shrine below the *śikhara* is adorned with numerous decorative carvings and figure sculptures, the latter representing Śivagaṇas, Bhairava, Śaiva, Brahmāṇī, Mahishamardinī, etc.

It appears that the main shrine with its *śikhara* was raised first, and the pillared-hall and porches were added to it a century or so later. This is clear from the divergent styles of the carving and ornamentations of the two. The roof of the *maṇḍapa* or hall, is supported on massive pillars covered all over with decorative patterns and figure sculptures. Its ceiling is much more elaborately and profusely carved, with beautiful lotus designs and rows of brackets shaped to represent female figures in different poses. The interiors of the hall and porches have been richly carved with figure sculptures and other carvings, such as Brahmā, Brahmāṇī, Gaṇeśa and Indrāṇī.

The Siddheśvara temple has a loftier and large *śikhara* than that of the Udayeśvara, with as many as nine vertical rows of turrets, but it lacks the grace and excellence of proportion of the latter. This temple represents a degenerate phase of the style, as is attested by the conventionalism of the plastic and decorative ornamentation and the repetition on the wall faces, of images of Śiva with identical attributes. As such, it is assignable to the twelfth century A.D.

Bilpank, situated at a distance of about twenty-one kilometres from Ratlam on Ratlam Mahu Road, is famous for its temple. Architecturally, it is a *Pañchāyatana* temple. The *śikhara* of this temple has disappeared, but the *garbhagṛiha* and the *sabhāmaṇḍapa* are intact. The *garbhagṛiha* is small and its doorjambs are highly decorated with Śaiva figures. In the *maṇḍapa* on both the right and left sides, there are balconies. This peculiarity is not generally found in Paramāra temples. In place of porches, there are balconies. Because of the balconies, the *sabhāmaṇḍapa* has been enclosed. The doorway of the *maṇḍapa* is narrow. It seems that there must be a porch in front of it. An inscription of Jayasiṁha Siddharāja, discovered in the neighbourhood, was probably from this temple. The other subsidiary temples in the area are intact, but consist only of *garbhagṛiha*. There are standing and sitting images on the outer face of the walls.

The temple of Badnawar belongs to the thirteenth century and hence is late Paramāra. From the remains, it seems that it was a huge temple, but now only the *garbhagṛiha* is left.

The Śiva temple at Ramgarh[1] near Kota, is about half a century later in time than the Udayeśvara temple, and has a similar plan and *śikhara* design. Its socle, however, is more ornate, showing bands of elephants, horses, lions and humans, while its sculptures reveal an unmistakable impress of Rajasthani plastic style. Only one of its four subsidiary shrines has survived, and shows a peculiar *śikhara*-design offering a new interpretation of the Bhūmija mode. However, this temple, must once have been a structure of considerable architectural merit.

The so-called Sun temple at Jhālrāpāṭan[1] (District Jhalawar) is orthogonal and *sapta-ratha* in plan, with a seven-storeyed elevation, but has a complicated *śikhara* design, combining a pair of half-leaning spires on each side over the central *ratha* (offset), with the characteristic turrets of the style. The temple introduces elaborate *toraṇas* at the entrance to the porch, and two bands of sculptures on the wall.

At Jhālarāpāṭan, there are some other temples[2] of this period. The temple dedicated to the *Varāha Avatāra*, or the boar incarnation of Vishṇu, is an open temple with four

1 Temples of North India, p. 69.
2. PRAS. WC., 1905-06, p. 56.

pillars supporting a canopy, under which the statue of a boar is enshrined. On the pedestal, there is an inscription in characters of the ninth or tenth century. The great Vaishṇava temple, the Sāta Sahelī, has been rebuilt at some late period. The shrine, and its *śikhara* and the *maṇḍapa*, up to beams above the pillars, are old. The Jaina temple of Śāntinātha is a rebuilding of an older temple. It was built by Sāha Pīpā in 1046 A.D., and its installation ceremony was performed by Bhavadevasūri.[1] The shrine and *śikhara* are old, but the *maṇḍapa* is new.

The Mahādeva temple, locally known as the Mālavī temple, near Alirajpur[2] (District Jhabua), is one of the latest examples, and belongs to the fifteenth century A.D.

This Bhūmija style of architecture of Malwa influenced some neighbouring regions where such temples[3] have been found. The earliest Bhūmija temple in Rajasthan is the Mahāvīra temple at Sewari (District Pali). Pañcha-ratha in plan and six-storeyed in elevation, the temple has a brick-built superstructure and is assignable to 1010-20 A.D. The next temple of this style is the Mahānāleśvara temple at Menāl (District Chitor), which appears to be contemporary with the Udayeśvara temple, and is likewise ornate, but only five-storeyed in elevation. The Undeśvara temple at Bijaulia is of this style, but it is nine storeyed in elevation. The Sun temple at Rāṇakpur (District Pali) and the Śiva temple known as the Adbhutnāth at Chitor, are late regional versions of the Bhūmija style, of the fifteenth century.

Only two Bhūmija temples are known in Gujarat. One of them is the Śiva temple at Limkheda (District Panchmahal), which is the earliest known triple-shrined Bhūmija temple, dating from the middle of the eleventh century. The other is the Ghaṭeśvara temple at Sarnel (District Kaira), assignable to the late twelfth century. Its sanctum is of a peculiar plan with eight offsets, and an exotic śikhara-design

1. *Anekānta*, XIII, p. 125.
2. Temples of North India, p. 68.
3. Ibid, pp. 68-69.

in the Bhūmija style. At Arang (District Raipur) in Mahakosala area, the Jaina temple known as Bhand Dewal, can be assigned to the late eleventh century. This temple has an ornate and lofty socle, and two bands of sculptures on the wall. The temple is five-storeyed and is stellate in plan, with six offsets, which is exceptional.

SECULAR ARCHITECTURE :—

This period was one of great prosperity, and therefore it was but natural that a large number of towns were founded and lakes and tanks excavated. Vākpati II (Muñja) is credited with the foundation of Muñjapura, and the excavation of Muñja Sāgara. Bhoja is said to have adorned Dhāra with many splendid buildings, and it became the premier city of India. Bhoja also founded the city of Bhojapura, now in ruins, situated twenty miles south of Bhopal.

Not far from Bhojapura to the west, is the Bhojapura Lake, which was the largest and the most beautiful in India.[1] It was situated in a valley, close to where two of the main branches of the Betawa unite in order to pass through a narrow gorge about twenty-nine kilometres to the south-east of Bhopal. The lake appears to have been twenty five or twenty six kilometres in length, and eleven or twelve kilometres in breadth. The remains of the embankments across the Betawa show that it may have been about a hundred feet in depth, and perhaps three hundred yards in length at the top. It was excavated by Bhoja for irrigational purposes.[2]

The Paramāra ruler Udayāditya, is credited with the foundation of Udaipur, which must have been a town of considerable importance during the rule of the Paramāras. Besides the temple of Nīlakaṇṭheśvara, Udayāditya also excavated a tank known as Udayasamudra. King Devapāla's name is connected with the construction of the city of Devapālapura, now only a village, about forty kilometres to the north-west of Indore. He also had excavated a lake known as

1. JASB, No. VIII, 1839, p. 814.
2. Ibid, No. XVI, 1847, p. 740.

Depālasāgara, which is a fine sheet of water, covering a space of several square miles.[1]

Some literary works composed during this period are especially concerned with secular architecture, and throw considerable light on this subject. In his *Samarāṅgaṇasūtra-dhāra*,[2] Bhoja discusses town-planning and house architecture. The *Pramāṇamañjarī* is concerned with domestic architecture.

The city, according to these works, was surrounded by circular wall which had watch-towers and four gateways. A moat encircled the entire city-wall. The city had main roads, and streets lined with shops and palaces and residential quarters. It also had parks, lakes, wells and banks, and artificially watered public baths (*Yantradhārāgṛiha*).

Different houses were meant for the different castes. From the *Samarāṅgaṇasūtradhāra*, it is known that Śūdras should not have more than a three and a half storey house; Vaiśya not more than five and a half storeys; Kshatriya not more than six and a half storeys, and a Brāhmaṇa not more than seven and a half storeys; kings, of various religious merit, not more than eight and a half storeys. The *Pramāṇamañjarī* also recommends that the number of storeys should depend upon the class of owners.

The *Samarāṅgaṇa*[3] also describes the construction of palaces, which were classified into three, namely, *Jyeshṭha* or the superior type, *Madhyama* or the intermediate type, and *Kanishṭha*, the inferior type. It also deals with public buildings like *Nyāya-śālā*, *Pustaka-śālā*, *Viddyābhavana*, *Nāṭaka-Saṁgīta-śālā*, *Mārgaśālā* (rest house), *Kūpas*, *Vāpis* and the *taḍāgas*, The *Pramāṇamañjarī*,[4] classifies houses according to their heights as *Kanishṭha*, *Madhyama* and *Jyeshṭha*, and these three are further sub-divided, making nine classes in all.

Wooden structures seem to have been quite popular for ordinary purposes. There were also buildings made of stone and brick. Sometimes their floors were studded with crystals. The house had small projecting balconies called *Vallabhikā*

1. PRAS. W.C., 1920, p. 102.
2. SS. Book I, Chap. X.
3. Ibid. I, XV.
4. PM, VV. 4, 41-45.

or *Vaḍabhi*. There were particular projections in the houses at certain heights, on which swans or pigeons were carved. The walls of the mansions were white-washed on the outside, but decorated within with pictures and precious stones. Courtyards and arches were built in the houses. The pillars were decorated with figures in dance-poses and dramatic gestures.

In royal palaces, special audience halls (*asthāna*) and pleasure pavilions (*Krīḍāmaṇḍapa*) were provided. The *Chandraśālās* were the special apartments on the terraces from which the moon rise was observed.[1] Pavilions (*vedikā*) and raised seats (*vitaṅka*)[2] were built in the grounds. These were decorated with precious stones. The most interesting feature was the *Yantra-dhārā-gṛiha*, which was an ideal resort for the summer season.[3] Generally, *Yantra-dhāra-gṛiha* was meant only for the royal family, but at Dhāra, it was accessible to the people.

SCULPTURE

It is not easy to get an idea of the sculpture of the seventh or eighth century A.D. from the few known examples. Generally, condensed plasticity, concentrated roundness, and terseness of treatment, seem to be the characteristics of the images of this period; which were influenced to some extent by contemporary Decannese art. As in Eastern India, a slow but gradual transition of the plastic conception was taking place in Middle India.

In the tenth century A.D. under the Paramāra ruler Bhoja, Paramāra art was prolific in sculptural output and at the stage of its highest development. But it did not achieve great aesthetic heights. Dhar, Mandu, Ujjain, Udayapur, Gyaraspur and Nemawar, were the main centres, where there are excellent specimens of Paramāra art. These figures were largely and vigorously conceived, and were modelled in ample dimensions. They are free from jerky movement and intense flexions, and the weight of the heavy roundness which characterises their

1. SMK, p. 80.
2. Ibid.
3. Ibid,

youthful body[1] does not seem to be felt. The face, fully and vigorously modelled, observes S.K. SARASWATI,[2] "wears an expression of blankness and is lighted up neither by any pleasure of the senses nor by any inner experience, urge or inspiration. The legs are slumpy, and ornamentation is characteristically medieval."

Several factors were responsible for the phenomenal rise in the worship of images from the eighth century onwards. With the gradual increase in the construction of temples, images were also modelled in large number. The new religious sects of this period introduced their own gods and goddesses, and their new forms and varieties were devised. The foreigners also introduced new changes in the form of worship to suit their own tastes. Syncreistic icons were introduced when attempts of reconciliation and rapprochement were made among these rival creeds.

BUDDHIST SCULPTURES :—

At Sanchi,[3] detached Buddhist sculptures have been found in the *bhūmi sparśa mudrā* (touching the earth attitude) and *dhyānamudrā* (meditative mood). Other images are of Avalokiteśvara, Maitreya and Mayūra Vidyārāja. These images are infused with the same spirit of calm contemplation, of almost divine peace, as the images of the earlier period, but they have lost the beauty of the latter. Though they are still graceful and elegant, they gradually tend to become stereotyped and artificial.

At Bhojapura[4] near Sanchi, there is an enshrined figure of a seated Buddha, with the soles of the feet turned up, the right hand lying over the knee, and the left placed in the lap. To the right and left of the head, there are representations of topes and other ornaments. Below is an inscription of the seventh or eighth century A.D.

At Dhamnar[5] in the Buddhist caves, there are rock-cut

1. The struggle for Empire, p. 658.
2. Ibid.
3. The Monuments of Sanchi, p. 254.
4. CBT, p. 211.
5. ASI, 1905-06, p. 107.

images of Buddha of the seventh or eighth century A.D. Most of them are mutilated, and it is difficult to interpret their *mudrās*. Some are in a benedictive attitude, in a teaching attitude, or in a meditative pose. There is a representation of Buddha attaining *Nirvāṇa*.

The seated Buddha image in *bhūmi sparśa mudrā* was found at Gyaraspur. There are folds of loin-cloth flowing down the crossed legs. The figure is carved in high relief, and is set in an ornamental frame with two mouldings. There were three more sculptures of the Buddha lying in the ruins. Each of the four occupied a niche in the four quadrants of the *stūpa*. The Buddhas in the east and north quadrants are in the *dhyāna mudrā* (meditative mood), and those on the south and west quadrants were respectively in the *bhūmi sparśa* and *dharmachakra Parivartana mudrās*. Each Buddha is flanked by two Bodhisattvas. From the style, these images[1] may be assigned to the ninth or tenth century A.D.

BRAHMANICAL SCULPTURES :—

Śiva—Different types of *Śiva* images have been found. The dancing Śiva of Jhalarapatan is a superb example of the sculptor's art of the Paramāra period.[2] In the temple of Dharmanātha at Dhamnar, a slab bears a representation of Śiva dancing a *tāṇḍava* with Nandi in the centre below him, surrounded by four dancing goddesses. The latter, from east to west, are Pārvatī with Nandi beneath her, Vaishṇavī with Garuḍa below, Indrāṇī with her elephant, and Brāhmī with the goose.[3]

An image of Śiva, the lord of dance, belonging to the eleventh century, was discovered from Ujjain, and is now in Gwalior Fort Archaeological Museum.[4] It is five feet high. This ten-armed image (arms on left proper are broken) is dancing in *Aindra* posture, the right arm thrown staff like (*daṇḍa-hasta*) across the body, and the left raised in *abhaya-mudrā*. The other arms on the right proper, show the

1. ARADGS, 1931-32, p. 3; 1935-36, p. 11.
2. Marg XII, p. 12.
3. ASI, 1905-06, p. 110.
4. Stella Kramrisch : The Art of India, p. 209.

trident (*triśūla*), emblem of the triple hierarchy of manifestation and three qualities (guṇa) of which the manifest world is made; the next hand is *patākā-hasta* and conveys power, at the same time it shows that the dance has just begun. The next upper hand holds *ḍamaru*, and the other holds a serpent. The back slab by which the arms are connected, suggests the expanse of the skin of the Elephant demon killed by Śiva.

Another ten-armed image of Śiva discovered in the Śiva temple in Ramgarh, is shown dancing after the total and simultaneous defeat of the Titans, in heaven, on earth and in the mid-region. Śiva, the universal, all-filling god, holds his bow high. To the right of Śiva is Gaṇeśa, his small son, who takes part in the dance. Although the image is in very high relief and partly carved in the round, it is badly damaged. There is triumph in the calm face, and in the bow wielding arm of the dancing god, and sovereignty in his crowned head which is thrown back and looking upwards.

At Agar, sixty-six kilometres north of Ujjain, there is an old sculpture of Śiva and Pārvatī seated on Nandi, which probably belonged to the original temple of the eleventh or twelfth century A.D.[1] Śiva slaying *Gajāsura*, or the elephant demon, was obtained from Gyaraspur.[2] Two panels bearing images of Tripurāri and Śiva with four hands, evidently formed lower parts of door-jambs.[3] The image of Śiva as Tripuarāri was found at Jhardia.[4]

On the slope of a hill at Udayapur, there is a gigantic unfinished sculpture carved in a single boulder of rock. It is twentysix feet tall, twelve feet and seven inches broad across the chest and hands, and four feet and six inches thick. It is six-handed. One of the right hands holds a sword, another a *ḍamaru* and the third an unfinished object, probably a *triśūla*. One of the left hands holds a skull crowned mace, another points a finger towards its left foot and the third is held in the *Abhaya-mudrā*. The feet are in a dancing posture. A human figure (some demon) is trampled under the left foot. A serpent, which

1. ARADGS, 1930-31, p. 30.
2. Ibid, Plate I, Photo 3.
3. PRAS. WC., 1920, p. 94.
4. Ibid, p. 100.

is entwined round the neck, has its hood on the chest, and the coils of its body hanging down. The head of the figure is covered with matted hair like a crown, with the sign of a crescent on it. The sculpture is locally known as *Rāvaṇa*, but in fact, it represents a terrible form of Śiva.[1]

On the lintels of the temple of Morī[2] there is an image of Lakulīśa, with a staff in his right hand and citron in his left hand. In the other temple, on the dedicatory block above the entrance, is an image of Lakulīśa whose hands are broken off. The staff is still retained in the left hand. The image of Lakulīśa in the centre of the lintel of the door frame of the temple of Sandhārā,[3] probably indicates that it was originally dedicated to Śiva.

The sculpture of Kaṭarmal Bhairava at Gyaraspur[4] is noteworthy. It is so called as it bears a *kaṭāra* (dagger). It is a four-armed standing figure. On either side of the image near the top corners, garlanded bearers are carved. The head has hair bound in tassels, and is set in a halo formed by seven serpent hoods. All the hands are broken off. There is a garland of skulls round the neck, and a girdle round the waist in which a dagger is stuck. It once had sandles on the feet. In the lower left corner a dog is carved, and in the lower right one is a female attendant. Figures of goblins are carved on both sides. In short, the sculpture represents Bhairava.

At Morī,[5] there is a life size nude figure of Bhairava with two hands, the right holding a scimitar, and the left a human skull. He bears a garland of skulls. The dog, his vehicle, stands to his left. There is also a second image of Bhairava of smaller size.

Vishṇu—The extant varieties of Vishṇu images found in Malwa are numerous, and they may be divided into several groups. A four armed standing image of Vishṇu of the eighth

1. ARADGS, 1923-24, p. 7.
2. PRAS. WC., 1913, pp. 55-56; 1920, p. 94.
3. Ibid, 1920, pp. 88-91.
4. ARADGS, 1923-24, p. 7.
5. PRAS. WC., 1913, pp. 55-56.

or ninth century A.D. was found at Bhilsa.[1] The lower left hand is broken, and the other three hands respectively hold a conch (*śaṅkha*), a wheel (*chakra*), and a club (*gadā*). The head wears a high hexagonal crown, and there is a halo behind the head. A garland (*Vaijayanti-mālā*) hangs round the neck. The god was flanked by two attendants. At Kāmed,[2] eight kilometres from Ujjain, there is a Chaturbhuja image from the tenth century or a little earlier.

At Mandu,[3] in the course of clearance, an elegantly carved black basalt image of Lakshmīnārāyaṇa was found. Vishṇu is shown riding on flying Garuḍa, with Lakshmī on his left thigh. The lower part of Garuḍa is badly mutilated, as is the pedestal, on which there is a badly damaged inscription of the tenth or eleventh century A.D. At Dhamnār,[4] in the temple of Dharmanātha, the dedicatory block over the doorway to the shrine, Vishṇu and Lakshmi are seated. He holds in his upper right hand the *gadā* and in his upper left, is seen between their faces, the *chakra*. The lower left hand is round Lakshmī's waist, and the right is uncertain. An image of Vishṇu with his consort (Lakshmī Nārāyaṇa) seated on his left thigh, was recovered from Dhar.

Various images illustrating the ten incarnations of Vishṇu have been found in Malwa. The ten incarnations of Vishṇu have been carved on the pillars of the Hindola gateway of Gyaraspur.[5] In the middle shrine on the north side of the Dharmanātha temple at Dhamnār is a slab bearing ten *avatāras* of Vishṇu. There are nine compartments, the first on the left containing two *avatāras*, the fish and tortoise. In the eighth compartment there is a full length figure of Vishṇu, a counterpart to that in the main shrine, which takes the place of one of the *avatāras*. At Panthera, near Oṁkāra images of incarnations of Vishṇu have been discovered.[6] One

1. ARADGS, 1936-37, p. 7.
2. ASI, 1934-35, p. 6.
3. Ibid, 1936-37, p. 33.
4. Ibid, 1905-06, p. 110.
5. ARADGS, 1932-33, p. 9.
6. ASI, 1935-36, p. 81.

of the finest images of Varāha was found in the temple of Kohala.[1] Sculptures of Varāha have been found at Badoh[2] and at Karohan.[3]

From Tongra,[4] a most important sculpture of Nṛisiṁha, the incarnation of Vishṇu killing the demon Hiraṇyakashyapa, of the eleventh century A.D., has been discovered. There is an image of Narasiṁha in the temple of *Varāha* at Kohalā.[5] The images of the Buddha *Avatāra* of Vishṇu have been obtained from Sunari[6] and Badoh.[7] A fine image of Balarāma was found at Badoh.[8] The temple of Dharmanātha at Dhamnar[9] contains a slab bearing Nārāyaṇa reposing upon the serpent Śesha, with Brahmā springing from his navel. Nārāyaṇa was attacked by the demons Madhu and Kaiṭabha, but he destroyed them. In the sculpture, they are represented as Vishṇu's feet and as if attacking each other. Below them, at the end of the serpent couch, Lakshmī sits on a low stool. A beautiful image of *Śeshasāyin* was found near the Lohāni cave Mandu.[10] A pedestal contains an inscription dated *Saṁ* 1258, and seems to record a gift of Khāvūka, the son of Lakshmīdeva. An image of Śesha, with attendant figures of Brahmā, ten *avatāras* etc. was recovered from Dhar.[11] A very fine, though mutilated, image of Nārāyaṇa on the *Anantaśayyā*, was found at Dūdhākheḍī,[12] and a Vishṇu on Śeshanāga was discovered at Jhardā.[13]

Scenes from the *Rāmāyaṇa* and *Mahābhārata* are found illustrated on the walls and pillars of the old temples. At

1. PRAS. WC., 1920, p. 83.
2. ARADGS, 1930-31, Plate V.
3. Ibid, 1934-35, p. 10.
4. Ibid, 1928-29, p. 11.
5. PRAS. WC., 1920, p. 83.
6. ARADGS, 1923-24, p. 8.
7. Ibid, 1930-31.
8. Ibid, 1933-34, Plate XII.
9. ASI, 1905-06.
10. Ibid, 1934-35, p. 60.
11. Ibid, 1930-34, p. 49.
12. PRAS. WC., 1920, p. 83.
13. Ibid, p. 101.

Sandhārā,[1] a large stone lintel has been covered with bas-reliefs which represent scenes from the *Rāmāyaṇa*. Some sculptures at Padholi[2] can be easily identified as scenes from the *Rāmāyaṇa*.

The shrine of the Gadarmal temple of Badoh[3] contains a composition, nearly life size of a newly born babe lying by the side of its mother. They have been surmised to be a Māyādevī Buddha by Belgar, Triśalā Mahāvīra by Cunningham and Yaśodā Kṛishṇa by Cousens. It is possible that the image now in the shrine of Gadarmal temple originally pertained to the Kṛishṇa fane. The old temple of Tumain[4] is decorated with vigorous and beautiful carving representing incidents in the life of Kṛishṇa. At Kukadeśvara[5], a large slab has been discovered with bas-reliefs which represent scenes from the life of Kṛishṇa. In the temple of Pārśvanātha at Morī,[6] numerous bas-reliefs in the *maṇḍapa* represent scenes from the life of Kṛishṇa.

Brahmā—The images of Brahmā were rare in ancient times. An inscribed sculpture of Brahmā of V.S. 1210 was found recovered from Bagh.[7] The inscription records the installation of the sculpture by Bhamini, sister of Śrī Yaśodhavala, a Paramāra Chief. At Mamon[8], an image of Brahmā was discovered. Brahmā has been depicted along with other gods in the panels of the temple at Phadhauli[9] and Dhundheri.[10]

Sūrya—The standing image of Sūrya five feet in height was discovered at Gandhawal.[11] The image of the Sun was found carved in the *maṇḍapa* of the temple at Jhardia[12] and at

1 ASI, 1919-20, p. 44; PRAS. WC., 1920, p. 91.
2. Ibid, 25-26, p. 189.
3. PRAS. WC., 1914, p. 64.
4. ASI, 1918-19, p. 22.
5. Ibid, 1919-20, p. 44.
6. PRAS. WC., 1920, p. 94.
7. ARADGS, 1926-27, p. 7.
8. ASI, 1925-26, p. 191.
9. ARADGS, 1925-26, p. 6.
10. PRAS. WC., 1920, p. 95.
11. Ibid, 1935-36, p. 83.
12. Ibid, 1920, p. 100.

Makla.[1] We find the representation of Nine Planets on the door-frames of the ancient temples of Dhundherī[2] and Modī.[3] At the end of the lintels of the ancient temple of Kāgpur,[4] the figures of eight *Dikpālas* are noticed. The head of the moon-god (*chandra*), with a crescent behind of the tenth century A.D., was recovered from Bhilsa.[5]

Mother Goddess—Worship of images of the mother goddess is found under different forms and names. Close to *Mata Kī Madhi* at Kāgpur, there is a well designed, and peculiarly posed, four armed goddess riding what looks like a horse. The head, hands and feet of the goddess, are lost. There are no traces of ornaments or clothing. From the style of sculpture, it may be assigned to the late Gupta Period.[6] A two-armed standing goddess or female devotee, with hands folded in salutation in front of the chest, and holding a garland between the two palms, was discovered at Bhilsa.[7] It has ear ornaments, a necklace, and bangles round the wrists, and carries a high basket on the head. It belongs to the eighth or ninth century A.D. It may be the goddess of Earth, the goddess of plenty. At Pantharia[8], near Oṁkāra, a broken image of charchikā, erroneously called Rāvaṇa, was discovered, and it may be assigned to the ninth or tenth century A.D. The image of Mahishamardinī has been noticed at Mammon[9], Gandharwal[10], Morī,[11] Jhardia[12] and Makla.[13] The image of Brahmāṇī is known from Suhania[14] and Morī,[15]

1. PRAS. WC., 1920, p. 100.
2. Ibid, p. 95.
3. Ibid, p. 94.
4. ARADGS, 1931-32.
5. Ibid, 1936-37, p. 7.
6. Ibid, 1931-32.
7. Ibid, 1936-37, p. 7.
8. ASI, 1935-36, p. 80.
9. Ibid, 1925-26.
10. Ibid, 1935-36.
11. PRAS. WC., 1920.
12. Ibid, p. 100.
13. Ibid, p. 120.
14. ARADGS, 1927-28.
15. PRAS. WC., 1920.

and of Kāli from Terahi[1], Dhamnar[2] and Jharda.[3] The sculpture of Pārvatī practising penance has been recovered from Kāgpur[4] and Suhania.[5] The images of Agni and Vāyu are known from Suhania.[6] Sometimes, doors are found carved with the figures of Gaṅgā and Yamunā.

The most important figure of the period is the famous image of Vāgdevī (goddess of speech), in the British Museum, which belongs to the reign of king Bhojadeva. It was executed in 1034 A.D. by the famous sculptor Manathala.[7] The goddess is in the *abhaṅga* pose. Of her four hands, the front pair are mutilated. She wears a crown and her ear-rings hang down to her shoulders. She wears a pearl necklace round her neck, and a pearl embroidered band encircles her breast. Her waist is decorated all around. She is attended by five subordinate figures, two above and three below. On the left, below, are a *ṛishi* and a dwarf, and on the right, probably Pārvatī on a lion. On the left above, is a flying female figure with a garland in her hand. The other figure is indistinct. Its *urumālā* (thigh ornament) and coronet are Drāvidian in style, and the ornaments of its arms are reminiscent of the early images of Bengal and Orissa.[8] In the opinion of D.C. GANGULY, the image is a *chef d'oeuvre* of rare beauty, in its exquisite serenity of pose, in its entrancing and balancing rhythm, in the elegance and suavity of its equiline features, and in the general restraint in the treatment of the anatomy, which is almost free from any exaggeration. The emotion of its static conception, alternating

1. ARADGS, 1934-35.
2. ASI, 1905-06.
3. PRAS. WC., 1930, p. 100.
4. ARADGS, 1931-32, p. 6.
5. Ibid, 1937-38, p. 11.
6. Ibid, 1927-28.
7. Rūpam, 1924, p. 2; GRAO, Elements of Hindu Iconography Vol., Pt II, pp, 377-78; R. P CHANDA, Medieval Indian Sculpture in the British Museum, p. 46; G.H.P., p. 272; S. SHIVARAMMURTI, Indian Sculpture, pp. 106-107.
8. GHPD, pp. 272-73.

between a *rājasika* and a *sāttvika*, is most appealing.[1] SHIVARAMMURṬI acclaims it as one of the most marvellous creations of the sculpture of the Paramāra realm patronised by Bhoja.[2]

Another master-piece of Paramāra sculpture is the grey-sandstone, ten-handed dancing Durgā, which is in the National Museum, New Delhi. It originally belonged to the Dabhoi fort. The Devī is in the *abhaṅga mudrā*. She is wearing *Karaṇḍa-mukuṭa*, whilst round her neck is a pearl necklace, and another hangs between he breasts. She is also wearing a *muṇḍa-mālā* which goes down to her thighs. She is wearing ornaments on her arms which resemble in style those of Vāgdevī of the British Museum. Her waist is covered with ornaments. On her left side is a figure which appears to be that of a lion, the *vāhana* of Durgā. Unfortunately, this important image is highly mutilated. The hands have disappeared completely.

Another Paramāra image discovered at Dhāra is carved out of hard white stone, and is in a perfect condition.[3] M. B. GARDE has identified this goddess as Pārvatī. She wears a necklace of pearls, a crown and ear-rings. Her four hands are adorned with ornaments. Her breast-band, drapery, and thigh ornaments, are similar to those of the Sarasvatī image. She is attended by eight figures. On the top are representations of Brahmā, Vishṇu, Gaṇeśa and Śiva; below are the female attendants with *chowries*. There are also sacrificial altars, two on each side. The goddess is immersed in deep meditation, with her hands in an attitude of prayer. Her face has an air of purity, and is expressive of divine serenity. M. B. GARDE suggests that she is engaged in performing the '*Pañch-āgnisādhanā*, which, according to the *Purāṇas*, was undertaken by Pārvatī for obtaining Śiva as her husband. It contains an inscription which falls within the reign of Udayāditya.

Vyantara Devatās—There are certain gods whose images were worshipped as the attendants of the chosen gods. One of such popular gods is Gaṇapati, the elephant-headed and pot-bellied god. The stone sculpture of Gaṇeśa with eight arms,

1. Rūpam, 1926, p. 1.
2. Indian Sculpture, p. 107.
3. ABORI, V, pp. ff., XXII, pp. 99 ff.

and another of Śakti of Gaṇeśa from Suhania,[1] are noteworthy. Near the Mānasarovara tank of Gyaraspur,[2] there is an old image of Gaṇeśa. In his left hand is *aṅkuśa*, and in the right hand *modakas*. The image of Gaṇeśa with his consort has been found at Udayapura.[3] At the village of Badoh,[4] there is an idol of Gaṇeśa dancing in Sātamarhi (or seven) shrines. The temple of Gaṇeśa at Makla contains an image of Gaṇeśa.[5] Another at Modī is remarkable.[6] At the ends of the lintels of the old temple of Kāgpur[7], the sculpture of Gaṇeśa has been carved. At Chirodia,[8] five kilometres to the east of Bhilsa, there are good sculptures of both Gaṇeśa and Yama.

On the bank of the reservoir Barā Talāv, of the village of Vaikheda[9], there is a colossal image of Kubera. The god of riches, sitting on his haunches, holds a bag in his right hand, and a wine cup in the left. There is a pointed head-dress on his head from the back of which long curls of hairs flow on to his back and shoulders. The image is four feet and five inches in height. An image of Kubera has also been found at Bhojapura[10] and at Terahi.[11]

In one of the Western niches of the old temple of Gandharwal, there is an image thickly bedaubed with paint, which may be of Hayagrīva.[12]

Syncretistic Icons—The composite sculptures of gods and goddesses found in Malwa indicate a spirit of reconciliation and rapprochement between the rival creeds. The Harihara *mūrti* emphasizes the reconciliation between the two major

1. ARADGS, 1937-38, p. 11.
2. Ibid, 1931-32.
3. Ibid, 1928-29, Pl. XII.
4. Ibid, 1930-31, p. 10.
5. PRAS. WC., 1920.
6. Ibid.
7. ARADGS, 1931-32, p. 7.
8. Ibid, 1923-24, p. 8.
9. PRAS. WC., 1920, p. 24.
10. ASI, 1027-28, p. 48.
11. ASIDGS, 1934-35, Plate V. C.
12. ASI, 1935-36, p. 83.

cults of Vaishṇavism and Śaivism. In this group of images, the left half of the male deity carries the usual weapons of Vishṇu, whereas the right depicts Hara. Such an image of Harihara was recovered from Ghusai[1]

Ardhanārīśvara is a composite aspect of Śiva and Pārvatī in one form. The archaeological museum at Jhalawar[2] preserves a beautiful statue in a standing pose, an image of Ardhanārīśvara has been recovered from Pali.[3]

The huge image of the Hindu Trinity found in the old temple of Makla,[4] is one of the best representations known. It is four feet in height and five feet in length. A bust of Trimūrti and a medallion with an inset of Trimūrti, have been recovered from Gyaraspur[5]. The image of Trimūrti from Padhavali is also remarkable.[6]

A large eight-armed image was discovered from Jhalarapatan.[7] It is a composite image, representing the four gods—Śiva, Vishṇu, Brahmā and Sūrya. The arms are all broken, but the figure is booted with long Persian boots, as is the case with Sūrya only. In front of it stands a *liṅga* with four images carved upon it, and they probably represent the same deities.

The beautiful figure of a celestial nymph or *Shālabhañjikā* from Gyaraspur, has attained world wide renown for its finely arranged coiffure, sharp and prominent facial features; and the delicately modelled contours. The upper part of her body is nude, while the lower is clad in a typical, *antarīya* or lower garment.

General—An image of Kārttikeya of the eighth century A.D. riding a bird, probably a peacock, was obtained at Kāgpur.[8] An image of Kapila *Muni* was found at Ujjain[9], and of a bearded *Muni* at Gandhaval.[10]

1. ARADGS, 1933-34, Pl. XII. b.
2. Marg, XII, p. 18.
3. ARADGS, 1928-29, Pl. XII. c.
4. PRAS. WC , 1920.
5. ARADGS, 1932-33.
6. Ibid, 1925-26.
7. PRAS. WC., 1904-05, pp, 31-32.
8. ARADGS, 1931-32.
9. Ibid, 1934-35.
10. Ibid, 1935-36.

The images of Nāga and Nāgini have been recovered from Ujjain.[1] There is a fine Nāga image of an earlier period at Vaikheḍa.[2]

There are figures of Kalpavṛiksha and Kāmadhenu at Modī.[3] The Kalpavṛiksha consists of a tree rising out of a round masonry enclosure, and the bust of a human figure is to be seen among its branches. Two human figures, too mutilated to be recognizable, are seated on each side of the trunk, while the nine planets (*Navagraha*) are found on the pedestal. The image of Kāmadhenu consists of a cow adorned with a neck-lace, suckling her calf, while in front of her is a raised receptacle containing round balls (*modakas*). A small image of Kāmadhenu, consisting of a cow suckling its calf (*Kāmadhenu*) under a tree, has been found at Dudākhedi.[4] Such an image has also been found at Jharda.[5]

In the temple of Vaikheda[6], there are two female figures exquisitely carved in relief on small pieces of stone. They hold stone lamps of antique shape in their hands, and resembling similar figures found in the interior of the Jaina temples at Kethuli[7] and at Mammon.[8]

JAINA SCULPTURES :—

In the period between the eighth and the twelfth century A.D., excellent large Jaina images of stone were made. Their design and execution are perfect. The facial expressions, the graceful poses, and the various moods, are chiselled in an exquisite manner. All the motifs are attractive and fascinating.

A big idol of a Tīrthaṅkara eight feet and ten inches in height, has been discovered at Mammon.[9] It is attended by two Yakshas, and five other smaller figures of Tīrthaṅkaras stand in the shrine. This principal idol, the halo behind the head

1. ARADGS, 1934-35.
2. PRAS. WC., 1920, p, 102.
3. Ibid, p. 94
4. Ibid, pp. 82-83.
5. Ibid, p. 100.
6. Ibid, p. 102.
7. Ibid, p. 92.
8. ASI, 1925-26, p. 191.
9. Ibid, 1925-26, p. 191.

of which is slightly damaged, is, on the whole, a good specimen of tenth century sculpture. The lintel of the shrine doorframe also bears images of Tīrthaṅkaras, and flanking the door on the north, is a fine sculpture of a seated Pārśvanātha. At Kāgpur[1], close to Matā Kī Medi, a *chaumukha*, has been found, which is the only Jaina relic so far recovered.

Inside the Jaina temple of Bhojapura,[2] there is a colossal standing image of Ādinātha about twenty feet in height, flanked on either side by images of Pārśvanātha accompanied by figures of Indra. Among the old relics of Gandhavāla,[3] mostly Jaina images have been found, some of which are ten feet high. In the two old Jaina temples of Ūṇ[4], a few colossal Jaina images of the twelfth or thirteenth century have been found.

A big figure of Jaina Tīrthaṅkara was found at Chainpur[5], and it is thirteen feet and three inches in length and three feet and eight inches in breadth. Jaina images of the twelfth century have been found at Bijawada[6] and Puragilana.[7] The Jaina temple in Chanderī[8] possesses some old images, namely, an image of Pārśvanātha dated V.S. 1252, and another idol of a Tīrthaṅkara dated V.S. 1316.

Besides Tīrthaṅkaras, the Jainas worshipped deities such as Sarasvatī, Ambikā and Padmāvatī. In a niche in the north-west corner of the exterior of the shrine of the temple at Mammon,[9] is a sculpture of Ambikā, and in the corresponding niche in the south-west corner, there is a figure of Chakareśvarī. The Jaina temple of Chanderi[10] contains a sculpture of the goddess Padmāvatī, dated in V.S. 1291.

There are two images of female Jaina deities under a tree inside Jharda.[11] Both of them are seated on thrones and

1. ARADGS, 1931-32.
2, ASI, 1927-28. p. 48.
3. Ibid, 1935-36, p. 83.
4. Ibid., 1918-19; PRAS. WC., 1919.
5. PRAS. WC., 1920, p. 87.
6. Ibid, p. 22.
7. Ibid, p. 81.
8. ARADGS, 1923-24, p. 11.
9. ASI, 1925-26, p. 19.
10, ARADGS, 1923-24, p. 11.
11. PRAS. WC., 1920, p. 100.

have eight hands. The first image, of V.S. 1229, is the more perfect. It holds a tree, a bow, an elephant goad (*aṅkuśa*) in its right hands, and a noose (*pāśa*) and rosary (*akshasūtra*) in a left hand. Two of the left hands and one right hand are missing. Below the goddess and to the right, a bull is standing, while two small attendant figures stand on each side of the pedestal, and small figures of two devotees have been carved in relief in front of the latter. The second image of V.S. 1229 (1172 A.D.) has lost its head, and the head of a Jina has been placed on its neck. Most of its hands are broken, but a bow and a rosary are discernible in two of its left hands. The figure of a goose is to be found below the right knee of the deity, and the pedestal is occupied with nine miniature figures of the planets.

At Pura-Gilana,[1] there are two images of Śāsana devīs, called Mahantārikā, as known from their inscriptions. Both images are headless. They represent a goddess seated on a throne with one leg drawn up and with four hands. In one of her right hands, she holds a child, and below her is a lion couchant. The emblems in the remaining hands are either broken or indistinct. One figure probably represents the parents of Mahāvīra. A male and a female are seated side by side under a tree, both headless. There is a female attendant on each side of them, and a row of horsemen on the pedestal.

In the Digambara Jaina Museum, Ujjain, a large number of Jaina images collected from different ancient sites, such as Ujjain, Badnawar, Guṇa etc. have been displayed. Among these some are quite important from the artistic point of view. The female torso of Badnawar, carved in white marble, is an excellent example of Paramāra art. The well modelled figure decked in the quaint jewellery of the period, is reminiscent of other similar sculptures studded in the Jaina temples at Abu. The icons of Pārśvanātha and Mahāvīra reveal the characteristic features of Paramāra art. Their hair is arranged in spiral curls, and their downcast eyes are full of spiritual ecstacy. They have bow-like eyebrows, thick lips and prominent chins.

1. PRAS, WC., 1920, p. 81.

Chapter—XIV

EDUCATION AND LITERATURE

During this period, Malwa achieved a high peak of greatness and fame in the spheres of éducation and literature. The system of education was efficiently organized; temples and *maṭhas* became seats of learning. The Paramāra rulers were great patrons, and therefore scholars from distant countries migrated to Malwa. Some of the ruling chiefs were themselves scholars. Among them, Bhoja is very important, and during his reign, the old literary traditions of Vikrama were revived. Under his patronage, there was remarkable development in every sphere of knowledge.

EDUCATION

Besides education given by private teachers, there were organized institutions managed both by the state and the public. Important holy places and towns became great educational centres. Some temples and *maṭhas* were converted into educational institutions. The Śaiva monasteries and temples of the *Mattamayūra sect* at Upendrapura, *Mattamayūrapura*, *Kadambaguha*, *Terambi*, *Āmardakatīrtha* (Ujjain), *Raṇod*, *Siyadoni*, *Bilhari*, *Sarwaya*, *Chanderi* and *Kundalapura*, acted as educational institutions where religious scriptures were studied. At the head of each monastery was a superintendent, highly distinguished for learning. The Āchāryas of the Mattamayūra sect were well-known for their scholarship, and they promoted learning.[1] There was a Śaiva monastery of established repute at Ujjain; known as *Chaṇḍikāśrama*.[2] The Śaiva monastery of Shergadh is also famous, and its head was *Bhaṭṭāraka* Nāg-

1. EI, I, p. 351; JMPIP, IV, p. 3.
2. IA, XI, p. 221.

naka.[1] Surwaya's old name, *Sarasvatīpattana*, indicates that it was a seat of learning. There are also the remains of old monasteries which were meant as residences for ascetics.[2]

The Jaina temple of Un, Chabutarā Deorā, was used as a school for children.[3] This is clear from the inscriptions found on the walls of the temple. One inscription consists of certain rules of Sanskrit grammar, while another is inscribed on the folds of the body of a snake and consists of various letters, both vowels and consonants, of the *Indian* alphabet, as well as the affixes used in the conjugation of Sanskrit verbs. There are some illustrations of the Kāmasūtra of Vātsyāyana on the wall of the sanctum. The Pārśvanātha-Jina-Vihāra at Dhāra, and the Nemichaityālaya of Nalachhā, also served as seats of learning.

The most important educational institution to impart education was the *Bhojaśālā* of Dhāra, the presiding deity of which was the goddess of learning, Sarasvatī. Numerous slabs of black stone with writings of the *Pārijātamañjarī* and Kūrmastotra, have been found, and also fragments of stone slabs containing two Prakrit poems, *Kodaṇḍa* and *Khadgaśatam*.[4] A *Sarpavandha* inscription containing the letters of the alphabet and the Sanskrit conjugational terminals, has been recovered.[5] Such an inscription has been also discovered at Ujjain.[6]

Mandu also seems to have been a seat of learning. One of the inscriptions[7] found begins with an invocation to Sarasvatī, the goddess of learning, to whose praise a few verses are devoted in the inscription. The way in which Sarasvatī is invoked, indicates that at Mandu, as in Dhar, a temple might also have existed dedicated to this deity, to which the slab originally belonged.

Sometimes, the Paramāra kings founded colonies of learned Brāhmaṇas by inviting them to settle, and providing

1. EI, XXIII, p. 34.
2. ASI, 1934-35, p. 25.
3. Ibid, 1918-19, p. 17.
4. Ibid, 1934-35, p. 60.
5. Ibid, 1918-19, p. 22.
6. EI, XXXI.
7. ASI, 1934-35, p. 60.

for their maintenance. Such villages were known as *agrahāra* villages, and they became centres of learning. Rājabrahmapurī has been mentioned in the Copper Plate Grant[1] dated V.S. 1192 of *Mahārāja* Jayavarmadeva. From this inscription, it is known that he granted a village to a person living at Rājabrahmapurī. From the Māndhātā plates[2] dated V.S. 1331 of Paramāra Jayasiṁha Jayavarman, it is known that Sādhanika Anayasiṁha, with the permission of the Paramāra king Jayavarman alias Jayasiṁha, together with his four sons, granted four villages in favour of a number of Brāhmaṇas residing in the Brahmapurī (Brāhmaṇa settlement). This Brahmapurī mentioned as the habitation of the Brāhmaṇa donees was at Maṇḍapadurga. It had a surrounding wall, a gate, a big shrine, and a pond, and contained sixteen temples endowed with golden jars. These localities are actually of the *Agrahāra* type.

The education of a child started at the age of six,[3] and generally continued for ten years. During this period, he studied the different branches of learning.[4] The initiation of a boy into reading and writing took place on an auspicious day.[5] The study of the *Vedas*, *Vedāṅgas*, *Purāṇas* and *Śāstras* was obligatory for the priestly class, as is evident from the various prefixes used by the Brāhmaṇas of the period. Grammar was an important subject in the curriculum. When Siddharāja Jayasiṁha triumphantly entered the city of Ujjain, he found all the students studying Bhoja's Grammar.[6] It is further proved by the inscriptions containing an alphabetical chart, and rules of Sanskrit grammar, from the time of Udayāditya and Naravarman, which have been found at Dhar, Un and Ujjain.[7] Astrology and Astronomy had their place in the system of education. Proficiency in History and Āyurveda was admired. Painting, music and dancing, were

1. EI, XIX.
2. Ibid, XXXII.
3. TM, pp. 64-65.
4. SMK, p. 19.
5. ABORI, XXXVI, p. 362.
6. P. Ch. pp. 156, 157, 185.
7. EI, XXXI, pp. 25 ff.

the fine arts which were taught to girls. For the purpose of specialization in a subject, it was necessary to move from one place to another.

The highest percentage of literacy was found among the Brāhmaṇas and the Jaina *Sādhus*. The princes received specialised education which made them scholar-statesmen. They were instructed in *dharma*, *artha*, *kāma*, *crafts*, archery, physical exercises, and in the science of administration and diplomacy. The Vaiśya's education was mainly concerned with accountancy and book-keeping. Among the Kāyasthas, literacy was essential because they were entrusted with the task of drafting the inscriptions. Those, who could not afford an expensive education, were imparted instruction at least in the three Rs.

Some other indirect methods also promoted education. We hear of literary *goshṭhīs* at this time. The religious discourses by the saints must have enlightened the laity on spiritual matters. The literary debates and discourses, which often took place in the royal courts, were attended by the people who must have been inspired by them. There was no examination system of the modern type, but knowledge was tested by oral means. For testing the knowledge of scholars, assemblies were sometimes convened, and in them, all sorts of questions were put by opponents as well as by experts.

The Brāhmaṇas generally acted as teachers. The *Rājagurus* or the preceptors of the kings, received large sums of money from the kings and feudatories. They were awarded clothes, land and even villages. On the whole, the income of the teachers was not enough, but they were held in high respect by society because of their high ideals. The Jaina Sādhus did not accept any gifts. Jinavallabhasūri refused to accept three lacs *pārutha drammas*, or three villages instead, granted by Naravarman Paramāra. He requested that two *pārutha drammas* from the customs house of Chitor should be granted for defraying the expenses of two temples of Kharatara Jainas.[1]

1. KB, p. 13.

LITERATURE

Literary activities continued in the Sanskrit, Prakrit and Apabhraṁśa languages during this period. There was an immense literary output in different branches of learning. A number of commentaries and sub-commentaries, and manuals and sub-manuals, were written. But there was a lack of vitality and originality in the whole range of literature. It became imitative, insipid, artificial, laboured and stereotyped. It was confined to the royal courts and lost touch with the masses. It became stagnant and lost a freshness of outlook because of the lack of contact with the outside world. Besides, this period also produced a large number of royal authors and patrons. Among them, the names of Vākpati Muñja, Bhoja and Naravarman are noteworthy.

Before the period of the Paramāras, there is some information about a few authors and their literary works. From the reference to Māhishmatī as '*agra-mahishī*' in Act VII of his play, KONOW[1] infers that Murārī was a protege of a Kalachuri prince at Māhishmatī prior to the middle of the eighth century A.D. He is the author of the *Anargha-rāghava*, a play of seven acts depicting the early life of Rāma up to his return from the forest. It bears ample testimony to the linguistic abilities of its author, though as a drama, it has obvious defects.[2] Vyomaśambhu, the Śaiva Āchārya of the Mattamayūra sect, wrote the *Vyomavatī*, a commentary on the *Padārthasaṁgraha* of Praśastapāda.[3]

The Paramāra period is remarkable from a literary point of view, because it produced a number of scholars of repute. The poetess Sītā, who composed a song eulogising the deeds of Upendra, the founder of the Paramāra dynasty, might have lived in his court.[4] The *Prabandhachintāmaṇi*[5] des-

1. Das Indische Drama, by STEN KONOW, Berlin, 1920, p. 83.
2. Sanskrit Drama by A. B. KEITH, Oxford, 1924, p. 229.
3. He is referred to by Udayana in his *Kiraṇāvalī* and is also cited by later writers like Guṇaratna, Vardhamāna and others. KEITH—Indian Logic and Atomism, p. 32.
4. NC, XI, V. 77.
5. PC, p. 43.

cribes Sītā as a contemporary of Bhojadeva. As she is referred to by Padmagupta in the *Navasāhasāṅkacharita*, she must have lived prior to Bhojadeva, and might have been a contemporary of Bhojadeva. Mānatuṅga, the famous author of the *Bhaktāmarastotra*, according to a *Paṭṭāvalī* of the Bṛihad-Gachchha, was a Minister of Vairīsiṁha of the Paramāra dynasty.[1] Devasena wrote the Darśanasāra in V.S. 990 (933 A.D.) while staying in the Pārśvanātha temple at Dhāra, probably during the reign of Vairīsiṁha.[2] This work deals with Jaina philosophy and is written in Prakrit. Two other works, viz. *Arādhanāsāra* and *Tattvasāra* are also attributed to Devasena.

Vākpati II (Muñja) was not only a patron of scholars, but he himself was endowed with poetic talents. The Udaipur *Praśasti*[3] extols Vākpati II (Muñja) as one who cultivated eloquence, lofty poetry, and mastery over the rules of the *śāstras*. Elsewhere, he has been described as *Kavivṛishaḥ*.[4] Though no independent work of his is available, his poetic ability is proved by various verses ascribed to him by contemporary and later authors.[5] Vākpati is said to have written a geographical description of India, known as *Muñja-Pratideśa Vyavasthā*.[6]

Vākpati II patronized scholars who made remarkable contributions to different branches of literature. Halāyudha, who originally lived at Mānyakheṭa, migrated to Ujjain and

1. The Age of Imperial Kanauj, p. 184. At the same time, we are told that he was a contemporary of Mayūra and Bāṇa at the court of King Harsha. Peterson, Fourth Report, p. xcii. (Mānatuṅga, author of the *Bhayaharastotra*)
2. RKJSB, p. 133.
3. EI, I, p. 235, v. 13.
4. IA, XVI, p. 23.
5. Dhanika quotes Muñja twice in his commentary on Daśarūpaka (vv. 66 and 67). The Kashmirian poet Kshemendra quotes three different stanzas composed by Utpalarāja (*Subhāshitāvalī*, vv. 3. 413, 3.414). In the *Rasikasaṁjīvinī*, Arjunavarman quotes a verse, the authorship of which is ascribed to Muñja (*Amaruśataka*, p. 23). Some other verses of the king were reproduced in the *Śārṅgadharapaddhati* (v. 126-127) and *Sūktimuktāvali*, p. 176.
6. AS. Res, Vol. IX, p. 176.

enjoyed the munificent patronage of Vākpati Muñja. In writing the *Abhidhānaratnamālā*, he followed the authority of Amaradatta, Vararuchi, Bhāguri and Vopālita.[1] The arrangement of this work is almost like that of the *Amarakośa*. The synonymous portion extends over four *Kāṇḍas* called *Svarga*, *Bhūmi*, *Pātāla* and *Sāmānya*, and is followed by the *Anekārtha-kāṇḍa*, the fifth and the last, which forms the homonymous portion including the indeclinables. He is also the author of the *Kavirahasya* and the commentary called the *Mṛitasañjīvinī* on Piṅgala's *Chhandaḥsūtra*. The former is an elaborate poem, meant to illustrate the modes of the formation of the present tense in Sanskrit literature, and is at the same time an eulogy of king Kṛishṇarāja III of the *Rāshṭrakūṭa* dynasty, who ruled over the Deccan between 939 and 967 A.D.; while the latter was composed in honour of king Muñja Vākpati between 974 and 995 A.D., probably at Ujjain.

Dhanañjaya, son of Vishṇu, was the court poet of king Vākpati Muñja. His masterly treatise on dramaturgy, the *Daśarūpa*, was composed in Malwa in the last quarter of the tenth century A.D.[2] This work is based on the time-honoured authority of Bhārata.[3] Dhanañjaya is, however, more precise, and restates the general principles in the form of a practical, condensed, and systematic manual.[4] His brother Dhanika, is said to have been the *Mahā-sādhyapāla* of Utpalarāja i.e. Vākpati II. His most famous work is *Avaloka*, a commentary on Daśarūpa. Dhanika quotes from Vākpati Muñja as well as Padmagupta's *Navasāhasāṅkacharita*, and is himself quoted by Bhoja in his *Sarasvatīkaṇṭhābharaṇa*.[5] His *Avaloka* must, therefore, have been written in the reign of Sindhurāja. From the *Avaloka*, we learn that its author composed poems in Sanskrit and Prakrit, and also wrote a treatise entitled *Kāvyanirṇaya*, which apparently dealt with general poetic topics.[6]

1. Ramavatara Sharma, *Kalpadrukośa*, Intro., p. XXV.
2. The *Daśarūpaka* Tr. by George CU. Hass, Intro. p. 1.
3. Ibid, p. XXVII.
4. De : *Sriṅgāraprakāśa*.
5. SK, pp. 123-24.
6. De : Sp. p. 125.

Dhanapāla was a contemporary of three Paramāra rulers, viz. Sīyaka II, Vākpati II and king Bhoja. He was originally a Brāhmaṇa, but later on he adopted Jainism. He was awarded the title of Sarasvatī by Vākpatī Muñja. He had complete mastery over Sanskrit and Prakrit. He composed the *Paiyalachchhīnāmamālā*, a Prakrit-Kośa in 972 A.D., when Sīyaka II sacked Mānyakheṭa. He also wrote the important Sanskrit Prose *Kāvya*, *Tilakamañjarī*, to satisfy the curiosity of King Bhoja about Jaina-*dharma*. It also sheds valuable light on the contemporary social and religious life of the people. His *Satyapurīyamahāvīra Utsāha* is a poem in praise of a Mahāvīra image at Satyapura. Incidentally, it throws some light on Mahmūd's route in his attack on Somanātha. The *Bhavisayattakahā* of Dhanapāla is a poem in twenty two *Sandhis*, and narrates the life of a merchant who suffered much on account of the jealousy of his step-brother. His *Chaturviṁśikā Ṭīkā* is a Sanskrit commentary on Śobhana's work *Chaturviṁśikā*. He also wrote the *Mahāvīra-Stuti*, and the *Ṛishabhapaṁchāśikā*, both in Prakrit.

Mahāsena was a court poet of king Vākpati II and the preceptor of Sindhurāja's *mahattama* Parpaṭa, at whose request, he wrote his *Pradyumnacharita*.[1] Harisheṇa is said to have written his *Dharmaparīkshā* in V.S. 1044=987 A.D., during the reign of Vākpati II.

Amitagati claims to have been honoured by Muñja, Sindhurāja and Bhojadeva. He has written books on various subjects in Sanskrit. He wrote the *Subhāshitaratnasaṁdoha*, an anthology in V.S. 1050=993 A.D., when Vākpati II was ruling. His other works are *Upāsakāchāra*, *Dharmaparīkshā*, *Paṁchasaṁgraha*, *Ārādhanā*, *Sāmāyikapāṭha* and *Bhāvanādvātriṁśatikā*. His Pañchasaṁgraha written in V.S. 1063 (1016 A.D.) at Masutikapura (Masuda vilanda), near Dhar, in mixed prose and verse, is a compendium of Jaina Philosophy, and it is almost a Sanskrit version of the *Gommatasāra*. Amitagati's *Dharmaparīkshā* composed in V.S. 1070 (1013 A.D.) may be regarded as a satire on popular Hinduism.

1. AJGPS.

Padmagupta or Parimala, the poet laureate of Vākpati II and Sindhurāja, was the son of Mṛigāṅkadatta. At the command of Sindhurāja, he wrote the famous *Kāvya Navasāhasāṅkacharita*. It describes in eighteen cantos the life and valour of king Sindhurāja Mavasāhasāṅka of Malwa. The author does not aim at history as is obvious from the fact that the work primarily deals with the mythical event of the winning of the Nāga princess Śaśiprabhā, by Sindhurāja. However, this work is of some interest as it gives the history of Sindhurāja's predecessors.

Muñja's nephew *Mahārājādhirāja Kavirāja Śishṭaśiromaṇi Dhāreśvara* Śrī Bhojadeva, was the first and foremost man of great learning—a versatile scholar, a polymath indeed, for he has been credited with works in almost every branch of knowledge. According to Ājaḍa, who wrote a commentary named *Padakaprakāśa* on Bhoja's *Sarasvatīkanṭhābharaṇa*[1], Bhoja wrote eighty-four works giving them names with his own titles or *birudas*. The *Prabhāvakacharita* refers to Bhoja's works in several branches of learning.[2]

Bhoja wrote on poetics, grammar, medicine, astrology and Yoga. His *Sarasvatīkanṭhābharaṇa*[3] is a voluminous work, but is more or less a compilation. It quotes profusely from Daṇḍin's *Kāvyādarśa*, and many other works, like *Dhvanyāloka*, *Agnipurāṇa* and *Avaloka* of Dhanika.[4] The *Śṛiṅgāraprakāśa* is at once both a treatise on poetics and on Dramaturgy.[5] The *Nāmamālikā* is a work on lexicography and is of the nature of a compilation.

The *Śṛiṅgāramañjarīkathā* has been written in Sanskrit prose with some of the peculiarities of the *Akhyāyikā* form of composition. It follows the same pattern, and resembles in style, the earlier prose romances, like the *Kādambarī*, and the

1. Des. Cat. of Sans. Mass in JBP. Vol. I. Intro., p. 48. Text. p. 37.
2. P. Ch. p. 300 vv. 75-78.
3. Kāvyamālā series, X., 94.
4. Rāmasiṁha and Ājada wrote commentaries on it. Rāmasiṁha's commentary is published along with S.K. in K.M. Series. For Ājada's commentary see Des. cat. of Sans. Mass. in JBP, Vol. I., p. 37, No. 50.
5. RBS, p. 9.

contemporaneous works like the *Tilakamañjarī*. The *Vyavahāramañjarī* is ascribed to Bhojarāja[1] and is referred to by Vimalabodha, a commentator of the *Mahābhārata*.[2]

The *Champūrāmāyaṇa*,[3] also called *Bhojachampū*, is a work divided into *kāṇḍas*; the first five are said to have been written by Bhojadeva, the sixth by Lakshmaṇa, and the seventh by Veṅkaṭādhvarin. The *Avanikumāraśataka*,[4] consisting of two Prakrit poems is engraved on the slabs at Bhojaśālā at Dhāra. Each poem consists of one hundred and nine stanzas in the *Ārya* metre, which are devoted to the tortoise incarnation of Vishṇu.[5] The *Kodaṇḍakāvya* of Bhoja was found engraved on the slabs in Bhojaśālā at Dhāra.[6]

The *Rājamārtaṇḍa* of Bhoja is a commentary on Pātañjala *Yogaśāstra*. His *Tattvaprakāśa* is one of the simplest and clearest manuals of the sect of Āgamic Śaivas. The object of Tattvaprakāśa[7] is to explain Śaiva Philosophy as found in the Śaivāgamas, mainly describing the categories of *Pati*, *Paśu*, and *pāśa*. His *Bṛihad-Rājamārtaṇḍa* seems to have been a work on *dharmaśāstra*, often quoted by later *dharmaśāstra* writers. Bhoja also seems to have written a book on music and dancing, for he is quoted by Mahārāṇā Kumbha as an authority on *Saṅgīta*, in the latter's work *Saṅgītarāja*.[8]

The *Rājamṛigāṅka* is a work on medicine. Bhoja wrote a book with the same title on astronomy in 1042 A.D.[9] The *Śālihotra* of Bhoja is an interesting book, giving information about horses, their diseases and the remedies.[10] His *Bhujabalabhīma* is a work on astrological matters. The *Vidvajjana Vallabha* is a work on *praśnajñāna* (science based on the prediction of

1. SILH, Vol. I, pp. 212 ff.
2. ABORI, XVIII, p. 194.
3. H. V. Trivedi doubts the identity of the writer with the Paramāra ruler Bhoja and also states that it is divided into six, and not seven, *Kāṇḍas*.
4. EI, VIII, pp. 241 ff.
5. Pischel doubts the authorship.
6. ASI, 1934-35, p. 60.
7. Published by T.S.S. and is translated by E. P. Javier, IA, LIV (1925), pp. 154 ff.
8. Vol. I, p. 6.
9. H. Dh I, p. 279.
10. Edited by E. D Kulkarni, Poona, 1953.

dreams), and is ascribed to Bhoja, who is represented as a powerful sovereign.[1]

The *Samarāṅgaṇasūtradhāra* of Bhoja is a voluminous treatise dealing with technical subjects like town-planning, house-architecture and sculptural subjects. His *Yuktikalpataru* deals mainly with architecture, arts and crafts. There are also references to *dūta*, *kosha*, *army*, alliance, town-planning and boats.

Bhoja tried to popularise almost all branches of knowledge and to systematise and simplify them. It seems that most of the works attributed to him, were written under his supervision by his court poets, because, as a ruler, he had little time to write. It is possible that some works were written in his name after his death, by those desiring to gain popularity.

Being a scholarly inclined, Bhoja was a patron of scholars. Pandita Chittapa, an inhabitant of the Bhilsa area, seems to have been a court poet of king Bhoja, and the latter perhaps conferred upon him the title of *Mahākavichakravartin.* He is the author of the *Khaṇḍakāvya*, in praise of the sun-god, inscribed on a stone at Bhāillasvāmin or Bhilsa.[2] This record which is written in the *Anushṭubh* metre, originally had twenty three stanzas. A number of stanzas of a poet named Chittapa are found in the Sanskrit anthologies and some other works.

It is known that king Bhoja of Dhāra showed his appreciation for the work named *Śyāmalādaṇḍaka*, by granting a hundred *agrahāras* in A.D. 1001 to its author, Purāntaka, son of Mahādeva, a worshipper in the temple of Mahākāli.[3] This work is in a peculiar variety of prose called Daṇḍaka which has a fixed melody.

Uvaṭa, the son of Vajraṭa of Anandapura, was a great Vedic scholar. He wrote the *Mantrabhāshya* in Avanti during the reign of Bhoja.[4] AUFRECHT ascribes the following works

1. Bh. Rep. on S. for Sans. Mss. 1882-83, p. 35.
2. EI, XXX, p. 251.
3. See Andhra Patrika, Annual Number (1917-18), p. 224 quoted by Krishnamachariar, HCSL, p. 492 and n. 1.
4. Bh. Rep. on Sans. Mss. 1882-83, App. II A, p. 191.

to Uvaṭa. (1) *Ṛigveda-prātiśākhya-bhāshya* or *Prāsādabhāshya* (2) *Mātrimodaka-Vājasaneyi Prātiśākhya-bhāshya* (3) *Vājasaneyi saṁhitā-bhāshya* or *Mantrabhāshya* (4) *Vedārtha-dīpikāsarvānu-kramabhāshya*.[1]

Jaina scholars also made remarkable contributions to the different branches of learning during the reign of Bhoja. Prabhāchandra was one of the leading literary figures under Bhoja I and Jayasiṁha I.[2] He wrote the *Prameyakamalamār-taṇḍa*, a work on Jaina Philosophy, during the reign of Bhoja. The *Nyāyakumudachandra*, *Ārādhanā-gadya-kathākośa*, *Samā-dhitantraṭīkā* and a commentary on *Mahāpurāṇa* of Pushpa-danta, were written during the reign of Jayasimha. Besides, he is the author of the *Pravachana-saroja-bhāskara*, *Pañchā-stikāya-pradīpa*, *Ātmānuśāsanatilaka*, *Kriyākalāpaṭīkā*, *Ratna-karaṇḍaśrāvakāchāra ṭīkā*, *Bṛihatsvayambhū stotra ṭīkā*, *Śabdāṁ-bhoja bhāskara*, *Tatvārtha-vṛitti-pada-vivaraṇa and Pratikramaṇa-pāṭhaṭīkā*.[3]

Vīra wrote the *Jambusvāmīcharita* in 1019 A.D. in Mālavā-deśa during the reign of Bhoja. His father, Devadatta, came from Guṇḍa Kheḍa and was the author of *Varaṅgacharita* and *Ambādevīrāsa*.[4] Śrīchandra is credited with the writing of the *Parāṇasāra*, *Mahāpurāṇa Tippana*, and a commentary on *Padmacharita* of Ravisenāchārya. Śrīchandra of Lālabāgaḍa Saṁgha, and of Balātkāragaṇa, a pupil of Śrīnandi, was a court poet of king Bhoja I. He is credited with writing the *Purā-ṇasāra* and *Mahāpurāṇa Tippana*, in V.S. 1080, and a commen-tary on *Padmacharita* of Ravisenāchārya in V.S. 1087. Nemi-chandra wrote the *Dravyasaṁgraha Ṭīkā* during the reign of Bhojadeva, at Āśramanagara, when Śrīpāla was *Māṇḍalika*. It is a brief exposition of Jaina philosophy in fifty-eight stanzas.[5]

1. Cata., p. 51; Peterson's 4th Report, Intro., p. 17.
2. RKJBKGS, p. 45.
3. Ibiḍ, pp. 101, 103, 145, 53, 21, 24, 82, 134, 192, 127, 216 and 434. See also JSI, p. 221.
4. AJGPS, No. 6.
5. *Sulabhajainagranthamālā*.

Nayanandi, a pupil of Māṇikyanandi of the Kundakunda line, wrote the *Sudarśana-Charita* while staying in the Jinavaravihāra at Dhāra in V.S. 1110=1043 A.D.[1] He narrates in twelve *sandhis* the life of a Jain hero. It is a Prakrit work in which the poet has made use of various *Chhandas* viz. *dohā*, *gāthā*, *dupadī*, *chaupadī*, etc.[2] Another work of his is the *Sakala-vihi-vihāna*. An apabhraṁśa work called *Ārādhanā* is also ascribed to Nayanandi.[3]

Śrutakīrti seems to have lived in the earlier period of Bhoja's reign. The *Kathākośa* mentions Śrutakīrti, the spiritual predecessor of Śrīchandra, who was honoured by kings Bhoja I and Gāṅgeyadeva.[4]

Śrī Sūtradhāra Malla was the son of Mauka, who was a favourite of king Bhānu of the dynasty of Srī Muñja and Bhoja. This Bhānu has been identified with king Udayāditya of the Paramāra dynasty, but this view does not seem to be correct.[5] He is the author of the *Pramāṇamañjarī*, which discusses the architecture of the houses of the common people.

The next poet king among the Paramāras was the '*Sukavibandhu*' king, Naravarman. The famous Nagpura *Praśasti*, which is a composition of this prince, shows that its composer was well-versed in rhetorics and possessed a fine imagination. The composition of the *Sarpabandha* inscription at Ujjain, Dhar and Una, is also attributed to Naravarman. Naravarman has displayed his mastery in the use of allegories, similes and other poetic embellishments, which go to make good *Kāvya*.

Jinavallabha, a contemporary of king Naravarman, lived at Chitrakūṭa. Once, two *Dākshiṇīya Paṇditas* came to the court of king Naravarman and put before the court *paṇditas* a *samasyā* (literary riddle) कण्ठे कुठारः कमठे ठकारः *Kaṇṭhe Kuṭhāraḥ Kamaṭhe ṭhakāraḥ*.[6] None of the scholars of Dhāra could solve

1. *Anekānta*, 1956, p. 98.
2 Ibid.
3. Cata. of Sans. Mss. in JBP, p. 61.
4 AJGPS, No. 7.
5. Bhāratīya Vidyā, XIX (1959), p. 31.
6. SJS. No. 42, p. 13.

the riddle of the South Indian scholars, except Jinavallabha. Jinavallabha himself left behind much literature. His chief works are the *Sūkshmārtha Siddhāntavichāra Sāra Shaḍaśīti Sārdhaśataka*, *Piṇḍaviśuddhi*, *Paushadhavidhi*, *Pratikramaṇa-samāchārī*, *Dharmaśikshā*, *Dvādaśakulaka Praśnottaraśataka* and *Śriṅgāraśataka*.

Some other contemporary Jaina scholars of Naravarman's reign are Samudraghosha, Vijayasiṁha Sūri and Ratnasūri. Samudraghosha, a pupil of Chandraprabha of Chandragachchha, answered the questions of king Naravarman and entertained the latter by his knowledge. Vijayasiṁhasūri was a pupil of Samudraghosha. Vijayasiṁhasūri was Samudraghosha's pupil, and wrote a commentary on *Upadeśamālāvṛitti*. Ratnasūri wrote *Amāsvāmicharita* at the request of Naravarman's Minister, Yaśodhavala, and his son. He was praised by Naravarman's courtiers for having defeated Vidyāśiva at Ujjain, in front of the image of Mahākāla.[1]

The Paramāra rulers Vindhyavarman and Arjunavarman also patronised several scholars. Bilhaṇa was the minister of peace and war of kings Vindhyavarman, Arjunavarman and Devapāla. He was a man of great learning and is called a poet of poets by Āśādhara.[2] The fragmentary Mandu inscription composed by Bilhaṇa contains a highly poetic description of the God Vishṇu in his various incarnations.[3] Another poet patronized by king Vindhyavarman was *kavi* Sulhaṇa, who lived at the king's court of Mandu. His only known work so far, is a commentary of Kedāra's *Vṛittaratnākara*, composed in V.S. 1226=1190 A.D.[4]

The Paramāra ruler Arjunavarman was himself a poet, whose inscriptions state that he was the repository of poetry and song, and relieved Sarasvatī of her book and lute.[5] His *Rasikamañjarī* is a very good commentary on the *Amaruśataka*.[6]

1. M.D. Desai; *Jaina Sāhitya no Ītihāsa*, p. 239.
2. ABORI, XI, p. 53.
3. Ibid, pp. 49-51.
4. BUJ, Vol. XX, pt. II.
5. JAOS, VII, p. 26.
6. EI, VIII, pp. 96.

Madana, on account of his great learning and poetic talent, is known as *Bālasarasvatī*, was the preceptor (*rājaguru*) of king Arjunavarman. His most famous *nāṭikā* is called *Pārijātamañjarī*[1] which originally consisted of four acts. Of these two have been discovered at Dhāra. The hero of the play is king Arjuna, and the heroine, his wife Pārijātamañjarī or Vijayaśrī.[2] Three inscriptions of king Arjunavarman were composed by *Upādhyāya* Madana.[3] He probably added his royal pupil in the compilation of the commentary on *Amaruśataka*.[4] AUFRECHT assigns the composition of *Bālasarasvatīyam* to Madana.

Āśādhara[5] belonged to the first half of the thirteenth century and was a contemporary of Paramāra kings Vindhyavarman, Subhaṭavarman, Arjunavarman, Devapāla and Jaituṅgideva. Originally, he belonged to Mandalgarh in Mewar, but settled in the town of Nalakachchhapura, which became the centre of his literary activity. He had a profound knowledge of Jainism.

Āśādhara's earliest known work is the *Ratnatrayavidhi Kathā* written in V.S. 1282, during the reign of the Paramāra ruler Devapāla. He wrote it for the wife of Nāgadeva, son of Malha, who was the customs officer. The most well known work of Āśādhara is *Dharmāmṛita*, which is divided into two parts, one dealing with the religion of *Sāgara*, and the other of the *Anāgāras*. Āśādhara himself wrote two commentaries on this work, *Svopajñapañjikā* or *Jñānadīpikā*, and *Bhavyakumāra chandrikā*, composed in V.S. 1300=1243 A.D. He wrote a work on Logic known as Prameyaratnākara. He also composed a small poem known as *Rājamativipralambha*. Besides these, he wrote commentaries on a number of works. His *Nityamahodyota* deals with the ceremonial bathing of the idol of Jina. His *Jinayajñakalpa* was composed in V.S. 1285=1228 A.D., and is commented on by Śubhachandra.

Āśādhara had a number of disciples, among whom Devendra, Viśālakīrti, Vinayachandra and Madanopādhyāya are

1. EI, VIII, p. 96.
2. Ibid, VIII, p. 96.
3. JAOS, VII, p. 25.
4. EI, VIII, p. 87.
5. *Jaina Sāhitya aura Itihāsa*, p. 342.

well-known. Devendra is said to have studied Grammar under Āśādhara; Viśālakīrti attained mastery over *Tarkaśāstra* sitting at his feet; Vinayachandra became well-versed in the doctrine of the Jainas under his careful supervision, and he taught Madana the art of poetry.[1]

The Jaina teacher Devendra, who lived at Ujjain, is mentioned as a pupil of Jagachandra, and a *guru* of Vidyānanda.[2] He is the author of *Karma-grantha* (a treatise in Prakrit *āryā* verse on the Jaina theory of the future influence of arts. His *Siddha-pañchāśikā* contains fifty Prakrit *āryā* verses on the beings who attain spiritual beautification.[3] He is also credited with the composition of *Śrāddha Jinakritya*, *Dharmaratnavṛitti*, *Sudarśana-charita*, *Chaityavandana-bhāshya*, *Siri-Usāha-Vaddhamānaprabhṛitistava* and *Siddhadaṇḍika-stava*.

Devendra was succeeded by Vidyānanda in the *Sūri-pada*, and he by Dharmaghosha, who enriched Jaina literature by various works. He died in 1330 A.D.[4]

The poet Dāmodara wrote the *Nemināthacharitra* in V.S. 1287 at the direction of Rāmachandra, son of Pṛithvīdhara and at the persuasion of Nāgadeva, son of Mālha at Salakhaṇapura.[5]

The *Rājaśekhara-charita*, a work believed to have been composed in the first quarter of the eleventh century, mentions the poetesses Kāmalatā, Kanakāvalī, Sunandā and Vimalāṅgī.[6] Of these, the last three are said to have hailed from Malwa.

1. Bh. R on S for Sans. Mss. (1883-84), p. 104.
2. Peterson's 4th Report, p. 57.
3. Ibid, p. 57 IA, XI, p. 255.
4. IA, XI, p. 255.
5. *Guru Gapāladāsa Varaiyā Smriti Grantha*, p. 551.
6. Great Women of India, p. 293.

CHAPTER—XV

SOCIAL CONDITIONS

This period is remarkable for changes in the social framework. The new religious movements considerably influenced society. The great prosperity under the Paramāras increased the comforts and luxuries of the people. Society gradually became more conservative in its beliefs and practices. The advent of Islam also had an indirect influence.

CASTE SYSTEM :—

During this period, old castes and *gotras* disappeared, and their place was taken by new ones whose origin is still not definitely known. Caste became hereditary, being determined by birth. The people generally followed professions according to their castes.

The population mainly consisted of Brāhmaṇas, Kshatriyas, Vaiśyas and Śūdras. The Brāhmaṇas occupied a position of great supremacy. The kings offered special privileges to them, and granted lands for their maintenance. During this period, a large number of Brāhmaṇa families migrated to Malwa from such places as *Ānandapura*, *Ahicchatrapur*,[1] *Chiñchāsthāna*,[2] *Sthāneśvara*, *Visālagrāma*, *Bādāvim* in Belluvalla of Karṇāṭa,[3] *Adriyalavidāvarī*[4] *Muktāvāsasthāna*,[5] *Takāristhāna*, *Śriṅgapura* in Madhyadeśa,[6] *Mahāvanasthāna*,

1. POC, 1924, p. 303; IA., VI, p. 52.
2. EI, XI, p. 812.
3. IA, VI, p. 55, XXXI, p. 365.
4. Ibid, XIX, pp. 350-51.
5. JASB, V, p. 379.
6. PRAS, WC, 1921, p. 54.

Tripuristhāna, *Akolāsthāna*, *Mathurāsthāna*, *Diṇḍvāṇakasthāna*, *Sarasvatīsthāna*, *Hastināpura*,[1] *Mutāvathū*.

The Brāhmaṇas continued to be mentioned along with their gotras,[2] such as *Chapalīya*, *Gopāli*, *Vasishṭha*, *Kauśika*, *Agastya*. *Bharadvāja*, *Kātyāyana*, *Kāśyapa*, *Parāvasu*, *Bhārgava*, *Gautama*, *Vatsa*, *Mudgala*, *Śāṇḍilya*, *Dhaumya*, *Harita-Kutsa*, *Mārkaṇḍeya*, *Kautsa*, *Parāśara* and *Audalya*.

Sometimes, the *Pravaras* of the Brāhmaṇas are found mentioned together with the *gotras*. The Betma plates of Bhojadeva[3] dated V.S. 1076 record that Bhojadeva granted a Brāhmaṇa, named Pandita Delha of the Kauśika-gotra, with three *Pravaras*, *Aghamarshaṇa*, *Viśvāmitra* and *Kauśika*. In the Kadambapadraka grant of Naravarman[4], dated V.S. 1167, the three *Pravaras* of a Brāhmaṇa named *Dviveda* Āśādhara, of Kātyāyana *gotra*, have been mentioned, namely, *Kātyāyana*, *Kapila* and *Viśvāmitra*. Mahākumāra Lakshmīvarmadeva in 1191 A.D., granted villages to Dhanapāla, a Karṇāṭa Brāhmaṇa from the south, who belonged to the Bhāradvāja *gotra*, and had the three *Pravaras*, *Bhāradvāja*, *Āṅgirasa* and *Bārhaspatya*.[5]

In the Modasa plate[6] of the time of Paramāra Bhoja, dated V.S. 1067, a Brāhmaṇa named Derdda, has been described as Vallotakīya and Chāturjātakīya, of the Upananya *gotra*. It is not found in early Indian literature, and it is difficult to determine whether it is a mistake for Aupamanyava. The expression *Vallotakīya* in the Brāhmaṇā's description, suggests that he was either, the inhabitant of a locality called Vallotaka, or that he belonged to a community of Brāhmaṇas known as Vallotaka.

There is also mention of the *Śākhās*[7] of the Brāhmaṇas in the Paramāra inscriptions, such as *Vājimādhyaṁdina*, *Śāṅkhāyana*,

1. EI, IX, pp. 115-16
2. Ibid, IX. pp. 115-16; JASB, XI, p. 221; JBBRAS, XXIII, p. 76; IA XLV, p. 78.
3. EI, XVIII.
4. Ibid, XX.
5. IA, XIX, p. 1.
6. EI, XXXIII.
7. Ibid, IX, pp, 115-16; Ibid XXIV, p. 256.

Āśvalāyana, *Rāṇāyani*, *Mādhyaṁdina*, *Kaṭha*, *Kauthuma* and *Vājasaneya*.

Sometimes the Brāhmaṇas bore titles of distinction, indicating their rank and the extent of their education, such as *Śrotriya*, *Śukla*, *Dikshita*, *Triveda*, *Pāṭhaka*, *Āvasathika*, *Paṇḍita*, *Agnihotrin*, *Rājan*, *Upādhyāya*, *Ṭhakkura*, *Mahārāja-Paṇḍita*, *Chaturveda*, *Dviveda* and *Yājñika*.[1] These prefixes were not hereditary or stereotyped during this period. The donee, his father and grand-father, do not have the same distinctive designation. In the Māndhātā plates[2] of Paramāra Jayasiṁha Jayavarman, dated V.S. 1331, *Avasthin* Vidyādharaśarman is stated to be the son of *Chaturvedin* Kamaḷādharaśarman, and the father of *Dikshit* Padmanābhaśarman and *Chaturvedin* Mādhavaśarman. The donees of the Bhopal grant[3] of M.K. Harischandra, include *Avasthika* Śrīdhara, who was the son of Agnihotrin; Bhāradvāja; Paṇḍita Madhusūdana, the son of *Avasthika* Delha; Paṇḍita Somadeva, who was a son of *Avasthika* Delha; and Ṭhakkura Vishṇu, who was the son of Paṇḍita Soṇḍala.

Some sub-castes were territorial in origin, such as the Nāgara Brāhmaṇas, Dākshiṇāṭya Brāhmaṇas and Śrīmālī Brāhmaṇas. The Ujjain stone inscription[4] of V.S. 1195, refers to Mahattama Śrī Dādāka of the Nāgara caste, who was appointed Governor of Ujjain by the Chālukya ruler, Jayasiṁha Siddharāja of Gujarata. Bhāṭuka, who composed the Arthuṇā inscription, was of the Valla family.[5]

With the advent of Muslim rule in India, the divisions and sub-divisions became more marked. The Brāhmaṇas tried to protect Indian Culture by laying more stress on ceremonial punctiliousness, and purity of birth and blood, than by referring to, and liberalizing, the tenets of Hindu *Dharma*. A Brāhmaṇa who had habitual contact with a Muslim was considered inferior to one who could keep himself aloof.[6]

1. EI, XIX, p. 241.
2. Ibid, XXXII, pp, 140-41.
3. Ibid, XXIV, p. 231.
4. IA. LXI.
5. EI, XXI.
6. Sachau II, pp. 134-35.

Learning (*adhyayana*), teaching (*adhyāpana*), acceptance of gifts (*pratigṛiha*) and conducting of sacrifices, were the special functions of the Brāhmaṇas.[1] A Brāhmaṇa boy was invested with the sacred thread and initiated into studies at the age of five. At the age of sixteen, he generally completed his studies and entered the next stage of his life.[2] The Brāhmaṇas devoted themselves to the study of the Vedas and the *Śāstras* as is indicated by such prefixes as *Dvivedin, Trivedin* and *Chaturvedin.*

The Brāhmaṇas mastered the different systems of Indian philosophy, and participated in literary and philosophic debates at the Royal Courts.[3] Some of them might have become *Sanyāsins*. Some became the heads of Śaiva monasteries, which were popular during this period. A few Brāhmaṇas acted as hereditary priests and *Rājagurus* of the kings. The lesser educated among them earned their livelihood by reciting *Svastivāchanā*, and by conducting temple worship.[4]

Under special circumstances, the Brāhmaṇas are known to have pursued professions which were traditionally meant for other castes. Some became rulers. The Paramāras might have originally been *Vāsishṭhi gotra* Brāhmaṇas. In the *Śṛingāramañjarīkathā*, we read of a Brāhmaṇa who became a king.[5] The Brāhmaṇas acted as *Sandhivigrahakas* and *Dūtakas* under the Paramāras. Mahāpaṇḍita Bilhaṇa was the *Mahasandhivigrahaka* of Vindhyavarman, Arjunavarman, and Devapāla.[6] Ṭhakkura Vishṇu was the *dūtaka* of the Harsola grants of king Sīyaka II.[7] Ṭhakkura Vāmanasvāmin and the Ṭhakkura Purushottama were the *dūtakas* of the Kalvan inscription of Yaśovarman.[8] Some of the Brāhmaṇas were composers[9] and

1. *Atri* S. 13; *Smṛitināma-Samuchchaya*, p. 15, 319.
2. SMK, p. 19.
3. *Tilakamañjarī*, *Prabandhachintāmaṇi* and *Śṛiṅgāramañjarīkathā.*
4. EI, XXXI, pp. 81 ff; IA, XLIII, p. 193.
5. SMK, p. 55.
6. JASB, V, p. 378; JAOS, VII, p. 33; EI, IX, p. 109.
7. EI, XIX, pp. 36 ff.
8. Ibid, pp. 76 ff.
9. Devapāla's Harsauda inscription composed by a Brāhmaṇa. IA, XX, p. 310; Brāhmaṇa Harshadeva composer of the Māndhātā inscription of Jayavarman II (EI, IX, p. 115).

engravers[1] of inscriptions. There were Brāhmaṇas who adopted the professions of the Vaiśyas. From the *Sṛiṅgāramañjarīkathā*,[2] we know that a certain Brāhmaṇa, named Mādhava, returned from *Siṁhaladvīpa* after doing good business.

The Rājapūta clans, such as the Pratīharas, Chauhānas, Paramāras, Chālukyas, Chandelas, Rāshṭrakūṭas, Kalachuris and Guhilas, were included among the Kshatriyas. These Rājapūta clans originated in different ways. Some of them might have descended from foreigners, while others were the descendants of the old tribes. It is also held that they came into existence through inter-caste marriages. From the Mahua inscription[3] of Vatsarāja, it seems that he came from a family of Brāhmaṇa Kshatriya inter-marriage. The common factor was the profession of a warrior, and hence they were called the Kshatriyas.

These Rājapūta clans had no independent *gotras* and *Pravaras*, but adopted those of the Brāhmaṇas. It is held by some scholars that Rājapūtas were originally foreigners, and while converting them to Hinduism the Brāhmaṇa *Purohitas* transmitted their own *gotras* and *Pravaras* to them. The Paramāras have the Vasishṭha gotra. From the Māndhātā plates[4] of Paramāra Jayasiṁha Jayavarman, dated V.S. 1331, it is known that Abhayasiṁha, of the Chahamāna family and Kshatriya community, was of the *Vatsa gotra*, and had the *Bhārgava Chyavana*, *Āpnavad*, *Aurva* and *Jāmadagnya pravaras*.

Some Rājapūtas became rulers and feudatories, while others worked as administrative officers. They joined the armies and fought on the battle-fields. Because of the influence of the teachings of Jainism; some of them gave up fighting and pursued the vocations of the Vaiśyas. Some Rājapūtas are known to have become members of the Osavālas, Śrīmālīs, Bagheravāla and Khaṇḍelavāla castes of the *Vaiśyas*.

1. Bhopal Inscription of Arjunavarman engraved by Pt. Bappaideva JAOS. VII, p. 33.
2. SMK, p, 28.
3. EI, XXXVII.
4. Ibid, XXXII,

Vaiśyas were not a homogenous group. They followed different professions and were divided into many castes and sub-castes. They were more conscious of their sub-castes than as their grouping as Vaiśyas. Trade and money lending were their main professions, and because of the influence of Jainism, they gradually gave up agriculture and cattle rearing, as these professions involved *hiṁsā*. These two professions in time passed into the hands of the Śūdras.

As a result of the development of trade and commerce, the *Vaiśyas* became rich men, and their status in society was determined by their wealth. The literature of this period reflects the general prosperity of the *Vaiśya* community. They contributed liberally to charitable and literary activities. Some of them built beautiful temples and installed images in them. They also patronized scholars.

Sometimes the *vaiśyas* took up the other occupations. They were influential in the royal courts. Some of them were appointed officers. The merchant guilds played an important part in town administration. They also acted as the trustees of the temples.

Some of the *Vaiśya* castes are found mentioned in the inscriptions. The Indragadha inscription of V.S. 767 records endowments made to Guheśvara, which appears to be the name of the deity enshrined in the temple, by Deullikā, Takshullikā and Bhoginikā, daughters of one Kumāra of the Prāgvāṭa caste.[1] From the Bhilsa inscription[2] of V.S. 935 (878 A.D.), it is known that Haṭiāka, a merchant of the *Poravāla* caste, made a permanent endowment to the Sun temple of Bhāillasvāmin at Bhilsa. These inscriptions prove that the people of the Prāgvāṭa or Poravāla caste, were originally followers of Brāhmanical religion, but later on, they were converted to Jainism. The *Lāra Baniās* were the inhabitants of Dhar. A person of this caste dedicated an image to Devī in V.S. 1138 (1081 A. D.).[3] Chillaṇa, who installed two Jaina images during the reign of Naravarman in V.S. 1157

1. EI, XXXII.
2. Ibid, XXX, p. 212.
3. ABORI, 1922-23.

at Bhojapura, belonged to the Vemaka family.[1] The inscription of V.S. 1206 on Jaina statues at Gudar, contains the name of the *Vabakanchuka* race.[2] Bhūshaṇa, who built the Jaina temple at Arthūṇā, was of the Nāgara family.[3]

Besides, there are some other castes of the Vaiśyas known from inscriptions, and some of them originally came from outside. The Khaṇḍelavāla caste has been mentioned in the inscriptions of V.S. 1216[4] and V.S. 1308.[5] The Poravāla Śrāvakas[6] are known to have performed the installation ceremony at Vardhanāpura, now known as Badnawar, in V.S. 1308. The Bagheravāla Śrāvakas[7] were also associated with this installation ceremony of images. These Khaṇḍelavāla, Bagheravāla and Poravāla castes, originated in Rajasthan in about the eighth century A.D., from Khaṇḍelā, Bagherā and Prāgvāṭa respectively, but in course of time, some of the Śrāvakas migrated even to Malwa. The Varkaṭa caste has been found mentioned in the inscription of V.S. 1231.[8]

The Śūdras consisted of agriculturists and members of many craftsmen's guilds. There are references to goldsmiths (*Svarṇakāras*), architects (*Sthapatīs*), carpenters, engravers *Sūtradhāras*), oilmen (*telīs*), potters, garland makers, sugar boilers, *rathakāras* and *rūpakāras*. In literary works, we also find mention of oilmen (*tailapas*), medical men (*Vaidyas*), agriculturists (*Kṛishakajanas*), Smiths (*lohakāras*), fortune tellers (*Śakunikas*) and persons proficient in magic (*Indra-jālika-vidyās)*, and mesmerists (*Mohana-vidyās*).

Though the Śūdras suffered from religious disabilities, their position seems to have improved from that of earlier times. As agriculture, cattle rearing, and handicrafts, were in their hands, they became prosperous. Their economic position

1. EI, XXXV.
2. ARADGS, 1929-30.
3. EI, XXI.
4. See appendix No. 6 for the text.
5. ,, ,, No. 7 ,, ,, ,,
6. ,, ,, No. 8 ,, ,, ,, inscriptions.
7. ,, ,, No. 2 ,, ,, ,, ,,
8. ,, ,, No. 9 ,, ,, ,, ,,

changed their social status. The new religious movements in Jainism and Śaivism brought about a change in the attitude of the people towards the Śūdras. Many of the Tantric teachers were themselves Śūdras.[1] This new change is reflected by the commentator Medhātithi, when he concedes to the Śūdras the right to private property, freedom from waiting on the three higher *Varṇas*, and he allows them to perform *Saṁskāras*, though without Vedic *mantras*.[2] These people were organized into guilds which generally looked after the social matters.

There were other castes known during this period whose exact position in society is uncertain. One such caste is that of the *Kāyasthas*.[3] They rose to high positions in the different branches of the administration. They were associated with the judiciary, general administration, the treasury, and other departments of the State. Some of the Paramāra grants were drafted by *Kāyasthas*[4]. From the Narwar inscription[5] it is known that Bhuvanapāla, the founder of a *Māthura* family of the *Kāyasthas*, was the minister of the Paramāra ruler Bhoja. The Victoria Hall Udaipur inscription[6] of the Paramāras of Malwa, refers to one Rudrāditya, and his grandson Mahīpati, as *Kāyastha-Kumāras* or prominent *Kāyasthas*. The *Kāyasthas* have been mentioned in the *Śṛiṅgāramañjarīkathā*, the *Kāyasthas* were also divided into sub-castes. One of them is *Māthura Kāyastha*, which is generally mentioned in the inscriptions. The Udaipur inscription[7] records the family of the *Nemakas*, who built some building.

1. KJN, Intro., p, 17.
2. Medhātithi's Comm. on MS III, 156 and VIII, 425.
3. There are three different versions tracing the descent of the Kāyasthas. In the first version, the Kāyastha family derived its descent from the sage Kaśyapa, through his son Kuśa. EI, XXVIII, 100 f. The second view is that they were Kshatriyas, EI, XXV, 276 f. The third view is that they were Śūdras. ARSIE, 1935-36, 229.
4. *Kāyastha* Guṇadhara drafted the Harsola inscription of Śīyak II (EI, XIX, p. 284); The Tilakawada inscription of Bhojadeva was written by Vallabha *Kāyastha* and the Charter of Maṇḍalika of Vāgaḍa was composed by a *Kāyastha* (EI, XXI, p. 50).
5. A.S.
6. Ibid, 1936-37, p. 124.
7. Ibid.

The lowest castes were known as *antyas* or *antyajātis*, who performed functions either dirty by nature, or involving cruelty to creatures. They may be divided into two categories. Firstly *Bhillas*, *Pulindas*, *Kirātas* and *Śavaras* who lived in the Vindhya hills and forests. These men lived by hunting, and plundered caravans passing through their forests. They dressed in tiger skin, drank spirits distilled from wine, and offered human victims before their goddess.

To the second category belonged those *antyajas* whose professions were : (1) Jugglar (2) Basket and shield maker (3) Sailor (4) Fisherman (5) Hunter (6) Weaver (7) Fuller (8) Shoe maker (9) Hāḍi (10) Domb (11) Chāṇḍāla and (12) Badhatan. These *Antyajas* had developed a class hierarchy, some being more depressed and despised than others. The weaver, sailor, jugglar and basket maker seem to have been higher in status. The most wretched among them were the chāṇḍālas. Not only is their touch included in a list of acts requiring purification of the body, but penances are prescribed for their approach within a certain distance, for the sight of, or for conversing with them.

POSITION OF WOMEN :—Generally, women occupied a position of supremacy in society. Many land-grants of the Paramāra kings were made in order to increase the spiritual welfare of the mother and father of the donor. King Yaśovarmadeva made a land-grant on the occasion of the annual funeral ceremony of his mother, Momalādevī, in 1135 A.D. We have no evidence of the Paramāra queens acting as regents. They lived in the inner apartment, or *antaḥpura*, which was guarded by eunuchs.

The girls of the higher classes had proper facilities for education, which included the study of religious books, and the arts of dancing, music and painting. Some of the ladies rose to high position by their abilities. Yogeśvarī was the head of a Śaiva Monastery at Ujjain. The poetess Sītā was well-known. Paṇḍita Harasukhā, the mother of Tannā Teli was the engraver of the Jhalarapatan inscription of the time of king Udayāditya.

There was a class of courtesans whose position seems to

have been superior to that of the common women. They were the privileged women in society whose company was sought by kings and wealthy merchants. In the *Śṛiṅgāramañjarīkathā* of Bhoja, a courtesan has been described as one who was accomplished in sixty-four arts, which included music, painting and dancing. She also took keen interest in intellectual pursuits such as *Pustaka-vāchana* and *Kāvya-Samasyā-pūrti*. She was clever in the science of erotics.

Though women were respected in society, the birth of a son was preferred, and was celebrated with great rejoicings. Parents worshipped gods to have a son. The birth of a daughter was regarded as a burden, which increased when the girl attained a marriageable age.

A woman occupied a position inferior to that of a male in the family. She was considered as one difficult to please, as one having bad intentions, fickle by nature, having to be protected, as one who became detached very easily and one who cherished love for the low-born. Her duties were confined to household work and looking after the children. Women could not inherit property, but they could possess *śtrīdhana*. The property of those without heir passed to the state.

MARRIAGE :—No direct evidence is available, but Somadeva puts the marriageable age of a girl at twelve. The husband's caste, *gotra*, *pravara*, learning, age, character and wealth, were the main deciding factors of the marriage.[1] This usually took place at the brides father's house. Large sums of money, gifts and jewellery, were given to the bride at the time of her marriage.

Sagotra and *Sapravara* marriages were not permitted. Marriages between people belonging to different religious sects were not favoured. *Anuloma* marriages became rare. Love marriages were not unknown during this period.[2] If the testimony of the *Dvyāśrayamahākāvya* and the *Pṛithvīrāja-vijayamahākāvya* be regarded as valid, *Svayaṁvara* marriages might also have been prevalent.[3] But society in general,

1. SN, III, 165-8.
2. Sindhurāja's marriage with the Nāga princess Śaśiprabhā.
3. DV. VII; E. Ch. D, pp. 124-26.

recognized the right of the father to find a suitable husband for his daughter. Even in the *Tilakamañjarī*, the couple, though in love with each other, received the parents sanction before marrying.[1]

The Paramāra rulers of Malwa established diplomatic relations with the contemporary ruling dynasties by matrimonial alliances. Such alliances were recommended to end *vigraha* by Dhanapāla.[2] Udayāditya's daughter was married to the Guhila king. Jagadeva gave his daughter in marriage to a Varman king of East Bengal. Arjunavarman's first queen was a daughter of a Kuntala king, and his second was a Chālukya princess. The Gaṅga king, Narasiṁha I (1253-1286 A.D.) married Sītādevī, the daughter of a Mālava king.[3] A Gujarat prince married a princess of the Paramāra dynasty.[4]

The marriage bond was considered to be indissoluble. The wife was dutiful towards her husband, and had to regard him not only as her master, but also as a deity. Under such circumstances, the Satī system became popular in the early medieval period as proved even from the Satī stones, and widow remarriages were discouraged. The widow who did not commit Satī, led a life of simplicity under the care of their male relatives.

Polygamy was an accepted practice. The Paramāra ruler Sindhurāja probably married Śaśiprabhā, when he was already the father of Bhoja. King Arjunavarman married a Gujarat princess as well as a Kuntala princess. The king's example must have been followed by the nobles and the rich. They may have kept harems. In the *Tilakamañjarī*, we read of Slave girls burning themselves on the funeral pyre when they heard of the death of their master.[5]

DRESS, ORNAMENTS AND COSMETICS :—

The *Tilakamañjarī*, *Śṛiṅgāramañjarīkathā* and a recently

1. TM, pp. 103-04.
2. Ibid, p. 243.
3. EI, V, Appendix p. 53, No. 362.
4. An. Rep. My. Arch. Dep. 1929.
5. TM, p. 156.

published inscription from Dhāra,[1] supply useful information about dress, ornaments and cosmetics. The usual dress consisted of *adhovasana* and *uttarīya* i.e. garments to cover the lower and the upper parts of the body respectively. Men also wore *pugrees*[2] on their heads. Women wore *Sārīs*, *cholīs*, *ghāghrās* and *pahiraṇa*[3]. They also wore a *kūrpāsaka* in winter.[4] The *kamyyūcholī*, which only partly covered the breasts, seems to have been the fashion of the day.[5] They also wore woollen petticoats in winter.[6] Wealthy women wore rich apparel.[7] Rich men used silk for their dress. China silk was very popular.[8] White coloured garments were popular, and they were put on all auspicious occasions.

The women had long hair, braided or knotted, which was always decorated with seasonal flowers.[9]

Taḍanka,[10] *dantapatra*,[11] *kamyyādi*,[12] *kuṇḍala*,[13] *śravaṇapāśa*[14] and *karaṇapūra*[15] were the ear ornaments. Sometimes the leaves of palm trees were used to adorn the ears.[16] There were various types of necklaces, viz. *Jāla-kaṇṭhī* (netted necklace),[17] the plain necklace,[18] *ekāvalī* (single string) necklace,[19] the *son-jāla* (golden net),[20] and *chañchal hāra* whose pendant

1. Bharatiya Vidyā, XVII, 1957, pp. 130-46; Dhirendra Verma Comm. Vol.; pp. 21ff.
2. TM, p. 130.
3. PWMI, 11, 38, 52.
4. TM, p. 136.
5. PWMI, II, 38,52.
6. SMK, p. 73.
7. Ibid, p. 74.
8. TM, p. 130.
9. SMK, p. 75; Description of *Śṛiṅgāramañjarī*, PMMI 11, 59, 61, 87.
10. Ibid.
11. TM, p. 301.
12. PWMI, 1.47.
13. Ibid, TM. p. 130.
14. Ibid, p. 226.
15. Ibid.
16. PWMI, I, 68.
17. Ibid, 11.5 and 48.
18. Ibid, 1.18, TM. p. 301.
19 PWMI, 1 111.
20. Ibid.

touched the *nābhi*,[1] and bejewelled necklaces and flower garlands adorned the necks of the Malwa women. The poor wore yarn necklaces only, and consequently there is reference to *gaṇṭhiā tagāu* (knotted thread), three stringed cotton yarn, and palm cotton yarn necklaces.[2] *Valaya*, *Kaṅkaṇa*, *Keyūra*,[3] *Chamdahai*,[4] *Rithās*[5] and gold bangles,[6] were worn on arms and hands. Dancer's feet resounded with the twinkling of the *nūpuras*.[7] Rings, studded with precious stones, were worn on the fingers.[8] *Padmarāgamaṇijhurmikā* (a foot ornament) was also worn.[9] *Māṇikyavalaya* was a thigh ornament.[10]

Women applied fragrant sandal, camphor, *kumkum* and *rodha* pollen to their bosoms.[11] Their palms and feet were painted with *alaktaka* dye.[12] Camphor powder (*karpūra chūrṇa*) was used in abundance.[13] Women applied a red round *ṭīkā* on their foreheads.[14] They applied collyrium to their eyes,[15] and sometimes dyed their hair.[16] Betel leaves were chewed for reddening the lips and the teeth.[17] Scented oils and perfumes were used by both men and women.[18]

FOOD AND DRINK :—Wheat, rice, barley, *til*, *vrihi*, *jowar*, *kodrava*, *mudga*, millet, oil, ghee, honey and meat, are among the food articles mentioned in the Paramāra inscriptions. Among the fruits, mango was popular. Because of the in-

1. TM, p. 130.
2. PWMI II 72-73, 74, 76,
3. Ibid.
4. PWMI 1, 119.
5. Ibid, 1.22.
6. Ibid, 1.119.
7. Ibid, 1.39; TM, p. 226.
8. Ibid, p. 130.
9. Ibid, p. 226.
10. Ibid.
11. TM.
12. Ibid, p. 47; PWMI, p. 127.
13. TM, p. 130.
14. PWMI, 11. 94, 45, 65, 66.
15. Ibid, 11.31, 46, 90.
16. Ibid, 1.89.
17. Ibid, 1.108.
18. Description of Aśokavatī in the Ninth Tale of the SMK.

fluence of Jainism, people began to incline towards vegetarianism. There is a solitary instance of a Brāhmaṇa eating meat in Bhojadeva's[1] inscription but in the Kshatriya's diet, meat formed an important element. Among vegetarians, milk, milk products, and sweets, were popular. If we are to believe the *Śṛiṅgāramañjarīkathā*, drinking was prevalent among the Brāhmaṇas and the women. Both men and women were fond of chewing betel leaves with a piece of camphor.[2]

FASTS AND FESTIVALS :—*Devoṭṭhāna*, *Ekādaśī* and *Śivarātri* are the only fasts referred to in the inscriptions. The occurrence of either a lunar or a solar eclipse was the occasion for making gifts to the Brāhmaṇas as we know from inscriptions.

A number of festivals were celebrated by the people and they have been mentioned in literary works. In the *Sṛiṅgāramañjarīkathā*, there is reference to the *Yātrā mahotsava* of Madana (*Madanotsava*), which fell on the fourteenth day of the bright half of *Chaitra*, and was celebrated with dancing, songs, and merry making.[3] Another important festival was *Vasantotsava*,[4] also known as *Chaityaparva*, which fell on the full-moon day of the month of *Chaitra*. Sachau describes it as the festival for women, who put on their ornaments and demanded presents from their husbands.[5] On this occasion, the drama *Pārijātamañjarī*, was staged at Dhāra[6] and the king was expected to participate in the festival.[7] Another well-known festival was the *Damanaka-Chaturdaśī* or *Damanakaparva*, which fell on the fourteenth Śukla of *Chaitra* and is referred to in the Sheragarh inscription of Udayāditya.[8] On this festival, a branch of Damana tree was offered to Śiva or Vishṇu, with a prayer to him and to Madana for the happi-

1. IHQ, VIII, p. 311.
2. TM, p. 130.
3. SEHNI, p. 275.
4. TM, p. 16.
5. *Tahakīka-ai-hinda,*
6. EI, VIII, p. 101.
7. TM, p. 16.
8. EI, XXIII, p. 134.

ness and felicity of the whole household.[1] The Bhopal plates of Mahākshatrapa Udayavarman refer to *Mahāvaiśākhīparva*, which fell in *Vaiśākha* on Sudi fifteenth.[2]

Another festival referred to in the inscription is (Gaṅgā) *Dashaharaḥ*,[3] which, according to Bhoja, fell on the tenth day of the month of *Jyeṣṭha*.[4] On this occasion, the Ganges is said to have descended to the earth. Those who bathed in the river and gave away gifts, became free from sins.[5] On *Jyeṣṭha Pūrṇimā* the *Sāvitri vrata* was observed, the performance of which, according to Bhoja, saved women from widowhood.[6]

In the month of *Bhādra*, on the eighth day *Kṛishṇajayantī*, was celebrated, that is, the birth day of Lord Kṛishṇa.[7] King Bhoja, like Jīmūtavāhana, declared that no fasts should be observed during the *Rohiṇakshatra*. On the fourth day of the bright half of *Bhādra*, the *Haritālikā* festival occurred, which was sacred to Pārvatī.[8] The eighth day of the light half of *Bhādrapada* was the day of *Indradhvajochchhrāya*, or the raising of the flag staff of Indra,[9] when the moon was in *Śrāvaṇanakshatra*, and the *Visarjana* was to take place at the end of *Bharaṇīnakshatra*.[10] It was the duty of the king to raise the flag staff with due ceremonies. Bhoja has given a pen picture of this festival in his *Rājamārtaṇḍa*.[11]

In the month of *Āśvina*, *navarātra* took place, in which Durgā was worshipped from the seventh to the tenth day of the bright half of *Śukla*. Another festival was *Nirājana*, which was of political significance. According to Bhoja's *Rājamārtaṇḍa*, it was to be celebrated on the eighth day of *Āśvina Śukla*.[12] The

1. *Smṛiti Kaustubha*, pp. 19-23.
2. IA, XVI, p. 254.
3. ABORI, XXII, p. 100.
4. Ibid, XXVI, pp. 335-36.
5. SEHNI, p. 281.
6. ABORI, XXXVI, p. 335.
7. Ibid, p. 323.
8. Ibid, pp. 323-27.
9. Ibid, pp. 323-27.
10. Ibid.
11. Ibid, XXXVI, pp. 323-27.
12. Ibid, XXXVI, p. 328, v. 188.

Yuktikalpataru gives a graphic description of the ceremony, and states that a big ornamental arch of some holy tree was to be erected in the north-east of the capital. Threads smeared with saffron paste were to be tied round the necks of horses.[1]

The *Tilakamañjarī*[2] refers to *Kaumudīmahotsava*, which fell on the full moon day of *Kārttika*. On this occasion, houses and shops were decorated with flowers and flags, and men and women bedecked themselves with garlands and festive clothes. At night, the streets and houses were illuminated with lights. Young men and women were expected to move in all directions, singing, dancing, laughing, and enjoying themselves. The festival was concluded with a grand feast, for which a number of animals were killed.[3] It is stated by Lakshmīdhara, that if a person fails to celebrate the festival according to the rites described above, the king must award him physical punishment.[4]

Bhoja refers to a festival called *Sukharātri*.[5] On this occasion, Lakshmī was worshipped at dusk and lamps were lit on trees, in temples, on roads, cremation grounds, river banks, tops of hills, and also in houses. It seems to be a festival like *Diwali*. The *Prabandhachintāmaṇi*[6] mentions *Diwālī* as being celebrated in Malwa. On the second day of the bright half of the *Kārttika*, the ceremony known as *Bhrātṛidvitīyā* was celebrated.[7] On this occasion, sisters fed their brothers, who in their turn, gave ornaments and clothes to their sisters. Its modern proto-type is *Bhāīdūja*.

The inscriptions of the Paramāra also refer to *Udyānaparva*,[8] *Pāvitraka-parva*,[9] *Bhūtarātriparva*, the ceremony of Saindha-

1. Yukti, pp. 178-79; SEHNI, p. 293.
2. TM, p. 220.
3. SEHNI, p. 376.
4. TM, p. 220.
5. ABORI, XXXVI, p. 329.
6. PC, p. 46.
7. ABORI, XXXVI, p. 329.
8. IA, VI, p. 53.
9. Ibid, XIV, p. 160; JASB, 1914, p. 242.

vadeva[1] and the *Yātrā festival* of god Jagatsvāmin.[2] The *Yātrā* festivals were common among the Jainas too.

There were also other occasions for celebrations. The birth of a child (*Janmotsava*)[3], the naming of a child (*nāmakaraṇa*), his first initiation to study (*Vidyārambha* or *Upanayana*) and weddings, were celebrated with great rejoicings. The anointment of a crown prince, the coronation of a new king, and the victory of the ruling king in the battle-field[4], were occasions of merry making. The consecration ceremony of temples and images was celebrated with pomp and show. Victory in literary discussions provided occasions for celebrations. These festivals and auspicious occasions were accompanied with dancing, singing, eating, sometimes even drinking, and prayers and worship of gods.

MEANS OF AMUSEMENTS :—The various festivals and functions provided ample opportunities to the people for entertainments. There were courtesans who entertained the wealthy people by their charms. There were institutions which afforded pleasure and entertainment to the public. Among them can be enumerated the gambling house (*tiṇṭā*), theatre (*raṅgaśālā*), pleasure house (*krīḍāgāra* or *krīdābhavana*), and temples (*devagṛiha*). Those who loved an out-door life, went out for swimming, hunting and playing. Singing and dancing were also means of entertainment. Parks were places of recreation.

1. IA, VI, p. 153.
2. Bomb. Gaz. I, pt. I, pp. 472-73.
3. TM, pp. 63-64.
4. Bhoja issued his Betma plates on the occasion of *Koṅkaṇavijaya-parva* in 1020 A.D. (EI, XVIII, p. 320) and issued his Banswara grant on the occasion of *Koṅkaṇa vijaya-grahaṇa parva*).

CHAPTER—XVI

ECONOMIC CONDITIONS

Malwa became prosperous during the reign of the Paramāras who established peace and order by their efficient administration. They adopted various measures to increase production. Trade and commerce developed greatly, and industries were well managed.

AGRICULTURE :—Land was irrigated by both natural resources and artificial water works. The ruling chiefs excavated lakes, canals, tanks and wells for the irrigation of land. Vākpati II, or Muñja, built a tank called Muñja-Sāgara. Near Bhopal, Bhoja excavated a large and beautiful lake which appears to have been sixteen or seventeen miles in length, and seven or eight miles in breadth. At Chitor, there is a tank named Bhojasāgara built by Bhoja. The Udayasāgara at Udayapura was named after the Paramāra ruler Udayāditya. The Āmera inscription records the construction of a water tank in the reign of king Naravarman. Mahākumāra Hariśchandra made a land-grant along with *Baolees*, wells and tanks.[1]

This example was followed by others. From the Gwalior inscription of Paṭaṅgaśambhu, it is known that he constructed five tanks at Raṇod.[2] In 1086 A.D., Janna, a Telī *Paṭel*, excavated a tank at Chirihitta, during the reign of King Udayāditya.[3]

The śūdras normally led an agricultural life. The Brāh-

1. JASB, VII, p. 735.
2. JMPIP, IV, p. 3.
3. JASB, 1914, p. 241.

maṇas were granted various royal land grants. They were given only the king's share, and the farmers who cultivated the land remained undisturbed.[1] The means of cultivation were plough and oxen.

The common agricultural products as known to us during this period, were rice, *Kodrava* (millet), *til* (sesame), *mūṅg* (*mudga,* bean), *vrīhi* (paddy) and *kaṇikā* (cummuni-seed).[2] Wheat and barley were produced in abundance.[3] Opium and indigo were also cultivated.[4] Among the commercial crops, sugarcane and cotton were the most important. In the *Śriṅgāramañjarīkathā*, there is a description of fields full of sugarcane. Contemporary literature and inscriptions refer to betel-leaves, coconut, palm, mango and *madhuka*.

Besides agriculture, cattle breeding was also the profession of a large number of people. Large pasture lands were attached to every village. Kings sometimes donated pasture land, or the right to graze cattle free.[5] Of pastural products, ghee, milk, and milk products were the most important. In contemporary literary works, there is often reference to the tinkling of the bells of the cows returning to the village in the evenings, after grazing in the pasture lands.

INDUSTRIES :—Some literary works, like the *Yuktikalpataru*, and inscriptions, give information about the flourishing state of industries. From references to weaver, thread and cotton, and the description of the various dresses of the people made of different materials, it can be inferred that the textile industry was in a flourishing state. In Malwa, according to Chau-fu-kua, cotton cloths were such a common product as to be the subject of a considerable export trade.[6] The sugar industry was important as can be inferred from the fact that inscriptions speak of *gur* and sugar being used by the king.[7]

1. CII, IV, p. clxxi.
2. EI, XXXIII, p. 195.
3. Ibid, XIV, p. 309.
4. Ibid.
5. IA, VI, p. 53.
6. Chu-fan-chi, p. 93.
7. EI, XIV, p. 310.

Iron and metal industries were pursued with great success during this period. The iron industry attained a high skill as is clear from the celebrated iron pillar at Dhar, now unfortunately, broken into three pieces. It has been estimated to have originally reached a height of fifty feet, being the highest pillar of its kind in the world[1]. The *Yuktikalpataru*[2] refers to the different varieties of iron, and their importance. Iron was used for manufacturing agricultural implements and weapons. The inscriptions refer to goldsmiths, blacksmiths, carpenters and architects, who were concerned with some metal in one way or another. Brass and copper were used for household utensils.

A high level of skill was attained in the Jewellery industry, as is clear from the fact that there is mention of different kinds of ornaments in the *Tilakamañjarī* and the *Śriṅgāramañjarīkathā*. Ornaments were made of precious metals like gold and silver, and were studded with various types of precious stones. The *Yuktikalpataru* refers to three varieties of mirrors, viz. *bhāvya*, *vijaya* and *paurusha*, which were made of metals other than glass.

House building was also a great industry during this period, as is known from literary works and archaeological remains. Dhāra, Ujjain, Mandu, Bhojapurā, Udayapura, and other cities, were full of residential buildings, beautiful temples, palaces, and places of public utility. The construction of these buildings required both skilled artisans and unskilled labourers.

Carpentary also progressed. Various kinds of furniture, such as chairs, stools, and bedsteads, were used for decorating the house as is known from the *Śriṅgāramañjarīkathā* and the *Tilakamañjarī*. The *Yuktikalpataru* mentions seats (*pīṭhas*) made of metal, stone and wood. Bhoja gives a detailed account about the pīṭhas and bedsteads, and types of wood used for them.

According to the *Yuktikalpataru*, different types of um-

1. P. Niyogi : Iron in Ancient India, pp. 21-30.
2. IC, XV, p. 32.

brellas were meant for kings, princes and ordinary people. The *Viśesha* type was to be used by the kings, and the *Sāmānya* type by ordinary people. The *Pratāpa* type was meant for the princes. On the occasion of marriage, the *Navadaṇḍa* type was to be used.

As in olden times, rivers and streams were used for communications, and boat-building became a developed industry. The *Yuktikalpataru* gives a vivid account of the various types of boats and the timber used for their making. Boats were manufactured in Malwa, as is clear from the fact that one of the sources of the royal revenue, was ferry tolls.

As both men and women used perfumes, it is obvious that the people were acquainted with the manufacturing process of perfumeries.

Besides these, there were other small industries. Mining was also carried out. One inscription records the granting of land with the right of mining gold.[1] The person who extracted oil was known as *Telī*. His industry was in a flourishing state as his name is found in inscriptions. The manufacture of leather and shoe-making was also developed. There were some other minor crafts, such as pottery, making of *yantras*, weapons, watches, musical instruments and iron works, all of which required specialised knowledge. These workers carried on their work in their own cottages, and there was no large-scale industry.

TRADE AND COMMERCE :—

Trade and commerce, both inland and foreign, developed greatly during this period. The merchants who carried on trade were known as *baniās* and *śreshṭhins*. They dealt in different articles, such as sugar, jaggery, madder, thread, cotton, clothing fabrics, coconut, butter, sesame oil, salt, grain, etc.[2]

The villages and towns were interrelated by routes, and the goods for trade passed through them. There was inter-provincial trade through these routes. For the purpose of

1. EI, XX, p. 106.
2. Ibid, XIV, pp, 309-10.

security, the merchants sometimes formed a caravan trail known as *Sārthavāha*, for trade to distant lands. Such a caravan of merchants has been described in the *Tilakamañjarī*.[1] Goods were also transported from one place to another through rivers.

The traders had their shops in the markets. There might have been arrangements for temporary markets on fixed days of the week and on festive occasions, when the traders from the neighbouring villages brought their commodities for sale. They carried on their mercantile activities after defraying the state dues, such as octroi duty, excise tax, ferry tolls, road cess and sales tax.

Foreign trade was by both land and water. As the Paramāra ruler Bhoja is known to have given encouragement to the shipping industry, it was but natural that foreign trade also prospered during this period. From a description of the *Śriṅgāramañjarī*[2] and the *Tilakamañjarī*,[3] it is known that some of the rich merchants might have gone by ship to the neighbouring countries of *Siṁhaladvīpa* (Ceylon) and *Suvarṇabhūmi* (East Indies).

The occupation of Lāṭa by the Paramāras brought Bharoch under their control. The port of Bharoch proved to be of great significance from the commercial point of view. It is situated where the river Narmada, after passing through Malwa flows into the sea; so the goods landed at Bharoch could be conveniently transported to Malwa by river, which could also be used for bringing goods down from Malwa.

GUILD SYSTEM :—Industries and trades were organised into guilds. Each guild had its own President, known as *Pradhāna*, *Pramukha*, *Mahattara*, *Mahara*, *Paṭṭakila* (Paṭela) etc., who may be compared to the Aldermen of the guilds in Europe in the early medieval period. These craft guilds and merchant guilds had their own rules, which were enforced on their members. They administered their own charities.

Because of the increase of wealth, the merchant guilds

1. TM, p. II7.
2. SMK, pp. 28,29.
3. TM, p, 103.

became influential. The merchants became members of the town committee. The Gwalior inscription[1] and the Shergarh inscription,[2] throw some light on the working of the guilds. The Gwalior inscription of 877 A.D. records that the guilds of oilmen and of gardeners, made some permanent endowments to the temple.

From the Shergarh inscription, it is known that three merchants, namely Narasiṁha, Gourīsha and Thirāditya, jointly made a daily grant of one *karsha* of ghee for the purpose of smearing the feet of *Bhaṭṭāraka* Nāganaka, from the income of the custom house in 1017 A.D. The three merchants constituted the town committee which was in charge of the collection of the market taxes of the custom house, which were usually collected in kind. There was a guild of oilmen at Shergarh, and its chief was Thāiyāka. The members of the guild used to supply oil for the lamps in the temple of Somanātha. From the Jhālarāpāṭan stone inscription[3] of Udayāditya dated V.S. 1143 (1086 A.D.), it is known that the head of the guild of oilmen was Janna, who built a temple of Śiva and dug a *vāpī* in the reign of Udayāditya. The sailors had their own associations. In the *Tilakamañjarī*, we read that Chandraketu made his son-in-law, Tāraka, chief of the sailors association.[4]

WEIGHTS AND MEASURES :—Literary works and inscriptions refer to the weights and measures which were prevalent in Malwa. These were made of iron and stones from Narmada,[5] which were hard and could not, therefore, easily be worn out.

For different types of articles, different weights and measures were used for convenience. *Dhāraka* was used for coconuts, candied sugar, jaggery, Bengal madder, thread, cotton and grain; *ghaṭaka* and *kumbha* for butter and sesame oil; *mūtaka* or *māṇaka* for salt; *Pulaka* for *Jāla* (flowers); *Karsha, Pala* or *Palika* and *Paṇaka* for oil and ghee; *santās* for *lagaḍā*;

1. EI, I, p. 159.
2. Ibid, XXIV, p. 137.
3. JASB, 1914, p. 241.
4. TM, p. 106.
5. JNSI, VIII, pt. II, p. 148.

Vumvuka for distiller's production; *Māṇī, Mūtaka, hāraka, Vāpa, mushthi,*[1] *sei*[2] and *Droṇakārī*[3] for grain and barley.

About the mutual relations of these weights and their modern equivalents, nothing can be said definitely. The *maṇa series*, according to BHANDARKAR, was as follows :— 4 *Pāila* =1 *Pāilī*; 5 *Pāilī*=1 *Maṇā*[4]; 4 *Maṇā*=1 *Sei* and 2 *Sei*= 1 *Maṇ*.

The system of weights and measures given in the *Gaṇitasāra* of Śrīdhara, is slightly different from the above. From the statement of the commentator of the *Gaṇitasāra*, it is clear that the system of weights and measures described by him was popular in the countries of Kanauj, Malwa and Gujarat. The weight standard given in the Gaṇitasāra is as follows :—

4	*pāvala*	=	1 *pālī*
4	*pālī*	=	1 *maṇā*
4	*maṇā*	=	1 *sei*
12	*maṇā*	=	1 *padaka*
4	*padaka*	=	1 *hārī*
4	*hārī*	=	1 *māṇi*[5]

The term *pulaka* meant a bundle. One *pala* was equal to four *karshas*, and a *karsha*, according to A. S. ALTEKAR was equal to three-fourths of a *tolā*.[6] *Mūtaka*, *Hāraka*, *Vāpa* and *Mushṭhi* seem to be handfuls. The term *Droṇakārī*, according to BISHESHWAR NATH, consisted of two Sanskrit words, i.e. *Droṇa* and *Khārī*, the respective meanings of which are thirty-two and ninety-six *seers*.[7] The term *Droṇa*, according to B. J. SANDESARA, was equal to one thousand and twenty-four Tolās, and Pāli or Pāili was equal to four pounds.[8]

Of land measurements, there is mention of *halavāha*[9] *nivarttana*,[10] *parva etc*. One *halavāha* meant that area of land

1. EI, XIV, pp. 309-10.
2. Ibid, XXXII, p. 157.
3. IA, XLV, p. 78.
4. IA, XI, p. 41.
5. JNSI, VIII, pp. 138 ff.
6. EI, XXIII, p. 318.
7. IA, XLV, p. 77.
8. JMSI, VIII, p. 148.
9. EI, XX, p. 106.
10. Ibid.

which could be tilled by one plough in a day. It is difficult to determine the exact size of land, because different types of *halas* were used in different areas and at different periods, and it was also determined by the capacity of the oxen.

Scholars gave different interpretations to the term *nivarttana*. PRAṆNATH VIDYALANKARA[1] says that it was almost equal to an *acre*. D. C. SIRCAR[2] calculates it to be two hundred and forty by two hundred and forty sq. cubits i.e. about three *acres*. The *Gaṇitasāra of* Śrīdhara gives *halavāha* as equal to eighty-three thousand, eight hundred and forty *yavas* i.e. a length not much more than one-third of a *Krośa*.

Land was measured by a rod, which was known as *parva*.[3] In the inscription of the Kadambapadraka plates, the term *parva* has been mentioned. This inscription records that twenty *nivarttanas* of land out of the forty-two *nivarttanas* of the village Kadambapadraka, were measured by the rod of ninety-six *parvas*. The exact *length* of *parva* is not clear.

COINAGE

From inscriptions and literary works, it is known that there were different types of coins prevalent for the purposes of exchange. The coins recovered in archaeological discoveries give an actual idea of the coinage system of the period under review.

The coins found mentioned in the Paramāra inscriptions[4] are *dramma*, *varāha*, *vṛishabha*, *rūpaka*, *ardharūpaka* and *Viṁśopaka*. From the *Kharataragachchha Paṭṭāvalī*,[5] we know that Naravarman of Malwa (1094-1133 A.D.), offered either 300,000 *pāruttha drammas* or three villages to the Jaina saint Jinavallabha Sūri, but the latter accepted only two *pāruttha drammas* daily from the custom house of Chitor, for the maintenance of two Kharatara temples. Merutuṅga refers

1. A Study in the Economic condition of N. India, p. 83.
2. Successors of the Sātavāhanas, p. 300 f n
3. EI, XX, p. 106.
4. Ibid, XIV, p. 310; Trans. of the Royal Asiatic Society Vol. I, p. 226; JASB, VII, p. 738 v. 6.; EI, XXIV, p. 131; IA, XLII, p. 78.
5. KB, p. 13,

to *Dināra in* connection with Vikramāditya of Ujjain, and *Tankah* with Paramāra Bhoja.[1] A number of coin types of Malwa are known from Ṭhakkura Pheru's work *Dravyaparīkshā*, written in V.S. 1375 (1318 A.D.),[2] though the names of the rulers who issued them are not definitely known.

The *gadahiyā* or Indo-Sassanian coins of Huzur Jawahir-khana, Indore,[3] have been obtained from the village of Kotha in the East Nimar District, and the coins with the legend '*Śrī Oṁkāra*' on them from their provenance, appear to have referred to Oṁkāra Māndhātā on the Narmada.[4] The coins of the Paramāra rulers Udayāditya,[5] Naravarman[6] and Arjunavarman have been also recovered.

Drammas :—From the numerous references to *dramma* in the inscriptions and literary works of the early medieval period, it seems that it was the most common coin. The term '*dramma*' is de ived from the Greek *drachma*, the weight standard of which is sixty-seven point five grams. As Gadahiyā coins were issued to this standard, the term '*dramma*' began to be applied to them. Later on, this term was applied to other coins, which adopted the *drachma* weight standard. It appears that not only the silver coins, but also the gold and copper coins of most of the dynasties of this period, followed the weight standard of the *drachma*.

Varāhas :—The Somanātha temple inscription of Shergarh mentions that the third donation of Devasvāmin, given in V.S. 1084 (1028 A.D.), was the monthly payment of two *Varāhas* to be made on the occasion of *Saṁkrānti*[7] These were obviously the *Ādivarāha* type of silver coins issued by the *Pratīhāra* king Bhoja, and they may be regarded as a sub-variety of the Indo-Sassanian series. These coins had the image of a boar on one side.

1. KB, p. 13.
2. *Dravyaparīkshā*, edited by V. S. AGRAWAL.
3. JNSI, VIII, p. 66.
4. JBBRAS, XII, p. 325.
5. JABB, 1920, Plate XIII, No. 2; NS, XXXIII, p. 208
6. JNSI, XXX, p. 208
7. EI, XXIII, pp. 133-34

Vṛishabhas :—Varāṅga, who was officer connected with the collection of tolls on roads, gave the donation of the five *vṛishabhas* for incense and sandal to the Somanātha temple of Shergarh in 1018 A.D. (V.S. 1075). These coins bore the emblem of an animal on one side.[1] They were probably issued by the predecessor of Mihira Bhoja, Vatsarāja, who was a devotee of Śiva.

Pāruttha drammas :—From literary and epigraphical references, it seems that *Pāruttha drammas* were circulating in Malwa, Rajasthan and Gujarat. It is not possible to explain the name of this coin or to identify it. From the *Lekhapaddhati*,[2] we know that these coins were minted at Śrīmāla. V. S. AGRAWAL[3] identified them with *Bhillamāla* or *Śrīmāliyadrammas*. The *Purātanaprabandha-saṁgraha*[4] states that one *Pārutthaka* was equal to eight *drammas*. The higher value attached to this coin was due to either the purity, or the superiority, of the metal.

Pañchīyaka drammas :—*Pañchīyaka-dramma* was current in the Malwa region in the early medieval period. In the Bhilsa inscription[5] of V.S. 935, there is written '*pa*' in lines 4, 6, 7 and 11. The mark, as well as the fact that the *akshara* in question is followed by a number, suggests that this '*pa*' is a contraction. Possibly, it stands for the coin called *pañchīyaka dramma*. The rent of the *vīthis* i.e. shops in the market, was realized in the currency known as *pañchīyaka dramma*, and paid by the donor to meet the expenses of the regular offerings to god and goddesses in the temple of Bhāillasvāmin. From the Siyadoni inscription[6], it is known that a *pañchīyaka dramma* was equal to a quarter *Ādivarāha dramma*.

Rūpaka :—*Rūpaka* was different from, and lower in value, than a *dramma*. There is no doubt that *rūpaka* stands for a silver coin. From the commentary on the *Gaṇitasāra*[7] of Śrīdhara,

1. EI, XXIII, pp. 133-34.
2. *Lekhapaddhati*, p. 114.
3. JNSI, XII, p. 201.
4. PPS, p. 53.
5. EI, XXX, p. 213.
6. Ibid, I, 169, II, 6,37.
7. Bomb. Gaz., I, Pt. I, pp. 47 f.

it is clear that five *rūpakas* stand for one *dramma*. If this is true, some of the silver coins weighing about thirteen point five grams were meant to be used as *rūpakas*.

Viṁśopaka :—The coin called '*Viṁśopaka*' was also popular. This was of considerably less value than a *dramma*. One inscription refers to a tax of one '*vi*' on every dramma. D. R. BHANDARKAR[1] regarded *Viṁśopaka* as a copper coin equal in value to one-twentieth of a *dramma*. The *Gaṇitasāra* of Ṭhakkura Pheru also equates twenty *viṁśopakas* with one *dramma*.[2] As suggested by V. V. MIRASHI,[3] the coin was so named because it formed the twentieth part of a *dramma*.

The *Dināra*, according to Ṭhakkura Pheru, was a gold coin equal to four *Māśakas*.[4] *Taṅkaḥ* was a silver coin, the standard weight of which, according to HABIBULLAH, was one hundred and seventy-two point eight grams.[5] According to ALTEKAR, the silver *Taṅkaḥ* was one *tolā*.[6]

Ṭhakkura Pheru refers to a number of coin types of Malwa. The *Chaukaḍīyamudrā* appears to have been a square billon coin. A hundred *Chaukaḍīyas* contained eight *tolās* of silver and its weight was one *taṅka* and ten *yavas*.[7] The *Diupālapurīmudrā* appears to have been issued by king Devapāla of Malwa. One hundred *Diupālapurīs* contained fifteen *tolās* and five *Māśās* of silver, though the gross weight of coin was only one *taṅka* and ten *yavas*.[8] *Kuṇḍaliyā* might have been round coin. A hundred *Kuṇḍa liyās* had four tolas and five and three by four *māśās* of silver.[9] One hundred *Vanliyāmudrā* had five *tolās* and eight and three by four *māśās* of silver. The *chhaḍḍa liyā* might have been a hexagonal coin. One hundred *chhaḍḍaliyās* contained seven *tolās* and four *māśās* of silver.[10]

1. EI, X, p. 19, f.n. 3.
2. E. Ch. D, p. 319.
3. CII, IV, p. clxxxix, f.n. 7.
4. *Dravyaparīkshā*, v. 61.
5. Foundations of Muslim Rule in India, p. 264.
6. JNSI, II, pp. 1-11.
7. DP, v. 94.
8. Ibid.
9. Ibid.
10. Ibid, v. 96.

It is difficult to know the shape of the *selaki-togaḍa* coin. One hundred of these contained five *tolās* and three *māśās* of silver.[1] The weight of these coins is the same i.e. one *taṅka* and ten *yavas*. Chitor had a coin of its own, which is known as *Jāniyā Chitorī*. One hundred of these coins had five *tolās* of silver.[2] There seems to have been no admixture of any other metal in it.

Some other silver coins of lower denomination and with a good deal of admixture of baser metals, have also been referred to by Pheru. One hundred of *Jakāriyā* coins contained four *tolās* and four and a half *māśās* of silver, one hundred of *Galahuliya* coins contained three *tolās* and four *māśās* of silver; one hundred of *Ravālgā* coins contained one *tolā* and eight *māśās* of silver, and one hundred of *Śivagaṇa* coins contained one *tolā* and three *māśās* of silver.

Pheru mentions another series of Mālava coins which seem to have merely been artistically stamped pieces of bullion. They do not seem to have been in common use in the market. Of these, there is reference to *Vāpadā*, *Malitā*, *Sīhamāra* and *Choramāra*. One hundred of *vāpadā* coins contained fourteen *tolās* of silver; one hundred of *Malītā* coins contained fourteen *tolās* and three *māśās* of silver and weighed one *taṅka*; one hundred of *sīhamāra* coins contained thirteen *tolās* of silver and weighed one *taṅka*; and one hundred of *Choramāra* coins contained thirteen *tolās* of silver and weighed one *taṅka*.[3] A fairly good idea of Malwa coins, referred to in the *Dravyaparīkshā*, can be had from the table on the facing page.

1. DP.
2. Ibid, v. 97.
3. Ibid, vv. 98-100

S. No.	Name of coin	Amount of silver contained in per hundred coins		Gross weight per coin	
		Tolās	Māśās	Taṅka	Yava
1.	Chaukaḍiyā	8	0	1	10
2.	Diupālapurī	15	5	1	10
3.	Kaṇḍaliyā	6	5¾	1	10
4.	Kauliyā	5	8¾	1	10
5.	Chhaḍḍaliyā	7	4	1	10
6.	Selaki Tongaḍa	5	3	1	10
7.	Jāniyā Chitorī	5	0	0	0
8.	Jakāriyā	4	4½	0	0
9.	Galahuliyā	3	4	0	0
10.	Ravālgā	1	8	0	0
11.	Śivagaṇā	1	3	0	0
12.	Vāpadā	14	0	0	0
13.	Malitā	14	3	1	0
14.	Sihamāra	13	0	1	0
15.	Choramāra	13	0	1	0

Some types of Indo-Sassanian or *gadhaiyā* coins remained confined particularly to Malwa. Coins with the legend '*Śrī Oṁkāra*' on them, and from their provenance, appear to have referred to Oṁkāra Māndhātā on the Narmada, and may have been a local type of *gadhaiyā coins* for Southern Malwa. BHAGWANLAL INDRAJI[1] suggested that these coins were issued by the authorities of the famous temple at Māndhātā. H. V. TRIVEDI[2] thinks that the issuer of these types of coins, might have put the name of the temple on them, instead of his own, which may be due to the remarkable influence wielded by the deity, or due to the honour paid by him to the deity. There is already such an instance of coins and inscriptions issued in the name of '*Ekaliṅga*', in Mewar.

Another variety of this coin type, bearing traces of a human head and the legend '*Śrīdāma*', was found in the Pich-

1. JBBRS, XII, p. 325.
2. JNSI, XIII, p. 205.

hore Pargana of the Bhilsa District,[1] and a new variety which resembles the *Ādivarāha* coins, was found at Bhat Pachlana in the District of Ujjain.[2] Some hoards were also recovered from places like Ghataoda (Dhar), Chanderi (Guna), Bardia (Mandsor) and Davalpura (Shajapur). Bhagwanlal Indraji published some Malwa coin types, which bear the figure of a well executed horse on one side, and some objects under its hoofs.

The *horseman reverse type*, which was found earlier only in the Huzur Jawahirkhana, Indore, *probably representing the finds of a hoard*, has now been reported from the village of Kotha in the East Nimar District.[3] Diskalkar[4] ascribed these coins to the Rāshtṛakūṭa king Govinda III, who was a famous horseman, but this theory is not quite convincing. It is equally likely that the type was started by some local opponents of the Gurjara Pratīhāras, to commemorate a local victory.[5] G. S. Tewari[6] describes it as a specific local type of the Nimar region. Some coins of the Paramāra dynasty were struck of Udayāditya,[7] Naravarman and Arjunavarman.[8] These coins resemble those of Kalachuri Gāṅgeyadeva. They bear an image of the seated goddess on one side, and a legend on the obverse. R. D. Benarji has published one coin of this type, and attributed it to Udayāditya. Gold and silver coins of his successors Naravarman (1097-1134 A.D.), and Arjunavarman (1210-1215 A. D.), have also been brought to light.

In the Shergarh inscription, there is a reference to a coin-denomination called '*Kapardaka-voḍī*'.[9] Altekar[10] regarded it as equal to the fourth part of a copper *paṇa*, and concluded that *Kapardaka-voḍī* must have been equal to twenty cowries.

1. ASI, 1913-14, p. 255.
2. ARADGS, 1927-28, p. 97.
3. JNSI, XX, p. 26.
4. Ibid, VIII, p. 70.
5. Ibid, p. 71.
6. Ibid, XXVIII, p. 214.
7. JASB, 1920, Plate XIII, No. 2; NS, XXIII, p. 203.
8. JNSI, XXX, 1968, p. 208.
9. EI, XXIII, 140. 1.6.
10. Ibid.

The Gujarātī commentary on the *Gaṇitasāra*,[1] equates twenty *kauḍas* with one *Kāginī* or *boḍī*. The term *kapardaka*, along with *voḍī*, makes it clear that *voḍī* was really calculated and paid in terms of *cowries*. This also suggests that *cowries* were the usual currency in Malwa. Besides *cowries*, barter also played an important role in medium of exchange, at least in the rural areas.

It is clear that this region became very rich, which enabled the rulers to make various grants. They could spend enormous amounts on literary and architectural activities, as well as in fighting wars. The names of the various types of coins, weights, and measures, as found in inscriptions and literary works, indicate the vigorous economic activity of this period.

1. JNSI, VIII, pp. 141 ff.

APPENDICES

1. Inscription on image in the Vikrama University Museum, Ujjain.

संवत् १३२३ वर्षे माघ सुदी ६ (सोमे) श्रीमूलसंघे............श्रीविशालकीर्ति-देवात् तत् शिष्य सुमन कीर्तिदेव मंडलाचार्य श्रीसागरचन्द्र तत् शिष्य रत्नकीर्ति श्री मेहतवालान्वये सा. मोगाभार्या सावित्री पुत्र माखिलभार्या विल्ह पुत्र परम भार्या (विसु पुत्र भार्या) पद्मश्री तथ प्रतिष्ठित वह्.य प्रणमति नित्यम् ।

2. Inscription on image No. 17 of the Digambara Jaina Museum, Ujjain.

संवत् १३०८ माघ सुदी ६ श्रीवागड़संघ आचार्यै श्री कल्याणवर्धन बधेरवाल सा. बाहरसुत कोका संधा वत्तुल सिरिसुतभार्या मागंदा द्वितीयभार्या काकु प्रणमति नित्यम् ।

3. Inscription on image No. 110 of the Digambara Jaina Museum, Ujjain.

संवत् १२२६ वैशाख वदी ६ वर्धनापुरे श्रीशांतिनाथचैत्ये सा. श्री सलन, सा. गोशल भा. ब्रह्मदि, भा. बहदेवादिकुण्डसुहितेन निजगोत्रदेव्या श्री अच्छुप्ता: रविकीर्ति कारिता: ।

4. Inscription on image No. 110 of the Digambara Jaina Museum, Ujjain.

संवत् १२२२ ज्येष्ठ सुदी ७ श्री खण्डेलवालान्वय सा. गोसलभार्या वासा...... ।

5. Inscription on image No. 273 of the Digambara Jaina Museum, Ujjain.

संवत् १२२८ वर्षे फाल्गुन सुदी ५ स्थापित—माथुरसंघे पंडिताचार्या श्री धर्म-कीर्ति तत् शिष्य आचार्यललितकीर्ति प्रणमति ।

6. Inscription on image No. 71 on the Digambara Jaina Museum, Ujjain.

संवत् १२२२ ज्येष्ठ सुदी ७ श्री खण्डेलवालान्वय सा. गोसलभार्या वासा...... ।

7. Inscription on image of the Vikrama University Museum, Ujjain.

संवत् १२६६ चैत्र सुदी ६ खंडिलवालान्वगे चनौ: शनि आवाम सा· कला भार्या गौरी श्रीसागररुद्रभार्या प्रणमति नित्यम् ।

8. Inscriptions on images in the Digambara Jaina Museum, Ujjain.

No. 129. संवत् १३०८ माघ सुदी ६ प्राग्वाटान्वये सहा सलका भार्या भट्टणि पुत्र साधु हाल प्रणमति नित्यम् ।

No. 130. संवत् १३०८ वर्षे माघ सुदी ६ बागड़ान्वय आचार्य श्रीकल्याणकीर्ति पौराचार्यान्वय साधुगणि रहसुच बांसदेवा भार्या लालान्त राउद चन्ना गृहे नचिद चन्द्र प्रणमति नित्यम् ।

No. 163. संवत् १३०८ वर्षे माघ सुदी ६ खोड़ श्री लाटवागड़संघे भट्टारक श्री कल्याणकीर्ति प्राग्वाटान्वय सा· सांडेल सुत नरदेव भार्या खमगिरि ।

No. 164. संवत् १३०८ वर्षे माघ सुदी ६ ... वागडान्वय पंडित श्री भानुकीर्ति पोरवालान्वय सा. कानभार्या सातभार्या सा. चहोभार्या पद्मिनी पुत्र सामा भार्या चान्द्र पुत्र वामविज भार्या वाहिणी खेम्मन सुत हरि चम्प प्रणमति नित्यम् ।

No. 127. संवत् १३०८ वर्षे माघ सुदी ६ ... श्री वर्धनापुरान्वय पंडित रतनुभार्या साधुसुत साहगभार्या कोड़े पुत्र सा. असिभार्या होन्तु नित्यम् प्रणमति ।

9. Inscription on image No. 171 of the Digambara Jaina Museum, Ujjain.

साधुनरपति साधुराता......संवत् १२३१ वैशाख सुदी ६ सोमे वर्कटान्वय सा· कुसोमति तस्य सुत आमदेव प्रणमति नित्यम् ।

GENERAL BIBLIOGRAPHY

ORIGINAL SOURCES

Texts and Translations

(1) Indian Sources

(A) BRAHMANICAL

(i) *EPICS*

Mahābhārata — Critically edited by SUKTHANKAR EDGERTON, BELVALKAR and others, Bhandarkar Oriental Research Institute, Poona, 1927-53

Rāmāyaṇā — Eng. Trans. by M. N. DUTT., Calcutta, 1892-94.

(ii) *PURĀṆAS*

Agni Purāṇa — Ed. by R. MITRA, BI. Calcutta, 1873-79.
Ed. Ass. Poona, 1900.
Eng. Trans. M. N. DUTT., Calcutta, 1901.

Bhāgavata Purāṇa — Ed. by V. L. PANSIKAR, Bombay, 1920.
Eng. Trans. M. N. DUTT, Calcutta, 1895.

Brahmāṇḍa Purāṇa — Pub. Venkatesvara Press, Bombay, 1913.

Matsya Purāṇa — Ass. Poona, 1907.
Eng. Trans. by a Taluqdar of Oudh. SBH. 2 Vols.
Allahabad, 1916-17.

Padma Purāṇa — Ed. V. N. MANDLIK,
Ass. 4 Vols. Poona, 1893-94.

Skanda Purāṇa — Pub. G. P. Raverkar, Bombay, 1909-11.

Śiva Purāṇa — Pub. Venkatesvara Press, Bombay.

Vishṇu Purāṇa — Bombay 1889. Eng. trans. by H. H. WILSON, 5 Vols. London, 1864-70.

Vishṇudharmottara Purāṇa — Pub. Venkatesvara Press, Bombay, 1912.

(iii) POLITY

Arthaśāstra — of Kauṭilya. Ed. by R. SHAMASASTRI, Mysore, 1919.

Nītisāra of Kāmandaka — Ed. by R. MITRA, BI, Calcutta, 1884.

Nītivākyāmṛita of Someśvara — Bombay, 1887-88, pub. MDJG. Series, Bombay

Nītisāra of Śukra — Ed. by G. OPPERT. Madras, 1882. Eng. trans. by B. K. SARKAR. 2nd. Ed. Allahabad, 1923.

(iv) DHARMAŚĀSTRA

Manubhāshya of Medhātithi — *Manu-smriti* with the comm. of Medhātithi, Ed. by G. JHA. BI. Calcutta, 1932-39.

(B) BUDDHIST

(i) CANONICAL TEXTS, COMMENTARIES AND TRANSLATIONS

Aṅguttara Nikāya — Ed. by R. MORRIS and E. HARDY. PTS. London, 1885-1900. Eng. trans. (The Book of gradual sayings) Vol. 1, II and V by F.L. WOODWARD, and Vol. III and IV by E.M. HARE. PTS. London.

Dhammapada — Ed. by S.S. THERA. PTS. London, 1914. Eng. trans. by F. MAX MULLER, SBE. Oxford, 1898.

Dīghanikāya — Ed. by T.W. RHYS DAVIDS and J.E. CARPENTER. 3 Vols. PTS. London, 1890, 1903, 1911.

Jātaka — Ed. by V. FAUSBOLL. 7 Vols. (Vol. 7 Index, by D. ANDERSEN). London, 1877-97. Eng. trans. under the Editorship of E.B. COWELL. 7 Vols. Cambridge, 1895-1913.

Majjhima Nikāya — Ed. by V. TRENCKNER and R. CHALMERS. PTS. London, 1888-1902. Eng. trans. (Further Dialogues of the Buddha) by Lord CHALMERS, 2 Vols. SBB, London, 1926-27.

Niddesa — *Mahāniddesa* Ed. by L. DELA VALLEE POUSSIN and E.J. THOMAS. PTS. London, 1916-17.

	Chullaniddesa. Ed. by W. STEDE. PTS. London, 1918.
Saṁyutta Nikāya	Ed. by LEON FREER. PTS. London, 1884-98. Indexes by Mrs. RHYS DAVIDS. London, 1904. Eng. trans. (Book of the Kindred Sayings or grouped Suttas) by Mrs. DAVIDS and F. L. WOODWARD. PTS. London, 1917-30.
Sutta-Nipāta	Ed. by D. ANDERSEN and H. SMITH. PTS. London, 1913. Eng. trans. by V. FAUSBOLL. SBE. Oxford, 1898.
Therī-gāthā	Ed. by H. OLDENBERG. PTS. London, 1883. Eng. trans. (Psa lms of the Brethren) by Mrs. RHYS DAVIDS. PTS. London, 1913.
Thera-gāthā	Ed. by R. PISCHEL PTS. London, 1883. Eng.trans. (Psalms of the Sisters) by Mrs. RHYS DAVIDS. PTS. London, 1909.
Vinaya Piṭaka	Ed. by H. OLDENBERG. PTS, London, 1879-83. Eng. trans. (Vinaya texts) by T. W. RHYS DAVIDS and H. OLDENBERG SBE, Oxford, 1881-85.

(ii) NON-CANONICAL TEXTS, COMMENTARIES AND TRANSLATIONS

Dhammapada	Commentary Ed. by H. C. NORMAN. 5 Vols. PTS. London, 1906-15. Eng. trans. (Buddhist Legends) by E. W. BURLINGAME. 3 Vols. HOS, Cambridge, Mass. 1921.
Dīpavaṁśa	Ed. and trans. by H. OLDENBERG, London, 1879.
Divyāvadāna	Ed. by E. B. COWELL and R. A. NEIL. Cambridge, 1886.
Lalitavistara	Ed. by S. LEFMANA, Halle, 1902-08. Ed. by R. MITRA. Calcutta, 1877.
Mahāvaṁśa	(earlier portion of the chronicle by Mahānāma) Ed. by W. GEIGER, PTS., London, 1908. Eng. trans. (The Great

Chronicle of Ceylon) by W. GEIGER assisted by MABEL H. BODE, London, 1912.

(C) JAINA

Bhagavatīsūtra — Pub. Jaina Sāhitya Prakāshan Trust, Ahmedabad, S. 1988. Tr. Becharadas Dosi.

Harivaṁśapurāṇa of Jinasena II — Pub. MDJG Series, Bombay, 1930.

Kharataragachchha Bṛihadgurvāvalī — of Jinapāla Upādhyāya, Ed. by JINAVIJAYA, Bombay, 1956.

Pariśishṭaparvan — Being an appendix of the *Triśashṭiśalākāpurushacharita* of Hemachandra. Ed. by H. JACOBI, BI. Calcutta, 1883-91. 2nd Ed. 1932.

Paṭṭāvalī Samuchchaya — Ed. by DARSHAN VIJAYA, Vikramgam (Gujarat), 1933.

Prabandhachintāmaṇi of Merutuṅga, — SJS, No. 3; Bombay, 1940.

Prabandhakośa of Rājaśekhara — Ed. by JINAVIJAYA, SJS. No. 6, Shantiniketan, 1935.

Purātanaprabandha Saṁgraha — Ed. by JINAVIJAYA, SJS. No. 2, Calcutta, 1936.

Vividhatīrthakalpa of Jinaprabha — Ed. by JINAVIJAYA, SJS, No. 10, Shantiniketan, 1934.

Uvāsagadasāo — Ed. in original Prakrit with Sanskrit Comm. of Abhayadeva and Eng. trans. by A. F. R. HOERNLE. BI. Calcutta, 1885-88.

(D) LITERARY WORKS

Amarakośa of Amarasiṁha — Ed. by T. GANAPATI SASTRI, 4 parts, 1914-17.

Ashṭādhyāyī of Pāṇini — Ed. by S. C. VASU, Allahabad, 1929.

Bṛihat-Saṁhitā of Varāhamihira — Ed. by H. KERN BI. Calcutta, 1865. Ed. with Eng. trans. and notes by V. SUBRAHMANYA SASTRI and M. RAMAKRISHNA BHAT. 2 Vols. Banglore, 1947.

Chaturbhāṇī	(Comprising Śūdrakas *Padmaprābhṛitaka*, Īśvaradatta's Dhūrta-viṭa-Saṁvāda, Vararuchi's *Ubhayābhisārikā* and Syamilaka's *Pādatāḍitaka*) Ed. by M. RAMAKRISHNA KAVI and S.K.RAMANATHA SASTRI, Patna, 1922. Tr. by MOTICHAND and VASUDEVA ŚHARAN AGRAWAL, BOMBAY 1959.
Daśarūpa of Dhanañjaya	Ed. with the comm. of Dhanika. by F. E. HALL. BI. Calcutta, 1865.
Dravyaparīkshā of Ṭhakkura Pheru	Ed. V. S. AGRAWAL.
Dvyāśrayamahākāvya of Hemachandra	Ed. by A.V.KATHVATE. 2 parts, Bombay, 1885, 1915.
Hammīramahākāvya of Nayachandrasūri	Ed. by N. J. KIRTANE, Bombay, 1879.
Hammīramadamardana of Jayasiṁha sūri	Ed. by C.D.DALAL, GOS, Baroda, 1920.
Harshacharita of Bāṇa	Ed. by P. V. KANE, Bombay, 1918. Eng. trans. by E. B. COWELL and F. W. THOMAS, London, 1897.
Kādambarī of Bāṇa	Ed. by P. PETERSON, Bombay, 1900. Eng. trans. by C. M. RIDDING, London, 1896.
Kāmasūtra of Vātsyāyana	with the commentary Jayamaṅgalā. Ed. by D. L. GOSWAMI, Benaras, 1929. Eng. trans. B. N. BASU. Revised by R. L. GHOSE and with a foreword by P. C. BAGACHI, 5th Ed. Calcutta, 1944.
Kāvyamīmāṁsā of Rājaśekhara	Ed. by C. D. DALAL and R. A. SASTRI GOS, 3rd Ed. Baroda, 1934.
Kīrtikaumudī of Someśvara	Ed. by A. V. KATHVATE, Bss. Bombay, 1883.
Kumārapālacharita of Hemachandra	Ed. by A. V. KATHVATE, 2 parts, Bombay, 1885, 1915.
Kumārapālaprabandha of Jinamaṇḍana	Ed. by CHATURVIJAYA, Bhavanagar, Sam. 1971.

Kuvalayamālā of Uddyotana	Ed. by A. N. UPADHYE, 1969.
Lekhapaddhati	Ed. by C. D. DALAL and G. K. SHRI GONDEKAR, Baroda, 1925.
Mālavıkāgnimitra of Kālidāsa	Ed. with the comm. of Kāṭayavema by S. P. PANDIT. Bss. 2nd Ed. Bombay, 1889. Eng. trans. by C. H. TAWNEY, London, 1891.
Meghadūta of Kālidāsa	Ed. by E. HULTZSCH, London, 1911; also NSP. 4th Ed., 1881; Trivendrum, 1919; Benaras, 1931. Gondal, 1935 etc.
Mṛichchhakaṭika of Śūdraka	Tr. RYDER, A. W., Cambridge. Mass., 1905.
Navasāhasāṅkacharita of Padmagupta alias Parimala	Ed. by V. S. ISLAMPURKAR. Bss. Bombay, 1895.
Paṃvāra-vaṁśa-darpaṇa of Dayāladāsa	Ed. by DASHARATHA SHARMA, Bikaner, 1960.
Pārijātamañjarī of Madana	Ed. by E. HULTZSCH. El, VIII, pp. 96 ff.
Pṛithvīrājavijaya of Jayānaka	Ed. by G. H. OJHA and C. S. GULERI, Ajmer, 1941.
Rājataraṅgiṇī of Kalhaṇa	Ed. DURGA PRASAD, 1892. Eng. trans. of M. A. STEIH, London, 1900.
Sarasvatīkaṇṭhābharaṇa of Bhojarāja	Ed. by JIVANANDA VIDYASAGARA, 2nd.ed. Calcutta, 1894.
Samarāṅgaṇasūtradhāra of Bhoja	Ed. by T. GANAPATI SASTRI, 2 Vols. GOS. Nos. XXV and XXXII, Baroda, 1924, 1925.
Śārṅgadharapaddhati	Ed. by PETERSON, Bombay Sanskrit Series No. 37.
Subhāṣitaratnasaṁdoha of Amitagati	Ed. by BHAVADATTA SASTRI and W. L. PANSHIKAR, K. M. Series, No. 82, 2nd Edition, Bombay, 1919.
Sukṛitasaṁkīrtana of Arisiṁha	Ed. by PUNYAVIJAYA, SJS, No. 32, Bombay, 1960.
Surathotsava of	Ed. by Pandit SIVADATTA, and PARAB.

Someśvara	NSP, Bombay, 1902
Sukṛitakīrtikallolinī of Jayasiṁha Sūri	Ed. by C. D. DALAL, GOS.
Shaḍdarśanasamuchchaya of Haribhadra	Calcutta, 1915.
Sṛiṅgāramañjarīkathā of Bhoja	Ed. by (Miss) K. MUNSHI, SJS. No. 30 Bombay, 1958.
Tilakamañjarīkathā of Dhanapāla	N. S. P. Bombay, 1903.
Vasantavilāsa of Bālachandra Sūri	Ed. by C. D. DALAL, GOS, VII, Baroda 1917.
Vikramāṅkadevacharita of Bilhaṇa	Ed. by G. BUHLER, Bombay Sanskrit Series, No. XIV, 1875.
Yuktikalpataru of Bhoja	Ed. by ĪSHVARACHANDRA, SASTRI, Calcutta Oriental Series, Calcutta, 1917.

(2) NON-INDIAN SOURCES

Megasthenes Fragments of Indica	Eng. trans. by MC. CRINDLE, Ancient India, as described by Megasthenes and Arrian, Calcutta, Bombay, London, 1877.
Periplus Maris Erythraei	Eng. trans. (The Commerce and Navigation of the Erythraean sea etc.) by J. W. MC-CRINDLE, Calcutta, Bombay, London, 1879.
Strabo Geographica	Ed. and trans. by W. MILLER, London, New York, 1914.
Hiuen Tsiang	Trans. by S. BEAL (Buddhist Records of the Western World, (London, 1884.
Yuan Chwang	Trans. by T. WATTERS (On Yuan Chwang's Travels in India) Ed. by T. W. RHYS DAVIDS and S. W. BUSHELL. 2 Vols. London, 1904-5.
Al Beruni's India	Trans. by E. C. SACHAU.
Khazain-Ul-Futūh.	Eng. trans. by M.HABIB, Bombay, 1931.
Tābquāt-i-Nāshirī of Minhaj-ud-dīn Siraj-ud-dīn	Eng. Trans. by H.G.RAVERTY, Calcutta, 1880.
History of India as told by its own Historians	Ed. by ELLIOT and DOWSON, London, 1906-07.

(3) BOOKS ON INSCRIPTIONS

Barua, B. M. and Sinha, G.	Barhut Inscription, Calcutta, 1926.
Bhandarkar, D. R.	List of Inscriptions of Northern India. Appendix to EI, XIX-XXIII.
Dvivedi. H. N.	*Gwalior Ke Abhilekha*, Gwalior, 1947.
Fleet, J. F.	Inscriptions of the Early Gupta Kings and their successors. CII, III, Calcutta, 1888.
Hiralal	Inscriptions in the Central Provinces and Berar, 2nd Ed. Nagpur, 1932.
Hultzsch, E.	Inscriptions of Aśoka, New Ed. CII, Vol. I. London, 1925.
Hultzsch, E.	South Indian Inscriptions 3 Vols. (ASI, NIS, Vols. 9, 10 and 29), Madras, 1890-1929.
Mirashi, V. V.	Inscriptions of the Kalachuri-Chedi Era, CII, Vol. IV, Ootacamund, 1955.
Ojha, G. H.	*Bhāratīya Lipimālā*, Ajmer, 1918.
Rice, Lewis	Mysore and Coorg from Inscriptions, London, 1909.
Sircar, D. C.	Select Inscriptions bearing on Indian History and Civilization, Vol. I, Calcutta, 1965.

Inscriptions have been published in the Epigraphia Indica, the Indian Antiquary, the Journal of the Asiatic Society of Bengal, PRAS, WC., etc.

(4) BOOKS ON COINS

Allan, J.	Catalogue of the Coins of Ancient India (in the British Museum), London, 1936.
Allan, J.	Catalogue of the Coins of the Gupta Dynasties, and of Śaśāṅka, King of Gauḍa (in the British Museum), London, 1914.
Bhandarker, D. R.	Carmichael Lectures on Ancient Indian Numismatics, Calcutta, 1921.
Cunningham A	Coins of Ancient India from the earliest

times down to the Seventh Century A.D., London, 1891.

Gopal Lallanji — Early Medieval Coin types of Northern India, Varanasi-5, 1966.

Rapson, E. J. — Indian Coins, Strassburg, 1897.

Rapson, E. J. — Catalogue of the Coins of the Āndhra dynasty, the Western Kshatrapas, the Traikūṭaka dynasty and the Bodhi dynasty (Cat. of Indian Coins in the British Museum Vol. IV)., London, 1908.

Singhal, C. R. — Bibliography of Indian Coins, Bombay, 1950.

Smith, V. A. — Catalogue of the Coins in the Indian Museum, Calcutta, including the Cabinet of the Asiatic Society of Bengal. Vol. I, Oxford, 1906.

Trivedi, H. V. — Catalogue of the Coins of the Nāga Kings of Padmāvatī, Gwalior, 1957.

(5) ON HISTORY IN ENGLISH

Agrawal, D. P. — The Copper Bronze Age in India, New Delhi, 1971.

Agrawal, V. S. — India as known to Pāṇini, Lucknow, 1953.

Agrawal, V. S. — Indian Arts, Varanasi, 1965.

Allchin B, and Allchin, F. R. — The Birth of Indian Civilization, Great Britain, 1968.

Allchin, F. R. — Piklihal Excavations, Andhra Pradesh Government Archaeological Series, No. 1, Hyderabad.

Allchin, F. R. — The Indian Middle Stone Age: Some New sites in Central and Southern India and their implications, BLUIA, No. II, pp. 1-36.

Altekar, A. S. — Rāshṭrakūṭas and their times, Poona, 1934.

Banerjea, J. N. — Development of Hindu Iconography, Calcutta, 1956.

Banerjee, K. D. Middle palaeolithic Industries of the Deccan, Poona.

Banerji, R. D. The Age of the Imperial Guptas, Benaras, 1933.

Bhandarkar, D. R. Aśoka, Calcutta, 1955.

Bhandarkar, D. R. Lectures on the Ancient History of India (Carmichael Lectures, 1918), Calcutta, 1919.

Bhargava, P. L. India in the Vedic Age, Lucknow, 1956.

Bhatia, Pratipal. The Paramaras (c. 800-1305 A.D.), New Delhi, 1970.

Bose, N. K. and Sen, D. Excavations in Mayurbhanj, Calcutta.

Buddha Prakash Studies in Indian History and Civilization, Agra, 1962.

Chakladar, H. Social Life in Ancient India, 2nd Edn., Calcutta, 1954.

Chattopadhyaya, Sudhakar Early History of North India, Calcutta, 1958.

Chattopadhyaya, Sudhakar The Śakas in India, Santiniketan, 1955.

Childe, V. G. Old world Prehistory, 1957.

Cunningham, A. Ancient Geography of India, Calcutta, 1924.

Deterra, H and Paterson, T.T. Studies on the Ice Age in India and Associated Human Cultures, Washington, 1939.

DE. N. L. Geographical Dictionary of Ancient and Medieval India, London, 1927.

Diwakar, R.R. (Ed) Bihar Through the Ages, Bombay, Calcutta, Madras, New Dehi, 1958

Fergusson, J. History of Indian and Eastern Architecture IInd Ed. Revised.

Fergusson, J. Tree and Serpent Worship, 2nd Ed. London, 1873.

Fergusson, J and Burgess, J. Cave Temples of India, London, 1880.

Fick, R. *Die sociale Gliederung im nordöstlichen Indien zu Buddha's Zeit*. Kiel, 1897. Eng. Trans.

by S. K. Maitra (The Social Organization in North-East India in Buddha's time). Calcutta, 1920.

Ganguly, D.C. History of the Paramāra Dynasty, Dacca, 1953.

Garde, M.B. Archaeology in Gwalior, Gwalior, 1934.

Gopal Lallanji The Economic Life of Northern India; Varanasi, 1965.

Habibullah, A.B.M. Foundation of the Muslim rule in India, Lahore, 1945.

Jain, K.C. Jainism in Rajasthan, Sholapur, 1963.

Jayaswal, K. P. History of India 150-350 A. D., Lahore. 1933.

J. Coggin Brown Catalogue o Pre-historic Antiquities in the Indian Museum, Simla, 1917.

Joshi, R.V. Pleistocene studies in the Malaprabha Basin, Poona, 1955.

Kane, P.V. History of Dharmaśāstra, 4 Vols. Poona, 1930-53.

Keith, A.B. History of Sanskrit Literature, Oxford. 1928.

Keith, A.B. The Sanskrit Drama, Oxford, 1924.

Keith, A.B. Indian Logic and Atomism, Oxford, 1921.

Khatri, A.P. Stone Age Cultures of Malwa, Ph. D. thesis, Poona, 1958.

Kramrisch, S. Indian Sculpture, London, 1929.

Krishna Deva. Temples of North India, New Delhi, 1969.

Law, B.C. Geography of Early Buddhism, London, 1932.

Law, B.C. Tribes in Ancient India, Poona, 1943.

Law, B.C. Ujjayini in Ancient India, Published by the Archaeological Department, Gwalior Govt. 1944.

Levi, S. Le theatre Inden, Paris, 1890.

Luard, C.E. and Lele, K,K. Paramāras of Dhar and Malwa, Bombay 1908.

Majumdar, A. K. History of the Chālukyas, Bombay, 1956.

Majumdar, R.C. The Vedic Age, London, 1951.

Majumdar, R.C.	The Age of Imperial Unity, Bombay, 1951.
Majumdar, R.C.	The Classical Age, Bombay, 1954.
Majumdar, R.C.	The Age of Imperial Kanauj, Bombay, 1955.
Majumdar, R.C.	The Struggle for Empire, Bombay, 1960.
Majumdar, R.C. and Altekar, A. S.	The Vākāṭaka Gupta Age, Benaras, 1954.
Marshall John and Alfred Foucher	The Monuments of Sanchi, 3 Vols.
Marshall John and Garde, M.B.	The Bagh Caves, Gwalior, 1927.
Mirashi, V. V.	Studies in Indology, Vol. I. Nagpur, 1960.
Misra, S.D.	Natural Regions of the Sub-continent India and Pakistan, (Typed Script)
Mookerji, R.K.	Hindu Civilization, London, 1936.
Mookerji, R.K.	Chandragupta Maurya and His Times. Madras, 1943.
Munshi, K.M.	The Glory that was Gurjaradeśa, Bombay, 1955.
Narain. A.K.	The Indo-Greeks, Oxford 1957.
Pandey, R.B.	Vikramāditya of Ujjayinī, Benaras, 1954.
Pargiter, F.E.	Ancient Indian Historical Tradition, Delhi, 1962.
Pargiter, F. E.	The Purāṇa Text of the Dynasties of the Kali Age, Varanasi, 1962.
Patil, D.R.	The Cultural Haritage of Madhya Bharat, Gwalior, 1952.
Pradhan, Sitanath	Chronology of Ancient India, Calcutta. 1927.
Peterson and Zeuner	Studies on the Ice Age in India and Associated human Cultures.
Puri, Baij Nath	India in the time of Patañjali, Bombay, 1957.
Puri, Baij Nath	India under the Kushāṇas, Bombay, 1965.

Piers, E.A. The Maukharis, Madras, 1934

Pusalker, A.D. Bhāsa. A Study.

Raghubirsingh Malwa in Transition, Bombay, 1936.

Rao, T.A. Gopinatha Elements of Hindu Iconography. 2 Vols. Madras, 1914, 16.

Rapson, E.J. Ancient India, Cambridge, 1914.

Rapson, E.J. Cambridge History of India, Vol. I, Cambridge, 1922.

Raychaudhuri, H.C. Political History of Ancient India, 5th Ed. Calcutta, 1950.

Ray, H.C. Dynastic History of Northern India, 2 Vols. Calcutta, 1932-36.

Rhys Davids, T.W. Buddhist India, London, 1902.

Saletore, B. A. Life in the Gupta Age, Bombay, 1943.

Sankalia, H. D. Prehistory and Protohistory in India and Pakistan, Bombay, 1962.

Sankalia, H. D., Subbarao, B. and Deo, S. B. The Excavations at Maheshwar and Navadatoli, Poona-Baroda, 1958.

Sankalia, H.D., Deo, S. B., Ansari, Z. D. and Ehrhardt, S. From History to Prehistory at Nevasa (1954-56), Poona, 1960.

Sankalia, H. D. The Godavari Palaeolithic Industry, Poona, 1952.

Saraswati, S. K. Survey of Indian Sculpture, Calcutta, 1957.

Sastri, K. A. N. The Cholas, Vols. I and II, Madras, 1925.

Sastri, K.A. N. The Nandas and the Mauryas, Benares, 1952.

Sharma, D. Early Chauhana Dynasties, Delhi, 1959.

Sharma, D. Rajasthan through the Ages, Bikaner, 1966.

Shastri, Ajay Mitra India as seen in the Bṛihatsaṁhitā of Varāhamihira, Delhi, 1969.

Sinha, B. P. The Decline of the Kingdom of Magadha Cir. 455-1000 A.D., Patna, 1954.

Sircar, D. C. The Successors of the Sātavāhanas in the Lower Deccan, Calcutta, 1939.

Sircar, D. C. Studies in the Geography of Ancient and Medieval India, Delhi, 1960.

Sircar, D. C. The Śākta Pīṭhas, Calcutta, 1965.

Sircar, D. C. The Guhilas of Kishkindhā, Calcutta, 1965.

Sircar, D. C. Ancient Malwa and the Vikramāditya Tradition, Delhi, 1969.

Smith, V. A. Early History of India, Oxford, 1924.

Spate, O. H. K. India and Pakistan, London, 1954.

Stevenson, Mrs. S. The Heart of Jainism, Oxford, 1915.

Tod, J. Annals and Antiquities of Rajasthan, Ed. by W. Crooke, 1920.

Tripathi, R. S. History of Kanauj, Benaras, 1937.

Upadhyaya, B. S. India in Kalidasa, Delhi, New Delhi, Jullundur, Bombay, Calcutta, Madras, 2nd Edition, 1968.

Vaidya, C. A. History of Medieval Hindu India, 3 Vols. Poona, 1921-1926.

Vidyalankar Prannath A Study in the Economic condition of North India.

Wheeler, R. E. M. Early India and Pakistan, London, 1959.

Zeitschrift für Indologie and Iranistik (211), 1922.

(6) MODERN WORKS IN VERNACULAR

Chauhsiang Kuang *Chīnī Baudhadharma Kā Itihāsa*, Prayag, V. S. 2013.

Desai, M. D. *Jaina Sāhityano Saṁkshipta Itihāsa*, Bombay, 1933.

Dvivedi, H. N. *Madhya Bhārat Kā Itihāsa*, Gwalior, 1959.

Jaina, Jagadish Chand *Bharat Ke Prāchīna Jaina Tirtha*, Benaras, 1952.

Jaina Tirtha Sarva-Saṁgraha Ahmedabad, 1953.

Moti Chandra *Prāchīna Bhāratīya Veśabhūshā*, Prayag, V. S. 2007.

Ojha, G. H. *Rājputānā Kā Itihāsa*, Ajmer, 1937.
Ojhā Nibandha Saṁgraha, Udaipur.

Premi, Nathuram *Hindī Jaina Sāhitya aura* Itihāsa, Bombay, 1942.

Reu, B. N. *Rājā Bhoja*, Allahabad, 1932. *Jaina tīrtha Sarva Saṁgraha*, Vol. I, Part I.

Upadhyaya, B. S. *Gupta Kālīna Bhārata*, Lucknow, 1969.

(7) GENERAL

(*A*) *COMMEMORATIVE VOLUMES*

Aiyangar Commemoration Volume.

B. C. Law. Volume.

Bhārat Kaumudī, Allahabad, 1945.

Gurugopāladāsa Vairayā Smṛitigrantha

Malaviya Commemorative Volume, Benaras, 1932.

Mirashi Felicitation Volume.

Pathak Commemorative Volume.

Vikrama Volume, Ujjain, 1948.

Vikrama Smṛiti Grantha, Ujjain, V. S. 2001.

(*B*) *GAZETTEERS*

Bombay Gazetteer, Vol. I, Part I.

Imperial Gazetteers, XVII and VIII.

The Central India State Gazetteer Series, Bhopal.

State Gazetteer, Vol. III, Compiled by C.E. LUARD, Calcutta.

Western States (Malwa) Gazetteer, Vol. V.

Part A, Text, compiled by C. E. LUARD, Bombay, 1908.

Gwalior State Gazetteer, Vol. I compiled by C. E. LUARD, Calcutta, 1908.

Gwalior State Gazetteer, Vol. I, Pt. IV by C. E. LUARD, Bombay, 1908.

Indore State Gazetteer, by C. E. LUARD, Calcutta, 1908.

(*C*) *REPORTS*

Annual Reports of the Archaeological Department, Gwalior State.

Annual Reports, Rajputana Museum, Ajmer.

Annual Reports of the Archaeological Survey of India.

Annual Report on the working of the Museum and Navaratna Mandir, Indore.

Annual Report of the Mysore Archaeological Department, Mysore.

Annual Bulletin of the Nagpur University Historical Society, Nagpur.

Annual Progress Report of Archaeological Survey of India, Western Circle, Poona-Bombay.
Archaeological Survey of India Reports by ALEXANDER CUNNINGHAM.
BHANDARKAR Report on Sanskrit Mss. 1882-83.
Bulletin of Ancient Indian History and Archaeology I, Saugar.
Bulletin National Institute of Science Vol. I, Delhi.
Epigraphia India, Ootacamund.
Indian Antiquary, Bombay.
Indian Archaeology—A Review.
Memoirs of the Archaeological Survey of India.
Memoir of Central India including Malwa and adjoining provinces with History and copious illustrations of past and present conditions of that country by Major General Sir JOHN MALCOLM, London, 1932.
Monthly Bulletin of the Asiatic Society, Calcutta.
PETERSONS Reports.
Proceedings of the Indian History Congress.
Proceedings and Transactions of the All-India Oriental Conference.

(*D*) *JOURNAL AND MAGAZINES*

English

Ancient India, Delhi.
Annals of the Bhandarkar Oriental Research Institute, Poona.
Indian Historical Quarterly, Calcutta.
Journal of the Asiatic Society of Bengal, Calcutta.
Journal of the Bombay Branch of the Royal Asiatic Society, Bombay.
Journal of the Bihar and Orissa Research Society, Patna.
Journal of the Bihar Research Society, Patna.
Journal of the Department of Letters, Calcutta University.
Journal of the Ganganatha Jha Institute.
Journal of Indian History, Trivandrum.
Journal of the Madhya Pradesh Itihāsa Parishad, Bhopal.
Journal of the Numismatic Society of India, Bombay.
Journal of the Oriental Institute, Baroda.
Journal of the Asiatic Society of Great Britain and Ireland, London.

Journal of the U.P. Historical Society, Lucknow.
Journal of the Palaentological Society, India, Lucknow, Benaras Hindu University Magazine.
Calcutta Review, Calcutta.
Man in India, Calcutta.
Zeitschrift der Deutschen Morgenlandischen Gesselschaft.
National Geographic, Oct. 1961.
Indian Forester, Dehra Dun.
Lalitakalā, New Delhi.
Marg, Bombay.

INDEX

A

Abhaya, 99.
Abhayadatta, 258, 269.
Abhayakumāra, 115.
Abhayasiṁha, 419, 484.
Abhayatilakagaṇi, 325.
Abhidhānaratnamālā, 470.
Abhimanyu, 384.
Abhinandanadeva, 404.
Abhinavagupta, 163.
Ābhīras, 19, 174, 176, 229, 230, 3^c3.
Abhisamayavibhaṅga, 399.
Abhonā, 264.
Aboḍa (Ābū), 200.
Ābū, 325, 329, 338, 350, 364, 441, 463.
Adamgarh, 58, 59.
Adhi-Droṇāchāryānvaya, 360, 366,409.
Ādinagar (Mukhaliṅgam), 345, 346.
Ādityasena, 259, 26c, 261.
Ādityavardhana, 245, 250, 254,258. 259, 267.
Ādityavarman, 261.
Adriyalavidāvarī, 497.
Africa, 36, 37, 45, 46, 47, 48, 54.
Agar, 451
Agāsiyaka, 360, 409.
Agastya, 89, 481.
Aghamarshaṇa, 481.
Āghāṭa (Ahar), 336.
Agni (Tributary of Narmadā), 57.
Agnihotrin, 482.
Agnimitra, 31, 32, 149, 150, 151, 188, 198.
Agnipurāṇa, 472.
Agrawal, V. S., 496.
Agsimā, (Agniśarmā), 196;
Ahara, 58, 68, 76, 77, 79, 82, 95.
Ahichchhatrā, 96, 183, 238, 293, 341
Ahichchhatrapura, 480.
Ahihol, inscription, 11.
Ahimita, 198.
Ahmedabad, 345.
Āin-ī-Akbarī, 327, 328.
Āin-ul-Multāni, 375.
Airikiṇa (Eran), 267, 268.
Ājaḍa, 472.
Ajadatta, 188.
Ajanta, 256, 282, 295, 301.
Ajātaśatru, 99, 100, 102, 207.
Ajay, 79.
Ajayadeva, 374, 382.
Ajayagarh, 359.
Ajayapāla (chālukya ruler,), 367.
Ajayapāladeva, 364, 385, 410.
Ajayavarman, 359, 362, 365, 368, 383.
Ajitiguṭa, 219.
Ajmer, 7, 166, 168, 362, 364, 440
Akālavarsha Krishṇa III, 327.
Ākara, 10, 168, 172.
Ākarāvanti, 224.
Akesines (chenab), 5.
Akolasthāna, 481.
Alamgirpur, 96, 97.
Alāuddīn Khilji, 375, 376.
Alexander, 4, 13.
Ālhaṇa ,360, 364.
Alirajpur, (Dist. Jhabua), 445
Alla, 415, 430.
Allahabad, 8, 251, 303.
Allan, J., 1, 3, 6, 7, 122, 146, 159, 240, 241, 243, 256.
Allchin, 53, 54, 62.
Altekar, A. S., 8, 88, 158, 160, 175, 178, 183, 185, 232, 239, 322, 330, 352, 395, 503, 510.
Alviḍagāṁva, 385.
Alvi-Mahadeo, 51.
Amaradatta, 470.
Amarakantaka, 50.
Amarakosha, 163, 298, 307, 314, 315.
Amarasiṁha, 161, 163, 216, 236, 298.
Amarāvatī, 280, 281.
Āmardakatīrtha, (Ujjain), 412, 413, 464.
Amaruśataka, 477, 478.
Amāsvāmīcharita, 477.
Ambādevīrāsa, 475.
Ambakheri, 78.
Ambashṭhas, 5.
Āmera, 497.
Amir Khusrau, 375.
Amitagati, 401, 471.
Amitasena, 188, 228.
Amoghavarsha, 327.
Āmrakārdava, 23, 245, 276.
Amrol, 428, 429.
Anāchāryakula, 201.
Aṇahila, 350.
Aṇahilapāṭaka, 350, 364, 370.
Ānandapāla (Shahi ruler), 347.
Ānandapura, 11, 474, 480.
Ananta, 158.

Anantapāla, 12.
Anargha-rāghava, 468.
Ānarta, 172, 173.
Anayasiṁha, 374, 387, 388, 466.
Ander, 201, 204, 205, 220.
Andhau, 169, 171.
Andhra, 45, 84, 169, 262.
Aṅga, 357, 358.
Aṅgadatta, 216.
Aṅgarāja, 198.
Aṅgirasa, 220, 481.
Antialcidas, 23, 151, 188, 194, 198, 201, 202.
Anu, 89.
Anūpa, 18, 91, 168, 172, 181, 245, 246.
Anuvinda, 94.
Anvalā, 195, 206.
Apāchyas, 94.
Āpagira, 201.
Apara, 132.
Aparājita, 343.
Aparānta, 165, 168, 172, 343.
Aparārka, 195.
Āpava Vasishṭha, 92.
Aphsad, 260, 261, 262.
Āpnavad, 484.
Ārādhanā, 471, 476.
Ārādhanāgadya Kathākośa, 475.
Ārādhanāsāra, 469.
Arang, (Dist. Raipur), 446.
Araṇipadra, 413.
Araṇyarāja, 338.
Ardhāṣṭamaṇḍala, 384.
Arhadāsa, 404.
Arikesarin alias Kesideva, 343, 346.
Arisiṁha, 361.
Arjuna, 90, 91, 92, 94.
Arjunavarman, 32, 368, 370, 371, 375, 382, 387, 392, 393, 403, 404, 416, 477, 478, 483, 490, 505, 510.
Arjunavarman, II, 374, 375.
Ārjunāyanas, 8.
Arṇorāja, 359, 363.
Arrian, 4, 5.
Arṭa, 166.
Arthaśāstra, 92, 105, 107, 109, 110, 139.
Arthūṇā, 388, 392, 403, 408, 416, 482, 486.
Ārya Āshāḍha, 120.
Āryabhāsa, 324.
Āryabhaṭa, 299.
Āryabhaṭīyam, 299.
Āryagrāma, 219.
Āryaka, or Ajaka, 102.
Aryan, 3, 83, 84, 86, 87, 88, 89, 92, 94, 95, 96, 97.
Āryarakshita, 120, 121.
Ārya Suhastin, 120.
Āryāvarta, 179.
Asāḍa, 224.
Āśādhara, 368, 369, 373, 403, 404, 477, 478, 479.
Āśādhara (A Brāhmaṇa), 481.
Āsala, 373.
Āśārāja, 360.
Asavatī, 200.
Ashta, 156, 164.
Ashṭādhyāyī, 5, 31.
Ashṭāṅgasaṁgraha, 301.
Aśmakas, 103.
Aśoka, 22, 104, 105, 106, 107, 108, 109, 111, 114, 116, 117, 118, 120, 122, 126, 127, 134, 136, 138, 139, 140, 141, 143, 145, 149, 152, 192, 198, 201, 202.
Āśramanagara (Keshoraipatan), 402, 475.
Assam, 341.
Āśvalāyana, 482.
Atigupta, 279.
Ātmānuśāsanatilaka, 475.
Atranjikhera, 78, 79, 96.
Atri, 220.
Atru, 374.
Atud-Khasa, 57.
Audalya, 481.
Aufrecht, 474, 478.
Aulikara, 9, 10, 17, 23, 24, 159, 250, 254, 258, 259, 261, 266, 267, 270, 273, 277, 302, 303.
Aurva, 484.
Avaloka, 470, 472.
Avanti, 1, 9, 10, 11, 15, 19, 31, 90, 91, 93, 94, 98, 99, 100, 101, 102, 103, 104, 105, 108, 115, 116, 118, 119, 121, 140, 141, 142, 146, 149, 168, 172, 188, 197, 214, 224, 225, 255, 256, 259, 274, 322, 323, 324, 330, 331, 349, 359, 360, 366, 407, 419, 474.
Avanti Sukumāla, 120, 198.
Avantijanāśraya, Pulakeśīrāja, 321.
Avantikumāraśataka, 473.
Avantimaṇḍala, 25, 362, 385.
Avantiputra, 101.
Avantisena, 102.
Avantivardhana, 324.
Avantivarman, 263, 333, 412, 413.
Avara, 22, 51, 64, 65, 67, 68, 69, 72, 73, 74, 75, 78, 95, 125, 126, 130, 132, 133, 134, 202, 210, 211, 213, 295.
Āvasathika, 482.
Āvaśyaka, Kathānakas, 102.
Avimāraka, 215.
Ayodhya, 88, 89, 90, 91, 92, 93, 150, 153, 154, 192, 239.

B

Bachirāja, 345.
Bactria, 235.
Bādāvim, 497.
Badnawar, 444, 463.
Badoh, 30, 289, 404, 405, 430, 431, 454, 455, 459.
Baḍvā, 8, 26, 187, 189, 193, 206.
Badwani, 144, 269, 404.
Bagh, 30, 269, 270, 281, 282, 290, 291, 292, 294, 295, 296, 301, 311, 313.
Bagherā, 400, 486.
Bagheravālas, 484, 486.
Bahadat (Brahmadatta), 196.
Bahadrabad, 78.
Bahal, 75, 76.
Bāhl, 371.
Bāhu, 93.
Baigas, 84.
Bailmān, 321.
Bajapai, K. D. 118, 128, 153, 156, 160, 232, 234, 235, 238,
Bala, 187, 189, 193.
Bālāditya, 247, 249, 258.
Bālāghāt plates, 9.
Balaka, 196.
Balamitra, 196.
Balarāma, 94.
Balarāma (brother of Kṛishṇa), 213, 273.
Bālasarasvatīyam, 478.
Balātkāragaṇa, 400, 475.
Balavāna, 374.
Bali, 221.
Balirāja, 337.
Ballāla (Hoyasāla chief), 369.
Ballāla, 363, 364, 365, 366, 389.
Baluchistan, 235.
Bamnāla hoard, 29, 239, 317.
Bāṇa, 10, 11, 31, 32, 152, 260, 265, 280, 297, 313.
Banas, 58, 77.
Bandhuvarman, 238, 252, 253, 259, 267.
Banerjea, J. N., 147.
Banerjee, K. D., 54.
Banerji, R. D., 241, 510.
Banganga, 41, 42, 65.
Banswara, 335, 345, 346, 347, 385, 391.
Bappairāja (Vākpatirāja I), 327. 331.
Baran, 400.
Bārappa, 339, 340, 343.
Bardia, 510.
Bārhaspatya, 481.
Barhināga, 184, 185.
Barkhera (Bhim Baithaka), 58.
Barli, 152.
Barnal, 8.
Barṇāla, 193.
Barṇāsa (Banas), 167.
Baro, 237.
Baroda Copper plate, 323.
Barulamisas, 219.
Basak, R. G. 262.
Basai, 40, 51.
Basarah (Vaiśālī) 237, 269, 293. 295.
Bastar, 84, 344.
Batesar, 428.
Bāvanagajā (Badawani), 405.
Bayālisa Parichachhedīyasūtra, 202.
Bayana, 239.
Beas, 41, 42.
Begumra, 330.
Belgar, 455.
Benaras, 93. 142, 293, 350.
Bengal, 323, 341, 357, 358. 457.
Berar, 320.
Besanagar, 22, 26, 143, 145, 151, 152, 194, 195, 204, 205, 206, 208, 222, 223, 289, 290, 291, 293, 294, 295.
Betma, 346, 347, 481.
Betwa, 39, 51, 65, 125, 141, 417, 446.
Bhaddalapura, 400.
Bhadra, 279.
Bhadrabāhu, 120.
Bhadraka, 151.
Bhadraka or Bhadragupta, 120, 121.
Bhadraśreṇya, 91.
Bhadravaṭa, 195.
Bhāgabhadra Kāśiputra, 23, 151, 152, 188, 194.
Bhagatrav, 65.
Bhāgavata, 151, 152, 206, 434.
Bhagavatīsūtra, 4.
Bhāgila, 148.
Bhāguri, 470.
Bhagwan Lal Indrajit, 509, 510.
Bhāilasvāmīgaḍha, 404.
Bhāillasvāmī Mahādvādaśaka, 364, 365.
Bhaillasvāmin (Bhilsa), 359, 372, 410, 417, 418, 474.
Bhaja, 288.
Bhaktāmarastotra, 469.
Bhāmāṇa, 320.
Bhāmana, 333.
Bhamini, 455.
Bhandarkar, D. R., 4, 102, 151, 157, 174, 237, 251, 319, 322, 326, 346, 503, 507.
Bhaṅgala (Bengal), 399.
Bhanpur, 437, 438.
Bhānu, 476.

Bhānugupta, 248.
Bhāradvāja, 255, 300, 481.
Bharadvāja gotra, 220.
Bhāraśiva family, 184, 185, 186, 193, 195, 196.
Bharata, 9, 98.
Bhārata war, 94.
Bhārata, (Writer), 470.
Bhāratas, (Tribe), 89, 100.
Bhāravi, 215, 236, 297, 298.
Bhārgava, 92, 93, 481, 484.
Bhārgava gotra, 220.
Bhargava, P. L. 88, 90.
Bharhut, 198, 208, 221, 223.
Bharoch, 316, 371, 501.
Bhartṛidāman, 177, 178, 227.
Bhartṛihari, 298.
Bharukachchha, 19.
Bhāsa, 31, 215, 216, 217, 297, 299, 308.
Bhāsvat (Bhilsa), 334.
Bhat Pachlana, 510.
Bhatia, Pratipala, 328, 330, 332, 333, 336, 338, 341, 342, 343, 354, 355, 363, 364, 368, 385, 396.
Bhatpura, 78.
Bhaṭṭi, 298.
Bhaṭṭimahara, 277.
Bhaṭṭisoma, 8, 188.
Bhāṭuka, 482.
Bhavabhūti, 296.
Bhavadatta, 182.
Bhāvanādvātriṁśatikā, 471.
Bhavanāga, 184, 185, 186, 193.
Bhāvaśataka, 186.
Bhavisayattakahā, 471.
Bhavyakumārachandrikā, 478.
Bheraghat, 38.
Bhīlas, 19, 84, 85, 488.
Bhillama, 369.
Bhilsa, 11, 27, 134, 166, 184, 229, 273, 283, 334, 335, 345, 364, 366, 372, 404, 417, 418, 453, 456, 459, 485, 506, 510.
Bhilsuri, 65.
Bhīma, 348, 350, 351, 354.
Bhīma II, 368, 369, 370.
Bhīmanāga, 183, 185, 186, 196.
Bhind, 70
Bhitargaon, 293, 295.
Bhitari Inscription of Skandagupta, 19, 238, 240.
Bhītarī seal, 243, 257.
Bhogavatī, 344.
Bhogin, 182.
Bhoginikā, 406, 485.
Bhoja, 20, 21, 24, 25, 27, 32, 33, 333, 341, 342, 345, 346, 347, 348, 349, 350, 351, 352, 355, 356, 357, 375, 376, 379, 381, 383, 385, 389, 390, 391, 396, 401, 402, 408, 417, 420, 4 6, 437, 446, 447, 448, 457, 464, 466, 468, 469, 470, 471, 472, 473, 474, 475, 476, 481, 489, 494, 495, 497, 501, 505.
Bhoja (Pratīhāra ruler), 505.
Bhoja II, 375.
Bhojas, 93.
Bhojapur, 30, 204, 205, 213, 352, 399, 401, 403, 405, 408, 436, 446, 449, 462, 486, 499.
Bhopal, 39,58, 227, 286, 287, 360, 364 365, 367, 387, 392, 393, 446, 482, 494, 497.
Bhṛigu gotra, 220.
Bhṛigukachchha (Broach), 167, 225.
Bhṛiguvardhana, 8, 187.
Bhṛiṁgārikā Chatuḥshashṭi, 385.
Bhujabalabhīma, 473.
Bhulunda, 245.
Bhūmaka, 156, 166, 167, 181.
Bhumara, 275.
Bhūmimitra, 153.
Bhūshaṇa, 403, 486.
Bhutra, 35.
Bhuvanapāla, 487.
Bihar, 84, 87, 341.
Bihār (Village), 399, 425.
Bihār, Koṭrā, 23, 250, 251, 252, 254, 267, 277.
Bijaulia, 359, 445.
Bijawada, 440, 462.
Bilaspur, 42.
Bilawali, 64.
Bilhaṇa, 371, 373, 382, 404, 416, 477, 483.
Bilhari, 412, 413, 464.
Bilpank, 443.
Bimbisāra, 99, 101, 104.
Binaika, 398, 425.
Bindunāga, 325.
Bindusāra, 105, 108.
Bisauli, 78.
Bisheshwar Nath, 503.
Bithla, 404.
Borkhedajhurd, 57.
Brahmāṇḍa Purāṇa, 183.
Brahmpuri, 466.
Brahmaśambhu, 413.
Bṛihad-Gachchha, 469.
Bṛihad-Rājamārtaṇḍa, 473.
Bṛihaddeśī, 217.
Bṛihadratha, 149.
Bṛihajjātaka, 300.
Bṛihaspati, 186.
Bṛihaspatināga, 185.
Bṛihatkathā, 102, 157, 162.
Bṛihatsaṁhitā, 13, 32, 255, 259, 300, 302, 313, 315.
Bṛihatsvayambhū stotra ṭīkā, 475

Broach, 167, 321, 322.
Buddha, 99, 101, 115, 116, 201, 202, 204, 207.
Buddha Pālita, 219.
Buddharāja, 264, 265.
Buddha Prakash, 254, 255.
Buddhi, Chanoleri, 404.
Buddhisāgara, 401.
Buddhodaya, 399.
Budhagupta, 23, 242, 243, 244, 245, 246, 247, 268, 273.
Budhasvāmin, 303.
Būhler, G. 196, 197.
Burhabalang river, 43.
Burhanpur, 56, 58,
Burma, 47, 49.
Burwas, 321.
Burzhom, 62.
Buxar, 154.

C

Cambay, 93, 162, 231, 369.
Campbell, 326.
Carlleyle, A. C. 1, 6.
Carmel (Mount), 45.
Ceylon, 117, 119, 357, 358.
Chachiga, 359.
Chachuroṇimaṇḍala, 385.
Chāhaḍa, 410.
Chakrakotya, 344.
Chakrapālita, 240.
Chakravarti, N. P. 366.
Chaityavandana-bhāshya, 479.
Chakrāyudha, 323, 330.
Chalap-Khurd, 57.
Chambal (river), 38, 46, 49, 51, 52, 63, 64, 65, 66.
Chambal Valley, 34, 40, 42, 51, 56.
Champūrāmāyaṇa (Bhojachampū), 473.
Chāmuṇḍarāja, 344, 350, 356, 414.
Chanchus, 84.
Chandana, 338.
Chandanagirimahāvihāra (Dhamnār), 398.
Chaṇḍapa, 342.
Chaṇḍarudra, 120.
Chanderi, 412, 462, 464, 510.
Chandigarh, 58.
Chaṇḍikāśrama, 411, 464.
Chandoli, 75, 76.
Chandragachchha, 477.
Chandragarbhaparipṛichchhā, 240.
Chandragupta (Maurya), 103, 104, 105, 120, 124, 141, 145.
Candragupta I, 229, 230.
Chandragupta II, 23, 28, 156, 168, 170, 171, 172, 178, 189, 215, 226, 231, 232, 233, 234, 235, 236, 237, 251, 252, 266, 267, 268, 272, 276, 280, 296, 297, 298, 306, 308, 313, 317.
Chandraketu, 2, 502.
Chandra Kshamāchārya, 234.
Chandrāṁśa, 182.
Chandraprabha, 477.
Chanera, 57.
Chapalīya, 481.
Charaka-Saṁhitā, 301.
Charchikā or Vijaya, 419.
Chārudatta, 215, 217, 297.
Chārudatta (Actor), 302, 304.
Chashṭana, 156, 168, 170, 171, 172, 178, 189, 226.
Chaturjātakīya, 481.
Chaturveda, 482.
Chaturvedins, 303.
Caturviṁśikā, 471.
Chau-fu-kua, 498.
Chāvoṭakas, 321.
Chehad, 373,
Chelukshamaṇa, 234, 279.
Chetaka, 100.
Chetiyagiri, 117.
Chhadanta Jātaka, 207.
Chhandaḥsūtra, 470.
Chharajanāga, 184, 185.
Chhatisgarh, 342.
Chhoṭisādri, 24, 254, 255, 267, 303.
Childe, 61, 74.
Chillana, 403, 485.
China, 47, 49, 160, 202.
Chiñchāsthāna, 480.
Chindwara, 56.
Chingleput District, 45.
Chinpur, 462.
Chirva, 349.
Chitor, 56, 195, 258, 270, 319, 345, 349, 400, 402, 403, 408, 445, 467, 497, 507.
Chitorgarh, 356.
Chitrakūṭa, 476.
Chitrodia, 459.
Chittapa, 27, 417, 474.
Cholaka, 316.
Cholas, 339, 343, 369.
Choli, 50.
Chudamoragiri, 200.
Chuṭukula, 182.
Chyavana, 484.
Cosmos, 249, 258.
Cousens, 455.
Cunningham, A., 5, 6, 122, 155, 204 455.
Cypras, 82.

D.

Dabhoi, 369, 458.
Dabok, 319, 320, 348.

Dādāka, 482.
Dādarapadra, 367.
Dadhikarṇa, 196.
Ḍāhala, 354, 422.
Ḍāhalamaṇḍala, 334.
Dāhanukā, 167.
Dahaz, 321.
Dahod, 404.
Daksha, 293.
Dakshamitrā, 219.
Dākshiṇātya (Brāhmaṇas), 482.
Dalal, M. L., 128, 129.
Dāmagada, 175.
Dāmaghasada or Dāmajadaśrī, 173, 217.
Dāmajada II, 175.
Dāmajada III, 176.
Damana, 167.
Dāmasena, 175, 176.
Dambarasiṁha, 331.
Dāmodara, 479.
Dāmodaragupta, 10, 262.
Dānarāśi, 406, 411.
Dāna-Śrījñāna, 399.
Daṇḍin, 472.
Dantidurga, 322, 323, 324.
Dārika, 399.
Darśanasāra, 401, 469.
Dāsa, 156.
Daśapura, 9, 17, 27, 119, 121, 167, 238, 252, 253, 254, 258, 259, 266, 267, 269, 270, 277, 281, 299, 303, 316, 317.
Daśaratha, 104.
Daśārṇa, 10, 17, 246, 301.
Daśarūpa, 470.
Dāsilakapatha, (Daswāḷia), 269.
Dasithakapalli, 277.
Dattabhaṭa, 241, 253, 277.
Dattasvāmin, 303.
Dattātreya, 92.
Davalpura, 510.
Dehgaon, 57.
Delha, 481, 482.
Delhi, 372, 375, 458.
Demetrius, 150.
Deo-Baranārk inscription, 263.
Deoguraria hill, 57.
Depālapur, 373.
Derdda, 396, 481.
De terra, 35, 36, 49, 50, 52.
Deullikā, 406, 485.
Deva, 406.
Devabhadra, 401.
Devabhūti or Devabhūmi, 152, 154.
Devachandra, 404.
Devadatta, 378, 397, 475.
Devadhara, 404.
Devagiri, 369, 371, 372, 373, 374, 377.
Devagupta, 11, 264, 265.
Devakachhar, 53.
Devamūrti, 158.
Devanāga, 185, 186.
Devapāla, 25, 26, 367, 368, 371, 372, 373, 385, 393, 403, 446, 478, 483, 507.
Devapāla (A Jaina Śrāvaka), 403.
Devapālapura, 409, 446.
Devapattana praśasti, 370.
Devasena, 401, 469.
Devasvāmin, 395, 505.
Devendra, 478, 479.
Devī, 104, 117, 127, 138, 143.
Devī Chandraguptam, 231.
Dewas, 64.
Dey, N. L., 343.
Dhamakas, 219.
Dhammapada, 141.
Dhammapāla, 115.
Dhamnār, 398, 414, 423, 425, 426, 427, 449, 450, 453, 454, 457.
Dhamutara, 219.
Dhanabhūti, 198.
Dhanadeva, 192.
Dhanañjaya, 327, 328, 340, 470.
Dhanapāla, 32, 335, 340, 381, 391, 400, 401, 471, 490.
Dhanapāla (A Karṇāṭa Brāhmaṇa), 481.
Dhandhuka, 350.
Dhaneśvara, 401.
Dhanika, 319, 320, 340, 408, 470, 472.
Dhanvantari 161, 163, 216.
Dhanyavishṇu, 247, 268, 273.
Dhāra, 27, 30, 186, 332, 333, 337, 341 351, 352, 353, 360, 361, 362, 363, 366, 368, 369, 373, 385, 387, 388, 390, 399, 401, 402, 404, 408, 419, 420, 421, 436, 448, 453, 454, 458, 465, 469, 471, 473, 474, 476, 478, 485, 491, 493, 499.
Dharaṇivarāha, 338.
Dharasena, 403.
Dharawada, 65.
Dhāreśvara, 421.
Dharmāditya, 265, 266.
Dharmaghosha, 479.
Dharmakīrti, 404.
Dharmāmṛita, 478.
Dharmapāla, 155, 323.
Dharmaparīkshā, 471.
Dharmapuri, 58, 341.
Dharma Rakshitā, 219.
Dharmaraksha, 202.
Dharmāraṇya vihāra, 278.
Dharmaratnavṛitti, 479.
Dharmasikshā, 477.
Dharma Śiva, 220.
Dharmavardhana, 200.
Dhaumya, 481.

Dhavagarta, 319.
Dhavala, 336.
Dhavalappa, 319, 320, 378.
Dhavalātman, 319.
Dholka, 370.
Dhruvadevī, 231, 232, 233, 308.
Dhruva Dhārāvarsha, 324.
Dhruvasena II, 12, 269, 303.
Dhruvasena Bālāditya, 266.
Dhruvasvāminī, 233, 237.
Dhūmarāja, 326.
Dhundheri, 455, 456.
Dhvanyāloka, 472.
Dikshita, 482.
Dinakara, 408.
Diṇḍvāṇakasthāṇa, 481.
Dion, 194.
Dionysus, 121.
Dīpavaṁśa, 118.
Diskalkar, D. B. 350, 510.
Divodāsa, 91, 93.
Dohaḍ, 362.
Dongergaon, 50, 355, 409.
Dooramela, 418.
Dorasamudra, 369, 477.
Douglas, R. D., 1.
Dravyaparīkshā 33, 505.
Dravyavardhana, 255, 256, 258. 299, 300.
Drishadvatī, 96.
Dṛishṭivadāṅga, 121.
Druhyu, 89.
Dubkuṇḍa, 348, 401, 404.
Dūdhākhedī 454, 461.
Dudubhisara, 201.
Dungarpur, 331, 345.
Durbalikāpushpamitra, 121.
Durdama, 91.
Durgāditya,406.
Durgagaṇa, 319, 320, 406.
Durlabharāja, 350.
Dūsala, 338, 339.
Durvāsārāśi, 411.
Dvādaśakulaka, 477.
Dvārikā, 360 .
Dviveda, 482.
Dvyāśrayamahākāvya, 325, 489.

E.

Edward, A. Piers, 260.
Egypt, 45.
Ekashashṭirātra, Sacrifice, 8, 187, 193.
Elorā, 322, 423.
Erakaṇa (Eran), 200.
Eran, 22, 23, 26, 28, 29, 62, 65, 66, 67, 68, 70, 73, 74, 95, 130, 131, 133, 134, 141, 143, 144, 145, 146, 147, 148, 155, 177, 179, 180, 181, 190, 210, 211, 230, 232, 233, 238, 244, 245, 247, 248, 263, 266, 267, 269, 272, 273, 283, 284, 286, 287, 289, 295, 304, 316.
Erythraean, Sea 33.
Europe, 47, 48.

F.

Fahien, 279.
Fergusson, J., 423.
Firishta, 375.
Fleet, J. F., 249, 256.
Forbes, 326.
France, 110.

Gai, G. S., 234.
Gājāyana Sarvatāta, 153, 158, 193, 219.
Gambhiri, 38, 40, 46, 49.
Gaṇaka Kālidāsa, 161, 216.
Gaṇapatināga, 185, 186.
Gandharvas, 88.
Gandharva, 404.
Gandhawal, 455, 456, 459, 460, 462.
Gaṅgdhāra, 23, 251, 252, 268, 272, 275.
Gangetic Valley, 70, 79, 86, 95, 186, 193.
Gāṅgeyadeva, 345, 348, 349, 351, 476, 510
Ganguli, D.C. 265, 322, 325, 327, 330, 332, 333, 334, 336, 337, 338, 342, 348, 349, 353, 354, 355, 358, 361, 362, 36[illegible], 368, 457.
Gaṇitasāra, 503, 504, 506, 507, 510.
Gaonari plates, 334, 337, 341, 407.
Garbardi, 57.
Gardabhilla, 7, 8, 159, 162, 163, 195.
Gardabhilla (King), 160, 163.
Garde, M. B. 430, 458.
Garga, 220.
Gargatrirātra sacrifices, 193.
Gārgīsaṁhitā, 150.
Garoth, 398.
Gāthāsaptaśatī, 157, 162.
Gauḍa, 160, 261, 262, 263, 265, 350
Gauḍadeśa, 406.
Gauri, 24, 254, 255, 267.
Gautama, 481.
Gautama-Gaṅgā, (Godāvarī), 345.
Gautamapura, 65,
Gautamīputra Sātakarṇi, 29, 156, 168, 169, 170, 172, 218, 219, 227.
Ghaṇṭoli, 408.
Ghaṭak, 58.
Ghaṭakarpara, 161, 163, 216.
Ghataoda, 510.
Ghaṭaprabha, 52,

Ghat-Bilod, 64.
Ghatiyalod, 65.
Ghaṭotkachagupta, 23, 233, 237, 238, 242, 267, 269.
Ghosh, 58.
Ghosh, J. C. 153.
Ghosh, N. C., 146.
Ghosūṇḍī, 153, 195, 219.
Gilunda, 58, 65, 77.
Girnar, 104, 216, 217, 224.
Girwar, 417.
Gobhaṭa, 254.
Godavari, 44, 52, 55, 67, 340, 345.
Goga, 375, 376.
Goggasthāna, 368.
Goggirāja, 334, 343.
Gokyāntī, 234, 279.
Gommaṭasāra, 471.
Gonarda, 31, 142, 214.
Goṇḍala, 355.
Gondarman, 28, 227.
Gondas, 84,
Gopā, 275.
Gopāla, 101, 102, 119, 160.
Gopāli, 481.
Goparāja, 26, 248, 308.
Gorakhpur, 333.
Gordon, D. H. 58.
Gośūrasiṁhabala, 277.
Gotiputa, 200.
Gourisha, 502.
Govardhana (Nasik), 168.
Govinda 256, 371, 510.
Govinda II, 324.
Govinda III, 323, 330.
Govinda, IV, 162.
Govindagupta, 23, 233, 237, 241, 267, 269.
Grace Morley, 82.
Grahavarman, 10, 265.
Greek, 3, 4, 6.
Guḍar, 486.
Gujrat, 10, 11, 41, 43, 87, 163, 166, 168, 169, 172, 175, 176, 178, 180, 236, 238, 331, 336, 339, 349, 350, 354, 361, 369, 370, 371, 372, 373, 435, 445, 482, 503, 506.
Guna, 463.
Guṇabhadra, 231, 278.
Guṇāḍhya, 157.
Guṇākarasena, 401.
Guṇāmbodhideva, 333.
Guṇaratna, 413.
Guṇaūrā, 367.
Gunda, 174.
Guṇḍakheḍa, 475.
Guṇḍamaya, 351.
Gupta, P. L., 229, 232,
Gupta, S. P. 82.
Gwalior, 24, 26, 275, 276, 348, 412, 414, 415, 422, 428, 429, 430, 434, 450, 497, 502.
Gyāraspur, 30, 366, 398, 404, 405, 414, 418, 419, 425, 431, 432, 440, 448, 450, 451, 452, 453, 459, 460.
Gyāta, 355.

H.

Habibullah, 507.
Haihaya, 30, 31, 88, 89, 90, 92, 93, 94, 95, 96, 97, 103.
Haimavata School, 200.
Haimendorf, 84.
Hāla, 157, 158, 162.
Halāyudha, 328, 340, 469,
Haldar, R. R., 245.
Haliddikāni, 116.
Hamīrapura, 41.
Hammīradeva, 374, 375.
Hammīramahākāvya, 372, 375.
Hamugama, 156.
Hansi, 348.
Harah, 262.
Harappa, 83.
Hari, 216.
Harischandra, 91, 21[illegible], 366, 367, 371, 417, 482. 497.
Hariśchandradeva, 25, 381.
Harisheṇa (Author.) 471.
Harisheṇa (The Vākāṭaka ruler), 256.
Harisvāmini, 277.
Hārīta-Kutsa, 481.
Harivaṁśapurāṇa, 322, 323, 324.
Harivarman, 261.
Harsha, 11, 261, 319.
Harsha, (Paramāra ruler Sīyaka II), 333.
Harshacharita, 11, 32, 186, 231, 263, 264.
Harshagupta, 259.
Harshapura, (A village called Harsauda in the Nimar Dist, 410.
Harshavardhana, 265.
Harsola copper, plate, 327, 328, 331, 333, 415, 483.
Harsud, 57.
Harsukhā, 488.
Haryaśva, 93.
Hasanpur, 65.
Hastikundi, 336.
Hastin, 244.
Hastinapur, 78, 89, 96, 481.
Hastyāyurveda, 301.
Haṭiāka, 417.
Haṭiāka, 485.
Haṭṭakeśvaratīrtha, 421.
Hayanāga, 185.
Heliodorus, 23, 26, 124, 151, 188, 194, 205, 206.

Hemachandra, 364.
Hemādri, 374.
Himadata, 197.
Himalayas, 90, 92, 360.
Hoernle, R., 249, 257, 260, 265.
Hoshangabad, 35, 37, 38, 39, 49, 50, 58, 364, 371.
Hṛidayaśiva, 407, 413.
Hṛidayeśa, 413.
Hsuam-tai, 279.
Hultzsch, E., 347.
Hūṇa, 1, 23, 85, 341, 342.
Hūṇa Maṇḍala, 334, 337.
Hunter, 58.
Hutiya, 57.
Huvishka, 154.
Hydaspes (Jhelum), 5.

I

Ikshvāku, 2, 103.
Iltutmish, 372.
Indore, 56, 57, 65, 440, 446, 505, 510,
Indra III, 330, 332.
Indragarh, 24, 320, 378, 395, 405, 406, 411, 485.
Indragupta, 155.
Indraratha, 345.
Indus, 5.
Inganapat (Ringod), 360, 409.
Ingnoda, 25, 360, 379.
Iran, 80, 81, 82, 84.
Isadata, 197.
Īśānamu, 406.
Īśānavarman, 262.
Īśidāsī, 115, 143.
Isidattā, 115, 142.
Īśvaradatta, 174, 175.
Īśvaramitra, 177, 180.
Īśvaraśiva, 407.
Īśvaravāsaka, 276.

J

Jagachandra, 479.
Jagaddeva, 353, 355, 358, 408, 409 417, 490.
Jagaddeva, (Pratīhāra) 368.
Jagadekamalla, 363.
Jainād, 355, 417.
Jaina Harivaṁśapurāṇa, 32.
Jaipur, 159.
Jaitrasiṁha, 374.
Jaitugideva, 373, 374, 403, 478.
Jalāluddīn, Khiljī, 376.
Jālor, 321, 338.
Jāmadagnya, 484.
Jamadagni, 90, 92.
Jamadhad, 57.
Jamli, 442.
Janaid, 321.
Jananātha, 353, 354.
Janārdana, (god Vishṇu), 273.
Janna, 409, 497, 502.
Janod, 51.
Jauval, 247.
Java, 47, 49.
Jayadāman, 171.
Jayadhvaja, 90, 92, 160.
Jayānanda, 404.
Jayanātha, 245.
Jayasena, 401.
Jayasiṁha, I (Paramāra ruler), 352, 353, 356, 381, 392, 408, 475.
Jayasiṁha, 24, 345, 352, 353, 372, 402, 418. 421, 475.
Jayasiṁha, (Chālukya ruler), 25, 352. 370.
Jayasiṁha Jayavarman, 27, 466, 482, 484.
Jayasiṁha, Siddharāja, 359, 360, 361, 362, 364, 390, 444, 482.
Jayasoma, 8, 187.
Jayaswal, K. P, 102, 158, 182, 183, 184, 193 257.
Jayatsena, 8.
Jayatvardhana, 187.
Jayavarmadeva, 25.
Jayavarman (Paramāra ruler), 362, 363, 364, 466.
Jayavarman, 179, 184, 251.
Jayavarman (Paramāra Mahākumāra), 365.
Jayavarman II, 373, 374, 375, 382, 385, 386, 387, 409, 416.
Jejākabhukti, 422.
Jetugi, 370, 416.
Jhalawar, 460.
Jhālrāpāṭan, 25, 28, 143, 145, 319, 320, 362, 405, 406, 409, 422. 444, 450, 488, 502.
Jhamphaithaghaṭṭa (Jhampaitghat on Chambal), 374.
Jharda, 439, 454, 457, 461, 462.
Jhardia, 451, 455, 456.
Jimūtavāhana, 494.
Jinadattasūri, 402, 403.
Jinapāla, 361.
Jinapatisūri, 404.
Jinaprabhasūri, 33, 158, 404.
Jinasena, 324.
Jinavallabhasūri, 361, 402, 467, 476, 477, 504.
Jinayajñakalpa, 478.
Jineśvarasūri, 401.
Jishṇu, 29, 216, 229, 230, 317.
Jīvadāman, 173, 174, 175, 226.
Jīvaka, 99, 207.
Jivantasvāmī, 119, 120.

Jīvitagupta, 260, 261, 262.
Jogalathembī, 168.
Jorwe, 69, 75, 76, 77.
Junagarh, 103, 172, 190, 191, 240, 241.
Jurz, 321.
Jyeshṭajarāsi, 411.
Jyotirvidābharaṇa, 161, 216.

K

Kabra Pahar, 58.
Kachchha, (Cutch), 172.
Kachchhelas, 321.
Kadambaguha, (Kadwāha), 412, 464.
Kadambapadraka, 385, 481, 504.
Kādambarī, 10, 11, 263, 280, 472.
Kadmali, 40.
Kadwāha, 405, 434.
Kagpur, 405, 420, 430, 456, 457, 459, 460, 462.
Kaivartas, 358.
Kāka, 229, 230, 364.
Kākanādaboṭa (Sanchi), 276, 277.
Kākanāva, 201.
Kākanvati, 433.
Kāladamana, 410.
Kālakāchārya, 160, 197.
Kālakāchāryakathā, 158.
Kālakāchāryakathānaka, 32, 156.
Kālakāleśvara tīrtha, 421.
Kalakunda, 57.
Kalegaon, 52.
Kalha, 333.
Kālī (Upāsikā), 115.
Kālibangan, 78.
Kālidāsa, 31, 150, 161, 163, 192, 215, 216, 236, 270, 273, 280, 288, 291, 297, 298, 306, 308, 313.
Kālindi (Yamunā river), 244, 268.
Kaliṅga, 15, 103, 256, 316, 322, 357, 358.
Kliṅgarāja, 343.
Kali Sind, 51.
Kalpi, 332.
Kalvan, 345, 349, 421, 483.
Kalyāṇa, 343, 346, 352, 363, 369 377.
Kalyāṇakīrti, 405.
Kalyāṇī, 336, 340, 345, 354, 363.
Kalyan Kumar Das Gupta, 2, 7.
Kalyanpur, 40.
Kamalādharaśarman, 482.
Kāmalatā, 479.
Kāmarūpa (Assam), 262, 332.
Kāmasūtra, 9, 10, 263, 302, 305, 465.
Kāmed, 453.
Kaṁka, (Chachcha), 335.
Kaṁsa, 220.
Kaṁtakanūya, 200.
Kanaka, 91,
Kanakāvalī, 479.
Kānakherā, 179, 180.
Kaṇaswā, 319, 414, 423.
Kanauj, 261, 323, 330, 332, 348, 349, 415, 428, 503.
Kānchī, 322.
Kāṇha, 353, 414.
Kanheri, 172.
Kanishka, 154, 165, 166.
Kāntipurī, 31, 182, 184.
Kāṇvas, 198.
Kanwan, 64.
Kānyakubja, 92, 93.
Kāpālika, 410, 411.
Kāpāsigāma (Kapasi), 200, 224.
Kapila, 481.
Kapiśā, 148.
Kapitha (Kāyathā), 32, 290.
Kapithaka (Kayatha), 275, 300.
Kapoteśvara (Modern kothār in-Kashmir), 352.
Kāpūr-āhāra (Kapura), 167.
Kārdamaka family, 169, 176.
Karkarāja, 323, 330.
Karkoṭa Nāgas, 91.
Karli, 203.
Karmagrantha, 479.
Karṇa, 351, 354, 356.
Karṇāṭa, 160, 339, 340 345, 351.
Karnatak, 44, 52.
Karohan, 454.
Karoti, 57.
Kārttikeyārjuna, 92, 93.
Kāsapagota, 200, 201.
Kāśeyas, 103.
Kashmir, 158. 160, 163.
Kāśi, 89, 91, 93, 248, 316.
Kāśikā, 5, 481.
Kasrawad, 119, 120, 125, 129, 130, 132, 134, 144.
Kāśya, 316.
Kāśyapa, 481.
Kāśyapa gotra, 207.
Katare, S. L. , 366.
Kaṭha, 482, 505, 510.
Kathākośa, 476.
Kathāsaritsāgara, 32, 102, 158, 160, 236, 240, 280.
Kathiawad, 32, 156, 166, 168, 172, 175, 176, 178, 180, 236, 324.
Katre, S. L. 147.
Kātyāyana, 481.
Kauravas, 6, 94.
Kauśāmbī, 93, 96, 97, 100, 101, 118, 148, 153, 154, 185, 239.
Kauthen grant, 337.
Kauthuma, 482.
Kauṭilya, 92, 105, 106, 107, 108, 110, 111, 112, 113, 139.
Kautsa, 481.
Kavachaśiva, 413.

Kavirahasya, 470.
Kāvyādarśa, 472.
Kāvyamīmāṁsā, 231, 296.
Kāvyanirṇaya, 470 .
Kāyastha, 489.
Kayatha, 22, 64, 65, 67, 68, 71, 72, 73, 78, 79, 83, 95, 141, 290.
Kedāra, 477.
Kedārarāśi, 411.
Kerala, 316, 339, 343.
Kethuli, 438.
Khadgaśatam, 465.
Khajurāho, 334, 442.
Khalimpur plates, 323.
Khaṇḍakāvya, 417, 474.
Khaṇḍelā, 405, 486.
Khaṇḍelagachchha, 405.
Khaṇḍelavāla, 484, 486.
Khandesh, 52, 435.
Khandwa, 56 ,57, 58.
Khanpura, 51.
Kharagraha, I, 266.
Kharaosta, or Prakharaosta, 166.
Kharaparika, 229, 230, 303.
Kharataragachchha Bṛihadgurvāvali, 361, 504.
Kharga Oasis, 45, 46.
Khatri, A. P., 37, 38, 46, 50, 54, 56.
Khāvūka, 454.
Khejaria, Bhop, 398, 425, 427.
Khera, 64, 65.
Kheṭa, 11.
Kheṭakamaṇḍala, 333, 335, 388.
Khilchipura, 291, 292.
Kholeśvara, 371.
Kholvi, 398, 425, 427.
Khor, 440.
Khoṭṭigadeva, 335.
Kielhorn, 158, 354, 413.
Kīkaṭa (Magadha), 200.
Kīra or Kīra Country (Kangra-valley), 357, 358.
Kirāḍu, 338, 339.
Kirāta, 19, 316, 488.
Kirātārjunīya, 298.
Kīrtikaumudī, 361.
Kīrtirāja, 346, 348, 434.
Kīrtivarman, 263.
Kodaṇḍa, 465, 473.
Kodaṇḍakāvya, 27.
Koḍiniputa, 201.
Kohla, 437, 454.
Koha, 375, 376.
Kolarian tribes, 84.
Konkaṇa, 167, 168, 172, 343, 344, 345 346, 347, 391, 435.
Kortalayar, 45.
Kośala, 9, 29, 98, 103, 144, 207, 241, 253, 341, 342 ,343.
Kosam, 295.
Kośavardhana, 357, 390, 403.
Kota, 290, 400, 444.
Koṭitīrtha, 195.
Koyali, 64.
Kramrisch, Stella, 288.
Krishṇa (Yādava), 373.
Kṛishṇa (Rāshṭrakūta ruler), 334, 335.
Kṛishṇagupta, 259, 260, 261.
Kṛishṇarāja, 330.
Kṛishṇarāja III, 470.
Kṛishṇaswami, 40.
Kṛita, (King), 160.
Kṛita era, 164, 187.
Kṛitavīrya, 90, 91, 92.
Kriyākalāpaṭīkā, 475.
Kshmāchārya, 279.
Kshapaṇaka, 161, 163, 216.
Kshudrakas, 4, 5, 166.
Kuberanāgā, 232, 235.
Kuḍugeśvara, 120.
Kuḍṁgeśvara, 404.
Kukadeśvara, 455.
Kukura, 168.
Kukusthavarmā, 306.
Kulāchala Parvata, 16.
Kulachanda, 350.
Kulāditya, 278.
Kulaipa, 173.
Kumāra, 368, 4 6, 485.
Kumāragupta I, 10, 29, 233, 237, 238, 239, 242, 243, 252, 267, 317.
Kumāragupta II, 242, 243, 244.
Kumāragupta III, 243, 257, 258.
Kumāragupta (Later Gupta ruler,), 262, 265.
Kumārapāla, 163, 356, 363, 364, 367.
Kumārapālacharita, 344.
Kumārapālapratibodha, 158.
Kumārasambhava, 297.
Kumārsena, 101, 121.
Kumārastotra, 436, 465.
Kumārasvāmin, 303.
Kumbha, 473.
Kumbharohaka, 388.
Kuṇāla, 104.
Kundakunda, 476.
Kundala (tributary of Narmada), 57.
Kuṇḍalapura, 412, 464.
Kunjarāvarta, 121.
Kunoor, 79.
Kuntala, 256.
Kuntalas (Rāshṭrakūṭas), 333, 342, 345.
Kupatākā, 418.
Kurara, 116.
Kuraraghara (Kuraghara), 141, 200.
Kūrmaśataka, 351.
Kurnool, 45, 84.

Kuru, 89, 103.
Kurukshetra, 90.
Kushāṇas, 13, 166, 184, 193, 199, 202.
Kuśika gotra, 220.
Kutch 55.
Kutsa gotra, 220.
Kutwal (Kāntipurī), 434.
Kutwar, 28, 228.
Kuvalayamālā, 247, 323, 324.

L

Lachure, 41.
Lāḍa Bāgaḍa Saṁgha, 401.
Laghudravya saṁgraha, 402.
Laghujātaka, 300.
Lahore, 348.
Lakshmadeva, 25, 357, 358.
Lakshmaṇa, 2.
Lakshmaṇa (Author), 473.
Lakshmasiṁha, 375.
Lakshmī, 404.
Lakshmīdeva, 454.
Lakshmīdevī, 331.
Lakshmīdhara, 495.
Lakshmīvarmadeva, 25.
Lakshmīvarman, 360, 365, 366, 367. 381, 385, 481.
Lakulīśa, 195, 406.
Lal, B. B. 86, 89, 96.
Lālabāgaḍa, Saṁgha, 475.
Lalitavistara, 101.
Lalitpur, 41.
Lambakarṇa, 407.
Langhrāj, 60.
Lāra Baniyas, 395, 419, 485.
Lāṭa. 11, 160, 195, 238, 264, 275, 317, 322, 330, 339, 340, 341, 343, 346, 369, 370, 371, 372, 390, 501.
Lauhitya (Brahmaputra), 257, 261.
Lavaṇaprasāda, 370.
Law, B. C. 11, 27, 263, 343.
Lekhapaddhati, 506.
Levi, 217.
Limkheda, (Dist. Panchamahal), 445.
Lokottara vihāra, 277.
Lolārka, 417.
London, 420.
Lothal, 79.
Lui-pā, 399.

M

Macburney, 47.
Machikunda, 57, 88.
Mackay, 74.
Madana, 27, 32, 349, 373, 383, 404, 478, 479.
Madanakīrti, 404.
Madanasiṁhadeva, 418.
Madanavarman, 359.
Madanikā, 304.
Madanopādhyāya, 478.
Madavika, 155.
Mādhava, 371, 484.
Mādhava community, 219
Mādhavagupta, 10, 260, 261, 265.
Mādhavaśarman, 482.
Mādhavasena, 149 .
Mādhavasena sūri, 401.
Madhurikā, 199.
Madhusūdana 482.
Madhuvana, 200.
Madhyadeśa, 87, 150.
Madhyamā, 258, 270.
Mādhyaṁdina, 482.
Madhyamikā, 31, 150, 152, 153, 188, 193, 195, 258.
Mādhyandina Vājasaṇeyas, 303.
Madhya pradesh, 4.
Madras, 4, 45, 55.
Magadha, 15, 98, 99, 101, 103, 104, 105, 188, 247, 259, 260, 261, 263, 332.
Magalakaṭiyas, 219.
Māghachandra II, 400.
Mahābhārata, 3, 5, 31, 90, 96, 213, 313, 454, 473.
Mahābhāshya, 31, 150, 192, 214, 215, 316, 220.
Mahadeo, hills, 58.
Mahadeo Piparia, 37, 46, 52, 55.
Mahādeva, 25, 119, 362, 374, 417.
Mahādvādaśakamaṇḍala, 365, 367, 385, 388.
Mahākachchāyana, 115, 116.
Mahākāla temple, 29, 101, 121, 122, 147, 195, 197, 332, 407, 408, 412, 421, 429, 477.
Mahākapi, Jātaka, 207.
Mahākumāra family, 25.
Mahākūṭa pillar inscription, 263, 264.
Mahāmālava, 10, 319.
Mahāmogalāna, 201.
Mahāpadma, 103.
Mahāpurāṇa, 402, 475.
Mahāpurāṇa Ṭippana, 475.
Mahārāshṭra, 44, 52.
Mahāsena, 401, 471.
Mahāsenagupta, 10, 11, 260, 261, 262, 263, 264, 265.
Mahata, 188.
Mahāvagga, 99.
Mahāvaṁśa, 117.
Mahāvanasthāna, 497.
Mahavanāya 201.
Mahāvīra, 119, 403, 404.
Mahāvīra stuti, 471.
Mahendra, 104, 117.

Mahendra Mountains (Ganjam District) 257.
Mahendrāditya, 234.
Mahendrapāla, 414.
Mahendrapāla II, 331.
Maheśvara, 22, 28, 36, 62, 65, 66, 69, 72, 73, 95, 118, 119, 123, 129, 130, 131, 132, 133 134, 143, 144, 145, 181, 210, 211, 293, 295, 341.
Mahi river, 11, 56.
Mahida, 196.
Mahidpur, 439.
Mahimekalai, 142.
Mahipāla, 325, 332, 333, 336, 415, 434.
Mahisati (Maheśvara), 200.
Mahisha dynasty, 181.
Māhishaka, 181, 182.
Mahishamaṇḍala, 119.
Mahishmanta, 88, 91.
Mahishmatī, 18, 28, 88, 90, 91, 92, 94, 98, 102, 118, 141, 142, 148, 172, 180, 182, 245, 277, 421, 468.
Mahlak Deo, 375, 376.
Mahmud, 358, 471.
Mahmūd of Ghazni, 347, 348.
Mahoba, 348.
Mahu, 156.
Mahuā, 24, 324, 405, 407, 428, 429 484.
Mahuḍa, 385, 386.
Māhukāna, 169.
Maināka mountains, 357.
Mainchuka, 406.
Maithilas, 103.
Maitraka dynasty, 12.
Majumdar, A. K. 363.
Makla, 439, 456, 459, 460.
Mala, 1.
Mālava, 1, 2, 3, 4, 5, 6, 7, 8, 9, 10, 11, 12, 13, 17, 242, 246, 253, 260, 263, 265, 302, 322, 334, 350, 363, 366, 369, 372, 375.
Mālavadeśa, 400, 475.
Malla, 476.
Māluśarman, 367.
Maitreya, (Bodhisattva), 210.
Majhima, 201.
Majmaluttavārikha, 231.
Majumdar, A. K., 339.
Majumdar, R. C., 170, 242, 245, 246, 322.
Majupa, 2.
Makanganja, 289.
Makaran, 235.
Maladhara, 374.
Malaprabha basin, 44, 52.
Mālatīmādhava, 296.
Mālavagaṇavishaya, 8.
Mālavaka Vishaya or Bhukti, 12, 97, 269, 413.
Mālavanagar, 6.
Mālavikāgnimitra, 31, 149, 150, 192. 297.
Mālavis (Community), 13.
Mālavī women, 11.
Mālavya, 3.
Mālaya, 1, 2, 47, 168.
Malayāchala, 360.
Malha, 478, 479.
Malibah, 321.
Malla people, 2, 207.
Mallarāshṭra, 2.
Malloi, 3, 4, 5.
Mambarus, 165, 166.
Mamlā (Poona), 167, 189.
Mamon, 455, 456, 461, 462.
Māna, 180, 181.
Managoli, 370.
Mānatuṅga, 469.
Māṇavāyaṇīs, 24, 254, 255, 267, 302
Mandal, 321.
Māṇḍalagarh, 369, 403, 478.
Māṇḍalika, 356, 408.
Maṇḍapadurga (Mandu) 369, 466 387, 388, 390.
Maṇḍāraka, 385.
Māndhātā, 26, 88, 152, 181, 352, 353 368, 370, 372, 373, 374, 385, 386, 393, 405, 416, 419, 421, 466, 482, 484, 509.
Mandla, 50.
Mandleshwar, 36, 40, 50.
Mandsor, 9, 22, 23, 24, 26, 27, 38, 40, 43, 51, 56, 64, 78, 158, 179, 195, 237, 238, 241, 242, 243, 245, 246, 251, 252, 253, 254, 256, 258, 259, 267, 274, 275, 277, 281, 285, 286, 289, 291, 292, 298 302, 304, 310, 315, 317, 334, 427.
Mandu, 333, 351, 352, 416, 419, 420, 448, 453, 454, 465, 477, 499.
Maṅgalāpura, 404.
Mangaleśa, 263, 264.
Mani, 216.
Maṇibhadra, 185, 196, 209, 212, 222, 223.
Māṇikyanandi, 401, 476,
Maṇittha, 216.
Manoti, 22, 51, 64, 65, 68, 83.
Manthala, 457.
Mantrabhāshya, 474.
Manupur, 78.
Mānyakheṭa 327, 332, 335, 469, 471.
Maori, 64, 65.
Marigalapura, 404.
Mārkaṇḍeya, 481.
Marmad, 321.
Marshall John, 197, 198.
Maru, 172.
Marwar, 337, 338.

Maser, 383.
Masutikapura (Masudavilanda), 471.
Mataṅga, 217.
Mataṅga Kāśyapa, 202.
Mathura, 89, 101, 105, 118, 150, 153, 154, 170, 182, 183, 196, 239, 292, 316.
Māthura family, 487.
Māthura Saṁgha, 401, 405.
Mathurāsthāna, 481.
Mātṛicheṭa, 275.
Mātrimodaka Vājasaneyi Prātiśākhya bhāshya, 475.
Mātrivishṇu, 244, 247, 268, 269, 273, 304.
Matsyapurāṇa, 31, 273.
Mattamayūrapura, 412, 413, 464.
Mattamayūra sect, 26, 405, 407, 412, 413, 464, 468.
Matupur, 57.
Mauka, 476.
Maukhari, 7, 8, 159, 187, 189, 193, 219, 259, 260, 261, 262, 265.
Mauneya Gandharvas, 88.
Maunirāśi, 411.
Maurya dynasty, 19, 21, 105, 114, 118, 188, 321.
Mayanalladevī, 361.
Mayūrākshaka, 252, 268, 272, 275.
Mayurbhanj, 43.
Mc Crindle, 5.
Medhātithi, 487.
Megasthenes, 105, 107, 112, 121, 124, 137, 191.
Megasthenes Indica, 105.
Meghadūta, 297, 308.
Meharauli, 235.
Mehgam, 65.
Mekala, 9, 241, 253.
Menāl (Dist. Chitor), 445.
Menander, 151.
Meṇṭha, 215.
Merutuṅgāchārya, 9, 158, 340, 341, 350, 370, 504.
Metwa, 64, 65.
Mewar, 336.
Mhow, 57.
Mihira Bhoja, 325, 430, 506.
Mihirakula, 24, 248, 249, 250, 257, 258, 274, 275.
Mirashi, V. V., 179, 180, 181, 182, 242, 245, 246, 253, 255, 258, 282, 320, 339, 343, 346, 348, 354, 355, 507.
Misra V. N., 61, 62.
Mitā, 196.
Mitra, S. L., 109.
Mirzapur, 43, 60.
Mitravindu, 94.
Moḍāsā, 396, 481.
Modi, 56.
Moga, 165.
Mogaliputa, 201.
Mogaliputra, Tishya, 117.
Mohenjodāro, 83.
Mojawaḍi, 57.
Mokhlapaṭaka, 358.
Mo-lā-p'o, 11, 265.
Momalādevī, 488.
Mookerji, R. K. 111, 151, 260.
Morajābhikaṭa, 189. 200
Mori or Modī, 405, 437, 452, 455, 456, 459, 461.
Morwan (Mayūravana) 40, 285.
Mosuka, 406.
Mṛichchhakaṭika, 32, 278, 297, 304. 310, 316.
Mṛigāṅkadatta, 472.
Mṛitasañjīvinī, 470.
Mudgala, 481.
Muhilaūndha family 410.
Muktāvāsasthāna, 497.
Mūla, 224.
Mūladatā, 224.
Mūlarāja, 336, 339, 350, 368.
Mūlasaṁgha, 400, 405.
Müller, F. Max., 88.
Multai, plates, 320.
Multan, 5.
Muṇḍas, 84.
Mūnja, 20, 33, 329, 330, 337, 340, 346, 376, 383, 396, 446, 471, 476, 497.
Muñja-Pratideśa Vyavasthā, 469.
Muñjapura, 341, 446.
Munshi, K. M., 338, 355.
Muralas, 341, 343.
Murārī, 468.
Mutāvathū, 481.
Mutgi, 369.
Mysore, 44, 120.

N

Nadiguta (Nandigupta), 196.
Nāḍol, 336, 337, 350, 356, 360.
Nāga, 3, 28, 29, 30, 31, 51, 84, 88, 95, 96, 176, 182, 183, 184, 185, 186, 187, 195, 196, 228, 229, 232.
Nāga (person) 196.
Nāgabhaṭa, 321.
Nāgabhaṭa II, 323, 330.
Nāgadaha (Nagda near Ujjain), 386.
Nāgadatta, 196.
Nāgadeva, 478, 479.
Nāgajhari near Ujjain, 349.
Nāganaka, 345, 411, 502.
Nāgara Brāhmaṇas, 482.
Nāgara family, 486.
Nagarkot, 348.

Nāgasena, 186, 187.
Nāgavardhana, 324.
Nagda, 22, 56, 64, 65, 66, 68, 76, 78, 83, 86, 133, 141.
Nagda (Udaipur, Rajasthan), 349.
Nāgila, 196.
Nagpur, 25, 355, 357, 358, 361, 385, 416, 476.
Nahapāna, 8, 28, 167, 168, 169, 170, 171, 172, 181, 219, 227.
Nahargaḍh, 38, 40, 51, 64.
Naigama family, 258, 303.
Nakhavat (Nahapāna), 182.
Nalachhā, 465.
Nalakachhapura (Nalcha), 478.
Nalanda seal, 243, 244, 257.
Nālandayaśasa, 279.
Nāmamālikā, 472.
Naṁdinagara (Nandner), 200.
Nānāghāṭ, 154.
Nanana grant, 360.
Nandigiri, 196.
Nandas, 103, 105.
Nandisoma, 8, 175, 187, 188, 189, 193.
Nandivardhana, 102, 103, 105.
Nandsa inscription, 2, 3, 8, 13, 26, 158, 187, 188, 189, 193, 206.
Maṇṇapa, 24, 320, 378, 395, 406.
Naṇṇarāja, 320.
Narain, A. K., 151, 233.
Narasiṁha, 421, 502.
Narasiṁha, I, 363, 490.
Narasiṁhagupta, 246, 247, 249.
Narasiṁhapurāṇa, 31, 273.
Naravāhana, 336.
Narvarmadeva, 358, 359.
Naravarman, 24, 25, 250, 251, 252, 254, 277, 357, 359, 360, 361, 379, 390, 402, 409, 413, 415, 416, 419, 466, 467, 468, 476, 477, 481, 485, 497, 504, 505, 510.
Nārāyaṇa, 153.
Nārāyaṇa (Chief Minister) 371.
Nārāyaṇavāṭikā, 195.
Narendrasena, 9, 241, 242, 246, 253, 254.
Naresar, 420, 428.
Narmada, river, 37, 38, 39, 42, 43, 50, 53, 54, 57, 63, 65, 75, 87, 88, 92, 119, 131, 239, 244, 340, 367, 407, 421, 440, 501, 505, 509.
Narmada (Name of princess) 88.
Narmadāpura, 386.
Narmada Valley, 34, 35, 37, 40, 42, 52, 55, 84, 89, 95, 96, 103, 502.
Narsinghpur, 35, 37, 39, 46, 49, 50, 51.
Nasik, 7, 167, 168, 172, 282.
Nāṭyadarpaṇa, 231.
Nāṭyaśāstra, 9.
Navadatoli, 22, 62, 65, 66, 68, 69, 71, 72, 73, 74, 75, 76, 77, 78, 79, 80.
Navagāma, 189.
Navagrāmaka, 12.
Navanāga, 184, 185.
Navanītakam, 310.
Navasāhasāṅkacharita, 32, 325, 329, 330, 331, 334, 341, 342, 343, 344, 408, 469, 470, 472.
Navsārī, 321.
Nayanandi, 401, 476.
Neemuch, 38, 285.
Nellore District, 45.
Nemakas, 487.
Nemāwar, 30, 56, 57, 295, 317, 405, 442, 448.
Nemichandra Saidhānika, 402, 475.
Nemichandra sūri, 402.
Nemināthacharitra, 479.
Nemisheṇa, 401.
Nesārikā grant, 323.
Nevasa, 49, 50, 52, 54, 55, 75, 76, 77, 85, 154.
Nichyas, 94.
Nigaṭa, 120.
Nighaṇṭu, 163.
Nīla, 94.
Nīlagirimaṇḍala, 385.
Nirmar, 56, 317, 371, 409, 416, 417, 505, 510.
Nimbara, 404.
Nirdosha, 258, 259.
Nirvāṇa Nārāyaṇa, 360.
Nisar Ahmad, 233.
Nishāda, 85, 172.
Nityamahodyota, 478.
Nṛivarman, 373.
Nyāyakumuda Chandra, 475.
Nyāyāvatāra, 298.

O

Ojha, G. H., 336, 344, 355.
Olduvai, Gorge, 46.
Omkāra Māndhātā, 341, 407, 409, 421, 435, 453, 456, 505, 509.
Orasang, 43.
Orissa, 43, 84, 457.
Osavāla, 484.
Oxydrakoi, 4.

P

Pabhaosa, 151.
Pachmarhi, 58.
Pāḍāriya (Parana), 200.
Padaprakāśa, 472.
Padārthasaṁgraha, 413, 468.
Pādatāḍitakam, 32, 236, 253, 298, 313 316, 318

Padhaoli, 404, 434, 455, 460.
Padmacharita, 402, 475.
Padmagupta, 32, 325, 326, 328, 337, 340, 341, 342, 343, 469, 470, 472.
Padmanābhaśarman, 482.
Padmanāga, 325.
Padmanandi, 401.
Padmaprābhṛitakam, 32, 278, 298.
Padmāvatī, 31, 176, 182, 183, 184, 185, 186, 187, 196, 296.
Pāḍukulikā, 200.
Pagāra, 386.
Paikuli inscription, 178.
Paithāna, 225, 316.
Paiyalachchhi, 335, 471.
Pālaka, 101, 102, 103.
Pālakāpya, 301.
Pālas, 358.
Palāsinī, 173.
Palestine, 45.
Palhaṇadeva, 387.
Palitaka, 169.
Pallavaram, 45.
Paṁchasaṁgraha, 471.
Pāṁsulakheṭaka (Pāṇāherā) 408.
Pañchadaṇḍachhatra prabanda, 158.
Pañchālas, 103, 150, 153, 154.
Pañchasiddhāntikā, 255, 300.
Pañchāstikāya Pradīpa, 475.
Pāṇḍavas (dynasty), 101.
Pandey, Raj Bali, 2, 6, 156, 157, 159, 160.
Pāṇḍu race, 219.
Pandu Rajar Dhibi, 80.
Pāṇḍuvaṁśa, 245.
Pāṇḍya country, 357, 358.
Pāṇḍyaka, 316.
Paṇherā, 353, 388, 392, 408.
Pāṇini, 5, 31.
Pañjikā, 413.
Panjtar, 165.
Pant, P. C., 41.
Panthera, 453, 456.
Pāradā, 167.
Paramāra, 11.
Parāśara, 481.
Parāvasu, 481.
Pārijātamañjari, 27, 32, 349, 370, 371, 436, 465, 478, 493.
Parīkshāmukha, 401.
Parmakherī, 56.
Parmarkheri, 64, 65.
Paramārtha, 278.
Parāśara gotra, 219, 303.
Paraśurāma, 90.
Parivrājaka Mahārāja, 244, 248.
Pāriyātra, 88.
Pāriyātra (Western Vindhyas) mountains, 258, 269.
Parkham, 208, 209.
Parṇadatta, 240.
Parpaṭa, 401, 471.
Partapgarh, 56.
Parva mountain, 370.
Parvati (tributary of Chambal), 56, 64.
Pāśupata, 410, 411.
Pāṭaliputra, 104, 105, 112, 118, 121, 124, 150, 151, 157, 158, 164, 188, 229, 236, 266, 316.
Patalpani, 56.
Pataṅgaśambhu, 26, 412, 414, 497.
Pātañjala Yogaśāstra, 473.
Patañjali, 5, 31, 108, 150, 192, 214, 215, 220, 221, 222, 223, 224, 351.
Paterson, 34, 35, 49, 50, 52.
Pāṭhaka, 482.
Paṭhārī, 275, 285, 286, 290.
Paṭṭāvalis, 32.
Pauliśa Siddhānta, 300.
Paurava, 91.
Paushadhavidhi, 477.
Pavanaputra, 195.
Pavvaiyā, 247.
Pawaya, 22, 28, 145, 146, 185, 188, 195, 202, 206, 212, 222, 223, 228, 229, 273, 284, 288, 289, 290, 291, 292, 293, 311, 312, 313.
Pekin, 49.
Periplus, 33, 165, 225.
Persia, 160.
Persians, 89, 95.
Perungadai, 142.
Phāguṇa, 224.
Pichore, 510.
Piklihal, 77.
Piṇḍaviśuddhi, 477.
Piṅgala, 470.
Piṅgalasūtravṛitti, 329.
Piparia, 36, 50.
Piparva, 128.
Piplinagar, 367.
Plato, 380.
Pokhara (Pushkara) 200.
Polāḍuṅgara, 398, 425, 426.
Poona, 167, 172.
Poravāḍa Community 417.
Poravāla caste, 485, 486.
Poṭhādevā, 224.
Poṭhak, 224.
Prabala, 414.
Prabandhachintāmaṇi, 33, 158, 333, 468, 495.
Prabandhakosha, 158, 372.
Prabhāchandra, 158, 401, 402, 475.
Prabhākara, 23, 241, 253, 254, 267, 277.
Prabhākaranāga, 185, 186.
Prabhākaravardhana, 10, 32, 264, 265.

Prabhāsa, 167.
Prabhāvakacharita, 32, 158, 472.
Prabhāvatī Gupta, 232, 235, 306.
Pradyota, 30, 98, 99, 100, 101, 102, 103, 104, 105, 114, 115, 119, 121, 123.
Pradyumnacharita, 471.
Prāgvāṭa Caste, 406, 485, 486.
Prakash, 75, 76.
Prakaṭāditya, 248.
Prākṛitaprakāśa, 163.
Pramāṇamañjarī, 447, 476.
Pramāṇapallava, 421.
Prameyakamalamārtaṇḍa, 475.
Prameyaratnākara, 478.
Prārjuna, 229, 230, 303.
Praśastapāda, 413, 468
Prasenjit, 207.
Praśnottaraśataka, 477.
Pratardana, 93.
Pratīhāras, 19,
Pratijñā Yaugandharāyaṇa, 216, 297.
Pratikramaṇapāṭhaṭikā, 475.
Pratikramaṇa-Samāchārī, 477.
Pratishṭhāna, 158, 167.
Pratiṭhāna, 200.
Pravachana-saroja-bhāskara, 475.
Pravara, 44, 52, 77.
Pravara valley, 76.
Pravarasena I, 178, 179.
Pravarasena II, 232, 297.
Pravāsagīti, 404.
Prayāga, 11, 316.
Prāyaśchitta Samuchchaya, 407.
Pṛithvīdhara, 479.
Pṛithvīpāla, 356, 360.
Pṛithvīrājarāso, 326, 327.
Pṛithvīrājavijayamahākāvya, 355, 489.
Pṛithvīsena, 175.
Pṛithvīsena II, 9, 241, 242, 246, 253, 254.
Pseva, 64, 65.
Ptolemy, 19, 33, 171.
Pubhāni, 418.
Pulakeśin II, 11.
Pulika, 98.
Pulindas, 19, 84, 85, 96, 488.
Punaghat Kala, 57.
Punjab, 3, 4, 5, 6, 35, 40, 41, 49, 87, 101, 164, 172, 229.
Puṇyasoma, 254.
Pura Gulana, 440, 462, 463.
Purāṇasāra, 402, 475.
Purandhara, 412, 413.
Purāntaka, 474.
Puri, B. N. , 170.
Pūrṇapāṭhakamaṇḍala, 384, 385.
Puru, 89.
Purugupta, 239, 242, 244.
Purukutsa, 88.
Purushadatta, 182.
Purushottama, 382.
Purushottama (Ṭhakkura) 483.
Pusa, 224.
Pusagiri, 224.
Pusaka, 224.
Pusalker, U. L., 216.
Pusani, 224.
Pusarakhita, 224.
Pushkalāvatī, 148.
Pushkara, 167, 168.
Pushkarasārin, 101, 105.
Pushpadanta, 402, 475.
Pushyagupta, 104, 141.
Pushyamitra, 31, 149, 150, 151, 153, 154, 163, 188, 192, 198, 215, 238.
Pushyamitras (Tribe), 19, 29, 238, 239, 303.

R

Rādhāgupta, 108.
Raghu, 358.
Raghuvaṁśa, 297, 358.
Rairh, 130, 166.
Rājabrahmapurī, 466.
Rājagṛiha, 99 100.
Rājamārtaṇḍa, 473, 494.
Rājamativipralambha, 478.
Rājamṛigāṅka, 473.
Rājarāja, 342.
Rajar Dhipi, 79.
Rājasayaṇa bhoga, 385.
Rājaśekhara, 158, 215, 298.
Rājaśekharacharita, 479.
Rājasthan , 3, 4.
Rājendra Chola, 345, 346.
Rajota, 64.
Rajpur, 398, 425.
Rajpur Parsu, 78.
Rājyādhidevī, 94.
Rājyapāla, 364.
Rājyavardhana, 10, 254, 265.
Rakhetra, 404.
Rālamaṇḍala, 334.
Rāma, 92 468.
Rāmachandra, 182, 231, 479.
Rāmachandra (the yādava ruler), 374, 375.
Rāmachandrasūri, 158.
Rāmadatta, 182, 183.
Rāmadeva, 415, 430.
Ramagarh, 444, 451.
Rāmagrāma, 207.
Rāmagupta, 26, 29, 231, 232, 233, 234, 267, 279, 317.
Ramnagar (Ahichchhatrā), 284.
Rāmanandi, 401.
Ramaṭhas, 333.
Rāmāyaṇa, 2, 313, 434, 454, 455.

Rāṇakpur (Dist. Pali in Rajasthan), 445.
Raṇathambhor, 372, 374, 375, 377.
Rāṇāyani, 482.
Rangpur, 79.
Raṇod, 26, 405, 412, 413, 414, 464, 497.
Rao, S. R., 82.
Rapson, 165, 174, 176.
Rapson, E. J., 6.
Rāshṭra, 254.
Rasikamañjarī, 477.
Ratañjana, 40.
Rathāvarta, 121.
Ratlam, 56, 269, 303, 360, 443.
Ratnakaraṇḍaśrāvakāchāra ṭīkā, 475.
Ratnakīrti, 405.
Ratnapāla, 337.
Ratnapur, 344.
Ratnasūri, 477.
Ratnatrayavidhikathā, 478.
Ratnavatī, 344.
Rāvaṇa, 91.
Rāvaṇavadha (Bhaṭṭikāvya), 298.
Ravi, 186.
Ravisenāchārya, 475.
Ravisheṇa, 402.
Raychaudhuri, H. C., 89, 260, 263, 264, 326, 332, 338, 375.
Ray, N., 262.
Rekhagupta, 278.
Retam, 51.
Revatimitra, 198.
Ṛigveda, 88, 96, 97.
Ṛigveda-prātiśākhya-bhāshya or Prāsādabhāshya, 475.
Rihand, 43.
Riksha, 88.
Ṛishabhadatta, 167. 168.
Ṛishabhapaṁchāśikā, 471.
Ṛitusaṁhāra, 297.
Robert Hatfield, 225.
Roḍapadī, 334.
Rohiṇī, 224.
Rojadi, 79, 82.
Romaka Siddhānta, 299, 300.
Ror, 41.
Ruḍapāṭī, 334.
Rudra, 119.
Rudra Bhaṭṭārikā, 177.
Rudradāman, 104, 171, 172, 173, 189, 191, 216, 217, 219, 224.
Rudradāman II, 179.
Rudradāsa, 245.
Rudradeva, 179.
Rudrāditya, 340, 382, 487.
Rudrasena, 175, 184, 186.
Rudrasena II, 177, 235, 306.
Rudrasena III, 28, 179, 227, 251.
Rudrasena IV, 180.
Rudrasiṁha, 174, 175, 179, 184, 277.
Rudrasiṁha II, 178, 179, 227.
Rudrasiṁha III, 180.
Rudraśiva, 412, 413.
Rudravarmā, 253.
Rūṇamaṇḍala, 384.
Rūpa, 215.

S

Sabalasena, 188, 228.
Śabaras, 19, 84.
Sabarkantha, 345.
Sabarmatī, 43.
Śabdāmbhojabhāskara, 475.
Śābha, 268.
Sachau, 493.
Sadāchandra, 182.
Sadāśiva, 413.
Sāḍha, 350.
Sādhumati, 418.
Sagara, 90, 93.
Sāgaranandin, 402.
Sagunghat, 37, 50.
Sāhañja, 91.
Sāhañjanī, 91.
Sāhasāṅka, 236, 296.
Sahasradhāra, 36.
Sahasrārjuna, 91.
Sāhavāna, 349, 350.
Saindhavas, 321.
Śaka, 1, 6, 9, 13, 19, 28, 29, 32, 147, 157, 162, 163, 165, 179, 181, 182, 189, 192.
Sākala (Sialkot), 198.
Sakala-vihi-vihāna, 476.
Śākambharī, 336, 349, 350, 355, 356, 359, 363, 377.
Śakapura (Shujalpur), 386, 409, 419.
Śakāra, 217.
Sāketa, 31, 150, 360.
Śākhānagara, 281.
Śakrāditya, 243.
Śaktikumāra, 160, 336.
Śakuntalā, 270, 297.
Salakhaṇa, 371, 382, 403.
Salakhaṇapura, 479.
Salakhaṇasiṁha, 370, 387.
Salakshaṇavarman, 359.
Saletore, B. A., 264.
Saletore, R. N., 260.
Śālihotra, 473.
Śālivāhanadeva, 350.
Śalivāhanakathā, 158.
Samādhitantraṭīkā, 475.
Samangad plates, 322.
Sāmantaśubha, 399.
Samarāṅgaṇasūtradhāra, 32, 351, 3[illegible]0, 420, 447, 474.

Samāsasaṁhitā, 300.
Sāmāyikapāṭha, 471.
Saṁghadāman, 175.
Saṁghamitra, 104.
Saṁghavaṭṭa, 410.
Saṁgrāmasiṁha (Saṁkha), 371, 372.
Sāmidata, 196.
Samika, 197.
Saṁkarshaṇa, 153.
Samprati, 104, 105, 120.
Samudraghosha, 477.
Samudragupta, 23, 162, 177, 179, 181, 186, 230, 231, 233, 235, 239, 251, 264, 266, 269, 272, 317.
Samudravijaya, 402.
Sanakānīka, 23, 229, 230, 235, 267, 272, 303.
Sanchi, 23, 25, 27, 30, 104, 117, 118, 126, 127, 128, 148, 154, 170, 179, 180, 181, 189, 198, 199, 200, 201, 202, 204, 207, 208, 209, 210, 212, 219, 220, 222, 223, 224, 225, 226, 227, 276, 277, 278, 283, 284, 285, 286, 291, 302, 318, 319, 399, 424, 425, 449.
Sandares, 165.
Sandesara, B. J., 503.
Sandhāra, 438, 452, 455.
Śāṇḍilya, 481.
Sāndīpani, 94, 213.
Sangaloda plates, 320.
Sangamakheṭaka Maṇḍala, 385.
Sangankallu, 62.
Saṅgītarāja, 473.
Sangli, 162, 231.
Saṅguna ghat, 54.
Sanjan, 231.
Sanjit, 51, 56, 64.
Śaṅka, 216.
Sankalia, H. D., 34, 37, 41, 50, 54, 58, 82, 89.
Śaṅkara, (A person), 406.
Śaṅkara, (Jaina Śrāvaka), 26, 279.
Śaṅkarāchārya, 412.
Śankaragaṇa, 264, 319, 406.
Śaṅkhapāla, 344, 408.
Śāṅkhāyana, 481.
Śaṅku, 161, 163, 216.
Sanmatitarka, 298.
Śāntisheṇa, 401.
Sapādalaksha, 369.
Sāphineyakas, 219.
Sapta Mālava countries, 12.
Saptasindhu, 88, 89, 90.
Sāraṅgadeva, 375.
Saranpur, 28, 134, 143, 145.
Sarasāpur, 375.
Sarasvatī, 96.
Sarasvatīgachchha, 400.
Sarasvatīkanṭhābharaṇa, 351.
Sarasvatīsthāna, 481.
Saraswati, S. K., 209, 449.
Sāriputa, 201.
Sārnāth, 118, 242.
Sarnel (District Kaira, Gujrat), 445.
Sarppasena Kshamaṇa, 234, 279.
Sarvanāga, 325.
Sarvania, 28, 227.
Sarvatāta, 153, 219.
Sarvavarman, 261, 262, 263.
Śarvilaka, 304.
Ṣarvva, 319.
Śāryātas, 93.
Śāsanachatustriṁśatikā, 404.
Śaśāṅka, 265.
Śaśiprabhā, 344, 408, 472, 490.
Sastri, K. A. N., 330.
Śatadhārā, 201, 204.
Sātakarṇi, 23, 159, 199.
Śatakas, 298.
Sātavāhana, 19, 23, 28, 29, 147, 154, 155, 163, 165, 167, 171, 198.
Sātavāhana (King), 154.
Sātila, 224.
Śatruñjaya, 400.
Sattasai, 157.
Satya, 216.
Satyadāman, 173, 217.
Satyagupta, 238.
Satyapura, 471.
Satyapurīyamahāvīrautsāha, 471.
Satyāśraya, 342, 343.
Sauma, 156.
Saurāshṭra, 9, 15, 55, 79, 89, 156, 168, 173, 184, 189, 197, 240, 244, 321.
Sauvīra, 172.
Savita, 155.
Sehore, 295, 317.
Seistan, 32.
Sellukamaṇḍala, 385.
Śesha, 182.
Śeshadatta, 182, 183.
Setubandha, 297.
Sevāḍi, 337.
Sewari (District Pali, Rajasthan), 445.
Sharma Dasharatha, 328, 336, 347.
Sharma, Y. D., 89, 97.
Shastri, Ajaya Mitra, 255.
Shergarh, 27, 325, 357, 378, 392, 395, 397, 403, 405, 409, 411, 464, 493, 502, 505, 506, 510.
Shivana valley, 34, 38, 39, 40, 42, 43, 44, 45, 51, 56, 79.
Shyamala hill, 39.
Sialk, 80, 81, 82.
Śibis, 5, 188.
Siddhadaṇḍika stava, 479.
Siddhapañchāśikā, 479.
Siddharāja Jayasiṁha, 466.

Siddhasena Divākara, 163, 197, 280, 298.
Siharāmaṇḍala, 385.
Śilāditya, 12, 265.
Śilāhāra family, 343.
Siṁha, 370, 371, 372.
Siṁhadantabhaṭṭa, 333.
Siṁhagiri, 121.
Siṁhaladvīpa (Ceylon), 484, 501.
Siṁhaṇa, 370, 371, 372, 373, 387.
Siṁhanandi, 400.
Siṁhāsanadvātriṁśikā, 32.
Siṁhasena, 177, 180.
Siṁhaśrīsena, 180.
Siṁhavarman, 251.
Simuka, 154.
Sind, 6, 32, 156, 157, 160, 321, 350.
Sindhu, 150, 172.
Sindhul, 359.
Sindhurāja, 32, 335, 337, 338, 339, 341, 342, 343, 344, 345, 379, 401, 408, 470, 474, 490.
Singrauli, 43.
Singrauli Basin, 60.
Sinha, B. P., 243, 249, 257, 258, 260, 263.
Śiprā river, 11, 64, 65, 123, 281, 421.
Sircar, D. C., 1, 7, 11, 150, 151, 157, 159, 161, 164, 169, 170, 179, 181, 182, 187, 233, 257, 259, 260, 263, 328, 347, 396, 504.
Siri-Usāha-Vaddhamānaprabhṛitis-tava, 479.
Sirsa valley, 41.
Śiśuchandradatta, 182, 183.
Śiśunāga, 102, 103, 105.
Śiśunandi, 182.
Sītā, 331, 468, 469, 488.
Sītādevī, 490.
Śivadāsa, 158.
Śivagaṇa, 319, 414.
Śivagupta, 155.
Sivanadi (Śivanandi), 197.
Sivanandi, 185, 196.
Śivapurāṇa, 31.
Siyadoni, 412, 464, 506.
Sīyaka I, 331.
Sīyaka II, 24, 327, 328, 330, 331, 333, 334, 335, 336, 381, 388, 407, 415, 471, 483.
Skandagupta, 19, 239, 240, 241, 242, 243, 244, 253.
Skanda Kārttikeya, 122.
Skandanāga, 183, 185, 186, 196.
Skandapurāṇa, 31, 274, 281, 419, 421.
Śmaśānapati, 399.
Smith, vincent, 1, 5, 6, 7, 109, 151, 241, 249.
Śobha, 273.
Śobhana, 340.
Śobhita, 337.
Sodhang, 128.
Sogin clan, 7, 8, 159, 187, 188, 193, 219.
Sohaḍa, 370.
Sohartrī, 219.
Solaṇadeva, 410.
Sollana, 359.
Somadeva, 32, 158, 482.
Somanātha, 79, 347, 471.
Somaprabha, 158.
Someśvara, 338, 351, 352, 353, 354, 361.
Soṇa Kutikaṇṇa, 115.
Sonarī (Sonāra), 200, 201, 204, 217.
Sonasiddha, 277.
Soṇḍala, 482.
Sonita, 38, 40.
Sonkutch, 51.
Sopara, 167.
Śrāddhajinakritya, 479.
Śravaṇa-belagoḷā, 120.
Śrāvasti, 19, 207, 225.
Śrībhagavadabhisamaya, 399.
Śrīchandra, 402, 475, 476.
Śrīdhara, 370, 482, 503, 504, 506.
Śrīdharavarman, 179, 180, 181, 182, 190.
Śrīkṛishṇa, 94, 213, 273.
Śrīmāla, 506.
Śrīmālī Brāhmaṇas, 483.
Śrīmālīs, 484.
Śrīmārga, 359.
Śrīnandi, 402, 475.
Śriṅgapura, 497.
Śṛiṅgāramañjarīkathā, 32, 394, 472, 483, 484, 487, 489, 490, 493, 498, 499, 501.
Śriṅgāraprakāśa, 231, 351, 472.
Śriṅgāraśataka, 477.
Śrīnivāsa, 409.
Śrīpāla, 402, 475.
Śrī śaila, 322.
Śrīsoma, 8, 175, 187.
Śrotriya, 482.
Śrutakīrti, 476.
Śrutasena, 216.
Sthalīmaṇḍala, 384, 385.
Sthāneśvara, 497.
Sthāvaraka, 304.
Strabo, 109.
Suara, 56.
Subāhu, 101.
Subandhu, 181, 182, 245, 269, 277, 282.
Subba Rao, 50.
Subbarao, B., 125.
Śubhachandra, 478.
Subhāshitaratnasaṁdoha, 471, 478.
Śubhaśila, 158.

Subhaṭavarman, 369, 370, 403, 416.
Sudarśanacharita, 401, 476, 479.
Sudarśana Lake, 141, 173, 191, 240,
Sudarśanapura, 141.
Sudāsa, 89.
Śuddhodana, 207.
Suddvāpa, 148.
Sudeva, 93.
Sudharma Svāmī, 119.
Śūdraka, 31, 32, 280, 297, 298, 308.
Suhania, 404, 420, 433, 456, 457, 459.
Sujyeṣṭha, 151.
Śukasaptati, 32.
Sukhadeva, 188.
Śukla, 482.
Sūkshmārthasiddhāntavichārasāra shaḍaśitisārdhaśataka, 477.
Sulhaṇa, 368, 369, 477.
Śulikas, 262.
Śulki chief, 383.
Sunandā, 479.
Sunandana, 160.
Sunari, 454.
Sundar Rajan, 40, 55.
Supārśva, 404.
Supekar, S. G., 37, 50, 51.
Sūra, 215.
Surāchārya, 401.
Surāditya, 352.
Śūrakula, 276, 302.
Śūrasenas, 101, 103, 105.
Suraśmichandra, 244, 267, 273.
Surat, 346.
Surathotsava, 361.
Suravīra, 355.
Sūrpāraka (Sopara), 167, 225.
Surwaya, 412, 433, 464, 465.
Sūryasiddhānta, 300.
Suśarman, 153.
Suśrutasaṁhitā, 301.
Susthitavarman, 262.
Sutlej, 42.
Śuva or Sucha, 263.
Suvarṇabhūmi (East Indies), 501.
Suvarṇasikatā, 173.
Suviśākha, 173, 189.
Śvabhra (the Sabarmati valley), 172.
Svāmidāsa, 245.
Svāmikarāja, 320.
Svapnavāsavadatta, 216, 297.
Svatiguṭa, 224.
Śvetapatha, 200.
Svopajñapañjikā or Jñānadīpikā, 478
Śyāma Jātaka, 207.
Śyāmalādaṇḍaka, 474.
Syāmilaka, 298.

T

Tagara, 225.
Tailapa II, 336, 339, 340, 342.
Tajikistan, 390.
Takāristhāna, 497.
Takraoda, 64, 65.
Takshullikā, 406, 485.
Tālajaṅgha, 90, 92, 93.
Tālanpur, 404.
Talavāḍā, 359.
Tamin, 321.
Tanjore, 345.
Ṭaṅka, 322.
Ṭannā, 488.
Tāpasa, 411.
Tāpasiyas, 219.
Tapti, 52, 56, 75.
Tāraka, 502.
Tattvasāra, 469.
Tattvaprakāśa, 408,4 73.
Tattvārtha-vṛitti-pada-vivaraṇa, 475.
Taxila, 101, 105, 108, 119, 133, 165, 194.
Tejapāla, 441.
Tejovardhana, 324.
Telangana, 154.
Tell Basak, 97.
Telod, 65.
Ṭeṇgi, 399.
Terahi, 291, 405, 420, 429, 457, 459.
Terambī (Terahi), 412, 464.
Tewari, G. S., 510.
Thāiyāka, 27, 502.
Ṭhakkura Pheru, 33, 505, 507, 508.
Ṭhākura Nārāyaṇa, 374.
Thāneśvara, 264, 265, 348.
Thapar, B. K., 62, 83.
Theravādins, 201.
Thirāditya, 502.
Thomas, 109.
Thomas, E. J., 4
Tigawa, 283, 284.
Tilakamañjarī, 32, 383, 401, 471, 473, 490, 495, 499, 501, 502.
Tilakawāḍā, 349, 408, 411.
Timingilas, 357.
Tingni, 64.
Tinnevelly, 60.
Tirabhukti, 269.
Tod, J., 326.
Toggala, 348.
Tongra, 415, 454.
Toramāṇa, 23, 246, 247, 248, 267, 268, 269, 273.
Tosaniya, 57.
Trailokayanandi, 401.
Trailokyavarman, 365, 366, 367, 410.
Trastenes (Chashṭana), 33, 171.
Tribhuvanapāla, 360.
Trigartas, 5.
Trilochana, 216.
Trilochanapāla, 346, 347.

Tripathi, R. S., 10, 260, 262, 263, 322.
Tripuri, 148, 339, 357, 358, 509.
Tripuristhāna, 481.
Trirātra sacrifice, 8, 187, 193.
Triśaṅku, 91.
Tritsus, 89.
Triveda, 482.
Trivedi, H. V. 147, 183, 185, 229, 253, 334, 347, 349, 415.
Trivedins, 303.
Tulsai, 51.
Tumain (Tumbavana), 118, 120, 128, 200, 210, 237, 238, 267, 269, 273, 277, 283, 289, 290, 291, 414, 430, 455.
Tuṇḍikeras, 93.
Tungipattan, 405.
Turushkas, 357.
Turvaśa, 89.
Tushāra, 390,
Tushāspha, 141.

U

Ububaraghara (Umner), 200.
Uchchakalpa, 245.
Udaipur, 24, 329, 330, 331, 332, 335, 339, 340, 341, 342, 345, 346, 348, 349, 350, 352, 354, 355, 356, 364, 371, 408, 415, 446, 469, 487.
Udari, 375.
Udayāditya, 25, 354, 355, 356, 357, 381, 402, 408, 409, 419, 440, 446, 466, 476, 488, 490, 493, 497, 502, 505, 510.
Udayāditya (Udayavarman), 367.
Udayagiri hill inscription, 23, 26, 204, 235, 272, 274, 275, 279, 281, 283, 286, 288, 289, 290, 291, 311, 312, 414.
Udayana, 413.
Udayana Vatsarāja, 100.
Udayapura, 30, 364, 405, 408, 410, 418, 440, 448, 451, 459, 497, 499.
Udayavarmadeva, 25.
Udayavarman, 365, 366, 367, 371, 381, 410, 494.
Udāyin or Udayabhadra, 102.
Uddahika, 148.
Uddyotanasūri, 247, 323, 400.
Udita, 324.
Udivisa (Orissa), 399.
Udumbaragarta (Umarbar), 269.
Uganda, 46.
Ujjeni, 200.
Ujjain, 9, 11, 12, 22, 25, 28, 29, 30, 31, 32, 33, 56, 64, 70, 86, 90, 95, 96, 97, 98, 103, 104, 105, 108, 112, 115, 117, 118, 119, 120, 123, 125, 126, 128, 130, 131, 132, 133, 134, 135, 140, 141, 142, 143, 144, 145, 155, 156, 159, 161, 164, 166, 171, 175, 177, 186, 188, 198, 190, 210, 211, 215, 216, 224, 226, 236, 237, 259, 263, 264, 266, 273, 274, 275, 276, 278, 279, 280, 293, 295, 297, 298, 300, 301, 304, 308, 313, 315, 316, 321, 322, 323, 332, 333, 336, 341, 349, 351, 357, 358, 360, 361, 362, 365, 366, 369, 372, 376, 399, 400, 403, 404, 405, 407, 408, 409, 411, 412, 419, 421, 439, 448, 450, 451, 453, 460, 461, 463, 464, 466, 469, 470, 476, 477, 479, 482, 488, 499, 505.
Ujjayinī, 10, 11, 33, 94, 98, 104, 108, 119, 121, 122, 133, 134, 142, 143, 145, 146, 147, 157, 162, 171, 173, 176, 187, 188, 189, 195, 197, 200, 213, 215, 216, 217, 219, 259, 273, 296, 322, 400, 407, 413.
Umarathā, 385, 410,
Un, 30, 357, 402, 408, 441, 442, 462, 465, 466, 476.
Undakhal, 51.
Undāna, 276.
Uniyārā, 159.
Upadeśamālāvṛitti, 477.
Upamanyu gotra, 481.
Uparahāḍamaṇḍala, 385.
Uparkot, 227.
Upāsakāchāra, 471.
Upasūnya, 278.
Upavinda, 94.
Upendra, 25, 329, 330, 331, 468.
Upendramaṇḍala, 384, 385.
Upendrapura, 412, 413, 464.
Upidaḍata (Upendradatta), 196.
Urjayat, 173.
Ushavadāta, 8, 219.
Uthavanaka, 365.
Uthūṇaka, 403.
Utpalarāja, 338, 339, 341.
Uttamabhadras, 7, 168.
Uttamadatta, 182.
Uttarakuru, 208.
Uttarapatha, 108.
Uttar Pradesh, 43.
Uvaṭa, 474.
Uzehe, 225.

V

Vaal river, 45, 46.
Vabakañchuka race, 486.
Vāchaspati, 334.
Vāchisuvijayita, 200, 201.
Vaḍajā, 335.
Vaḍanagara, 344.
Vaḍaūda, 365.

Vāddiga, 366.
Vāgaḍa, 331, 335, 341, 342, 356, 387, 388, 403.
Vāgaḍa Saṁgha, 405.
Vāgbhaṭa, 301, 372.
Vāhlikas, 235.
Vaidya, C. V., 260.
Vaikheḍa, 459, 461.
Vainyāditya, 248.
Vairīsiṁha, 329, 331, 379.
Vairīsiṁha II, 332, 333, 469.
Vaiśālī, 93, 100, 116.
Vājasaneya, 482.
Vājasaneyi Saṁhitā bhāshya (Mantra-bhāshya), 475.
Vājimādhyaṁdina, 481.
Vajjaḍa, 343.
Vajjuka, 344.
Vajra, 120, 121.
Vajrāṅkuśa, 344.
Vajraśākhā, 121.
Vajrasattvasādhana, 399.
Vajrasvāmī, 121.
Vajraṭa, 474.
Vajraṭasvāmin, 332.
Vākalarāśi, 411.
Vākiliyas, 219.
Vākpati I or Bappairāja, 331, 332.
Vākpati II, 24, 327, 328, 329, 330, 331, 334, 335, 336, 336, 337, 338, 339, 340, 341, 342, 343, 378, 379, 381, 382, 387, 401, 407, 415, 446, 468, 470, 471, 472, 497.
Vākyapadīya, 298.
Valāka, 156.
Valka (Vāghli), 245.
Valla family, 482.
Vallabharāja, 350.
Vallāla, 441.
Valloṭaka, 481.
Valloṭakīya, 481.
Vālmīki, 2.
Vāmanasvāmin, 483.
Vaṅga country, 235, 332.
Vaṇika, 337.
Vaṅkshu, 358.
Vappakadeva, 319, 320, 406.
Varāha (person), 258, 270.
Varāhadāsa, 258.
Varāhamihira, 31, 32, 161, 163, 216, 255, 259, 300, 301, 302, 303, 304, 307, 308, 314, 315, 318.
Vārāṇasī, 93, 103, 148.
Varaṅga, 392, 506.
Varaṅgacharita, 475.
Vararuchi, 161, 163, 216, 470.
Varddhamānapura (Badnawar), 362, 386, 405, 486.
Vardhamāna, 413.
Varkaṭa, 486.
Vartivardhana, 102.
Vasumitra, 32, 150.
Vasamanadatā, 196.
Vasantāchārya, 341.
Vasantapāla, 410.
Vasantasenā, 280, 304.
Vasishka (Vāsudeva), 170, 199.
Vasishṭha, 200, 325, 481.
Vasishṭha Gotra, 329.
Vaśishṭha Siddhānta, 300.
Vāsishṭhīputra, 172.
Vāsishṭhīputra Pulumāvī, 228.
Vāsishthīputra Sātakarṇi, 228.
Vastupāla, 372, 441.
Vāsudeva, (ruler), 124, 153.
Vāsula, 27, 298.
Vasumitra, 150, 151.
Vasunāga, 185, 186.
Vaṭapadraka, 385.
Vatsa, 93, 98, 481.
Vatsabhaṭṭi, 27, 281, 298.
Vatsarāja (Pratīhāra ruler), 322, 323, 506.
Vatsarāja of Kauśāmbī, 105.
Vatsarāja of Mahua inscription, 24, 322, 323, 407, 484.
Vātsyāyana, 9, 10, 31, 217, 302, 304, 305, 307, 308, 309, 312.
Vāyupurāṇa, 183.
Vāyurakshita, 237, 241.
Vedārtha-dīpikā sarvānukrama bhāshya, 475.
Vejaja, 200.
Velankar, H. D., 163.
Velugrāma (Veṇagrāma), 142.
Vemaka family, 403, 486.
Veṅgī, 353.
Veṅkaṭādhvarin, 473.
Veṅkaṭaramayya, M., 8.
Vera, 199.
Vesantara Jātaka, 207.
Vessanagara (Vaiśyanagara, Modern Besanagar), 143.
Vetāla-bhaṭṭa, 161, 163, 216.
Vetālapañchaviṁśati, 32.
Vetravatī, (Betawa), 11, 335.
Vichāraśreṇi, 9.
Vidarbha, 32, 149, 320.
Vidiśā, 17, 22, 23, 26, 28, 29, 30, 31, 104, 117, 118, 119, 123, 124, 131, 141, 143, 151, 154, 155, 176, 182, 183, 184, 188, 193, 194, 195, 196, 200, 205, 210, 212, 219, 224, 226, 232, 233, 234, 235, 236, 252, 264, 267, 275, 279, 301, 315, 316.
Vidvajjana Vallabha, 473.
Vidyādhara, 348.
Vidyādharaśarman, 482.
Vidyalankara Prananath, 504.
Vidyānandasūri, 404, 479.

Vidyāpurī, 404.
Vidyāśiva, 477.
Vigrahapāla, 337.
Vigraharāja III, 355, 356.
Vijayapāla, 336.
Vijayapāladeva, 25, 360, 379, 409.
Vijayarāja, 388, 403.
Vijayasena, 176, 227.
Vijayasiṁhadeva, 366.
Vijayasiṁhasūri, 477.
Vijayaśrī, 32.
Vijayavarman, 160.
Vikrama, 157, 160, 161, 162.
Vikramacharitra, 158.
Vikrama Chola, 361.
Vikrama-Cholānula, 361.
Vikramāditya, 6, 9, 12, 21, 32, 156, 157, 158, 159, 160, 161, 162, 163, 164, 195, 197, 216, 236, 275, 280, 297, 351, 464, 505.
Vikramāditya II, 353, 354.
Vikramāditya V, 337.
Vikramorvaśīya, 270.
Vilapadraka, 357, 409.
Vimalabodha, 473.
Vimalāṅgī, 479.
Vinayachandra, 478, 479.
Vinayapiṭaka, 116.
Vinda, 94.
Vindaballa, 160.
Vindhya, 87, 90, 421.
Vindhyabhūbhṛit, 369.
Vindhyamaṇḍala, 384.
Vindhyaśakti, 177.
Vindhyavarman, 368, 369, 403, 404, 416, 477, 478, 483.
Vindhyaśakti, 177
Vinhuka (Vishṇudatta), 196.
Vinītarāśi, 406, 411.
Vinītaruchi, 279.
Vīra, 475.
Vīracharita, 158.
Vīradāman, 176, 177.
Vīrapurushadatta, 177.
Vīrarājendra, 353, 354.
Vīrasena, 23, 149, 185, 235, 274.
Vīrasena (Buddhist Śrāvaka), 277.
Vīrasenanāga, 184.
Vīravarman, 359.
Vīryarāma, 349, 350.
Viśākhadatta, 231.
Viśākhayūpa, 102.
Viśālā, 215.
Vīsāladeva, 373, 375.
Visālagrāma, 497.
Viśālakīrti, 404, 478, 479.
Vishṇu (Person), 470.
Vishṇu (Ṭhakkura), 482, 483.
Vishṇudharmottara, 3,13.
Vishṇunandi, 401.
Vishṇuvardhana, 229, 256, 257, 258, 269.
Viśvabhū, 98.
Viśvadeva, 196.
Viśvadharman, 238, 250.
Viśvāmitra, 194, 481.
Viśvanandi, 401.
Viśvasena, 177, 178, 227.
Viśvasiṁha, 177.
Viśvavarman, 251, 252, 267, 268, 273, 275.
Vītahavyas, 93.
Viṭhalpur, 438.
Vītihotras, 93, 94, 98, 103.
Vivāhavṛindāvana, 300.
Vividhatīrthakalpa, 33, 158, 404.
Vonones, 164.
Vopālita, 470.
Vratakhaṇḍapraśasti, 374.
Vṛisha (ruler), 184.
Vṛishabhanandi, 401.
Vṛittaratnākara, 368, 477.
Vṛittipañjikādi Lakshaṇaśāstra, 402.
Vyāghrahela, 324.
Vyāghranāga, 185.
Vyapuramaṇḍala, 358, 384.
Vyavahāramañjarī, 473.
Vyomaśambhu, 468.
Vyomaśiva, 413.
Vyomavatī, 413, 468.

W

Wakankar V. S. 38.
Watson, 326.
Wheeler, M., 62, 89, 97.
Winternitz, 88.

Y

Yādavas, 83, 89, 95.
Yadu, 89, 94.
Yaduvaṁśa, 88.
Yagata, 228.
Yajñadhara, 367.
Yajña Sātakarṇi, 171, 174, 228.
Yajñasena, 31, 149.
Yājñika, 482.
Yakhadāsī, 197.
Yakhadina, 197.
Yakhi, 197.
Yakhila, 197.
Yama rakhitā, 196.
Yaśagupta, 254.
Yaśaḥkarṇa, 358.
Yaśamotika, 169.
Yaśodāman, 176.
Yaśodāman II, 178, 179.

Yaśodharman, 24, 25, 27, 156, 229, 249, 250, 254, 256, 257, 258, 259, 263, 274.
Yaśodharman Vishṇuvardhana, 255, 256, 267, 303.
Yaśodhavala, 364, 455, 477.
Yaśorāja, 359.
Yaśovarmadeva, 25, 488.
Yaśovarman, 334, 360, 361, 362, 365, 382, 390, 421, 483.
Yatga, 188.
Yaudheyas, 8, 173.
Yavanas, 150.
Yayāti, Mahāśivagupta, 343.
Yogarāja, 333.
Yogasūtras, 351.
Yogayātrā, 300.
Yogeśvararāśi, 411.
Yogeśvarī, 411, 488.
Yoginīsaṁcharyā, 399.
Yuanchwang, 11, 12, 33, 248, 249, 263, 265, 279, 281.
Yudhāsura, 320.
Yuktikalpataru, 32, 351, 352, 389, 390, 474, 495, 498, 499, 500,
Yuvarāja, 339.

Z

Zeuner, 34, 47.

*

Plate I

1. Mandsor, Palaeoliths of Series 1. (p. 38)

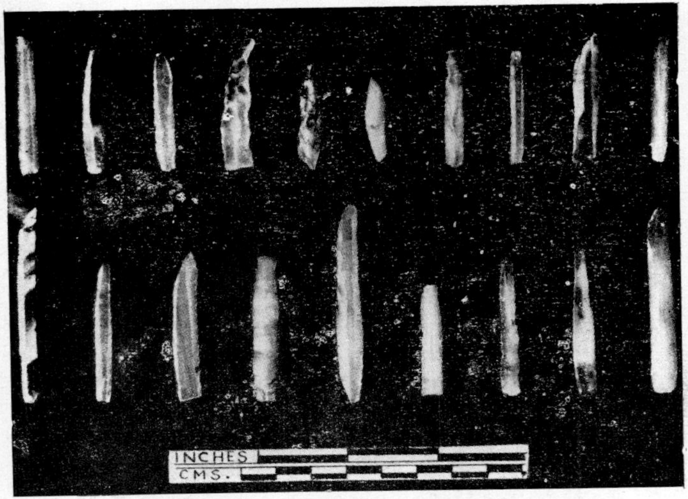

2. Nagda, Microliths. (p. 56)

Plate II

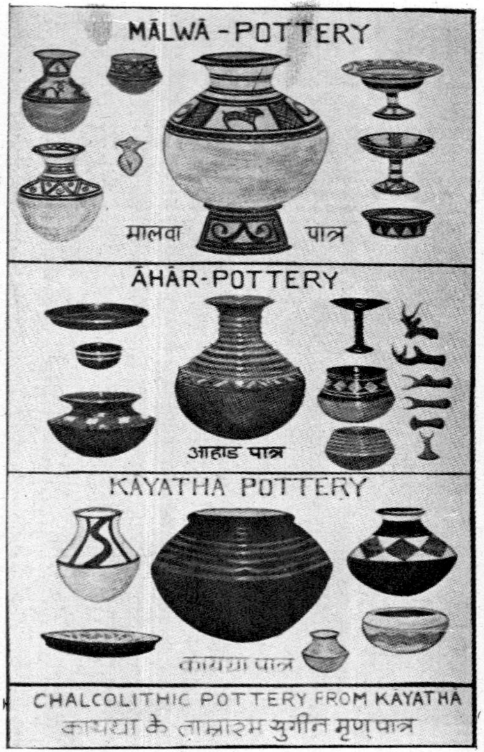

3. Kayatha, Chalcolithic pottery and other objects. (pp. 67-74)

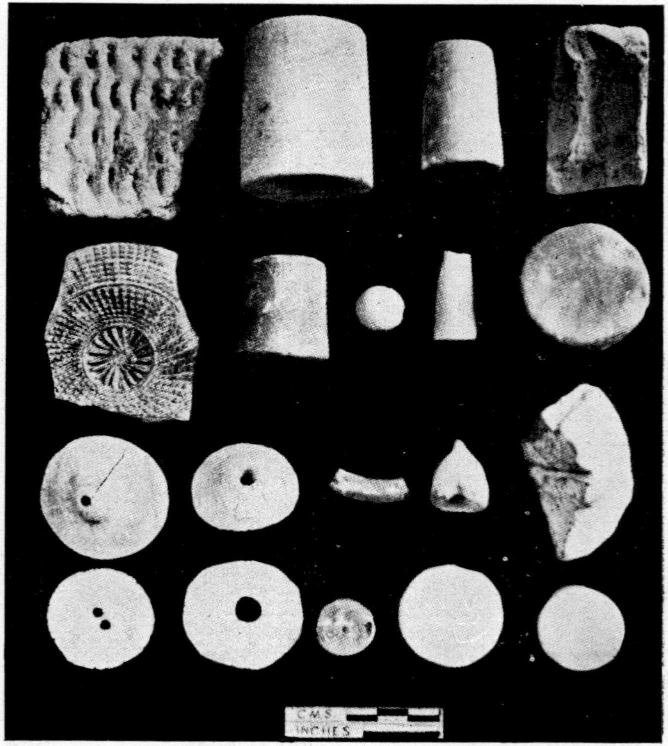

4. Eran, Beads, food-rubber and other minor antiquities from Chalcolithic period 1. (pp. 73-74)

Plate III

5. Navdatoli, Painted potteries. (pp. 68-70)

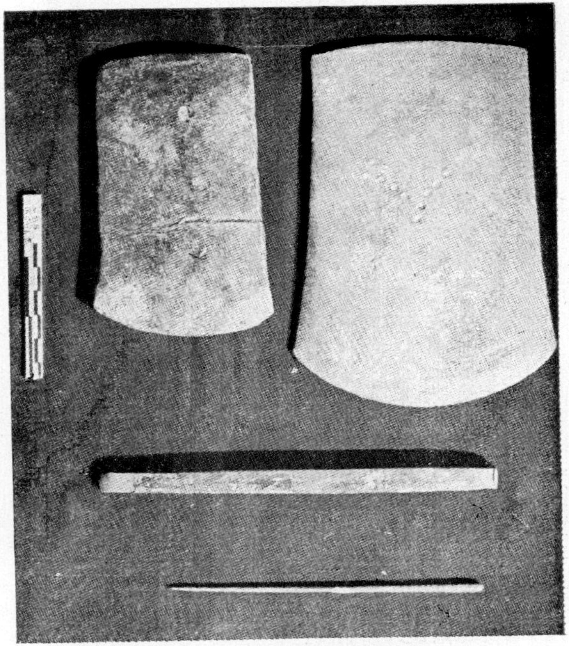

6. Navdatoli, Copper implements. (p. 72)

Plate IV

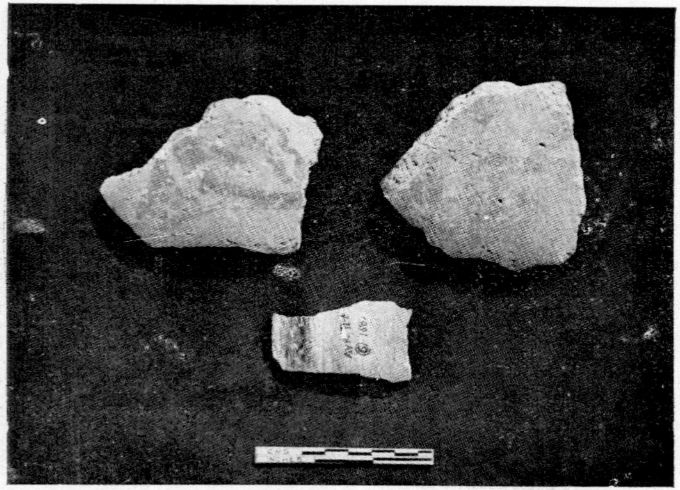

7. Avara, Chalcolithic pottery. (p. 64)

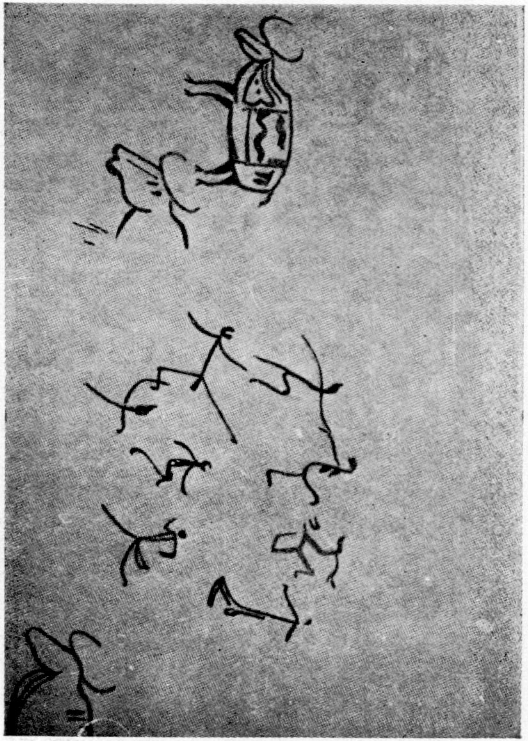

8. Bhim Baithaka, Pre-historic painting from the rock-shelter. (p. 59)

Plate V

9. Ujjain, View of a massive brick structure. (pp. 123-124)

10. Ujjain, Wooden structure in the make up of the rampart. (p. 124)

Plate VI

11. Ujjain, Section of roads of different periods. (p. 125)

12. Ujjain, Ironsmith's furnace. (pp. 141-142)

Plate VII

13. Sanchi, General view of stūpa 1. (p. 126)

Plate VII

14. Sanchi, Stūpa 1 North gate. (p. 203)

Plate VIII

15. Sanchi, Lion Capital. (p. 127)

Plate IX

16. Sanchi, Ajātaśatru and his women meeting Buddha at the mango grove at Rājagṛiha. (p. 207)

17. Sanchi, Prasenjit going out of his palace to witness the miracle of Śrāvasti. (p. 209)

Plate X

18. Sanchi, Top bar : Carriage of ashes to Kusinagar. Middle bar : War for relics. Lowest bar :

Plate X

19. Sanchi, Śālabhañjikā. (p. 208)

Plate XI

20. Besanagar, general view of the pillar of Heliodorus. (p. 206)

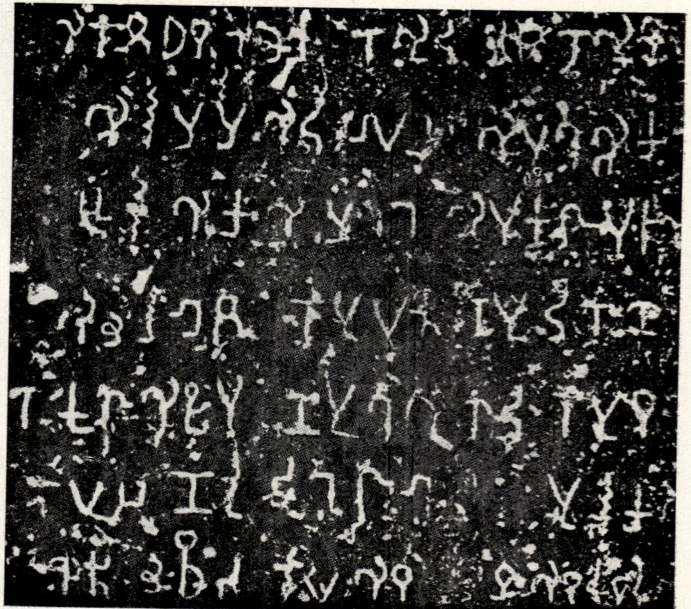

21. Besanagar, Inscription of Heliodorus. (p. 206)

Plate XII

22. Besanagar, Yakshī. (p. 208)

23. Besanagar, Kalpavṛiksha. (p. 208)

Plate XIII

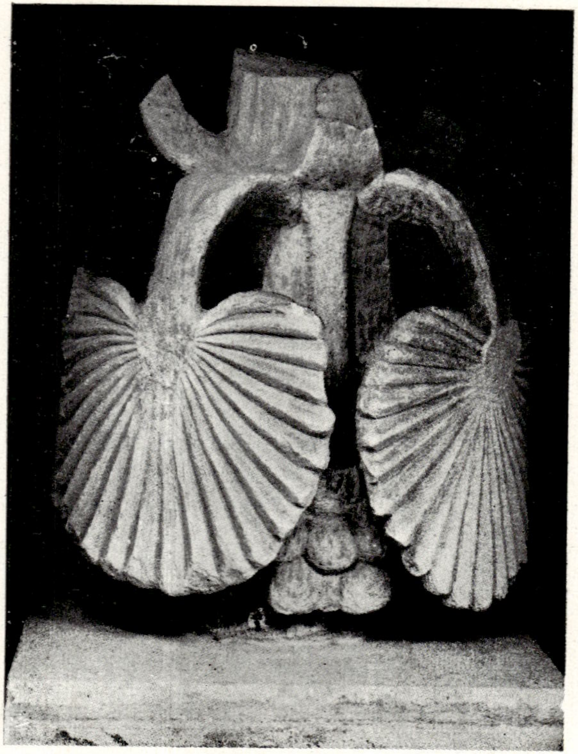

24. Besanagar, Palm Capital. (p. 206)

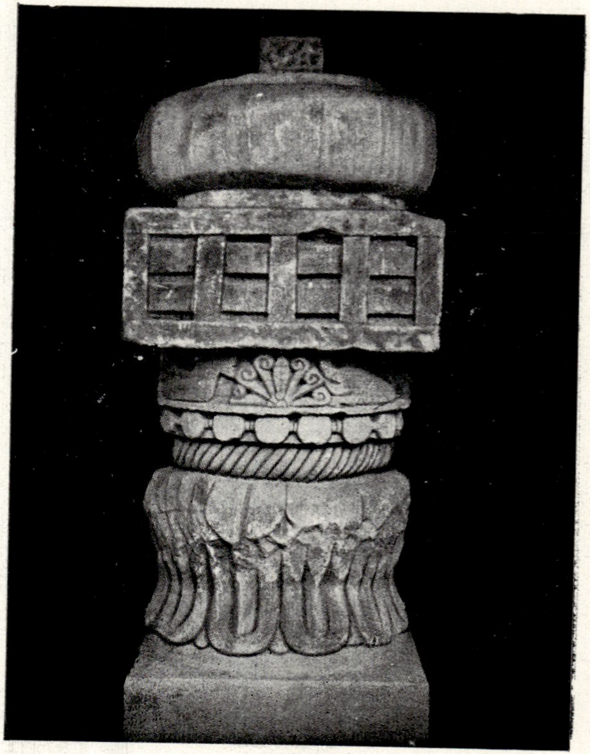

25. Besanagar, Abacus of Makara. (206)

Plate XIV

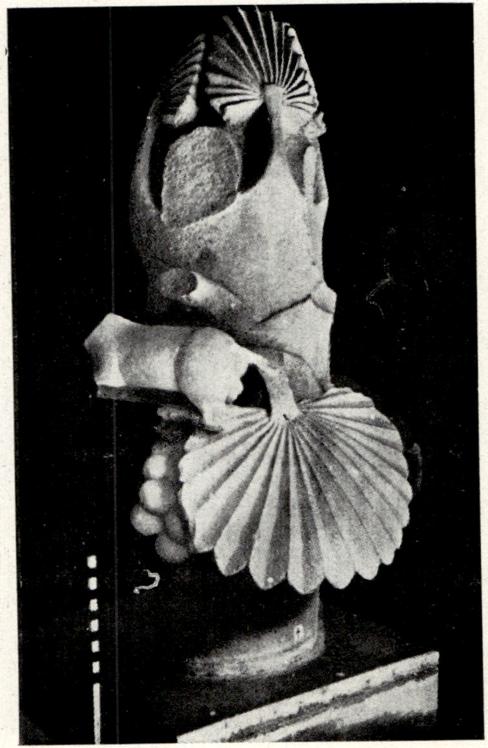

26. Pawaya, Fan palm capital. (206)

27. Pawaya, Yaksha Maṇibhadra. (p. 209)

Plate XV

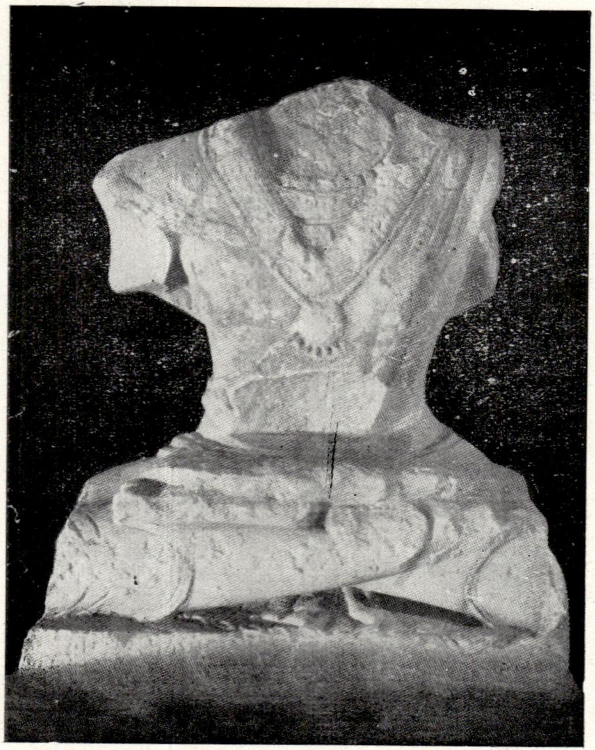

28. Sanchi, Bodhisattva. (p. 209)

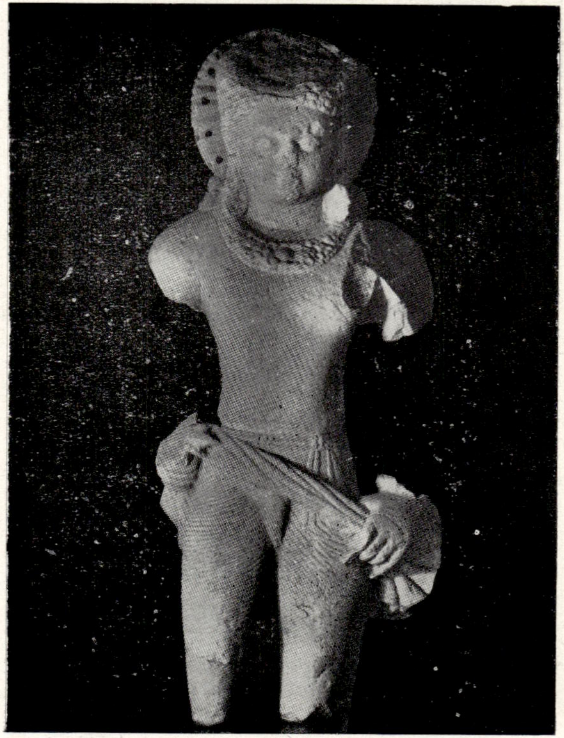

29. Sanchi, Bodhisattva vajrapāṇi. (p. 252)

Plate XVI

30. Sanchi, Buddha seated in meditation. (p. 209)

31. Sanchi, Nāgarāja. (p. 209)

Plate XVII

32. Pawaya, Dance panel. (p. 292)

33. Sondani, Flying gandharvas. (p. 291)

34. Udaigiri, Varāha. (288)

35. Udaigiri, Nāga near Varāha. (p. 288)

Plate XIX

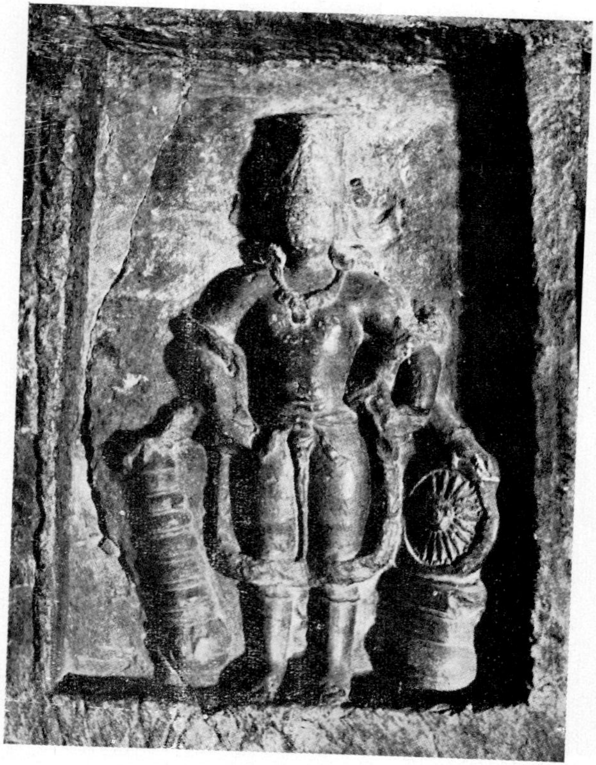

36. Udaigiri, Vishṇu. (p. 288)

37. Udaigiri, Seshaśāyī Vishṇu. (p. 288)

Plate XX

38. Udaigiri, Sivaliṅga. (p. 289)

39. Udaigiri, Gaṇeśa. (p. 290)

Plate XXI

40. Udaigiri, Gaṅgā and Yamunā. (p. 291)

41. Udaigiri, Umā-Maheśvara. (p. 290)

Plate XXII

42. Udaigiri, Mahishāsuramardinī. (p. 290)

43. Kayatha, A torso of the Sun image.

Plate XXIII

44. Eran, Varāha. (p. 289)

45. Bagh, Head of Dvārapāla. (p. 292)

Plate XXIV

46. Udaigiri, Jaina image of Pārśvanātha. (p. 292)

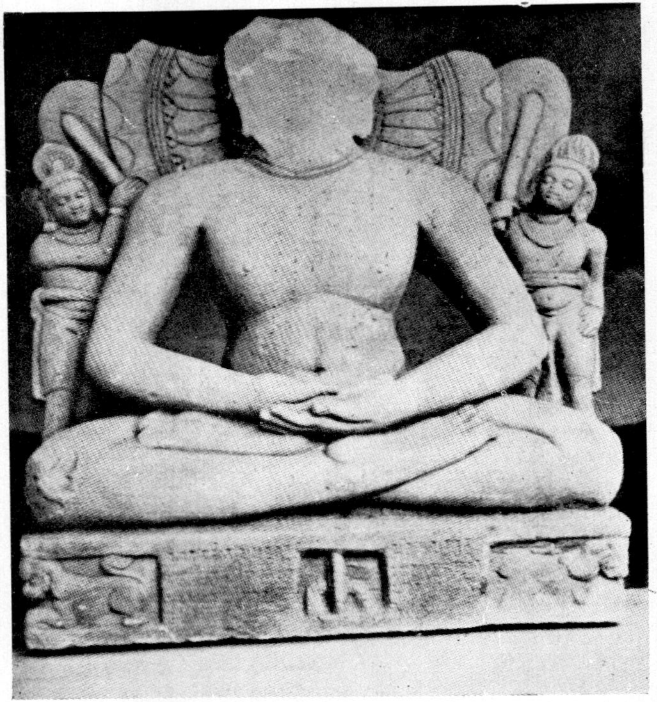

47. Vidiśā, Inscribed image of the time of Rāmagupta.

Plate XXV

48. Eran, Pillar of a temple. (p. 287)

49. Eran, Ruined temple of the Gupta period. (p. 284)

Plate XXVI

51. Udaigiri, Gupta temple. (p. 283)

50. Sanchi, Gupta temple. (p. 284)

Plate XXVII

52. Bagh, Cave IV Chaitya. (pp. 282-283)

53. Sanchi, Late Gupta temple. (284)

Plate XXVIII

54. Sanchi, Buddha standing in Varada pose. (p. 291)

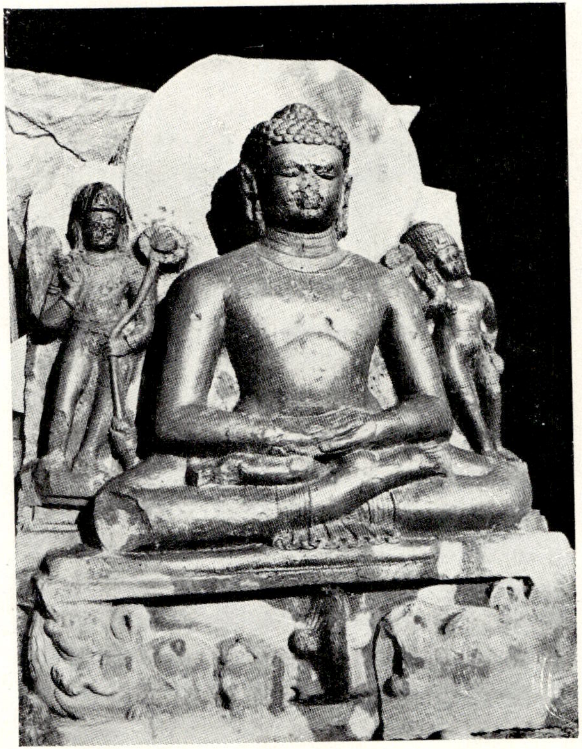

55. Gyaraspur, Buddha. (450)

Plate XXIX

56. Jhalrapatan, Maṇḍapa of Sītaleśvara Mahādeva temple. (pp. 422-423)

57. Jhalrapatan, General view of the Sun temple, from South-east. (p. 444)

Plate XXX

58. Gyaraspur, Hindola toraṇa (p. 432)

59. Gyaraspur, Aṭhakhambā. (p. 432)

Plate XXXI

60. Gyaraspur, Bajramaṭha temple. (432)

61. Gyaraspur, Maladevi temple Sikhara. (431-432)

Plate XXXII

62. Gwalior, Teli kā Mandir. (pp. 429-430)

63. Gwalior, Sasa bahu temple. (pp. 434-435)

Plate XXXIII

64. Surawaya, Vishṇu temple. (p. 433)

65. Surawaya, Vishṇu temple, partial view of the maṇḍapa.

Plate XXXIV

66. Eran, Remains.

Plate XXXV

67. Dhar, Bhojaśālā, interior view. (p. 436)

Plate XXXV

86. Dhar, Bhojaśālā, ceiling of the Central dome. (436)

Plate XXXVI

69. Bhojpur, Bhojeśvara temple, portion of the front doorway. (p. 436)

Plate XXXVIII

Plate XXXVI

70. Udayapur, Nīlakaṇṭheśvara temple. (pp. 440-441)

Plate XXXVII

Plate XXXIX

75. Udayapur, Dancing Śiva. (p. 451)

76. Ujjain, Naṭarāja Śiva. (pp. 450-451)

Plate XL

77. Indore Museum, Umā-Maheśvara.

78. Gwalior Museum, Bust of Śiva and Pārvatī.

79. Dhar, Image of Vishṇu. (p. 453)

80. Gandhawal, Harihara.

Plate XLII

81. Modi, Brahmā, with four heads. (p. 455)

82. Torso of a female figure.

83. Gandhwal, Dancing Kālī. (p. 456)

84. Udaipur, Udayeśvara temple sculpture.

Plate XLIV

85. Badoh, Yośodā with kṛishṇa. (p. 455)

86. Dhar, Vāgdevī (p. 457)

Plate XLV

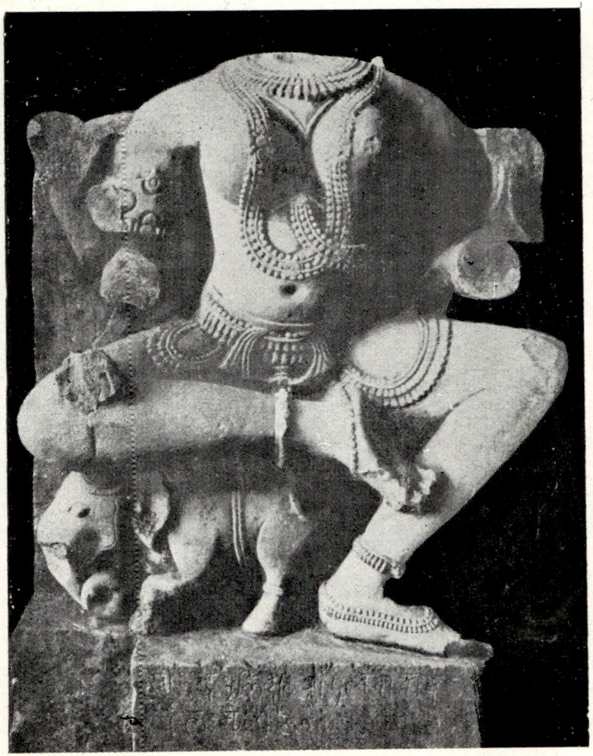

87. Naresar, Indrāṇī.

88. Badnawar, A female Jaina deity. (p. 463)

Plate XLVI

89. Dhar, A fragmentary sculpture showing Lokapālas.

90. Gwalior, Rahu and Ketu.

91. Un, Jain sculpture. (p. 462)

92. Gandhawal, Sun. (p. 455)

Plate XLVIII

93. Gwalior Museum, Kārttikeya. (p. 460)

94. Gwalior Museum, Kubera (p. 459)

Plate XLIX

95. Sohania, Skanda.

96. Dhar, Iron pillar. (p. 499)

Plate L

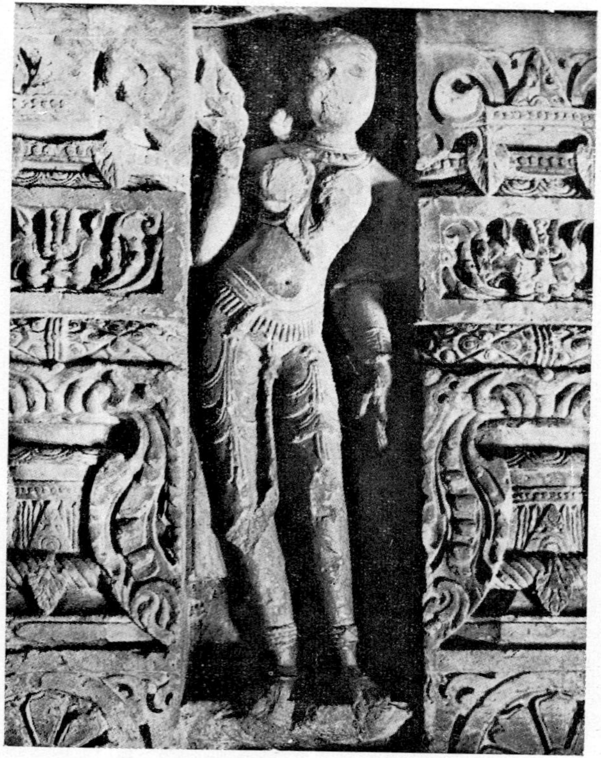

97. Udayapur, Deity of the Udayeśvara temple. (p. 440)

98. Nemawar, Dvārapāla at the entrance of the Sabhā maṇḍapa (p. 443)

99. Ancient coins of Malwa.

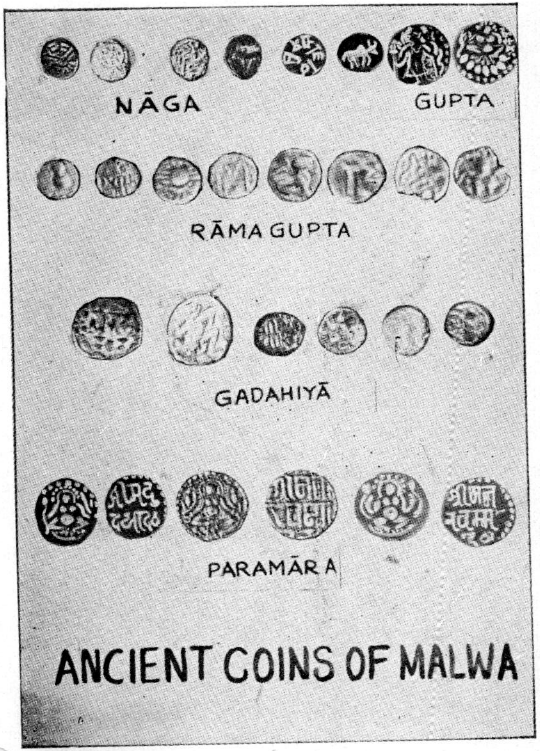

100. Ancient coins of Malwa.

LOCATION OF MALWA IN INDIA

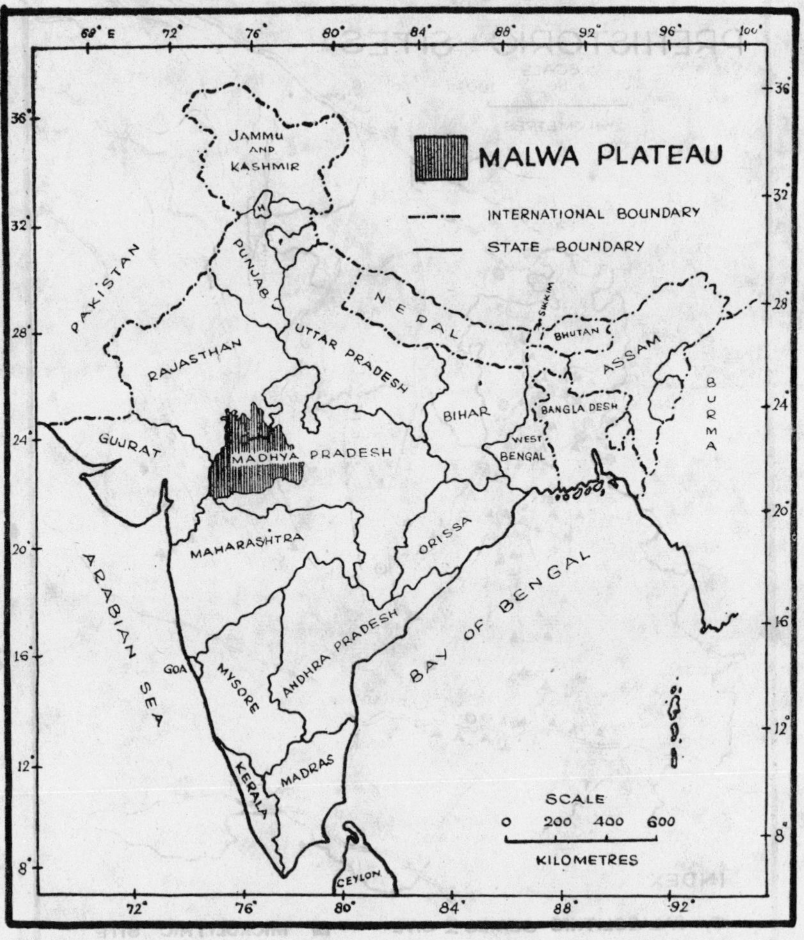

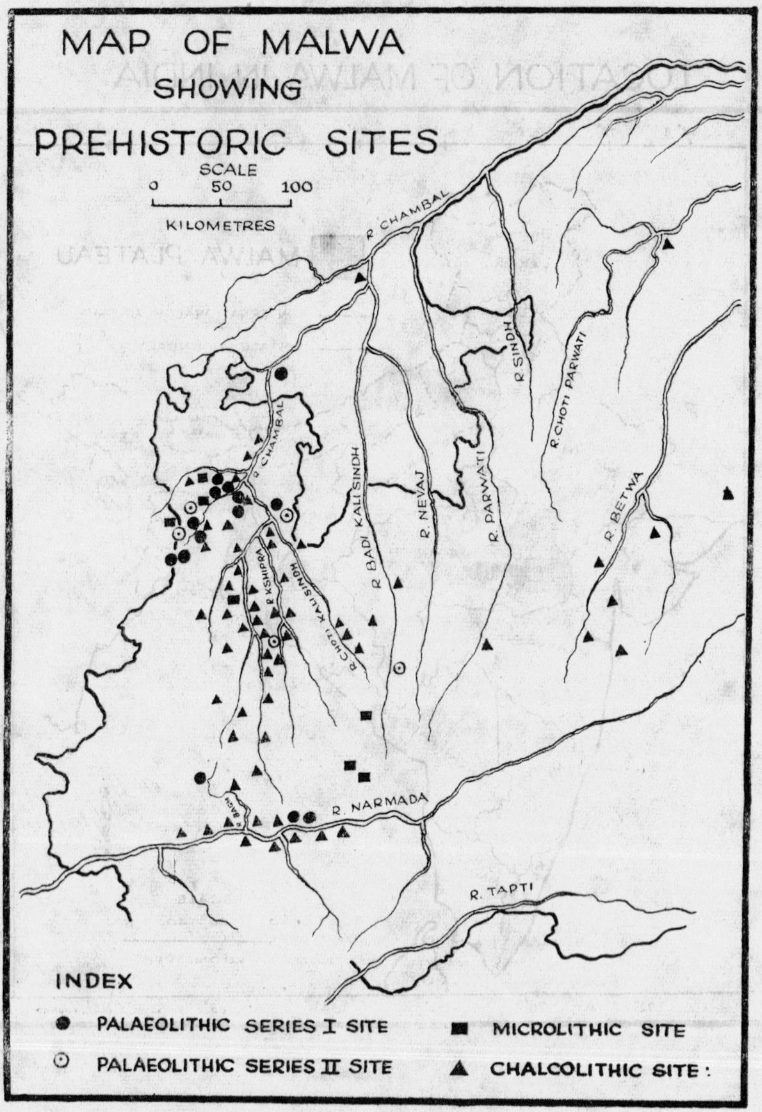
MAP OF MALWA
SHOWING
PREHISTORIC SITES
SCALE
0 50 100
KILOMETRES
R. CHAMBAL
R. CHAMBAL
R. SINDH
R. CHOTI PARWATI
R. BADI KALI SINDH
R. NEVAJ
R. PARWATI
R. BETWA
R. KSHIPRA
R. CHOTI KALI SINDH
R. BAGH
R. NARMADA
R. TAPTI
INDEX
PALAEOLITHIC SERIES I SITE
PALAEOLITHIC SERIES II SITE
MICROLITHIC SITE
CHALCOLITHIC SITE

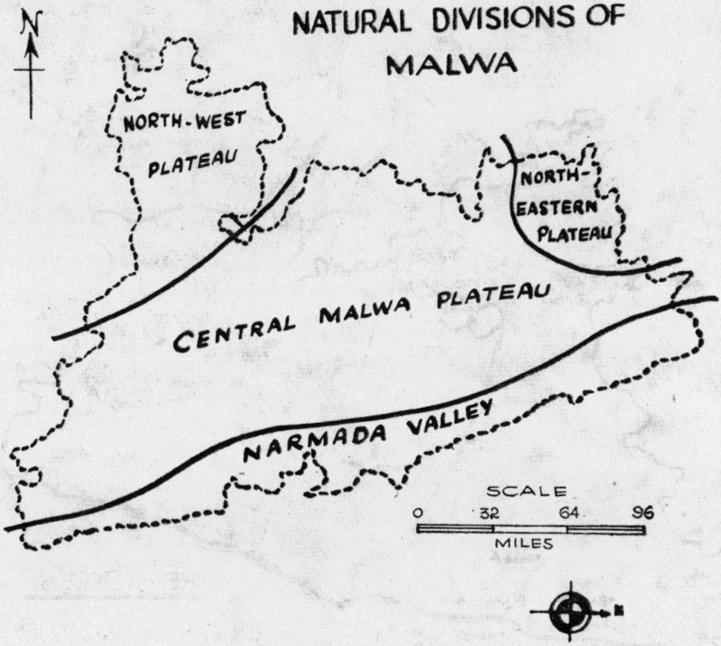
NATURAL DIVISIONS OF MALWA
N
NORTH-WEST PLATEAU
NORTH-EASTERN PLATEAU
CENTRAL MALWA PLATEAU
NARMADA VALLEY
SCALE
0 32 64 96
MILES

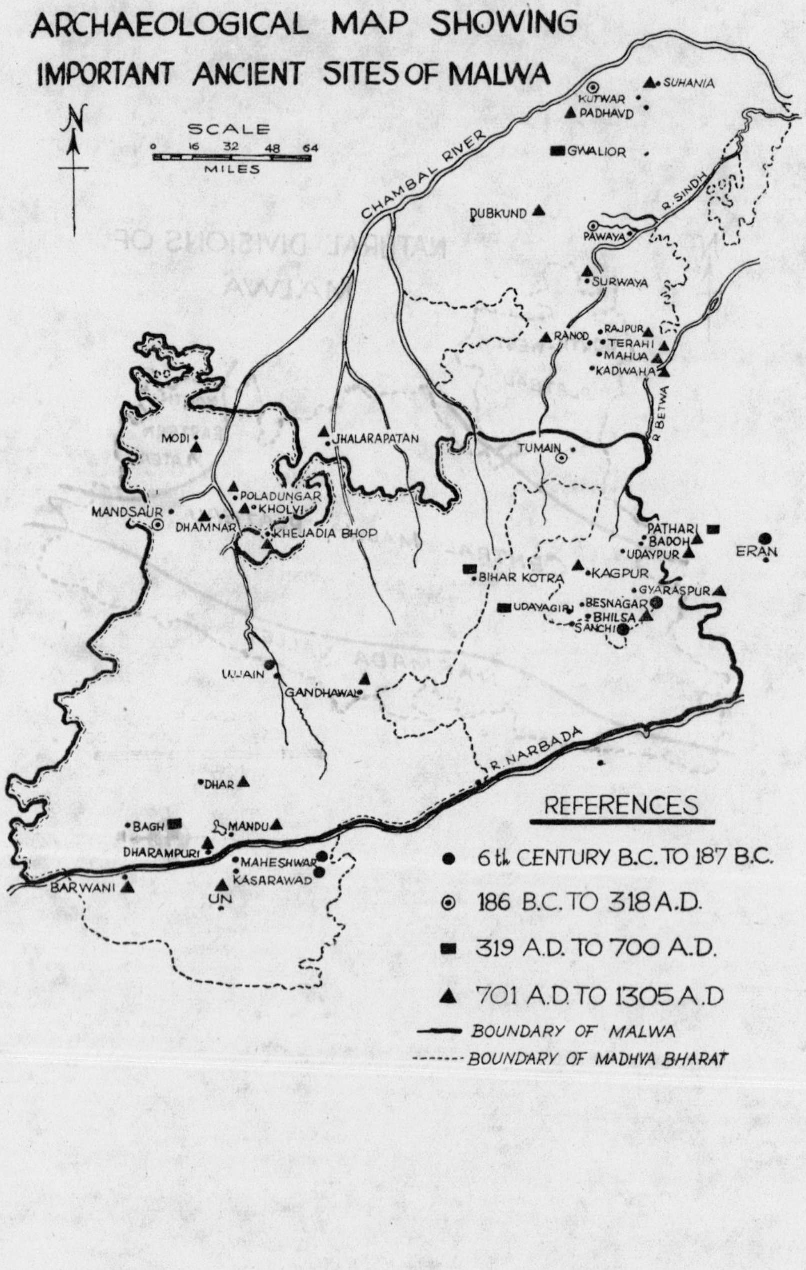
ARCHAEOLOGICAL MAP SHOWING
IMPORTANT ANCIENT SITES OF MALWA
N
SCALE
0 16 32 48 64
MILES
CHAMBAL RIVER
KUTWAR
SUHANIA
PADHAVD
GWALIOR
R. SINDH
DUBKUND
PAWAYA
SURWAYA
RANOD
RAJPUR
TERAHI
MAHUA
KADWAHA
R. BETWA
MODI
JHALARAPATAN
TUMAIN
POLADUNGAR
KHOLVI
MANDSAUR
DHAMNAR
KHEJADIA BHOP
PATHARI
BADOH
UDAYPUR
ERAN
BIHAR KOTRA
KAGPUR
GYARASPUR
UDAYAGIRI
BESNAGAR
BHILSA
SANCHI
UJJAIN
GANDHAWAL
R. NARBADA
DHAR
REFERENCES
BAGH
MANDU
DHARAMPURI
MAHESHWAR
KASARAWAD
BARWANI
UN
6 th CENTURY B.C. TO 187 B.C.
186 B.C. TO 318 A.D.
319 A.D. TO 700 A.D.
701 A.D. TO 1305 A.D
BOUNDARY OF MALWA
BOUNDARY OF MADHYA BHARAT